Dictionary of Policing

Dictionary of Policing

Edited by

Tim Newburn and Peter Neyroud

WILLAN
PUBLISHING

Published by

Willan Publishing
Culmcott House
Mill Street, Uffculme
Cullompton, Devon
EX15 3AT, UK
Tel: +44(0)1884 840337
Fax: +44(0)1884 840251
e-mail: info@willanpublishing.co.uk
website: www.willanpublishing.co.uk

Published simultaneously in the USA and Canada by

Willan Publishing
c/o ISBS, 920 NE 58th Ave, Suite 300,
Portland, Oregon 97213-3786, USA
Tel: +001(0)503 287 3093
Fax: +001(0)503 280 8832
e-mail: info@isbs.com
website: www.isbs.com

First published 2008

Paperback
ISBN 978-1-84392-287-2

Hardback
ISBN 978-1-84392-288-9

British Library Cataloguing-in-Publication Data

A catalogue record for this book is available from the British Library

Project managed by Deer Park Productions, Tavistock, Devon
Typeset by Pantek Arts Ltd, Maidstone, Kent
Printed and bound by T.J. International Ltd, Padstow, Cornwall

Contents

List of entries

List of contributors

Professor Laurence Alison, Centre for Critical Incident Research, University of Liverpool.

Alan Beckley, formerly Head of Management Development Training, West Mercia Constabulary.

Professor Trevor Bennett, Centre for Criminology, University of Glamorgan.

Jan Berry, Chairman, Police Federation.

Professor Ben Bowling, School of Law, King's College London.

Professor Mike Brogden, Lancaster University.

Professor Jennifer Brown, Department of Psychology, University of Surrey.

Dr Robin Bryant, Department for Studies in Crime and Policing, Canterbury Christ Church College.

Tom Bucke, Independent Police Complaints Commission.

Professor Ray Bull, School of Psychology, University of Leicester.

Dr Elizabeth Burney, Institute of Criminology, University of Cambridge.

Professor Rob Canton, School of Applied Social Sciences, De Montfort University.

Professor Ed Cape, School of Law, University of the West of England.

Dr Claire Corbett, Centre for Criminal Justice Research, Brunel University.

Inspector David Coulson, Staff Officer to the Acting Assistant Chief Constable, West Mercia Constabulary.

Dr David J. Cox, Research Institute for Law, Politics and Justice, Keele University.

Professor Adam Crawford, Centre for Criminal Justice Studies, University of Leeds.

Professor Hazel Croall, School of Law and Social Sciences, Glasgow Caledonian University.

Dr Pamela Davies, Sociology and Criminology Division, Northumbria University.

Jenny Deere, Former Head of Leadership Academy, National Policing Improvement Agency.

Professor Jason Ditton, Scottish Centre for Criminology.

Paul Evans, Director, Police and Crime Standards Directorate.

Professor Roger Evans, School of Law, Liverpool John Moores University.

Professor Graham Farrell, Midlands Centre for Criminology and Criminal Justice, Loughborough University.

Dr Emily Finch, Law School, Brunel University.

Kate Flannery, Her Majesty's Inspectorate of Constabulary.

Professor James Fraser, Centre for Forensic Science, University of Strathclyde.

Professor Nicholas Fyfe, School of Social Science, University of Dundee, and Scottish Institute for Policing Research.

Sharon Gernon-Booth, Associate Director, Audit Commission.

Detective Chief Inspector Stan Gilmour, Head of Field Intelligence, Thames Valley Police.

Professor Barry Godfrey, Research Institute for Law, Politics and Justice, Keele University.

Professor Barry Goldson, School of Sociology and Social Policy, University of Liverpool.

Professor Peter Grabosky, Research School of Social Sciences, Australian National University.

Professor John Grieve, John Grieve Centre for Policing and Community Safety, London Metropolitan University.

Dr Nathan Hall, Institute of Criminal Justice Studies, University of Portsmouth.

Dr Peter Hall, Faculty of Health and Life Sciences, Coventry University.

Dr Simon Hallsworth, Department of Sociology, London Metropolitan University.

Dr Clive Harfield, John Grieve Centre for Policing and Community Safety, London Metropolitan University.

Mark Harron, School of Law and Social Science, University of Plymouth.

Professor Frances Heidensohn, Mannheim Centre for Criminology, London School of Economics.

Giles Herdale, Head of Policing Policy and Practice, National Policing Improvement Agency.

Professor Alex Hirschfield, Applied Criminology Centre, University of Huddersfield.

Professor Simon Holdaway, School of Law, University of Sheffield.

Sophie Holmes, Department of Applied Social Science, University of Lancaster.

Professor Mike Hough, Institute for Criminal Policy Research, King's College London.

Dr Carolyn Hoyle, Centre for Criminology, University of Oxford.

Dr Anthea Hucklesby, Centre for Criminal Justice Studies, University of Leeds.

Professor Gordon Hughes, School of Social Sciences, Cardiff University.

Richard Ives, Pompidou Group Project, Drug Prevention Support Network.

Leonard Jason-Lloyd, Department of Criminology, University of Leicester.

Professor Yvonne Jewkes, Department of Criminology, University of Leicester.

Dr Tim John, University of Glamorgan.

Professor Les Johnston, Institute of Criminal Justice Studies, University of Portsmouth.

Ken Jones, President, Association of Chief Police Officers.

Trevor Jones, School of Social Sciences, Cardiff University.

Peter Joyce, Department of Sociology, Manchester Metropolitan University.

Paul Kernaghan, Chief Constable, Hampshire Constabulary.

Professor Gloria Laycock, Jill Dando Institute of Crime Science, University College London.

Dr Maggy Lee, Department of Sociology, University of Essex.

Professor Mike Levi, School of Social Sciences, Cardiff University.

Stuart Lister, Centre for Criminal Justice Studies, University of Leeds.

Dr John Locker, Department of Criminology, Keele University.

Barry Loveday, Institute of Criminal Justice Studies, University of Portsmouth.

Professor Laurence Lustgarten, Independent Police Complaints Commission.

Sir Ken MacDonald QC, Director of Public Prosecutions, Crown Prosecution Service.

Deputy Chief Constable Alex Marshall, Thames Valley Police.

Dr Mario Matassa, Mannheim Centre for Criminology, London School of Economics.

Dr Rob C. Mawby, Centre for Criminal Justice Policy and Research, UCE Birmingham.

Professor Rob I. Mawby, Criminology and Criminal Justice Department, University of Plymouth.

Tiggey May, Institute for Criminal Policy Research, King's College London.

Larry Mead, School of Law and Criminology, University of Derby.

Dr Aogán Mulcahy, Sociology Department, University College, Dublin.

Chief Superintendent Rick Naylor, former President, Police Superintendent's Association.

Professor Tim Newburn, Mannheim Centre for Criminology, London School of Economics.

Peter Neyroud, Chief Constable and Chief Executive, National Policing Improvement Agency.

Louise Nicholas, Midlands Centre for Criminology and Criminal Justice, Loughborough University.

Liz Owsley, National Co-ordinator, British Association for Women in Policing.

Kate Pearce, Head of Analysis, National Centre for Policing Excellence.

Professor Jill Peay, Department of Law, London School of Economics.

Ian K. Pepper, School of Social Sciences and Law, University of Teesside.

Martyn Perks, formerly Chief Inspector, Association of Chief Police Officers' Firearms Secretariat.

Dr Joanna Phoenix, School of Applied Social Sciences, Durham University.

Professor Maurice Punch, Mannheim Centre for Criminology, London School of Economics.

Paul Quinton, National Policing Improvement Agency/Home Office.

Professor John Raine, School of Public Policy, University of Birmingham.

Dr Brian Rappert, Department of Sociology and Philosophy, University of Exeter.

Dr Jerry H. Ratcliffe, Department of Criminal Justice, Temple University, USA.

Professor Mike Redmayne, Department of Law, London School of Economics.

Professor Robert Reiner, Department of Law, London School of Economics.

Dr Colin Rogers, School of Applied Sciences, University of Glamorgan.

Dr Mike Rowe, Institute of Criminology, Victoria University of Wellington, New Zealand.

Professor Stephen P. Savage, Institute of Criminal Justice Studies, University of Portsmouth.

Dr Ken Scott, Centre of Police Studies, Bell College, Scotland.

Professor Douglas Sharp, Centre for Criminal Justice Policy and Research, UCE Birmingham.

Georgie Sinclair, School of History, University of Leeds.

Dr Graham Smith, School of Law, University of Manchester.

Peter Smith QC, formerly of the Independent Commission on Policing for Northern Ireland/Judge of the Court of Appeal, Jersey and Guernsey, Deputy Judge of the High Court of Justice, Northern Ireland.

Emeritus Professor Keith Soothill, Applied Social Science Department, University of Lancaster.

Julie Spence, Chief Constable, Cambridgeshire Constabulary.

Professor Betsy Stanko, Strategic Research Unit, Metropolitan Police.

Peter Stelfox, Head of Investigative Practice, National Policing Improvement Agency.

Professor Philip Stenning, Research Institute for Law, Politics and Justice, Keele University.

Bill Taylor, formerly Commissioner of the City of London Police and Her Majesty's Inspector of Constabulary (Scotland), now of the Elmley Partnership Limited.

Professor Nick Tilley, School of Social Sciences, Nottingham Trent University and Visiting Professor at the Jill Dando Institute of Crime Science, University College London.

Dr Steve Tong, Department of Crime and Police Studies, Canterbury Christ Church University.

Rachel Tuffin, National Policing Improvement Agency.

Paul Turnbull, Institute for Criminal Policy Research, King's College London.

Professor P.A.J. Waddington, Policy Research Institute, University of Wolverhampton.

Dr Alison Wakefield, Department of Sociology, City University.

Professor Clive Walker, Centre for Criminal Justice Studies, University of Leeds.

Professor David S. Wall, Centre for Criminal Justice Studies, University of Leeds.

Steve Warner, Her Majesty's Inspectorate of Constabulary.

Dr Colin Webster, School of Social Sciences, Leeds Metropolitan University.

Professor Robin Williams, School of Applied Social Sciences, University of Durham.

Alan Wright, formerly Keele University.

Professor Emeritus Michael Zander QC, Mannheim Centre for Criminology, London School of Economics.

The above list of contributors shows the position they held at the time of writing their entry.

Table of cases

About this book

This Dictionary has been compiled for those working within policing or who are involved in educational or training courses linked with policing. The project has developed in part from the academic and commercial success of the *Handbook of Policing* (Newburn 2003). We have sought to build upon the glossary provided in the Handbook – to map out in alphabetical form many of the major terms and concepts used in discussion of contemporary policing. The volume is part of a major new series of Dictionaries from Willan Publishing covering other aspects of criminal justice and the criminal justice system. Two of these – the *Dictionary of Probation and Offender Management* (Canton and Hancock 2007) and the *Dictionary of Prisons and Punishment* (Jewkes and Bennett 2007) – have already been published with great success, and we very much hope the *Dictionary of Policing* will help build on this.

There are some 200 entries in this Dictionary. They have been contributed by a very wide range of academics and professionals in or connected with the Police Service. The contributors are all experts in their particular fields and the entries represent their views of particular topics – there is no editorial line adopted in this volume, other than that we have striven to maintain high standards both in terms of the clarity of the language used and in relation to the substance provided in each of the items. Individual entries are of varying length. They vary from 500 to 1,500 words according to the nature and importance of the particular topic. You will find that the entries have a standard format. Each starts with a short definition. The main substance of the entry follows, and there is a set of 'Key texts and sources' at the end. This includes key website references as well as more standard forms of publication. Full citations are contained in the 'List of references' at the end of the Dictionary. The 'Key texts and sources' point the reader to the next steps that might be taken in exploring a particular area, both in terms of further reading and in identifying some of the more useful and reliable web-based resources that exist. In addition, wherever relevant, we have also provided an indication of where there are related entries in the Dictionary.

The primary focus of the Dictionary is policing within the UK, although attention has been paid wherever possible to international issues and to topics that bear in some important way on policing in the UK. At an early stage we decided against attempting to make this Dictionary truly international and comparative in focus. We did so as we judged that such a task – though potentially valuable – was extraordinarily difficult to achieve successfully. Moreover, there are some very significant changes taking place in relation to the education and training of police officers in the UK, and it seemed to us that this was a propitious moment at which to launch a Dictionary that would meet the needs of people on the new courses in criminal justice and police studies that have proliferated in the last decade or so, together with those studying on now well established courses. This is an exciting time to be involved in, and to be studying, policing, and we hope this volume will help elucidate many of the issues that arise in contemporary debates.

Tim Newburn
Peter Neyroud

Acknowledgements

The compilation of this volume, which represents the work of almost 120 authors and comprises some 200 entries, would obviously not have been possible without the support and assistance of many colleagues. It has been a privilege to work with each and all of the contributing authors who, despite being busy, still managed to retain good humour and to observe tight deadlines throughout the editorial and production process.

The editors would also like to thank Iman Heflin and Pam Taylor for their work in helping manage the complex and lengthy process of communicating with authors and collating the entries. Particular thanks are due to David Kershaw for the enormous skill that went into the reading and editing of the text. He saved us from many errors and considerably eased the final stages of production. The production process itself was handled with great efficiency by Michelle and Bill Antrobus at Deer Park Productions. A number of colleagues read and commented on elements of the dictionary. We thank them all, but wish to acknowledge a particular debt to Rob C. Mawby. Finally, as always, our thanks to Brian Willan and everyone associated with Willan Publishing for their support and professionalism.

Introduction and overview

It is perhaps unusual to begin a dictionary with an essay. Most dictionaries simply begin with some instructions about how individual entries should be read and what the abbreviations and other textual signs and markers mean (we have done that elsewhere). However, for a number of reasons we felt that a short introductory piece was important in this volume. In part, we wanted to explain why we felt there was a need for a *Dictionary of Policing* – and we will come to this shortly. At least as importantly, however, we wanted to take the chance to put what follows into some sort of historical, political and professional context. This Dictionary, like any other document on policing, is a product of its times. In what follows, therefore, we will reflect a little on the nature of these times and what they have to say about policing as it is currently organized and practised.

THE HISTORY OF POLICING

We are fast approaching the 200th anniversary of the introduction of the New Police in London. We have already passed similar anniversaries marking the emergence of formal police forces in various parts of Scotland and in Ireland. Not surprisingly, these last two centuries have seen some far-reaching changes in the nature and organization of policing in the UK and beyond. Arguably, however, it is in recent decades that the greatest and most sustained changes have occurred. These changes, some of the detail of which we will come to in a minute, present some profound challenges for modern policing. As a consequence, policing itself has been changing markedly. Moreover, there is every likelihood that it will continue to change at a fairly rapid pace in coming years.

When we use the term 'policing' here we are referring in the main to the duties carried out by officers employed by public constabularies. Of course, policing activities are carried out by a much broader range of officials, and this has been the case for far longer than we have had public constabularies. The term 'constable' emerged in Norman times. The medieval officer-holder with this title was responsible for maintaining the peace, though it has been argued that some of these responsibilities were usurped by justices of the peace from the fourteenth century onward (Critchley 1978 though see Emsley 1991 for a counter-view). The gradual formalization of policing throughout the eighteenth century and the creation of what we now recognize as police forces throughout the first half of the nineteenth century occurred for complex reasons. Although Whiggish historians have portrayed the emergence of the New Police as a largely functional response to growing problems of crime and disorderliness, one doesn't have to be a fully fledged Marxist to appreciate that the importance, for both the state and capital, of imposing order upon, and controlling the behaviour of, the working poor in a rapidly industrializing Britain was a major task.

Two important points arise from this. First, *policing* is about far more than just *the police*. Secondly, although public constabularies continue to secure high levels of public confidence and support, it is important to remember that the introduction of police forces was both a controversial measure and one that was subject to a certain amount of both political and popular resistance. This is important because policing is something that is never without controversy and, arguably, should never be accepted uncritically. However vital one considers policing to be in the maintenance of order, one must always remember that it also carries with it the potential for repression.

When thinking about the introduction of policing in the early nineteenth century, it is also important to remind ourselves of the mandate they were given. The first instruction book for the Metropolitan Police suggested that every effort of the police was to be directed towards the prevention of crime. It went on: 'The security of person and property, the preservation of public tranquillity and all other objects of a police establishment will thus be better effected than by the detection and punishment of the offender after he has succeeded in committing the crime.' There are two aspects of this description of police duties that are important. The first is the primacy it gives to prevention over other activities – even though prevention was fairly narrowly conceived at the time. The second concerns the very broad range of tasks encompassed by these first instructions, including not only crime prevention but also the keeping of the peace and the detection and punishment of offenders. To this day, the existence of a myriad of contrasting, sometimes overlapping and even occasionally contradictory, responsibilities represents one of the major challenges for the police.

These are just two of the many long-standing themes that continue to affect policing and to infuse contemporary debates around policing. The ways in which these things are played out differ, often markedly, from how they would have been seen and disputed in previous eras. Nevertheless, in very general terms much of what constitutes controversy in modern policing has, in some form or other, been a source of friction and debate for much of the period in which we have something that we recognize as policing in its modern, bureaucratic form. The best discussion of these issues is still to be found in Robert Reiner's (2000) classic book, *The Politics of the Police*. There he examines the emergence, development and construction of British policing as both a practical and ideological project. As he goes on to show, it was a hugely successful project, partly as a result of a number of thoughtful strategic decisions taken by the main architects of the New Police. Crucially, however, it was also aided and abetted by the very specific historical circumstances pertaining at that moment – not least the consolidation of the modern nation-state and the twentieth-century project that gave rise to a very particular form of citizenship – which together provided fertile ground upon which this quintessentially modern institution could flourish.

However, as modern social theorists are so fond of pointing out, our world is no longer quintessentially *modern*. It is, they argue, *post*-modern or *late*-modern. We live in very changed – and still quickly changing – social circumstances. These affect the way we live, interact, communicate, and think. These changed circumstances also, of course, have a potentially profound effect upon our major institutions, including the police. Crucially, they change, often in very marked ways, the circumstances under which such institutions operate. Let us look in slightly greater detail at the nature of some of these major controversies.

CURRENT DEBATES AND CONTROVERSIES

Reiner identifies eight separate strands to the police legitimation project:

- *Bureaucratic organization*: an emphasis on professionalism, training, high standards of discipline and a quasi-military command structure.
- *Rule of law*: the impression that police behaviour was governed by the criminal law in much the same way as the behaviour of any other citizen.
- *Strategy of minimal force*: the police force was largely unarmed and was believed to use the minimum of force necessary to settle disputes and resolve conflicts.
- *Non-partisanship*: that police forces were not directed by politicians and had a degree of freedom from political control.
- *Accountability*: that the police were accountable to the law, on the one hand, and, on the other, were subject to scrutiny and oversight by outside bodies.
- *Service role*: the police engaged in a broad range of activities – services – beyond merely dealing with those matters that required the use of coercive force.
- *Preventive policing*: as we have seen, from the first instruction book onward, a central part of the police mandate concerned visible preventive patrol and a deliberate playing down of plain clothes and covert activities.
- *Police effectiveness*: the creation of an image of effectiveness in the delivery of the key objectives of maintaining order and controlling crime.

Just as each of these formed an important part of the process by which police legitimacy was gradually established and embedded, each has also come under challenge over the past 30 or 40 years, and these challenges collectively provide much of the explanation for the apparent decline in police legitimacy from its high point in the decade and a half after the Second World War. Thus, for example, police misconduct and corruption scandals have led to a questioning of standards of conduct and the extent to which the police are subject to the rule of law. Police activity, particularly in the public order sphere, has led to accusations of paramilitarism and, in the case of some disputes, such as the 1984–5 miners' strike, of political partisanship. The tripartite system of accountability as conceived in the 1960s has been under stress, initially by the perceived inability of the local police authorities to hold their chiefs to account, but more recently and more fundamentally by the shift towards more national accountability.

As government-inspired managerialism gradually took hold, crime control objectives increasingly took on greater and greater importance and centrality – apparently at the expense of the service role so important to the development of police legitimacy. As is visible in many aspects of contemporary criminal justice, the current emphasis on risk-oriented thinking has led to a substantially increased emphasis within the police on proactive, often covert, action. Such approaches are given further impetus by the crime-fighting mandate and through reliance on managerialist target-setting. Finally, the rise and rise of crime rates – at least until the mid-1990s – led to a growing cacophony of voices questioning police effectiveness. Crucially, of course, the social circumstances in which policing takes place have also changed. The relatively deferential nature of the post-war social order has given way progressively to a more complex, fast-moving world in which the ideals of inclusive citizenship have come under pressure from various directions. Policing has once again become the subject of considerable discussion and no little controversy.

Over the last decade or so debates over policing have been dominated by three primary issues: the relationship between the police and minority communities; the shape and structure of the Police Service itself; and the police role in the delivery of security and reassurance. We will take each briefly in turn.

Police and minority communities

From the Notting Hill 'race riots' of the late 1950s – captured by Colin McInnes in his 1959 novel, *Absolute Beginners* – through Stuart Hall and colleagues' analysis of the developing moral panic around mugging in the 1970s and the Scarman Inquiry into the Brixton riot in the early 1980s, to the Stephen Lawrence Inquiry in the late 1990s, problems in police–minority community relationships regularly punctuated the last half century.

Indeed, the shadow of the Stephen Lawrence Inquiry still hangs over British policing. Lord Justice Macpherson's use of the term 'institutional racism' in his analysis of the shortcomings of the investigation of the murder of Stephen Lawrence continues to resonate in public debates whenever the nature of the Police Service's relationship with minority communities is called into question. Although the Police Service embarked on a massive programme of activity in the aftermath of the inquiry, research suggests that evidence of positive change is at best mixed (Foster *et al.* 2005).

Though the pace of change in the Police Service may have been slower than some would wish, the Lawrence case certainly had an appreciable impact on the political climate. Reiner (2000: 211) suggested that the inquiry's report had 'transformed the terms of the political debate about black people and criminal justice…what had not [previously] featured in public awareness and political debate was the disproportionate rate at which black people suffered as victims of crime'. This remains one of the greatest challenges facing a modern police service: dealing with the perception among minorities that they are over-policed and under-protected.

The shape of the Police Service

Centralization has arguably been the dominant trend in British policing in recent decades. The growing power and influence of central government is the most visible aspect of this transformation. Driven in part by managerialist changes imposed by central government, the Police Service has itself become more homogeneous in its aims, objectives and tactics. Indeed, as Robert Reiner presciently argued some time ago, we are close to having a national police service in all but name. For this reason and others, it is clear that the debate about the size and number of police forces is unlikely to go away.

It is not long ago now that it was very seriously mooted that the current 43 constabularies in England and Wales be merged and regionalized to create a new structure of somewhere between 17 and 24 forces. The proposed changes did not go ahead – largely because of the funding consequences of the changes and problems of negotiating them through Parliament – and they have not seriously re-emerged for public scrutiny since. Instead, a more piecemeal process of stronger encouragement for collaboration, supported by enhanced provisions for collaborative working in the Police and Justice Act 2006, is taking shape. It remains to be seen whether this will stave off the need for a more fundamental appraisal of the structure of policing.

The second danger is that regionalization or some other form of reorganization will take policing even further away from local communities. The vast bulk of policing is local in character, and yet there have been many developments since the 1960s that have had the effect of increasing citizens' sense that they have little positive connection with local policing. Much effort in recent times has gone into 'neighbourhood policing' – the latest attempt to re-embed policing within local communities. There is a clear risk that such a programme could be undermined by an approach that did not consider very carefully the consequences for the whole of policing, from neighbourhoods to national.

The third, and related, danger is that reorganization swings the pendulum even further towards central government domination of police activities. The strongest area for consensus between the political parties is that there is a need to consider reforms to local governance to strengthen the local ownership of policing, particularly at the neighbourhood level. This is widely seen as an important counterbalance to greater national involvement in performance standards and areas of more obvious national interest, such as counter-terrorism, organized crime and serious crime.

The delivery of security

In large part because of the perceived and actual threat of international terrorism, security has become an ever-present theme of contemporary social policy. Increasingly, a wide array of government activity – from immigration policy to international aid – is seen through the lens of security. The police are in the unenviable position of being the agency most closely associated with what one might think of as 'everyday security' concerns linked with the protection of person and property against criminal acts, as well as playing a very significant role in what hitherto have been defined as 'national security' concerns – threats that are generally perceived to come from beyond the nation-state.

This environment pulls the police in radically different directions simultaneously. First, and as previously discussed, there are very substantial pressures on the police both to provide a visible presence within local communities and to be the lynchpin in localized crime prevention, investigation and control efforts. In part, neighbourhood policing arose from the identification of what became known as the 'reassurance gap': the fact that, despite apparently falling crime rates, a majority of citizens continued to believe that crime – nationally and locally – was rising. Public belief that things are getting worse drives up both demands upon, and expectations of, the police. A series of inquiries in the 1980s (the Sheehy Inquiry [1993]; the Core and Ancillary Tasks Review [1995]; and, the Cassels Inquiry [1994], among others) were all driven, in part, by a concern to explore how limited police resources might best be managed and used to deal with the array of demands facing the service. Although not stated quite so explicitly, such concerns also underpin the more recent review of policing undertaken by Sir Ronnie Flanagan (2007).

Notwithstanding the great many inquiries, change in the last 20 years has been rather piecemeal and reactive. There have been a succession of waves of reform that have focused only on one or two dimensions of policing at a time. Moreover, reform has tended to avoid any real application of principles to police reform. To the extent that they have been met, public demands in relation to policing have been managed in large part by pressure from the Police Service for increased resources and by extending the 'policing family'. In the midst of this proliferation of policing bodies and agents, it remains the case that we lack a clear statement which clarifies what is considered to be the core role of the public constabularies and which distinguishes them from others – whether they be partners or competitors. It is nearly 50 years since the last Royal Commission on Policing. Whether the time has come for another one or not, it is certainly time for a careful debate on the whole of policing, from neighbourhood through to national, with future reforms considered carefully against the whole, supported by the sustained development of evidence and as wide a consensus as possible.

EDUCATION AND TRAINING

The social and educational backgrounds of senior police officers have changed markedly in the course of the last half-century (Reiner 1991; Wall 1998). Indeed, the socio-economic and educational backgrounds of police officers generally have altered in recent times (Lee and Punch 2006). A graduate entry scheme was created in the late 1960s and the numbers of officers with higher educational qualifications has been expanding rapidly.

There has been an accelerating push to codify and professionalize practice, which began to take shape seriously in the mid-1980s with the creation of national codes for the police use of firearms and the standardization of procedures for investigating major crime. Over the last 10 years, the Association of Chief Police Officers (ACPO) and the National Centre of Policing Excellence (now part of the Policy and Practice Directorate of the National Policing Improvement Agency – NPIA) have codified over 80 areas of practice, using the codes and guidance as the basis of national learning programmes and the framework for an emerging national approach to the accreditation of practice. On top of this, the Skills Sector Council, Skills for Justice, has worked with the Police Service to develop a national competency framework for policing.

With the creation of the NPIA, police education, training and development have now moved into a single agency, which has been designed to be 'Police Service led and owned'. The responsibility for the governance of the development of police leadership and training has shifted out of the Home Office and into the NPIA, with a board chaired by ACPO providing oversight. For the first time since the original National Police Staff College was set up in the 1960s, the Police Service has assumed responsibility for its own leadership development, a possible prelude to a new phase of professionalization and modernization. The NPIA has an openly declared aim of developing 'evidence-based practice' and linking this to the learning programmes and personal development of police officers and staff.

It is these and other changes that we believe make the publication of a *Dictionary of Policing* particularly timely. Our hope is that it will provide a reliable guide to many of the key concepts and ideas that students and practitioners regularly encounter, and our intention is that it should complement the wider reading undertaken by all those involved in police-related education and training.

Tim Newburn
Peter Neyroud

ACCOUNTABILITY AND GOVERNANCE

There are two distinct forms of accountability within writing on policing and the police. The first is *policy accountability* – the degree of influence exercised by external democratic bodies over police organizational policies concerned with overall goals, resource allocation and policing styles. The second is *individual accountability* – the extent to which, and the ways in which, individual police officers are held to account for their behaviour as they go about their day-to-day activities (Reiner 1995).

In writing on policy accountability, the term 'police governance' has been used to denote the constitutional and institutional infrastructure for framing and directing the policies of the police (Lustgarten 1986). There is now a substantial body of research on the policy accountability of the police in the UK, most of which has focused on England and Wales (though see Walker 2000 for an analysis that also includes the distinct systems in Scotland and Northern Ireland). In England and Wales, the Police Act 1964 divided responsibility for policing policy in the 41 provincial police forces (outside London) between the three parties of the 'tripartite structure': police authorities (including a majority of locally elected councillors), central government (the Home Office) and chief constables. The Metropolitan Police – Britain's largest and most influential force – operated with the Home Secretary as its police authority until the Greater London Authority Act 1999, which introduced a statutory police authority for London, including local government representation. Policing policy was thus supposed to be balanced between a combination of local, national and professional interests. The tripartite structure contained a good deal of studied ambiguity about the relative powers of each party and became the subject of heated controversy during the 1970s and 1980s when local Labour authorities challenged the jealously guarded 'operational independence' of chief constables. These arguments were repeatedly resolved in favour of chief constables, supported by the courts and central government. There was, however, some recognition that local police commanders – the senior officers in charge of the local geographical units of policing, or 'basic command units' (BCUs) – needed to consult more closely with their communities.

From the late 1980s onwards, the challenge to chief constables' policy-making autonomy came increasingly from national rather than local government. The key factor underpinning the increasingly terse relationships between chief constables and central government ministers (of both main parties) was successive government attempts to reform the Police Service along the same centrally driven performance model that has been applied to other public services. In effect, this has served to continue a longer-term trend towards growing national control over policing policy. Home Office influence has expanded in a variety of ways in recent decades, through issuing policy circulars in a range of areas, greater control over the training and career paths of senior police officers, the increased proportion of police funding that comes from central government and, from the late 1980s onwards, the development of an increasingly vigorous national performance framework. Increasingly, managerial and contractual forms of police accountability have come to displace political forms (Jones 2003).

A further illustration of growing central control over policing policy is the emergence of national policing organizations, the most recent example being the establishment of the Serious and Organized Crime Agency (SOCA) in 2006. Part of the justification for the establishment of SOCA was that many provincial forces were considered too small to be able to provide these functions effectively. In 2005, it seemed that further radical centralization of control over policing was imminent, when the then Home Secretary stated his strong support for a restructuring of police organization in England and Wales into a much smaller number of large regional forces. This raised grave concerns among some police chiefs and local authorities about the lack of local accountability in the proposed structures, though supporters of the restructuring argued that accountability mechanisms would be most effectively developed at BCU level. However, a combination of local bodies' lack of statutory powers and the likelihood that local police chiefs would be constrained by regional and national influence cast doubts on how accountable to the local democratic process such large forces would be. In the event, the proposed restructuring became mired in controversy and was postponed indefinitely following a change of Home Secretary in 2006. In a striking reversal of party positions during the 1980s, calls for more direct control of policing by locally elected bodies have most recently come from Conservative sources, who have attacked the Labour government for its centralizing tendencies (Loveday and Reid 2003).

Turning to individual accountability, there is a substantial literature about the mechanisms used to regulate and control the activities of individual police officers and the systems of complaint and redress against them (Goldsmith and Lewis 2000). A formal system for dealing with complaints against the police in England and Wales was introduced by the Police Act 1964, though it lacked any independent element in the investigation and adjudication of complaints. This independent element in the oversight of the complaints process (if not the investigation) was gradually introduced with the establishment, first, of the Police Complaints Board in the 1970s and then the Police Complaints Authority (PCA) in 1984. The PCA supervised the investigation of more serious incidents referred to it by the police. It also provided regular official comment on certain police policies and practices. Research has cast doubt on the effectiveness of this complaints system, from the viewpoint both of police officers and from those who made complaints (Maguire and Corbett 1991). A key source of criticism concerned the fact that those undertaking the investigation were still police officers, albeit from another division or force. The PCA was abolished by the Police Reform Act 2002 and replaced with the Independent Police Complaints Commission (IPCC). Unlike its predecessors, the IPCC has its own independent investigators, enabling it to oversee police investigations into serious complaints or, alternatively, to investigate them itself. Although most discussion of individual forms of police accountability focuses on formal complaints systems, Dixon and Smith (1998) demonstrate how the civil law has increasingly been used as a remedy for police misconduct. In particular, civil actions appear to be growing in popularity as an alternative to the police complaints systems as a means of redress for police misconduct in particular instances.

The majority of existing literature on accountability concerns the public police. This appears increasingly anomalous in the light of the pluralization of policing that has occurred over recent decades. Policing is now both authorized and delivered by diverse networks of commercial bodies, voluntary and community groups, individual citizens, and national and local governmental regulatory agencies, as well as the public police (Bayley and Shearing 2001). These developments echo an influential body of thinking in political science concerning the changing ways in which societies are governed. In particular, the term governance has been used – in a different way from the use of the term 'police governance' as outlined above – to capture the ways in which the governing process has become more complex and fragmented and cannot be regarded as the preserve of state institutions. Rather, it is increasingly characterized by 'inter-organizational networks', including commercial, community and voluntary bodies as well as state institutions (Rhodes 1997). These changes have been linked to a range of developments associated with neoliberal reform programmes, such as privatization, contracting out and the creation of semi-autonomous service delivery agencies. Such developments have, it is argued, led to a fragmentation of the state, reducing central state's control over the implementation of policy and further encouraging the development of inter-organizational networks.

Recent work has applied this broader notion of governance to the context of policing (Johnston 2000). Some authors have argued that the fragmented nature of contemporary policing requires new ways of thinking about what policing is and what it is for. It has been suggested that 'security governance' provides a more appropriate term for thinking about these issues than does the term 'policing', which remains strongly associated with the institutions of the state (Johnston and Shearing 2003). In particular, it is argued that we need to develop ways of bringing these increasingly influential 'security networks' under the direction and control of democratic governance. Loader (2000) has proposed the establishment of local, regional and national 'policing commissions' with a statutory responsibility to monitor and direct policing policy as exercised by a wide range of 'policing' agencies and institutions. This kind of thinking was influential in shaping the recommendation of the Patten Commission on policing reform in Northern Ireland for the establishment of 'district policing partnership boards'. These would be a committee of the local authority with the power to 'buy in' extra local policing resources from providers other than the public police. It also recommended that, at force level, a 'policing board' (not a 'police board') should be established that would have substantially more powers than the existing police authority (Shearing 2000). It was suggested that this body might be given responsibility for regulating all policing providers, including commercial firms, and for co-ordinating provision across policing networks. The government's legislative response to the Patten Commission ultimately held back on some of these elements. However, although perhaps its time had not yet come, the model laid down by Patten provided an interesting way of approaching the problem of governing local security networks. This requires the effective management of the diversity of policing provision and the maintenance of standards of accountability and equity (Johnston 2000).

Trevor Jones

Related entries

Bichard Inquiry; Constabulary independence; Corruption (police); Deaths in police custody (DPCs); Ethics in policing; Independent advisory groups; Legitimacy; National security; New public management (NPM); Patten Report; Plural policing; Police Act 1964; Police and Magistrates' Courts Act 1994; Police authorities; Police powers; Police Reform Act 2002; Royal Commission on the Police (1962).

Key texts and sources

Goldsmith, A. and Lewis, C. (eds) (2000) *Civilian Oversight of Policing: Governance, Democracy and Human Rights.* Portland, OR: Hart Publishing.

Jones, T. (2003) 'The governance and accountability of policing', in T. Newburn (ed.) *Handbook of Policing.* Cullompton: Willan Publishing.

Walker, N. (2000) *Policing in a Changing Constitutional Order.* London: Sweet & Maxwell.

See also **http://www.crimereduction.gov.uk/active communities/activecommunities49.htm** for a Home Office report into public perceptions of police accountability. The Police Federation's website also contains a page on accountability (**http://www. polfed.org/we_stand_accountability.asp**). The Independent Police Complaints Commission's website is at **http://www.ipcc.gov.uk/**.

ANTI-SOCIAL BEHAVIOUR

> Anti-social behaviour is defined in law as '[a person acting] ... in a manner which caused or was likely to cause, harassment, alarm or distress to one or more persons not of the same household as himself' (Crime and Disorder Act 1998, s. 1).

Dealing with anti-social behaviour is a policing target, yet what is meant by this term? The phrase has always been familiar to psychologists and psychiatrists, but until recently was not otherwise in common use. Through government agency it is now widely applied to social and environmental incivilities in public space, yet definitions remain entirely subjective. Section 1 of the Crime and Disorder Act 1998 created a legal definition as cited above, which is far from precise: the legal wording copies existing public order legislation, and it is largely in connection with public order that the police will be called upon to exercise their powers against 'anti-social behaviour'.

One consequence has been a large expansion of police powers. The best known instrument is the anti-social behaviour order (ASBO), provided in s. 1 of the Crime and Disorder Act 1998. Police or local authorities (but local authorities only in Scotland, having consulted the police) can apply to magistrates for ASBOs. The Anti-social Behaviour Act 2003 (s. 30) provided the dispersal order, giving the police the power to designate local areas where groups can be banished for displaying anti-social behaviour, and with a power – suspended following a successful legal challenge – to impose curfews for under 16-year-olds. Summary closure of crack houses became available in Part 1 of the Act. Penalty notices for disorder have been introduced, covering a wide range of misbehaviour, from public urination to underage drinking. These powers have been taken up by many police forces with enthusiasm.

What has driven the New Labour government's crusade against bad behaviour, expressed not only in legislation but also in aggressive marketing by the Home Office? It stems from a recognition by local politicians and MPs in deprived areas that there are poor communities where harassment and nuisance behaviour severely affect people's quality of life. As this often takes the form of repeat low-level crime, the criminal courts, it was alleged, were unable to deal adequately with the cumulative effect, and the police were anyway unlikely to take action. Simultaneously, some local authority landlords were keen to expand the disciplinary powers available under housing legislation.

From his days as shadow Home Secretary, former Prime Minister Tony Blair expressed a personal commitment to protecting communities from unwanted behaviour, inspired by beliefs in communitarian ideas and reinforced by the American zero-tolerance approach. While still in opposition, New Labour drafted the controversial policy which led to the introduction of the ASBO.

The ASBO is a controversial instrument for several reasons. It is a civil order but becomes an individual crime, imprisonable for up to five years, if its terms are breached. It takes the form of prohibitions tailored to the individual case, and these must run for at least two years. The terms are supposed to limit the capacity of the recipient to repeat the behaviour in question and often involve territorial bans – not only exclusion from streets affected by the conduct but also sometimes from whole local authority areas or even the whole country (making enforcement even more difficult). Associations with named persons or types of venue are also often forbidden. There is no limit to the number or type of prohibitions, although proportionality is supposed to be observed. The Court of Appeal has stated that criminal acts should not be included, since there is an obligation on everyone to obey the law.

ASBOs are undoubtedly popular with the public but have attracted criticism on grounds of legitimacy and human rights. An appeal to the House of Lords on the issue of hearsay evidence (which circumvents witness intimidation) was rejected on the grounds that the order was a civil one and therefore not subject to the right of a fair trial in criminal cases. However, it was ruled that courts should be 'sure' of the evidence of anti-social behaviour – a standard equivalent to the criminal 'beyond reasonable doubt'.

Concern has been expressed about the imposition of ASBOs on juveniles: some 40 per cent are imposed on 10–17-year-olds, and many receive custody for breach. The order severely disrupts the lives of young people, including family life, and recipients are not allowed the normal protection of anonymity accorded to young offenders.

The Police Reform Act 2002 gave courts the power to impose ASBOs ancillary to criminal convictions. These 'CRASBOs' rapidly became the main element pushing up the volume of orders. Some police forces have deliberately used them against persistent offenders because breach is easier and quicker to prove than repeat offending.

Young people are widely perceived as the main perpetrators of anti-social behaviour. 'Youths hanging about' comes top of the list of aggravation in the British Crime Survey and many local polls. The British Crime Survey also confirms that people living in council estates and other poor housing neighbourhoods are by far the most likely to complain of serious anti-social behaviour, including drug dealing and use. The anti-social behaviour label is attached to many plainly criminal acts, as well as to those that are just a nuisance.

Although personal aggression, especially 'nasty neighbours', was the main focus when the ASBO was introduced, the campaign against anti-social behaviour has been widened to include many environmental nuisances and incivilities (e.g. graffiti, public drinking). Many local practitioners prefer a problem-solving approach rather than automatic enforcement. For instance, the removal of abandoned cars reduces perceptions of anti-social behaviour (this reflects the broken windows theory that visible disorder creates a sense of insecurity and damages community confidence). A hierarchy of responses – such as warnings, mediation, situational prevention or the informal acceptable behaviour contracts – may suit individual cases.

Neighbourhood policing and, in particular, reassurance policing, are meant to involve police officers directly throughout the anti-social behaviour spectrum. The more police officers are required to listen to community concerns, the more they encounter demands based on a range of tolerance levels. If people are encouraged to complain about anti-social behaviour, they are likely always to find things to complain about. Until clearer definitions and boundaries are set around the notion of anti-social behaviour, it may cause problems for local police.

Elizabeth Burney

Related entries

Audit Commission; Broken windows; Community safety; Community support officers (CSOs); Crime and Disorder Act 1998; Crime prevention (situational and social); Dispersal orders; Neighbourhood policing; Youth and policing.

Key texts and sources

Ashworth, A. (2004) 'Social control and "anti-social behaviour": the subversion of human rights?', *Law Quarterly Review*, 120: 263–91.

Burney, E. (2005) *Making People Behave: Anti-social Behaviour, Politics and Policy.* Cullompton: Willan Publishing.

Flint, J. (ed.) (2006) *Housing, Urban Governance, and Anti-social Behaviour.* Bristol: Policy Press.

Squires, P. and Stephens, D. (2005) *Rougher Justice: Anti-social Behaviour and Young People.* Cullompton: Willan Publishing.

See also the Crime Reduction website (http//www.crimereduction.gov.uk) and http//www.community-safety.net. The Home Office's web page regarding anti-social behaviour is at http://www.homeoffice.gov.uk/anti-social-behaviour/. The Home Office's web page regarding ASBOs is at http://www.homeoffice.gov.uk/anti-social-behaviour/penalties/anti-social-behaviour-orders/.

ARREST

An arrest is an overt restriction on a citizen's liberty and must therefore conform to many safeguards and procedures. The vast majority of summary arrest powers are contained in the Police and Criminal Evidence Act 1984 (PACE). Arrest powers may also be conferred on officers outside the Police Service (e.g. officers serving with the Serious Organized Crime Agency), and, under certain circumstances, an ordinary citizen may make an arrest.

The power to make arrests is the most important and well-known aspect of police powers. An arrest also constitutes a very overt restriction on the liberty of a citizen and must therefore conform to the many safeguards and procedures that have evolved in modern times. This has become especially important in view of the Human Rights Act 1998. According to Code of Practice G under the Police and Criminal Evidence Act 1984 (PACE): 'The right to liberty is a key principle of the Human Rights Act 1998. The exercise of the power of arrest represents an obvious and significant interference with that right.'

Arrests are made under the authority of a warrant or summarily without a warrant. Arrests under warrant are made far less frequently than those without. Some of the most common arrest warrants are issued by magistrates where a person has failed to appear in court to answer a summons, or where a person aged at least 17 years is concerned in an imprisonable offence or whose address cannot be established.

The vast majority of summary arrest powers are to be found under ss. 24 and 24A of PACE. Section 24 states that a police officer may arrest without a warrant anyone who is about to commit, or is committing, an offence, or where there are reasonable grounds to suspect either. If an offence has been committed and the suspect is guilty of it, or this is reasonably suspected, a police officer may arrest the suspect. A police officer has a further arrest power where he or she has reasonable grounds to suspect that an offence has been committed and there are reasonable

grounds to suspect a person to be guilty of it. Section 24 of PACE then provides that these summary arrest powers may be exercised only where there are reasonable grounds for believing that any of the following conditions are fulfilled: to enable the suspect's name and/or address to be ascertained; and to prevent the suspect from suffering physical injury or causing physical harm to him or herself or another person, or causing loss of or damage to property, or committing an offence against public decency, or causing an unlawful obstruction of the highway. The arrest conditions also include the protection of a child or other vulnerable person from the suspect; allowing the prompt and effective investigation of the offence or of the suspect's conduct; or preventing any prosecution for the offence being hindered by the suspect's disappearance. Police arrest powers are now subject to Code of Practice G under PACE that came into force on 1 January 2006. This was the first time that codes of practice were formulated with regard to police powers of arrest, and these may be amended from time to time, as are the other codes under PACE.

A relatively small number of police arrest powers exist under other statutory provisions, although these relate to specific purposes, such as s. 41 of the Terrorism Act 2000 which states that a police officer may arrest without a warrant a person whom he or she reasonably suspects to be a terrorist. There is also the common law power to prevent or deal with a breach of the peace. Among other things, this enables the police (and ordinary citizens) to arrest persons who are causing or threatening violence, or damage to property. This definition of a breach of the peace was stated in R v. Howell and therefore goes beyond mere noisy or exuberant behaviour. It may not always be necessary to arrest a person who is committing or threatening a breach of the peace, as the law permits temporary restraint, such as holding a person back to enable the person to calm down (see Albert v Lavin).

Arrest powers are not only conferred on officers in the Police Service. Officers serving in the Serious Organized Crime Agency may be designated the powers of a police officer for specific duties, whereas others may be given the powers of an immigration officer or the customs powers of an officer of HM Revenue and Customs.

There is also the citizen's arrest power, which is largely enshrined in s. 24A of PACE (plus the common law power to prevent or deal with a breach of the peace). Section 24A enables any ordinary citizen to make an arrest where an indictable offence is being committed or where there are reasonable grounds to suspect this. Furthermore, an ordinary citizen may make an arrest where an indictable offence has been committed and the suspect is guilty of it, or where there are reasonable grounds for suspecting the person to be guilty of it. Note the much narrower range of circumstances compared with those available to the police. Also, the citizen's arrest power is confined to *indictable* offences and not all offences. Indictable offences are those crimes that must be tried before a judge and jury in the Crown court, or those offences that are triable either way and may be tried before a magistrates' court or the Crown court. The surrounding circumstances that may justify a citizen's arrest under s. 24A of PACE are to prevent the suspect causing physical injury to him or herself or to any other person; to prevent the suspect from suffering physical injury; to prevent the suspect causing loss of or damage to property; or to prevent the suspect from making off before a police officer can assume responsibility for him or her. These may only apply where it appears to the person making the arrest that it is not reasonably practicable for a police officer to make the arrest instead.

Arrest procedures must conform to the provisions stated in PACE and Code G. These include informing the suspect that he or she is being arrested and the reason why, followed by the administration of the caution. This should be accompanied by the police officer making a clear indication that the suspect is under legal restraint. Words alone may be sufficient, although it is more common for the police officer to take a firm hold of the suspect, especially if there is some resistance and/or the likelihood of escape. The use of handcuffs may be necessary where the latter is occurring or is likely to occur, and any further force must be reasonable in all the circumstances.

Leonard Jason-Lloyd

Related entries

Constabulary independence; Criminal investigation; Custody; Defendants; Drugs and policing; Police and Criminal Evidence Act 1984 (PACE); Police powers; Warrants.

Key texts and sources

Clark, D. (2004) *Bevan and Lidstone's 'The Investigation of Crime: A Guide to the Law of Criminal Investigation'* (3rd edn). Oxford: Oxford University Press.
English, J. and Card, R. (2005) *Police Law* (9th edn). Oxford: Oxford University Press.
Jason-Lloyd, L. (2005) *An Introduction to Policing and Police Powers* (2nd edn). London: Cavendish Publishing.
Sampson, F. (2005) *Blackstone's Police Manual. Volume 4. General Police Duties.* Oxford: Oxford University Press.
Zander, M. (2005) *The Police and Criminal Evidence Act 1984* (5th edn). London: Sweet & Maxwell.
See also the Home Office's PACE web page (http://police.homeoffice.gov.uk/operational-policing/powers-pace-codes/pace-code-intro/).

ASSOCIATION OF CHIEF POLICE OFFICERS (ACPO)

The Association of Chief Police Officers (ACPO) is 'An independent, professionally led strategic body. In the public interest and, in equal and active partnership with Government and the Association of Police Authorities, ACPO leads and co-ordinates the direction and development of the police service in England, Wales and Northern Ireland. In times of national need ACPO, on behalf of all chief officers, co-ordinates the strategic policing response' (*ACPO Statement of Purpose 2006*).

The Association of Chief Police Officers (ACPO) has its origins in two chief constables' clubs dating back to the late 1800s which focused mainly on social contact, albeit their roles gradually changed to providing better co-operation between police forces and the Home Office and, increasingly, to addressing matters of national policing policy. In 1948, the Association of Chief Police Officers of England and Wales was finally formed as a unified body. The association adopted its present title of the Association of Chief Police Officers of England, Wales and Northern Ireland after the (now) Police Service of Northern Ireland joined in 1970.

Although for much of its history ACPO has, in formal terms, been merely a staff association, in practice it has become a national police organization. Through its role in the establishment of the National Reporting Centre from the 1980s onward, ACPO (and its Scottish counterpart, ACPOS) has emerged as one of the primary authoritative voices in British policing, influencing not only service-level developments but also, increasingly, national policing and criminal justice policy-making (Savage *et al.* 2000). A marked change occured when, in 1996, the Chief Police Officers' Staff Association was created to represent the interests of chief officers in the Home Office forces over salaries and conditions of service. At the same time, ACPO became a private company limited by guarantee, with a more clearly defined role to promote the effectiveness, efficiency and professionalism of the Police Service in England, Wales and Northern Ireland.

The association now has a membership consisting of police officers or senior police staff who hold the rank or appointment above that of chief superintendent or equivalent police staff grade, in the 44 police forces in England, Wales and Northern Ireland governed by the Police Act 1996, as well as in national police agencies and a number of other non-Home Office forces.

In recent times, the need to respond swiftly to demands from government, to facilitate an extensive police reform programme and to influence the policing agenda has proved to be of critical importance and has caused members to commission a fundamental review of the purpose and structure of the organization to ensure that it remains fit for purpose and can meet the demands of twenty-first-century policing.

The association now focuses on the following:

- Providing strong and visible leadership.
- Developing policing doctrine in a professional and co-ordinated manner.
- Acting as the principal voice of the service.

- Co-ordinating the strategic policing response in times of national need.
- Supporting the continuous professional development of members and the achievement of the highest standards of performance.
- Developing its business activities to ensure that the ACPO brand is recognized globally as a mark of excellence in policing.

Ken Jones

Related entries

Chief constables; Doctrine; International Association of Chiefs of Police (IACP); Police Federation; Police Superintendent's Association (PSA); Politics (police involvement); Rank structure.

Key texts and sources

The Association of Chief Police Officers' website is at **www.acpo.police.uk/**.

ATTRITION

Attrition in criminal justice refers to the disparity between the number of crimes that are committed and the number that end with a conviction.

There are a number of stages involved in the prosecution of crime. Crimes are weeded out at each stage so that only a small proportion of known crime ends in a caution or conviction. Police practices have a significant bearing on this attrition rate. In order for a crime to be investigated, it has first to be reported to the police, and attrition is initially caused by the non-reporting of crime. The perception that the Police Service was unsympathetic to such crimes as sexual, racial or domestic violence resulted in victims being reluctant to report their experiences. This produced a number of reforms (such as the formation of domestic violence units, specialist rape centres and community safety units) designed to make the Police Service more victim oriented.

The Police Service may also have influenced the attrition rate by not recording some of the crimes reported to it. One way to do this was 'cuffing', whereby a reported crime was either not recorded at all or was downgraded to an incident that did not have to be included in the official crime statistics. To address this problem the National Crime Recording Standard was introduced by the Association of Chief Police Officers and the Home Office in 2002 to provide for a greater degree of reliability and consistency in the collection and recording of crime data.

Crimes reported to the police and recorded by them are investigated, and the investigation forms the basis of the decision on whether a prosecution should be mounted. Historically, there has been a high attrition rate between crimes recorded by the police and the conviction rate. This has been a major issue for such crimes as domestic violence and sexual assault, where women are commonly the victims. Kelly *et al.* (2005) stated that, in 2002, 11,766 allegations of rape resulted in only 655 convictions (5.6 per cent).

Police practices can contribute to this attrition rate in a number of ways. The calibre of investigations is integral to a successful outcome. Imperfections in investigation and evidence presentation may result in the Crown Prosecution Service declining to prosecute or in the courts throwing out the case. Shortcomings of this nature have been criticized in a number of high-profile cases that include the murder of Stephen Lawrence. Attrition undermines public confidence in the criminal justice system, as guilty persons escape sanction for the crimes they have committed. Accordingly, in 2001, the government announced its intention to close the justice gap and to bring more offenders to justice. Attrition has thus become associated with this policy objective.

There are numerous ways whereby the Police Service can contribute to the attainment of this goal. Good intelligence is the basis on which crime may be successfully prosecuted, and the Police Service must establish good relationships with communities in order to gather it. Neighbourhood policing is an important underpinning of this strategy, one aspect of which is to encourage people to report crime in order to generate a greater number of incident reports and intelligence to guide future police operations. Specific police operations directed

at prolific offenders may also result in more offenders being convicted. The Home Office estimated in 2001 that 100,000 offenders committed around half the recorded crime in England and Wales, and police actions directed at prolific offenders (either working in isolation or with other agencies) may have a major impact on the conviction rate.

Peter Joyce

Related entries

Sexual offences/sexual violence.

Key texts and sources

Coleman, C. and Moynihan, J. (1996) *Understanding Crime Data: Haunted by the Dark Figure.* Milton Keynes: Open University Press.

Garside, R. (2004) *Crime, Persistent Offenders and the Justice Gap. Discussion Paper* 1. London: Crime and Society Foundation.

Home Office (2001) *Criminal Justice: The Way Ahead* (Cm 5074). London: HMSO.

Kelly, L., Lovett, J. and Regan, L. (2005) *A Gap or a Chasm? Attrition in Reported Rape Cases.* London: Home Office.

Macpherson, Sir W. (1999) *The Stephen Lawrence Inquiry: Report* (Cm 4262). London: HMSO.

AUDIT COMMISSION

The Audit Commission is an independent body responsible for ensuring that public money in England is spent economically, efficiently and effectively.

The Audit Commission helps local government, health, housing, community safety and fire and rescue services deliver high-quality local and national services for the public. As an independent regulator, the Audit Commission ensures public services are good value and that public money is properly spent. The Audit Commission's remit covers 11,000 bodies that, between them, spend nearly £180 billion of public money every year.

The Audit Commission has subjected various aspects of policing to rigorous scrutiny. From the mid-1980s onwards, it published a series of papers that applied private sector business management principles to policing. Through studies such as *Helping with Inquiries* (1993), its general approach was to recommend the delayering or flattening of police organizational structures, together with the devolution of responsibility and financial delegation. Much such change paralleled the new public management principles that have increasingly come to influence public services since the early 1990s.

Supporting delivery and improvement of police services is an integral part of the Audit Commission's role in helping local community safety partners, such as councils, housing providers and probation and health services, to work together to build safer, stronger and more sustainable places. This role includes working with local social services to deliver value-for-money solutions to local problems of crime and anti-social behaviour. Through comprehensive performance assessment, the commission assesses how well councils, together with their Crime and Disorder Reduction Partnership partners, are delivering safer, stronger communities. Community safety inspections are undertaken on a risk basis. Inspectors routinely involve police partners in interviews and focus groups during the on-site stage of inspections to gather evidence to assess how well local councils fulfil their statutory duties as responsible authorities under the Crime and Disorder Act 1998.

The Audit Commission appoints auditors to police authorities in England and Wales who work within the *Code of Audit Practice* to deliver a range of financial, stewardship and governance audits. Auditors make an annual assessment of police use of resources and report specifically on how well police authorities are achieving value for money. The Audit Commission works in partnership with the Police and Crime Standards Directorate to review police crime data quality and 'activity-based costing'.

As an independent regulator, the commission provides input and challenge to government consultations on key national developments relating to policing and community safety. This includes the implementation of the review of the Crime and Disorder Act, police modernization, revision of the Policing Performance Assessment Framework and the development of the 'Assessments of policing and community safety'.

The Audit Commission works closely with HM Inspectorate of Constabulary on a range of performance assessment activities. Developments in policing and community safety that will support police modernization are a high priority for the commission. In the future, the commission will take a lead role as the Local Services Inspectorate and will engage closely with the Justice, Community Safety and Custody Inspectorate to deliver cross-cutting assessments of local services.

Sharon Gernon-Booth

Related entries

Accountability and governance; Best value; Crime and Disorder Act 1998.

Key texts and sources

Audit Commission (2002) *Community Safety Partnerships: Learning from Audit, Inspection and Research.* London: Audit Commission.

Audit Commission (2006) *Neighbourhood Crime and Anti-social Behaviour: Making Places Safer through Improved Local Working.* London: Audit Commission.

Audit Commission and Wales Audit Office (2006) *Crime Recording 2005: Improving the Quality of Crime Records in Police Authorities and Forces in England and Wales.* London: Audit Commission.

The Audit Commission's website is at http://www.audit-commission.gov.uk.

B

BAIL

Bail is the releasing of a person suspected or charged with an offence while awaiting the outcome of an investigation or trial. If suspects or defendants are refused bail, they are either detained in police custody or remanded in custody by courts, depending on the stage their case has reached.

Decisions about whether to bail suspects/defendants are taken at different stages of the criminal justice process – namely, pre-charge and post-charge by the police and courts when defendants are awaiting trial or sentence, or when offenders appeal against their convictions or sentence. Most bail decisions are taken when suspects/defendants are legally innocent. It is for this reason that bail decisions are of paramount importance to perceptions of the fairness and legitimacy of the criminal justice process and are a significant indicator of civil liberties. Bail decisions are important for other reasons – for example, their impact on the prison remand population, which has been rising steadily in recent years, and their impact on subsequent decisions, including pleas and sentencing (Hucklesby 2002). The margin for error in bail decisions is high because they require an assessment of likely future behaviour, and a small minority of decisions are proved wrong with the benefit of hindsight as they result in serious offences being committed.

The law governing bail is contained in the Bail Act 1976. The Bail Act has been amended considerably since its enactment, mainly to make the granting of bail more difficult for certain groups of offenders (i.e. serious offenders and offenders who have allegedly committed offences on bail)

(Hucklesby 2002). Consequently, the right to bail has been significantly eroded. Nevertheless, in most cases, there is a presumption in favour of bail, except in certain circumstances. Bail may be refused if the court considers there are substantial grounds for believing that defendants may abscond, commit offences on bail or interfere with witnesses. The presumption in favour of bail is reversed for defendants who, the court believes, were on bail when the alleged offence was committed (Bail Act 1976, Sch. 1, Part 2A). In these circumstances, defendants may be refused bail unless the court is satisfied that there is no significant risk of offences being committed on bail. This is one of a number of measures introduced to tackle the problem of offending on bail, which has been identified as making a significant contribution to the crime problem, despite the lack of systematic evidence to support this or agreement about how to measure it (Hucklesby and Marshall 2000). When bail is refused by a court, defendants are remanded in custody for seven days after the first hearing and for up to 28 days thereafter. Custodial remand rates vary between courts, which raises questions about the consistency and fairness of bail decision-making (Hucklesby 1997a). There is also limited evidence that both police and court bail decisions vary for different groups of suspects/defendants and that suspects/defendants from minority ethnic groups are more likely to be subject to pre-charge bail and are less likely to be bailed subsequently in the process (Phillips and Brown 1998; National Audit Office 2004).

Both the police and courts may grant bail with or without conditions. Conditions may be attached to bail on similar grounds to those which enable bail to be refused (Bail Act 1976, s. 3(6)). There are no guidelines about which conditions may be used in what circumstances, but they should relate to the grounds that have been applied. In practice, a limited range of conditions are applied, which include residence, curfews, exclusion zones and no-contact conditions (Hucklesby 1994; Raine and Willson 1996). The Criminal Justice Act 2003 introduced restriction on bail, which only courts may impose. This requires identified drug users to undergo a drugs assessment and any recommended follow-up (Hucklesby *et al.*, 2005). The use of conditional bail has recently increased, which, along with research that indicates that conditions are used differently by different courts, has heightened concerns about its purpose, effectiveness and necessity (Hucklesby 1994; Raine and Willson 1994, 1996). Breach of conditions is not an offence but may result in bail being refused, whereas failing to appear in court to answer bail is an offence.

Police bail is governed by the Police and Criminal Evidence Act 1984 (PACE). Section 37(7)(b) of PACE enables the police to release suspects on bail prior to charge. The purpose of this provision is to allow further inquires to be made. Currently, no conditions may be attached to this type of pre-charge bail. The Criminal Justice Act 2003 amended PACE in relation to pre-charge bail to accommodate the new charging procedures. Under s. 37(7)(a), bail may be granted in order for the Crown Prosecution Service to make decisions about whether or not suspects should be charged. Bail conditions may be applied in such cases. Section 47 of PACE requires the police to release suspects on bail after charge, in accordance with the Bail Act 1976. Bail after charge may be subject to conditions but not those requiring suspects to reside at bail hostels or to seek the advice of a solicitor. Custody officers make police bail decisions, although the Crown Prosecution Service may have a greater input into pre-charge bail decisions in the future. Information about the use of police bail is limited, especially pre-charge (see Hucklesby 2001 for review of research). Research on post-charge bail concentrates on the use of conditions and suggests that there are variations in the use and range of conditions applied between different police stations and forces (Raine and Willson 1995a; Hucklesby

2001). Police decisions about whether or not to release suspects on post-charge bail and on which conditions to impose are particularly important because they influence subsequent court remand decisions (Hucklesby 1996).

Anthea Hucklesby

Related entries

Arrest; Evidence; Frankpledge; Youth and policing.

Key texts and sources

Corre, N. and Wolchover, D. (2004) *Bail in Criminal Proceedings.* Oxford: Oxford University Press.
Hucklesby, A. (2002) 'Bail in criminal cases', in M. McConville and G. Wilson (eds) *The Handbook of the Criminal Justice Process.* Oxford: Oxford University Press.
See also the bail guidance page of the Crown Prosecution Service's website (http://www.cps.gov.uk/legal/section14/chapter_l.html#03). Liberty's guide to human rights website is at http://www.yourrights.org.uk/your-rights/chapters/the-rights-of-defendants/bail/bail.shtml.

BASIC COMMAND UNITS (BCUs)

A basic command unit (BCU) is a territorial policing unit within a police force area.

Most police forces have an organizational structure that comprises a headquarters tier and an operational tier of units known variously as areas, districts, divisions or boroughs. Generically, these territorial policing units are all basic command units (BCUs). The BCU has become the key unit of operational policing, with the role of providing basic policing services within a fixed geographical area. Each BCU has its own headquarters, which is the base for the area's command team and support and operations units. It is from here that the area's commander (a chief superintendent), oversees the delivery of policing across the sub-units of the BCU.

The term 'basic command unit' can be traced back to the 1991 Audit Commission report, *Reviewing the Organisation of Provincial Police*

Forces, which argued the case for devolving power to allow local discretion and flexibility in the use of resources. Thereafter BCUs grew in significance, and government efforts to measure performance and to improve standards of policing have focused on BCUs as the unit of analysis. The 2001 police reform white paper, *Policing a New Century* (Home Office 2001b), put the BCU at the heart of its vision to modernize the service by devolving more power to BCUs across England and Wales. The Police and Justice Bill 2006 subsequently proposed to put BCUs on a statutory footing, requiring them to be coterminous with local authority boundaries. However, this clause was withdrawn once it was established that all but six (of approximately 225) BCUs had already achieved coterminosity. This matching of borders facilitates partnership working under the Crime and Disorder Act 1998 and has the purpose of strengthening the accountability of BCUs to local people. Some commentators have argued that devolution of responsibility should go further. Loveday (2006b: 33), for example, has argued that BCUs should be empowered to set their own priorities and that BCU commanders should be 'hired and fired by local politicians' or elected police boards.

BCUs are subject to considerable scrutiny: their performances are compared with the aim of spreading good practice and improving policing nationally. The Police Standards Unit has a specific mandate to focus on BCUs and, in addition, between 2001 and 2006, HM Inspectorate of Constabulary (HMIC) undertook a five-year BCU inspection programme, 'Going local again'. At the beginning of this, 318 BCUs existed in England and Wales that varied in size – from less than 100 to more than 1,000 police officers; in number and diversity of population policed from 4,000 to 300,000 residents; and in physical area from one square mile to several hundred (Audit Commission 2001). HMIC published in 2002 a summary of the emerging inspection findings (*Getting Down to Basics*) and later reported the existence of fewer, but larger, BCUs, attributing this enlargement process to 'pressures to achieve resilience, financial efficiency and coterminosity' (HMIC 2005b: 25).

Although in recent years there has been much debate and controversy concerning the restructuring of police forces, it seems likely that BCUs will retain their importance as the 'critical building blocks' (HMIC 2005b: 63) of the current, and possibly future, framework of policing in England and Wales.

Rob C. Mawby

Related entries

Intelligence analysis (previously crime analysis).

> **Key texts and sources**
>
> HMIC (2002) *Getting Down to Basics: Emerging Findings from BCU Inspections in 2001*. London: HMIC.

BEAT

> Historically, a beat is a geographical area that one police officer has responsibility for patrolling on foot.

The 'bobby on the beat' remains a touchstone of British policing, invoking the image of the uniformed officer patrolling the streets night and day, deterring crime through performing a 'scarecrow function' and providing a benign reassuring presence to local residents and businesses. At the centre of this symbolic form of policing is the notion of a geographical area for which one officer is responsible for patrolling – namely, the 'beat'.

The origin of the beat lies in the design of the Metropolitan Police District in 1829 by Richard Mayne and Charles Rowan, the first commissioners of the Metropolitan Police. They organized the Metropolitan Police District into divisions, which were made up of subdivisions, which in turn comprised sections, each of which contained a number of beats. Each sergeant was given charge of a section, and each constable was responsible for a beat within a section. At the start of each duty the sergeants would march the constables to their respective beats, where they would remain until relieved by the next shift, at which time the sergeant would march them back to the station, for inspection and dismissal.

The *General Instructions,* issued to all members of the Metropolitan Police in 1829, detailed the duties of police officers and, for police constables, advised:

> *A particular portion of the Section called a Beat, is committed to his care: he will have previously been informed by his Serjeant of the names of the streets, &c., forming his Beat. He is responsible for the security of life and property within his Beat, and for the preservation of the peace and general good order, during the time he is on Duty.*

Ascoli (1979: 92) records that Rowan defined the beat 'as a stretch or area which could be covered in fifteen or twenty minutes at a steady pace of 2.5 miles per hour', and Emsley (1996: 225) notes that beats were carefully measured. The average Metropolitan day beat was 7.5 miles and the night beat was 2 miles. Each beat was numbered and its boundaries were clearly defined. As policing spread outside London, this organizational pattern was repeated, though beats varied considerably in size and character.

To keep the police constable accountable, the sergeant constantly patrolled the section, visiting each beat and taking each constable's report at appointed times. In some forces this was organized through the 'fixed points' system (Chatterton 1979), in which each beat had four specified points and the patrolling officer had to be at each point at fixed times during the shift in order that the sergeant could make contact. The sergeant was expected to meet each beat officer twice during a shift at one or more of these points.

Although the bulk of police time was spent on the routine patrolling of beats well into the 1960s (Emsley 1996: 224), in the postwar period the role of the 'beat bobby' became increasingly marginalized following the introduction of police patrol cars, improvements in communications technology and operational innovations such as unit beat policing in the second half of the 1960s. In this context the resource efficiency of deploying officers on foot (see Patrol) was increasingly questioned. Nevertheless, the idea of police officers being responsible for specific beats has endured, and forces still deploy officers in roles with titles similar to 'community beat officer'. These uniformed officers may each have personal responsibility for maintaining links with people and for problem-solving in a beat area. These areas are typically aligned to ward boundaries and, in some forces, are subdivided to create 'micro-beats'. The public and media demand for reassurance over public safety and for 'bobbies on the beat' suggests that the notion of a beat will remain. However, with the introduction of (police) community support officers and neighbourhood policing teams, increasingly the beat is no longer the exclusive domain or responsibility of the 'bobby'.

Rob C. Mawby

Related entries

Community policing; Neighbourhood policing; Patrol; Rank structure; Rowan and Mayne; Unit beat policing (UBP).

Key texts and sources

Chatterton, M.R. (1979) 'The supervision of patrol work under the fixed points system', in S. Holdaway (ed.) *The British Police.* London: Edward Arnold.

Emsley, C. (1996, 2nd edn) *The English Police: A Political and Social History.* London: Longman.

BEST VALUE

The avowed aim of best-value arrangements is to secure continuous improvement in the performance of functions by public service organizations.

The concept of 'best value' in local public services was promoted and introduced by the New Labour government shortly after its election in 1997. Prior to that election, New Labour had promised to abolish the regime of compulsory competitive tendering (CCT) introduced under the preceding Conservative administration, which had forced outsourcing and privatization on many local public services. The idea of best value, the concept of which had been developed in the USA, appeared to provide a ready means by which the discipline of efficiency and effectiveness might be sustained while also honouring the political commitment to end CCT.

As a result, the Local Government Act 1998 imposed a duty on all principal local authorities, police authorities and the larger town councils 'to provide best value' for their citizens and to satisfy the Audit Commission on an annual basis in this regard. Under the legislation, the affected public authorities were also required to conduct annual programmes of best-value reviews, with the aim of covering all aspects of their service provision responsibilities within a five-year period. The reviews would normally be conducted on an 'in-house' basis (typically by a best-value team) but would be subject to external inspection by the Audit Commission, which would provide a follow-up assessment in two main respects: first, 'how good is the service?'; and, secondly, 'how good are its prospects for improvement?'

The methodology for best-value reviews was largely established in guidance from the government and involved the '4Cs' of 'compare', 'consult', 'challenge' and 'compete'. Under the first 'C', organizations were expected to *compare* their performance with other similar authorities (and for which a suite of national best-value performance indicators (BVPIs) was developed by the government). Under the second 'C', authorities were expected to *consult* widely with service users and other stakeholders. The third 'C' required them to subject their services to critical *challenge*, asking fundamental questions about the need for provision, about strengths and weaknesses in the current arrangements, and about how best the services might be provided. The fourth 'C' required the organizations to demonstrate the capacity of their service to *compete* with alternative providers and to test

that 'in-house' provision was indeed both efficient and effective – in short, providing best value for the community.

Between 1998 and 2005, several hundreds of best-value reviews were undertaken by best-value authorities – some focusing on particular aspects or themes of the overall operation (for example, procurement, administrative support, specialist services or call-handling), others taking a wider, more 'cross-cutting' perspective (for example, focusing on inter-agency arrangements for information sharing and communication between the police and other criminal justice services).

Almost from the outset, criticisms were levelled at the cost and time involved in conducting such reviews, and about the value for money involved. Such criticisms eventually led the government to relent somewhat, particularly by removing the requirement to review all services every five years and by encouraging the Audit Commission to adopt a 'lighter touch' and more selective inspection process.

For local government, the introduction in 2002 of a new regime of assessment – comprehensive performance assessment – was generally viewed as the replacement, in effect, for best value, even though formally the phrase lived on in the key legislation. Within policing, similarly, while best-value reviews continued to be undertaken, their number and significance tended to diminish with time and as attention shifted more towards other assessment processes – notably that of policing performance by HM Inspectorate of Constabulary and in response to the development of a Policing Performance Analysis Framework. Indeed, the Police and Justice Act 2006 repealed the earlier legislation – from 2007–8, police authorities are no longer required to produce best-value performance plans.

John Raine

Related entries

Audit Commission; Patten Report; Scotland (policing).

Key texts and sources

Halachmi, A. (ed.) (2000) 'Symposium on value for money, best value and measuring government performance', *International Review of Administrative Sciences*, 66: 393–526.

Martin, S. (2000) 'Implementing best value: local public services in transition', *Public Administration*, 781: 232–45.

Information on the best value initiatives is available from the Scottish Executive's website (http://www.scotland.gov.uk/Publications/2004/04/19166/35253).

BICHARD INQUIRY

The Bichard Inquiry was a government-initiated investigation following the conviction of Ian Huntley in 2003 for the murders of two 10-year-old girls the previous year. Its critical findings have significance for the national dimension of policing and for the operation of the tripartite structure of police accountability.

Ian Huntley committed the murders of Jessica Chapman and Holly Wells in August 2002 while employed as a school caretaker in the Cambridgeshire village of Soham. He was sentenced to life imprisonment on 17 December 2003. The trial raised concerns over how Huntley had been able to secure a job as a school caretaker in 2001 in Soham, despite allegations of eight separate sexual offences being made against him in Humberside between 1995 and 1999. After Huntley's conviction, the Home Secretary announced an inquiry, chaired by Sir Michael Bichard, with the following terms of reference:

Urgently to enquire into child protection procedures in Humberside Police and Cambridgeshire Constabulary in the light of the recent trial and conviction of Ian Huntley for the murder of Jessica Chapman and Holly Wells. In particular to assess the effectiveness of the relevant intelligence-based record keeping, the vetting practices of those forces since 1995 and information sharing with other agencies, and to report to the Home Secretary on matters of local and national relevance and to make recommendations as appropriate.

The inquiry issued its report on 22 June 2004. It found 'errors, omissions, failures and shortcomings which are deeply shocking' across all the organizations that had contact with Ian Huntley. The report identified both organizational and systemic failures: Humberside Police's intelligence system was 'fundamentally flawed'; the force's senior officers were unaware of the problems; the social services' decision-making over sexual abuse allegations made against Huntley was questioned; Cambridgeshire Constabulary made record-keeping and vetting errors; and Soham Village College failed to check adequately Huntley's employment history. At a systemic level, no national information technology (IT) system for recording police intelligence existed, and the Home Office was criticized for not doing more to establish such a system.

Bichard made 31 recommendations covering 1) child and vulnerable adult protection; 2) enhanced vetting procedures; 3) IT-related issues; and 4) information management issues. Recognizing the national dimension to policing, key recommendations included the establishment of a national IT intelligence system for England and Wales and a national code of practice for police forces on record creation, review, retention, deletion and sharing. The government accepted the recommendations, which were endorsed by stakeholders, including the Association of Chief Police Officers.

The inquiry issued its final report in March 2005. This acknowledged 'impressive progress' towards implementing the recommendations. However, it also noted that much remained to be done, particularly relating to the introduction of a national IT intelligence system. The government published further progress reports in November 2005 and May 2006, the latter claiming that 21 of the 35 recommendations had been 'substantially delivered'. A further progress report was expected during 2007.

The Bichard Inquiry is also significant as an example of the operation of the tripartite structure of police accountability following the

Police Reform Act 2002. In the wake of the inquiry's findings, the Home Secretary, using new powers under the Act, instructed Humberside Police Authority to suspend the Chief Constable, David Westwood, for the maintenance of public confidence. The authority initially refused, before acquiescing following a High Court injunction. Westwood returned to duty in September 2004 as part of a deal he negotiated with the Home Secretary that involved him not making substantive public comment about the suspension and his taking early retirement in March 2005.

Rob C. Mawby

Related entries

Accountability and governance; Intelligence-led policing; National Intelligence Model (NIM); Police National Computer.

Key texts and sources

Bichard, Sir M. (2004) *The Bichard Inquiry Report (June 2004)* (HC 653). London: HMSO.
Bichard, Sir M. (2005) *The Bichard Inquiry: Final Report (March 2005)*. London: HMSO.
The Bichard Inquiry website is at **www.bichard inquiry.org.uk**. See also the Home Office's 'Bichard recommendations implementation' website (http://police.homeoffice.gov.uk/operational-policing/bichard-implementation/?version=2).

BLACK POLICE ASSOCIATIONS

Black police associations represent the interests of 'black' officers and police support staff, which usually means people who define their ethnic origin as Afro-Caribbean or south Asian.

Black police associations have been established in the majority of UK constabularies, as well as other European and North American police forces. The birth of these associations can be traced back to the USA during the 1950s, when Afro-American officers responded to the experience of open discrimination in their employment (Leinen 1984). Recruitment into police forces was a particular pressure point, especially in cities with large Afro-American populations. Black police associations took chief officers to court to enforce recruitment quotas and, therefore, positive discrimination.

Recruitment has been one of a number of concerns to UK black police associations. A challenge to racial prejudice and discrimination in police occupational culture was their initial focus. The first association in the UK was formed in the London Metropolitan Police Service to eschew the racism it identified as central to it. This was one aspect of a process that defined the employment experience of a black officer as being distinct from that of a white officer, not least through the affirmation of different values and the rejection of racism (Holdaway and O'Neill 2004).

Impetus was given to the development of associations nationwide when the Home Secretary accepted a Stephen Lawrence Inquiry recommendation that associations should be established in each constabulary (Macpherson 1999). Association officers became members of committees and other groups concerned with the recruitment and retention of minority ethnic staff; they assist in race relations training; they act as a conduit between minority ethnic communities and constabularies; they support their members; they review policies and practices for negative discrimination; and, generally, they represent the interests of their members.

A related aspect of the Home Secretary's acceptance of the recommendation was to require chief constables to manage race relations more clearly and to meet a range of related targets. Black police associations remain a ready resource for this work as, at the national level, there is the National Black Police Association, which supports its member associations and consults with the Home Office on a wide range of subjects.

Black police associations are an example of a police organization developing from the 'bottom up'. They pose the question of whether the categorization of their members as 'black' can capture the identities and interests of officers from many minority ethnic groups. Associations representing officers with Asian, Italian, Jewish and other backgrounds have developed. Some of these focus on racial discrimination and prejudice, some increasingly on their shared, distinct culture, including religious beliefs. A national Muslim Police Association has now been established in England.

These developments present a dilemma for associations and chief officers. Do they emphasize the single experience of 'black' officers or the diverse and distinct experiences of officers with different cultures, including religious beliefs? The former unifies a black police association membership; the latter requires recognition of cultural diversity. Whatever their stance, these associations have highlighted how ethnicity is managed within constabularies and, importantly, they have made strategic use of 'race' and 'ethnicity' as political resources.

Simon Holdaway

Related entries

Politics (police involvement).

Key texts and sources

Holdaway, S. and O'Neill, M. (2004) 'The development of black police associations in the UK', *British Journal of Criminology*, 44: 854–65.
Leinen, S. (1984) *Black Police: White Society*. New York, NY: New York University Press.
Macpherson, Sir W. (1999) *The Stephen Lawrence Inquiry: Report of an Inquiry by Sir William Macpherson of Cluny*. London: HMSO.
The National Black Police Association's website is at http://www.nationalbpa.com. The Metropolitan Black Police Association's website is at http://metbpa.cfclientzone.net/.

BOW STREET 'RUNNERS'

The Bow Street 'Runners' were a police force with both detective and preventive elements that operated from 1748–1839 from Bow Street Public Office, Westminster.

The Bow Street 'Runners' (originally consisting of just seven men) were created in 1748 by the novelist, Henry Fielding (1707–54), who was appointed as a magistrate for Westminster in the same year. Bow Street was the original Public or Police Office, consisting of a chief magistrate and two other stipendiary magistrates, three clerks and other officials, including 'Runners' and various patrols. In 1792 seven other public offices were created (Great Marlborough Street, Hatton Garden, Lambeth, Queen's Square, Union Hall, Westminster and Worship Street), but Bow Street remained *primus inter pares*. Fielding was keen to have his embryonic force put on an official footing and, in August 1753, after a series of highway robberies had generated widespread fear throughout London, he successfully petitioned for £600 of government money to fund the force. The Home Office subsequently held the purse-strings and assumed overall financial control, but the day-to-day functioning of Bow Street was left in the hands of successive chief magistrates. Henry Fielding was succeeded in 1754 by his half-brother, Sir John Fielding (1721–80), who further developed the role of the 'Runners' through persuasive advertising in publications such as *Hue & Cry* (which eventually became the *Police Gazette*).

Senior Bow Street personnel preferred to be known as 'principal officers', considering the term 'Runner' to be both derogatory and demeaning. They were sworn in as constables of Westminster and also had constabulary powers in the four surrounding counties. They had no uniform (their only badge of office being a small tipstaff) and they did not have patrol duties, spending a considerable proportion of their employment involved on provincial investigations.

Never numbering more than a dozen at any given time, they were complemented by other personnel. The *foot (Night) patrol* (established by 1790) was a non-uniformed body of men that eventually consisted of one inspector and 82 patrol constables split into 17 patrols, each with a patrol conductor. It patrolled the city of Westminster at night on regular 'beats'. Two patrol members remained on call at Bow Street to respond to crimes reported by the public. The foot patrol was disbanded in 1829 with the advent of the Metropolitan Police.

The *horse patrol* was created in 1805 in order to patrol the major turnpiked roads leading into the

Metropolis. This patrol was the first uniformed police force in London, with scarlet waistcoats and blue trousers, and normally operated at a distance of between 10 and 15 miles from central London. By 1828 it consisted of two inspectors, four deputy inspectors and 54 patrol men in four divisions. It functioned under Bow Street's jurisdiction until 1836, when it passed into the control of the Metropolitan Police. The *dismounted horse (Day) patrol* was created in 1821 to patrol in daylight around the area between the jurisdiction of the foot patrol and the horse patrol. This force, consisting of 89 patrol constables, eight sub-inspectors and four inspectors, divided into four divisions, was transferred to the authority of the Metropolitan Police in 1829.

David J. Cox

Related entries

Metropolitan Police/New Police; Patrol.

Key texts and sources

Babington, A. (1999) *A House in Bow Street: Crime and the Magistracy, London 1740–1881* (2nd edn). London: Macdonald.

Cox, D. (2003) '"A certain share of low cunning" – the provincial use and activities of Bow Street "Runners", 1792–1839', *ERAS Online Journal*, 5 (available online at www.arts.monash.edu.au/eras/edition_5/coxarticle.htm).

Fitzgerald, P. (1888/1972) *Chronicle of Bow Street Police Office: With an Account of the Magistrates, 'Runners' and Police.* London: Chapman & Hall (reprinted Montclair, NJ: Patterson Smith).

BRITISH ASSOCIATION FOR WOMEN IN POLICING (BAWP)

The British Association for Women in Policing (BAWP) was founded in 1987 as a support group for women officers but, as the police family has broadened, the organization has become all inclusive. Members include women and men from all ranks and levels of the Police Service, plus representatives from police authorities and police-related organizations and anyone with a professional interest in supporting the development of women in policing.

The British Association for Women in Policing (BAWP) aims to raise awareness and understanding of issues that affect women working in the Police Service; to provide a women's perspective on matters that affect police and police staff personnel; to help share information on developments in policing, particularly those affecting women; to develop a national and international network of professional and social contacts; and to contribute to the continuous professional development of its members. Committee members represent women's views at Home Office and Police Service meetings, ensuring women have a voice in national discussions and decisions. The BAWP's quarterly magazine, *Grapevine*, is supplemented by information leaflets on issues such as networking, flexible working, working with the media and domestic violence.

The BAWP was a key player in the development and launch of the 'gender agenda' in August 2001, and the association (through its work) has become the lead organization for progressing its aims and objectives. Lobbying has ensured this agenda forms part of government policy, and it was embraced in the Police Reform Programme, the National Policing Plan and HM Inspectors' inspection regime. In 2001, only 16 per cent of officers were women, and the BAWP campaigned to ensure recruitment had an appropriate representation of women, robustly challenging the fitness test to ensure it took its rightful, not dominant, place in the selection process. The old fitness test focused on upper body strength, and only 47 per cent of women passed. The new non-discriminatory fitness test has resulted in 84 per cent of women being successful. In 2006, the BAWP undertook a review of the gender agenda and, after consulting women and men of all ranks and grades across the UK, developed 'Gender agenda 2', which established good practice, highlighted areas for improvement and set the challenge for the following five years.

To further understanding of the issues for women in policing, the BAWP commissioned ground-breaking research on 'work and the menopause', to ensure that, with more women remaining in the service for longer, it was better able to support women through this key life event. Additionally, the BAWP has commissioned research on attitudes to operational deployment by both officers and the public, an exploration of the attributes of a well conducted constable and research into positive discrimination as a means to gender equality.

The BAWP has excellent links with all British police forces via regional and force networks that includes a virtual network for women involved in, or wanting to be involved in, specialist roles (e.g. firearms, dogs, criminal investigation department, Special Branch). It also works with statutory staff associations and unions, support associations, the European Network of Policewomen and the International Association of Women Police.

Julie Spence

Related entries

European Network of Policewomen; Gender and policing.

Key texts and sources

Blok, D. and Brown, J. (2005) *The Gendered Nature of Policing among Uniformed Operational Officers in England and Wales.* Guildford: University of Surrey.
Brown, J., Di Franco, C. and O'Neill, D. (2006) *The Well Conducted Constable.* Guildford: University of Surrey.
Brown, J., Hegarty, P. and O'Neill, D. (2006) *Playing with Numbers – a Discussion Paper on Positive Discrimination as a Means for Achieving Gender Equality.* Guildford: University of Surrey.
University of Nottingham (2006) *Work and Menopause.* Nottingham: University of Nottingham.
See also the following websites: **www.bawp.org**; **www.enp.nl**; **www.iawp.org**.

BROKEN WINDOWS

'Broken windows' is shorthand for the theory that neglect of relatively minor incivilities can create a permissive environment for anti-social behaviour, which can lead to a tipping point where crime problems become serious and out of control.

The broken windows hypothesis was formulated by James Q. Wilson and George Kelling. They presented it in an article that first appeared in 1982 in the magazine, *Atlantic Monthly*, though it has since been widely reprinted. The broken windows thesis has been discussed and debated extensively in criminological circles. It has also had a major influence on the policing of some areas on both sides of the Atlantic. In terms of impact, Wilson and Kelling's article is one of the most significant pieces of criminological analysis to have been written. It is also one of the most commonly misunderstood and misrepresented.

The literal significance of broken windows, the source of the more general metaphor, is that, 'if a window in a building is left unrepaired, all the rest of the windows will soon be broken' (Wilson and Kelling 1982: 31). This, Wilson and Kelling argue, 'is as true in nice neighbourhoods as in run-down ones'. Furthermore, 'Window-breaking does not necessarily occur on a large scale because some areas are inhabited by determined window-breakers...rather, one unrepaired window is a signal that no one cares, and so breaking more windows costs nothing'.

The more general metaphor is that turning a blind eye to embryonic signs of incivility creates a permissive context in which anti-social behaviour can become commonplace and increasingly difficult to control. Anti-social behaviour comes to be expected – it becomes normal. The neighbourhood deteriorates, people become frightened, families move out and single adults move in. Increases in littering, hanging around on street corners, drunkenness and begging take place. A spiral of physical and social decline and disorder occurs.

This process of decline, Wilson and Kelling stress, is not inevitably accompanied with rapid increases in serious crime. Those living in such neighbourhoods may adopt strategies to reduce the risks they perceive they face from the others they see. Many, including in particular the old, confine themselves to their own homes. In this way people avoid one another and become atomized. As a result of this, informal controls will wither and the area will be more 'vulnerable to criminal invasion' (1982: 32) – for example, from prostitution, drug dealing and street robbery.

In the eyes of the police who, from time to time, may be called to incidents to exert some control in communities that have experienced a spiral of decline, Wilson and Kelling argue that 'the residents are animals who deserve each other' (1982: 33). Where this happens citizens are likely to stop calling the police, not least on the grounds that they can apparently do nothing to help.

Wilson and Kelling argue that order maintenance and crime prevention are closely linked to one another, but that this connection had been lost in modern policing with its emphasis on crime fighting and law enforcement. They advocate policing involving direct contact with the community as a means of sustaining informal social control and the conditions for it to thrive. They thus state that:

The essence of the police role in maintaining order is to reinforce the informal control mechanisms of the community itself. The police cannot, without committing extraordinary resources, provide a substitute for that informal social control. On the other hand, to reinforce those natural controls the police must accommodate them

(p. 34).

And accommodation of local controls involves the use of discretion in relation to similar acts

leading, in some contexts, to arrests and, in others, to ignoring them or dealing with them informally, bringing with it the obvious attendant risks of discrimination.

For Wilson and Kelling, policing is less about enforcement in relation to individual infractions of laws than it is about serving the community's needs intelligently by working with it, where needed, to help it exert controls that create a liveable environment for its members. More particularly, in relation to broken windows, it is about helping to ward off the dangers that spiralling processes of decline will take hold, precipitating intolerable conditions for local citizens. It is here that, Wilson and Kelling argue, police resources need to be concentrated.

In *Fixing Broken Windows*, George Kelling and Catherine Coles (1996) describe and defend what they see as the wide-ranging and successful application of broken windows policing in New York in the 1980s and 1990s. Efforts began on the subway system and then moved to the streets. A remarkable improvement in the safety of both seems to have taken place.

Notwithstanding its surface plausibility and claims made about its effectiveness when put to use, the broken windows thesis and the policing strategies emanating from it have been highly controversial. The theory and its implications have also, arguably, been widely misconstrued by followers and critics alike. In particular, broken windows policing has often been associated with zero-tolerance policing. 'Zero tolerance' does not form part of Wilson and Kelling's lexicon. Any association with harsh, intolerant policing in which officers are given licence to ride roughshod over community wants and interests runs counter to what Wilson and Kelling ostensibly say they would prefer.

Two major empirical questions arise in relation to the broken windows thesis. The first has to do with the causal relationship between disorder and crime. Some strong research suggests that the level of collective efficacy (or social capital) is crucial to the level of violent crime in neighbourhoods, independent of the disorder emphasized by Wilson and Kelling. The second has to do with the effectiveness of policing inspired by broken windows. Claims that the reduction in crime in New York is attributable to it have been challenged. Other factors may have been at work, and falls have been observed in other cities that have not embraced the broken windows thesis. The jury is still out on both these important issues.

Nick Tilley

Related entries

Anti-social behaviour; Community policing; Neighbourhood policing; Signal crimes; Zero-tolerance policing (ZTP).

Key texts and sources

Bowling, B. (1999) 'The rise and fall of New York murder', *British Journal of Criminology*, 39: 531–54.

Kelling, G. and Coles, C. (1996) *Fixing Broken Windows*. New York, NY: Free Press.

Sampson, R. and Raudenbusch, S. (2001) *Disorder in Urban Neighbourhoods: Does it Lead to Crime? National Institute Research in Brief*. Washington, DC: US Department of Justice Office of Justice Programs, National Institute of Justice.

Wilson, J.Q. and Kelling, G. (1982) 'Broken windows', *Atlantic Monthly*, 249: 29–36, 38.

For an article by the Center on Juvenile and Criminal Justice detailing a crime reduction initiative in San Francisco using alternative crime policies, see http://www.cjcj.org/pubs/windows/windows.html.

BURGLARY

Normally considered to entail unauthorized access to property in order to steal, in English criminal law burglary also includes any unauthorized access to commit an offence.

Unlike in many other countries, where burglary comprises forced entry to premises, in English criminal law access in order to burgle may also be through an open or unlocked door or window, or through subterfuge. The latter, generally termed 'distraction burglary' and targeted at older people, has received considerable attention in recent years. Burglary is subdivided into burglary (dwelling) and burglary (other), which includes both burglary of corporate property and burglary of outbuildings, garages, etc., making it difficult to identify rates of recorded burglary against households or commercial premises. Victim surveys, however, suggest that the risk of commercial burglary is higher. In 2005–6, 2.4 per cent of households experienced a burglary (Walker *et al.*, 2006), while the second Commercial Victimisation Survey reported that 25 per cent of retailers and 22 per cent of manufacturers had experienced a burglary in the previous year (Taylor 2004). Repeat victimization is also common, especially among commercial victims.

That said, there is little evidence that burglars form a coherent group of offenders. Many burglars commit other offences, while some types of burglar, for example ram-raiders (Donald and Wilson 2000) and possibly distraction burglars, are somewhat distinctive. Research on burglars has also tended to focus on decision-making – i.e. why burglars target particular property in particular areas. It is generally the case that burglars travel relatively short distances (Wiles and Costello 2000), but they may burgle properties they pass en route to somewhere farther afield – for example, between their home and the city centre (Cromwell *et al.*, 1991). The reasons why burglars choose particular properties within these areas suggests a degree of limited planning and has implications for designing out crime.

From a policing perspective, burglary is difficult to detect. Burglaries are usually committed when the property is empty and in the absence of witnesses. In England and Wales in 2005–6, only about 13 per cent of burglaries were cleared up. This has resulted in a number of initiatives, including Operation Bumblebee, introduced in the Metropolitan Police force area in the early 1990s (Stockdale and Gresham 1995), and efforts to improve rapid response to incidents (Blake and Coupe 2001). It is also notable that early recognition of the difficulties endemic to burglary detection contributed to the development of Neighbourhood Watch.

Most especially, though, both the government and the police have supported burglary reduction initiatives. Burglary reduction formed a key part of the Safer Cities programmes (Ekblom *et al.*, 1996) and Secured by Design (Pascoe and Topping 1997; Armitage 2000). The Burglary Reduction Initiative (subsequently renamed the Reducing Burglary Initiative) was launched in 1998 as a major element of the Home Office's Crime Reduction Programme (Tilley *et al.*, 1999; Hamilton-Smith 2004). Recent initiatives aimed at older people include Locks for Pensioners (Mawby and Jones 2006) and the creation of a National Distraction Burglary Taskforce (Home Office 2003). While evaluations of these initiatives have produced mixed findings, they suggest that, given the low detection rate, burglary reduction through education and target hardening may be more effective than sentencing changes.

Rob I. Mawby

Related entries

Crime scene examiners (CSEs); Geographical information systems (GIS); Hotspots; Neighbourhood Watch; Volume crime.

Key texts and sources

Cromwell, P.F., Olson, J.N. and Avary, D'A.W. (1991) *Breaking and Entering.* Newbury Park, CA: Sage.
Mawby, R.I. (2001) *Burglary.* Cullompton: Willan Publishing.
For current Home Office definitions of burglary, see **www.homeoffice.gov.uk/rds/pdfs06/ countburglary06.pdf**. The government's crime reduction toolkit for burglary is available online at **http://www.crimereduction.gov.uk/toolkits/ db00.htm**.

BYFORD REPORT

The Byford Report was published following a review undertaken in the early 1980s of the police investigation into the Yorkshire Ripper murders.

In May 1981, the Home Secretary requested Lawrence Byford, one of HM Inspectors of Constabulary, to review the police investigation into the Yorkshire Ripper murders. In December 1981, *The Yorkshire Ripper Case: Review of the Police Investigation of the Case* was presented to the Home Secretary. This is more generally known as the Byford Report.

Between July 1975 and January 1981, a series of 13 linked murders and 7 attempted murders were committed across towns and cities in West Yorkshire and Greater Manchester. The victims were lone females, many of whom were working as prostitutes. They were generally attacked with a hammer, and those who died were mutilated with a knife. The similarities between these crimes and the murders of prostitutes by 'Jack the Ripper' led to the offender being dubbed the 'Yorkshire Ripper'. Crimes of this type are rare, and so they generated a great deal of press interest as well as public fear.

The five-and-a-half-year investigation into the crimes was described by Byford as 'undoubtedly the largest-scale police investigation ever conducted in this country'. However, it was widely criticized at the time for its failure to identify the offender. He was eventually arrested by two uniformed officers as the result of routine patrol work. His name was Peter Sutcliffe and he was arrested because the vehicle he was in was displaying false number plates. He was with a prostitute, and suspicion fell on him when a hammer and a knife he had tried to conceal were discovered. He subsequently admitted all the offences. On 22 May 1981, Sutcliffe was convicted at the Central Criminal Court and was sentenced to 20 concurrent life terms.

The level of criticism of the police investigation led the Home Secretary to request a report from Byford to identify any lessons that might be learnt. The report paints a picture of a Police Service that was poorly organized, badly led and under-resourced. The series of amalgamations of police forces in England and Wales that had occurred in 1969 and 1974 had resulted in 43 police forces, each of which had its own arrangements for managing homicide investigations. These relied on the manual processing of information using card-index or similar filing systems. Few of them were compatible with each other and, in some cases, different areas of the same force used different systems. Normally this did not cause a problem as most homicides are single events that are investigated where they occur. However, because Sutcliffe's crimes were committed in different towns, cities and force areas they exposed the inability of the police to share information and to co-ordinate investigative efforts effectively. Eventually, a central major incident room (MIR) was established to co-ordinate the records built up by the individual investigations. By that time the task was enormous and, in Byford's opinion, it merely added to the difficulties. Some sense of the nature of the problem is provided by statistics from the MIR:

- Number of records for people (known as nominals): 267,962.
- Number of actions (the individual tasks investigators carry out): 115,297.
- Number of statements : 30,926.
- Number of vehicle sightings in red-light districts: 5,468,514.

Byford also criticized the way in which lines of inquiry were managed. In particular, he highlighted the decision to accept three letters and a tape recording purporting to come from the killer as genuine. These were received between March 1978 and June 1979 and contained information which, it was thought, could only have come from the killer. They appeared to offer a way of narrowing down the number of people of interest to the investigation by providing a blood group (from saliva on the envelopes), a handwriting sample and an accent (which experts said belonged to someone from the north east of England). Despite the reservations of some detectives about their authenticity, they were given wide publicity. This not only overwhelmed the already struggling MIR with information from the public but the decision to use the blood group, handwriting and accent as eliminating criteria also meant that Sutcliffe, who did not fit these criteria, was not considered as a potential suspect. This was despite the fact that he featured in several lines of inquiry. In all, Sutcliffe was interviewed in relation to the investigation on nine separate occasions and on three further occasions for unrelated matters. Because of the difficulty of sharing information, many of the interviewing officers were unaware of the level of information that was held about him or the fact that he had been previously interviewed.

The conclusion drawn from the Byford Report was that a better organized, led and resourced investigation would have arrested Sutcliffe earlier and would undoubtedly have saved lives. Despite calls for the dismissal of the Chief Constable of West Yorkshire over the failings, no action was taken against individuals.

The lasting legacy of the Byford Report lies in the development of the following:

- The standardization of documents, procedures and roles within MIRs that are contained in the Major Incident Room Standardized Administrative Procedures (MIRSAP).
- The computerization of records in the Home Office Large Major Enquiry System (HOLMES).
- Improved training of senior investigating officers.
- Standard procedures for appointing an officer in overall command to co-ordinate inquiries in linked-series investigations.
- The practice of independent officers reviewing lines of inquiry and the use of senior scientific advisers in complex investigations.

All these developments are now considered to be standard practice in the investigation of homicide and have their origin in the Byford Report.

The report was not published in full at the time and only became available in 2006, following an application by a newspaper under the Freedom of Information Act 2000. In the same year, DNA tests on the envelopes used to send the letters and tapes, which were by then known to be hoaxes, led to the conviction of John Humble for perverting the course of justice.

Peter Stelfox

Related entries

Home Office Large Major Enquiry System (HOLMES).

Key texts and sources

Copies of the Byford Report can be obtained from http://www.cabinetoffice.gov.uk/foi/reading_room/topic/previous_administration.asp.

C

CALL MANAGEMENT

> Call management is the rational allocation of police resources in response to public calls for assistance.

Police encounters with members of the public are usually initiated by the public. With the growth of telephone ownership and technical developments (e.g. mobile phones), a large proportion of public-initiated police activity is via the telephone. Police control rooms are crucial intermediaries in this process. Despite its role in linking the public with the police, call management is a topic that has largely eluded research.

Control rooms perform the following tasks. First they receive the call. Calls are usually received through dedicated emergency lines (e.g. 999, 911) or through more generally accessible non-emergency channels that may be available to different control rooms (e.g. central force-wide control rooms or locally). Some callers have dedicated lines (e.g. security companies who report alarm activations and hospitals and other premises that have 'panic buttons').

Next, the call is interpreted and assessed. The control-room staff must determine and assess what is occurring. Much will rely on assessing the caller's credibility: is he or she a hoaxer? Is the caller drunk or drugged? What is his or her emotional state? Ambient noise (e.g. background shouting, breaking of glass, sniggering accomplices, etc.) may add to or detract from the caller's credibility. Some calls may lack credibility but still acquire high priority because of the status of the source (e.g. activated burglar alarms – a high proportion of which are false alarms).

Depending on the assessment of the call, a response will be allocated and given a priority rating. Allocation may involve deciding what kind of police response is appropriate. Most commonly, this will be a routine patrol, but it could be a public-order reserve unit or a specialist response (e.g. a dog handler or firearms). Rarely will it require a wider mobilization – e.g. to a disaster, a serious crime, etc. Many forces operate systems of 'graded response' in order to prioritize the allocation of police resources to situations that either call for urgency or are most likely to result in arrest for serious criminal offences.

Dispatchers will then notify patrols of the nature, location and priority of the incident. Economy of transmission dictates that descriptions of incidents are truncated and often stereotyped (e.g. crime 'in progress', 'violent/non-violent domestic', etc.). Dispatchers will also indicate if similar calls have been received from the same location and whether there are any 'warning signals' displayed on the command-and-control computer – e.g. people known to be violent.

Finally, control rooms monitor incidents with varying attentiveness, depending on their initial assessment of the call. Officers will normally report their arrival on the scene and will give an initial appraisal. Sometimes officers at the scene will ask for additional resources or backup, which dispatchers will need to provide, often in haste.

Call management aspires to rationalize the allocation of scarce resources by limiting control-room staff's discretion in handling calls through the use of rules and procedures. However, at each of the stages identified above, there is still ample scope for discretion to influence decision-making.

P.A.J. Waddington

Related entries

Computer-aided despatch (CAD); Graded response; Home Office Large Major Enquiry System (HOLMES); Scotland (policing); Unit beat policing (UBP).

Key texts and sources

Audit Commission (1990) *Calling All Forces: Improving Police Communications Rooms.* London: HMSO.

Manning, P.K. (1988) *Symbolic Communication: Signifying Calls and the Police Response.* Cambridge, MA: MIT Press.

Waddington, P.A.J. (1993) *Calling the Police.* Aldershot: Avebury.

For a Scottish study of police call-management strategy, see http://www.audit-scotland.gov.uk/audit/pdfs/PBpolicecall.pdf. For the Thames Valley Police report on call management, see http://www.thamesvalley.police.uk/news_info/freedom/policies_procedures/pdf/Contact%20Management%20Strategy.pdf.

CAUTION

A police caution is a formal warning usually delivered by a senior officer in uniform at a police station. It is an alternative to prosecution, normally for first or second-time offenders committing less serious offences. A caution should be recorded by the police and is citable in court as part of the offender's antecedent criminal history.

A formal police caution has been used as an alternative to prosecution since the inception of organized police forces, along with other forms of diversion from court, such as no further action and informal warnings. The police should only caution when there is sufficient evidence for a realistic prospect of conviction if the case went to court or for a full admission of guilt. In the case of a juvenile, parental consent to caution will be required.

Caution rates (cautions as a percentage of all cautions and prosecutions) increased significantly in the 1980s and 1990s, particularly for juveniles. The Children and Young Persons Act 1969 and Home Office Circulars 14/85 and 59/90 drove the increased use of cautions, as well as the emergence of a practitioner orthodoxy of 'non-intervention' and 'systems management', originally attributed to Tutt and Giller (1987). Circular 59/90 introduced national standards for cautioning which remain in force, although they do not appear to be widely complied with or enforced. In 1993 the cautioning rate for 10–13-year-old males and females was 90 and 97 per cent, respectively, and that for 14–16-year-olds 69 and 87 per cent. It was presumed that adults would be prosecuted and therefore they were not cautioned, unless they were in an 'at risk' group, such as the elderly or mentally disordered.

Cautioning circulars advised chief constables that prosecution should be used as a last resort for juveniles to avoid the stigma, labelling and development of criminal careers resulting from a court appearance. Cautioning was considered a serious step, and in many cases it was thought more appropriate to give an informal warning. Although the decision to caution was a police decision, for juveniles, if the police were in doubt or there were indications of social or domestic problems, then they consulted with other agencies, such as social services, education or the Probation Service. This led to the development of inter-agency decision-making structures, including juvenile liaison panels and bureaux. Cautioning also appeared to work and to be a 'value for money' when these considerations were rising up the government's public sector policy agenda. *Home Office Statistical Bulletin 8/94* found that 85 per cent of those cautioned in 1985 and 1988 were not convicted of a 'standard list' offence within two years of their caution. This has to be treated with care because reconviction rates are not the same as re-offence rates.

Towards the mid-1990s, the caution rate for juveniles started to decline as a consequence of a reversal of Home Office policy (Circular 18/94). New Labour's Crime and Disorder Act 1998 replaced the juvenile caution with a system of reprimands and warnings. Decisions remain the responsibility of the police but now in conjunction with youth offending teams operating locally within a framework established by the national Youth Justice Board. It was envisaged that a 'rehabilitation and change programme' would accompany a 'final warning' in the majority of cases – partly as a reaction to the non-intervention approach – and that this would be based on a youth offending team risk assessment tool, the ASSET.

The Criminal Justice Act 2003 introduced a 'conditional caution' for adults, requiring participation in a rehabilitative programme or some form of reparation. The decision to give a conditional caution lies with the Crown Prosecution Service (CPS) rather than the police. This reflects the transition to joint working between the police and the CPS and provisions in the Criminal Justice Act 2003 to ensure that the CPS will now be responsible for most decisions on charging, rather than the police. Prior to reprimand and warning and conditional cautions there was no legislative basis for a caution, although this now only remains the case for a 'simple' adult caution. Nevertheless, much police cautioning practice is still unregulated, and the exact roles in practice of the police and CPS across a range of diversion decisions remain unclear.

There is a lack of cautioning research, and what there is has been mainly concerned with juveniles. The early research focused on explanations of the differences in caution rates between police forces that gave rise to accusations of 'justice by geography' (Ditchfield 1976; Laycock and Tarling 1985). While inconsistencies in outcomes might be due to legally relevant variables, 'justice' and 'equality' demand a uniformity of approach. This research suggested that, while some of the differences in rates could be accounted for by the proportion of first offenders or patterns of offending, social variables such as class, age, sex and race also played their part, as did differences in the implementation of policy. The Association of Chief Police Officers introduced a 'gravity factor matrix' in the late 1980s in an attempt to improve the consistency of decision-making. These have been refined and are now widely referred to in policy, though research suggests that their use in practice is variable.

Another focus of early research was on the net-widening thesis, whereby it was argued that an increasing number of young people were included in the criminal justice system and accelerated up tariff. Ditchfield (1976) concluded that juveniles were being cautioned when previously they would have been dealt with by informal warnings or no further action. Tutt and Giller (1987) argue that the increased numbers both prosecuted and cautioned in the period from 1980 to 1985 could only be accounted for by net widening, given the fall in the juvenile age population.

More recent research has focused on the impact of Home Office circulars on policy and practice (Evans and Wilkinson 1990; Evans and Ellis 1997). In contrast to previous research, this drew on national survey data. It found that, despite Home Office attempts to encourage greater consistency, significant differences in caution rates between and within police forces still remained. These were best explained by differences in the extent to which forces, and basic command units within forces, utilized different pre-court options, including unrecorded and recorded informal warnings, instant cautions, cautions after inter-agency consultation and 'caution plus'. Research has also examined the reliability of confession evidence in relation to cautions (Evans 1993a) and evaluations of young adult diversion schemes (Evans 1993b). The research into reprimands and warnings has been based on small samples or case studies rather than on national samples (Holdaway 2003). The most recent Home Office circular, *The Final Warning Scheme* (14/06), continues to express concern about inconsistency between forces, although reconviction studies claim they are an effective intervention (Hine and Celnick 2001).

Roger Evans

Related entries

Crown Prosecution Service (CPS); Drugs and policing; 'Judges' Rules'; Restorative justice/restorative cautioning; Right of silence.

Key texts and sources

Ditchfield, J.A. (1976) *Police Cautioning in England and Wales*. London: HMSO.

Evans, R. and Ellis, R. (1997) *Police Cautioning in the 1990s. Home Office RDS Research Findings* 52. London: Home Office.

Evans, R. and Wilkinson, C. (1990) 'Variations in police cautioning policy and practice in England and Wales', *Howard Law Journal*, 29: 155–76.

Holdaway, S. (2003) 'The final warning: appearance and reality', *Criminal Justice*, 3: 351–67.

See also the Home Office's website (**http://www.homeoffice.gov.uk/science-research/ RDS/**) and the website of the Youth Justice Board (**http://www.youth-justice-board.gov.uk/**).

CHIEF CONSTABLES

Chief constables are the chief officers of the UK police forces outside the police areas of London – the Commissioners of the City and Metropolitan forces have different constitutional and legislative histories. They are the highest rank of officer to hold the office of constable in their police force and are responsible to their police authority for its direction and control.

From their respective origins in the Municipal Corporations Act 1835 and County Police Act 1839, the borough and county police forces were locally controlled. This principle of local governance remained more or less unchallenged until after the First World War. Some oversight by the Home Office, through HM Inspectorate of Constabulary, was introduced by the County and Borough Police Act 1856. However, the management of the police was not organized along professional lines, and the local nature of policing was also reinforced by the Home Office's minimalist approach to policing during Victorian and Edwardian times. Chief constables were little more than 'gifted amateurs' and, in some cases, not so gifted.

The county chiefs (about 55) tended to be ex-military officers who were appointed mainly because they shared a similar social position and outlook to the county police authority. Borough chiefs, on the other hand (about 110), tended to have been serving police officers, chosen more for their trustworthiness rather than for their policing abilities or achievements (see Stallion and Wall 1999). Moreover, their position, unlike the county chief, had no statutory basis until 1919, and control over the police was placed in the hands of the Watch Committee. The role of borough chief, therefore, developed through practice.

Labour unrest during the late nineteenth century, the police strikes of 1916 and 1918 and the fear of Bolshevism, combined with the bureaucratic inconvenience of dealing with 180 or so individual organizations, encouraged the Home Office to (re)consider its position over the police. So, following the Desborough Committee Report in 1919, but in the absence of full statutory authority, the Home Office sought to increase its influence over policing. This was achieved by reframing the rules under the Police Act 1919 to require chief constables to have held prior police experience (esp. Regulation 9). The wartime practice of centrally directing the police with instructive circulars was continued, and the development of a 'professional' relationship between the police forces was promoted. Finally, chief police officers were encouraged to see themselves both as part of a wider policing function and as operationally independent of their police authority. These strategies strengthened both the formal and informal links between the police and the Home Office and had the long-term effect of weakening the power of the police authorities. They changed police management from being an amateur activity which relied on local models of management and practice into a professional activity informed by a shared knowledge and underpinned by centrally determined core values, yet locally responsive, even if in an account-giving rather than account-taking form (Reiner 1991).

Consequently, the type of person who became a chief constable after the 1920s changed. They were chosen more for their police and management experience. Though ever distrustful of central government, the county police authorities resisted the policy of internal recruitment by recruiting their chiefs from the colonial police because these officers satisfied the police regulations and were socially acceptable. This pattern of resistance did not continue after the Emergency Powers (Defence) Act 1939 increased the Home Secretary's direct powers over the police. The county police authorities subsequently sought to recruit the graduates of Lord Trenchard's short-lived officer-class scheme.

A national police staff college was opened in 1948 at Ryton-on-Dunsmore and moved to Bramshill in 1960. The broad function of this college was to sustain the policy of internal recruitment by educating potential senior officers and training them for command – a function it retains today. Currently, the main vehicles for training chief constables are the Senior Police National Assessment Centre and the Strategic Command Course.

Underlying the development of the police in the UK has been a powerplay between local and central government over control of the police. During the past 170 years, they have changed from being a distinct instrument of local governance to becoming an instrument of central government policy. The policy of internal recruitment has contributed to the realignment of the mechanisms that effect control over police management. It has reconfigured the social structure of police management so that, as chief constables have changed from gifted amateurs into professional bureaucrats, they have also ceased to be part of the local ruling elite and have become, instead, a very special, self-selecting and internally accountable, professional elite with links to the police policy-making process (Wall 1998).

Perhaps one of the most significant policing changes in recent years has been the increasing nationalization of policing through the centralization of police policy-making and the corporatization of the police forces. This process was strengthened by the *de facto* restructuring of the Association of Chief Police Officers (ACPO) and the introduction of the principle of assuming compliance unless a chief officer specifically stated that he or she was dissenting (Savage *et al.* 2000). It was also strengthened by the *de jure* formation of national police forces, such as the Serious Organized Crime Agency in April 2006.

Today there are 50 chief constables of geographic forces set up in the UK following the Local Government Act 1973 reorganizations (37 in England, 4 in Wales, 8 in Scotland and 1 in Northern Ireland). All are career police officers and most are university educated. Some non-geographic forces (such as the British Transport Police and the Civil Nuclear Constabulary) also have chief constables. All chief officers above the rank of chief superintendent are represented either by ACPO or ACPO Scotland. Recent plans to reduce the number of independent police forces, and therefore chief constables, were abandoned in June 2006, so the number of chief constables remains constant.

David S. Wall

Related entries

Accountability and governance; Association of Chief Police Officers (ACPO); HM Inspectorate of Constabulary (HMIC); Police Act 1964; Police and Magistrates' Courts Act 1994; Police authorities; Police Reform Act 2002; Politics (police involvement); Rank structure; Scotland (policing).

Key texts and sources

Loader, I. and Mulcahy, A. (2003) *Policing and the Condition of England: Memory, Politics and Culture.* Oxford: Oxford University Press.
Reiner, R. (1991) *Chief Constables: Bobbies, Bosses or Bureaucrats?* Oxford: Oxford University Press.
Savage, S., Charman, S. and Cope, S. (2000) *Policing and the Power of Persuasion: The Changing Role of the Association of Chief Police Officers.* London: Blackstone Press.
Stallion, M. and Wall, D.S. (1999) *The British Police: Forces and Chief Officers, 1829–2000.* Bramshill: Police History Society.
Wall, D.S. (1998) *The Chief Constables of England and Wales: The Socio-legal History of a Criminal Justice Elite.* Aldershot: Ashgate/Dartmouth.
See also ACPO's website (**http://www.acpo.police.uk/**).

CHILD ABUSE

> Child abuse is one form of the maltreatment of a child or young person under 18 years of age.

Four major categories of child abuse can be identified. First is physical abuse and, among the forms this can take, are hitting, shaking, throwing, poisoning, burning or scalding, drowning and suffocating. Secondly, sexual abuse involves forcing or enticing a child to take part in sexual activities. The persistent ill-treatment of a child can also be by way of emotional abuse, whereas a more passive form of child maltreatment is neglect. The former causes severe adverse effects on the child's emotional development, whereas the latter represents a failure to meet a child's basic physical and/or psychological needs and can result in the serious impairment of a child's health or development.

Extent and seriousness

As suggested above, there are various forms of child abuse, and the risks to the very young of being seriously and repeatedly abused are staggeringly high. There are also complex links between domestic violence and child abuse. Children under the age of 1 are more at risk of being murdered than any other age group. One National Society for the Prevention of Cruelty to Children (NSPCC) estimate suggests that 1 in 10 young adults have suffered serious abuse or neglect in childhood.

All children are most at risk to all these forms of abuse from those who care for them. Some 600 children are added to the child protection register every week. Children in local authority care are also at risk of serious forms of abuse, and deaths and suicides have resulted in these residencies. Parents, however, are the principal suspects in the vast majority of all child homicides. Child sexual abuse also occurs more frequently in the familial context than it does in public spaces and by predatory paedophile strangers.

Working together to prevent and protect: multi-agencyism

Following the death of Maria Colwell in 1973, the problem of child abuse is said to have been redis-covered. This was an era when the role of the police as an investigatory body was less central than that of social services. By the mid-1980s there was a further resurgence of widespread concern about child abuse tragedies following Jasmine Beckford (1984), Kimberley Carlile (1986) and the Cleveland Affair (1987).

In 2000, Victoria Climbié died. While multi-agency work has now become firmly recognized as fundamental to the prevention of child abuse and to its investigation, this did not prevent this terrible child abuse ordeal. Interagency communication and co-ordination, as well as inter-professional co-operation, have long been seen as essential to the effective prevention and policing of all forms of child abuse and to tackling victimization and bringing perpetrators to account. Indeed, the conclusions of the Victoria Climbié Inquiry (Laming 2003) confirmed that the legislative framework for the well-being and safety of children was sound. Fundamental and radical changes in the way the key public services are managed was central to its 108 recommendations.

In many instances, it is teachers, health professionals and social workers who are first alerted to and suspicious of child abuse. However, the Police Service has a range of responsibilities in preventing and detecting child abuse and protecting children (see Department of Health 1999, 2000). The police also have responsibilities in connection with the policing of domestic violence, which can cut across issues concerning child abuse. At one level, therefore, the police have a duty and responsibility to investigate criminal offences committed against children. The police also have a responsibility to co-ordinate and lead the risk assessment and management process for the exchange of information about all those dealt with by the courts for a sexual offence.

Child victims, abuse and the criminal justice system

The roles and responsibilities of various agencies that are formally connected to the criminal justice system impact variously upon the effective prevention, policing and experiences of child victims. The criminal justice system (the police, in particular) is pivotal in gathering sufficient evidence to bring criminal charges and to achieving criminal justice. Concomitant to this, the police, the courts and criminal proceedings generally are potential sources of further negative experiences for child victims as witnesses. This can amount to secondary victimization where victims of child abuse are especially vulnerable to experiencing reactions and responses from individuals, groups or agencies that add to their suffering.

It is only recently that children have been recognized as vulnerable victims and witnesses who deserve special status and supportive provisions when preparing for and giving evidence in adult criminal courts. Some special information is now available for parents and carers of children due to give witness evidence in court, as well as for practitioners. There are also special co-ordinator personnel (for example, child witness officers) and, in some cases, there may also be intermediaries to facilitate communication. Changes can be made to the courtroom environment (e.g. judges and lawyers may remove wigs and gowns), and other measures have also been introduced to enable child witnesses to give their best evidence, either in private or in court (including screens to shield witnesses from the accused, communication aids, video and live television links). Recently, significant issues have been raised in respect of vulnerable victims and witnesses, as well as intimidated victims, in the context of expanding the role of the volunteer appropriate adult (Williams 2000). Both vulnerable and intimidated victims are likely to qualify for an enhanced service under *The Code of Practice for Victims of Crime* (Home Office 2006f).

Concern for victims and witnesses has shaped legislative and policy changes over the last 30 years. Criticisms of police interviewing and training and an inquisitorial style of cross-examination in the courts, as well as controversy surrounding the inter-agency child protection 'policing' function more generally, have all contributed towards changing methods of investigating, evidencing and prosecuting in child abuse cases. Specific changes have been brought about following serious case reviews and inquiries. Following Jasmine Beckford's death, this included pressure on the police to introduce more sympathetic means of dealing with child victims. Following 'Cleveland' in 1987, the report (Butler-Sloss 1988) made a number of detailed recommendations, including procedures for the joint investigation of child abuse cases by police officers and social workers, the joint training of police and social workers, new interviewing techniques and a network of communication between all the involved agencies.

Over the last 30 or so years there have been over 40 major inquiries, with an estimated 90 serious case reviews per year (Redner and Duncan 2004), yet the Beckford and Cleveland cases, clearly illustrate several marked differences. There are contrasts in the type of child abuse. In the former, physical abuse and neglect were seriously overlooked whereas in the latter child sexual abuse was uncovered but, in some instances, social workers were over-zealous in their desire to take action to protect the children. Despite parental participation in serious case reviews and major inquiries having become increasingly more common since the early 1990s, many parents still feel they are unfairly labelled as child abusers.

Balancing the rights of parents and the needs of children has been 'a perennial problem for the state throughout the history of child abuse prevention' (Corby 2006: 151). The Victoria Climbié Inquiry (Laming 2003) brought together three earlier, independent statutory inquiries into her death. Lord Laming referred to 'a catalogue of administrative, managerial and professional failure by the services charged with her safety'. While the established approach is to police child abuse through multi-agencyism, the police work to standards of proof that are 'beyond reasonable doubt'. Social services seek to investigate whether child abuse has taken place and whether there is a risk to children. Into the twenty-first century, both these agencies are risk-oriented services, and there continues to be a precarious balance between the rights of children and those suspected of inflicting abuses who, for the most part, tend to be the children's primary carers.

Pamela Davies

Related entries

Crime prevention (situational and social); Domestic violence; Interagency policing; Policing; Repeat victimization; Sexual offences/sexual violence; Victim and witness support.

Key texts and sources

Corby, B. (2006) *Child Abuse: Towards a Knowledge Base*. Maidenhead: Open University Press.

Department of Health (1999) *Working Together to Safeguard Children*. London: HMSO (available online at http://www.doh.gov.uk/quality5.htm).

Department of Health (2000) *Assessing Children in Need and their Families: Practice Guidance*. London: HMSO.

Home Office (2006) *The Code of Practice for Victims of Crime: A Guide for Victims*. London: Office for Criminal Justice Reform.

Redner, P. and Duncan, S. (2004) 'Making the most of the Victoria Climbie Inquiry report', *Child Abuse Review*, 13: 95–114.

Williams, J. (2000) 'The inappropriate adult', *Journal of Social Welfare and Family Law*, 22: 43–57.

For general information on child abuse, see the websites of the NSPCC (http://www.nspcc.org.uk/) and Childline (http://www.childline.org.uk/Child abuse.asp).

CIVILIANIZATION

> Civilianization refers to a process through which staff (employed in the Police Service) do not take the oath of constable or hold a warrant but yet perform a variety of functions at various levels in the organization, up to the equivalent of assistant chief officer rank.

The first wave of civilians were employed by the Police Service at its inception in relatively low-grade clerking roles and tasks, such as cleaning and catering. On occasion, some chief officers were appointed from persons outside the service. In the modern era, Home Office Circular 114/83 provided the main impetus to what was to become a rapid expansion of civilians employed by the Police Service. The rationale offered then was that the increased demands on police services were not being met, even though there had been a progressive increase in the numbers of police officers and expenditure. In 1984, the Police and Criminal Evidence Act (PACE) required the presence of a designated sergeant to supervise the custody process, which involved the redeployment of considerable numbers of operational officers into this role. These pressures and the Conservative government's Financial Management Initiative, which sought to improve public services with the application of private sector management methods, added to the incentives to increase the rate of civilianization. Circular 114/83 had explained that there was unlikely to be any increase in the numbers of police if existing officers occupied posts that could 'properly and more economically be filled by civilians.' Such civilianization was a significant move from the earlier servicing and clerking functions to one in which warranted police officers were to be substituted by specially trained civilians in such operational roles as scenes of crime or control-room call handling. The purpose was that police officers could be released from support tasks into front-line policing. This, in turn, would be more economic and also a more efficient and effective use of resources. In addition, higher-grade posts, such as research, information technology, human resources and finance, were also the subject of a professionalization of functions with the appointment of appropriately qualified civilians.

Bodies such as the Audit Commission advocated the extension of civilianization (e.g. the setting up of administrative support units to relieve police officers of their paperwork burdens). A further Home Office Circular (105/88) developed a checklist of functions suitable for civilianization, including station inquiries, detention officers and driver training. The terminology evolved from one of civilians to 'police staff'. Thus by the 1990s, civilians made up 30 per cent of the police workforce.

Further developments in what has come to be known as the 'extended police family' involved the civilian in uniform concept. Sue Davies (1989), in commenting on the office of constable, had suggested a civilian alternative to the apparently insatiable demand from the public to have a visible policing presence. She proposed that uncommitted foot patrol is not a policing priority and that resources were unlikely to permit officers to deal with street annoyances and to take the time to talk to the public. She advocated that street wardens should perform many street tasks, without exercising the powers of a constable. This was not to be addressed until the Police Reform Act 2002, which made way for the introduction of police community support officers (PCSOs). PCSOs are support staff employed by police authorities to complement the work of police officers by performing high-visibility patrolling. They can proactively assist in crime prevention and local intelligence gathering. They help minimize the low-priority demands on police officers' time, ensuring that their attention can be directed to activities that require greater levels of training and skill. In comparison with police officers, PCSOs are endowed with limited powers. However, their exact role can vary between communities and police forces, as do the powers they are granted (Johnston 2005) – a situation that was addressed by the Police and Justice Act 2006 (see Community support officers (CSOs)). Present government plans aim to increase their number to 16,000 by 2008.

Loveday (2006) comments on the current police workforce modernization project that seeks to expand further the role of civilians, and he argues that this represents a fundamental reconsideration of the roles and status of police staff. He notes that over 70,000 police staff are currently employed, whose tasks span manning control rooms, inquiry desks and custody suites, and whose remits have expanded into crime pattern analysis and suspect interviewing. These staff represent a third of the police workforce. The Serious Organized Crime and Police Act 2005 provides for the civilianization of the role of the custody sergeant created by PACE, which stimulated the earlier phase of civilianization. This is currently contested by the Police Federation and is indicative of some tensions as to the perceived limits of the civilianization process. HM Inspectorate of Constabulary (HMIC) (2004) also noted problems between regular officers and police staff with respect to some operational functions, and especially where the latter are supervising the former.

Loveday (2006a) concludes that it is inconceivable that the police can function without civilian staff. Research by Dick and Metcalfe (2001) suggests that organizational commitment is similar for both police staff and police officers, but that work will have to be undertaken to address the work, pay, conditions and career prospects of police staff – as recommended by HMIC (2004) and as aspired to under the 'workforce modernization' programme – and the potential tensions that are likely to arise from further civilianization.

Jennifer Brown

Related entries

Community support officers (CSOs); Police powers.

Key texts and sources

HM Inspectorate of Constabulary (2004) *Modernising the Police Service: A Thematic Inspection of Workforce Modernisation.* London: Home Office.

Home Office (1983) *Manpower, Effectiveness and Efficiency in the Police Service* (Circular 114/83). London: Home Office.

Johnston, L. (2005) 'From "community" to "neighbourhood" policing: police community support officers and the "police extended family" in London', *Journal of Community and Applied Social Psychology*, 15: 241–54.

Loveday, B. (2006) 'Workforce modernisation: implications for the Police Service in England and Wales: evaluating HMIC Thematic Modernising of the Police Service', *Police Journal*, 79: 105–24.

CIVIL LIABILITY

> While police officers are personally liable for their unlawful acts, omissions and negligence, under the Police Acts 1964 and 1996, a chief constable is ultimately liable for the torts committed by an officer under his or her direction and control.

Like everyone else, police officers are liable for their unlawful acts and omissions. Under English common law, civil actions for damages in tort have served as an important constitutional safeguard against abuse of power by public officials and they played a large part in regulating police powers before their codification under the Police and Criminal Evidence Act 1984. For example, during the course of the last two centuries, the concept of reasonable suspicion has been developed by the civil courts when ruling on claims for the tort of false imprisonment as a consequence of allegations that a police officer unlawfully arrested the claimant.

In the landmark judgment of *Fisher* v. *Oldham Corporation*, it was ruled that an individual officer was personally liable for his tortious conduct when serving in the office of constable. This position was changed by s. 48 of the Police Act 1964 (now s. 88 of the Police Act 1996). A chief constable is vicariously liable for torts committed by an officer (whether a constable or police authority employee) under his or her direction and control in the performance or purported performance of the officer's functions. Although a claim can still be made against an individual officer, it is common practice for claimants to sue the chief constable for damages. The intentional torts of assault (and battery), false imprisonment and malicious prosecution (also referred to as malfeasance cases) have attracted the most publicity in recent years after civil actions developed as a popular remedy for police misconduct in the 1980s and early 1990s. In that period, success in the civil courts compared with the infrequency

with which complaints were substantiated was taken as evidence of the inadequacy of the complaints system (Smith 2006). The Metropolitan Police Commissioner appealed against a series of high-profile six-figure awards in the summer of 1996, and the Court of Appeal issued guidelines in the test case of *Thompson* v *Commissioner of Police of the Metropolis*, which capped the amount of damages juries could award.

The police are also liable in negligence, and there have been important recent developments regarding the police's duty of care to witnesses and victims of crime. At common law the courts have been reluctant to impose a duty of care on the grounds that fear of litigation would interfere with the police's capacity to investigate crime and to enforce the law. The Human Rights Act 1998 imposes additional responsibilities on the police and allows those who allege that they were responsible for a breach of their rights to sue for damages. In *van Colle* v. *Chief Constable of the Hertfordshire Police*, £50,000 was awarded to the parents of a prosecution witness shot dead by the defendant shortly before the criminal trial commenced. It was ruled in the High Court that, despite knowing that threats had been made against the deceased, the police failed to respond to the intimidation of a witness and to protect his right to life and privacy.

Graham Smith

Related entries

Accountability and governance; Constabulary independence.

Key texts and sources

See the Home Office's Police and Criminal Evidence Act web page (**http://police.homeoffice.gov.uk/ operational-policing/powers-pace-codes/pace-code-intro/**). For the Human Rights Act 1998, see **http://www.crimereduction.gov.uk/hra.htm**. For the Police Act 1996, see **http:www.opsi.gov.uk/acts/ acts1996/1996016.htm**.

CLEAR-UP RATES

In its simplest form, the clear-up rate is a measure of offences that meet the criteria for detection as defined by Section H of the Home Office Counting Rules and expressed as a percentage of total recorded crime.

The Chief Officer of Police of every police force shall at such times and in such form as the Secretary of State shall direct, transmit to the Secretary of State such particulars with respect to offences, offenders, criminal proceedings and the state of crime in the area for which the force is maintained as the Secretary of State may require (http://www.countingrules. homeoffice.gov.uk/output/Page1.asp).

Recorded crime and detection data form part of the statutory data requirement described in the paragraph above. The Home Office Counting Rules for Crime (HOCR) detail those offences contained within the notifiable crime series and define the rules for both recording and detecting crime. The notifiable crime series includes 'indictable only', 'either way' and a limited number of summary offences.

Over the decades, recorded crime and the clear-up rate became a simplistic indicator of police performance, and many forces were judged, or chose to be judged, on the way they had reduced crime or the number of crimes they had cleared up. The clear-up rate regularly attracts attention from the media as a measure of police effectiveness. The reliability of the clear-up rate as a performance indicator is vulnerable to variations in crime recording. In 2000, HM Inspector of Constabulary undertook a major review of police crime-recording practices and, in its report, *On the Record*, it was recommended that the Home Office and the Police Service should work together to develop a more consistent approach to crime recording to ensure comparability between forces.

As a response to the recommendations, the Association of Chief Police Officers (ACPO) developed the National Crime Recording Standard (NCRS) which was adopted by all police forces in England and Wales in April 2002. The NCRS is now embedded within the HOCR. ACPO, working together with the Home Office, established a governance regime for crime recording through the National Crime Recording Steering Group.

The introduction of the NCRS coincided with the development of the Policing Performance Assessment Framework (PPAF). This method of recording crime provided the Home Office with an opportunity to refine the accountability framework. While crime detection rules include both prosecution and non-prosecution clear-ups, PPAF introduced the concept of sanction and non-sanction detections. Sanction detections include those offences where an offender is charged, summoned and receives a caution (including reprimands and final warnings) and, more recently, penalty notices for specified offences and formal warnings for cannabis. Non-sanction detections became effectively excluded from the performance management regime.

The sanction detection clear-up rate continues to be measured as a statutory performance indicator to show how effective forces are in the investigation of crime, and it provides a proxy indicator for the offences that are brought to justice.

Steve Warner

Related entries

Crime statistics; Detectives; National Intellingence Model (NIM); Tasking and co-ordinating groups (TCGs).

Key texts and sources

See http://www.homeoffice.gov.uk/rds/countrules. html for files containing the Home Office's rules for counting and classifying notifiable offences in England and Wales.

CODE OF CONDUCT/ETHICS

In the past, what members of police forces were prohibited from doing was set out in a 'discipline code'. This code described the unacceptable behaviour on which a charge and disciplinary hearing were based. More recently there has been a shift away from a code of discipline to a 'code of conduct' or 'set of standards'. These standards describe the type of police behaviour that is acceptable and unacceptable in specific contexts.

The modern Police Service (post-1829), as a disciplined service, has always had some form of rules, regulation or guidance in respect of conduct by its officers. The first and enduring models were based on 'military' regimes, although it was always recognized that the police were a 'civilian force'. For the most part, the approach to defining conduct focused on describing what members of police forces were prohibited from doing, and this was enshrined in some form of 'discipline code'. This code then provided the basis for describing unacceptable behaviour, on which a charge and disciplinary hearing were based. A simple example of this is an officer being 'drunk on duty'.

The Police (Discipline) Regulations 1985 was an example of this approach, and it set out 17 'offences' in a 'discipline code'. This code, in keeping with its predecessors, contained an 'offence' of *discreditable conduct*, which had the appearance and impact of a failure that was comprehensive in its potential application.

By 1999 there was a subtle but important difference to the way in which behaviour and misconduct were expressed. There was a philosophical shift from a 'discipline code' to a 'code of conduct'. There were now only 12 elements, and they were rather more general in tone and content as against the 'offences' model of 1985 and earlier. This change received a mixed reception in police forces, mainly due to the fact that the new approach did not contain specific offence classifications, and this made formulating charges for a disciplinary hearing a more demanding and detailed task. Developments about roles and behaviours in policing also exist on an international front, and of particular interest is the Council of Europe's work on the European Convention on Human Rights with regard to the *European Code of Police Ethics*. This code comprises 65 elements and is more strategic and generic in application than individual police officer behaviour, but it does set out some general principles in this area.

In the UK a further development in the approach to police officer behaviour was signalled by the creation of the Police Service of Northern Ireland (replacing the Royal Ulster Constabulary), when the opportunity was taken to create a code of ethics. In 10 articles, this code draws from a number of sources, including the United Nations and the Council of Europe.

In England and Wales in 2004, the Home Secretary instigated a review of police disciplinary procedures. There were a number of drivers to this, which included a desire to simplify matters and to make the control of misconduct by police officers more aligned to that of the public at large. The particular legal position of police officers (as servants of the Crown rather than simply employees), their role and their responsibilities (including the potential for exercising lethal force under the law) mean they merit some singular treatment.

The opportunity of a review was taken to refine further the concept of a code of conduct and to create a set of standards (entitled *Standards of Professional Behaviour*) that combines the ethos of ethics with a code of conduct. The *Standards of Professional Behaviour* will be issued as part of the new Police (Conduct) Regulations issued by the Secretary of State in accordance with s. 87 of the Police Act 1996. The standards describe acceptable and unacceptable behaviour for police officers in specific areas and are written in a positive tone to reflect the expectation of the behaviour of officers. They are clustered under 10 headings, which are then expanded on in guidance and example. This guidance will support the new disciplinary framework that will be brought in when the Police (Conduct) Regulations 2007 become law.

Bill Taylor

Related entries

Corruption (police); Ethics in policing; European Convention on Human Rights (ECHR); Patten Report.

Key texts and sources

See the Independent Police Complaints Commission's website (http://www.ipcc.gov.uk/index/complainants/who_complaint/pol_codeconduct.htm) for the current police code of conduct. For the Police Service of Northern Ireland code of ethics, see http://www.psni.police.uk/nipb-ethics-nonotes-1.pdf. For the European code, see http://www. legislationline.org/legislation.php.?tid=155&lid=4886.

COLONIAL POLICING

Colonial policing is an *armed* rather than a *civil* style of policing that evolved throughout the British Empire. It operated within a framework of 'policing by strangers' – imperialistic and elitist in nature, where the notion of policing by coercion overshadowed policing by consent.

The 'colonial policing model' emerged alongside its 'English' counterpart in the early part of the nineteenth century. Sir Robert Peel created a semi-military police force in Ireland where the maintenance of order was perceived as a priority. The Irish Constabulary, founded in 1836, was more akin to the 'continental' models that had appeared in western Europe than to the civil style of the 'new' Metropolitan Police created in 1829. This Irish model of policing was subsequently transported throughout the British Empire and Commonwealth.

Colonial police forces were similar to a gendarmerie: armed police officers living in barracks with an emphasis on foot and arms drill. The structure of each force was divided between the gazetted ranks, or 'European' (the imperial term for 'white British') officer corps, and the rank-and-file drawn from the local population and, often, other parts of the empire, leading to the concept of *policing by strangers*. While these colonial forces varied from one colony to another in terms of their traditions and police practices, their underlying role was the colony's first line of defence, with the maintenance of law and order relegated to second place. Policing colonial peoples was facilitated by the widespread use of coercion to establish and maintain colonial rule, after which the principles of policing by consent could occur (Jeffries 1952).

Efforts to regulate colonial police forces resulted in the creation of the Colonial Police Service in 1936. This brought all the colonial police forces under one roof, bar a few notable examples (including the Indian Police, accountable to the India Office). By 1948, the authorized regular establishment of the Colonial Police Service stood at 1,040 gazetted European officers, 120 non-European gazetted officers, 659 European inspectors and 56,253 other ranks. At about this time came a call for standardization in an attempt to transform, at independence, colonial constabularies into their 'English' counterparts. This was foiled by the crisis of decolonization that occurred after 1945, which saw a return to paramilitary styles of policing. In such colonies as Palestine, Malaya and Kenya, the police operated in the front line, developing auxiliary units, strike forces and intelligence systems to ensure that colonial rule was maintained. This paved the way for newer forms of counter-insurgency policing that would appear in Northern Ireland in the 1970s.

The concept of colonial policing has contributed to the evolution of professional policing worldwide. Former colonial policemen stayed on in the post-colonial era to manage the police forces of newly independent states, or they moved to Commonwealth countries, taking their expertise and experiences with them. Those who returned to the UK included Sir Kenneth Newman, who used his Palestine police experiences to inject colonial policing notions into the management of public disturbances in London in the 1960s.

Georgie Sinclair

Related entries

Chief constables; Military policing; Models of policing; Paramilitary policing; Transnational policing.

Key texts and sources

Anderson, D.M. and Killingray, D. (1991) *Policing the Empire: Government, Authority and Control, 1830–1940.* Manchester: Manchester University Press.

Anderson, D.M. and Killingray, D. (1992) *Policing and Decolonisation: Politics, Nationalism and the Police, 1917–1965.* Manchester: Manchester University Press.

Jeffries, C. (1952) *The Colonial Police.* London: Max Parrish.

Sinclair, G.S. (2006) *Colonial Policing and the Imperial Endgame, 1945–1980: 'At the End of the Line.'* Manchester: Manchester University Press.

COMMUNITY AND RACE RELATIONS

Since the late 1960s, the British Police Service has consciously sought to nurture positive community and race relations. Initially this predominantly related to police relations with black communities in Britain, although this has broadened more recently to include other minority ethnic groups and a wide range of other interest groups.

Although the term 'community and race relations' might encompass almost any aspect of police work, in practice the phrase has had a more precise focus and has become something of a euphemism for police interactions with minority communities of various kinds. In that sense the term does not usually refer to the broad sweep of police–public relations but more narrowly to consultation and communication with those perceived in some way to have particular interests.

Police relations with minority ethnic communities have often tended to be problematic, and the recent position of black and Asian communities in Britain was foreshadowed by the experiences of Maltese, Irish, East European and Jewish migrants going back to the nineteenth century. For much of this period these relationships were conceptualized in terms that suggested that the problems were rooted within minority communities themselves: either they were particularly prone to commit certain types of crime, or they were culturally different and misunderstood the benign, almost mythical, status of the bobby in British society. For either reason, minority ethnic communities tended to be regarded as inherently problematic for the Police Service.

This model tended to conceive of the police as the impartial enforcer of the law: although individual officers might occasionally act in a prejudicial manner, this did not reflect fundamental flaws in the Police Service as an institution. The challenge for senior ranks was either to prevent 'rotten apples' from joining in the first place or to ensure that they were identified, disciplined or dismissed thereafter. Organizationally, the role of the Police Service in tackling racism was relatively narrow: to prevent racism from occurring within the ranks and to ensure that an equal level of policing was delivered to all sections of the community. This model has been labelled as 'colour blind' policing – policing delivered without reference to ethnicity.

More recently, this model has been replaced incrementally by one predicated around the development of a more proactive role for the police. In the wake of the Stephen Lawrence Inquiry, the Police Service has sought to become a positively anti-racist organization, challenging prejudice and discrimination at every turn. These ambitions have been stated in a plethora of policy documents produced by the Association of Chief Police Officers (ACPO), HM Inspectorate of Constabulary (HMIC), the Home Office and individual police services, and have been given added impetus by the Race Relations (Amendment) Act 2000, which placed a statutory duty on public bodies, including the Police Service, actively to promote good race relations and to consult with minority ethnic communities. Internally within the Police Service, this model of anti-racism led to the introduction of targets for individual police services to recruit more minority ethnic staff and to the proliferation of ethnic and religious staff associations intended, in part, to help shift the normative whiteness of police culture. The extent that these, or related, efforts have been successful is far from clear. Home Office (2006e) data show that, in 2005, 3.5 per cent of all police officers were of a black and minority ethnic (BME) background, which was a modest increase on the previous year, when the proportion was 3.2 per cent. However, this figure still lagged behind the stated target of 4.0 per cent, and it remains the case that the BME population is less well represented in more senior ranks, with only 2.3 per cent of ACPO officers being from a BME background. Both the proportions of police civilian staff and of community support officers that are of a BME background are closer to their representation in the overall population: at 5.9 per cent and 14.3 per cent, respectively. Against this context of very modest progress, ACPO requested in 2006 that the Home Office abandon minority ethnic employment targets as they were likely to be unrealizable. Since it is widely claimed that the recruitment of a diverse workforce will communicate the Police Service's genuine commitment to a progressive and inclusive organizational culture and a willingness to embrace diversity in the wider community, lack of progress on these matters seems particularly serious (Rowe 2004).

In addition to internal reforms, there have been other efforts to liaise more effectively with an increasingly diverse and fragmented population. Although some police operations against terrorism have proved controversial since the bomb attacks in London in July 2005, there does seem to have been concerted effort to liaise with minority communities in a manner that would previously have been unthinkable. One of the difficulties facing such practices is that the Police Service has not proved adept at dealing with fragmented and internally differentiated communities. Although the Police Service has made efforts to improve dialogue with those outside mainstream community organizations, it is clear that examples of good practice in this respect are often not widely spread across the Police Service (HMIC 2003b).

Central to this development has been another important shift in police discourse, which has been the recognition that social diversity encompasses more than race and ethnicity. Many of the debates and developments that have sought to improve police relations with minority ethnic communities have been extended as it has been recognized that other groups also have particular policing needs, although these too have often had mixed success. An HMIC report (2003b) identified a wide range of variables that the Police Service needed to recognize in order to provide a professional service to a heterogeneous population. Among these were the elderly, those with mental and physical disabilities, young people, older people and lesbian, gay, bisexual and transgender communities. The proliferation of staff groups within the Police Service also indicates an increasing recognition that distinct interests have particular policing needs, and that a modern ethical organization ought to meet specific needs, rather than pursue the delivery of a uniform level of service equally available to all. Disputes between some religious minorities and the Gay Police Association over the legitimacy and status of homosexuality, to take a recent example, indicate that the Police Service, like any other organization, might find that the beliefs, interests and values of a multitude of minority groups cannot always be reconciled, and that embracing diversity raises fundamental challenges.

Mike Rowe

Related entries

Black police associations; Independent advisory groups; Institutional racism; Scarman Inquiry; Stephen Lawrence Inquiry.

Key texts and sources

Cashmore, E. and McLaughlin, E. (eds) (1991) *Out of Order? Policing Black People.* London: Routledge.

Foster, J., Newburn, T. and Souhami, A. (2005) *Assessing the Impact of the Stephen Lawrence Inquiry.* Home Office Research Study 294. London: Home Office.

HM Inspectorate of Constabulary (2003) *Diversity Matters.* London: Home Office.

Home Office (2006) *Statistics on Race and the Criminal Justice System, 2005.* London: Home Office.

Rowe, M. (2004) *Policing, Race and Racism.* Cullompton: Willan Publishing.

The Home Office's web page on race relations and the police is at **http://www.homeoffice.gov.uk/ police/about/race-relations/**. The Independent Police Complaints Commission's website also contains a page about race relations (**http://www.ipcc. gov.uk/index/resources/race_equality_scheme/ restools/restools_ref/restools_rra.htm**). See also the National Black Police Association's website (**http://www.nationalbpa.com/**).

COMMUNITY POLICING

Community policing is decentralized. It involves strong, two-way communication between the local citizenry and the police. Priorities are defined by the community, and the community plays an important part in determining and implementing locally relevant and acceptable solutions to its problems.

The main impetus for community policing both in the USA and Britain was large-scale urban disorder associated with heavy-handed policing that was insensitive to the wants and needs of minority groups. The police had become detached and distant from those they were supposed to serve. In the USA the community policing movement has been very strong, in terms both of the range of police organizations embracing the concept and in the significance it is supposed to have for the organization. It is widely treated as the key organizing principle for police work. As one commentator put it: 'Community policing, or variations of it, has become the national mantra of the American Police' (Greene 2000: 301).

In Britain, community policing has never had the influence it enjoys in the USA. Though community beat officers had been in existence since the 1960s and community policing as an approach to policing was already being advocated by John Alderson in the late 1970s, Lord Justice Scarman's report on the Brixton disorders of 1981 made engagement with the community a priority. The Scarman Report led to the establishment of police community consultative groups, which comprise regular public meetings where police and residents talk together about local issues and about what is being done about them. In practice, public attendance rates, as with other community initiatives, have characteristically been low, and those attending have not been representative of local people. Older, white and middle-class people have been over-represented. Chief constables in the early 1990s were found to give only muted support to ideas of community policing. Furthermore, community policing roles enjoyed relatively low regard within police services, making it difficult to attract the most energetic and able officers.

What has been meant by 'community' and what has been included in practice within community policing has been variable. The term 'community' is notoriously slippery, referring sometimes to those with common interests regardless of place of residence, sometimes to specific, local, self-defined neighbourhoods, sometimes to beats or wards and sometimes to whole cities. It is sometimes treated as an ideal to be aspired to and sometimes as a descriptive term to refer to a given population. Community policing has involved, for example, newsletters, meetings, advisory groups, Neighbourhood Watch, direct community action, youth clubs, joint police–community operations, zero-tolerance policing and the provision of intelligence to the police. It is hard to determine what precisely is entailed in delivering community policing or what precisely constitutes the community focus.

Neighbourhood policing is planned for the whole of England and Wales by 2008. This promises higher status and more support than previous community policing initiatives. It will involve teams of police officers and community support officers working in local areas to deliver a British version of community policing.

Nick Tilley

Related entries

Chief constables; Neighbourhood policing; Scarman Inquiry.

Key texts and sources

Greene, J. (2000) 'Community policing in America: changing the nature, structure and function of the police', in J. Horney (ed.) *Criminal Justice 2000: Policies, Processes, and Decisions of the Criminal Justice System*. Washington, DC: US Department of Justice.

Scarman, Lord (1982) *The Scarman Report: The Brixton Disorders, 10–12 April 1981*. Harmondsworth: Penguin Books.

Skogan, W. (ed.) (2004) *Community Policing: Can it Work?* Belmont, CA: Thomson Wadsworth.

Tilley, N. (2003) 'Community policing, problem-oriented policing and intelligence-led policing', in T. Newburn (ed.) *Handbook of Policing*. Cullompton: Willan Publishing.

The Home Office's web page on community policing is at http://police.homeoffice.gov.uk/community-policing/. See also the Home Office's web page on neighbourhood policing (http://police.homeoffice.gov.uk/community-policing/neighbourhood-police).

COMMUNITY SAFETY

'Community safety' is a term used in policy circles to describe a local, multi-agency partnership approach to the reduction of crime and disorder. It also refers to attempts to reduce the fear of crime among local people and, more contentiuosly, the promotion and achievement of public safety.

Community safety emerged in the UK in the 1980s among several metropolitan local authorities as a *local* governmental strategy that sought to move beyond the traditionally police-driven agenda of formal crime prevention. It gained nationwide institutional recognition in the so-called Morgan Report emanating from the Home Office (1991). Apart from seeking to involve other 'social' agencies in crime prevention, community safety has also made more ambitious claims both to generate greater participation and possibly leadership from all sections of the community, geographically defined, and to target social harms from all sources in the locality and not just those classifiable as 'crimes'.

Definitions of community safety – such as 'crime prevention' and 'crime and disorder reduction' – will always remain the subject of intense debate, not least given that crime is a socially and historically contingent category. Few academic commentators would dissent from the starting point that there is no universally accepted definition of either community safety or crime prevention (Hughes 1998; Crawford 2007). However, for the purposes of government and governance, it tends to be associated with public actions aimed at a broad range of crimes and, increasingly since the Crime and Disorder Act 1998, at 'disorder' or acts of 'anti-social behaviour' in specific localities and communities. In a broad sense, it is a form of crime prevention and safety promotion policing that involves the participation of community members alongside formal agencies of the local state and quasi-formal voluntary and private agencies (Johnston and Shearing 2003). In reality, research to date indicates that community safety 'work' is both 'owned' and driven by local government and public police-dominated crime and disorder reduction partnerships (CDRPs) or community safety partnerships, set up under the terms of the Crime and Disorder Act 1998 in England and Wales (similar trends are evident in Scotland and Northern Ireland). As the institutional manifestations of community safety, CDRPs appear to sit closer to the ambition of the new public management discourse than the politics and practice of community activism.

According to a growing number of criminological scholars (Crawford 1997; Johnston and Shearing 2003; Hughes 1998, 2006), governmental logics, such as community safety, crime prevention and security, all necessarily involve political and normative and not just technological and administrative questions, despite the pretensions of the new so-called 'crime sciences' and 'what works' experimentalists (Sherman *et al.* 1997). In accordance with the famous distinction by C. Wright Mills (1959), questions of prevention and safety are both 'private troubles' for many individuals and 'public issues' related to the very structure and dominant processes at work in specific social structures. The potency –

instrumental and symbolic – of debates about crime and community safety, and policies designed respectively to reduce and increase their prevalence, is difficult to ignore. In this context it is crucial to emphasize that community safety, like security, often becomes a metaphor for much wider moral and political questions about justice, social order and the 'good society'.

Gordon Hughes

Related entries

Audit Commission; Crime and Disorder Act 1998; Crime reduction; Home Office; Plural policing; Police and Crime Standards Directorate (P&CSD); Special branch (SB); Youth and policing.

Key texts and sources

Crawford, A. (1997) *The Local Governance of Crime.* Oxford: Clarendon Press.

Crawford, A. (2007) 'Crime prevention and community safety', in M. Maguire et al. (eds) *The Oxford Handbook of Criminology.* Oxford: Oxford University Press.

Hughes, G. (1998) *Understanding Crime Prevention: Social Control, Risk and Late Modernity.* Buckingham: Open University Press.

Hughes, G. (2006) *The Politics of Crime and Community.* Basingstoke: Palgrave.

Johnston, L. and Shearing, C. (2003) *Governing Security.* London: Routledge.

For the Home Office's *National Community Safety Plan, 2006–09,* see http://www.crimereduction. gov.uk/communitysafety01.htm. See also the National Community Safety Network's website (http://www.community-safety.net/).

COMMUNITY SUPPORT OFFICERS (CSOs)

> Community support officers (CSOs) are uniformed, civilian employees of the police authority who are directed and controlled by the chief officer of the force and who possess a range of limited and discretionary police powers.

The introduction of 'community support officers' (CSOs), under s. 38 of the Police Reform Act 2002, constitutes one of the New Labour government's most significant modernization reforms of the police. Sometimes referred to as 'police community support officers' (PCSOs) to indicate their organizational affiliation, they have become central to the concept of the 'extended police family' – the widely used metaphor for policing delivered by a plurality of different personnel. Acting in an auxiliary capacity to police constables, with a focus predominantly on providing high-visibility patrol, the arrival of CSOs heralds an important further degree of civilianization and specialization in the police division of labour. The Police Federation opposed their introduction by raising concerns that CSOs would encroach on both the role and funding of police officers. As CSOs receive substantially less training, have fewer powers and earn less salary than constables, their opponents have also criticized them for being representative of a 'two-tier' system of policing, as well as a form of 'policing on the cheap'.

Funded mostly by a combination of central and local government, there are currently over 6,750 CSOs deployed across the 43 local police forces of England and Wales, equating to 3 per cent of all Police Service strength and 8 per cent of all police staff (Clegg and Kirwan 2006). The government's annual spending review of 2004 outlined plans to increase the number of CSOs to 16,000 by 2008 – a target that, if met, will transform the current ratio of CSOs to police officers from approximately 1 in 22 to almost 1 in 9. As such, CSOs are likely to become the public face of community policing, with an integral role in the delivery of 'neighbourhood policing'. The introduction of CSOs, and the planned expansion in their numbers, can be linked to a series of governmental agendas.

First, and primarily, CSOs have been introduced to enhance the visible patrol capability of local police forces. Public anxiety about crime and disorder has become entwined with widespread concerns over the demise of community-orientated, police foot patrols. The advent of CSOs is, therefore, strongly linked to political imperatives to reduce the fear of crime, to provide reassurance to local communities and to improve public confidence in the police. The appearance of CSOs in local neighbourhoods is an expedient and concrete, if largely symbolic, way by which government has been able to demonstrate that it is taking action on law and order.

Secondly, CSOs have gained much operational responsibility for the policing of 'anti-social behaviour' in public spaces in residential and commercial areas. While on patrol, CSOs are routinely tasked not only with community engagement and crime prevention but also increasingly with enforcement-orientated duties, such as dealing with physical and social incivilities, undertaking surveillance of 'problematic' groups and gathering intelligence on anti-social behaviour. As the powers chief officers can confer on CSOs are mostly restricted to dealing with anti-social behaviour, some commentators have identified the rationale for their introduction as the creation of 'quasi-police officers' to police 'quasi-crimes' (Ormerod and Roberts 2003: 157).

Thirdly, the recruitment of CSOs is linked to the Home Office's 'diversity agenda', in which the police are required by 2009 to be representative of the communities they serve (Johnston 2006). In the Metropolitan Police area, where the concentration of CSOs is greatest and the requirement for greater diversity among police is arguably most pressing, 35 per cent of CSOs are of ethnic minority origin. Nationally, 15 per cent of CSOs are of ethnic minority origin, a higher proportion than other police staff and police officers (Clegg and Kirwan 2006). Similarly, CSOs are improving the gender balance within the police, with 42 per cent being female.

Fourthly, CSOs constitute part of the Home Office's 'workforce modernization' programme in which civilians perform tasks previously undertaken by constables. This agenda aims to improve organizational efficiency by releasing constables from low-level tasks, allowing them instead to concentrate their activities on higher-priority duties that require their greater depth of training and broader powers. This goal, however, may be undermined if constables are routinely tasked to respond to the increased volume of intelligence about crime and anti-social behaviour that CSOs generate while on patrol.

Fifthly, CSOs have been identified as a key strategy by which the police aim to maintain 'policing within the police'. In response to the increasing marketization and pluralization of policing, the police argued that the introduction of CSOs would help them compete more effectively against other providers of visible policing in the emerging market for security-orientated patrols (see Blair 1998). Importantly, CSOs can be not only recruited, trained and deployed to police divisions more speedily than constables and at a lower cost but they are also less likely to be abstracted from geographically aligned patrol work.

Recent developments, however, identify that the role is undergoing a process of professionalization, which may endanger the contribution of CSOs in these agendas. Although conceived as 'dedicated patrol officers', the broadening and deepening of CSO training regimes, the standardization and extension of their legal powers, and their greater integration within the bureaucratic command and control system are combining to foster a more flexible use of the resource by police managers. In this respect, CSOs are often deployed to various low-level policing tasks – for example, traffic duties and victim contact work, as well as scene preservation and generic guarding duties (Crawford *et al.* 2005b). This reduces the extent of CSOs' reassurance-based patrols and risks, according to the role, a low status within the police hierarchy. Integrating CSOs into the institutional fabric of the police, such that they do not become a maligned 'organization within an organization', represents a key challenge for the service (Crawford *et al.* 2004).

The extension of CSOs' legal powers contained in recent legislation may have a more fundamental impact on the nature of the role. Powers introduced by the Anti-social Behaviour Act 2003, such as those to disperse groups in designated dispersal zones and to issue penalty notices for an increasingly broad array of low-level offences, have brought a more coercive edge to the role. Further, the Police and Justice Act 2006 standardizes the majority of their available powers and so introduces greater consistency over what CSOs can legally do. The standardized menu will comprise a range of security and enforcement-orientated powers, including (in specified circumstances) the powers to detain persons for 30 minutes, to stop and search, to seize alcohol, to search and enter premises and vehicles, and to issue fines for anti-social behaviour (see Jason-Lloyd 2006). This may reduce any uncertainty among the public over the differential access of CSOs to legal powers, but it risks drawing the latter into more confrontational encounters with the former. Such an outcome is likely to undermine not only the consensual and community-focused style of policing initially envisaged for CSOs but also efforts to recruit high numbers of ethnic minority people into the role.

The concept of the CSO chimes with the lay imagery of Sir Robert Peel's 'citizen in uniform' dedicated to patrol, but like their police constable predecessors they may find that pressures within and without the police bureaucracy impinge on the extent to which they are able to remain true to the vision of their architects.

Stuart Lister

Related entries

Beat; Civilianization; Community policing; Dispersal orders; Neighbourhood policing; Neighbourhood wardens; Plural policing; Police and Criminal Evidence Act 1984 (PACE); Police powers; Police Reform Act 2002; Public attitudes to the police; Reassurance policing; Roads (policing of).

Key texts and sources

Cooper, C., Anscombe, J., Avenell, J., McLean, F. and Morris, J. (2006) *A National Evaluation of Community Support Officers. Home Office Research Study* 297. London: Home Office.

Crawford, A. (2003) 'The pattern of policing in the UK: policing beyond the police', in T. Newburn (ed.) *Handbook of Policing*. Cullompton: Willan Publishing.

The Home Office's community support officers web page is at **http://police.homeoffice.gov.uk/ community-policing/community-support-officers/**. See also the website of Police Community Support Officers UK (**http://www.pcsos-national.co.uk/**).

COMPSTAT

Compstat (short for computerized statistics) is a police managerial accountability mechanism. It is designed to be a process by which police commanders can be made accountable for the crime levels in their command areas, and it aims to reduce crime and quality-of-life problems by making commanders answerable to the executive level of the Police Service.

The crime reduction component of the Compstat process revolves around four principles: timely and accurate intelligence, effective tactics, rapid deployment and relentless follow-up and assessment. The basic aim is to provide commanders with regular detailed intelligence on crime hotspots so that they can determine an appropriate crime reduction strategy.

Compstat originated in the early 1990s in the New York City Police Department under Police Commissioner William Bratton. At regular meetings, maps of crime were projected on to a wall. This crime-mapping system allowed meeting participants to concentrate on crime hotspots, and precinct commanders were asked not only to address emerging crime hotspots but also to review the effectiveness of previously employed tactics. Accurately or not, Compstat was associated with a significant reduction in crime in New York City. As a result, Compstat was rapidly adopted in other cities and countries, sometimes under a different name (for example, Australia's New South Wales Police called their Compstat process the 'Operations and Crime Review').

The name (sometimes also referred to as computerized statistics) does tend to be a little misleading. While geographical information systems do play a substantial role in the process, Compstat is a marriage of crime mapping, operational strategy and accountability among mid-level commanders. The crime mapping of local hotspots forms the focus for the timely and accurate intelligence, and it then falls to the commanders to devise effective tactics to combat existing and new crime problems. The local area commanders are next required to deploy appropriate resources rapidly in an attempt to capitalize on the timely intelligence. The last part of the process often takes place at subsequent Compstat meetings, where the review of the crime patterns after the deployment of resources indicates the success (or not) of the previously adopted tactics. This relentless follow-up and assessment is a key part of the process.

Reviews of Compstat appear to be mixed. Some question whether Compstat was responsible for the crime reduction in New York City in the early to mid-1990s, citing other possible explanations, such as increased recruitment of police in the city, a levelling of the crack cocaine market, an improvement in the national economy and the introduction of zero-tolerance policing, all of which occurred over the same period. Evaluations of Compstat have also noted that it tends to drive short-term thinking. Attempts to alleviate long-established crime and disorder problems are expected to be effective over a few weeks, thus forcing commanders to employ target patrol strategies that rarely address the long-term causes of crime. Other evaluations have also noted that Compstat has a distinctly 'theatrical' component, where style and delivery to a large audience are more important than substance, and where the crime reduction aspects can play a secondary role in the meeting.

However, Compstat has also been described as a paradigm in police organizational management and has been cited as responsible for moving the police towards a more data-driven and intelligence-led approach to crime reduction. There have, as yet, not been sufficient evaluations of

Compstat in enough locations to provide the empirical evidence to state definitively that the introduction of Compstat reduces crime or not. However, this has not stopped adaptations of Compstat reaching police departments worldwide.

Jerry H. Ratcliffe

Related entries
Zero-tolerance policing (ZTP).

Key texts and sources

Moore, M.H. (2003) 'Sizing up Compstat: an important administrative innovation in policing', *Criminology and Public Policy*, 2: 469–94 (reprinted in Newburn, T. (ed.) (2005) *Policing: Key Readings*. Cullompton: Willan Publishing).

Weisburd, D., Mastrofski, S.D., McNally, A.M., Greenspan, R. and Willis, J.J. (2003) 'Reforming to preserve: Compstat and strategic problem solving in American policing', *Criminology and Public Policy*, 2: 421–56 (reprinted in Newburn, T. (ed.) (2005) *Policing: Key Readings*. Cullompton: Willan Publishing).

COMPUTER-AIDED DESPATCH (CAD)

Computer-aided despatch (CAD) is the use of technology to support and enhance the way that calls for service are managed.

Up until the late 1980s, the resourcing and management of incidents reported to the police were dealt with by means of paper-based systems. With the increase in demand, systems with a much greater capacity were needed. Coupled with advances in computerization, electronic solutions become possible and affordable. Such systems are not universally referred to as computer-aided despatch (CAD). Terms such as 'command and control', and 'operational information systems' are among the others used. Improvements and enhancements are constantly becoming available, so that CAD systems now include features such as mapping systems (to show the location of the incident, the caller or the whereabouts of resources), as well as access to contingency plans for specific sites or types of incident.

By integrating CAD with other computer systems, the availability of wider information about locations and people gives real-time access to relevant historical information, as well as warnings to assist the officers attending. This plays a key role in tailoring an appropriate response as well as in helping to ensure officer safety. CAD has also made a wide range of management information available. Future challenges include the further integration of systems so that information can be accessed at one hit rather than needing to repeat requests. Information security is also becoming an important issue. As more information becomes available, it is imperative that disclosure of that information is carefully monitored to ensure that only necessary information is released and that there are no information leakages.

David Coulson

Related entries

Call management; Graded response; Home Office Large Major Enquiry System (HOLMES); Scotland (policing); Unit beat policing (UBP)

Key texts and sources

Audit Commission (1990) *Calling All Forces: Improving Police Communications Rooms.* London: HMSO.

Manning, P.K. (1988) *Symbolic Communication: Signifying Calls and the Police Response.* Cambridge, MA: MIT Press.

Waddington, P.A.J (1993) *Calling the Police.* Aldershot: Avebury.

CONSTABLES

Today, the constable is the entry rank to the Police Service. Historically, however, the office of constable was a locally elected role undertaken by 'worthy' men of the community.

The position of constable grew from the idea of 'men of superior birth' defending the homeland. At the very start of the thirteenth century, every adult free man was encouraged to arm himself against invasion from France or against local threats. Sheriffs took charge of the militia of a hundred (an area of land) under the general charge of a constable. This improvement in the frankpledge system was reinforced in 1252 when royal writ reiterated the role of the constables, reinstated 'hue and cry' and, additionally, established local watches to patrol parishes after dark. Anyone falling foul of the watchmen was interrogated by the constable in the morning and, if needed, delivered to a local lock-up. Strictly speaking, constables were officers of the king, but they were elected locally from and by local 'worthies', and they answered to local magistrates. Some of the duties of constables were taken over by justices of the peace after 1360, but essentially they retained the responsibility of keeping law and order and, until the eighteenth century, were usually men with military experience.

The constables at that time often took up the 'honour' very reluctantly. The office could prove costly. Provisioning a group of watchmen, chasing down offenders, executing warrants from the local magistrates, keeping the defendant in a lock-up or even in their homes until trial and then delivering them to petty or quarter sessions (sometimes some distance away) could, as one might imagine, cost a lot of money. If one adds to this the unpopularity of collecting local taxes, it is easy to see why many attempted to evade this position.

The efficiency of constables was therefore variable, as it fell to those who could not avoid it or who attempted to make the position pay through collection of fees and expenses. The constables became, in some areas, despised and a symbol of corruption in government. It is a wonder, then, that the idea of the constable is still held with such affection. This is partly due to the creation of a constabulary by the County Police Acts 1839 and 1840. The downgrading of the position of constable was coincident with an attempt to professionalize the post. Although mid-nineteenth-century constables were also of variable quality, many being dismissed for drunkenness and many being corrupt, by the end of the century the introduction of police pensions, the grading of officers and (slightly) better recruitment and training incrementally improved the reputation of police constables. The police constable, of course, became associated in the 1950s in the public mind with George Dixon of *The Blue Lamp* fame, and this no doubt helped improve the general public image of police constables. That dominant image was scarcely challenged until the last quarter of the twentieth century.

Barry Godfrey

Related entries

Beat; Civilianization; Civil liability; Constabulary independence; Dixon of Dock Green; Frankpledge; Hue and cry; Plural policing; Police powers; Rank structure; Royal Commission on the Police (1962); Special Constabulary; Unit beat policing (UBP).

Key texts and sources

Bartlett, R. (2000) *England under the Norman and Angevin Kings, 1075–1225.* Oxford: Oxford University Press.
Godfrey, B. and Lawrence, P. (2005) *Crime and Justice, 1750–1950.* Cullompton: Willan Publishing.
See also the Police Federation's website (http://www.polfed.org/default.asp).

CONSTABULARY INDEPENDENCE

Constabulary independence concerns the idea that there should be a distance between the police and the government, as well as a degree of autonomy and freedom for the police from political or other external interference and direction in the enforcement of the law.

Ever since the 'new police' were established in Britain in the nineteenth century, the relationship between the police and politicians and governments has been a source of controversy and, sometimes, concern. From the outset, opponents of the 'new police', expressed fears that they would perform a role as 'government spies', as the French police of the time were perceived to do, or that they would be deployed to serve particular partisan interests rather than some more generic 'public interest'.

The nineteenth-century police reformers adopted two key strategies to try to allay these fears. The first was to suggest that the 'new police' were not really 'new' but simply a more organized, efficient incarnation of the old police whom they replaced. A hundred or so years later, in summarizing what he described as the 'nine principles' on which the 'new police' were established, Charles Reith (1952: 163) summarized this strategy in the following terms: [The seventh principle]:

> *To maintain at all times a relationship with the public that gives reality to the historic tradition that the police are the public and that the public are the police; the police being only members of the public who are paid to give full time attention to duties which are incumbent on every citizen, in the interests of community welfare and existence.*

The second strategy was to urge a distancing between the police and the government, as well as a degree of autonomy and freedom for the police from political or other external interference and direction in the enforcement of the law. It is this second strategy that gave rise, especially during the twentieth century, to the notion or doctrine (as it has come to be regarded) of 'police independence'. Modelled on the similar idea of 'judicial independence', which also emerged during the nineteenth century in Britain, the idea behind the notion of police independence was that freedom from external influence or direction was essential to ensure that the police enforced the law equally and impartially with respect to all citizens, regardless of any partisan political or personal considerations. As such, the notion of police independence, like that of judicial independence, can be regarded as an essential element of the broader concept, propounded particularly by the nineteenth-century jurist, Alfred Dicey, of 'the rule of law'.

For much of the nineteenth and early twentieth centuries, the principle of police independence in Britain was reflected as much in its breach as in its observance. Indeed, several writers on the topic, such as the political scientist, Geoffrey Marshall (1965), and the lawyer, Laurence Lustgarten (1986), have argued persuasively that the doctrine has no legitimate historical pedigree, either in constitutional law or in practice, and in his book, *A History of Police in England and Wales* (1967), Thomas Critchley provided numerous examples of circumstances in which the police were specifically directed by their watch committees as to how and against whom the law should be enforced (see Brogden 1982).

A number of authoritative statements about the relationship between the police and governments in the twentieth century, however, lent support and credibility to the idea of police independence as a fundamental constitutional principle. In its report in 1929, the Royal Commission on Police Powers and Procedures commented that duties are imposed upon every constable by law and 'cannot be widened or restricted by any superior officer or administrative authority' (1929: 15). The commission also wrote, however, that it was the duty of a chief constable to direct the activities of members of his force to ensure that they properly discharged the duties of their office. It added that 'the chief constable is responsible to his police authority' and should direct the activities of the force with its approval. This seemed to leave little room for any broad immunity for the police, either as individual officers or as an institution, from direction as to the performance of their duties and role.

A year later, however, the decision of Mr Justice McCardie in the case of *Fisher* v. *Oldham Corporation* gave a huge boost to the idea of police independence. Fisher claimed that he had been falsely arrested by members of the Oldham Police, and sued the Oldham Corporation, as the police's employer, for damages. In dismissing the case, McCardie held, citing decisions in some earlier Australian cases, that for purposes of civil liability the relationship between the police and the corporation could not be considered one of master and servant, because:

If the local authorities are to be liable in such a case as this for the acts of the police with respect to felons and misdemeanours, then it would indeed be a serious matter and it would entitle them to demand that they ought to

secure a full measure of control over the arrest and prosecution of all offenders

(Fisher v. Oldham Corporation at 372–3).

In its report some 30 years later, the Royal Commission on the Police invoked the judgment in the *Fisher* case in support of its assertion that, with respect to their 'quasi-judicial' law enforcement functions of investigation, arrest and prosecution in individual cases, 'it is in the public interest that a chief constable …should be free from the conventional processes of democratic control and influence' (1962: 30). Nevertheless, the commission emphasized that this did not detract from the ultimate political *accountability* of the chief constable for such decisions.

It was in the words of Lord Denning, in his judgment in the case of *R* v. *Metropolitan Police Commissioner ex parte Blackburn* in 1968, that the doctrine of police independence found its most expansive and most often quoted modern expression:

I have no hesitation…in holding that, like every constable in the land, the Commissioner should be, and is, independent of the executive. He is not subject to the orders of the Secretary of State, save that under the Police Act 1964 the Secretary of State can call on him to give a report, or to retire in the interests of efficiency. I hold it to be the duty of the Commissioner of Police, as it is of every chief constable, to enforce the law of the land. He must take steps so to post his men that crimes may be detected; and that honest citizens may go about their affairs in peace. He must decide whether or not suspected persons are to be prosecuted; and, if need be, bring the prosecution or see that it is brought; but in all these things he is not the servant of anyone, save of the law itself. No Minister of the Crown can tell him that he must, or must not, keep observation on this place or that; or that he must, or must not, prosecute this man or that one. Nor can any police authority tell him so. The responsibility for law enforcement lies on him. He is answerable to the law and to the law alone

(R v. Metropolitan Police Commissioner at 769).

Despite its evident confounding (in the last sentence) of independence (freedom from direction and control) and accountability (requirements to account for one's decisions), and despite the fact that it has subsequently been criticized by many leading police and constitutional scholars – Lustgarten (1986: 64) commented that 'seldom have so many errors of law and logic been compressed into one paragraph' – this statement of the doctrine of police independence has now come to be accepted as definitive by police, politicians and commissions of inquiry in almost all countries of the Commonwealth (Stenning 2006) and has been endorsed by superior courts in several subsequent cases in these countries, including the House of Lords in England (see *R v. Chief Constable of Sussex, ex parte International Trader's Ferry Ltd*).

Philip Stenning

Related entries

Accountability and governance; Police authorities; Politics (police involvement); Scotland (policing).

Key texts and sources

Critchley, T. (1967) *A History of Police in England and Wales*. London: Constable.

Jones, T. (2003) 'The governance and accountability of policing', in T. Newburn (ed.) *Handbook of Policing*. Cullompton: Willan Publishing.

Lustgarten, L. (1986) *The Governance of Police*. London: Sweet & Maxwell.

Stenning, P. (2006) 'The idea of the political "independence" of the police: international interpretations and experiences', in M. Beare and T. Murray (eds) *Police and Government Relations: Who's Calling the Shots?* Toronto: University of Toronto Press.

See also HM Inspectorate of Constabulary's website (**http://inspectorates.homeoffice.gov.uk/hmic/**).

CONSULTATION

> Alongside formal mechanisms to control and oversee policing have developed a range of mechanisms intended to provide for direct liaison and consultation between the Police Service and the public. The extent to which these have given members of the public direct input into policing, however, is much debated.

For most of its history the Police Service has not been expected to liaise or consult with the public. Fear of being compromised by sectional interests seems to have prevented the Metropolitan Police, for example, from consulting the community during the 1950s and 1960s (Whitfield 2007). Formal channels incorporating local and national interests have had a legitimate role in the democratic oversight and direction of the Police Service for many decades, but mechanisms to liaise directly with the public have only developed since the mid-1980s.

It was following a recommendation of the Scarman Inquiry into the 1981 Brixton riots that the Police and Criminal Evidence Act 1984 required that police services establish police community consultative committees (PCCCs), designed to provide an opportunity for the police and public to discuss issues of concern in local areas. For a variety of reasons the PCCCs did not provide for robust consultation: they tended not to attract much public interest and lacked power in terms of having an influence on police practice. Keith's (1988) study of PCCCs in London did suggest, though, that they were a useful 'safety valve' on occasion and may have prevented issues of concern escalating into more serious conflict.

Since then other measures have been developed requiring police consultation with the public. Developments in the 1990s, such as the Police and Magistrates' Courts Act 1994 and the Police Act 1996, required chief constables and police authorities to consult more closely with local communities and to encourage scrutiny by becoming more transparent. Commentators have noted that the development of performance indicators and the broader regime of new public management have owed more to a desire to extend the power and reach of central government, especially in fiscal terms, than to a desire to enhance local accountability (McLaughlin *et al.* 2001). Public consultation has been a recurring theme in New Labour's rolling programme of police reform. The flagship Crime and Disorder Act 1998 requires that crime and disorder reduction partnerships (CDRPs) conduct crime audits of local areas and consult with local communities to produce a strategy to tackle issues of concern. A review of the first round of audits found that CDRPs tended to rely on official sources of data and only rarely conducted surveys of local communities or used other methods to consult the public (Phillips *et al.* 2000). A subsequent review suggested that CDRPs widely consulted with the public and that such engagement had a significant impact on establishing priorities (Newburn and Jones 2002). However, it also noted that consultation had a limited impact because, among other things, the results arrived at were sometimes at odds with targets and priorities imposed internally, locally or by central government. This illustrates a fundamental limit of processes of consultation, which is that they do not necessarily entail any transference of power to those being consulted. In this context, control remains in the hands of the Police Service, police authorities, the Home Office and the myriad agencies involved in police governance.

Mike Rowe

Related entries

Community and race relations; Doctrine; Police authorities; Stephen Lawrence Inquiry.

Key texts and sources

Keith, M. (1988) 'Squaring circles? Consultation and "inner city" policing', *New Community*, 15: 63–77.
McLaughlin, E., Muncie, J. and Hughes, G. (2001) 'The permanent revolution: New Labour, new public management and the modernisation of criminal justice', *Criminal Justice*, 1: 301–18.
Newburn, T. and Jones, T. (2002) *Consultation by Crime and Disorder Partnerships. Police Research Series Paper* 148. London: Home Office.
Phillips, C., Considine, M. and Lewis, R. (2000) *A Review of Audits and Strategies Produced by Crime and Disorder Partnerships in 1999. Briefing Note* 8/00. London: Home Office.
Whitfield, J. (2007) 'The historical context: policing and black people in post-war Britain', in M. Rowe (ed.) *Policing Beyond Macpherson.* Cullompton: Willan Publishing.

CORONERS

Coroners are independent judicial officers whose role is to ascertain the medical cause of death in cases where this is not known and to investigate whether this arose from violence or other unnatural causes.

Coroners are usually lawyers but, in some cases, are doctors. The office of coroner dates from 1194, and the basis of the modern office was created by the Coroners' Act 1887. The current legislation governing coroners is the Coroners' Act 1988.

The coroner has the duty to investigate the circumstances of sudden, unnatural or uncertified deaths. These are usually reported by the police or a doctor. If the coroner decides that a medical examination of the deceased is required, a pathologist will carry it out and, if this shows that death was not due to natural causes, an inquest will be convened. This constitutes an inquiry to determine how, when and why the deceased person died but not to determine who was to blame for the death. Juries are sometimes used at inquests, including deaths occurring in prison or in police custody. When used, it is they who make the final decision as to whether death arose from unlawful killing, misadventure or accident.

Historically, the independence of the coroners made for critical scrutiny of police actions. This was displayed early in the life of the Metropolitan Police when a police baton charge at a political rally organized by the National Political Union of the Working Classes resulted in an officer, PC Culley, being fatally stabbed. The inquest jury returned a verdict of justifiable homicide. More recently, the verdict of an inquest jury in 1997 into the murder of Stephen Lawrence that he had been 'unlawfully killed in a completely unprovoked racist attack by five white youths' emphasized the shortcomings of the police investigation into his murder.

The investigation of deaths in police custody form an important aspect of coroners' work. However, verdicts of unlawful killing do not automatically result in the prosecution of officers who were involved in the death. The Butler Report (1999) argued that the Crown Prosecution Service (CPS) should prosecute officers when there was a case to answer, but this agency has remained loathe to do so, for reasons of the higher burden of proof required in a criminal court and the unlikelihood of conviction. The CPS, therefore, often effectively overturns the verdict of an inquest.

This situation has prompted calls for reform designed to improve the way in which deaths of this nature are investigated and to improve police practices to prevent them from arising in the first place. Liberty (2003) proposed a number of changes to the manner in which deaths in custody were investigated. These included investigating every death in custody as a possible homicide and investigating all deaths in custody independently. In 2004 the Joint Parliamentary Committee on Human Rights noted that, although some forces had established procedures designed to prevent and reduce the number of deaths in custody, there was a wide variation in practice across the country. Accordingly, it proposed the establishment of a multi-agency body specifically to focus on deaths in custody. In 2006 the Forum for Preventing Deaths in Custody was set up, which represents 14 organizations (including coroners and the Police and Prison Services) who work together to reduce the number of deaths in custody.

Peter Joyce

Related entries

Crown Prosecution Service (CPS); Stephen Lawrence Inquiry.

Key texts and sources

Butler, G. (1999) *Inquiry into Crown Prosecution Service Decision-making in Relation to Deaths in Custody and Related Matters.* London: HMSO.
Joint Parliamentary Committee on Human Rights (2004) *Deaths in Custody: Third Report. House of Lords Paper* 15, House of Commons Paper 137. London: HMSO.
Liberty (2003) *Deaths in Custody – Reform and Redress.* London: Liberty.
The Coroners Society's website is at **http://www.coroner.org.uk/**. See also the Department of Constitutional Affairs' web page on coroners (**http://www.dca.gov.uk/corbur/coronfr.htm**).

CORRUPTION (POLICE)

> Police corruption generally refers to officers who do something against their duty, or who do not do something, in return for some gain or promise, though it may also refer more broadly to police abuse of power.

The idea of corruption as acts of commission or omission in return for some gain or promise focuses principally on bribery and on financial arrangements for not enforcing the law: it reflects legal definitions relating to a briber, a bribee and reciprocation from the bribee. But the policing literature conveys evidence of widespread and even systematic deviation from rules and laws by officers (Simpson 1977; Duchaine 1979). There is reference to internal disciplinary offences and criminal offences (such as excessive violence, the abuse of human rights, burglary and perjury), while in some societies the police become involved in political violence, drug trafficking and torture. Corruption is, then, also often used as a broad label to refer to police abuse of power. This wider definition enables researchers to examine the entire range of police deviance and misconduct, and it raises profound questions as to why police officers, who are meant to abide by the law, break the law. Furthermore, there is the key issue of police accountability: 'who controls the controllers'?

Institutional responses to corruption scandals frequently adopt the imagery of isolated incidents or of a few 'bad apples' (Punch 2003). Yet in his overview, Newburn (1999) maintains that conventional corruption is found in virtually all forces, at every level of the organization and in all countries at some time. In short, corruption needs to be viewed as an inherent and universal facet of policing: it cannot simply be the product of 'bad apples'. Indeed, when we scrutinize the spectrum of police corruption, with officers seriously abusing the trust in them to engage in grave offences against citizens, suspects and criminals, then we can only conclude that this is 'police crime'.

The police may collude with external groups, such as politicians and/or organized criminals, to engage in serious crime, including the drug trade. And while we associate police death squads with South America, it is clear that the police in Northern Ireland co-operated with British security services to leak information about people suspected of supporting the Republican cause to Protestant, paramilitary groups who then murdered innocent citizens. And in Spain a covert unit assassinated people associated with the Basque separatist movement, ETA.

However, most research into corruption has looked at practices that are largely internal to the police organization. These can be roughly classified into four categories. *Grass eaters* passively accept the perks of free meals and gifts. This low-level corruption may involve some implicit reciprocation, such as turning a blind eye to minor offences, may be widespread and may be viewed as perfectly acceptable (perhaps also among police researchers!). The *meat eaters* are proactive, corrupt entrepreneurs who regulate 'graft' by effectively licensing criminal and legitimate enterprises, by demanding money and by co-operating with certain criminal groups. Generally, this will be found in detective units with close links to organized crime. Here the police are plainly the regulators of corruption.

Noble cause corruption represents activities where officers rationalize that, to secure a conviction, they 'must' bend the rules. There is no corruptor and no direct financial gain but, rather, a determination to achieve results. In Britain, a series of miscarriages of justice were uncovered, involving suspected terrorists, where detectives had falsified statements, interfered with evidence, pressurized suspects to give false confessions and had lied in court (also referred to as 'process corruption'). The justification was doubtless that these were high-profile cases with intense public pressure to secure a conviction – and police culture may support this. But it also emerged that the deviant techniques were employed more widely in routine cases, suggesting that the practice was widespread. The fourth category relates to the criminal behaviour of *super-predators*, who are into gratuitous violence, stealing drugs from suspects and recycling them, burglary, selling cases, sexual offences, collusion with criminals and even murder. They have become criminals.

In short, police corruption takes many forms, is a reoccurring and tenacious element in policing and can be highly pernicious. Revelations about it can have considerable implications within and beyond the police organization (Sherman 1978). It cannot be dismissed as individualistic human failure or as episodic because it can be engrained and systemic. And it cannot easily be dealt with by a 'quick-fix', reform programme. Indeed, many senior officers and others appreciate this, and increasing attention is paid to ethics, integrity and governance as well as to assertive counter-corruption measures in proactive 'professional standards units'. Persistent, well resourced, intelligence-led strategies are employed to anticipate and locate corrupt officers and to tackle them as serious criminals within the organization. The strengthening of external oversight, with the Independent Police Complaints Commission in England and Wales and the Police Ombudsman in Northern Ireland, has also enhanced the emphasis on accountability.

Inevitably, the subject of corruption raises painful issues for the police, but these cannot be denied or ignored. Police agencies are changing and reforming. If they claim to be in the business of public service, policing by consent, tackling crime, creating security and establishing client-friendly relations with the public, then they cannot abuse people's rights, physically assault them, distort evidence and collude with criminals. For if policing is essentially about the rule of law, due process, respect for citizens' rights, professional ethics, transparency and accountability, then it cannot tolerate corruption. Yet the first step in tackling corruption is to acknowledge that the research evidence graphically illustrates that policing and corruption are inseparable.

Maurice Punch

Related entries

Constables; Criminal investigation department (CID); Detectives; Ethics in policing; Independent Police Complaints Commission (IPCC); Media and policing; Police culture; Specialist squads.

Key texts and sources

Newburn, T. (1999) *Understanding and Preventing Police Corruption: Lessons from the Literature.* London: Home Office.

Sherman, L.W. (1978) *Scandal and Reform: Controlling Police Corruption.* Berkeley, CA: University of California Press.

COVERT POLICING

Covert policing refers to the conduct of a police investigation of which the subject of the inquiry is unaware, or may be assumed to be unaware, and which infringes or potentially infringes a person's right to a private life. It also refers to a covert strategy designed to investigate offences, to gather evidence, to prevent or disrupt criminal activity, or to obtain intelligence.

The police have probably always used covert methods of investigation but, for a variety of reasons, covert policing has taken on greater significance in the past decade or so. In its seminal report, *Helping with Enquiries: Tackling Crime Effectively*, published in 1993, the Audit Commission encouraged the police to develop proactive, intelligence-led, investigative strategies,

particularly because of their perceived effectiveness, especially in terms of cost and resources. Other factors that have promoted an increased use of covert policing include the need to tackle the growth in serious, organized crimes that often cross jurisdictional borders; the development of new technologies that facilitate both new forms of crime and new forms of investigative techniques; and the creation or development of international policing organizations, such as Interpol, that rely on the gathering and exchange of intelligence. More recently, the growth of national and international terrorist activity has created a further need to develop covert policing strategies.

For many years, covert policing was largely unregulated by statute, but the Interception of Communications Act 1985, governing the interception of postal and telecommunications, was enacted following an adverse finding by the European Court of Human Rights (ECtHR) in the case of *Malone* v. *UK*. This was followed a decade later by the Police Act 1997, which regulated surveillance involving entry on or interference with property or with wireless telegraphy, and which was enacted in anticipation of another adverse judgment by the ECtHR in the case of *Khan* v. *UK*. However, these statutes still left a variety of forms of covert policing unregulated (e.g. surveillance not involving entry on or interference with property, and the use of informants and undercover police operations), and the incorporation of the European Convention on Human Rights (ECHR) into domestic law by the Human Rights Act 1998 led to a growing awareness that covert policing methods were at risk of challenge, particularly under ECHR Article 8 (the right to respect for private and family life). Thus the Regulation of Investigatory Powers Act 2000 (RIPA) was passed following consultation on many of its provisions.

The Police Act 1997 and RIPA do not provide a comprehensive, or satisfactory, regulatory regime governing covert policing. RIPA does not cover covert surveillance that is not conducted in respect of a specific investigation or operation and, while the interception of communications that is not authorized under RIPA is a criminal offence, unauthorized covert surveillance or the use of a covert human intelligence source is not, although it is unlawful for the police and other law enforcement agencies (such as public authorities) to act in a way that is incompatible with a convention right (Human Rights Act 1998, s. 6). Furthermore, it does not adequately protect against interference with communications that are subject to legal professional privilege (see *R* v. *Grant*).

Ed Cape

Related entries

Criminal investigation; Criminal investigation department (CID); Ethics in policing; European Convention on Human Rights (ECHR); Evidence; Intelligence-led policing; National Intelligence Model (NIM); Police powers; Regulation of Investigatory Powers Act 2000 (RIPA); Special branch (SB).

Key texts and sources

Audit Commission (1993) *Helping with Enquiries: Tackling Crime Effectively.* London: Audit Commission.

Harfield, C. and Harfield, K. (2005) *Covert Investigation.* Oxford: Oxford University Press.

Justice (1998) *Under Surveillance: Covert Policing and Human Rights Standards.* London: Justice.

See also the Crown Prosecution Service's web page on covert surveillance (**http://www.cps.gov.uk/ legal/section20/chapter_d.html**).

CRIME

According to the *Concise Oxford Dictionary*, crime may be defined as 1) a serious offence punishable by law; 2) illegal acts as a whole; or 3) a shameful act.

Dictionary definitions of crime such as the above refer to a number of important features. Crime is generally seen as punishable by law and as somehow shameful (or immoral). To criminologists, however, these definitions are problematic. To define crime, for example, as

behaviour punishable by law emphasizes the law and how activities are censured rather than the specific elements of the activities. What, it can be asked, do 'offences punishable by law' have in common, other than that Parliament has felt it necessary to criminalize them? The word 'serious' could be taken to imply that 'criminal' law is somehow symbolically different from those illegal activities subject to civil or administrative law. But how is 'serious' to be defined? Moreover, what one society sees as 'shameful' (or 'immoral') at any one time may be tolerated in another society or at a different time. Not all 'immoral' acts are prohibited by law and, in any event, considerations of 'morality' differ within and between cultures. This was reflected, for example, in changes in the criminal and legal status of such activities as homosexuality and drug 'use' and 'abuse' throughout the twentieth century, as well as in changing public and legal perceptions of racial, sexual and family violence and the recent criminalization of 'anti-social behaviour'. Legal definitions of crime can therefore be seen as the result of political processes, and activities defined as crime must be viewed within their specific social, economic, cultural and historical contexts.

Crime is therefore generally viewed as a socially constructed category (Croall 1998), indicated in the commonsense meanings attached to the word and reflected in point 3 in the definition above. Phrases such as 'that's criminal' or 'it ought to be a crime' reflect a sense of outrage or condemnation, and euphemisms such as 'pilfering', 'fiddling' or 'con' ('softer' words than crime) are used to describe activities that, while legally criminal, are subculturally tolerated (Mars 1982). These commonsense notions of crime are associated with criminal justice – crime is dealt with by 'the police' and leads to prosecution, trial and punishment. By contrast, such activities as breaches of health and safety regulations, which are subject to criminal proceedings, are often seen as 'technical' matters, as 'not really crime', subject to 'regulation', 'law enforcement' by inspectors (as opposed to policing) and 'sanctions' (Croall 2001).

The definition and processing of incidents as crime are also highly dependent on the situation in which they take place. The police play a crucial role as definers of crime through their exercise of discretion, which involves a series of decisions involving whether to take action in a specific incident (which could potentially be defined as 'criminal') and what action to take. Will, for example, a disorderly incident result in a warning? An arrest? What will the charge be? These decisions are influenced by a host of factors: how the behaviour is interpreted by participants, victims, witnesses and individual police officers, which will in turn be influenced by local subcultural norms and the local police culture, and by local, regional and national crime and policing policies, central government targets and community safety initiatives. What is viewed as 'disorderly' or 'anti-social' behaviour in one community may be seen as relatively normal behaviour in another, and levels of community tolerance vary considerably.

While these could be seen as low-level crimes involving high amounts of situational discretion, more serious crimes are equally problematic. 'Murder', rape, assaults and fraud would be regarded as serious crimes in most societies and historical periods, yet their definitions are highly contestable and culturally contingent. Definitions of rape are extremely contestable, with rape within marriage being only recently criminalized and trials often hinging on the credibility of the victim and the situation in which the alleged offence took place. Recurrent cases involving the use of (legitimate) 'force', which causes injury or death by the police or armed forces in the course of their duties, reveal the very narrow line between such force and (illegitimate) 'violence'. Conceptions of homicide are intricately associated with notions of intent and individual responsibility, notions rendered problematic by considerations of corporate homicide where mass deaths result from inattention to criminally enforced regulations within companies – often the result of managerial failure to enforce regulations strictly or of a lax attitude to such regulations sanctioned within a corporate culture (Tombs and Whyte 2007). Are these cases any less serious than other forms of homicide?

Property crimes, such as fraud, are no less contestable. Criminologists involved in the study of white-collar crime have pointed to the narrow line between 'misleading' advice to clients or information about products and 'fraud' (Croall 2001). Fraud is often associated with dishonesty, yet when does a sales 'pitch' become dishonest? Again, such distinctions are highly dependent on the cultural and social context of the activities in question and on prevailing commercial and marketing practices.

These kinds of considerations have led critical criminologists to argue not only that the criminal law is socially constructed but also that the definition of crime is ideological – in that it is likely to reflect the interests and influence of the most powerful and to criminalize the least powerful. Feminist criminologists, for example, have pointed to the way in which definitions and the legal processing of rape and violence against women have been affected by the relative powerlessness of women and the legal institution of marriage. Others point to the way in which it is more likely to be the 'anti-social' or disorderly behaviour of largely poorer inhabitants of 'crime prone' areas that attracts media, political and criminal justice attention, whereas the harmful activities of corporations or the violence or terrorism of states and their agencies are less likely to be subject to criminal law and proceedings. Indeed, to define state activities as 'criminal' is likely to be criticized as 'political'.

Crime is, therefore, a highly contested concept, which means that attempts to count it (such as criminal statistics or crime surveys) must be treated with considerable caution. Technically, care must be taken to ascertain which, out of the potential range of activities definable as 'crime', they refer to, and how, for the purposes of such figures, 'crime' has been defined. They may be interpreted more as accounts of the operation of law enforcement agencies, such as the police, than as accurate counts of 'crime'. To some critical criminologists, the ideologically constructed nature of crime provides such insuperable difficulties as to suggest abandoning the concept altogether and focusing instead on the different ways in which social harms are generated and subjected to different forms of legislative intervention (Hillyard and Tombs 2004).

Hazel Croall

Related entries

Crime statistics; Discretion; Force (police use of); Fraud and policing; Murder; Sexual offences/sexual violence.

Key texts and sources

Croall, H. (1998) *Crime and Society in Britain.* London: Pearson.

Lacey, N. (2002) 'Legal constructions of crime', in M. Maguire *et al.* (eds) *The Oxford Handbook of Criminology* (3rd edn). Oxford: Oxford University Press.

Muncie, J. (2002) 'The construction and deconstruction of crime', in J. Muncie and E. McLaughlin (eds) *The Problem of Crime* (2nd edn). London: Sage.

CRIME AND DISORDER ACT 1998

The Crime and Disorder Act 1998 was the first and most important piece of criminal legislation of the New Labour administrations of the late 1900s and early 2000s. This Act establishes for the first time statutory responsibilities for crime and disorder reduction in local authority areas in England and Wales.

The Crime and Disorder Act 1998 may be viewed as feeding off two interconnected features of neoliberal government thinking – namely, a political discourse of populist communitarianism and a modernizing new public management project. The importance of the Act in the populist communitarian discourse of New Labour is best captured in the speech made by Home Secretary, Jack Straw, during the Crime and Disorder Bill's second reading, when he argued that 'The Bill represents a triumph of community politics over detached metropolitan elites'. Particularly central to this communitarian crusade was the intent to tackle disorder and

anti-social behaviour through the use of civil law standards of proof, associated with the eventual establishment of such exclusionary measures as child curfews and parenting and anti-social behaviour orders. It is important to note that moral or social transgressions, as well as law breaking, came under the scope of the new powers vested in the local crime and disorder reduction partnerships (CDRPs). This ambitious national political project, and intended programme of local policy implementation, was also structured by the development of a 'what works', evidence-based paradigm for crime and disorder reduction policy and practice which speaks to the logic of the new public management.

The Crime and Disorder Act stressed that, for successful outcomes to be achieved, statutory responsibility for crime and disorder reduction and the management of youth crime should be devolved ('at a distance', if not 'hands off') from the central state to a series of local partnerships. Both youth offending teams (YOTs) and the Youth Justice Board (the national board which monitors the local operation of the system and sets national standards) were also established as a result of this Act. 'Youth justice' became linked primarily and principally to the prevention of offending by young people and children rather than the welfare of the child. Its local delivery arm was the YOT, made up of social services, probation, education, youth workers and the police, and whose goal was to provide a 'joined up' delivery of the service. In terms of crime and disorder reduction (and/or community safety), the Act gave both the local authority and the police new duties and powers to develop multi-agency and (supposedly) community-based strategic partnerships to help reduce crime and disorder in their locality. Since 1998, all 376 statutory CDRPs in England and Wales have had to:

● carry out audits of local crime and disorder problems;
● consult with all sections of the local community;
● publish three-year crime and disorder reduction strategies based on the findings of the audits;
● identify targets and performance indicators for each part of the strategy, with specified timescales;

- publish the audit, strategy and the targets; and
- report annually on progress against the targets.

There is limited research evidence with regard to the workings and outcomes of these partnerships, but 'official' findings from the Home Office and quasi-government Audit Commission reviews suggest that there is limited proof of successful 'outcomes'. Put bluntly, it is not clear that CDRPs have been an 'evidence-based' success. Independent criminological research across the country has also revealed that tensions and conflicts and political struggles between 'partners' remain, alongside the pressure to be seen publicly as 'happy' and united partners working with 'communities' (Gilling 2005). Furthermore, most partnerships have adopted a narrow crime reduction agenda rather than promoting a broader 'community safety' approach in the first two phases of local implementation (1999–2002, 2002–5). Local CDRP strategies have thus remained driven by a centrally imposed performance management agenda in which cost-effective measures for the realization of (largely central government) reduction targets are prioritized, and yet CDRPs have still not been able to prove their success in performance management terms (see Crime reduction) (Hughes 2006).

In 2006, the Home Office undertook a review of the workings of CDRPs – the *Crime and Disorder Act Review* – in response to the ongoing concerns over the performance of local partnerships (and, by implication, but *sotto voce*, the Home Office's own failures of strategic leadership). The stated objective of this review was to strengthen the visibility, responsibilities, membership and the role of local partnerships in this work, all of which were be institutionalized in the Police and Justice Act 2006.

Gordon Hughes

Related entries

Anti-social behaviour; Audit Commission; Basic command units (BCUs); Caution; Community safety; Consultation; Crime reduction; Drugs and policing; Interagency policing; Neighbourhood wardens; Plural policing; Problem-oriented policing; Racially motivated offending; Restorative justice/restorative cautioning; Stephen Lawrence

Inquiry; Victim and witness support; Youth and policing.

Key texts and sources

Gilling, D. (2005) 'Partnership and crime prevention', in N. Tilley (ed.) *Handbook of Crime Prevention and Community Safety*. Cullompton: Willan Publishing.
Home Office (2006) *Crime and Disorder Act Review* (available online at **http:www.crimereduction. gov.uk/partnerships60**).
Hughes, G. (2006) *The Politics of Crime and Community*. Basingstoke: Palgrave.
The Crime and Disorder Act is available online at **http://www.legislation.gov.uk/acts/acts1998/1998 0037.htm**.

CRIME MAPPING

Crime mapping involves the mapping and spatial analysis of offences, offenders and victims of crime using geographical information systems (GIS) and dedicated mapping software. Typical approaches include the identification of geographical clusters of crime incidents (or 'hotspots') by offence category and time of day, and the monitoring of changes in crime.

Crime incidents potentially have three geographies: the location of the victim (e.g. the householder who has had a car stolen and burnt out), the offence location (e.g. where the vehicle was dumped) and the offender (e.g. where the perpetrator lives). Geographical information systems (GIS) can be used to explore the relationships between any two or all three. Alongside this are the scales of people (offenders, victims), property (dwellings, businesses) and places (town centres, streets, 'crime corridors').

Crimes can be mapped using territorial units, such as wards or police beats (e.g. aggregate analyses displaying crime rates on a map), or by the use of grid-referenced individual records that pinpoint the precise crime location (e.g. disaggregate analyses plotting offences as a series of dots on a map).

The mapping may be concerned solely with the characteristics of the offences, known offenders and victims of crime (crime-centred analyses) or may be undertaken to relate the geography of crime to the physical, social and policy environment (crime environment analyses – Hirschfield 2005). Examples of the former might be maps showing repeat victims, the distribution of burglaries by specific modus operandi or assaults by time of day. Examples of the latter might show, for example, burglaries in relation to street layout and open space, or night-time assaults in relation to pubs, bus stops and taxi ranks.

A range of techniques can be used for mapping crime:

- Calculating and mapping crime rates for administrative policy areas and different types of neighbourhood. Outputs here might include maps with symbols or shading.
- Mapping the distribution of individual incidents (offence, victim, offender locations).
- Mapping the distribution of repeat incidents (multiple incidents, repeat victims).
- Identifying clusters /'hotspots' from points.
- Exploring space-time clustering (when crimes occur, where do they occur? Where crimes occur, when do they occur?).
- Relating offence locations to those of previous offences and the residences of offenders and known suspects (geographic offender profiling).
- Conducting specific site and RADIAL analyses (e.g. mapping robberies within 500 m of a tube station).

It is also possible, using a GIS, to define concentric buffer zones surrounding a target area that can be used to search for evidence of displacement. This might involve, for example, drawing a series of rings 50 m apart around streets that have had properties target-hardened and counting the number of burglaries within each ring. These rings can be plotted to mimic the shape of the target area and to contain a population of similar size in order to maximize the chances of being able to detect displacement.

There are several methods for identifying crime hotspots:

- *Spatial overlap analysis*: superimposing shaded maps to reveal the location of areas with the highest rates of, for example, burglary, vehicle crime and assault.
- *Nearest neighbour analysis*: a test to distinguish random from non-random crime distributions.
- *Plotting of hotspot ellipses*: these identify clusters of crime that are close in both space and time.
- *Kernal density estimation*: a process that detects hotspots by slowly moving a user-defined search window across an entire map, repeatedly searching for clustering.

A number of advances have been made in hotspotting techniques in recent years. Several GIS products have been developed that have embedded software for defining spatial and temporal hotspots (for example, 'Hotspot Detective' in MapInfo). The US National Institute of Justice 'Mapping and analysis for public safety' initiative provides crime analysis freeware, including the CrimeStat spatial statistics program that contains software for generating hotspot ellipses, the Crime Analysis Spatial Extension for ESRI's ArcGIS and other products (see http://www.ojp.usdoj.gov/nij/maps/).

Other refinements in crime mapping are currently being explored. These include the development of techniques for forecasting future hotspots, known as prospective hotspotting (Johnson *et al.* 2005), and computer-based mapping methods for profiling offenders and prioritising suspects (the Interactive Offender Profiling Project; see **http://www.i-psy.com/conferences/conference_8th/conference_programme.htm**).

Data quality, particularly the standard of geocoding, has always been important. Fortunately, the quality of police recorded crime data has improved considerably in the last 10 years. However, recorded offences can be highly variable in the way in which addresses and locations are geographically referenced. The precision of the location reference is highly dependent on the crime category. Pinpointing the location of residential burglaries is, for example, easier than identifying crimes against the person – robbery, theft and assault are particulary difficult to map because of the, often, high degree of uncertainty about where they occurred. In many information systems, their location is assigned to the nearest landmark or street intersection but, in many cases, it is difficult to obtain a reliable spatial reference for them.

Alex Hirschfeld

Related entries

Compstat; Computer-aided despatch (CAD); Geographical information systems (GIS); Geographic(al) profiling; Hotspots; Intelligence analysis (previously crime analysis).

Key texts and sources

Bynum, T.S. (2001) *Using Analysis for Problem-solving: A Guidebook for Law Enforcement.* Washington, DC: COPS/US Department of Justice.

Leipnik, M.R. and Albert, D.A. (eds) (2002) *GIS in Law Enforcement: Implementation Issues and Case Studies.* London: Taylor & Francis.

Ratcliffe, J. (2004) 'The hot spot matrix: a framework for the spatio-temporal targeting of crime reduction', *Police Practice and Research*, 5: 5–23.

See also **www.cops.usdoj.gov**. The Home Office's report on data exchange and crime mapping is available online at **http://www.crimereduction. gov.uk/technology/technology01.htm**.

CRIME PREVENTION (SITUATIONAL AND SOCIAL)

Crime prevention is a generic term incorporating a range of techniques designed to stop crimes from happening or to reduce their probability. These techniques fall loosely into social or situation measures, or a combination of the two.

Crime prevention can be regarded as any action that results in the reduced likelihood of a criminal act occurring (be it a burglary, anti-social behaviour or disorder, or a terrorist attack). Crime prevention can range from careful parenting to preventive detention in prison. With such a broad definition, crime prevention risks becoming a meaningless concept from both an academic and practical perspective. In an attempt to bring some semblance of utility to the notion, Brantingham and Faust (1976) suggested a useful analogy with medicine, and offered a primary, secondary and tertiary typology of prevention. Primary prevention is aimed at the general population with the purpose of pre-empting offending. Secondary prevention is targeted at those at risk of offending, and intervenes, for example, with after-school clubs in high-risk areas. Tertiary prevention is aimed at offenders who might be dealt with through the criminal justice system and, for example, offered some form of rehabilitation during imprisonment. The distinctions offered by Brantingham and Faust are not universally accepted. For example, Van Dijk and de Waard (1991) and Tonry and Farrington (1995) have suggested similar but alternative schemes.

The definition of crime prevention suggested here starts with the Brantingham and Faust distinctions and is focused on primary prevention. Primary crime prevention is divided into situational and social measures to prevent crime. The following discussion of situational measures draws on the definitions used by Clarke (2005), while the definition of social prevention adopts the distinctions from Tonry and Farrington (1995), who divide social prevention into developmental and community-based interventions. There is general agreement that both situational and social controls are necessary (but not always sufficient) for a properly rounded approach to crime prevention at local, regional and national levels.

Various techniques of situational crime prevention (SCP) have been developed over the past 25 years and, indeed, the definition itself has developed over that period (and continues to do so). Currently, SCP comprises a theoretical framework, a methodology for diagnosing a crime problem, a series of techniques aimed at affecting potential offenders' decision-making processes and a range of evaluation or assessment strategies.

The theoretical framework draws on 'opportunity theories', including the rational choice perspective, routine activity theory and crime pattern analysis. The general methodology conforms to the SARA process of Scanning, Analysis, Response and Assessment, as frequently adopted in problem-oriented policing, but it is typically the techniques of SCP that are seen as central to the approach. These techniques fall under five headings – increasing risk, increasing effort, reducing reward, removing excuses and reducing provocation. They have been expanded considerably over the past decade or so, and examples of their use are published in the *Crime Prevention Studies* series of books edited by Clarke. These approaches are presumed to operate by affecting the decision-making process of the offender, which is presumed to be rational. Although these presumptions can and have been challenged, empirical work suggests that they form an adequate basis for the development of practical interventions. It is important to note that it is the offender's perceptions that are influenced by any interventions, rather than the reality of risk, effort, etc.

Although SCP is sometimes seen as little more than target hardening, the techniques now go far beyond reducing the opportunity for offending in this way. They are seen to apply to the design of goods (e.g. mobile phones), services (e.g. the provision of bank credit), management practices (e.g. stock control systems) and legislation (e.g. in preventing 'loopholes' that can provide new opportunities for offending). They also apply to the design of the environment in the broadest sense. This area has become known as 'crime prevention through environmental design' (CPTED) and includes consideration of the ways in which housing layout, lighting schemes, CCTV provision and building design can offer opportunities for crime prevention.

SCP techniques have not been without their critics. A pervasive criticism has been that of potential displacement. It is virtually impossible to prove that displacement does not occur following an SCP initiative, but the overwhelming evidence is that, if it does occur, it is to a relatively limited extent and that, in practice, a diffusion of benefits (i.e. the benefit of the

initiative spreads beyond the target area, crime, etc.) is equally likely.

Finally, SCP has been accused of promoting a fortress society, with images of oppressive CCTV systems, bars, locks, gates and so on. Proponents of the approach argue that these excesses are the result of poorly thought-out schemes and that there is nothing inherent in SCP itself that should lead to a threatening, technology-driven environment.

A characteristic of SCP is that it aims to deliver immediate reductions in the targeted behaviour. In this respect it can be contrasted with social crime prevention, which addresses the motivation of the potential offender and generally operates on a longer time frame. Dividing social crime prevention into its constituent parts, developmental prevention is defined by Homel (2005) as an approach that 'involves the organized provision of resources in some fashion to individuals, families, schools or communities to forestall the later development of crime or other problems'. Community crime prevention 'refers to actions intended to change the social conditions that are believed to sustain crime in residential communities' (Hope 1995).

Considering each approach in turn, developmental prevention has claimed some success where effort has been concentrated on 'early intervention'. These programmes are aimed at children from birth to 5 years and their families, with the intention of reducing the risk factors (such as inconsistent parental discipline, child maltreatment and abuse, and low levels of parental supervision) associated with later delinquency. In the UK, for example, there has been considerable investment in the Sure Start programme, which targets children and families in at-risk communities (and could therefore be characterized as secondary rather than primary prevention). These programmes not only reduce the risk of later offending but also improve life skills, health and general well-being. There is also increasing evidence that initiatives addressing risk factors but targeted at children over the age of 5, even into early teenage years, can be effective in reducing offending behaviour.

Community crime prevention, in contrast, relates to efforts to prevent crime that derive from the dynamics of the local community and which would apply to members of that community. Encouraging this kind of community activity has proved quite difficult to achieve (Hope 1995), although the area has received renewed academic interest through the pioneering work of Sampson and colleagues in Chicago. They argue that a mechanism through which community crime prevention might be exercised is collective efficacy (Sampson *et al.* 1997). A community with high levels of collective efficacy would be characterized by effective informal social control, social cohesion and trust.

In some contexts, particularly in parts of the USA, community crime prevention is closely associated with a particular style of policing. The work of Kelling and colleagues (2005), focused on New York, and that of Skogan and associates (2003) working in Chicago, exemplifies this approach.

Although it is clearly possible to describe social and situational crime prevention as separate activities, they do, in practice, overlap considerably. To take a simple example, 'removing excuses' is now included as a category in the matrix of SCP options and could be construed as a social rather than a situational mechanism in effecting a change in offender behaviour, drawing, as it does, on socially acceptable justifications for specific acts. Similarly, it can be argued that situational improvements (such as mending broken windows) can increase community confidence and the likelihood of informal social control. Nevertheless, the distinctions remain useful in facilitating the development of practical preventive activities and in offering some conceptual clarification of what is otherwise a complex mêlée of ideas and approaches.

Gloria Laycock

Related entries

Broken windows; Community safety; Crime reduction; Geographical information systems (GIS); National security; Neighbourhood Watch; Plural policing; Police Service of Northern Ireland (PSNI); Repeat victimization; Special Constabulary; Youth and policing.

Key texts and sources

Brantingham, P.J. and Faust, F.L. (1976) 'A conceptual model of crime prevention', *Crime and Delinquency*, 22: 284–98.

Tilley, N. (ed.) (2005) *Handbook of Crime Prevention and Community Safety.* Cullompton: Willan Publishing.

Tonry, M. and Farrington, D. (eds) (1995) *Building a Safer Society. Crime and Justice: A Review of Research. Volume 19.* Chicago, IL: University of Chicago Press.

See also Clarke, R.V. (ed.) *Crime Prevention Studies.* New York, NY: Criminal Justice Press, and Cullompton: Willan Publishing (some volumes available online at **www.popcenter.org**) – a series of 20 or so publications covering a broad range of crime and social problems that takes an SCP perspective.

CRIME REDUCTION

At its simplest, crime reduction is any measure or variety or measures aimed at reducing crime. The term has become associated chiefly with targeted and relatively short-term situational and policing measures put in place by a variety of local agencies and in line with central government performance targets. More accurately in the contemporary UK context, crime reduction is an approach that gives primacy to technical and numerical measurement and the trappings of a 'scientific' evaluation of effectiveness.

Crime reduction came to prominence in government circles in the UK with the publication in 1998 of a set of Home Office evaluation reviews of 'what works' in reducing crime. Owing much to a US-based 'scientific' review of what works in crime prevention by Sherman *et al.* (1997), these findings of a Home Office-based administrative criminology then gained support from the newly elected Labour government to undertake and evaluate the nationwide and seemingly research-driven and evidence-led Crime Reduction Programme (CRP) (1999–2002) across a number of chosen localities and sites in England and Wales.

The three-year CRP based at the Home Office, which was financed through £250 million made available following the 1999 comprehensive spending review, was intended to build on the Crime and Disorder Act 1998 and to 'harness' the activities of local crime and disorder reduction partnerships (CDRPs). As noted above, it was premised on the conclusions of *Reducing Offending*, a Home Office report that highlighted the 'scientifically proven' interventions most likely to provide the basis for a cost-effective, sustained reduction in the long-term rise in crime (Goldblatt and Lewis 1998). Questions considered by the authors in this report included: how effective is an intervention and can the benefits be quantified? What evidence is available on the likely costs of implementation? What is the likely timescale for the costs and benefits? And how strong is the available evidence on effects, costs and timescales? These questions underpinned the subsequent institutionalization of this reductive logic in the CRP, which was extended in April 1999 with the announcement of an extra £153 million for CCTV initiatives and other interventions aimed at reducing vehicle crime. This ambitious, nationally directed 'evidence-led' programme was also to be applied to interrelated programmes across the criminal justice system that received funding under the comprehensive spending review (for example, the £211 million allocated to drug use and related crime and the £226 million provided for 'constructive' prison regimes).

The CRP was intended to make a significant contribution by ensuring that the Home Office was achieving maximum impact for money spent and that the impact was progressively improved. The programme hoped to promote innovation, to generate a significant improvement in knowledge about effectiveness and cost effectiveness and to encourage the mainstreaming of emerging knowledge about 'best practice'. The CRP thus emphasized the need for local policy-makers and practitioners to act primarily on evidence-based 'scientific' research that establishes 'what works' and to ignore alternative approaches considered uneconomic and inefficient in preventing crime and disorder. As Edwards and Stenson (2004: 225) note: 'At worst this may pressure local policy makers towards a naïve emulation of measures that in very different settings have, it is claimed, been shown to have "worked".' In the eyes – viewed retrospectively – of many of the academic researchers involved in this programme of evidence-based crime reduction, the programme did not live up to its promise, not least due to problems of theory and policy implementation failure and the wish for ministers to get 'quick' wins – at times turning 'evidence-based policy' into 'policy-based evidence' (*Criminal Justice* 2004).

Despite the 'failure' or, viewed more sympathetically, the limited proven success of the CRP, the term 'crime reduction' has largely replaced the more ambitious ones of crime prevention and community safety in official discourses. Although the 'reductive' success of both CDRPs and the CRP has been questioned by academic critics and government officials alike, the term 'crime reduction' remains pervasive in the new public management culture of formal crime control in the UK.

Follett (2006) has noted that there are two crucial assumptions underpinning the administrative criminological discourse of crime reduction: first, that crime cannot be prevented but merely reduced – in other words, crime is viewed pragmatically as an inevitable part of everyday life – and, secondly, there is an assumption that cost effectiveness is pivotal to judging success, failure and 'what works'. In other words, crime reduction is associated with an economic calculus of 'what works'. Its advantage for policy-makers and politicians alike is that it is seemingly less 'fluffy' than either crime prevention or community safety, which are both notoriously difficult to 'measure' in terms of outcomes. Crime reduction measures thus hold the promise of being subject to 'before and after' experimental evaluations and, therefore, both scientifically measurable and resulting in proven cost-effective outcomes. However, as an instance of evidence-based policy, crime reduction runs the risk of being dominated by counting solely that which is easily measurable. Perhaps we would do well to remember Albert Einstein's words of caution about numbers and counting: 'Not everything that can be counted counts, and not everything that counts can be counted.'

It may have been noticed that this discussion has pointed to three different terms that interconnect, overlap and compete in the broad field of local crime control (namely, crime prevention, community safety and crime reduction). It is important to note that the different terms used to depict the local policies, practices, politics and theories geared towards the 'prevention' or, failing that, the 'reduction' of crime, and those strategies aimed at the promotion of 'community safety', are indicative of the changing and hybrid nature of the policy field under scrutiny here. In part these different governmental logics arise out of criticisms of traditional 'reactive' criminal justice responses to crime, such as punishment and individualistic treatment approaches. Both situational and social prevention approaches, which came to the fore in the 1980s, share a preoccupation with preventing 'criminality' *before* the event. Next, 'community safety' strategies appear to call for multi-agency partnership and community-based approaches in which a more expansive and broader project of social regeneration, social inclusion and communal 'responsibilization' is sought. Meanwhile, targeted 'crime reduction' approaches, based on the pragmatic evaluation of what can be measured and counted in terms of 'what works', have come to prominence since the late 1990s. The latter appear to be less concerned with 'prevention' and more focused on the manageable and seemingly 'rational', 'scientific' reduction of unacceptably high levels of crime and disorder (Hope 2001; Hughes 2004; Crawford 2006).

Such strategies should not be read as linear steps towards greater 'success' by the state in alleviating the problems of crime, disorder and insecurity. Instead, it is vital to note the coexistence of these logics and their hybridization in specific policy and political contexts. Current practices in the UK and other late modern societies in this field, for example, are simultaneously predicated on some of the following (often contradictory) techniques and strategies:

- Techniques of 'rational' risk management.
- Responsibilizing strategies towards private citizens, corporations and communities.
- Emotive and symbolically reassuring 'zero-tolerance' policing of the 'anti-social' and 'disorderly', often drawing on popular, mass media-'mediated' fears of the dangerous and predatory 'outsiders'.
- Multi-agency, 'joined-up' partnerships aiming to counter social and economic degeneration and exclusion and to promote social regeneration and inclusion.
- A focus on targeted reductive projects and initiatives.

Gordon Hughes

Related entries

Burglary; Compstat; Crime and Disorder Act 1998; Hotspots; Neighbourhood policing; Police and Crime Standards Directorate (P&CSD); Volume crime; Zero-tolerance policing (ZTP).

Key texts and sources

Edwards, A. and Stenson, K. (2004) 'Policy transfer in local crime control', in T. Newburn and R. Sparks (eds) *Criminal Justice and Political Cultures*. Cullompton: Willan Publishing.

Follett, M. (2006) 'Crime reduction', in E. McLaughlin and J. Muncie (eds) *The Sage Dictionary of Criminology*. London: Sage.

Hope, T. (2001) *Perspectives on Crime Reduction*. Aldershot: Ashgate.

Hughes, G. (2004) 'Crime prevention, community safety and crime and disorder reduction', in J. Muncie and D. Wilson (eds) *Student Handbook of Criminal Justice and Criminology*. London: Cavendish.

See also the special issue of *Criminal Justice* (2004) on the Crime Reduction Programme. The Home Office's crime reduction website is at http://www.crimereduction.gov.uk/.

CRIME SCENE EXAMINERS (CSEs)

Crime scene examiners (CSEs) attend scenes of crime, victims and suspects as requested in order to record photographically, search for and recover physical, forensic and fingerprint evidence. They also provide scientific advice on scene protection and evidence preservation. CSEs are also known as crime scene investigators (CSIs) and scenes of crime officers (SOCOs).

Alphonse Bertillon (1853–1914) is generally acknowledged as being among the first to act as a crime scene examiner (CSE), recording evidence at crime scenes photographically and using finely ground graphite powder to recover fingerprints. Although there is controversy over who first developed a system for the identification of offenders using fingerprints, a pupil of Bertillon, Dr Edmond Locard (1877–1966), published the principle of exchange of evidence that suggests how evidence can be moved between the crime scene and the offender, and vice versa. It is still important for the CSE to know and understand Locard's principle.

Contemporary CSEs can be either police officers or civilian specialists, and they can be employed by an individual police force or law enforcement agency, forensic science services or private companies. The military also have their own CSEs. There are about 3,000 CSEs nationally. They attend scenes ranging from major incidents, such as a murder, post-mortem or disaster, to volume crime scenes, such as burglary, criminal damage or theft.

The perception of the roles, responsibilities and capabilities of the modern CSE is often shaped by the mass media. The reality, however, can be somewhat different. Such perceptions may be reinforced by the general availability of academic texts that focus on practices in the USA (Nickell and Fisher 1999; Fisher 2002). However, a number of practices and procedures in the UK do differ from those of the USA.

The CSE has a range of roles and responsibilities, which were first recognized nationally by a Touche Ross report (1987) and developed by the Association of Chief Police Officers/Forensic Science Service (1996). The role has continued to evolve so that the CSE today has the knowledge and skills to record the scene of a crime, a victim or offender using still digital or traditional wet photography. The CSE can recover a range of physical evidence types, including fibres, footwear and instrument marks, glass, hairs, paint and sources of DNA, such as blood, semen and saliva. A range of different powders can be applied with different types of brushes in order to recover fingerprints from varying surfaces. All the evidence must be carefully packaged, thoroughly sealed in the packaging, correctly labelled and then stored or forwarded for forensic investigation. The CSE must keep comprehensive notes of his or her actions, write statements and present evidence in court. The integrity of all the evidence recovered must be maintained, from its recovery at the crime scene to presentation at court. The CSE's role has 'an even greater emphasis on ensuring that contamination of the evidence cannot take place' (Pepper 2005: 9).

National training, non-compulsory national registration on a register of forensic practitioners and the ability of a chief constable (under the Police Reform Act 2002) to designate CSEs as investigators have done much to raise the status of the CSE as an integral member of the team conducting the criminal investigation.

Ian K. Pepper

Related entries

DNA profiling; Fingerprints; Forensic and investigative psychology; Forensic investigation; Offender profiling; Technology and policing.

Key texts and sources

Pepper, I.K. (2005) *Crime Scene Investigation: Methods and Procedures.* Maidenhead: Open University Press.

Touche Ross Management Consultants (1987) *Review of Scientific Support for the Police. Volume III.* London: Home Office.

CRIME STATISTICS

> The two mains sources of statistical information about crime are the Recorded Crime Statistics and the British Crime Survey (BCS). Both measures have strengths and weaknesses, and neither can claim to be a full and complete index of crime.

There are two main sources of information about crime in England and Wales: the Recorded Crime Statistics compiled by the police and the British Crime Survey (BCS). The police statistics necessarily cover only those crimes that are reported to the police and those that the police themselves encounter. While they are often used as an index of crime, they are better thought of a measure of police workload – the crimes that are brought to police attention. They can mislead as an index of crime because the proportion of crime reported to the police, and recorded by them, can change over place and time.

For this reason, the BCS was introduced as a complementary measure of crime. It interviews a large sample of the population in England and Wales, asking about their experience of crime in the previous year. This allows estimates to be made of crimes committed against people and their personal property, *including* unreported and unrecorded offences.

Recorded Crime Statistics

The police in England and Wales have collated statistics on crime since 1857. Before then, judicial statistics of offenders convicted by the courts were the only available criminal statistics. The police are required to collate crime statistics by law, and the Home Secretary is required to publish these. The Recorded Crime Statistics, as they are known, are published annually as *Criminal Statistics, England and Wales*. Similar arrangements apply to Scotland and Northern Ireland.

Police statistics were, for many years, regarded as a reliable indicator of crime. However, they can sometimes prove misleading. The proportion of crimes reported to the police changes over time, as relationships between the police and the public change and as the technologies for communicating with the police change. It has also been shown that police forces vary in the proportion of crimes reported to them that they record.

Police statistics of recorded crime can be misleading for other reasons. For example, the rules for counting crimes can change over time. If two offenders jointly assault two victims, this could be treated as one crime, two crimes or four crimes, for example, under different counting rules. The police can also apply different rules at different times about the evidence needed for recording. Parliament may also create new offences, and the Home Office can extend (and has extended) the list of offences for which statistics have to be recorded.

The procedures for recording crime have changed substantially since 1998, when new counting rules were introduced to ensure that police across the country compiled statistics in a consistent – and inclusive – way. The biggest changes were the inclusion of offences of common assault and harassment and to count one crime per victim when the same offender had committed offences against several victims. Both these changes increased the numbers of crimes recorded by the police considerably. Even more far-reaching changes to the statistics were made in 2002, when the 'National Crime Recording Standard' was introduced. This required the police to adopt a 'victim-led' approach to crime recording, in which victims' accounts of crimes were taken at face value. Previously the police had exercised considerable discretion in deciding whether and how to record crimes reported to them. The National Crime Recording Standard further inflated the count of crime and had a particular impact on the recording of violent crime.

These various changes have taken several years to bed in, the result being that, since 1998, police statistics have been a more unreliable guide than usual to real crime trends. Now that the system is beginning to settle down again, the police statistics may once more offer a reasonable guide to trends – provided that no further changes are made to recording procedures.

The British Crime Survey (BCS)

The British Crime Survey (BCS) was set up in 1982 as a complementary measure of crime. It relies on large population samples of adults in England and Wales, who are asked directly whether they have been the victim of crime over the last 12 months. The BCS provides a count of crime that includes *unreported* offences and reported offences that have gone *unrecorded*. As the survey's methodology has been fairly stable over time, it is thought to provide an index of crime trends that in some ways is better than police statistics.

However, the BCS also has limitations. Its estimates of crime levels are based on samples and are thus subject to sampling error. Not everyone selected for interview agrees to take part, and thus there is scope for sample bias. And not everyone who has been the victim of a crime will choose to provide details to an interviewer. Despite these limitations, the survey is thought by government statisticians and by academic criminologists to provide a better guide to crime trends than police statistics. All are agreed, however, that the two sources of information provide a better picture of crime than could be obtained from either series alone.

The BCS has provided a reasonably comprehensive account of crimes against individuals and their property since 1982. There have been similar surveys in both Scotland and Northern Ireland. The BCS was modelled in part on the US National Crime Victimization Survey, which began in the 1970s. The first sweep of the survey was conducted in early 1982, with a nationally representative sample of 10,905 respondents in England and Wales (Hough and Mayhew 1983). The basic format of the questionnaire remains unchanged:

- A 'main questionnaire' asking a fixed series of screening questions about victimization.
- A number of 'victim forms' collecting details about victims' experiences.
- Various 'follow up' questionnaires asking questions about crime-related topics, some of which are changed from sweep to sweep.

Following the first BCS, the survey was repeated in 1984, 1988 and 1992. It was then conducted in alternate years until 2000, when the sample size doubled – to about 20,000. In 2001 it moved to being a continuous 'rolling' annual survey, with 40,000 interviews conducted throughout the year. One reason for the increased sample size was to provide more reliable measures of different forms of violent crime. Another was the perceived need for numerical 'performance indicators' relating to levels of public confidence in the police in each of the 43 police force areas in England and Wales. The much larger sample size allows tolerably precise survey estimates for overall household and personal crime at individual police-force level.

What can be said about crime trends?

In combination, the BCS and the Recorded Crime Statistics can tell us a great deal about crime trends. It is clear that crime rose throughout the 1980s, peaking in the mid-1990s. In the 1980s the police statistics *overstated* the rate of increase because a larger proportion of crimes committed were reported to the police over time. (The reasons for this include the increasing availability of phones and the greater prevalence of household insurance.) In the mid-1990s, the police statistics showed signs of *under-recording*, possibly reflecting the introduction of new performance targets for policing.

From 1995 the overall trend, as indicated by the BCS, has been downward. The police statistics initially mirrored this trend but, as the new changes to the counting rules were introduced, trends for some categories of recorded crime were upward – notably crimes of violence. At the time of writing, it appeared that, overall, crime trends were fairly steady. The increase in recorded crimes of violence since the turn of the century is, in part, a statistical artefact. However, it seems likely that some forms of violent crime, especially crimes of violence in public space and those associated with drug markets, are actually rising.

The BCS not only collects information about crime but also asks people about their experience of, and attitudes towards, the police and other parts of the criminal justice system. The survey is one of the main sources of information about public ratings of the police in England and Wales.

Mike Hough

Related entries

Attrition; Compstat; Crime; Defendants; Police performance indicators.

Key texts and sources

Hough, M. and Maxfield, M. (2007) *Surveying Crime in the Twenty-first Century*. Cullompton: Willan Publishing.

Smith, A. (2006) *Crime Statistics: An Independent Review, Carried out by the Crime Statistics Review Group for the Secretary of State for the Home Department*. London: Home Office (available online at http://www.homeoffice.gov.uk/rds/ pdfs06/crime-statistics-independent-review-06.pdf).

Walker, A., Kershaw, C. and Nicholas, S. (2006) *Crime in England and Wales, 2005/06*. Home Office Statistical Bulletin 12/06. London: Home Office (available online at http://www.homeoffice.gov.uk /rds/pdfs06/hosb1206.pdf).

See also the Home Office's crime statistics web page (http://www.homeoffice.gov.uk/rds/crimeew0607. html).

CRIMINAL INVESTIGATION

Criminal investigation is the scientific collection, examination and preservation of evidence. Because it is a costly and resource-intensive procedure, a thorough investigation cannot be applied to all reported crimes. Hence, the strategic categories of 'volume' and 'serious crime' are used to determine where and how investigation resources are allocated.

Crime management 'desks' receive reports of volume crime (some with little prospect of detection) by telephone, thus gathering crime pattern intelligence that may inform subsequent investigation strategy if patterns of offending are identified and attributed to identifiable suspects. This is not intended to minimize the importance of such crimes, particularly to the victims, but necessarily focuses efforts where success is most likely to be achieved.

Criminal investigation management can be divided into six generic determinants. *Intelligence-led policing*, expressed theoretically in the National Intelligence Model (NIM), is used to determine which crimes should be investigated (and by whom) or whether other interventions are more suitable. Since there is rarely an option not to investigate serious crime, in reality the NIM process articulates how volume crime investigation can be accommodated with the investigation of serious crime. The wider concept of knowledge-based policing redirects NIM application away from merely delivering volume crime performance targets back to the original concept of informing a holistic approach to policing.

The next determinant is the *statutory framework of investigative powers*, which can be divided into pre-arrest and post-arrest investigation. Human rights law overarches both these phases, protecting citizens from abuse of state power and reinforcing proportionality decisions about which investigative techniques can be appropriately applied in which investigations. The most intrusive tactics and techniques available to investigators are reserved for only the most serious crimes, and then only when appropriate (proportionate) in the circumstances.

Managing evidence acquired through investigative authority, citizens' co-operation and coercive powers involves, in major inquiries, mechanisms to understand and act on large volumes of evidence (which in turn determine further lines of inquiry); procedures to ensure the safeguarding and forensic examination of exhibits for use at trial; and the disclosure of all relevant material to the defence in order to ensure fairness of the trial procedure.

Closely connected with the securing of evidence is the *management of the key resources* of skills and staff. Relatively minor volume crime is unlikely to require enhanced detective skills, yet criminal investigation is an increasingly skilled profession and the requirement for enhanced skills has consigned the omni-competent detective to history. Statement taking, statement reading (i.e. further action identification), scene searching, suspect interviewing and victim interviewing are ever more specialist in their application.

Major inquiries absorb large numbers of personnel on work such as scene-access management (often perceived as tedious but crucial for evidential preservation, minimizing contamination and demonstrating continuity in the evidential chain) and house-to-house inquiries (which, in an increasingly cosmopolitan society, often demand language skills that investigators do not possess: a rural murder investigation in 2005 necessitated house-to-house inquiries in an urban tower block where 50 different languages were spoken). Some of this work necessarily has to be outsourced to partner agencies with the requisite skills: forensic scientists, pathologists and criminal or behavioural psychologists. In child abuse cases, witnesses and victim may be interviewed jointly with social services.

Partnership is also key in the fifth determinant when managing criminal investigation: *the community*. Community perceptions of crime influence what is investigated. The adverse economic significance of white-collar crime is often unappreciated by communities because large-scale commercial fraud appears victimless. Community reaction to the murder of Sussex schoolgirl Sarah Payne generated a press campaign naming and shaming (often erroneously) suspected paedophiles, resulting in mob vigilantism. The high-profile murders of Stephen Lawrence and Damilola Taylor prompted the development of community impact assessments and critical incident management skills in recognition of the fact that investigating serious crime is no longer merely a matter of identifying the culprit.

Community expectations of protection have complicated the investigation of dangerous offenders because such individuals must now be risk assessed and managed on release at the conclusion of their sentence. Such risk management is informed by the original criminal investigation and subsequent offender evaluations.

Communities also feature in the final determining element: *third-party oversight*. This often identifies good practice to be fed back into knowledge-based policing. Mechanisms to achieve this include 'gold groups' (independent experts and lay advisers to those in strategic command of investigation); independent advisory groups drawn from the community advising on wider issues; HM Inspectorate of Constabulary thematic inspections; cold-case reviews; and, a particularly influential stimulus of good practice, learning derived from the trial process and miscarriages of justice.

Much of the above has been distilled into core investigative doctrine from which are derived five principles required of any investigation (ACPO/NPIA 2005: 22):

1. An overview of the investigative process and planning required to conduct an investigation.
2. Decision-making reviewed to improve application of the investigative mindset.
3. Investigative and evidential evaluation to determine the value of material gathered during an investigation.
4. Core investigative strategies employed (victim, witness, scene and suspect management).
5. Sound resource management skills applied.

No longer merely a process to deliver a suspect to trial, criminal investigation offers opportunities for deeper community insight and better informed policing. Enhanced investigative professionalism benefits policing in general: senior investigating officers have to be more than just good detectives.

Clive Harfield

Related entries

Criminal investigation department (CID); DNA profiling; Evidence; Fingerprints; Forensic and investigative psychology; Forensic investigation; Home Office Large Major Enquiry System (HOLMES); Volume crime.

Key texts and sources

ACPO/NPIA (2005) *Practice Advice of Core Investigative Doctrine.* Bramshill: NPIA.
Harfield, C. and Harfield, K. (2005) *Covert Investigation.* Oxford: Oxford University Press.

Newburn, T., Williamson, T. and Wright, A. (eds) (2007) *Handbook of Criminal Investigation.* Cullompton: Willan Publishing.

Zander, M. (2005) *Police and Criminal Evidence Act 1984* (5th edn). London: Sweet & Maxwell.

See also **www.acpo.police.uk/policies.asp**.

CRIMINAL INVESTIGATION DEPARTMENT (CID)

In 1878, the Metropolitan Police established a Criminal Investigation Department (CID) with a director who reported to the Home Secretary rather than the Commissioner. This arrangement created an elite group of detectives associated with corruption scandals and miscarriages of justice. While controls have been introduced to curb such malpractice, concerns are still expressed that investigators are able to avoid these safeguards when pressures dictate.

The Metropolitan Police Act 1829 established the Metropolitan Police, the first of the modern police forces and a model that was subsequently applied nationally. To mitigate concerns within the establishment and rising middle classes that a French 'spy' system would be introduced in Britain, the Metropolitan Police Act explicitly created a uniformed constabulary whose remit was to prevent crime by visible presence through patrol. In 1842, a small Detective Department was established in the Metropolitan Police to perform a specialist, plain-clothes investigative role, albeit with strict controls to limit its activities and its ability to associate with criminals (Hobbs 1988). Nevertheless, Ascoli (1979) notes that three of the four chief inspectors in the department were found guilty of corruption.

In 1878, the Metropolitan Police established a Criminal Investigation Department (CID) with a staff of 250, and with a director who reported to the Home Secretary rather than the Commissioner for the first 10 years of the CID's existence. This arrangement essentially allowed for a 'force within a force' to develop, 'with a structure and hierarchy bearing little resemblance to the uniform branch' (Hobbs 1988: 41) and based on the continental structures that had exercised such concerns, apparently now abated, about the introduction of the police.

Within these early developments two persistent, related and central issues that have dogged the CID's history are found – the tensions within the police organization arising from the creation of an elite and less controlled group (detectives) and, resulting from the latter point, associations with corruption scandals and miscarriages of justice. Maguire and Norris (1992: 15) note the impact of the specialized tasks that the CID performs: 'obtaining information ("intelligence") about the movements and activities of "known criminals"', with the need for detectives to 'get close to them'; and 'gathering sufficient evidence to convict such people of specific offences…being extremely difficult if strict attention is paid to their rights and civil liberties'. Sir Robert Mark's period as Commissioner for the Metropolitan Police (1972–7) is associated with concerted efforts to tackle endemic corruption within the CID. However, the 1990s again saw extensive concern about corruption in the CID, accompanied by operations to tackle it (McLagan 2003).

Research on CID subculture is less comprehensive than that conducted on uniformed police officers. The typical view, arising largely from research conducted in the 1980s (e.g. Holdaway 1983; Hobbs 1988), is one in which the solidarity, suspicion and machoistic aspects identified in uniformed subcultures are heightened. As Innes (2003) notes, there is some evidence that these elements are waning, although at what pace is difficult to gauge. Controls, legislative and managerial, have been introduced that fetter previous practices associated with the CID – for example, the Police and Criminal Evidence Act 1984 and its restraints on detention and questioning, or safeguards to ensure that informant (covert human intelligence source) handling is professionalized and line managed effectively. Considerable concerns have, however, been expressed by commentators – notably by McConville *et al.* (1991) – that investigators are able to avoid these safeguards when pragmatic or cultural pressures dictate.

Tim John

Related entries

Detectives; Evidence; Murder.

Key texts and sources

Ascoli, D. (1979) *The Queen's Peace*. London: Hamish Hamilton.

Hobbs, D. (1988) *Doing the Business: Entrepreneurship, Detectives and the Working Class in the East End of London*. Oxford: Oxford University Press.

Holdaway, S. (1983) *Inside the British Police*. Oxford: Blackwell.

Innes, M. (2003) *Investigating Murder*. Oxford: Oxford University Press.

Maguire, M. and Norris, C. (1992) *The Conduct and Supervision of Criminal Investigations*. Royal Commission on Criminal Justice Research Study 5. London: HMSO.

McConville, M., Sanders, A. and Leng, R. (1991) *The Case for the Prosecution*. London: Routledge.

McLagan, G. (2003) B*ent Coppers: The Inside Story of Scotland Yard's Battle against Police Corruption*. London: Weidenfeld & Nicholson.

CRITICAL INCIDENTS

> A critical incident is any event where the effectiveness of the policing response is likely to have a significant impact on the confidence of the victim, his or her family and/or the community.

It can be argued that policing critical incidents has been part of mainstream policing since its inception. However, it was the Stephen Lawrence Inquiry that focused particular attention on the concept of critical incidents, with one quarter of the recommendations relating specifically to families and communities and their confidence. More recently it has been acknowledged that trust in policing needs to be enhanced among all communities, particularly when policing an incident is likely to have a considerable impact on the confidence of the community it polices. Communities perceive police intention through action, response and priorities.

A critical incident can be characterized by fast-time pressure, incomplete information and rapidly changing circumstances that are complex and are often policed 'in action'. Critical incidents can also be protracted and gradual, with events being aggregated over a period of time. Thus while not all incidents are dramatic and fast moving, they share similar characteristics. Critical incidents can occur in both the external operational or internal police environment. An internal critical incident, for example, may involve a grievance by a police officer on race, gender or sexual orientation grounds that mirror tensions in the community.

Managing critical incidents is challenging, requiring an understanding of the context and complexities of the incident while being able to make decisions in an uncertain and untested environment. The decisions made under these circumstances must have the potential to affect positively both the progress and outcome of the investigation, as well as to balance the needs of the police, the community, the family, the media and other parties.

Communication failures with the victim, family, community and officers, and real or perceived policing or investigative failures can have an adverse effect in managing critical incidents. This can be exacerbated by the 'culture of blame' that can develop and that can make policing very painful. The appointment of independent, specially trained officers can help alleviate these difficulties.

Accepted wisdom in responding to critical incidents involves the following considerations:

- Management structures, which include groups to consider strategy and operational issues and to establish minimum standards of supervision.
- Family liaison officers and arrangements to deal with the concerns of the family or victim.
- Community impact assessments which look at how events may be experienced by differing communities.
- Decision logs for recording and justifying decisions taken and any changes made.

- Communication strategies and debriefing processes.

Developments in understanding and conceptualizing critical incidents have refined the original definition as follows:

> *an incident or event which has, or is perceived to have, an effect upon a specific or non-specific community resulting in significant impact on the confidence or consciousness of victims, their families and/or the community. The proficiency of the response to such an incident or event will have a quantifiable variance on the level of tension that is present in the community* (http://www.acpo.police.uk/asp/policies/Data/critical_incident_management_17X08X07.pdf).

John Grieve

Related entries

Criminal investigation; Family liaison; Forensic and investigative psychology; Independent advisory groups.

Key texts and sources

Grieve, J., Crego, J. and Griffiths, W. (2007) 'Critical incidents', in T. Newburn, T. Williamson and A. Wright (eds) *Handbook of Criminal Investigation.* Cullompton: Willan Publishing.
Hall, N. (2005) *Hate Crime.* Cullompton: Willan Publishing.

CROWN PROSECUTION SERVICE (CPS)

The Crown Prosecution Service (CPS) is the independent public prosecution service of England and Wales.

The Crown Prosecution Service (CPS) was established in 1986 by the Prosecutions of Offences Act 1985 to prosecute criminal offences investigated by the 43 regional police forces in England and Wales and by a number of specialist forces and investigative agencies. It is headed by the Director of Public Prosecutions (DPP), who is supported by the Chief Executive. The Attorney General, who is the superintending minister, answers for the CPS in Parliament.

The CPS is divided into 42 areas, each headed by a chief Crown prosecutor and coterminous with regional police force boundaries. These areas are supported by a headquarters, within which is located operational and administrative support directorates, as well as specialist casework functions, including the Counter Terrorism and Serious and Organized Crime Divisions and a Specialist Crime Division (for the prosecution of high-profile or complex casework).

The primary aim of the criminal justice system is to reduce crime and the fear of crime, and to bring more offenders to justice. Within this, the role of the CPS is to determine whether or not criminal offences identified by the police should proceed to a criminal prosecution or be diverted to a non-court disposal. A non-court disposal includes a conditional caution. This involves offering offenders activities of a rehabilitative, reparative or penal nature if it would be appropriate to do so, but would also involve prosecution for the original offence if not completed satisfactorily.

Charging or diversion judgements are made by applying a two-part (evidential and public interest) test contained in the *Code for Crown Prosecutors* – a document issued by the DPP to guide Crown prosecutors. The evidence in the case must be such that there is a realistic prospect of conviction in court – i.e. a conviction is more likely than not. Examples of public interest factors favouring or tending against prosecution are contained in the code. The code applies equally to the police when they make a charging decision in cases delegated to them to charge by the DPP in his charging guidance.

The CPS prepares and presents all its cases in the magistrates' courts and, increasingly, presents more of its cases in the Crown court through in-house higher court advocates. However, the Private Bar is instructed to present the majority of Crown court cases. In order to fulfil its charging role, CPS prosecutors are located in 374 charging centres throughout

England and Wales to provide face-to-face advice and to decide what charges offenders should face in court. 'Out-of-office hours' (24 hours a day, every day) legal advice and charging cover are provided by CPS Direct, a specialized on-call service where duty prosecutors respond to calls from any force as required.

It was through this close working that the concept of the prosecution team was developed. The two agencies – the police and the CPS – while maintaining their independence, decided that much closer co-operation was necessary in the preparation and prosecution of cases in order for the criminal justice system to fulfil its objectives better.

Ken MacDonald

Related entries

Arrest; Bail; Clear-up rates; Custody; Police and Criminal Evidence Act 1984 (PACE); Police powers.

Key texts and sources

Ashworth, A. and Redmayne, M. (2005) *The Criminal Process.* Oxford: Oxford University Press.
Sanders, A. and Young, R. (2007) *Criminal Justice.* Oxford University Press.
The CPS's website is at http://www.cps.gov.uk/. The *Code for Crown Prosecutors* is available online at www.cps.gov.uk/victims_witnesses/code.html. *The Director's Guidance on Charging* is available at www.cps.gov.uk/publications/directors-guidance/dpp-guidance.html. See also the websites of the Attorney General (www.attorneygeneral. gov.uk), HM Court Services (http://www.hm courts-service.gov.uk/infoabout/ cps/index.htm) and the CPS Inspectorate (http://www.hmcpsi. gov.uk/).

CUSTODY

> **Custody is a short-term secure holding facility for persons under arrest or otherwise in police detention.**

Custody suites are principally used to detain arrested people for the purpose of investigating an offence they are suspected of committing. They may also be used as a designated 'place of safety' to accommodate people who have been detained under the Mental Health Act 1983 for the purpose of conducting a mental health assessment.

The Home Office-approved design for police cells is known as the Lambeth model. Cells are unisex, designed for single occupancy and equipped with washing and toilet facilities. Suites may also have a small number of 'dry' or 'trap' cells that are used to prevent the loss of evidence, particularly forensic evidence. All cells, including fittings and fixtures, are designed to minimize the availability of ligature points or other features that could be used by a detainee to self-harm. Some cells may be equipped with CCTV, or otherwise adapted, to provide additional protection for vulnerable detainees. In most modern suites, cells are arranged in corridors to ensure that men, women and juveniles are kept separate. Custody suites should also be equipped with exercise areas, medical rooms, interview rooms and solicitor consultation rooms.

The custody officer (the Serious Organized Crime and Police Act 2005 civilianized this role – it need no longer be undertaken by a police officer of the rank of sergeant) is responsible for authorizing the continued detention of people brought to the custody suite following arrest. They are independent of the investigation, and their role is to provide for the ongoing care and welfare of all people detained in the suite and to ensure they are treated in accordance with the Police and Criminal Evidence Act 1984 (PACE) and the codes of practice. The custody officer will normally be assisted by one or more detention officers. Where people are detained for more than six hours, their continued detention must be reviewed. The reviewing officer, a police officer of the rank of inspector or above, must also be independent of the investigation.

Other people to be found working in custody include healthcare professionals, solicitors, appropriate adults and interpreters. Healthcare professionals conduct medical assessments and provide treatment where appropriate. They may also be called upon to take forensic samples from detainees. Everyone is entitled to free legal advice while in police detention. Solicitors are independent of the police, but where a person does not have a solicitor, the custody officer can arrange for the duty solicitor to be called. Appropriate adults must be called for all detainees aged 17 years or under. Their role is to help the detainee to understand what is happening to him or her, to ensure the detainee is treated properly and fairly, and to assist his or her communication with the police. Interpreters are provided for detainees who are unable to communicate in English. In some circumstances, interpreters may provide their services by telephone.

Independent custody visitors (ICVs) are volunteers whose role is to check on the treatment of detainees and the conditions in which they are held. ICVs can visit a police station at any time and must be given immediate access, unless doing so would place them in danger.

Alex Marshall

Related entries

Bail; Civilianization; Coroners; Deaths in police custody (DPCs); Police and Criminal Evidence Act 1984 (PACE); Police powers.

Key texts and sources

PACE and the codes of practice are available online at www.police.homeoffice.gov.uk/operational-policing/powers-pace-codes/pace-code-intro/?version=3. The Association of Chief Police Officers/Home Office *Guidance on the Safer Detention and Handling of Persons in Police Custody* is available online at www.police.homeoffice.gov.uk/operational-policing/powers-pace-codes/safer-detention/?version=1.

CYBERCRIMES

Cybercrimes are illegal acts committed with the assistance of or by means of computers, computer networks, the Internet and web-based information and communications technologies (ICTs).

Cybercrimes are usually classified into two categories: crimes that cannot be committed in any other way or against any other type of victim (i.e. where the computer or online service is the target of the offence – for example, tampering with data and planting viruses) and familiar or conventional crimes that are facilitated by information and communication technologies (ICTs) ('cyber' versions of identity theft, stalking, paedophile activities and trading counterfeit goods, among others). Additionally, some behaviours that are not strictly cybercrimes in so far as they are not illegal may constitute what most people would consider harmful (e.g. some forms of pornography, gambling, unsolicited email, unregulated sales of medicines and prescription drugs, etc.).

Cyberspace is one of the fastest-growing sites of crime and transgression and presents numerous difficulties for law enforcers. Much policing of cyberspace is actually carried out by non-police bodies (Internet service providers, global interest groups, hotline providers and private security firms set up specifically to protect business interests) and, while 'the police' do have a mandate to investigate cybercrimes, they are becoming part of a more diverse assortment of bodies with regulatory and investigating functions. For example, the most recent initiative in the UK is the establishment of the Child Exploitation and Online Protection (CEOP) Centre which has brought together specialists from the NSPCC, Microsoft, AOL and Internet charities, as well as the police. Supported by the Serious Organized Crime Agency, CEOP is also linked to counterparts in Australia, Canada and the USA via an organization called the Virtual Global Taskforce.

Despite these initiatives, many academic commentators are scathing about the success of law enforcement agencies in tackling cybercrime. The main obstacles to its effective policing are the sheer volume of material generated and the global scope of the problem. Downloaded Internet content (e.g. hate mail or child pornography) will frequently originate on sites hosted elsewhere, making it virtually impossible for a police force in one country to investigate or bring a successful prosecution against individuals in another. This problem is compounded by the differing sizes and structures of national police forces; any difficulties faced by police officers trying to co-operate within geographical boundaries in the 'real' world are infinitely magnified in the borderless world of cyberspace. A further obstacle concerns the inadequacy of legislation. For example, the UK police are authorized only to search for, and seize, tangible evidence (Computer Misuse Act 1990). This requirement can be counterproductive to the investigation and prosecution of cybercrimes where evidence may be regarded as intangible. In addition, some critics question the police's commitment to the task, arguing that officers lack adequate, ongoing training in computer technologies and are part of an organizational culture that is resistant to change (Jewkes 2003; Jewkes and Andrews 2005).

While initiatives such as the Virtual Global Taskforce demonstrate that not all law enforcers are Luddites seeking to thwart progress, the challenges for the police are set to intensify as the next generation of ICTs promises to integrate online digital technology ever more closely into everyday life, raising new problems concerning governance, security, surveillance and vulnerability.

Yvonne Jewkes

Related entries

Europol; Fraud and policing; Pornography (child).

Key texts and sources

Jewkes, Y. (2003) 'Policing cybercrime', in T. Newburn (ed.) *Handbook of Policing*. Cullompton: Willan Publishing.

Jewkes, Y. and Andrews, C. (2005) 'Policing the filth: the problems of investigating online child pornography in England and Wales', *Policing and Society*, 15: 42–62.

See also www.virtualglobaltaskforce.com.

D

DANGEROUS OFFENDERS AND DANGEROUSNESS

'Dangerous offenders' and 'dangerousness' are related, but not interchangeable, concepts. Certain violent and sexual offenders are considered 'dangerous offenders', but the concept of 'dangerousness' is potentially much wider. There are important definitional, practical and ethical issues to consider.

The issue of 'dangerous offenders' has a long history, but it has recently become much higher on the political agenda. This is partly because political terrorism has had a higher profile in western nations and also because, more parochially in the UK, some horrific crimes have had extensive media coverage, which has raised public concern. The focus needs to be both on 'dangerous offenders' and on 'dangerousness', which are related but not interchangeable concepts.

There have been many attempts to define dangerousness, but Gunn's (1982) identification of three elements that stand out – destructiveness, prediction and fear – still captures the spirit of present concern. However, it needs to be recognized from the outset that 'dangerousness' is a relative concept, informed by public attitudes and values to crime and punishment as well as being shaped by the laws introduced to govern the dangerous. Those classified as dangerous have varied across time, but they all have represented similar threats to the values of normal society – the 'ungovernables' (Pratt 1997).

While the repetitively violent criminal largely embraces the 'commonsense' definition of the dangerous offender, this can be regarded as rather a narrow focus. Crimes of omission can be just as dangerous as crimes of commission. In his seminal paper, Bottoms (1977) pointed out that any adequate theory 'must take seriously the offences of the powerful as well as those of the powerless'. There remains no adequate justification as to why certain types of offenders are deemed 'dangerous' when others who pose the same or greater level of harm are not labelled as such. Grave harms are often the result of negligent and avoidable actions.

Multinational corporations, for example, may be responsible for endangering the public by polluting rivers and water supplies, often in the name of profit. These corporations may deliberately seek countries with lax regulatory controls in order to maximize their profits. The Bhopal disaster in India is an example of this different kind of dangerousness, when thousands of people were killed – many more victims than the worst psychopath on a shooting spree – after a gas leak at the Union Carbide factory. The company was fully aware of the potential disaster stemming from chemical leaks and did nothing to avert it. However, apart from the problem of challenging the powerful, it is probably easier to find and detain individuals who are overtly violent at the personal level. Indeed, it is the overtly violent from whom the public normally want protection.

The imperative of protecting the public from harm, combined with a wish to be seen as being tough on crime, has shifted the emphasis for politicians from considering how to defuse dangerous situations to a focus on allegedly dangerous individuals. The focus on dangerous *offenders* is largely about considering what to do with offenders who have already exhibited dangerous behaviour (usually personal violence towards others). However, there are also moves to try to predict which children might become dangerous offenders or, similarly, which petty offenders might become serious offenders in the future. The important ethical concerns that can be raised about dealing with known dangerous offenders are even greater when one is trying to predict who might become 'dangerous offenders'.

Public protection was explicitly introduced into the law for the first time with the Prevention of Crime Act 1908. This new penal concept meant the state had a duty to intervene and protect its subjects from those who endangered them (Pratt 1997). However, in England and Wales there is no actual crime of 'dangerousness'; instead, legislation has been passed to extend the powers given to the courts to deal with offenders who are deemed dangerous.

Protective sentences can be imposed under a number of provisions, which include s. 80(2)(b) of the Powers of Criminal Courts (Sentencing) Act 2000, by which courts may extend the 'normal sentence' that may be appropriate for a serious 'violent' or 'sexual' offence if of the opinion that only such a sentence would be adequate to protect the public from 'serious harm' from the offender. The prospective harm must be of a grave nature, and s. 31(3) of the Criminal Justice Act 1991 further provides that 'serious harm' for the purposes of these sections means 'protecting members of the public from death or serious personal injury, whether physical or psychological, occasioned by further such offences committed by [the defendant]'. Section 109 of the Powers of Criminal Courts (Sentencing) Act 2000 also provides for automatic life sentences for offenders who commit a second 'serious offence'. 'Extended sentences' are also used under s. 85 of the Powers of Criminal Courts (Sentencing) Act 2000, as well as discretionary life sentences. The Criminal Justice Act 2003 has, however, recently repealed the provisions of the Powers of Criminal Courts (Sentencing) Act 2000. But because the new provisions only came into force on 4 April 2005, the old provisions still apply to relevant offences committed before that date (Thomas 2006). Routinely, dangerous people who have committed an offence have been dealt with in one of the aforementioned ways, while individuals in need of treatment have been processed through the mental health system. There is, however, one other category that has emerged: the dangerous person with a severe personality disorder (DSPD) who is untreatable and can also be subject to indeterminate sentencing (McAlinden 2001). The criteria laid out in the legislation still leave unanswered questions, such as how likely and how serious the predicted harm must be before it is justifiable to lengthen a prison sentence beyond its proportionate term, and how prospective psychological harm should be interpreted (Ashworth 2004a).

Unless social control agents predict with total accuracy which offenders will be dangerous in the future, the problem of 'false positives' and 'false negatives' will always be a key consideration in this area. 'False positives' are where a social control agent falsely predicts someone will be dangerous when, in fact, he or she will not be. In contrast, 'false negatives' are where a social control agent predicts someone will not be dangerous when he or she will be. There is always a tension between these possibilities in trying to balance ethical and practical considerations. The more the importance of public protection is emphasized, the more likely there will be 'false positives', and more offenders will be detained unnecessarily. The more that the importance of the civil liberties of offenders is stressed (that is, to argue that it is wrong to continue to lock up 'dangerous' offenders once their original sentence has been served), the spectre of more 'false negatives' arises.

In brief, the notion of 'dangerous offenders' raises definitional, practical and ethical considerations that have not been solved and that are perhaps irresolvable.

Keith Soothill and Sophie Holmes

Related entries

Criminal investigation; Forensic and investigative psychology.

Key texts and sources

Ashworth, A. (2004) 'Criminal Justice Act 2003. Part 2. Criminal justice reform – principles, human rights and public protection', *Criminal Law Review*, 516–32.

Bottoms, A.E. (1977) 'Reflections on the renaissance of dangerousness', *Howard Journal of Penology and Crime Prevention*, 16: 70–96.

Brown, M. and Pratt, J. (eds) (2000) *Dangerous Offenders: Punishment and Social Order*. London: Routledge.

Gunn, J. (1982) 'Defining the terms', in J.R. Hamilton and H. Freeman (eds) *Dangerousness: Psychiatric Assessment and Management*. London: Gaskell.

McAlinden, A. (2001) 'Indeterminate sentences for the severely personality disordered', *Criminal Law Review*, 108–23.

Pratt, J. (1997) *Governing the Dangerous: Dangerousness, Law and Social Change*. Sydney: Federation Press.

Thomas, D.A. (2006) 'Sentencing: dangerous offenders – Criminal Justice Act 2003 – "significant risk of serious harm"', *Criminal Law Review*, 174–9.

DEATHS IN POLICE CUSTODY (DPCs)

> Deaths in police custody (DPCs) may be evidence of system failure or weakness in the provision of policing services: people detained in police custody are in a vulnerable condition, particularly detainees with mental health problems. There is great concern, therefore, to ensure that information on the extent and patterns of DPCs is properly gathered and profiled.

Deaths in police custody (DPCs) are instances of individual tragedy, but they may also be symptoms of something even more fundamental. DPCs are events interwoven with questions about the quality and transparency of policing, police culture, the effectiveness of mechanisms for police accountability, the status of police–community relations – often relations with minority ethnic communities – and, in some cases, the quality of justice and the rule of law. The death of Steve Biko in 1977 in South Africa, who died in hospital after injuries sustained during interrogation in a security police headquarters, was a tragedy that not only symbolized the hollow nature of the 'rule of law' in apartheid South Africa but also served to galvanize further the movement against apartheid itself. In Australia, such has been the concern over the high rates of DPCs of indigenous Australians that a royal commission into the issue was set up in 1989 (Wooten 1991). In Britain, the death of Jimmy Kelly, who died in 1979 in police custody after being arrested by Merseyside Police in a drunken state and who had sustained serious injuries while in a police transit vehicle, served to expose much deeper political tensions between the local police chief and his police authority, and this became part and parcel of a wider debate about the adequacy of the machinery of police accountability in Britain.

At the very least, DPCs may be evidence of system failure or weakness in the provision of policing services and, possibly, of the quality of co-operation between the police and other public services. For this reason there is great concern to ensure that information on the extent and patterns of DPCs is properly gathered and profiled, particularly as there has been concern that the problem has been growing. In Britain, these tasks are undertaken by both the Home Office, as part of its annual statistical recording process, and the Independent Police Complaints Commission (IPCC; prior to 2004, the Police Complaints Authority) as part of its monitoring of police activity. The statistics are gathered under the broader heading of 'deaths during or following police contact' (Teers and Bucke 2005), which also includes road traffic fatalities, fatal shootings and deaths following any other contact, but deaths 'in or after custody' are separately identifiable.

For example, in the year 2004–5 in England and Wales there were 106 deaths during or following police contact, of which 36 were deaths in or after police custody (Teers and Bucke 2005: 7). Of these 36, 29 were white males, 2 were males of black African origin and 5 were white females; the average age of those who died was 43. Seven were declared dead in the custody suite; one died while being arrested; 28 died after they had been transferred to hospital; and two died as a result of suicide in the police cell. Some 25 of the 36 were reported to have been intoxicated or to have consumed drugs.

Monitoring and analysis of DPCs are also undertaken by the campaigning group Inquest, which was set up in the wake of the death of Jimmy Kelly and other deaths in state custody. Inquest has supported campaigns for official inquiries into deaths in police custody on many occasions. One high-profile case was the death of Roger Sylvester, a 30-year-old black man who died after going into a coma following his arrest by Metropolitan Police officers. Up to six officers were involved in forcefully restraining him after he was arrested for banging on doors naked. The coroner's court jury reached a verdict of unlawful killing, although a high court subsequently overturned the verdict. Similar controversy has surrounded the death of Christopher Adler, a black paratrooper who was choked to death on the floor of Hull police station while officers talked and joked around him. In Adler's case, the IPCC report into the incident concluded that four police officers were guilty of the 'most serious neglect of duty'.

In an attempt to detect systemic factors behind DPCs, the Home Office conducted research on 360 cases between 1990 and 1996 (Leigh *et al.* 1998). The research concluded that:

- DPCs were rare;
- the most common cause was deliberate self-harm;
- substance abuse and medical conditions accounted for over half the deaths;
- although a disproportionate number of deaths involved black detainees, this could be explained by the proportionately higher arrest rate for black people.

Particular concern lies with detainees with mental health problems, which account for around 50 per cent of all DPCs. Police cells are frequently used as 'places of safety' under mental health legislation, in the absence of alternative, health-based accommodation. Furthermore, there is a question over the adequacy of the training of custody officers in enabling officers to recognize the signs of mental health problems in other detainees, which would allow them to know when to call on the services of a forensic medical examiner (or 'police surgeon'). Even medical practitioners may not have had the appropriate training to recognize mental disorder.

In these respects a number of policy initiatives have been taken to tackle DPCs (Home Office 2004c: 80–3), which include the following:

- The better design of custody suites to prevent suicides, including monitoring equipment.
- Fully independent investigation of DPCs and enhanced independent custody visiting.
- The use of nurses in custody centres to work alongside officers and doctors, and better training for forensic physicians in the mental health area.
- Better interagency working between police and health-based organizations.
- More guidance and training for custody officers on health issues, the signs of self-harming and substance misuse.

People detained in police custody are in a vulnerable condition, and DPCs act as one index of how that vulnerability is handled by policing services. There is now greater awareness among practitioners and policy-makers of how that level of vulnerability can turn itself into a death during or soon after a person is placed in police custody. Nevertheless, it is difficult to deny that, in virtually every case of a death in police custody, something might have been done to prevent it.

Stephen P. Savage

Related entries

Coroners; Custody; Independent Police Complaints Commission (IPCC).

Key texts and sources

Home Office (2004) *Deaths During or Following Police Contact: Statistics for England and Wales, April 2003 to March 2004.* London: HMSO.
Leigh, A., Johnson, G. and Ingram, A. (1998) *Deaths in Police Custody: Learning the Lessons.* London: HMSO.
Teers, R. and Bucke, T. (2005) *Deaths During or Following Police Contact: Statistics for England and Wales, 2004/5.* London: IPCC.
Wooten, J. (1991) *Royal Commission into Aboriginal Deaths in Custody.* Canberra: Australian Government Publishing Service.
See also www.inquest.org.uk and the Home Office's police custody web page (http://police.homeoffice. gov.uk/operational-policing/powers-pace-codes/ custody.html). For reports on DPCs that have appeared in the *Guardian*, see http://www.guardian. co.uk/celldeaths/archive/0,,195393,00.html.

DEFENCE LAWYERS

A defence lawyer is a solicitor or barrister who acts on behalf of a person suspected or accused of crime. The term is also used to describe staff employed by solicitors, particularly those who advise clients at police stations.

The term 'defence lawyer' (sometimes known as 'a brief'), although in common usage, is not a legal term and, while it is frequently used to denote a person who is qualified as a solicitor or barrister who acts for suspects or defendants, it is also used to describe a person who is not so qualified, such as a legal executive or representative. It is a criminal offence for an unqualified person to act as, or to pretend to be, a solicitor (Solicitors Act 1974, ss. 20 and 21). However, for the purposes of the right to legal advice at police stations under the Police and Criminal Evidence Act 1984 (PACE), s. 58, Code of Practice C (para. 6.12) provides that the term solicitor includes an accredited or probationary representative. All lawyers providing publicly funded legal advice at police stations must either be a duty solicitor or accredited (or working towards accreditation) under a scheme run jointly by the Legal Services Commission (LSC) and the Law Society.

Barristers who act for criminal defendants are generally self-employed, although they normally work with other barristers, sharing common services and resources. They have rights of audience in all criminal courts, although more experienced barristers tend not to appear in magistrates' courts. Under the so-called 'cab-rank' rule they should be prepared to act for the prosecution or defence, and some are specialists in certain areas of criminal law. They do not qualify as a solicitor for the purposes of giving police station advice.

Solicitors may be self-employed, although they normally work as partners in, or employees of, firms of solicitors. A small number are employed by the Public Defender Service, which is run by the LSC. Solicitors do not have rights of audience in the Crown court unless (as an increasing number do) they have a 'higher rights' qualification. Only those firms that have a contract with the LSC can act for suspects or defendants under legal aid.

Barristers and solicitors, and legal executives who are members or fellows of the Institute of Legal Executives, are subject to the professional conduct rules of their professional bodies, and may be disciplined for breach of those rules. Those firms that have a contract with the LSC are also subject to the quality requirements of the contract, and may lose their contract if they are found to be in breach. The conduct rules impose a range of obligations on lawyers (including defence lawyers), including the requirement to act in a client's best interests, a duty to keep their client's affairs confidential, a duty of full disclosure to their client and a duty not to act where there is a conflict of interests. In the case of lawyers advising a client at a police station, PACE Code of Practice C (Note for Guidance 6D) provides that the 'solicitor's only role in the police station is to protect and advance the legal rights of their client'.

While past research evidence tends to suggest that defence lawyers are not sufficiently adversarial, policy-makers and successive governments have tended to criticize them for being too adversarial and for acting in a way designed to inflate their fees.

Ed Cape

Related entries

Defendants; Right of silence.

Key texts and sources

Cape, E. (2004) '50th anniversary article: the rise (and fall?) of a criminal defence profession', *Criminal Law Review*, 401–16.

McConville, M., Hodgson, J., Bridges, L. and Pavlovic, A. (1994) *Standing Accused: The Organisation and Practice of Criminal Defence Lawyers in Britain*. Oxford: Clarendon Press.

See also the Public Defence Solicitors Office's website (http://www.pdso.org.uk/).

DEFENDANTS

> A defendant is a person against whom formal criminal proceedings have been commenced and who has not yet been sentenced.

The terms 'defendant' and 'accused' tend to be used interchangeably, and some legislation refers to the former (e.g. the Criminal Justice Act 2003, Part 11, ch. 1) while other legislation uses the latter term (e.g. the Criminal Justice and Public Order Act 1994, ss. 34–38). Both should be distinguished from 'suspect' which, although not appearing in the Police and Criminal Evidence Act 1984 (PACE) or the PACE codes, is commonly used to denote a person who is suspected of committing a criminal offence, but against whom formal criminal proceedings have not been commenced.

In recent years about 1.3 million people per annum have been arrested in respect of notifiable offences (*see Statistics on Arrests for Recorded Crime (Notifiable Offences) and Operation of Certain Police Powers under PACE*). Not all people who are arrested are subsequently detained at a police station, but statistics are not routinely collected on the number of people detained following an arrest. About 2.2 million people appear in magistrates' courts each year, either as a result of having been arrested and charged or as a result of having been summoned for a criminal offence (see the *Criminal Statistics*). Defendants initially appear in a magistrates' court even if they are ultimately tried or sentenced in the Crown court. The police and Crown prosecutors have been granted a number of powers to impose fixed penalties and other forms of punishment without initiating formal criminal proceedings, and the government has signalled its intention to extend these powers further.

Suspects and defendants have a number of rights. Suspects' rights are principally governed by PACE, and they include the right to legal advice if the suspect is arrested and held in custody at a police station or the suspect voluntarily attends a police station in connection with the investigation of an offence (PACE s. 58 and Code of Practice C, s. 6). Defendants have a common law right to legal advice and

representation, and this is also guaranteed by the European Convention on Human Rights (ECHR), Article 6(3)(c). A defendant is presumed to be innocent until proved guilty according to law (ECHR, Article 6(2)), and defendants are said to enjoy the privilege against self-incrimination, although some have argued that these rights have been restricted, if not abrogated, by the inference provisions of the Criminal Justice and Public Order Act 1994 and the disclosure requirements of the Criminal Procedure and Investigations Act 1996 (see, e.g., Ashworth and Redmayne 2005).

Suspects who are vulnerable as a result of youth or mental vulnerability are subject to special measures, especially the requirement that they should normally only be interviewed in the presence of an appropriate adult (PACE Code of Practice C, para. 11.18). However, there are no similar provisions for vulnerable defendants, and the special measures provisions for vulnerable witnesses introduced by the Youth Justice and Criminal Evidence Act 1999 do not apply to defendants.

While there is a wealth of research evidence on suspects' and defendants' rights (especially the former), little recent research has been carried out in respect of the experience of suspects and defendants of the criminal process. For an early example, see Bottoms and McClean (1976).

Ed Cape

Related entries

Bail; Defence lawyers; European Convention on Human Rights (ECHR); Evidence; Police and Criminal Evidence Act 1984 (PACE).

Key texts and sources

The *Criminal Statistics*, which show the number of defendants appearing in the criminal courts, are published by the Home Office annually. *Statistics on Arrests for Recorded Crime (Notifiable Offences)* and the *Operation of Certain Police Powers under PACE* are also published annually by the Home Office. They are both available online at the Home Office Research, Development and Statistics Directorate website (http://www.homeoffice.gov.uk/rds/). For an account of the legal process from the defendant's point of view, see the Criminal Justice System's web page (http://www.cjsonline.gov.uk/defendant/walkthrough/index.html).

DETECTIVES

A police detective in the UK is associated with the criminal investigation department. The role of the detective has typically been to investigate specific crimes, particularly serious crime, retrospectively.

in the archetypal case, the investigator undertakes inquiries in order to (i) determine whether, in fact, an offence has been committed and (ii) gather sufficient evidence to establish a set of possible suspects, to eliminate those responsible, and to support criminal charges against any who might be

(Maguire and Norris 1992: 7).

The investigative priority, in contrast to the crime prevention mantra of the uniformed police, coupled with particular working norms (plain clothes, working outside the established shift system), has provided detectives with a distinct but varying identity both within the police and in media and fictional accounts (Reiner 2000). Detectives are characterized by individualism, by combining craft ('working on a hunch') with science and by a close working knowledge of internal administrative, and external legal, rules and regulations. Detectives are associated with a close working relationship with criminals and those on the periphery of criminal organizations, through the development of informants and sources of information. At various points in the history of detection, it has been demonstrated that detectives have been able to manipulate the system to produce required results (so-called 'noble cause corruption') or to work outside it through corruption for personal gain.

Measuring the impact of detective work has proven problematic. Clear-up and detection rates vary across crime classifications, typically being high for violent crimes and low for property crimes. The existence of witnesses/victims and the gravity of violent crimes are seen to be a more important determinant of the relative success than the investigative efforts of the police. Indeed, research has consistently demonstrated that investigative activity, in the absence of clear leads from the public, is relatively unproductive (e.g. Ericson 1993).

In the context of the factors considered above, it is generally accepted that the role of the detective is changing. Responses to detectives' associations with criminal networks and to the dangers of corruption have led to shorter-term periods of 'tenure' in criminal investigation departments, raising subsequent concerns about the core investigative skills and experience of senior investigating officers to conduct their roles effectively (e.g. Kinchen 1996). More generally, exhortations by influential bodies such as the Audit Commission (1993) to 'target the criminal, not the crime' have resulted in intelligence-led policing becoming prioritized, as exemplified in England and Wales through the National Intelligence Model. Such developments have subtly moved investigation away from a reactive model, where individual crime incidents are investigated. The processes of crime screening and prioritization remove detective input from more minor cases. Consequently, detective work deals with remaining cases and, in collaboration with intelligence units, focuses on series and patterns of crime, thus becoming problem focused and more future oriented.

Tim John

Related entries

Corruption (police); Criminal investigation; Criminal investigation department (CID); Police culture; Special branch (SB); Unit beat policing (UBP).

Key texts and sources

Hobbs, D. (1988) *Doing the Business: Entrepreneurship, Detectives and the Working Class in the East End of London.* Oxford: Oxford University Press.

Innes, M. (2003) *Investigating Murder.* Oxford: Oxford University Press.

Maguire, M. and Norris, C. (1992) *The Conduct and Supervision of Criminal Investigations. Royal Commission on Criminal Justice Research Study* 5. London: HMSO.

DISCRETION

In the context of policing, the term 'discretion' denotes the freedom of the individual officer to act according to his or her own judgement in particular situations.

Public police organizations have traditionally been viewed as rule-bound bureaucracies, structured around a rigid hierarchy of military-style ranks and disciplinary codes. This suggests that policing involves a relatively straightforward and mechanistic enforcement of the law, with little room for discretion by police officers (Allen 1976). However, the overwhelming conclusion of empirical research since the 1960s has been that one of the defining features of public policing is the very wide degree of discretion that characterizes much front-line police decision-making. Furthermore, a particular feature of the police organization is that 'within it, discretion increases as one moves down the hierarchy' (Wilson 1968b). In the context of England and Wales, Lord Scarman famously concluded that 'the exercise of discretion lies at the heart of the policing function' (1981). This discretion arises from a number of factors.

First, a significant degree of police discretion flows from the nature of the law and its application. Given limited police resources and the infinite possibilities for law enforcement, decisions have to be made about which laws to enforce and when to avoid recourse to formal police powers. Once decisions have been made about which laws to enforce, further decisions must then be taken about methods and styles of enforcement (Jones *et al.* 1994).

Secondly, the broad nature of the police mandate (Bittner 1974) is predicated upon the necessary existence of a significant degree of discretion for police officers. The idea of full enforcement is a myth because of the sheer breadth and complexity of situational exigencies which police officers are required to deal with. Thus, police officers must constantly make decisions about which laws to enforce and how

to do this. It is clear that law enforcement is only one part of what police officers actually do in practice. A significant part of police activity involves order maintenance or peacekeeping: the containment of incidents that might lead to law breaking (Reiner 2000). This is reflected in the fact that a range of police powers relates to offences that are deliberately framed broadly, such as 'breach of the peace', in order to provide police officers with a flexible resource that can be deployed in attempting to achieve the broader objectives of order maintenance.

Thirdly, police discretion is *de facto* enhanced by the low social visibility of front-line policing. Adversarial police contacts are disproportionately experienced by relatively powerless marginal groups ('police property') and often take place away from the eyes of supervisors and/or the wider public (Reiner 2000). Thus, while the law and organizational policies provide an important broader framework for the pattern of policing, within these there remains considerable decision-making autonomy for police officers (Smith 1986).

A traditional concern of police reformers has been to limit the degree to which the operation of this discretion is shaped by the more negative features of occupational police cultures. Two broad responses to this problem have been attempted by policy-makers. First, there have been various attempts to restrict the extent of police discretion via more restrictive and detailed legal regulation and retrospective review of police decisions, as well as attempts to render operational policing process more 'visible'. Secondly, reformers have tried to counter, through training and ethical guidelines, the negative influence of occupational cultures that have been viewed as a key factor in shaping discretionary policing in problematic ways.

Trevor Jones

Related entries

Crime; Ethics in policing; Force (police use of); 'Judges' Rules'; Police and Criminal Evidence Act 1984 (PACE); Police culture; Stop and search.

Key texts and sources

Brooks, L.W. (2001) 'Police discretionary behaviour: a study of style', in R.G. Dunham and G.P. Alpert (eds) *Critical Issues in Policing* (4th edn). Prospect Heights, IL: Waveland.

Smith, D.J. and Gray, J. (1986) *Police and People in London.* Aldershot: Gower.

Wilson, J.Q. (1968) *Varieties of Police Behaviour: The Management of Law and Order in Eight Communities.* Cambridge, MA: Harvard University Press.

DISPERSAL ORDERS

Dispersal orders are new powers to remove groups of two or more people from areas that have been designated as dispersal zones due to a history of persistent anti-social behaviour.

Part 4 of the Anti-social Behaviour Act 2003 (ss. 30–36) gives the police in England and Wales new powers to disperse groups of two or more people from areas where there is believed to be persistent anti-social behaviour and a problem with groups causing intimidation. In Scotland, a very similar power was introduced by Part 3 of the Antisocial Behaviour, etc., Scotland Act 2004. (In Scotland, however, orders may last only three months (renewable), and there is no discretionary power to exclude those dispersed from the area for up to 24 hours.) With local authority agreement, a senior police officer (superintendent) can designate an area as a 'dispersal order' zone. This decision must be published in a local newspaper or by notices in the area. Designation can be for a period of up to six months and may be renewed. The designated area must be clearly defined, but may be as small as a shopping arcade or as large as a city centre or whole local authority area. Within a designated zone, a police constable or community support officer (CSO) may disperse groups where their presence or behaviour has resulted, or is likely to result, in a member of the public being harassed, intimidated, alarmed or distressed. Individuals who do not reside within the designated area can then be directed to leave the locality and may be excluded from it for up to 24 hours. A person does not commit an offence because an officer has chosen to use the power to disperse, but if individuals refuse to follow the officer's directions, they will be committing an offence.

The 2003 Act (s. 30(6)) also creates a power to remove to his or her home any young person under 16 who is out on the streets between 9 p.m. and 6 a.m. and not under the control of an adult. In an early judgment in July 2005, the High Court ruled that this power did not allow the use of reasonable force (*R(W)* v. *Metropolitan Police and the London Borough of Richmond*). Consequently, police forces around the country suspended the use of what colloquially became known as the 'curfew' element of dispersal orders. This power is not available in Scotland under equivalent legislation passed in 2004, partly because of concerns raised about its coercive nature. In May 2006 the Court of Appeal overturned the earlier judgment but laid down two strict conditions for the exercise of reasonable force in relation to the original power (*R (on the application of W)* v. *Commissioner of Police of the Metropolis*). Young people can only be removed to their home from a dispersal order zone if they are either: 1) at risk or vulnerable from anti-social behaviour and crime; or 2) causing, or at risk of causing, anti-social behaviour. In the light of this judgment, new guidance on the use of dispersal powers was published (Home Office 2006d) and the Home Office Minister, Tony McNulty, challenged police and practitioners 'to take a more robust and unremitting approach to tackling anti-social behaviour by making maximum use of the dispersal powers available to them'.

These powers have been available since 20 January 2004. The Home Office (2005c) estimated that, by 30 June 2005, over 800 areas were designated for the purpose of dispersal order powers. The data suggest that the use of dispersal orders reflects considerable local variations. Three forces accounted for a quarter of all areas designated, whereas four forces had designated no areas and five had designated only one area. Dispersal orders have been used to address a wide variety of local problems, including prostitution, aggressive begging and illegal street vending, but are most commonly used in relation to groups of young people. In a similar vein, 'designated public places orders' (DPPOs) allow for controlled drinking zones in areas that have experienced alcohol-related disorder or nuisance. DPPOs provide police and CSOs with powers to require people to stop drinking or to confiscate alcohol.

Controversially, the dispersal order only requires that the group's *presence* is sufficient to be *likely* to offend a member of the public. While groups gathering in dispersal zones are not *per se* in violation of the law, they can fall foul of the legislation where their demeanour, comportment or dress may be sufficient to frighten others. Appearance, as much as specific behaviour, is potentially caught by the power. In this sense, the dispersal order has a pre-emptive logic: the intervention is justified, despite the lack of any necessary criminal incident, if it either pacifies other people's subjective fears or halts the potential escalation of behaviour. It conforms to a type of 'preventive exclusion', at least for a specific period of time (Von Hirsch and Shearing 2000). Hence, the power potentially bypasses the agency of the individuals concerned. It implies that assumptions are made about what they might do, not merely what they have done.

The discretionary nature of the powers places considerable pressures of professional judgement on individual police officers, and more worryingly CSOs, in situations that may precipitate rather than reduce conflict. This leaves considerable scope for inconsistent implementation in ways that may impact negatively upon perceptions of procedural fairness on the part of those (young) people dispersed. Research demonstrates that experiences of procedural justice – the appropriate manner in which the police exercise their authority, being treated fairly and with respect – can significantly affect perceptions of legitimacy and public confidence in the police, as well as legal compliance (Sunshine and Tyler 2003). Ominously, Skogan's (2006) research shows the

impact of having a bad experience in contact with the police – of which being treated unfairly is a major factor – is 4 to 14 times as great as that of having a positive experience. Consequently, effective policing will often demand non-recourse to formal dispersal order powers, except as a last resort.

There are concerns about the displacement of problems from dispersal zones to neighbouring areas, the extent of the police resource necessary to implement dispersal zones, the raised expectations that designation can generate and about what should occur beyond the end of the designated period. Experiences of implementing dispersal orders suggest the powers provide a short-term intervention that, where used creatively, may precipitate more extensive and longer-term problem-solving and preventive work through local partnerships between relevant agencies and local communities, rather than a stand-alone solution to anti-social behaviour.

Adam Crawford

Related entries

Anti-social behaviour; Community support officers (CSOs).

Key texts and sources

Home Office (2005) *Use of Dispersal Powers* (available online at **http://www.together.gov.uk/article.asp?c=185&aid=3463**).

Home Office (2006) *Respect and Dispersal Powers*. London: Home Office.

Skogan, W. (2006) 'Asymmetry in the impact of encounters with the police', *Policing and Society*, 16: 99–126.

Sunshine, J. and Tyler, T. (2003) 'The role of procedural justice and legitimacy in shaping public support for policing', *Law and Society Review*, 37: 513–48.

Von Hirsch, A. and Shearing, C. (2000) 'Exclusion from public space', in A. Von Hirsch *et al.* (eds) *Ethical and Social Perspectives on Situational Crime Prevention*. Oxford: Hart Publishing.

See also the Chartered Institute of Environmental Health's web page on dispersal orders (http://www.cieh.org/asb/the_law5.html).

DIXON OF DOCK GREEN

Originally created by Ted Willis for the film *The Blue Lamp*, PC (later Sergeant) George Dixon was the central character of the long-running BBC television series, *Dixon of Dock Green*. Dixon represented the quintessential ideal of the British bobby, practising community policing long before the term was coined in the 1970s. Standing for an ideal of policing that has continuing resonance today, Dixon is regularly evoked by those seeking to reform policing practice.

Dixon of Dock Green was a long-running BBC television series, launched in 1955 and continuing until 1976 for 434 episodes. Its eponymous hero was PC (later Sergeant) George Dixon, played by Jack Warner. Dixon represented the quintessential ideal of the British bobby, as summed up succinctly some 40 years earlier by a *Times* editorial: 'not merely guardian of the peace; he is the best friend of a mass of people who have no other counsellor or protector.' Dixon practised community policing long before the term was coined in the 1970s in an attempt to recreate what he had represented. The series was set in a working-class milieu, portrayed as fundamentally consensual, with a shared ethical code. This was made explicit when Dixon addressed the audience at the end of each episode to draw out the moral of the story. Policing was represented as primarily service work, though there was some crime and deviance and even an occasional bent copper. But the veneer of the cosy community constable cloaked a murkier reality of widespread brutality, abuse and corruption behind the scenes during the supposed 'Golden Age' of British policing, as memoirs and oral histories of the period reveal.

The George Dixon character had originally been created by author, Ted Willis, for a film *The Blue Lamp* made by Ealing Studios in 1949 and released in 1950 with considerable commercial and critical success. Ealing Studios had become celebrated during the war for films evoking the spirit of Britain's finest hour, embodying an ethos of public service and of the people as heroes. They continued producing films evoking these values in the postwar decade, and *The Blue Lamp* is a characteristic example. PC George Dixon and the other officers working out of Dock Green station were stalwart representations of the virtues of honesty, compassion, courage, community. But the opening of the film dramatically conveys a burgeoning threat to this Durkheimian organic solidarity. A montage of newspaper headlines and violent scenes, and a sombre voice-over, warns of a growing wave of violence and gangsterism. In the course of the film we encounter a young Dirk Bogarde as a harbinger of a new embryonic youth culture, restless for excitement and quick wealth. In the course of a robbery about midway through the film he shoots Dixon dead. The rest of the narrative depicts the hunting down of the killer. In a perfect illustration of Durkheim's analysis of crime uniting all healthy consciences, the whole of London seems to co-operate in this – even the professional underworld who, in a rousing final sequence at White City racetrack, help the police find Bogarde.

The character of Dixon was widely seen as an embodiment of English national virtue, and he was resurrected in 1955 for 21 more years of being 'just an ordinary copper' (the series' theme tune). It is usual to regard the series as quaintly old-fashioned and increasingly anachronistic as the television image of the police shifted in the 1960s and 1970s to more morally ambiguous, action-oriented series like *The Sweeney*. But in fact the appeal of the Dixon model increased rather than diminished over time. During the 1950s, supposedly its heyday, the programme never featured in the monthly lists of the most popular shows. It first appeared there in 1968, the *annus mirabilis* of countercultural revolution! In the 1970s it was regularly in the top 20. Its demise was due to Jack Warner's age (he was still on the beat in his 80s!) rather than a lack of an audience. Dixon stood for an ideal of policing that has continuing resonance and remains regularly evoked by politicians and police chiefs seeking reform (e.g. 'It's time to bring back Dixon, says Met', *Guardian* 28 February 2003: 15).

Robert Reiner

Related entries

Constables; Media and policing.

Key texts and sources

Aldgate, A. and Richards, J. (1999) 'The thin blue line', in J. Richards and A. Aldgate (eds) *Best of British*. London: Taurus.

Mason, P. and Leishman, F. (2003) *Policing and the Media*. Cullompton: Willan Publishing.

McLaughlin, E. (2005) 'From reel to ideal: *The Blue Lamp* and the popular construction of the English "bobby"', *Crime, Media, Culture*, 1: 11–30.

Reiner, R. (2003) 'Policing and the media', in T. Newburn (ed.) *Handbook of Policing*. Cullompton: Willan Publishing.

DNA PROFILING

DNA (deoxyribonucleic acid) is the genetic material of living organisms that determines each individual's hereditary characteristics, and exact copies of this material are found in every living cell. A DNA profile comprises a set of highly polymorphic genetic markers that can be used to compare the origins of biological samples found at crime scenes with those taken from known individuals.

The initial discovery of DNA-based methods for human individuation was made by Alec Jeffreys in 1985. It was first used to support a criminal investigation a year later when Jeffrey's original techniques were used to compare DNA profiled from semen recovered from the bodies of Linda Mann and Dawn Ashworth who had been raped and murdered, in 1983 and 1986, respectively. Since then a series of technological innovations has meant that DNA profiling (known also as DNA fingerprinting and DNA typing), based on polymerase chain reaction amplifications of a varying number of short tandem repeat loci found at different locations on the human genome, has become the 'gold standard for identification' in a range of contexts. It has also been described as the most significant advance in forensic science support to policing since the introduction of fingerprinting more than 100 years ago.

DNA extraction methods have now advanced to the point that profiles can be obtained from very small numbers of human biological cells recovered from scenes of crime (in, for example, blood, semen, saliva, hair roots and scalp detritus, flesh, skin, vaginal fluids and nasal secretions). It is also increasingly possible to distinguish multiple contributors to mixed biological samples and thus more easily to identify possible perpetrators of crimes in which genetic material from both victims and offenders is co-mingled.

While the initial uses of DNA profiling were largely confined to reactive forensic casework, the subsequent ability to construct digital representations of profiles and store them in continuously searchable computerized databases has made possible a vastly expanded role for DNA profiling in many criminal investigations. An increasing number of criminal jurisdictions have established such databases, which include both profiles obtained from crime scenes and those obtained from individuals during the course of criminal investigations.

The largest such database, containing more than 4 million subject sample profiles (comprising more than 5 per cent of the population and almost one quarter of a million crime scene profiles), is the National DNA Database of England and Wales (NDNAD). Current legislation (the Criminal Justice Act 2003) empowers the police to take and retain samples from all those arrested on suspicion of involvement in a recordable offence and to retain samples regardless of whether the individual in question is subsequently charged or convicted of the offence in question. Records contained on the NDNAD and referred to as SGM+TM profiles comprise measurements of 11 genetic loci, each of which is on a different chromosome. It is currently calculated that the chances of two unrelated individuals sharing the same measurements for this set of loci are less than one in a billion.

Patterns of crime scene attendance and the availability and potential significance of biological evidence mean that DNA profiling is used in less than 1 per cent of criminal investigations. However, in cases when DNA is recovered from scenes of crime, detection rates are markedly improved – e.g. in 2004–5 the overall detection rate rose from 25 per cent to 40 per cent when DNA profiles were recovered, and the domestic burglary detection rate rose from 16 per cent to 41 per cent. It is generally agreed that an understanding of exactly how the availability of DNA impacts on the investigative process needs more detailed research in order that its full potential is maximized.

There is increasing interest in the genetic analysis of biological material found at crime scenes in order to infer the physical characteristics of the person who left such material. The most advanced of such methods utilize arrays of single nucleotide polymorphisms to characterize the 'biogeographic ancestry' of individuals, but there are other efforts to analyse genetic data capable of predicting eye and hair colour, as well as height and other phenotypical attributes.

Robin Williams

Related entries

Crime scene examiners (CSEs); Evidence; Fingerprints; Forensic and investigative psychology; Forensic investigation; Offender profiling.

Key texts and sources

Butler, J. (2001) *Forensic DNA Typing: Biology and Technology behind STR Markers.* London: Academic Press.

HM Inspectorate of Constabulary (2000) *Under the Microscope.* London: Home Office.

McCartney, C. (2006) *Forensic Identification and Criminal Justice.* Cullompton: Willan Publishing.

National DNA Database Board (2006) *The National DNA Database Annual Report, 2004–2005.* London: HMSO.

See also the Home Office's web page on the NDNAD (http://www.homeoffice.gov.uk/science-research/using-science/dna-database/). The Parliamentary Office of Science and Technology postnote on the NDNAD is available online at http://www.parliament.uk/documents/upload/postpn258.pdf.

DOCTRINE

> Doctrine – in the form of guidance and advice – is an attempt to bring structure and consistency to the strategy and tactics employed by the police forces of England and Wales. It encompasses policing policy, business processes and professional practice.

Prior to the establishment of the National Centre for Policing Excellence (NCPE) in 2002, the development of operational strategy and the tactics to be applied across the Police Service in England and Wales occurred on an ad hoc and inconsistent basis. The establishment of the NCPE – a direct result of the Police Reform Act 2002 – provided the opportunity for this type of work, in the form of doctrine, to be undertaken by one agency adopting a structured and consistent approach. The development of doctrine follows a hierarchy that reflects different levels of status for the Police Service. This hierarchy is, in turn, influenced by the Police Reform Act 2002. The NCPE has now been absorbed into the National Policing Improvement Agency's (NPIA) Directorate of Policy and Practice.

Regulations

Regulations are created under a specific statutory basis drawn from primary legislation and, therefore, they are legally binding (e.g., Police and Criminal Evidence Act 1984 (PACE) codes of practice). To date, the NPIA has not been commissioned to produce any of these.

Codes of practice

By revising the Police Act 1996 through the insertion of a new s. 39(a), the Police Reform Act 2002 introduced for the first time a power for codes of practice to be issued to chief officers covering any aspect of their functions and responsibilities. Such codes are laid before Parliament by the Home Secretary and provide a framework that chief officers are required to 'have regard to'. The NCPE/NPIA has been commissioned to produce such codes in areas where a nationally consistent framework is deemed necessary (e.g. codes of practice on the National Intelligence Model and the Police National Computer).

Guidance

The Association of Chief Police Officers (ACPO) has had a long-standing responsibility to produce guidance on operational policing matters. The NPIA has formalized this process so that the product commissioned by ACPO is endorsed by the Police Service through the inspection framework adopted by Her Majesty's Inspectorate of Constabulary (HMIC).

Practice advice

Also commissioned by ACPO, practice advice is a relatively new concept. It is often supplementary to guidance and focuses on specific areas where the Police Service would benefit from evidence-based good practice. Adherence to the final product is discretionary on the part of chief officers.

The majority of doctrine development focuses on the production of guidance and practice advice. There are, however, key processes that influence doctrine, regardless of its status:

- *Consultation*: this is conducted during the development of doctrine and will encompass statutory consultees (e.g., police authorities) and consultees that are relevant to the subject matter.
- *Evidence-based good practice*: the combination of research and consultation with subject-matter experts allows for the identification and evaluation of good practice that can be disseminated across England and Wales in the form of doctrine.
- *Maintenance*: all doctrine is subject to review on a biennial basis to incorporate, for example, changes in legislation or emerging good practice. This ensures that the doctrine is contemporary and maintains relevance.

Doctrine is disseminated to forces and other relevant agencies in hard copy and electronic format. The final product is also subject to in-house legal and diversity checking and to a process of product authoring to ensure consistency prior to dissemination.

Since the establishment of the NCPE/NPIA, approximately 30 doctrine products have been developed and disseminated across the intelligence, investigative and operational business areas of policing. Examples include the following:

- *Code of Practice on the National Intelligence Model.*
- *Code of Practice on Police Use of Firearms and Less Lethal Weapons.*
- *Guidance on the Management of Police Information.*
- *Guidance on the Safer Detention and Handling of Prisoners.*
- *Practice Advice on Core Investigative Doctrine.*
- *Practice Advice on the Use of Immigration Powers against Crime.*
- *Practice Advice on Professionalising the Business of Neighbourhood Policing.*

It is anticipated that the term doctrine, and the concepts and processes underpinning it, will form a central component of the National Policing Improvement Agency, established in April 2007.

Giles Herdale

Related entries

Association of Chief Police Officers (ACPO); Constabulary independence; Forensic investigation; Leadership; Politics (police involvement); Professionalization; Training (police).

Key texts and sources

Neyroud, P.W. (2003) 'Policing and ethics', in T. Newburn (ed.) *Handbook of Policing*. Cullompton: Willan Publishing.
See also the website of the National Policing Improvement Agency (www.npia.police.uk)

DOMESTIC VIOLENCE

Domestic violence, in its widest definition, includes criminal, controlling and other harmful behaviour committed by intimates against intimates, which commonly threatens other family members, especially children.

By naming the ranges of behaviour that enabled domestic violence to work as a form of social control, feminist campaigns emphasized the complexities of 'loving one's abuser' (Ferraro 2006). Domestic violence is currently the 'official' term to name a common type of violence. Domestic violence includes a wide variety of behaviour, some of which is defined as criminal. Domestic violence may include physical violence, rape, sexual abuse, stalking, emotional belittling and bullying, and financial hardship.

The British Crime Survey has documented the extent of domestic violence in England and Wales since 1982. This survey suggests that there has been a fall in domestic violence between 1995 and 2004–5. The survey captures four forms of domestic violence: partner abuse (non-sexual), family abuse (non-sexual), sexual assault and stalking. Women are more likely than men to report having experienced intimate violence across all four forms since the age of 16 (Finney 2006). Research demonstrates how very serious, damaging criminal behaviour is often minimized by the victim, often because psychological ties bound in personal, social and cultural expectations are so great. Many victims come to believe that violence is triggered by what they do and how they behave, rather than the acts and actions of the assailant. In blaming themselves for the violence, many victims find it difficult to seek help and confide in others.

Family and friends are the main support for those suffering domestic violence. When victims do seek help, the police and health workers, in particular, are critical partners in challenging domestic violence. This is especially important when thinking about the debate about the causes of domestic violence. There is clearly a strong association of alcohol abuse, drug misuse and mental illness with situations of domestic violence. This does not mean that individual treatment for any of these factors will stop the violence. For the police, however, the co-presence of any of these issues does increase the risk of greater harm from the abuser. The research also highlights the highest predictor of child abuse is the abuse of the woman in the family.

Given the above complexities, recent Home Office research suggests that advocacy is one of the best approaches to stopping domestic violence. For those facing higher risk, advocacy enhances the work of the police and the courts by allowing victims to engage with a criminal justice process while, at the same tie, dealing with the emotional upheaval of 'managing' and 'exiting' an intimate relationship. Not surprisingly, problems in taking action against perpetrators (bringing criminal charges and conviction) and in resolving child contact issues were found to create real barriers for women and children in being able to move on in their lives.

Finally, never underestimate the social damage domestic violence costs the UK. Many of those in prisons have histories of lives blighted by experiences of violence at home. A 2004 study places the total cost of domestic violence for the state, employers and victims at around £23 billion (Walby 2004).

Betsy Stanko

Related entries

Attrition; Child abuse; Drugs and policing; Gender and policing; Repeat victimization; Sexual offences/sexual violence; Victim and witness support.

Key texts and sources

Ferraro, K. (2006) *Neither Angels nor Demons*. Boston, MA: Northeastern University Press.

Finney, A. (2006) *Domestic Violence, Sexual Assault and Stalking: Findings from the 2004/5 British Crime Survey. Home Office Online Report 12/06*. London: Home Office.

Walby, S. (2004) *The Cost of Domestic Violence*. London: DTI Women and Equality Unit.

See also the Home Office's web page on domestic violence (http://www.homeoffice.gov.uk/crime-victims/reducing-crime/domestic-violence/). For general information on domestic violence, see http://www.adviceguide.org.uk/index/family_parent/family/domestic_violence.htm.

DRUG EDUCATION AND PREVENTION

Drug prevention measures in the form of educational programmes target vulnerable groups and attempt to reduce the risk factors for their involvement in drugs and crime. Drug prevention strategies generally can be divided into three main categories: 'universal' prevention (which aims to stop people from starting to use drugs in the first place), 'targeted' or 'selective' prevention (for groups especially vulnerable to drugs problems) and 'indicated' prevention (for established drug users).

Although it is universally recognized that 'prevention is better than cure', less money is spent on preventing drug misuse than on attempting to control supply or on treating drugs problems. This is partly because prevention outcomes are long term, and the benefits do not accrue directly to the services providing them (for example, schools do drug education but the potential benefits of reduced drug use in adult life do not affect them to any great extent).

Prevention can be divided into three categories:

1. *Universal prevention*: this type of prevention is for everyone, and generally aims to stop people starting using drugs or at least to delay the onset of drug use. Most universal prevention, therefore, focuses on children and young people (e.g. drug education in schools). A wide range of professionals is involved.
2. *Targeted (or selective) prevention*: This is for particular groups especially vulnerable to drugs problems (e.g. 'chill-out' rooms in nightclubs giving help and advice). Specialist professionals and volunteers are involved.
3. *Indicated prevention*: This prevention is for drug users, especially those using drugs that are particularly dangerous. It aims to encourage less dangerous use (e.g. advice to injecting drug users about the dangers of blood-borne diseases and about how to reduce the risk). Conducted by professional drugs workers.

In relation to universal prevention, especially that provided in schools, different methods of prevention have been tried (such as mass media campaigns and different types of drug education). Following the realization that 'just say no' approaches did not work (and neither did fear and shock tactics nor information on its own), two main approaches have found favour in UK schools. The 'social influence approach' 'seeks to achieve "psychological inoculation" and aims to encourage anti-drug use attitudes, counteract beliefs that using illegal drugs is normal, and develop the ability to resist offers of drugs'. The 'social competence', or life skills approach, seeks to 'develop a broader range of personal and social skills in addition to tactics to refuse offers of drugs' (Advisory Council on the Misuse of Drugs (ACMD 2006).

'Unfortunately,' the AMCD continues, 'there is little evidence that any are effective, and many have been found to be ineffective or even counter-productive.' For example, mass campaigns (on their own), are ineffective and may even stimulate interest, and, to have any chance of success, school drug education must be carried out in accordance with the research evidence.

What is this evidence? Guidance from the Department for Education and Skills (2004: para. 2.3) states:

effective drug education programmes ... [are] ones which:

- *address knowledge, skills and attitudes*
- *provide developmentally appropriate and culturally sensitive information*
- *challenge misconceptions that young people hold about the norms of their peers' behaviour and their friends' reactions to drug use ...*
- *use interactive teaching techniques such as discussion, small-group activities and role play*
- *involve parents/carers as part of a wider community approach.*

The role of the police in school-based drugs education has been clearly set out in an Association of Chief Police Officer's (ACPO) document that gives practical and strategic guidance for police forces. It states: 'Drug education for young people is most effective when it is delivered within a whole school, whole community approach to drug prevention, where different partners work together to convey coherent messages about the risks of drug taking' (2006c: para. 1.9). Drug education in schools should be teacher led, and the police can provide support for schools. The guidance explains:

In some cases this support is extensive and delivered by police officers who have had comprehensive training in school liaison (e.g. the All-Wales Core Programme and Hampshire Constabulary's 'Getting it Right' Programme). Some of this work is delivered by ... police officers working with or for not-for-profit organisations (e.g. DARE UK – Drug Abuse Resistance Education; and RIDE – Resistance in Drug Education)

(2006c: para. 1.9.1).

While there is no evidence that police involvement in drug education in schools has any advantage over teacher delivery, it is appreciated by teachers and pupils and seen as useful in giving accurate information about the law on drugs and about the consequences of breaking the law. There are also wider benefits, such as the development of good relations between students and pupils and the police and helping them to understand more about the role of the police.

With an increasing focus on whole-school and whole-community approaches, the police have an important role in helping to link school and community – through, for example, ensuring that schools' concerns about the underage sale of tobacco, alcohol or volatile substances are addressed, and contributing to the development of healthier schools and communities. The police also have a role in school or community-based targeted drug prevention, reaching vulnerable groups and attempting both to reduce the risk factors for their involvement in drugs and crime and to develop the protective factors through, for example, sporting and other activities.

The police role in prevention can sometimes become entangled with its role as law enforcer. All schools should have a policy on handling drug-related incidents in school, and some incidents will involve the police. These operational aspects need to be separated from preventive work. One tricky area is in the use of sniffer dogs in schools. The ACPO guidance is unequivocal on this point: 'drugs dogs should not be used for searches where there is no evidence for the presence of drugs on school premises. Demonstration and educational visits should not be used as a covert detection exercise' (2006c: para. 4.7.2). Another difficult area is drug testing in schools: 'We recommend that drug testing and sniffer dogs should not be used in schools. We consider that the complex ethical, technical and organisational issues, the potential impact on the school–pupil relationship and the costs would not be offset by the potential gains' (ACMD 2006: para. 5.45).

Tackling drugs issues is a complex challenge that must involve a wide range of professionals and other interested parties. Prevention in various forms, including (but not limited to) drug education in schools, is an important part of the response. Addressing drugs issues in schools should take place within the context of a whole-school approach that 'is supported by consistent messages from family and community' (DfES 2004: para. 2.4). 'Drugs' must include not only illegal drugs but also medicines, volatile substances, alcohol and tobacco.

Richard Ives

Related entries

Crime reduction; Drug Intervention Programme (DIP); Drugs and policing; Police and Crime Standards Directorate (P&CSD).

Key texts and sources

ACMD (2006) *Pathways to Problems: Hazardous Use of Tobacco, Alcohol and other Drugs by Young People in the UK and its Implications for Policy.* London: COI.

ACPO (2006) *Joining Forces: Drugs Guidance for Police Working with Schools and Colleges.* London: ACPO in association with the Home Office and the DfES.

DfES (2004) *Drugs: Guidance for Schools.* London: DfES.

The Home Office's drugs website is at http://drugs.homeoffice.gov.uk/. Advice for young people and families affected by drug problems is available online at http://talktofrank.com/home_html.aspx and http://www.adfam.org.uk/.

DRUG INTERVENTION PROGRAMME (DIP)

The Drug Intervention Programme (DIP) integrates measures targeted at drug-using arrestees and offenders at different stages of the criminal justice system. These measures – known as 'interventions' – seek to encourage drug-using arrestees and offenders into drug treatment.

The Drug Intervention Programme (DIP) was launched by the Home Office in 2003 in 20 high-crime areas and has since been rolled out across England and Wales. Its stated aim was to break the cycle of drug misuse and crime by making every stage in the criminal justice system an opportunity for drug-using offenders to engage in treatment. This objective was to be achieved through a number of integrated interventions, including drug treatment referral schemes at point of arrest and at court, and community-based drug services on release from prison. Over its short life additional elements have been added, including drug testing on arrest and restrictions on bail for drug users.

Central to the work of DIP is a system of throughcare and aftercare. Throughcare seeks to promote continuity of approach from arrest to sentence and beyond. Aftercare allows those receiving help to get access to further drug treatment and other forms of support, such as assistance with finding housing and employment and education or training courses in order to help their reintegration into the community. This element of DIP is delivered by criminal justice integrated teams (CJITs). Policy guidance recommends that each offender who is assessed by a CJIT and taken on to its caseload is allocated a case manager. This case manager will then develop a care plan with the offender for the delivery of, or referral to, appropriate services.

The Home Office provided general guidance on the delivery of CJITs, although teams have developed different ways of working. They are drawn from a range of professional backgrounds, including the Police and Probation Services, the National Health Service and voluntary sector drug treatment services. This is a complex intervention working across health and criminal justice sectors and, needless to say, it has faced considerable service delivery challenges.

To date there is little published work on the effectiveness of this approach to providing drug treatment and associated care. Early findings from an evaluation of the national programme (Matrix and ICPR, 2007) suggest that established routes of referrals (arrest and court referral) have continued to work best, identifying 86 per cent of the 24,000 referrals between May 2005 and February 2006. The numbers coming on to the programme via the Probation and Prison Services have been low. Once referred, about 40 per cent of drug-using offenders lose contact before an assessment of their needs can be undertaken. There is a further dropout before individuals are assigned a case manager, and this resulted in about 4,000 clients being taken on to the CJIT caseload between July and December 2005.

DIP is estimated to cost about £165 million per year and questions have been raised as to whether it can offer value for money. Such interventions are based on the assumption that tackling problem drug use will lead to reductions in offending behaviour and, as some commentators have pointed out, this may not be the case. Others have argued that drug treatment should be entered into voluntarily in order for it to be effective, and that the quasi–coercive approach of DIP will inevitably result in a high rate of failure. However, many commentators agree that the DIP approach of providing access to 'end-to-end' services tackling the range of needs and problems drug-using offenders have is entirely appropriate.

Paul Turnbull

Related entries

Bail; Drug education and prevention; Drugs and policing.

Key texts and sources

Matrix and Institute for Criminal Policy Research (2007) *Evaluation of Drug Interventions pilot programmes for children and young people*, Home Office Online Report 07/07, London: Home Office

McSweeney, T. and Hough, M. (2005) 'Drugs and alcohol', in N. Tilley (ed.) *Handbook of Crime Prevention and Community Safety*. Cullompton: Willan Publishing.

Seddon, T. (2006) 'Drugs, crime and social exclusion: social context and social theory in British drugs – crime research', *British Journal of Criminology*, 46: 680–703.

Turnbull, P.J., Hickman, M. and Fernandez, J.L. *et al.* (2007) *National Evaluation of Criminal Justice Integrated Teams: Summary*. London: Home Office (available online at http://www.homeoffice.gov.uk/rds).

Further information about the DIP is available from www.drugs.gov.uk/drug-interventions-programme.

DRUGS AND POLICING

Policing illicit drugs is one of the greatest challenges facing modern policing today. The cost to society of illicit drug use continues to escalate, as does the pressure to reduce drug-related crime. The police – who, until relatively recently, worked in isolation – now work across a number of partnerships tackling all aspects of drug use and supply.

In the last 50 years, drugs policing has undergone significant change. Up until the late 1950s it received little attention, as few perceived illicit drugs as a problem that needed addressing (Downes 1977). However, in 1961 the UN Single Convention on Narcotic Drugs was passed, which required all signatories to declare illegal the cultivation, manufacture, export, import, distribution, sale and possession of many plant-based drugs. In 1971 a further UN Convention on Psychotropic Substance added many psychoactive pharmaceutical drugs to the list of those to be controlled and, in 1988, the Convention against Illicit Traffic in Narcotic Drugs and Psychotropic Substances legislated to strengthen the existing provisions against money laundering and for the seizing drug-related assets.

In Britain, the UN obligations are fulfilled through the Misuse of Drugs Act 1971 (MDA), which regulates controlled drugs. All illegal drugs are classified under one of three categories: Class A, B or C. Class A drugs are treated by the law as the most dangerous and include heroin, cocaine and crack, ecstasy, LSD, methadone, methamphetamine, magic mushrooms and injected Class B drugs. Class B drugs include amphetamine, barbiturates and codeine, and Class C drugs include cannabis, anabolic steroids and minor tranquillizers. It is illegal to possess, supply, produce, cultivate, manufacture, offer to supply, allow premises you occupy to be used for any illegal drug-related activity and to import or export any controlled drug. All offences are punishable by a fine and/or imprisonment.

In 2005–6 there were a total of 178,502 drug offences recorded by the police (of which 152,627 were possession offences), which represented a 23 per cent increase from the previous year (Roe and Man 2006). The increase, for the most part, was due to a rise in the number of cannabis possession offences being recorded by the police, which coincided with an increase in the number of cannabis warnings issued by the police. The introduction of cannabis warnings was perhaps the most significant – and controversial – change to drugs policing since the introduction of the MDA.

Prior to reclassification, many people were of the view that the police rarely took formal action against offences involving cannabis. In fact, of the 513,000 known indictable offenders in England and Wales in 1999, just under one in seven (69,377) was cautioned or convicted for possession of cannabis. Although cannabis possession offences declined between 1998 and 2002, this downward trend was abruptly stalled following the announcement of a possible reclassification. From 2002 until reclassification took effect, formal police action against possession offences steadily rose (May *et al.* 2002, 2007).

Pressure on successive governments to reclassify cannabis had been building since the introduction of the MDA. This pressure continued to mount with the publication of the Independent Inquiry into the Misuse of Drugs Act 1971 (Police Foundation 2000), which recommended that cannabis be reclassified from Class B to Class C, partly because it would make possession of cannabis a non-arrestable offence (Police Foundation 2000) (the Serious Organized Crime and Police Act 2005 made all offences arrestable). It was envisaged that, by removing the power of arrest, a considerable source of friction between the police and cannabis smokers would also be removed and the criminalization of large numbers of young people would be avoided.

In the first half of 2002, both the Home Affairs Committee and the Advisory Council on the Misuse of Drugs recommended that cannabis be reclassified (ACMD 2002; Home Affairs Committee 2002). While there appeared to be considerable will for reform, a number of well placed senior police officers were resistant to the proposition that they would lose their power of arrest. However, after much discussion, in 2003 the government announced a compromise: cannabis would be reclassified but the power of arrest would be retained (Home Office Drug Strategy Unit 2002). Juveniles (17 and under), however, would continue to be arrested and processed in accordance with the Crime and Disorder Act 1998. The contorted process that led to reclassification ended up creating maximum confusion about what the new reform actually meant, even among some police officers (May et al. 2007). However, in the first year of policing cannabis as a Class C drug (2004), arrests dropped and, while street warning data were unavailable for the first three months of 2004, in the last nine the police issued 27,520 cannabis warnings.

In 2005–6 just over a quarter (27 per cent) of all possession offences recorded by the police were for possession of a Class A or B drug. It is widely recognized that most problematic Class A users will come into contact with the police not for a possession offence but for an offence committed to fund their use. The precise proportion of crime that is committed to fund illicit drug use is not known – and, indeed, is probably unknowable (Coid et al. 2000; MacGregor 2000; Best et al. 2001; Hough et al. 2001; McSweeney and Hough 2005). However, it is well established that problem drug users often commit crime to finance their drug use

(Inciardi and Pottieger 1994; Parker and Bottomley 1996; French et al. 2000). For example, the National Treatment Outcome Research Study (NTORS), a longitudinal study of 1,100 opiate users attending drug treatment services, found nearly two thirds had committed a crime in the three months before treatment (Gossop et al. 1998). The NEW ADAM survey (Bennett 1998, 2000) which drug tests and interviews samples of arrestees, found that 65 per cent tested positive for some form of illicit drug (24 per cent for heroin and 15 per cent for cocaine), with the main funding sources coming from acquisitive crime. In committing these crimes many problematic users will – almost definitely – come into contact with the police. For many offenders, getting arrested can act as the trigger point to tackling their misuse.

Since the mid-1990s the government has pursued a policy of ensuring that problem users caught up in the criminal justice system are offered treatment to help them address their drug use. To complement the range of intervention programmes offered post-arrest (probation orders with drug rehabilitation requirements and prison-based treatment), there are a number of interventions at the point of arrest. These interventions now form part of the Drug Intervention Programme (DIP) and include arrest referral (AR) and Tough Choices.

AR workers in police custody areas approach potential drug-misusing arrestees and offer assessments and referrals to appropriate treatment services. Evaluation of a number of early pilot schemes found reductions in expenditure on drugs and reductions in acquisitive crime among those contacted after arrest (Edmunds et al. 1998, 1999).

The Criminal Justice and Court Services Act 2000 introduced police powers to drug test detainees in police custody. Testing is for specified Class A drugs for those charged or convicted of 'trigger' offences aged over 18. Trigger offences include offences drawn from the Theft Act 1968, the MDA and the Vagrancy Act 1824. The introduction of the Drugs Act 2005 extended the testing powers of the police and established compulsory drug testing of arrestees and 'required assessment'. The police are now able to test on arrest where they have 'reasonable grounds' for believing Class A drugs are involved in the commission of an offence. Failure to comply with testing is an offence in itself, and positive tests can lead to a compulsory drug treatment order. Required assessments enable the police to compel those who test positive on arrest or charge to attend an assessment of their drug use, know as Tough Choices. The two measures are designed to increase the number of assessments and ultimately propel greater numbers of drug users into treatment and out of offending.

Further to encourage drug users to seek treatment, police officers, in accordance with the provisions of the Criminal Justice Act 2003, can attach conditions to a police caution. Where the condition is not met, the offender may be charged with the original offence. A conditional caution requires an offender to carry out actions that either address his or her offending behaviour (rehabilitative condition) or make reparation to the victim or the community. There are limitations to which offences may be disposed of by a conditional caution, and the local Crown Prosecution Service makes the final decision on approving any conditional caution proposed by the police. Conditional cautioning is considered to provide early intervention to prevent the escalation of drug use to problematic levels.

Policing drug dealers and traffickers is the responsibility of a number of agencies, including local police forces, the Concerted Inter-agency Drugs Action Group (CIDA) and the Serious Organized Crime Agency (SOCA). Local police forces tend to concentrate their efforts on disrupting local drug markets, CIDA maintains responsibility for co-ordinating operational policing activity across all intelligence and enforcement agencies, and SOCA tackles trafficking, importation and exportation. Supporting their work are the Asset Recovery Agency, the Police Standards Unit, HM Inspectorate of Constabulary and numerous other government and non-governmental agencies. In recognition of the work of local police forces, the Home Office also organizes the 'Tackling Drug Supply' awards ceremony each year. The event is designed to highlight best practice among police forces and to disseminate good practice across force areas. In 2005 Operation Crackdown – a national operation –

successfully recovered £3 million in cash assets, closed 170 dealing houses, seized 483 firearms and arrested over 3,000 people for the supply of Class A drugs. Despite the intensity of work currently being undertaken to tackle trafficking and supply, in 2005–6 recorded trafficking offences accounted for only 14 per cent of all recorded drug offences. This did, however, represent a 5 per cent increase from the previous year (Walker *et al.* 2006).

In 2005–6, 10.5 per cent of adults disclosed that they had used one or more illicit drugs in the previous year, a decrease of 1.6 per cent from 1998. However, despite the range of interventions available for drug users and the efforts in place to intercept suppliers and traffickers, the 2005–6 British Crime Survey reported that the use of any Class A drug had increased from 2.7 per cent in 1998 to 3.4 per cent (Roe and Man 2006).

Tiggey May

Related entries

Anti-social behaviour; Domestic violence; Drug education and prevention; Drug Intervention Programme (DIP); Entrapment; Europol; Home Office; Intelligence-led policing; International police co-operation; Interpol; National Intelligence Model (NIM); Organized crime; Police powers; Scotland (policing); Specialist squads; Street crime; Transnational policing.

Key texts and sources

Home Office Drug Strategy Unit (2002) *Updated Drug Strategy.* London: Home Office.

Hough, M., McSweeney, T. and Turnbull, P. (2001) *Drugs and Crime: What Are the Links? Evidence to the Home Affairs Committee of Inquiry into Drug Policy.* London: DrugScope.

May, T., Duffy, M., Warburton, H. and Hough, M. (2007) *Policing Cannabis as a Class C Drug: An Arresting Change?* York: Joseph Rowntree Foundation.

South, N. (2007) 'Drugs, alcohol and crime', in M. Maguire *et al.* (eds) *The Oxford Handbook of Criminology* (4th edn). Oxford: Oxford University Press.

The Home Office's drugs website is at http://drugs.homeoffice.gov.uk/.

ENTRAPMENT

> Entrapment involves actions taken by a state agent, such as a police officer or police-instigated informant, to encourage a person to commit a criminal offence with a view to prosecuting the person for the offence.

The emphasis on intelligence-led policing in recent years has brought into sharp focus the issues and problems associated with entrapment although, as an investigative method, it is far from new. The term 'entrapment' has been used to describe a variety of investigative activities, ranging from encouraging the commission of an offence (e.g. by a police officer asking a person to supply him or her with drugs), or facilitating the commission of an offence (e.g. by flagging down an unlicensed taxi or deliberately leaving items of value in a public place to 'test the virtue' of passers-by) to 'test purchases' (which are authorized, for example, by the Trade Descriptions Act 1968, s. 27, and the Criminal Justice and Police Act 2001). It is also sometimes used to describe a process of gathering evidence in relation to an offence that has already been committed (most notably in the Colin Stagg case in 1994 where, in the course of a murder investigation, an undercover police officer befriended a suspect with the intention of obtaining incriminating evidence from him).

Unlike in the USA, entrapment does not amount to a defence to an allegation of crime in English law, although it may be taken into account in determining sentence (*R* v. *Sang*). However, whether the police should use investigative methods involving entrapment, and whether a prosecution should be permitted to proceed on the basis of evidence obtained by

entrapment, has exercised the minds of both the judiciary and academic lawyers. On the one hand, entrapment may be the most efficient, and sometimes the only, way of securing evidence in respect of certain kinds of offences (ranging from serious offences, such as contract killing and drug supply, to regulatory offences, such as selling liquor to children). On the other hand, entrapment that involves police officers in encouraging or engaging in criminal activity risks creating crimes that otherwise would not have been committed and compromising the moral integrity of the criminal justice system.

The response of the courts has not always been consistent and, as Ashworth (2002) has pointed out, has left a number of grey areas in terms of what is legitimate investigative activity. Generally, the evidential use of information obtained by deceptive methods in respect of crimes already committed is governed by the Police and Criminal Evidence Act 1984 (PACE), s. 78 (e.g. *R* v. *Mason* and *R* v. *Christou and Wright*). With regard to entrapment in the sense defined above, the leading case is *R* v. *Looseley* in which it was held that the normal remedy for unlawful entrapment is a stay of proceedings for abuse of process. Although the line between lawful and unlawful entrapment is not entirely clear, providing a person with an 'unexceptional opportunity' to commit an offence, especially a regulatory offence, will normally be acceptable, although in the case of serious offences such as drug dealing, conspiracy to rob, etc., there should normally be reasonable suspicion in respect of the person targeted, and adequate supervision of the operation. On the other hand, a prosecution will normally be stayed if the court is satisfied that the accused had only committed the offence because he or she 'had been incited, instigated, persuaded, pressurised or wheedled into committing it' (*Nottingham City Council* v. *Amin*).

Ed Cape

Related entries

Ethics in policing; Intelligence-led policing; Police and Criminal Evidence Act 1984 (PACE).

Key texts and sources

Ashworth, A. (2002) 'Re-drawing the boundaries of entrapment', *Criminal Law Review*, 161–79.
Ashworth, A. and Redmayne, M. (2005) *The Criminal Process*. Oxford: Oxford University Press.

ETHICS IN POLICING

Police ethics includes both the values that underpin professional and democratic policing together with the moral decisions faced by police officers at all levels of the organization in the course of their work and the basis on which these are resolved.

It is in the nature of the tasks involved in policing that the ethical dilemmas presented to officers and their managers are sometimes intractable. The mission to protect life may need to be balanced with the need to take life to do so. Preventing serious crimes may require the police to act deceptively, to intrude in citizens' lives and homes. There is now considerable evidence to suggest that a Police Service that is viewed as acting 'ethically' may well have significant advantages in securing legitimacy with those whom it serves, potentially adding to its effectiveness (Tyler 2004).

Although the definition above applies very much to the everyday as well as to times of crisis, much of the debate has tended to focus on questions of ethics in policing from a crisis perspective. There have been, broadly, three areas for debate: the styles of policing, the institution of policing and police culture. With styles of policing, the focus has been on areas such as the impact of 'crime-fighting' approaches, with their potential for 'noble cause corruption', often driven by police officers frustrated by the 'system' which they seek to short-cut. In particular, a number of studies have looked at the ways in which tactics such as covert policing can lead to entrapment and the creation of crimes that might otherwise not have happened. The challenge for police in this instance is to manage deception 'ethically'.

Corruption has been the primary institutional focus. This has ranged, from the early twentieth century, where concerns about political and economic corruption produced a literature about 'professionalism' and studies of the extent and causes of corruption, to more recent concerns about administrative corruption resulting from the extensive focus on performance managerialism.

The focus on police culture has looked at the ways in which the occupational culture of policing has acted as an inhibitor of ethical behaviour. Studies have shown that officers tend to be driven by informal values that are often at odds with the more formal values the organization is overtly committed to. This becomes particularly important in the context of the considerable discretion that police officers have about the exercise of powers, such as arrest and detention. An occupational culture that appears to be insular, masculine and white raises significant questions about the impact the exercise of those powers has on different citizens.

A key issue related to culture has been the challenge of diversity and, in particular, of race and gender equality. As has frequently been observed in the research, the police treat different communities in different ways, which has tended (across the world) to create cultures and workforces that represent the majority community, with a strong male gender bias. This has posed awkward questions about the equality of policing and its legitimacy with minority communities. The increasingly complex diversity of local communities in the UK has made this a particularly challenging area, posing significant dilemmas for officers trying to square the circle between sensitivity to different cultures and values and enforcing a law that may not be flexible or working with communities that are not supportive of such flexibility (such as settled communities towards travellers).

There has been considerable debate about how to ensure the police act ethically. The proposed solutions have fallen into three broad areas: external regulation and oversight; internal controls and management; and recruiting, developing and rewarding 'virtuous' officers. In the UK a series of royal commissions and other inquiries have tended to promote structural solutions to problems of malpractice. In the main these have involved proposals to improve systems of accountability and governance, together with the creation of bodies capable of the independent investigation of complaints. Faced with such problems, the alternative to structural reform has generally been to exhort officers to behave professionally. There had been less enthusiasm, until the Patten Commission in Northern Ireland, for a more overtly 'ethics'-based approach, incorporating a formal code of ethics and a strong emphasis on training based around ethical dilemmas. The seeming reluctance to embrace ethical codes in the UK stands in contrast to the approach in the USA, where the International Association of Chiefs of Police has a well established code of ethics and online training materials. Equally, there have been serious attempts to create a European model, including a *European Code of Police Ethics*.

More recently, however, there has been considerable interest in the values of individual officers and the potential for developing a new professionalism, shaped around a commitment to ethics and human rights. Neyroud and Beckley (2001a) have tried to frame a more normative framework for ethics in policing, which encompasses the range of ethical dilemmas that policing – particularly operational policing areas, such as the use of force or covert operations – presents. A helpful starting point for policing would be a set of ethical principles, drawing on human rights and ethical theory, which could be situationally applied. Arguably, there are four areas for development if 'ethical policing' is to be achieved: the development of the 'professionalism' of policing; a properly balanced approach to performance; public participation in policing to enable the police to 'negotiate' their priorities

and to ensure they are responsive to community needs; and, lastly, strong frameworks for ethical compliance in critical operational areas, such as the police use of force or covert policing. Neyroud and Beckley (2001) concluded that 'good policing in the 21st century requires more than "good performance". It needs a renewal of the contract between the police officer and the citizen, which, in turn, requires greater openness and scrutiny, continuously improving professional standards and a new commitment to ethics at the core of policing'.

Peter Neyroud

Related entries

Accountability and governance; Code of conduct/ethics; Corruption (police); International Association of Chiefs of Police (IACP); Legitimacy; Patten Report; Police culture.

Key texts and sources

Kleinig, J. (1996) *The Ethics of Policing*. Cambridge: Cambridge University Press.

Neyroud, P.W. and Beckley, A. (2001) *Policing, Ethics and Human Rights*. Cullompton: Willan Publishing.

Tyler, T.R. (2004) 'Enhancing police legitimacy', *The Annals*, 593: 84–99.

See also the Home Office's web page on police ethics (http://www.homeoffice.gov.uk/rds/policeethics. html).

EUROPEAN CONVENTION ON HUMAN RIGHTS (ECHR)

The European Convention on Human Rights (ECHR) is an international human rights convention that has been agreed by all governments within the Council of Europe. It is enforced by access to the European Court of Human Rights and by domestic courts.

The European Convention on Human Rights (ECHR) was created in the 1950s as a European human rights framework that could underpin the new, post-Second World War democracies.

Its signatories are those countries who are part of the Council of Europe – a 'club' that has, since the fall of the Berlin wall, expanded to include Europe from the Atlantic to the Urals. The convention is underpinned by the European Court of Human Rights and a number of specific instruments, including the European Code of Ethics for Policing.

In the UK, the ECHR was of growing influence through the 1980s in the field of policing, particularly though cases that dealt with the interception of telecommunications (*Malone* v. *UK*) and terrorism. However, since the passage of the Human Rights Act 1998, UK citizens have been able to enforce their rights under the convention through the domestic courts, and public authorities, such as the police, have been under a duty to ensure that they comply with the convention.

The ECHR has had a significant impact in policing post-1998. The Police Service devoted a considerable amount of effort to auditing its policy and practices to ensure compliance (Neyroud and Beckley 2001a). In particular, policies relating to the police use of force and firearms (because of the right to life), to public order (rights of assembly and association) and to covert policing (the right to respect for private and family life) were subjected to careful review. In the case of covert policing, the Human Rights Act led directly to the Regulation of Investigatory Powers Act 2001 and the provision of a statutory basis for this area of policing (Neyroud and Beckley 2001b).

The ECHR has led to an important debate about the ethics of policing and the education of police officers in human rights and ethics. This has been reflected in the development of a European common curriculum on ethics by CEPOL (Collège européen de Police) – the EU-funded network of police colleges. The development of the European Code of Ethics for Policing has been an important feature of this.

However, the ECHR has not been without its critics. Critics have suggested that the rights-based framework means that citizens are less focused on their responsibilities. Furthermore, there have been a number of cases that have provoked protests that the law is being driven by minority interests and that there is a need to 'rebalance' the system. The UK government responded to this with a white paper, *Rebalancing the Criminal Justice System* (Home Office 2006g).

Peter Neyroud

Related entries

Ethics in policing; Human rights.

Key texts and sources

Freeman, M. (2002) *Human Rights*. Cambridge: Polity Press.
Gearty, C. (2007) *Civil Liberties*. Oxford: Oxford University Press.
Neyroud, P.W. and Beckley, A. (2001a) *Policing, Ethics and Human Rights*. Cullompton: Willan Publishing.
Neyroud, P.W. and Beckley, A. (2001b) 'Regulating informers: the Regulation of Investigatory Powers Act, covert policing and human rights', in R. Billingsley *et al.* (eds) *Informers*. Cullompton: Willan Publishing.
See also the websites of the ECHR (**http://www.echr. coe.int/echr/**), Justice (**http://www.justice.org.uk/**) and Statewatch (**http://www.statewatch.org/**).

EUROPEAN NETWORK OF POLICEWOMEN

The European Network of Policewomen is an international organization that promotes 'quality through equality'.

The European Network of Policewomen was founded on 23 March 1989 at the International Conference for Policewomen held in the Netherlands. The founders envisioned the creation of a professional network that could provide an information channel through which both policewomen and policemen could work together in the field of equal opportunities within the police services of Europe.

The network is a non-profit-making organization and, due to its growth, it became a foundation under Dutch Law in 1994. It acts independently of any government, political party or group and, in 1996, was officially granted the status of a non-governmental organizations. The initial aim of the network is to optimize the position of women in European police and/or law enforcement organizations. The general management of the network is the responsibility of the general board, which appoints an executive board and a president. The executive board conducts the network's daily management. Both boards are composed of representatives from European police forces.

The further aims of the network are to:

- raise awareness and understanding of issues affecting women in the European police services;
- facilitate and contribute towards discussions on issues of concern to both male and female police officers;
- provide, wherever possible, the female perspective;
- stimulate and deliver a contribution towards equal representation of men and women in every layer of the police organization;
- exchange best practice on current issues, new approaches and initiatives;
- contribute to the continuous professional development of all its members;
- support and assist the establishment of new national networks;
- deliver specific support for each associated country; and
- synchronize co-operation between various police organizations as well as the relevant networks in Europe in the working field of gender, the management of diversity and equality issues.

Liz Owsley

Related entries

British Association for Women in Policing (BAWP); Gender and policing.

Key texts and sources

The European Network of Policewomen's website is at **www.enp.nl**. See also the British Association of Policewomen's website (**http://www.bawp.org/index.php**).

EUROPOL

Europol is the European Union law enforcement organization that handles criminal intelligence. Its aim is to improve the effectiveness of the co-operation between the competent authorities of the member states in preventing and combating serious international organized crime and terrorism.

The platform for the launch of Europol was the Trevi Group, formed in 1976. Originally established as a European intergovernmental forum to tackle terrorism, its remit was extended to look at the mechanics of police co-operation in the European Community across the whole range of crime. At the European Council meeting in Luxembourg in 1991, the group presented plans for a common information system that was able to compensate for the erosion of borders and with the capacity to tackle international organized crime (Hebenton and Thomas 1995: 85). In a meeting later that year, references were incorporated into the Treaty on Political Union under Article K.1(9) for the creation of a European Police Office – or Europol as it is more commonly known.

Police co-operation was formally integrated into the EU with the passing of the Maastricht Treaty on European Union of 7 February 1992. Based in The Hague, the Netherlands, Europol is accountable to the Council of Ministers for Justice and Home Affairs. The council appoints the director and the deputy directors. The Europol Management Board comprises one representative from each member state and has responsibility for supervising the activities of the organization. Europol is funded by contributions from the member states according to their GNP. The budget allocated for 2006 amounted to €63.4 million. Approximately 600 people work at the Europol premises, including 90 European liaison officers (ELOs) representing a variety of law enforcement agencies (including police, customs, immigration services and gendarmerie, etc.).

Europol started limited operations on 3 January 1994, specifically in relation to drugs (following the creation of the Europol Drugs Unit in 1993). Its mandate was extended in 1998 to include counterterrorism and, as of 1 January 2002, to deal with all serious forms of international crime. Europol commenced full activities in July 1999. Its mandate covers:

- illicit drug trafficking;
- illicit immigration networks;
- terrorism;
- forgery of money (counterfeiting the euro) and other means of payment;
- trafficking in human beings (including child pornography);
- illicit vehicle trafficking; and
- money laundering.

Additionally, crimes against the person, financial crime and cybercrime fall within Europol's remit where there is evidence of organized criminal activity and where two or more member states are affected. Europol supports member states by:

- facilitating the exchange of information, in accordance with national law, between ELOs; ELOs are seconded to Europol by the member states as representatives of the national law enforcement agencies;
- providing operational analysis in support of operations;
- generating strategic reports (e.g. threat assessments) and crime analysis on the basis of information and intelligence supplied by member states and third parties;
- providing expertise and technical support for investigations and operations carried out within the EU, under the supervision and legal responsibility of the member states concerned (**www.europol.eu.int**).

Mario Matassa

Related entries

Interpol; Organized crime; Transnational policing.

Key texts and sources

Hebenton, B. and Thomas, T. (1995) *Policing Europe: Co-operation, Conflict and Control.* London: Macmillan.
See also Europol's website (**www.europol.eu.int**).

EVIDENCE

> Police investigations gather evidence for use in court. Various legal rules, however, restrict the sort of evidence that is admissible. These rules of evidence are designed to regulate the reliability of evidence and the fairness of trials.

At a general level, police investigations are about gathering and preserving evidence. Evidence may come in many forms: physical evidence, such as blood stains and fingerprints; documentary evidence; and witness statements. But evidence may be more abstract than these examples suggest. One definition of 'evidence' is that it is anything that makes a fact of interest more likely to be true. Thus the fact that a person has previous convictions for burglary is evidence that he or she has committed the burglary he or she is now being investigated for. The fact that there are rumours that this person has committed the burglary is also evidence that he or she has done so. But with these last two examples, the evidence might not be admitted by a court to prove the person's guilt. There are complex legal rules of evidence which sometimes result in relevant evidence being excluded by a court. This entry will concentrate on sketching these rules and the constraints they impose on criminal investigation.

The courts take a general interest in ensuring that evidence gathered by the police is reasonably reliable. Two types of evidence that experience has shown can be unreliable are confessions and eyewitness evidence. With these examples, the Police and Criminal Evidence Act 1984 (PACE) codes of practice (Codes C and D, respectively) lay down rules governing the way in which confessions and eyewitness evidence are gathered. The courts take breach of these rules seriously and will often exclude evidence gained in breach of these codes. It is not easy to say precisely when a breach will lead to exclusion, because s. 78 of PACE gives judges a degree of discretion in this matter. But even if a breach of the rules occurred in good faith, it is likely to lead to exclusion if it was a 'significant and substantial' breach or if the defendant has been disadvantaged by it.

In the common law tradition, considerable emphasis is placed on orality: witnesses should come to court to give evidence in person, rather than having their evidence read in court in the form of a written statement. A general concern for reliability is one reason for this preference: if the witness cannot be cross-examined, it may be difficult to tell what weight to put on his or her evidence. The rule against 'hearsay' or second-hand evidence is one manifestation of this preference for orality. Historically, the hearsay rule has meant that evidence of absent witnesses has been excluded by the courts. However, in recent times the rule against hearsay has been somewhat relaxed, most significantly by reforms contained in the Criminal Justice Act 2003. The position today is that if a witness is dead, cannot be found, is too scared to come to court or is abroad and it is impracticable to secure his or her attendance, then the court has a discretion to admit hearsay evidence of what the witness said. Fairness to the defence is a major concern in the exercise of this discretion: the more important the evidence to the prosecution's case, the more likely it is to be excluded. A relaxation of the orality principle can also be seen in recent rules allowing children and other vulnerable witnesses to give evidence by television link or in a pre-recorded form.

One concern of the law of evidence has been that certain forms of evidence are 'more prejudicial than probative'. Given the use of lay decision-makers (juries and magistrates), it is thought that some types of evidence are best excluded, because to include them would risk prejudicing the decision-maker. The defendant's previous convictions are a prime example of evidence that has traditionally been seen in this way. Again, however, the Criminal Justice Act 2003 introduced significant relaxation of the traditional exclusionary rule. Previous convictions will still often be excluded, but where a defendant has a previous conviction for the same type of crime as the one for which he or she is now on trial, it is now likely to be admitted. Fairness to the defendant, however, remains a concern that may tip the scales against admissibility.

The rules described so far might generally be thought to have as their concern the promotion of accurate decision-making. The concern with previous convictions and with hearsay evidence is, roughly, that the decision-maker may give them too much weight. This may also occur if an unreliable confession or identification is admitted. But sometimes the courts will exclude evidence simply to promote fairness, even where the evidence in question is a reliable indication of the defendant's guilt. Section 78 of PACE gives judges a general power to promote trial fairness. On occasion, judges have excluded DNA evidence linking a person to a serious crime because a breach of the rules governing the destruction of DNA samples has been thought to render the trial unfair. The Human Rights Act 1999, which incorporates the European Convention on Human Rights into English law, has probably increased this overall concern with trial fairness: Article 6 of the convention guarantees the right to a fair trial. Article 6, for example, may have implications for the admission of hearsay evidence because it gives a defendant the right to examine witnesses against him or her. However, it remains unclear how strong this right is, and the English courts have so far been cautious of its use to exclude hearsay evidence that is otherwise admissible under the Criminal Justice Act 2003. Article 8 of the convention guarantees the right to privacy; the implications of this for criminal trials remain uncertain, but Article 8 may add weight to calls for the exclusion of evidence gained in breach of the rules on covert investigations in the code of practice issued under the Regulation of Investigatory Powers Act 2000.

The rules of criminal evidence are complex, and this entry has done no more than sketch the most significant of them. The complexity of the rules can sometimes lead outsiders to conclude that criminal trials are more about lawyers' clever games than about a search for the truth. One should not draw that conclusion too quickly. The rules of evidence regulate the reliability of evidence and the fairness of trials – difficult issues that are bound to lead to rules of some complexity.

Mike Redmayne

Related entries

Arrest; Bail; Crown Prosecution Service (CPS); Police and Criminal Evidence Act 1984 (PACE; Police powers.

Key texts and sources

Choo, A. (2006) *Evidence.* Oxford: Oxford University Press.

Munday, R. (2005) *Evidence* (3rd edn). Oxford: Oxford University Press.

F

FAMILY LIAISON

Family liaison describes the practice of providing specially trained police officers to
support the family of a deceased in cases of
unexplained or violent death or in other
stressful situations.

Traditionally, unexplained or violent death
meant homicide, road deaths or mass disaster,
but family liaison is increasingly being used in
non-fatal situations where the police need to
establish effective relationships with families in
stressful circumstances – often referred to as
critical incidents. This may occur, for example,
in cases of very serious wounding or when children may have been abducted.

In such cases the police usually have an
urgent need for information to progress their
investigations, and the victim's family are often
the only source of this. If not handled sensi-
tively, police inquires can add to the trauma of
the incident for the family. Additionally, people
often need a great deal of practical support at
these times, and the police have traditionally
seen the provision of this support as one of
their roles. Family liaison officers (FLOs) receive
training to carry out the roles of gathering
information for the investigation and offering
practical support to the bereaved. This latter
role includes explaining investigative and legal
procedures to them and providing a communication channel to senior investigating officers
which enables the family to be kept informed of
the progress of the investigation.

The Association of Chief Police Officers'
Family Liaison Strategy Manual (2003b) identifies the main objectives of Family Liaison as to:

- provide information to and facilitate care
  and support for the family, who are themselves victims, in a sensitive and
  compassionate manner in accordance with
  the needs of the investigation;
- gather evidence and information from the
  family in a manner that contributes to the
  investigation and preserves its integrity; and
- secure the confidence and trust of the family,
  thereby enhancing their contribution to the
  investigation.

FLOs are all volunteers who undergo nationally
accredited training. The nature of the role
means that it is often very stressful and requires
a high degree of sensitivity. This is particularly
so in the case of homicide, where a high proportion of victims are killed by a relative or
associate, meaning that FLOs are often dealing
with people who know both the victim and the
offender. In cases where more than one FLO is
deployed, a family liaison co-ordinator will be
appointed. Some forces also have a family liaison adviser to provide advice and support to
senior investigating officers during the initial
period of investigation or at other particularly
challenging stages.

The role of the FLO is now well established
in the UK. Bereaved families find the support of
FLOs to be beneficial, and most police forces
can cite instances where families have drawn on
the support of an FLO for many years after the
event. However, where family liaison breaks
down, as it did in the investigation of the death
of Stephen Lawrence, the results can be cata-
strophic for both the police investigation and
for the well-being of the family and even the
wider community.

Peter Stelfox

Related entries

Critical incidents; Gay Police Association; Stephen Lawrence Inquiry; Victim and witness support.

Key texts and sources

ACPO (2003) *Family Liaison Strategy Manual* (not published outside the Police Service).

Office for Criminal Justice Reform (2005) *Code of Practice for Victims of Crime*. London: Office for Criminal Justice Reform.

The ACPO *Family Liaison Strategy* document (2000), which contains guidance on good practice, is available online at **www.acpo.police.uk/asp/ policies/Data/family_liaison_strategy.doc**.

FEAR OF CRIME

The fear of crime is generally taken to mean the personal worry about becoming a crime victim, although it is sometimes seen more vaguely as the feeling of being unsafe, particularly when out alone at night.

Unknown in Britain before the early 1980s – when questions on fear were included in the first British Crime Survey – fear of crime has since been extensively researched and, more recently, the object of corrective social policy. Fear of crime began life in America in the mid-1960s as a by-product of attempts to improve crime counting. Disillusion with official crime statistics led the Presidential Commission on Law Enforcement and Administration of Justice to commission three crime surveys. Their goal was to count unrecorded victimizations, but all three also included novel questions relating to the degree of public alarm about crime in general.

Their finding that there was, indeed, widespread public anxiety about crime became a rallying cry for the white middle class who had become alarmed by the extension of basic civil rights to the poor and black. Fear of crime thus began as fear of black people. Subsequently, it has gradually been transformed from being a *reason* for conducting criminological inquiry into being the *object* of that inquiry, and from being a national concern about crime into a local fear of victimization. In sum, gradually over the last thirty years, general – if bigoted – societal concern about crime has been transmuted into a personal problem of individual vulnerability.

Since its birth, fear of crime has chiefly been investigated by questionnaire-based social surveys. The chief goal of these has been to test various propositions that might account for why some people are more fearful than others. There is no agreed underlying theory at stake – indeed, it has never been forcefully explained why people shouldn't worry about crime (or what they should worry about instead) or why we should try to make them worry less.

Demographic characteristics were obvious candidate correlates of fear and were the first to be investigated. Gender, age and race analysis indicated that women, the old and the non-white were most fearful, although this was somewhat paradoxical – at least for women and the elderly – as they were the least likely to be victimized. Those who had already been a crime victim were hypothesized to be more fearful than those who had not, but research findings are surprisingly inconclusive on this issue.

The media are widely believed to be the villain of the piece. However, although it is easy to demonstrate that the mass media concentrate on precisely those crimes (personal ones of violence) that are least likely to occur, it has proved difficult to correlate this with individual fear. Consumption of media messages is so ubiquitous it has proved impossible to discover a sufficient number of non-consumers to test the proposition. One fairly common finding is that people rely on their own experience in their evaluations of their own neighbourhoods, but on the media for descriptions of places further afield. Christopher Hale's magisterial review of the research literature (1996) has yet to be bettered, and Ditton and Farrall's (2001) edited collection of original articles is the only one available.

In the 1990s, fear of crime entered mainstream politics, typically singeing those politicians unwise enough to touch it. At the turn of the century, however, fear of crime became a key issue for the Home Office. At this point, and for the first time, a competent theoretical understanding of why people fear the things they do, and how these fearful things might be eliminated, was developed. Known as the 'signal crimes perspective', this was developed from the successful American Chicago Alternative Policing Strategy by Martin Innes (Ditton and Innes 2005). Hitherto, crimes had been rated for seriousness in legal terms, with murder thus being seen as more significant and more to be feared than, say, graffiti. From the new perspective, and building on an earlier understanding that police officers must be visible, accessible and familiar, an attempt was made to discover what aspects of the local environment people perceived to be the sources of anxiety and, accordingly, for them, 'signalled' crime and created fear. The final strand of the policy, known as 'reassurance policing', was to be the co-production of solutions through engaging community-based informal social control.

This approach was trialled in the National Reassurance Policing Programme (NRPP), and the results were published in Tuffin *et al.* (2006). Independently, other academic research had shown that people's fearful self-rating often varied over time, and was responsive to local environmental and other changes. The NRPP research was unusually robust, surveying respondents in trial (or experimental) areas and in matched non-trial (or control) ones both before and after locally managed intervention. Crucially, the same respondents who were interviewed initially were also interviewed afterwards, so the before and after samples were exactly matched. Crime, perceptions of safety and confidence in the police showed significant improvements in the experimental areas and, although the NRPP is quietly winding down, its legacy programme, Neighbourhood Policing, is continuing the good work, initially in one pathfinder basic command unit for each police force, but eventually to be rolled out to the whole country.

Jason Ditton

Related entries

Community support officers (CSOs); Intelligence-led policing; National Intelligence Model (NIM); Neighbourhood wardens; Police performance indicators; Restorative justice/restorative cautioning; Signal crimes.

Key texts and sources

Ditton, J. and Farrall, S. (eds) (2001) *The Fear of Crime. International Library of Criminology, Criminal Justice and Penology*. Aldershot: Dartmouth.

Ditton, J. and Innes, M. (2005) 'The role of perceptual intervention in the management of crime fear', in N. Tilley (ed.) *Handbook of Crime Prevention and Community Safety*. Cullompton: Willan Publishing.

Hale, C. (1996) 'Fear of crime: a review of the literature', *International Review of Victimology*, 4: 79–150.

Tuffin, R., Morris, J. and Poole, A. (2006) *An Evaluation of the Impact of the National Reassurance Policing Programme. Home Office Research Study* 296. London: Home Office Research, Development and Statistics Directorate.

The government's crime reduction toolkit for fear of crime is available online at http://www.crime reduction.homeoffice.gov.uk/toolkits/fc00.htm.

FEDERAL BUREAU OF INVESTIGATION (FBI)

The Federal Bureau of Investigation (FBI) is one of the largest and best known crime-fighting agencies in the world. It operates across the USA and has agents based in a number of other countries around the world. It deals with the enforcement of federal law across the USA and all aspects of international crime and terrorism.

The Federal Bureau of Investigation (FBI) developed from a small team of 'special agents' first established in 1908 during the presidency of Theodore Roosevelt. From those early days, when agents were relatively few in number and had a restrictive remit of investigation, the organization grew in numbers as its responsibilities increased. Its most well-known head, J. Edgar Hoover, was appointed in 1924. Hoover was seen as a 'progressive' and introduced a more defensible system of appointments (based on merit) and a new training regime. His appointment – in what are seen as the 'lawless years' because of prohibition and gangsterism – was significant and long-lived. During his time as Director, the 'Bureau of Investigation' became the FBI; new techniques for the investigation of crime were developed; the largest collection of fingerprints was established; the staff complement grew; and the FBI laboratory was established.

Hoover's time in office was not without its critics. He was noted for his concern about subversion and, under his leadership, the FBI spied upon tens of thousands of suspected subversives and radicals. Several US presidents were inclined to sack him but, for various reasons, this never came about. Some of the techniques used by the FBI in their pursuit of communists, civil rights activists and the Ku Klux Klan were questionable to the point of being illegal and brought the FBI into considerable disrepute when they were revealed. Despite these considerable criticisms and some allegedly scandalous aspects of his private life (by the standards of the day), his influence over the FBI and its development was enormous. Hoover died in 1972 at the age of 77 after almost 48 years as the FBI Director. The FBI building in Washington, DC, is named after him, and he remains a larger-than-life figure in the history of the bureau.

Following his tenure, a series of FBI directors concerned themselves with establishing the integrity of the bureau. The notion of 'quality over quantity' was introduced, and three national priorities were established: foreign counter-intelligence, organized crime and white-collar crime. Subsequent years saw this remit expand to include counterterrorism, drug investigations and violent crime. Over the period the FBI also invested in the greater recruitment of women and minority ethnic groups, it increased its efforts to deal with economic and computer crime, and it established a DNA database.

The FBI Academy at Quantico trains agents and police officers from all over the world. It also houses the Investigative Support Unit, which provides advice on offender profiling – an approach developed by the FBI although interpreted differently by other academics and based on the assumption that offender characteristics can be inferred from the nature of the offence. This is seen as a particularly useful technique in the investigation of series crimes, such as stranger rape and homicide.

From 1993 the FBI's mission and resources expanded to address the increasingly international nature of crime. The FBI's budget grew by more than $1.27 billion as the bureau hired 5,029 new agents and more than 4,000 new support staff. Following the attacks of 11 September 2001, the FBI was restructured to focus effort on the prevention of terrorist attacks, countering foreign intelligence and addressing cybercrime-based attacks and other high-technology crimes.

During its history the FBI has carried out a number of highly successful operations, including investigations of the World Trade Center bombing in New York City (1993) and the bombing of the Murrah Federal Building in Oklahoma City (1995). There have also been some serious errors, such as the way in which the siege in Waco, Texas, was handled, which resulted in the death of 80 individuals (1993). This led to a review of the FBI's capacity to handle crisis situations and the subsequent establishment of a Critical Incident Response Group (CIRG).

Not least because of the portrayal of the FBI agent in popular fiction and the media more widely, which began in Hoover's time, the FBI is probably one of the best known national and international policing agencies.

Gloria Laycock

Related entries

International Association of Chiefs of Police (IACP); International police co-operation; Offender profiling; Transnational policing.

Key texts and sources

Marx, G.T. (1998) *Undercover – Police Surveillance in America.* Berkeley, CA: University of California Press.
See also the FBI's website (**http://www.fbi.gov/home page.htm**).

FINGERPRINTS

A fingerprint is an impression of the friction ridges of all or any part of the finger. Fingerprints may be recovered from crime scenes where they have been deposited in natural secretions from friction ridge skin. They are then compared with inked impressions taken of the fingers and thumbs of known individuals.

The analysis of highly individualized – often assertedly unique – 'friction ridge skin patterns' found at the ends of fingers and elsewhere on the hand as a method of identification has a very long history. Its use in modern policing practice is widespread and its evidential acceptability is well established in all criminal jurisdictions. Fingerprints have been used regularly in the UK to record the identity of known offenders and to assist in the identification of individuals who have left their fingermarks at scenes of crime since the establishment of the Fingerprint Branch of Scotland Yard in 1901, following the Belper Report on *The Working of the Method of Identification of Criminals by Measurement and Fingerprints*.

A series of photographic and chemical methods can be used to enhance the quality of partial fingermarks retrieved from crime scenes, and there is constant innovation in supplements to the human visualization of these biometric traces. In the last ten years there have also been important advances in the computer-assisted storage and comparison of fingerprints. In England and Wales, the National Automated Fingerprint System (NAFIS), now known as IDENT1, funded by central government, is now the main repository of such records. It holds digital copies of previous paper records of fingerprints and also receives and automatically compares with existing records new electronic fingerprints taken from suspects by the use of new LIVESCAN technology. The computerization of fingerprint submission and comparison greatly facilitates both the corroboration of arrestees' identities and more effective speculative searching of the national collection when fingermarks have been recovered from scenes of crime. However, the results of such computer searches are subsequently examined by trained experts before identifications can be pronounced and acted upon. In the UK, and unlike other forensic disciplines, expertise in the analysis and comparison of fingerprints remains largely located within police forces themselves. Every police force in England and Wales has its own fingerprint bureau staffed by expert fingerprint examiners.

Current Home Office research shows that fingermarks are recovered from about one third of all crime scenes attended by crime scene investigators in England and Wales. One quarter of these recovered fingermarks are identified thorough comparison with existing records, and one half of these identifications are designated as having contributed to the detection of the crime in question. However, despite the long history of the use of fingerprints in support of criminal investigations, the advent of DNA profiling and its grounding in empirical studies of molecular variation within human communities have also contributed to a more critical theoretical appraisal of the scientific basis for the categorical identifications traditionally claimed by fingerprint experts. In addition, several recent high-profile cases in the UK and elsewhere (e.g. the acquittal of Shirley McKee on charges of perjury in Scotland in 1999 and the erroneous implication by the Federal Bureau of Investigation of Brandon Mayfield in the Madrid bombing in 2004) have also raised questions about the routine practice and occupational culture of fingerprint examiners. While some see this appraisal as serving to undermine the established certainties of fingerprint evidence, it may be more useful to engage with it as a stimulus for improving an understanding of both the usefulness and limitations of fingerprint comparison as a central forensic support to criminal investigations.

Robin Williams

Related entries

Crime scene examiners (CSEs); DNA profiling; Forensic investigation.

Key texts and sources

Ashbaugh, D. (1999) *Quantitative-qualitative Friction Ridge Analysis*. Boca Raton, FL: CRC Press.

Cole, S. (2001) *Suspect Identities: A History of Fingerprinting and Criminal Identification*. Cambridge, MA: Harvard University Press.

Morgan, H.B. (2004) *The Processing of Fingerprint Evidence after the Introduction of the National Automated Fingerprint Identification System (NAFIS)*. Online Report 23/04. London: Home Office.

FIREARMS (POLICE USE OF)

The police use of firearms is one of a number of tactics that may be utilized in an endeavour to enable a peaceful resolution to a policing operation, mounted to achieve a legitimate aim and using effective conflict management.

Historically, the availability and use of firearms by the police were at the discretion of each force's chief officer, and any associated policy and procedures were imposed by them. This lack of national co-ordination continued until March 1983, when the Home Office issued ten guidelines for the police on the use of firearms. Much of what was contained in these guidelines was already in existence in individual force policy, but this was the first time that these had been drawn together into one document to be followed by each force in England and Wales. Also in March 1983, utilizing these Home Office guidelines, the Association of Chief Police Officers (ACPO) published a new manual of guidance on the police use of firearms. Comprising 12 chapters and 11 appendices, it addressed issues relating to the selection and training of officers, through to authorization, command and tactics.

Maintained initially by a joint standing committee, and now by an ACPO working group, the ACPO manual, *Police use of Firearms*, has been progressively developed, updated and improved through the inclusion of good practice and by the enactment of the Human Rights Act 1998. It is now truly a national document, having been adopted for use by the Police Service of Northern Ireland and the Association of Chief Police Officers for Scotland. While the ACPO manual contained programmes of training, these were deemed insufficient and, with the development of national occupational standards in policing, a National Police Firearms Training Curriculum (NPFTC) was published in February 2004. Through the NPFTC, national standardized procedures, terminology and accredited training packages have been enabled.

Policy and procedure have been greatly influenced through two major reviews of operations where officers have discharged firearms. In 1996, on behalf of the Joint Standing Committee on the Police use of Firearms, a review was produced entitled *A Review of the Discharge of Firearms by Police in England and Wales 1991–1993*. The review contained 42 recommendations, in respect of policy and operational, equipment and training issues. The second review, published in 2003, was conducted by the Police Complaints Authority and was entitled *Review of Shootings by Police in England and Wales from 1998 to 2001*. This review contained 48 recommendations in respect of the need for further ongoing research, through to learning from the outcomes of investigations.

The police use of firearms is also likely to encompass the use of less lethal weapons which, together, and in accordance with the Home Office *Code of Practice on Police Use of Firearms and Less Lethal Weapons*, are classified as 'weapons requiring special authorization'. This code, made under s. 39 of the Police Act 1996 and s. 73 of the Police Act 1997, came into effect in December 2003. The code imposes sanctionable requirements on chief officers related to the use of 'weapons requiring special authorization', in respect of responsibility, control, equipment, tactics, training, post-incident procedure, the promulgation of good practice and communication strategy.

Martyn Perks

Related entries

Association of Chief Police Officers (ACPO); Force (police use of); Less lethal weapons; Technology and policing.

FORCE (POLICE USE OF)

Force is the exercise of physical coercion by the police in the performance of their duties.

The use of force is perhaps one of the most central and contentious aspects of state policing. Famously, Bittner (1990: 125) defined the police as 'nothing more than a mechanism for the distribution of situationally justified force in society'. While in general terms the potential need for officers to resort to physical force is widely taken for granted, the legitimacy of specific acts raises the thorny question of exactly what coercive action is justified. The police often struggle for legitimacy because they are required to undertake acts that would be extraordinary or even illegal if done by others (Waddington 1999b). This is perhaps no more so than in the use of force.

Despite or perhaps because of the contention about the legitimacy of the police use of force, the understanding of it is deficient in key respects. Outside the use of firearms, historically, basic official Police Service data about the frequency and character of force employed by and against the police have been sparse and assembled according to diverse criteria. In addition, the 'low visibility' of many police functions has made it difficult to gather information independent of official agencies. What information

has been available, though, has suggested that, in the UK and the USA, the use of significant force by and against the police has been fairly rare as a percentage of public encounters. Some functions, such as custody arrest, are more likely to involve force than others. With the difficulties associated with studying force in day-to-day encounters, much of the academic and policy commentary has been given to well-known public order events that turned violent.

What is evident in relation to major public order and other incidents is that assessments of the appropriateness of specific instances of force often vary. While it is routinely said that force should be necessary and reasonable, it is often much more difficult to reach agreement on what these terms mean in practice. Various studies have pointed to the diverse administrative, lay, professional and legal standards employed to make appraisals. Although dispute is not inevitable, no well defined distinctions exist between what counts as necessary and reasonable force and what counts as unnecessary and unreasonable force, as well as what distinguishes unnecessary and unreasonable force from outright police brutality.

While determinations of appropriateness often turn on the factual details of particular incidents, what should be included as the relevant facts to any case is open for debate (for instance, in questions about the relevance of wider police relations with ethnic minorities for understanding specific incidents). Public assessments of police action are highly indebted to mass media portrayals – a condition that raises questions about who gets to participate in producing such accounts (Lawrence 2000). Reactions to the apprehension of Rodney King in Los Angeles in 1991, as well as to the shooting of Jean Charles de Menezes in London in 2005, attest both to the scope for disagreement about appropriate conduct and to the scope for disagreement about what considerations are relevant to judging police actions. Analyses of public order events or paramilitary policing exhibit such contrasting assessments as well – in particular, in relation to whether police actions diminished or escalated conflict (see, for instance, the Scarman Inquiry). Given these considerations, it is hardly surprising that much less analysis exists on the extent of police brutality than on the use of force in general.

Disagreement about police use of force is often difficult to resolve – in part because it raises fundamental questions about the role of discretion and rules in relation to police accountability. For many years, analysts of police practices have argued that discretion in the adherence to rules is of central importance in understanding the actions of officers. This recognition has happened in tandem with the importance of distinguishing between formal organizational rules and informal practices. While discretion enables a flexible approach to individual situations, it also provides grounds for criticism regarding the consistency and appropriateness of actions. In relation to the use of force short of firearms, the mix of discretion and rules can be especially problematic. Rules too open ended can invite criticisms of lax controls, whereas rules too prescriptive can be deemed unworkable. Different policies have been introduced to set out advised police responses. In the USA, most agencies have in place a 'use of force continuum', whereas in UK the preference is for a less prescriptive 'conflict resolution model'.

In recent years in the UK, significant attention has been given to the police use of force. This has in part stemmed from further high-profile cases and from the growing importance of health and safety requirements, as well as from the findings of key bodies such as the Patten Commission concerned with the ethics of policing. Greater documentation of force incidents is taking place, and there has been an active search for new tactics and technology to aid officers, such as less lethal weapons (Rappert 2002).

Brian Rappert

Related entries

Arrest; Code of conduct/ethics; Crime; Dispersal orders; Ethics in policing; Legitimacy; Less lethal weapons; Military policing; Paramilitary policing; Police culture; Policing; Public order; Scarman Inquiry.

Key texts and sources

Lawrence, R.G. (2000) *The Politics of Force: Media and the Construction of Police Brutality.* Berkeley, CA: University of California Press.
Rappert, B. (2002) 'Constructions of legitimate force: the case of CS sprays', *British Journal of Criminology,* 42: 689–709.
Waddington, P. (1999) *Policing Citizens: Authority and Rights.* London: UCL Press.
See also the Independent Police Complaints Commission's website (http://www.ipcc.gov.uk/).

FORENSIC AND INVESTIGATIVE PSYCHOLOGY

Forensic and investigative psychology is a diverse discipline that covers such topics as eyewitness testimony, deception, the risk assessment of dangerousness and offender profiling.

Forensic psychology is a varied discipline that covers a range of areas of research, consultancy and advice relevant to the criminal and civil justice system. These include such diverse topics as eyewitness testimony, deception, the risk assessment of dangerousness and offender profiling, among many others. The American Psychology–Law Society defines forensic psychology as 'the professional practice by psychologists within the areas of clinical psychology, counselling psychology, neuropsychology, and school psychology, when they are engaged regularly as experts and represent themselves as such, in an activity primarily intended to provide professional psychological expertise to the judicial system.' Although no obvious equivalent defining statement has been set by the Division of Forensic Psychology (a division of the British Psychological Society), the majority of forensic psychologists in the UK tend to be employed in the Prison Service and they focus on assessment, intervention and throughcare.

The Daniel M'Naghten case (1843, who shot and killed the secretary of the prime minister, and in which an expert evaluated the mental state of a defendant for the purposes of the court) is used as an insanity defence in many countries. This case reflects the clinically oriented, specialist form of forensic psychology used in the UK. This type of forensic work concentrates on the causes, consequences and methods of treatment of criminal behaviour. However, the origins of forensic psychology lie in areas that more obviously connect with investigative processes and detection. For example, Hugo Munsterberg might arguably be considered the first forensic psychologist as a result of his book, *On the Witness Stand*, which mainly considers eyewitness testimony. This work also reflected some of William Stern's (1901) earlier observations on the questionable accuracy of eyewitness recall. Further, many other academics who were *not* prison psychologists figured prominently in the development of ideas now widely used to assist the police and the courts. These include Binet's test for intelligence; Cesare Lombroso, William Marston, John Larson and Leonard Keeler's developments in notions of lie detection and the polygraph; and personality theorists such as Hans Eysenck, who made major contributions to the notion of individual differences. Many of these ideas have informed the type of forensic psychology that is directly relevant to policing and other law enforcement professionals. Topics include police interviewing, the selection of police officers, offender profiling and advancing our understanding of police decision making and stress responses in critical incidents. Indeed, in the USA at least, forensic psychology would not be considered the exclusive domain of individuals engaged in prison work but, rather, would reflect a more pluralistic church in which the broader focus is on advice for the courts.

Despite the UK's clear emphasis on risk assessment and the rehabilitation of offenders, a key figure in forensic psychology in the UK is David Canter, who coined the term 'investigative psychology' in the early 1990s to reflect the many diverse ways in which psychology could contribute to criminal and other investigations. Canter's objective was to bring coherence to an otherwise diverse range of contributions to law enforcement and to demarcate it from the clinical input noted above. Further, this activity reflected a commitment to involve those who work with law enforcement problems at the 'coal face'. As a consequence, many of the students who emerged from investigative psychology had a law enforcement background and continue now to be centrally involved in criminal investigation, either as senior police officers, crime analysts or behavioural profilers.

Investigative psychology should be considered as distinct from the more narrowly defined term, 'offender profiling', which entered common parlance in the 1970s with the development of the Behavioural Science Unit (BSU) at the Federal Bureau of Investigation Academy in the USA. The BSU fostered the belief that trained 'profilers' could attend a crime scene and use it 'Like a fingerprint … to aid in identifying the murder' (Ressler *et al.* 1986). Recent research has seriously questioned this claim and given a more balanced view of what is possible, as well as indicating the necessary conditions and scientific backing required to support such claims (Alison 2005).

In the UK at least, a broader definition of offender profiling has emerged, where behavioural advisers can contribute to DNA intelligence-led screens, risk assessments, interview advice, linking crimes, media strategy and a plethora of other domains in which an understanding of psychological principles can assist an inquiry team. The UK arguably boasts some of the highest professional standards of behavioural science contributions, based largely on an almost wholly exclusive UK-based research agenda, which began with some of Canter's earliest comments on the need for a scientific basis for such an approach.

Investigative psychology as a whole has now grown significantly and, since those early studies, other areas of psychology have been applied to the investigative process, including leadership, decision-making and organizational/occupational aspects of behaviour (Alison in press). This emerged partly as a response to the recommendations of the white paper, *Police Training: The Way Forward* (2000), and its objective of enhancing leadership and decision-making in the Police Service. Thus, while studies continue to develop on the psychological processes of offenders, it has become increasingly apparent that attention to what the police do is also of great academic and practical interest.

Thus, current work in investigative psychology can be argued to adopt two central themes. The first issue involves developing our knowledge of criminal behaviour – how it emerges, develops and changes; how people get involved in crime and why they stop; and the identification of the interpersonal significance of criminal behaviour. In doing so, the purpose is to identify whether there are identifiable geographic, behavioural or temporal patterns that may increase our ability to link offences, to predict an offender's home location or to prioritize suspects in police databases. The second theme connects with police decision-making, problem-solving and the management of major investigations. This may include psychological methods for improving information collection (including interviewing, documentation and archiving), making decisions and enhancing leadership and management styles.

The main advances in investigative psychology in recent years include the following:

- Greater awareness of the potential for profiling offenders (as well is its limits).
- Developments in geographic profiling and IT systems to facilitate this process.
- Greater recognition of the importance of linking offences.
- Theoretical developments to assist in explaining models of offender behaviour – especially with regard to sex offending.
- Recognizing the importance of police decision-making as a key area of research.
- The identification of individual differences in effective police decision-making.
- The identification of the key skills required in critical investigative incidents.
- Recommending training procedures to enhance performance.
- Establishing how environmental factors impact upon effective investigations.
- Assisting in the development of evidence-based decision support systems.
- Identifying how group cohesion, leadership and effective communication influence decisions.
- Assisting in the incorporation of expert systems into effective practice.

- Evaluating debriefing methods for critical incidents.
- Providing quality assurance and an evidence-based approach to major investigations.
- Evaluating costs/benefits analyses for decisions made in major investigations.
- Promoting an academic and practitioner-based commitment to effective policing, reducing crime and assisting in building a safe and secure community.

Compared with many other areas of psychology, investigative psychology is only just beginning to emerge from its infancy, particularly in the realm of police decision-making and leadership, offender profiling and behavioural investigative advice. However, some of its earliest origins hark back to the 1900s, and it continues to thrive in academic and practitioner circles. Increasingly, its impact is felt in the forensic arena in the UK, and it has found favour with police forces and other law enforcement agencies at an international level.

Laurence Alison

Related entries

Crime scene examiners (CSEs); Criminal investigation; Forensic investigation; Offender profiling; Technology and policing.

Key texts and sources

Alison, L. (2005) *The Forensic Psychologist's Casebook: Psychological Profiling and Criminal Investigation.* Cullompton: Willan Publishing.

Alison, L. (in press) *The Psychology of Critical Incident Management in Policing.* Cullompton: Willan Publishing.

Blackburn, R. (1995) *The Psychology of Criminal Conduct: Theory, Research and Practice.* Chichester: Wiley.

Canter, D. (1995) *Criminal Shadows: Inside the Mind of the Serial Killer.* London: HarperCollins.

Hugo Munsterberg's *On the Witness Stand* is available online at **http://psychclassics.yorku.ca/Munster/ Witness/detection.htm**. See also the Centre for Critical Incident Research's website (**http://www. liv.ac.uk/psychology/ccir/ introduction.html**) and the website of the Centre for Investigative Psychology (**http://www.i-psy.co.uk/**).

FORENSIC INVESTIGATION

> Forensic investigation is the integration of a range of scientific and technological evidence and intelligence in support of a criminal investigation (the identification or elimination of individuals, the identification of productive lines of inquiry or the rejection of a particular hypothesis in the reconstruction of a crime). Forensic investigation requires structured co-operation between police investigative teams and a range of specialists to ensure effective outcomes.

The investigation of crime, in particular major and serious crime, is a dynamic process that requires structured management to ensure the effective use of resources, to manage risks and to optimize outcomes. Forensic science and related areas of activity, such as forensic pathology, present an extensive range of opportunities from which investigative objectives can be met. These include key areas such as the identification or elimination of individuals, the identification of productive lines of inquiry or the rejection of a particular hypothesis in the reconstruction of the crime. Recent scientific, technological and legal developments, particularly in relation to DNA profiling and the National DNA Database, now provide previously unavailable means of investigating crime (particularly volume crime) and more efficient means to meet investigative objectives. The process by which this potential is harnessed is forensic investigation. Fraser (2000) sought to describe forensic investigation in an organizational and developmental context, distinguishing it from traditional models in use at the time. In essence, he considered forensic investigation to be a new development in response to a changing environment. This was partly because effective forensic investigation brings additional challenges to the traditional investigative approach for a number of reasons, including:

- the range and complexity of forensic opportunities;
- the mode of delivery of forensic science;
- lack of knowledge of the parties involved (police and scientists); and

- the need to align specific scientific analyses with investigative outcomes.

A typical homicide inquiry is likely to include a wide range of specialist examinations and analyses, such as shoemarks, fingerprints, blood, DNA, toxicology and pathology. It could also include highly specialist areas such as entomology, anthropology, archaeology or many other scientific disciplines. These disciplines are only relevant inasmuch as they have the potential to resolve an investigative problem and, therefore, central to forensic investigation is the clear definition of the relevant problem to be explored or resolved and the relevant scientific analyses that have a bearing on this.

With the exception of fingerprints, virtually all forensic services are provided to the police from external agencies. The nexus between the external organizations and police investigators is usually via the scientific support department (SSD), particularly the crime scene management unit or its equivalent. Most crime scene mangers will be familiar with investigative processes and the broad potential of scientific evidence that may be available. However, SSDs will rarely have a detailed understanding of the scientific potential available in individual case examinations. An external strategic supplier of forensic science, such as a major laboratory, will be necessary to provide the range of services, together with the benefits of accredited scientific standards and considerable experience. However, no single organization covers the entire range of disciplines, and there is a bewildering range of niche services available from small, highly specialist groups or individuals. While these niche suppliers may represent the only source of some specific techniques, they are unlikely to have the experience of larger laboratories or formal accreditation. As such, they present a higher risk to the investigator that must be assessed and managed.

Despite the dramatic increase in use of forensic science in recent years, numerous reports (e.g. ACPO/FSS/Audit Commission 1996) have identified a range of barriers to its effective use, including:

- poor knowledge of forensic science on the part of the police;

- poor knowledge of investigative processes and intelligence on the part of forensic scientists; and
- failure to integrate forensic science into the overall investigation.

Fraser (2000) identified the integration of scientific examinations into the overall investigation as the central issue and proposed a problem-solving model by which to achieve this. Integration is not solely an issue in relation to external specialists but also for those in the Police Service itself. Williams (2004) found that, where SSDs were seen as 'expert collaborators' in an investigation, they contributed more effectively to the process.

Recent years have seen considerable developments in investigative methodologies that recognize the above difficulties (among others) and that have sought to ensure that forensic science is an effective part of any investigation. The most sophisticated published source is the *Core Investigative Doctrine* (*CID*) (ACPO/NPIA 2005), which provides definitive national guidance on the principles of criminal investigation. At the heart of the *CID* is a model of investigation that describes the activities, decision-making processes and outcomes in criminal investigations taking into account legal, ethical, procedural and conceptual aspects. The vehicle for forensic investigation proposed by the *CID* is the forensic strategy. This is developed and managed via formal meetings during the course of the investigation and involves all relevant personnel: investigators, scientists, pathologists and any other necessary specialists. The purpose of the forensic strategy, in management terms, is to:

- define specific problem areas;
- engage the wide range of skills and knowledge necessary;
- support and develop effective teamwork;
- structure the scientific aspects of the investigation;
- identify a logical series of specific scientific and related examinations;
- prioritize scientific examinations and anticipate outcomes;
- communicate and inform the investigative team; and

- compel reflection and overcome prejudice and irrationality.

In addition, the *CID* details some of the investigative issues that are capable of being addressed and resolved by an effective forensic strategy:

- Clarification of involvement and activities of suspects and witnesses.
- Elimination of individuals from an inquiry.
- The significance of forensic intelligence – such as partial DNA or partial fingermarks.
- Identification of individuals by inceptive intelligence from DNA or fingerprints.
- Corroboration or elimination of events.
- Establishing the sequence of events.

The fundamental challenge of forensic investigation is the seamless integration and maintenance of alignment between scientific activities and investigative objectives in the complex and dynamic environment of a criminal inquiry. The range, complexity and continual development of scientific potential require formal management via a forensic strategy in order to optimize benefits, manage risks and meet legal requirements.

James Fraser

Related entries

Crime scene examiners (CSEs); Criminal investigation; Forensic and investigative psychology; Offender profiling; Technology and policing.

Key texts and sources

ACPO/NPIA (2005) *Practice Advice on Core Investigative Doctrine*. London: Association of Chief Police Officers/NPIA.

ACPO/FSS/Audit Commission (1996) *Using Forensic Science Effectively*. London: HMSO.

Fraser, J.G. (2000) 'Not science. Not support: forensic solutions to investigative problems', *Science and Justice*, 40: 127–30.

Williams, R. (2004) *The Management of Crime Scene Examination in Relation to the Investigation of Burglary and Vehicle Crime. Home Office Online Report*. London: Home Office.

See also the websites of the Forensic Science Society (http://www.forensic-science-society.org.uk/) and the Forensic Science Service (http://www.forensic. gov.uk/forensic_t/inside/about/index.htm).

FRANKPLEDGE

> Frankpledge was a system of guaranteeing the good behaviour of citizens that developed in late Anglo-Saxon times and that became fully functional after the Norman Conquest. Although amended several times, the frankpledge finally fell into disuse under the Tudors.

Late Anglo-Saxon law required, in most parts of England, every commoner (unless part of the household of a lord) to be a member of a 'tithing' – 'ten people' – and groups of tithings were associated together in wards, or 'leets'. The tithings were jointly responsible for ensuring that any of their group accused of a crime appeared in court to answer for it (if the man did not appear, the entire group could be amerced – fined – to compensate the injured party). The group could also pledge to act as compurgators (men who attested to the good character of an accused and thereby 'cleared' him in the absence of other evidence). This was the precursor to the notion of bail. The system also served as self-protection for its members and, if a law was broken, the members of the group could make a 'hue and cry' in order to activate the local people to apprehend fleeing offenders.

After the Norman invasion, essentially the same system of guaranteeing good behaviour became known as 'frankpledge'. William the Conqueror restated that everyone who wished to be regarded as free must be in a pledge, and that the pledge must hold and bring him to justice if he commited any offence. Laws passed by Henry I ordered every person of means over the age of 12 years to be enrolled in a frankpledge and so, subsequently, unfree men were admitted. At this time the idea of the collective fine was expanded.

By 1166, every man in a tithing was compelled to be a pledge for the appearance before the king's justice of every other member of the tithing. There were no local or nationally appointed police agencies to carry out these duties, so the practical responsibility for arresting and holding offenders rested with the tithing group. The man chosen to take the law-breaker before the hundred court became known as the 'tithing man', and was eventually known as the constable.

In time, the office of constable took on some extra duties of governing in addition to the general duties that came with the ancient system of frankpledge. From the late 1200s, the frankpledge began to fall into decay. There were complaints that the sheriff abused his power, often for financial gain. Royal power also had an interest in curbing the power of the sheriff. It seems that the frankpledge was still operating in 1376, and its final denouement came only with the new ideas of government introduced by the Tudors.

Barry Godfrey

Related entries

Constables; Hue and cry.

Key texts and sources

Baker, J.H. (1990) *An Introduction to English Legal History* (3rd edn). London: Butterworths.
Jewell, H.M. (1972) *English Local Administration in the Middle Ages*. Newton Abbot: David & Charles.

FRAUD AND POLICING

> Fraud is the obtaining of financial advantage or the causing of loss by implicit or explicit deception. It is the mechanism through which the fraudster gains an unlawful advantage or causes unlawful loss.

Fraud covers everything from cheque/plastic fraud (and, arguably, 'distraction burglary') at the low, individual loss end to multi-million pound international scams at the other – against private individuals, financial services and other firms, and against the government/taxpayers. Along this spectrum, it is mainly investigated reactively by divisional criminal investigation departments or fraud squads (sometimes linked in with specialist prosecutors at the Serious

Fraud Office), but the growth of interest by national and international crime networks in fraud and in corrupting financial services insiders has led to some proactive interest by the police, the Serious Organized Crime Agency and HM Revenue and Customs.

Frauds – only a minority of which currently *require* the Internet – cost more than all other property crimes combined, and tax fraud is the largest single component. Over 10,000 people in HM Revenue and Customs, the Deparment for Work and Pensions and the National Health Service investigate fiscal, benefit and health service fraud, but the police response to fraud declined by 2005 to about 524 officers in fraud squads (of whom over a quarter were in the City of London) and others distributed in units and divisions where fraud is not a priority. A small number of officers in the City of London/Metropolitan Police District (MPD) Dedicated Cheque and Plastic Crime Unit and in the MPD Vehicle Fraud Unit are wholly funded by the private sector and, elsewhere, limited funds are given for operations. The government's *Fraud Review 2006* recommended a major boost to regional and local forces' fraud resources and a national fraud reporting system (as well as more analysis).

Fraud policing has been little studied compared with many other areas, but investigative difficulties vary (Levi 2003; Doig 2006). Some frauds are known about in advance or in progress via intelligence-led policing (including information from regulators – e.g. of gaming and solicitors – as well as from the Credit Industry Fraud Avoidance System and financial institutions on 'identity frauds'), while others are discovered only after they are completed, sometimes many years afterwards. Although most frauds are local or regional in nature (e.g. payment card, insurance and cheque frauds), in some cases, evidence may have to be obtained from many countries. This has been facilitated in recent years because of international

attempts to suppress money laundering and terrorism, which have led to the growth of mutual legal assistance. It is not difficult to obtain financial information through Police and Criminal Evidence Act 1984 production orders, and stored and timed CCTV footage has the potential to make offenders more identifiable in the future. The Serious Fraud Office (which deals with about 60 cases a year) has the power to require from anyone – including suspects – documents and answers to questions, and varied powers are possessed by the Department for Trade and Industry (who can apply to wind up companies) and the Office of Fair Trading. Contrary to popular belief, only a minority of frauds are committed by high-status people, in whom the media have a particularly keen interest. 'Partnership' – both public–private and inter-public sectors, and internationally – is needed to ensure fuller and better-quality reporting and evidence gathering, and faster proactive leads in cases where frauds can be known about in advance. In addition, the police (e.g. the MPD's Operation Sterling and the North-East Fraud Forum) can play a role in encouraging collective fraud prevention and in offering a backup investigative service.

Mike Levi

Related entries

Crime; Cybercrimes; Identity theft; Organized crime; Specialist squads.

Key texts and sources

Doig, A. (2006) *Fraud.* Cullompton: Willan Publishing.

Levi, M. (2003) 'Organised and financial crime', in T. Newburn (ed.) *Handbook of Policing.* Cullompton: Willan Publishing.

See also the Home Office web page on fraud (**http://www.homeoffice.gov.uk/crime-victims/reducing-crime/fraud/?version=2**).

GAY POLICE ASSOCIATION

The Gay Police Association was established to represent gay Police Service employees.

The Gay Police Association exists to:

- work towards equal opportunities for gay Police Service employees;
- offer advice and support to gay Police Service employees; and
- promote better relations between the Police Service and the gay community.

The association was formed in 1990 by a group of Metropolitan Police officers. It is now a formally recognized staff association with members in all 52 UK police forces. The association is mandated by the Home Office to assist the development of gay policing issues and is the only national organization that specifically represents the needs and interests of gay police staff in the UK.

As of late 2006, the association had no full-time workers. However, it now has regional and force co-ordinators in many UK forces. These are assocation members who identify as gay and are appointed by the national co-ordinator to represent association national policy and practice at a local level. In addition to their full-time job, the role of the force co-ordinator is to help alleviate feelings of isolation often experienced by many gay police employees. Recent research (Foster *et al.* 2005), however, suggests many forces may still be without local co-ordinators.

In addition to its work in supporting gay staff, the association also works to educate the Police Service and central government on all issues connected with sexual orientation and policing. This includes policy development, the investigation of homophobic hate crime, victim care and family and community liaison. The association's training activities have included contributions to the Senior Command Course at Bramshill Police College, trainer development for Centrex, the training of family liaison officers in several forces and contributions to initial criminal investigation department courses, community safety unit training and senior investigating officer development.

Since 2004, police forces have sought to monitor the sexual orientation of their recruits. Initially introduced in three pilot areas, the nationwide scheme now means that, on non-attributable equal opportunities monitoring forms, police recruits are asked to tick a box to indicate if they are heterosexual, bisexual, gay, lesbian, or if they would prefer not to say. Forces may also collect such data for inclusion on officers' personnel records (with their permission).

Tim Newburn

Related entries

Community and race relations.

Key texts and sources

The Gay Police Association's website is at http://www.gay.police.uk/index_flash.html. The Scottish Gay Police Association's website is at http://www.gpascotland.com/.

GENDER AND POLICING

Policing has traditionally been seen as an occupation for men. Women have, however, served as police officers since the start of the twentieth century, and the female contribution to law enforcement has been distinctive and important and, in the twenty-first century, growing in significance.

The first female officers entered policing in the UK in 1915, during the First World War. The upheavals of wartime, especially the movement of large numbers of troops and refugees, were putting vulnerable women and naive recruits at risk. Pressures to introduce policewomen as agents of control into this situation came from outside the police and government. An international alliance promoting the cause of females in law enforcement had flourished for several decades. Its origins lay in various nineteenth-century moral reform societies that had campaigned for such causes as the employment of prison matrons in the USA and of women as Poor Law guardians in Britain. By the early 1900s, women had already become police officers in several US states and in a number of German cities. A group of well connected women, who had been associated with first-wave feminism and the suffrage movement, pressed for volunteer policewomen to patrol British cities and garrison towns. When they achieved this, the pioneers funded and provided training for these first policewomen.

Although this experiment was deemed successful and attracted considerable support, there were many conflicts and a long and hard-fought struggle before women finally gained full attested status and powers as officers in 1931. This victory was also a limited one and was to have a lasting effect on women's participation in the field. First, they undertook a highly *specialized* role, carrying out distinctive work, after specific training, with female offenders and victims and juveniles. Secondly, their origins in *moral and welfare reform* movements and associations with feminism marked them out from their male counterparts. This was also reflected

in considerable *inequalities* in their position: women faced restrictive recruitment quotas, lower pay, a marriage bar, limited career opportunities, and a ban on handling weapons. Numbers stagnated in the 1930s, although they almost doubled to 418 during the Second World War and increased thereafter, reaching 4,000 (4 per cent of national strength) before integration in the 1970s.

Integration

The gendered composition of British police forces was first altered in the early twentieth century through the influence of external factors, notably the groups campaigning for policewomen and the particular circumstances of wartime. In the 1970s, more far-reaching changes were achieved when women were very rapidly, and with little preparation, integrated into mainstream policing. Again, outside pressures brought this about with the passing of laws against sex discrimination, from which the police, despite active resistance, were not exempted. As with the first steps towards women's entry into law enforcement, there were parallel developments in the USA, following the Civil Rights Act 1964, and agencies around the world have since pursued similar courses of action.

Integration in Britain and elsewhere meant, in practice, that women officers undertook the same duties and received the same pay and career openings as men. These moves were evaluated in the USA during the early 1970s in a series of studies comparing women's performance on patrol with that of their male colleagues. Few differences of note were found; more significant were the set of assumptions that lay behind the list of evaluated items – these were at the extremes of stereotypyed masculine values and emphasized danger, aggression and physical powers.

Another strand of research, however, followed a different set of themes and, starting with Martin's path-breaking 1970 study in Washington, revealed the problems women officers faced within the police department and the strategies they used to cope with them. By the 1990s, women formed 15 per cent of officers in Britain, were widely deployed in non-traditional tasks (from dog handling to serious crime squads) and several had been promoted to Association of Chief Police Officers' ranks, including to posts as chief constable. In the USA, overall percentages were lower and even in decline, although the proportion of black and ethnic minority females was much higher.

Research

Twenty-first century research by Brown and Heidensohn (2000) has shown a worldwide pattern of the increased recruitment of women in law enforcement. This trend reflects heightened awareness of 'gendered agendas' in policing, focusing on domestic violence, child abuse, rape and serious sexual assault, as well as trafficking for sexual purposes. These topics were all among the chief concerns that the pioneer policewomen brought to the occupation in the early part of the last century, and they now feature much more significantly in public concerns and in policy priorities. Harassment in police organizations remains an issue, as does promotion. These matters are the focus of the many policewomen's organizations, national and international, which provide networking support and professional development for their members.

Current and future issues

In 2005, women constituted 21 per cent of police numbers in Britain, a slight increase on 2004. They are under-represented in higher ranks. Gender parity is far off, unless more active steps in recruitment and retention policies, such as those introduced to increase the numbers of Catholics in the Police Service of Northern Ireland, are taken. Questions still arise about their deployment in traditional or more 'male' duties. Research commissioned by the British Association for Women in Policing (BAWP) showed few gender deployment differences between constables, but other analyses show females in child protection and men in guns, cars and horses sections.

The murder of a woman officer in 2005 again led to queries about policing as a suitable job for a woman. Questions about physical fitness selection tests, their appropriateness and discriminatory effect are also still current. In some jurisdictions (e.g. Brazil and India), women-only police stations have been set up to make it easier for women victims to report crime and to gain help.

Policing has always been a highly gendered occupation, but its masculine ethos has been challenged by the entry of women who brought a mission – to protect and control – to law enforcement. In order to survive and flourish in policing, women had to adapt to the cop culture they encountered. As their numbers grow and the policing agenda changes, it is police organizations themselves that will need to integrate and draw upon the full range of all the possibilities of diversity.

Frances Heidensohn

Related entries

British Association for Women in Policing (BAWP); Community and race relations; Ethics in policing; European Network of Policewomen; Police culture.

Key texts and sources

Brown, J. and Heidensohn, F. (2000) *Gender and Policing*. Basingstoke: Palgrave Macmillan.

Carrier, J. (1988) *The Campaign for the Employment of Women as Police Officers*. Aldershot: Avebury.

Heidensohn, F. (1992) *Women in Control? The Role of Women in Law Enforcement*. Basingstoke: Palgrave Macmillan.

See also the websites of the National Centre for Women and Policing (**www.womenandpolicing.org**), the British Association for Women in Policing (**http://www.bawp.org/index.php**), the European Network of Policewomen (**http://www.enp.nl/**) and the International Association of Women Police (**http://www.iawp.org/**).

GEOGRAPHICAL INFORMATION SYSTEMS (GIS)

> A geographical information system (GIS) is a system of hardware, software and procedures designed to support the capture, storage, retrieval, analysis and display of geographically referenced information.

A geographical information system (GIS) is a database with a wide range of data-processing and analysis functions that uses geographical identifiers to bring different layers of information together (e.g. recorded crime records, incident data, census variables, transport routes) and to explore relationships between them. A GIS does this by superimposing or 'overlaying' different data sets upon each other to generate new information that cannot be produced with ease, accuracy or speed by other means.

An essential function of all GIS is the ability to explore the relationships between the various data layers. For example, a GIS containing data on recorded crime (offence category and date) and the location of licensed premises could be used to identify how many incidents of criminal damage or violence against the person occur on Saturday nights between 1 a.m. and 2 a.m. within 100 m of a particular pub. Clearly, the complexity of these inquiries increases with additional data. If CCTV camera positions are included together with taxi ranks, nightclubs and bus stops, then queries can be answered bringing all these factors together.

The visualization of disaggregate crime data can be further enhanced by the superimposition of digital aerial photographs. These provide valuable information about the presence of factors that can significantly increase or significantly decrease the risk of victimization. For example, the picture gained by using a GIS to plot domestic burglaries for individual properties by time of occurrence and modus operandi can be enhanced considerably if aerial photographs identify those dwellings that back on to an open space or situations where trees and shrubs are blocking the natural surveillance of properties.

Crime patterns can be placed into a socio-demographic context by adding social indicators (e.g. deprivation score, unemployment rates) and geo-demographic (residential area) classifications. The latter identify similar types of residential neighbourhoods in terms of their demographic, socioeconomic, ethnic and housing composition. It has been long recognized that certain types of residential neighbourhood are more criminogenic than others. The British Crime Survey, using the ACORN geo-demographic classification, showed that the areas of highest risk for residential burglary included low-income areas (i.e. including social housing) and areas with a mixed social status and an over-representation of single people. Burglary rates in these areas were over twice the national average (Dodd *et al.* 2004). In short, area classifications provide a more sophisticated spatial framework than purely administrative units (e.g. electoral wards, census tracts), which are unlikely to contain socially homogeneous populations.

A GIS can also be used to produce aggregate crime counts for any area that has a digital boundary (e.g. police beats or census output areas (OAs)). This involves using GIS functions to count how many points (e.g. individual burglaries) fall within a particular boundary. This operation is carried out by intersecting one data set with another. For example, intersecting grid-referenced burglary locations with OA boundaries would resulting in an OA code being appended as an additional variable to each burglary record. The individual burglaries can then be aggregated by OA to give an overall count of the number of residential burglaries within each OA. Burglary rates can then be derived by relating the burglary count to the households in each OA.

Clearly, crime mapping and crime analysis are key uses of GIS in a policing context. However, there are broader, more strategic roles for GIS in policing, such as the following:

- Producing force-wide area profiles to inform neighbourhood policing strategies.
- Defining new areas for operational policing (e.g. redrawing police beat boundaries).

- Producing strategic impact assessments (e.g. identifying vulnerable communities, housing stress and anti-social behaviour).
- Using data sets from a range of agencies (fire, probation, health, education, housing) to help local communities.
- Interactive web mapping to share information with the public (see www.beatcrime.info).
- Mapping crime prevention.
- Mapping crime opportunities and potential hotspots (crime generators and attractors).
- Identifying addresses for targeting crime prevention advice/campaigns.
- Crowd control and traffic management.
- Enabling the better co-ordination of services.

Alex Hirschfield

Related entries

Compstat; Crime mapping; Forensic and investigative psychology; Geographic(al) profiling; Hotspots; Intelligence analysis (previously crime analysis).

Key texts and sources

Clarke, R. and Eck, J. (2003) *Becoming a Problem-solving Crime Analyst in 55 Steps.* London: Jill Dando Institute of Crime Science, University College London (available online at www.jdi.ucl.ac.uk).

Hirschfield, A. and Bowers, K. (eds) (2001) *Mapping and Analysing Crime Data: Lessons from Research and Practice.* London: Taylor & Francis.

Tilley, N. (ed.) (2002) *Analysis for Crime Prevention. Crime Prevention Studies* 13. Cullompton: Willan Publishing.

See also the following websites:
www.ojp.usdoj.gov/nij/maps/
www.iaca.net
www.crimereduction.homeoffice.gov.uk/toolkits
www.neighbourhood.statistics.gov.uk
www.agi.org.uk

GEOGRAPHIC(AL) PROFILING

Geographic(al) profiling is the process of estimating the geographic locations relating to a particular offender by using the recorded locations of past offences and associated events.

Maps used by the police, showing the locations of offences with coloured pins and photographs, are familiar to many of us, if only through media and fictional portrayals. There is a long cultural history of believing that the location of offences in both space and time can provide 'clues' to the identity and location of an offender or offenders. We assume (with some justification) that an individual does not usually commit offences that are randomly located over vast expanses of space, but that the distribution of locations is due in part to decisions taken (albeit often unwittingly) by an offender. Geographic (or geographical) profiling is an attempt to work this phenomenon backwards – that is, based upon certain assumptions about criminal behaviour, *post hoc* estimations can be made concerning the locations familiar to the offender (a profile of his or her 'ecological niche'). Of particular interest is the offender's home base or centre of activities (sometimes referred to as the 'anchor point'). Most geographic profiles will not only be based on the geographic locations of offences themselves (such as where a rape occurred) but also on other spatial features of the case (such as where a weapon used during the rape was subsequently found abandoned).

Geographic profiles are usually employed to inform police inquiries (for example, in terms of prioritization of suspects) rather than as a means of attempting to identify the precise location of an offender. Much of the literature surrounding geographic profiling is concerned with its application to serious and serial interpersonal crimes, such as stranger rape and murder. However, there have also been a number of studies of the application of geographic profiling to serial 'volume' crimes, such as burglary and credit card fraud.

Perhaps the simplest models of geographic profiling are those based solely on the principle of least effort, and the parallel geographical equivalent of distance decay. The least effort principle predicts that offenders will expend the minimum possible energy in achieving their goals, such as travelling the least distance possible to commit a crime (as suggested by rational choice theory). This approach ignores any complexities such as constructed geographic features (road networks or bridges), natural barriers (rivers and cliffs) and any detailed consideration of the offender's motivation. Mathematically, the principle of least effort (if a linear model of distance decay is used) 'predicts' that the offender is most likely to be located close to the imaginary 'centre of gravity' of all the points representing the locations of offences (in fact, the arithmetic unweighted mean of the latitude and longitude or other geo-reference of each point). An early example of this centrographic approach was Stuart Kind's geographic profile of the 'Yorkshire Ripper' (Peter Sutcliffe) case in the UK (Kind 1987). More sophisticated variants on this model will build in the supposed existence of a 'buffer zone' around the offender's location (where the offender is less likely to commit offences) and introduce weighting into the calculation of the arithmetic mean. With computer-based systems, a variety of distance-decay functions can also be applied (for example, a negative exponential function replacing the simpler linear approach).

The development of geographic profiling has been heavily influenced by the work of environmental criminologists (most notably Paul and Patricia Brantigham) and by research conducted into journey-to-crime behaviours. Canter and Larkin (1993) examined serial rape by strangers and identified the existence of two distinct forms of journey-to-crime behaviour that may be of use in geographic profiling: 'marauding' (with the offender's home location forming the anchor point and increasing distances being travelled to commit crime) and 'commuting' (an offender travelling to another location which then forms a temporary anchor point for activity).

The concept of the mental map (or cognitive map) has also proved important to geographic profilers (Canter and Hodge 2000). For example (and perhaps simplistically), the locations that offenders choose (e.g. a location they take a prostitute to commit rape) rather than those that are chosen for them (e.g. where they 'pick up' a street-walking prostitute) are more likely to feature within their mental map and, hence, to be more important when performing a geographic profile.

In terms of the practical application of geographic profiling, a number of considerations arise. First, there is some debate concerning the minimum number of linked offences (though five is often taken as the absolute minimum) and, perhaps more fundamentally, how individual offences may be seen to be linked (e.g. through forms of common case analysis). Secondly, the way in which the underlying geography of the region is modelled requires careful consideration and working through (the so-called 'Manhattan metric' being a particularly common approach). Lastly, there are the inevitable technical geographical limitations to take into account, ranging from inaccuracies in the recording of the locations of crimes, to geo-coding errors when these locations are converted to a format suitable for mathematical analysis.

A number of algorithmic geographic profiling computer-based techniques have been developed, notably 'Rigel' (Kim Rossmo), 'Dragnet' (David Canter) and specific functions within 'CrimeStat' (Ned Levine). Most can be linked with geographic information systems to produce visual representations of profiling results. Despite their mathematical sophistication, all use algorithms based on a number of fundamental theoretical assumptions. For example, Rigel employs the distance-decay model, whereas CrimeStat uses the travel demand model (adapted from transportation research). However, these underlying assumptions are not always apparent to either the user or the researcher. There is currently a lively debate concerning the advantages and disadvantages of the three main computer-based techniques, and whether they are actually any more effective than human judgement alone (Snook et al. 2002).

In terms of the effectiveness of geographic profiling, the work of Santilla *et al.* (2003), Snook *et al.* (2004, 2005) and others has raised a number of points requiring careful consideration. Geographic profiling software appears to work best when it has been calibrated to match a particular environment (e.g. the specific layout of roads, traffic systems, residential and business locations, etc.). Furthermore, different geographic profiling systems seem better suited to different crimes (e.g. for serial rape, the models built on research into animal roaming and selection may provide the more accurate results). However, the debate continues among researchers concerning whether any of the software currently available performs any better than simple centrographic alternatives.

Robin Bryant

Related entries

Crime mapping; Forensic and investigative psychology; Geographical information systems (GIS); Hotspots; Intelligence analysis (previously crime analysis).

Key texts and sources

Ainsworth, P. (2001) *Offender Profiling and Crime Analysis.* Cullompton: Willan Publishing (ch. 5).

Brantingham, P.J. and Brantingham, P.L. (1981) *Environmental Criminology.* Prospect Heights, IL: Waveland Press.

Snook, B., Zito, M., Bennell, C. and Taylor, P. (2005) 'On the complexity and accuracy of geographic profiling strategies', *Journal of Quantitative Criminology,* 21: 1–26.

For the CrimeStat Spatial Statistics program (Version 3.0), see **http://www.icpsr.umich.edu/CRIMESTAT/**. For ESRI Environmental Criminology Research Inc.'s 'What is Rigel?' web page, see **http://www.geographicprofiling.com/rigel/index.html**. For Dragnet software, see the website of the Centre for Investigative Psychology (**http://www.i-psy.com/publications/publications_dragnet.php**).

GLIDEWELL

> Glidewell was a review of the Crown Prosecution Service conducted between 1997 and 1998.

During the period July 1997 to May 1998, Sir Iain Glidewell conducted a comprehensive review of the Crown Prosecution Service (CPS) at the request of the Attorney General, with support from Sir Geoffrey Dear QPM DL, HM Inspector of Constabulary and Robert McFarland.

Sir Iain and his team were invited to assess the extent to which the CPS had contributed to the falling number of convictions and to consider:

- the manner in which the CPS had influenced its relationship with the police;
- the validity of criticisms that the CPS had led to unjustified downgrading of charges; and
- the cost recommendations to enable the service to function within existing provision.

At the time of the review, the government had already made the decision to restructure the CPS so that it became coterminous with police force areas. Each of the new CPS areas was to be headed by a chief Crown prosecutor with support from an area business manager.

The review team found that improvements in efficiency and effectiveness could be realized, particularly in relation to judge-ordered and judge-direct acquittals, and concluded: 'There has not been the improvement in effectiveness and efficiency of the prosecution process which was expected to result from the setting up of the Crown Prosecution Service in 1986'.

The key recommendations arising from the review fell into three clear categories:

1. A change in priority of the workload of the CPS to concentrate effort on serious crime and the work of the Crown court.
2. Coterminosity with police force areas.
3. The adoption of a strong position as an integral part of the criminal justice process.

The review went on to recommend that the CPS should take responsibility for the prosecution process after charge to arrange the initial hearing at the magistrates' court and take on a greater role with victim and witness care.

The review prompted the establishment of a steering group, chaired jointly by the Association of Chief Police Officers (ACPO) and the CPS, that went on to install criminal justice units in all police force and CPS areas to handle the administrative support for the investigation and prosecution processes which saw, for the first time, CPS lawyers sited in police stations.

The recommendation that the CPS should take responsibility for the prosecution process from the point of charge was rejected by ACPO and the CPS in favour of a greater collaboration between the police and the CPS at the local level.

The Glidewell Review fundamentally changed the way in which the CPS viewed itself. The founding principle of independence that had been interpreted as meaning separate from the policing operation was recast as independence of mind. The placing of CPS lawyers in criminal justice units at police stations removed the need for prosecution files to be transported between police stations and CPS offices and, in doing so, brought to an end the 'memo culture' that had been the principal way in which the two organizations communicated and conducted business. In so doing, the Glidewell Review embarked both the CPS and the police on a course to closer and more collaborative team working.

Finally, Sir Iain and his team made a number of far-reaching recommendations about the way in which the CPS should be managed, with particular regard to human resources, information technology and the overall accountability and funding for the organization.

Peter Hall

Related entries

Crown Prosecution Service (CPS); Victim and witness support.

Key texts and sources

See the CPS's website (http://www.cps.gov.uk/) for information and news regarding the Glidewell Report.

GRADED RESPONSE

> Graded response is the method by which the Police Service selects the response to incidents reported.

The need to grade responses arose particularly when it became apparent that public demand was outstripping the availability of police resources to the point where it was not physically possible to attend all requests for service. Current thinking among contact management industries suggests that 80 per cent of calls for service ought to be dealt with at the first point of contact. Albeit that public expectation is continually raised, it should be possible to meet demand by the appropriate management of resources.

The National Call Handling Standards state that calls for service should be divided into either an emergency or a non-emergency contact. An emergency contact is defined as one that is reporting an incident which poses:

- danger to life;
- use, or immediate threat of use, of violence;
- serious injury to a person; and/or
- serious damage to property.

Further definition specific to certain incident types are listed in the document.

Non-emergency contacts are further divided into three levels of response:

1. priority;
2. scheduled; and
3. resolution without deployment.

A priority response is defined as an incident in which the police contact-handler acknowledges that there is a degree of importance or urgency associated with the initial police action, but an emergency response is not required. For a scheduled response, it is accepted that the needs of the caller can be met by scheduling an attendance at an agreed time.

Resolution without deployment is used when the needs of the caller can be adequately met through telephone advice or the help desk, access to a database of frequently asked questions, the involvement of another and more appropriate agency or service, or through some other method.

David Coulson

Related entries

Call management; Computer-aided despatch (CAD); Home Office Large Major Enquiry System (HOLMES); Unit beat policing (UBP).

Key texts and sources

Association of Chief Police Officers (2005) *National Call Handling Standards.* London: ACPO.

Home Office (2006) *Improving Call Handling – Good Practice Guide.* London: Home Office.

The government's crime reduction toolkit for graded response is available online at **http://www.crime reduction.gov.uk/toolkits/rv0401.htm.**

HATE CRIME

Hate crime was defined by the Stephen Lawrence Inquiry as 'a crime where the perpetrator's prejudice against any identifiable group of people is a factor in determining who is victimised'.

Over the past 25 years or so, western democracies in particular have, by a variety of processes, come to recognize officially an offence commonly known as 'hate crime'. At the most basic level, hate crimes are criminal offences motivated by hatred in which the offender's hatred of the victim or the victim's group plays some part in victimization. But this simplicity masks a number of important issues that are central to a true understanding of hate crime.

Defining hate crime is fraught with difficulties. Barbara Perry (2001) suggests that it is very difficult to construct an exhaustive definition of 'hate crime' that is able to take account of all its facets. Crime is socially constructed and means different things to different people and different things at different times, and what constitutes a crime in one place may not in another. As Perry suggests, crime is therefore relative and historically and culturally contingent, and this is particularly true of hate crime. Given this inescapable complexity it should not come as any surprise that numerous academic and professional definitions exist around the world.

As an object of academic study, hate crime is a relatively new and under-explored issue, particularly in Britain. Despite a long history of what we now label as 'hate crimes', it was the murder of black teenager, Stephen Lawrence, in London in 1993 and the subsequent public inquiry that followed in 1999 that served as a catalyst for raising the profile of hate crime as a social and political problem deserving of serious attention in its own right. While the Stephen Lawrence Inquiry focused on the issues of race and racism, the debate that followed served to draw attention to the experiences of other targets of hate-motivated offending. This in turn has sparked significant interest among policy-makers, academics and criminal justice practitioners in all forms of hate crime and, in particular, in how the problem might best be responded to.

Following the Stephen Lawrence Inquiry, in England and Wales, the Association of Chief Police Officers (ACPO) (2000: 13) defined hate crime as 'a crime where the perpetrator's prejudice against any identifiable group of people is a factor in determining who is victimised'. This was further broken down by the category of prejudice so that a racist or homophobic incident is defined as 'any incident that is perceived to be racist/homophobic by the victim or any other person' (ACPO 2000: 13).

In 2005, however, ACPO revised its definitions of a hate incident and a hate crime. A hate incident is now defined as 'Any incident, which may or may not constitute a criminal offence, which is perceived by the victim or any other person, as being motivated by prejudice or hate' (ACPO 2005b: 9). A hate crime is defined as 'Any hate incident, which constitutes a criminal offence, perceived by the victim or any other person, as being motivated by prejudice or hate' (ACPO 2005b: 9).

These definitions acknowledge that hate crimes are not always about hate but about prejudice. However, prejudice is a far more expansive concept than hate, covering a far wider range of human emotions, and this rather complicates our understanding of hate crimes. By adopting deliberately broad and inclusive definitions that include the phrases 'any identifiable group' and 'perceived by the victim or any other person', ACPO's definitions, adapted from the recommendations of the Stephen Lawrence Inquiry, unquestionably accept that anyone can be a victim of hate crime if he or she believes him of herself to be so. But if anyone can be a victim of hate crime, and if any crime can be a hate crime, there is a danger that the concept will lose its meaning.

It is therefore important that, when attempting to define and conceptualize 'hate crime', a number of key questions are considered:

- What prejudices, when transformed into action, are we going to criminalize?
- How will we know if these actions truly constitute a hate crime?
- What crimes are we going to include in our definition?
- Which groups will be acceptable to us as victims?
- How strong must the relationship between the prejudice and the offence be?
- Must that link be wholly or just partially causal?
- Who will decide?
- How will we decide?
- How can we guard against hatred without impinging upon people's basic democratic freedoms?
- And, of course, why is it important to consider these questions?

The answer to this last question is crucial. As Jacobs and Potter (1998: 27) suggest: 'how much hate crime there is and what the appropriate response should be depends upon how hate crime is conceptualised and defined.'

Nathan Hall

Related entries

Community and race relations; Community policing; Gay Police Association; Stephen Lawrence Inquiry.

Key texts and sources

Association of Chief Police Officers (2000) *ACPO Guide to Identifying and Combating Hate Crime.* London: ACPO.
Association of Chief Police Officers (2005) *Hate Crime: Delivering a Quality Service. Good Practice and Tactical Guidance.* London: ACPO (available online at http://www.acpo.police.uk/asp/policies/Data/Hate%20Crime.pdf).
Hall, N. (2005) *Hate Crime.* Cullompton: Willan Publishing.
Jacobs, J.B. and Potter, K. (1998) *Hate Crimes: Criminal Law and Identity Politics.* New York, NY: Oxford University Press.
Perry, B. (2001) *In the Name of Hate: Understanding Hate Crimes.* New York, NY: Routledge.
See also the Home Office's web page on hate crime (http://www.homeoffice.gov.uk/crime-victims/reducing-crime/hate-crime/).

HM INSPECTORATE OF CONSTABULARY (HMIC)

HM Inspectorate of Constabulary (HMIC) is independent of both government and the Police Service. Its core role is to promote the efficiency and effectiveness of police forces and policing organizations in England, Wales and Northern Ireland through inspection and assessment. It also provides impartial professional advice to ministers, chief constables and police authorities.

HM Inspectorate of Constabulary (HMIC) was established under the County and Borough Police Act 1856. At a time of high crime and poorly organized policing, this statute made it compulsory for every county and borough to establish and maintain a police force. The inspectorate's role was to ensure the efficiency of these forces through regular inspection and, subject to a declaration of efficiency, to recommend the payment by central government of financial grants to support each force.

Although 'efficiency' was never defined, the work of the early inspectors concentrated on assessing police officer numbers – both absolute and in proportion to the local population – the levels of supervision, the degree of co-operation between neighbouring forces and the state of repair of police stations, cells and lock-ups. In addition, the inspectors set themselves objectives to encourage the amalgamation of the tiny, inefficient borough forces and to help achieve national uniformity in police pay and pensions.

The direct influence of HM inspectors of constabulary (HMIs) has varied over the years. The appointment under royal warrant has ensured that the post of HMI has achieved a high status in policing and has attracted candidates with the highest operational and intellectual qualifications and expertise. During the first 100 years of the HMIC, the numbers of concurrent post-holders has varied from two to eight, dependent largely on the level of political concern over police efficiency and effectiveness.

In the midst of a move to greater controls over policing, following the Royal Commission (1960), the first HM Chief Inspector of Constabulary (HMCIC) was appointed in 1962 and the inspectorate took on a structure that set the trend to the present day – regionally based HMIs with assistants, staff officers and support staff, carrying out regular force inspections and addressing specific issues of importance to policing nationally.

In 2007, HMCIC remains the principal adviser to the Home Secretary on professional policing matters and co-ordinates the work of one functional and four regional HMIs. Each regional HMI takes responsibility for the inspection and assessment of a number of police forces, as well as associated organizations such as the Serious and Organized Crime Agency and HM Revenue and Customs. The functional HMI has national portfolio responsibility for the inspection of police training, development and diversity issues. HMIs are also asked to lead targeted reviews commissioned by the government following high-profile cases or perceived failures in policing – for example, re-examining the investigation of the Soham murders in 2003.

Since 2004, HMIC has also undertaken the baseline assessment of performance of every police force across a wide range of policing services. This assessment provides a published grade for each service area in each force, allowing comparison of service delivery and improvements.

Around half the 130 staff at HMIC are police officers seconded from forces throughout the UK – ranging from chief inspectors to deputy chief constables – who bring operational and specialist expertise to the work of the inspectorate, supporting focused or themed inspection of forces and the production of public reports.

Kate Flannery

Related entries

Accountability and governance; Association of Chief Police Officers (ACPO); Audit Commission; Best value; Home Office; Police performance indicators.

Key texts and sources

Cowley, R. and Todd, P. (2006) *The History of Her Majesty's Inspectorate of Constabulary: The First 150 years, 1856 to 2006.* London: Home Office.
HM Chief Inspector of Constabulary (2005) *Annual Report, 2004–2005.* London: HMSO.
HMIC's website is at **http://inspectorates.home office.gov.uk/hmic/**.

HOME OFFICE

The Home Office is the government department with lead responsibility for law and order and for the UK's borders. Its core purpose is the protection of the public. The Home Secretary and five other ministers head the department.

The Home Office originated in the late eighteenth century when two secretaries of state – one for the north and one for the south of England – were consolidated within one department: the Home Department. The King or Queen's peace – initially through the magistracy and military and, after 1829, through the police – was always a central responsibility of the new department, which became officially known as the Home Office in the 1840s.

The Home Office has national responsibility for the Police Service in England and Wales. The Immigration and Nationality Directorate, the Identity and Passports Agency and the Office for Security and Counter-terrorism fall within its remit, as do a number of agencies and non-departmental public bodies, including the Serious Organized Crime Agency, the Independent Police Complaints Commission, the National Policing Improvement Agency (NPIA), the Security Industry Authority and the Criminal Records Bureau. The Home Office has a group headquarters that sets the strategic framework for its key services, provides common support services and drives the delivery of the department's agenda.

The Home Office describes its key priorities as:

- protecting the nation from terrorist attack;
- cutting crime, especially violent and drug-related crime;
- enabling people to feel safer in their homes and local communities, particularly through more visible, responsive and accountable local policing; and
- securing the UK's borders, preventing the abuse of immigration laws and managing migration to the UK's benefit.

The Home Office manages its relationship with the police in a tripartite manner, working with chief officers and police authorities. The Home Secretary:

- has overall responsibility for ensuring the delivery of an efficient and effective Police Service in England and Wales;
- sets the key priorities for policing and the means by which the achievement of these will be measured. These are set out in an annual National Community Safety Plan;
- through the Police and Crime Standards Directorate, monitors the performance of the Police Service and, where necessary, offers support and, ultimately, intervention where performance is falling;
- prescribes nationally certain policing approaches (e.g. the National Intelligence Model) and technology where this is necessary to ensure consistency and economies of scale;
- has national responsibility for counter-terrorism and the Security Service and consequent oversight of force-level input to the national counter-terrorist effort;
- with the Secretary of State for Communities and Local Government, ensures there is adequate provision in the local government settlement for the central police grant; and
- sets police pay and conditions, pensions and regulations.

The Home Office went through a period of significant change in 2006–7. A series of problems relating to foreign criminal records and to managing immigration caused the then Home Secretary, John Reid, to describe the department (which, at that stage, included prisons and probation) as 'not fit for purpose'. The Home Office's response was to implement a Reform Action Plan (July 2006). A wider debate across government culminated in the decision to change the responsibilities of the Home Office, focusing the reconfigured department more tightly on public safety while moving prisons and probation to a newly created Ministry of Justice.

The combined effect of these changes has been to create a dual structure of Home Office and Ministry of Justice that is recognizably European. As regards policing, it has meant the following:

- The Home Office now has its core focus on protecting the public.
- The structure and organization of the Home Office have been radically changed, reducing the size of the headquarters and devolving more responsibilities and resources to front-line operations and services. The aim is more accountable, better performing front-line services, working to clear priorities and performance targets set by a smaller, but more influential, strategic policy function.
- The Home Office has devolved responsibility for supporting police modernization and improvement to the NPIA, which came into place in April 2007.

Tim Newburn

Related entries

Accountability and governance; Association of Chief Police Officers (ACPO); Ministry of Justice; Politics (police involvement).

Key texts and sources

Gibson, B. (2007) *The New Home Office: An Introduction.* Winchester: Waterside Press.

The Home Office's website is at http://www.home office.gov.uk/.

HOME OFFICE LARGE MAJOR ENQUIRY SYSTEM (HOLMES)

The Home Office Large Major Enquiry System (HOLMES) is the computer software used by police to manage homicide and major incident investigations.

The Home Office Large Major Enquiry System (HOLMES) was first introduced in 1986 to replace the manual card index systems that were then in use. Work had started in the 1970s to find ways of computerizing information management in criminal investigation. In 1981 this was given added impetus by the Byford Report into the investigation of the Yorkshire Ripper murders. This found that the systems in use were inefficient in handling large amounts of information and, because they were often incompatible with each other, sharing information was difficult.

HOLMES was conceived as a national system that would solve these problems, but this was not simply a matter of introducing a common computer system. To ensure that data entry was consistent, HOLMES rules and conventions were developed, and the *Major Incident Room Standardised Administrative Procedures* (MIRSAP) were introduced to provide common standards for documents, procedures and roles in major incident rooms (MIRs). It has been argued that the real benefit of these developments has come from the standardization of practice they have brought about, rather than simply the computerization of information gathered by investigations. Even on those investigations where HOLMES is not used, which is frequently the case (see below), the principles of MIRSAP are still followed.

The Police Information Technology Organization manages the technical development of HOLMES on behalf of the Police Service, and the Association of Chief Police Officers' HOLMES Working Group develops policy for its use. Every force in the UK uses HOLMES but few forces have permanent MIRs because homicide and major investigations are relatively infrequent events. The usual practice is to have a central HOLMES unit that provides the capability to set up an MIR near to the scene of an incident, usually in the nearest police station. These use portable HOLMES terminals which are connected over a telephone network to a central server.

Excluding the roles of the senior investigating officer (SIO) and the team of investigators who carry out the inquiry, MIRSAP identified 21 roles that could be employed in an MIR. Not all these are required in every case and, in some cases, one person can perform multiple roles. However, MIRSAP illustrates that the effective management of information and adherence to common standards are resource intensive. Of more immediate concern to many SIOs is the time it takes to populate HOLMES with sufficient information for it to be of use to an inquiry. Many homicides are solved relatively quickly and do not involve large amounts of information or many lines of inquiry. In these cases, many SIOs prefer to use card index systems, which are often called 'paper systems', as they believe they are quicker to establish than HOLMES and are equally capable of managing small inquiries.

In 1994 work started on the development of a system to replace the first version of HOLMES. This provided the opportunity to update the technology, which had become dated by then. HOLMES 2 was launched in 1999. It is Windows based and is compatible with the range of analytical and other software that has become available for use in MIRs. HOLMES 2 provides the following functions:

- *Document management* enables all documents to be monitored by the MIR and shows what is happening to each one at any point in the investigation.
- *Workflow management* enables the system to be tailored to the working practices in the MIR.
- *Graphical indexing* provides the facility for users to index directly from a typed copy of a document rather than having to re-key the data.
- *Record management* enables data to be retrieved for research and analysis and provides a range of search facilities.
- *Task management* allows actions to be allocated and manages their progress.

- *Exhibit management* manages and tracks the movement of all relevant property throughout the investigation.
- *Research and analysis* provides links to commercial analytical software.
- *Disclosure management* helps to manage disclosure material.
- *Court preparation* enables a file to be produced for court.

A laptop version of HOLMES 2 has recently been launched with the same functionality to provide a more portable version that can be used by one operator. If this proves successful, it may encourage SIOs to use HOLMES 2 on all investigations, thus making the 'paper system' redundant.

The Casualty Bureau function is a recent development using HOLMES' capacity to manage large amounts of information. Where incidents involving mass casualties occur, the police are faced with many calls from the public concerned about the welfare of relatives who may have been involved. Each of these reports is entered on to a specially adapted version of HOLMES, and the police use these to identify casualties from the incident. Because Casualty Bureau uses HOLMES' technology, the data can be quickly linked to the MIR established to investigate the incident.

Peter Stelfox

Related entries

Byford Report; Murder.

Key texts and sources

ACPO (2005) *Major Incident Room Standardised Administrative Procedures (MIRSAP)* (not published outside the Police Service).
See also the web page of the Unisys Corporation (**http://www.holmes2.com/holmes2/whatish2/**) on HOLMES 2.

HOTSPOTS

Hotspots are geographical areas with significantly higher rates of recorded crime and disorder than surrounding areas.

It has long been observed that episodes of recorded crime in an area are not evenly distributed in either space or time. Put simply, some locations appear more prone to crime than others (particularly 'volume crime', such as theft or burglary), either in terms of repeat victimization or as a general level of crime and disorder. Similarly, there are particular times of the day or week when crimes are more likely to take place, compared with other times. Furthermore, this clustering in space and time can remain relatively consistent and persistent over a number of years. These locations are often referred to as crime hotspots (an early use of the term may be found in Sherman *et al.* 1989). Hotspots have been the subject of considerable interest, notably among crime analysts, and there is a burgeoning academic literature on the subject, particularly in relation to crime reduction strategies. However, the term hotspot may also be encountered in other policing contexts, such as hotspots of deprivation, where it has the more general meaning of 'significantly different from the average'.

Although crime hotspots tend to be areas of a few square kilometres, within a hotspot there may be specific locations (a few adjacent streets or even individual residential addresses) which account for particularly high levels of reported crime (sometimes referred to as 'hotpoints' or 'hotdots'). The existence of these hotpoints and the hotspot itself may be partly explained by repeat victimization. In addition, from an epidemiological perspective, victimization may be seen as a form of contagious disease that might spread from one geographical area to surrounding ones (Johnson and Bowers 2004 in the case of burglary). Through these mechanisms, a hotpoint may enlarge to form a hotspot. There are, however, a number of more general theoretical perspectives (particularly those with a 'spatial' dimension) that suggest possible reasons for the existence of hotspots, such as routine activity theory and social disorganization theory.

Inevitably there is some debate concerning how hotspots are identified. For example, a police officer's impressions gained from regularly patrolling a particular neighbourhood may not always be reflected in recorded crime figures (Chainey and Ratcliffe 2005). Another question concerns the units of measurement used to take the 'temperature' of a supposed hotspot. If we choose to use an absolute scale (e.g. the number of thefts from motor vehicles compared with last month) rather than a relative one (e.g. the number of crimes per 1,000 of population), this may affect whether we decide that the data relating to a particular location have reached a threshold and if that location should be classified as a hotspot. This is particularly important when we make comparisons with a certain periodicity, such as a week, month or year. On the technical level, there is often discussion concerning the choice of the kernel density function (a way of measuring the density per unit area). Although these may appear to be rather arcane and technical discussions, they do in fact reflect some fundamental issues concerning how we define and subsequently identify crime hotspots.

In terms of crime reduction, there is perhaps an important distinction to be made between operational-level hotspots (identified by an analysis of data and intelligence on a week-by-week basis) and more persistent hotspots identified for tactical intervention. For example, some hotspots are relatively transient in nature, perhaps due to specific and changing circumstances (such as the release of a prolific car thief from prison). Other hotspots are more ingrained and persistent, perhaps due in part to such factors as the layout of local housing and pedestrian walkways. Crime analysts may use a variety of statistical techniques (of varying degrees of sophistication) to attempt to differentiate between these two broad forms of hotspot.

Hotspots are familiar to most practitioners as a visual representation using geographic information systems (such as 'ArcView' or 'MapInfo') linked with crime data. Areas of higher incidence of crime are usually shaded in a darker colour, such as red, when compared with surrounding areas. In the UK, the identification of hotspots is normally the task of a crime analyst working at basic command unit level in a police force. The existence of a hotspot will often influence police actions at the tactical and operational levels. Indeed, hotspot management is part of the UK's National Intelligence Model adopted by all police forces.

Strategies designed to tackle crime hotspots must take into account that each area or location has a unique combination of social and environmental factors. There is a danger that geography alone may be used by the unwary as the single explanatory variable of a hotspot, ignoring the existence of 'lurking' variables, such as demography. The aetiology of a particular hotspot may reside, for example, in distraction burglars targeting elderly people whose accommodation also happens to cluster spatially in a certain part of town.

More recent research has focused on the possibility of predicting future hotspots (e.g. Johnson *et al.* 2004). One key criticism of more 'traditional' approaches is that hotspot identification has become an exercise in identifying past events and that it provides only a limited guide to the future. 'Predictive hotspotting', on the other hand, derived from disciplines as diverse as behavioural ecology (optimal foraging theory), epidemiology and criminology, attempts to predict where burglary is likely to occur in the future and thus, by extension, how best to deploy police resources or to 'harden' the possible targets.

Robin Bryant

Related entries

Compstat; Crime mapping; Geographical information systems (GIS); Geographic(al) profiling; Intelligence analysis (previously crime analysis); Stop and search.

Key texts and sources

Bowers, K.J., Johnson, S.D. and Pease, K. (2004) 'Prospective hot-spotting: future of crime mapping?', *British Journal of Criminology*, 44: 641–58.
Chainey, S. and Ratcliffe, J. (2005) *GIS and Crime Mapping*. Chichester: Wiley.

Tilley, N. (ed.) (2006) *Handbook of Crime Prevention and Community Safety*. Cullompton: Willan Publishing.

Mapping Crime: Understanding Hot Spots (Eck, J., Chainey, S., Cameron, J., Leitner, M. and Wilson, R. (2005)) is available online at **http://www.ncjrs. gov/pdffiles1/nij/209393.pdf**. The government's crime reduction toolkit for hotspots is available online at **http://www.crimereduction.gov.uk/ toolkits/p0313.htm**.

HUE AND CRY

> Hue and cry was a way of catching offenders who had evaded the night watchmen and constable. On hearing the call to hue and cry, everyone in the neighbourhood was expected to join in the pursuit of the offender. Hue and cry was repealed in 1827, being relegated to the name of a news-sheet that advertised wanted men and newly released prisoners.

Hue and cry – literally meaning a loud clamour or public outcry – originated in the Anglo-Saxon period in order both to advertise crimes and to apprehend offenders, but it fell away as a practice after the Norman invasion. It was reinstated by the Statute of Westminster in 1285 as a means of dealing with offenders who had evaded the night watchmen and the constable. Since the maintenance of law and order was nominally the responsibility of all subjects of the Crown, the statute called for offenders to have hue and cry 'levied against them, and such as keep the watch shall follow with hue and cry, with all towns near'. Everyone in the locality was immediately to join in the pursuit, with those who were reluctant to do so being viewed, at best, with suspicion and, at worst, as being as bad as the fleeing offender.

This system was somewhat haphazard and, while it could work tolerably well in small rural communities or as part of the network of private prosecution agencies, it was a system that could not cope with the development of large towns in the eighteenth century. In the eighteenth century, therefore, hue and cry was modified so that the call for an offender to be arrested now passed through the hands of a justice of the peace, who would examine the case and then grant an arrest warrant that called for the constable to execute it. However, the large urban communities and anonymous populations that were created by industrialization in the early nineteenth century called for a more organized system of policing. There was also a move away from victims attempting to get their property back (i.e. through the Associations for the Prosecution of Felons) towards more preventative policing.

Earlier systems of policing, such as the parish watches and constables, were swept away by the introduction of the New Police in 1829 (around the same time as the provisions of hue and cry were repealed, in 1827), and hue and cry was relegated to being used as the name of a news-sheet advertising wanted men and newly released prisoners. While there is considerable debate among historians as to whether the New Police provided a more efficient form of crime control than the parish watches, there is a consensus that hue and cry was always an imperfect system that could not cope with the demands of the 'modern age'.

Barry Godfrey

Related entries

Constables; Frankpledge.

Key texts and sources

Critchley, T.A. (1967) *A History of Police in England and Wales, 900–1966*. London: Constable.
Godfrey, B. and Lawrence, P. (2005) *Crime and Justice, 1750–1950*. Cullompton: Willan Publishing.

HUMAN RIGHTS

The Universal Declaration of Human Rights states that 'Everyone shall be subject only to such limitations as are determined by law solely for the purpose of securing due recognition and respect for the rights and freedoms of others and of meeting the just requirements of morality, public order and the general welfare in a democratic society'.

One of the major commitments in the political manifesto of the Labour government, before it was voted into power in 1997, was that of the introduction of legislation to promote human rights. Subsequently, a government white paper, *Rights Brought Home: The Human Rights Bill* (1997), was circulated to canvass opinions on the most appropriate way to bring in legislation, as there were many models around the world from which to choose and as a number of cases had already been taken against the UK through the European Convention on Human Rights (ECHR) and the European Court of Human Rights (ECtHR). The Human Rights Act 1998 (HRA) was given Royal Assent in November 1998, but commencement was delayed until 2 October 2000. The HRA was merely a vehicle to introduce the existing ECHR into the UK's legal system.

ECHR

Following the Second World War, British lawyers drew up the provisions of the ECHR, and the text of the convention was adopted in 1950. The UK government formally ratified the convention in March 1951, but the articles were not assimilated into the English or the Scottish legal system until the introduction of the HRA. Section 1 of the HRA defines which convention rights the UK has adopted. The articles and protocols give citizens of the UK and visitors to the UK the rights and freedoms contained within them:

- *Article 2*: right to life.
- *Article 3*: prohibition of torture.
- *Article 4*: prohibition of slavery.
- *Article 5*: right to liberty and security.
- *Article 6*: right to a fair trial.

- *Article 7*: no punishment without law.
- *Article 8*: respect for private and family life.
- *Article 9*: freedom of thought, conscience, religion.
- *Article 10*: freedom of expression.
- *Article 11*: freedom of assembly.
- *Article 12*: freedom to marry.
- *Article 14*: prohibition of discrimination.
- *Articles 16, 17, 18*: political activity of aliens, abuse of rights, restriction on rights.
- *First Protocol*: protection of property, right to education, right to free elections.
- *Sixth Protocol*: abolition of the death penalty, death penalty in time of war.

Section 3 of the HRA informs courts how to interpret *all* legislation – i.e. which is to be read and given effect in a way compatible with the principles of the ECHR. Section 6 defines what a 'public authority' is. People who believe that their rights have been infringed can take action against a public authority in two ways described in s.7. Police officers are covered by the HRA, as are all other public sector organizations, such as local authorities, courts, the Prison Service, social services and many others.

Legal principles of the ECHR

Every action of the Police Service (as a 'public authority') must be compatible with convention rights, and this introduces explicit human rights dimensions into:

- policy-making and procedures;
- the exercise of discretion; and
- decisions that affect people.

Every use of police powers (stop, search, arrest, seizure, etc.) affects the human rights of others and many other areas and functions of the Police Service as an employer and a licensing authority.

Categories of articles

The articles are defined by three different categories: *absolute rights* are regarded as sacrosanct rights and are not to be diminished by state actions; *derogable* (or strong) *rights*, from which states may make specific legal exemptions; and *qualified rights*, in which states may interfere with the rights of the individual under specified circumstances. It is important to remember that, whenever a public authority or state interferes with the rights of an individual, this will be unlawful unless the act or omission can be justified with reference to a specific exemption or qualification.

Compatibility and compliance

In deciding whether police actions are compatible and compliant with the ECHR articles, the following tests of compatibility are utilized:

- Legality.
- Proportionality.
- Relevance/necessity.
- Equality of arms.
- Accountability/independent public remedy.

Developments since the introduction of the HRA

Since commencement in 2000, there have been a multitude of cases heard in magistrates' courts and Crown courts around the UK. In the main, decisions based on the ECHR have been made without the difficulties that had been envisaged by some prior to its introduction. There have been a number of decided cases that the courts have subsequently followed as legal precedent.

There have also been several high-profile cases relating to privacy, and it is likely there will be an amendment to the law to introduce a provision specifically in this area. There has also been considerable discussion on the law regarding legislation to require all UK citizens to have identity cards (i.e. the costs and whether such cards are truly 'voluntary'). Similarly, there has been concern about the proportionality of collecting DNA samples from any person (whether adult or not) when arrested for a criminal offence. Finally, the crime of 'identity theft' is becoming more prevalent, leading to many problems for individuals who have their financial or passport identity stolen.

Under the provisions of terrorism law, several people were detained in prison without charge or trial and, as a result of a subsequent court case (*R v. Abu Hamza*), the Prevention of Terrorism Act 2005 was enacted. However, the sections on 'control orders' are still under discussion. There have been a number of cases relating to maternity rights, to the turning off of the life-support systems of dangerously ill patients and to conjoined infants. Under Article 3 of the ECHR, controversially, nine Afghan men who highjacked an aircraft could not be returned to their country because they faced a serious risk of death or torture. Finally, there have been many other cases concerning immigration and 'asylum seekers'.

Alan Beckley

Related entries

Code of conduct/ethics; Ethics in policing; Right of silence.

Key texts and sources

Beckley, A. (2000) *Human Rights: The Guide for Police Officers and Support Staff.* Goole: New Police Bookshop.

Neyroud, P. and Beckley, A. (2001) *Policing, Ethics and Human Rights.* Cullompton: Willan Publishing.

Starmer, K. (1999) *European Human Rights Law: The Human Rights Act 1998 and the European Convention on Human Rights.* London: LAG.

House of Lords' judgments are available online at **www.parliament.uk**. Court service judgments are available online at **www.courtservice. gov.uk/ judgments/judg_home.htm**. See also the Human Rights Unit's website (**www.humanrights. gov.uk**) and Liberty's website (**http://www.liberty-human-rights. org.uk/**).

HUMAN TRAFFICKING

> Human trafficking refers to the trading and systematic movement of people by various means, potentially involving a variety of agents, institutions and intermediaries. It typically involves coercion, deception and the exploitation of those who are moved within or across borders.

The activity of human trafficking is not new; indeed, it has historical parallels with the trading of people as commodities for the colonial slave trade. In the contemporary context, human trade has been described as a form of new slavery in the global economy. The growth of trafficking in persons has been variously linked to the development of transnational organized crime networks, exploitative cultural practices and broader processes of political repression, civil conflict and unequal access to resources and employment opportunities in some of the world's poorest and most unstable regions.

There are competing understandings of, and approaches to, human trafficking. When the problem is defined as a moral, crime or illegal migration issue, there is a tendency to opt for solutions that involve control and punishment and that risk the stigmatization and penalization of trafficked victims; when the problem is defined as a social, labour or human rights issue, strategies of empowerment may be preferred. While trafficking has been most closely associated with prostitution and state interventions to regulate the sex trade, critics have argued that the problem is evident in multiple processes and sites of work. Indeed, there have been recent attempts to broaden the understanding of trafficking to include other forms of exploitation (e.g. forced labour, debt bondage, the removal of organs), notably under the UN Convention against Transnational Organized Crime (Protocol to Prevent, Suppress and Punish Trafficking in Persons, especially Women and Children) (2000).

There are three main stages in the trade in women, children and men: the recruitment of irregular migrants; their movement to countries of transit and destination; and the control and exploitation of migrants once their journey has ended. Different intermediaries or criminal groups may be involved in each of these stages. These fall on a continuum ranging from freelance criminals or entrepreneurs providing a single service (for example, transportation, fake documents), to (semi-)legitimate travel agencies, migration brokers, labour recruitment agents and other service providers in hidden economies, to more structured criminal organizations controlling the trafficking process. Significantly, critics have pointed out that human trade would not thrive as it does in particular regions without the collusion and corruption of public officials.

In the UK in 2006, a unit with dedicated facilities covering enforcement, intelligence gathering, training, victim care and research functions was established. The UK Human Trafficking Centre is an initiative led by the Association of Chief Police Officers and is a multi-agency centre involving academic experts, victim care organizations, the Crown Prosecution Service, the Serious and Organized Crime Agency and the Immigration and Nationality Directorate, as well as experienced police officers.

International responses to human trafficking and the development of state policies and specific anti-trafficking initiatives also reflect conflicting agendas and priorities raised by this issue. While there is obvious concern to protect victims and to prevent a range of trafficking harms, states tend to conflate trafficking control with asylum and migration control. Official discourses of a 'war' against human trafficking tend to regard all those who cross borders without authorization as a threat to state sovereignty and national security, and have generally led to tighter border controls, the extension of quasi-judicial functions to civil regulatory agencies and, increasingly, punitive measures of policing, detention and exclusion. Many of these sanctions and intensified enforcement practices have been highly contentious and ineffective and, arguably, only serve to return trafficked persons to the same conditions from which they originally fled or to push a greater percentage of human traffic into more hazardous journeys or into the hands of exploitative criminal groups.

Maggy Lee

Related entries

Corruption (police); Organized crime; Prostitution; Transnational policing.

Key texts and sources

Bales, K. (2005) *Understanding Global Slavery: A Reader*. Berkeley, CA: University of California Press.

Di Nicola, A. (2005) 'Trafficking in human beings and smuggling of migrants', in P. Reichel (ed.) *Handbook of Transnational Crime and Justice*. Thousand Oaks, CA: Sage.

Kempadoo, K. (ed.) (2005) *Trafficking and Prostitution Reconsidered: New Perspectives on Migration, Sex Work, and Human Rights*. Boulder, CO: Paradigm Publishers.

Kyle, D. and Koslowski, R. (2001) *Global Human Smuggling – Comparative Perspectives*. Baltimore, MD: Johns Hopkins University Press.

Salt, J. (2000) 'Trafficking and human smuggling: a European perspective', *International Migration*, 38: 31–56.

Weber, L. and Bowling, B. (2004) 'Policing migration: a framework for investigating the regulation of global mobility', *Policing and Society*, 14: 195–212.

See also the Home Office's human trafficking action plan (**http://www.homeoffice.gov.uk/documents/ human-traffick-action-plan**) and the website of Anti-slavery, an organization concerned with modern-day slavery (**http://www.antislavery.org/ index.htm**).

IDENTITY THEFT

> Identity theft is a broad label used to describe the assumption of the legal identify of another person, living or dead, done on either a temporary or permanent basis. Although it has come to be viewed as synonymous with financial fraud, the wrong that characterizes identity theft is the impersonation of another, irrespective of the purpose that motivates the fraudster.

Identity theft has emerged in the public consciousness as a pressing and prevalent social problem in recent years and has come to be seen as synonymous with financial fraud. The prototypical construction involves the theft or cloning of a credit card that is used by the fraudster to make unauthorized purchases that are attributed to the account holder. There are variations that involve the use of identity information to open a new credit card account or to obtain a loan, but the central theme of the popular perception is firmly based on financial gain.

The essence of the problem is that identity theft has come to be seen as a two-stage process: the initial stage is the acquisition of the identity of another person, and this is followed by the commission of an unlawful act while using that identity. There are two problems with this two-stage conceptualization of identity theft. First, it sees the appropriation of another's identity as a means to an end, and this focuses attention on the end result – i.e. the outcome achieved while using a false identity as the essence of the harm involved in identity theft. This renders the actual assumption of another's identity as an invisible, almost peripheral, element of the overall problem. The second problem with the prototypical construction is that it creates an erroneous expectation that the wrongful act will involve fraudulent financial transactions.

Although a significant percentage of fraudsters are motivated by financial gain, many are driven by other, equally compelling, motivations. The cloak of anonymity offered by the assumption of another's identity offers the impostor a broad range of criminogenic opportunities, as it allows the consequences of one's actions to be attributed to another person. There is a range of situations in which an offender has used the name of another person in order to divert responsibility for his or her criminal wrongdoing. A common example is the acquisition of a 'spare' identity for driving, particularly popular in the light of the relatively recent proliferation of speed cameras as a means of avoiding the penalties associated with the contravention of road traffic legislation.

In addition to the misuse of identity for criminal ends, there are further examples that demonstrate the assumption of another's identity as a means to improve a tainted or otherwise unsatisfactory identity. Here, the assumption of the alternative identity is permanent – the impostor lives life as the victim – and so often involves the appropriation of a dead person's identity. One such example is the assumption of the identity of Christopher Buckingham (who died in childhood) by an as yet unknown man who adopted this identity in order to pass himself off as the Earl of Buckingham, a title which fell into misuse in 1689.

Despite its seemingly inextricable association with financial fraud, the true locus of the harm in identity theft lies in the misappropriation of the identity of another, living or dead, irrespective of the purpose for which it was assumed. However, until the misconceptions that surround identity theft are dispersed, understanding of the problem will remain incomplete, and this will operate as an impediment to understanding the problem and, consequently, to its prevention and the formulation of detection strategies.

Emily Finch

Related entries

Cybercrimes; Fraud and policing; Human rights; Transnational policing.

Key texts and sources

Finch, E. (2003) 'What a tangled web we weave: identity theft and the Internet', in Y. Jewkes (ed.) *dot.cons: Crime, Deviance and Identity on the Internet.* Cullompton: Willan Publishing.
Finch, E. (2006) 'Stolen identity and the Internet', in Y. Jewkes (ed.) *Crime Online.* Cullompton: Willan Publishing.
The government's crime reduction toolkit for identity theft is available online at **http://www.crimereduction.gov.uk/theft1.htm**. See also the Home Office's identity theft web page (**http://www.identity-theft.org.uk/**).

INDEPENDENT ADVISORY GROUPS

Independent advisory groups are mechanisms through which citizens advise the Police Service on policy and operational practice in 'critical incidents'.

It is axiomatic that police legitimacy and policing 'by consent' rest on accountability. Independent advisory groups are one mechanism through which the police can account to local communities, in an 'explanatory and co-operative' sense (Marshall 1987), by providing a way for engaged and active citizens to advise on police practice.

During the Stephen Lawrence Inquiry, the police were criticized for having inadequate local measures to consult with communities – especially those from ethnic minorities – in much the same way that the Scarman Inquiry concluded that a cause of the Brixton riots was a failure of police–public communication. While Scarman

led to the creation of community police consultative groups, independent advisory groups emerged in the aftermath of Lawrence.

The first such group – initially named the Lay Advisory Group – was formed by the Metropolitan Police Racial and Violent Crime Task Force a few months prior to the publication of the Stephen Lawrence Inquiry to advise on the implementation of 'anti-racist policing' measures and live investigations into racist murders and other 'critical incidents' (e.g. David Copeland's 1999 nail-bombing campaign). Inviting the Metropolitan Police's 'sternest critics' into the inner world of Scotland Yard to engage with police attempts to reform its operational response to London's diverse communities was a bold move that brought about organizational change in such spheres as the response to racist violence.

When Operation Trident was set up by the Metropolitan Police in 2000 to respond to gun crime in London's black communities, an independent advisory group was established. Trident provides oversight and monitoring of operations, conducts monthly case reviews in murder inquiries, liaises with victims' families and maintains links between local communities and the police. Local Trident groups have been established in Hackney, Haringey, Lambeth, Brent and Southwark.

HM Inspectorate of Constabulary stimulated the nationwide development of independent advisory groups following its favourable assessment of them in the inspection report, *Policing London: Winning Consent*, in 2000 and later by including the 'good use of IAG [independent advisory group] advice in strategic planning and tactical operations' in its baseline assessment of police forces. By 2004, four out of five police forces had established a force-wide independent advisory group, seven in ten had groups at a divisional (basic command unit) level and two thirds had one for specific operations (Foster *et al.* 2005).

There is a strong view among senior police officers and independent advisory group members that such groups have improved consultation at a strategic level. However, it remains unclear how these groups fit with other structures of police accountability and consultation, such as community police consultative groups, community safety partnerships and local police authorities. Independent advisory groups also struggle to retain their independence, to avoid conflicts of interest and to avoid 'burn out' suffered by community members advising on high-profile cases.

Ben Bowling

Related entries

Accountability and governance; Criminal investigation; Stephen Lawrence Inquiry.

Key texts and sources

HMIC (2000) *Policing London: Winning Consent.* London: HMIC.
Marshall, G. (1987) 'Police accountability revisited', reprinted in T. Newburn (ed.) (2004) *Policing: Key Readings.* Cullompton: Willan Publishing.

INDEPENDENT POLICE COMPLAINTS COMMISSION (IPCC)

The Independent Police Complaints Commission (IPCC) is responsible for overseeing the handling of complaints against the police in England and Wales, with the ability to undertake its own investigations into incidents where police misconduct may have occurred.

Created by the Police Reform Act 2002, the Independent Police Complaints Commission (IPCC) came into operation in April 2004. Headed by a chair, deputy chair and 15 commissioners, the IPCC is a 'non-departmental public body', which allows it to function independently from government, the police, interest groups and political parties. Its responsibilities cover all 43 'Home Office' police forces, as well as non-territorial forces, such as the British Transport Police, the Ministry of Defence Police and the Serious Organized Crime Agency.

The IPCC has stronger powers than the Police Complaints Board (1977–85) and the Police Complaints Authority (1985–2004). A key power requires police forces to refer all cases to the IPCC which are of a particular level of severity. This includes complaints or incidents involving deaths, serious injuries, assault or corruption. Police forces can also make voluntary referrals, and the IPCC has the power to 'call in' specific cases where, for example, there are particular public concerns. The IPCC then assesses the circumstances of each case and decides on one of the following forms of investigation:

- *Independent investigations*: conducted by IPCC staff into incidents with a high level of public concern, the potential to impact on communities or serious implications for the reputation of the police.
- *Managed investigations*: conducted by the police under the direction of the IPCC. The IPCC sets the terms of reference for the investigation, approves the choice of lead investigator and manages the investigation.
- *Supervised investigations*: conducted by the police with the IPCC agreeing the terms of reference, the investigation plan and the choice of lead investigator.
- *Local investigations*: conducted when the IPCC decides that the case has a low level of seriousness or public interest, and the police have the necessary resources and experience to carry out an investigation without external assistance.

During its first year of operation, the IPCC initiated 31 independent investigations, 126 managed investigations and 598 supervised investigations, and it referred back 684 cases to be dealt with locally by police forces.

The IPCC also has responsibility for a range of other activities. Under the Police Reform Act 2002, complainants have the right of appeal to the IPCC if they are dissatisfied with the way in which their complaint was handled by the police. The IPCC also has responsibility for judging applications from police forces who consider no action should be taken about a complaint. These 'dispensations' may be granted for a number of reasons, including when a complaint is deemed to be vexatious or repetitious.

Police forces also apply to the IPCC when they wish to end an investigation that has not been fully completed. Applications for 'discontinuance' may occur when a complainant will no longer co-operate with investigators. In the IPCC's first operational year it dealt with 1,033 appeals, 4,737 dispensations and agreed to 70 investigations being discontinued.

Beyond its operational responsibilities, the IPCC has a wider role. The Police Reform Act 2002 places a responsibility on the IPCC to increase and maintain public confidence in the police complaints system. This 'guardianship function' has been defined to include setting standards for the complaints system, promoting confidence in it, ensuring access and feeding back learning (IPCC 2005). In practice there is a great deal of overlap between guardianship and operational activities, such as investigations and appeals. For example, lessons may emerge from investigations that need to feed back to police forces.

It is important to note that the central focus of the IPCC is on *police misconduct*. Many of the IPCC's investigations examine incidents where there has been no complaint about the police. Examples here would include deaths in police custody, fatal shootings and fatal car chases. Furthermore, the IPCC does not deal with public complaints about the general operational policy of police forces. These 'direction and control' matters are handled locally by the police. Examples may include complaints about a lack of officers conducting foot patrols in a neighbourhood or the length of time officers are expected to take to attend particular incidents.

Concerns about the handling of police complaints date back to at least the 1959 Royal Commission on the Police. Central to these has been the issue of whether an independent element should exist with regard to the handling of police complaints and, if so, what it should look like. The Police Complaints Board, Police Complaints Authority and the IPCC all mark the growth of this independent element. They also reflect a wider process of reform leading to greater civilian oversight, which has been occurring across western societies over the last 25 years (see Goldsmith 1991). However, with serious complaints and allegations of misconduct *about* the police still being investigated *by* the police, the IPCC's predecessors faced questions about credibility and public confidence. The need for reform reached a critical point in the late 1990s with the parliamentary Home Affairs Committee (1997) and, most significantly, the inquiry into the death of Stephen Lawrence (Macpherson 1999) both recommending that investigations should be made independent of the police.

While the creation of the IPCC was a direct response to those recommendations, it remains to be seen whether debates about how to deal with police complaints and misconduct will recede. In 2004–5 there were 22,898 complaints made against the police (Gleeson and Bucke 2006). Yet fewer than 100 officers received either a misconduct sanction or a criminal conviction. Such a differential is likely to continue to stimulate debate between complainant representatives, police forces and police staff associations about how proportionate the complaints system is and what an efficient and fair system should look like.

Tom Bucke

Related entries

Accountability and governance; Corruption (police); Deaths in police custody (DPCs); Police Reform Act 2002.

Key texts and sources

Gleeson, E. and Bucke, T. (2006) *Police Complaints: Statistics for England and Wales, 2004/05*. London: IPCC.

Goldsmith, A. (1991) *Complaints against the Police: The Trend to External Review*. Oxford: Clarendon Press.

Home Affairs Committee (1997) *Police Disciplinary and Complaints Procedures (First Report)*. London: HMSO.

IPCC (2005) *Annual Report, 2004/05*. London: IPCC.

The IPCC's website is at **www.ipcc.gov.uk**.

INSTITUTIONAL RACISM

> 'The collective failure of an organisation, to provide an appropriate and professional service to people because of their colour, culture, or ethnic origin... [Institutional racism] can be seen or detected in processes, attitudes and behaviour which amount to discrimination through unwitting prejudice, ignorance, thoughtlessness and racist stereotyping which disadvantage minority ethnic people' (Macpherson 1999: 28).

The notion of institutional racism raises fundamental, analytical questions for social science and, therefore, for its application to the police. We are used to thinking about individuals acting but not institutions. Individuals are conscious: they can reason, change their minds and act in ways that have a deliberate or unintended effect on others, including racial discrimination. We can identify the outcomes of individual action and, if needs be, measure them. Institutions seem to be different and elusive when we assess them against these criteria.

Furthermore, the notion of 'racism' is contested: it infers that people (and institutions) discriminate negatively on the grounds of race, but other criteria (demeanour, skin colour, custom, social class, for example) may be as or more relevant. For example, how can we know if 'race' is the major criterion used when an institution acts? And when it is said that institutional racism is evident in an organization, will this impact differently on different groups, depending on how particular groups are defined in terms of 'race' (Williams 1985)?

The origins of this concept lie in the USA in the work of the political activists, Stokely Carmichael and Charles V. Hamilton (1986). They argued that the social structure of American society (and therefore by definition, its police) is ordered to facilitate the dominance of white Americans and, logically, the absolute subordination of their black peers. The underlying view is of a zero-sum power game that blacks cannot win. Further, it assumes that all black people have the same interests and, indeed, it brings together different people (south Asians, Afro-Caribbeans, and Arabs, for example) into a political unity. That appearance of cohesion may, of course, betray fundamental diversity. A key point of Carmichael and Hamilton's view is that, if American society is of the order described, its police and all other institutions *must* be institutionally racist.

Two major watersheds in English policing have provoked discussion about institutional racism. These were Lord Scarman's report about the disturbances in Brixton, London, in 1981 and, more recently, Justice Macpherson's report about the Stephen Lawrence murder (Scarman 1981; Macpherson 1999).

Scarman rejected the notion that English society and, by definition, its police, is an example of institutional racism. For him, institutional racism required the policies and related practices of English civil society and, therefore, of the London Metropolitan Police Service, to be explicitly discriminatory, to the clear disadvantage of an ethnic group. He could not find any such intention and therefore rejected the idea that the Metropolitan Police Service was institutionally racist. Put another way, to uphold the allegation of institutional racism, Scarman would have had to find the policies and practices of the Metropolitan Police to be similar to those of the South African police during the period of apartheid. There was an open intention to discriminate on the ground of race in this context.

Macpherson took a very different view. He defined institutional racism as:

The collective failure of an organisation to provide an appropriate and professional service to people because of their colour, culture, or ethnic origin. It can be seen or detected in processes, attitudes and behaviour which amount to discrimination through unwitting prejudice, ignorance, thoughtlessness and racist stereotyping which disadvantage minority ethnic people
(1999: 28).

Note how many facets of institutional racism are included here. They have made the precise identification of racism rather difficult, not least because any differential outcome of police action for an ethnic or culturally based minority can be evidence of institutional racism when placed within Macpherson's schema. Macpherson's definition lacks precision. In the light of these considerable difficulties, it is interesting that the government and the Association of Chief Police Officers accepted without question Macpherson's view that the police was an example of institutional racism. This signals us to the symbolic, political connotations of the notion.

Apart from the definitional problems posed by Macpherson, research has indicated that there are widely differing interpretations of institutional racism in constabularies (Foster *et al.* 2005; Holdaway and O'Neill 2005). Some officers, for example, have understood it to mean that all individuals are racists, which is precisely not what it means. Others have focused on differential outcomes of policy that disadvantage minority ethnic groups, thus neglecting processes that lead to the outcomes. And others have viewed it as a reflection of wider structures of racism in English society, therefore failing to consider the occupational culture that mediates wider structural constraints. As far as policy is concerned, it has encouraged officers to look simultaneously in opposite directions. 'Race' discrimination is concerned with ethnic minorities' common experience within an institution; cultural discrimination is concerned with their diverse experiences. Institutional racism cannot be both.

The basic question is: 'How does an institution act?' Drawing on Richard Jenkins' (1996) view that institutions 'are emergent products of what people do as much as they are constitutive of what people do', Holdaway (1999) has suggested that an analysis of institutional racism should focus on officers' taken-for-granted actions and related assumptions about how one performs police work. This relates institutional action to the occupational culture of the police. To argue that the police is an example of institutional racism is to say that the routine, taken-for-granted views, values and related actions of officers include racially prejudicial and, at times, discriminatory actions, and, crucially, that such views are embedded in the occupational culture, which mediates wider societal structures of race inequality.

Simon Holdaway

Related entries

Black police associations; Community and race relations; Hate crime; Police culture; Racially motivated offending; Racial profiling; Scarman Inquiry; Stephen Lawrence Inquiry.

Key texts and sources

Holdaway, S. (1999) 'Understanding the police investigation of the murder of Stephen Lawrence: a mundane sociological analysis', *Sociological Research Online*, 4(1).
Holdaway, S. and O'Neill, M. (2005) 'Institutional racism after Macpherson: an analysis of police views', *Policing and Society*, 16: 349–69.
Williams, J. (1985) 'Redefining institutional racism', *Ethnic and Racial Studies*, 8: 323–48.
See also the Home Office's web page on police equality and diversity (http://www.homeoffice.gov.uk/police/about/police-equality/).

INTELLIGENCE ANALYSIS (PREVIOUSLY CRIME ANALYSIS)

Analysis is the process of collecting, reviewing and interpreting a range of data and making inferences and recommendations. Intelligence analysts use defined analytical techniques to identify and explain patterns of crime and incidents and to infer who might be responsible. Analysis supports strategic decision-making and the tactical deployment of resources to prevent crime, and to detect and disrupt criminal activity.

Analytical techniques have been used in policing for many years. However, specifically employed intelligence analysts have been supporting UK law enforcement only since the late 1980s. Intelligence analysts now work in all police forces and partner agencies, including the Serious Organized Crime Agency, HM Revenue and Customs and the UK Immigration Service. Analysts are also employed locally in crime and disorder reduction partnerships. Further, many telecommunications companies and the finance industry use analytical skills and techniques to analyse an increasingly wide variety of information.

Worldwide, analysts are variously described as crime analysts, intelligence analysts and criminal intelligence analysts. In the USA this has led to two quite distinct professions. In the UK, however, the terms have not been divisive and, together with common occupational standards and a limited, easily identifiable community, have led to an increasingly cohesive profession. The majority of police analysts are deployed locally in basic command units. There are, further, increasing numbers of analysts employed regionally and in specialist departments, including special branch, road policing and major incident investigation units.

Intelligence analysts work to the intelligence cycle, which is widely used in UK law enforcement to understand and develop the continuous process of information management, analysis and tasking. The stages of the cycle are direction, collection, collation, evaluation, analysis, dissemination and back to direction, which is the tasking stage of the process and directly links to tasking and co-ordination as defined in the National Intelligence Model (NIM). Tasking and co-ordination is a decision-making mechanism for the management of policing business, both strategically and tactically. The mechanism uses the assessment of local policing issues to define priorities and to allocate resources. Collection covers the focused gathering of information from a wide variety of sources to support the tasking, and collation is the organization of that material so that it is secure and searchable and can be easily retrieved. These parts of the process, together with dissemination, are controlled by a nationally mandated *Management of Police Information Code.*

Collected information is then evaluated with regard to the initial task and the information already available. The risk of using the information in relation to the source, the likely 'truth' of the information and any restrictions on its use are also assessed. The analysis part of the process identifies premises and draws conclusions and inferences from the information, making recommendations for further data collection, reduction opportunities or enforcement activity. These findings are usually disseminated in written form, but may include a verbal briefing and may be supported by charts and maps. The outcome of the cycle may lead to further tasking in response to the findings and, as such, the cycle is a continuous process.

The basic premise on which intelligence analysis is based is unchanged and has been understood by policing for many years – that crime is not a random event and that people are predictable in their habits and behaviours. With this in mind, the most fundamental analytical technique is crime pattern analysis. This uses crime and incident data to identify patterns. These patterns may be trends – the changing nature of crime and incidents, which repeat over time. A pattern is, therefore, to some degree a predictable series of crimes or incidents that are linked by a common element. This pattern may suggest these crimes or incidents are committed by the same individual or group of individuals in a geographically defined area (hotspot) that is victim to a disproportionately high level of crime or incidents. Problem-solving responses can then be focused on this area.

For a crime or incident to occur, an offender and a suitable target must come together in a specific location and a number of decisions must be made by a potential offender in relation to the opportunity (such as the desirability of a particular commodity or the likelihood of being caught). These three elements (victim, offender and location), form the points of the problem analysis triangle, which focuses responses in each of these areas. By analysing the incident or crime information and gaining a clearer understanding of the problem, responses may, for example, be focused on the location in which an offence occurred and the recommendation made that street-lighting be improved. Victim-focused responses may recommend that the public are warned to lock their vehicles when parked in this location, and offender-focused recommendations might be to identify the perpetrator and to remove his of her motivation to commit such offences.

Crime pattern analysis underpins the majority of the work of the analyst, but techniques have been developed to describe and assess the criminal market and business, criminal communications and associations, and the environmental context in which crime and incidents occur. The analytical process will first identify what is and is not known about an individual or problem using the questions what, where, when, how, who and why (known as the five WH). This may be supported by collating the gathered information in chart form. For example a timeline may show how events are linked over time, and an association chart may identify networks of individuals or organizations graphically by showing the links between them. Inferences are then made by the analyst (hypotheses, predictions, estimations or conclusions) that aim to go beyond the facts to explain what might be occurring. As such, the analytical process is both logical and progressive.

The outcomes of analysis support the development of intelligence products by the local or departmental intelligence unit. These products are used to inform immediate and long-term decision-making in relation to policy and resource allocation and to inform directly ongoing operations related to an individual or group of individuals, or to a specific priority issue. Intelligence products are also defined elements of the NIM.

As well as sophisticated graphical and mapping software, analysts use crime and intelligence management databases, spreadsheet packages and other task-specific software and, therefore, require advanced IT skills. Analysts are also typically curious and confident individuals. The specific skills required are identified in the National Occupational Standards, alongside the other standard law enforcement roles.

Kate Pearce

Related entries

Compstat; Crime mapping; Geographical information systems (GIS); Geographic(al) profiling; National Intelligence Model (NIM); Terrorism.

Key texts and sources

ACPO (2005) *Guidance on the National Intelligence Model.* Wyboston: NCPE.
Fisher, A. (2001) *Critical Thinking: An Introduction.* Cambridge: Cambridge University Press.
Osbourne, D. and Wernicke, S. (2003) *Introduction to Crime Analysis: Basic Resources for Criminal Justice Practice.* New York, NY: Haworth Press.
Ratcliffe, J. (ed.) (2004) *Strategic Thinking in Criminal Intelligence.* Cullompton: Willan Publishing.

INTELLIGENCE-LED POLICING

Intelligence-led policing aims to reduce crime through the informed direction of enforcement agencies. Information is collected from a variety of sources, to produce 'intelligence'. This is then used to direct the activities of enforcement agencies in ways that enable them to disrupt, disable or undermine criminal behaviour.

Intelligence has a very long history in the prevention of crime and terrorist behaviour. An early English example comes from the Gunpowder Plot of 1606. Among the Roman Catholic dissidents at the time who were planning to blow up Parliament and thereby assassinate King James and his Protestant government was one informant (whose name is still uncertain) who wrote to Lord Monteagle to advise him not to attend Parliament on 5 November, saying:

> *I would advise you…to devise some excuse to shift of your attendance of this Parliament, for God and man hath concurred to punish the wickedness of this time. And think not slightly of this advertisement but retire yourself into your country, where you may expect the event in safety, for though there be no appearance of any stir, yet I say they shall receive a terrible blow, the Parliament, and yet they shall not see who hurts them.*

Lord Monteagle showed the letter, which he received ten days before the explosion was planned, to Robert Cecil, who was the Secretary of State. Following this the Privy Council, the relevant authority at the time, eventually decided to search the vaults under the Houses of Parliament where they found the gunpowder and Guy Fawkes. The plot was thwarted and the crime/terrorist act prevented. Though in this case the information became available fortuitously rather than from covert activities of any kind, the remainder of the story illustrates well the principles of intelligence-led policing: the intelligent use of information received to work out what might be happening in ways that would allow the enforcement authorities to act to pre-empt the threat.

The tragic events of 9/11 in 2001 spurred the Americans to embrace intelligence-led policing mainly in the interests of forestalling terrorist acts, as had been achieved successfully in England in November 1606. The American enforcement authorities are now being urged to collect intelligence from a variety of sources, including the community as well as covert ones, to build accounts of potential threats in order that they can be forestalled by informed targeted activity. Local intelligence is collated and passed upwards for processing to inform the work of the security services.

The actual term 'intelligence-led policing' originated in Kent Police in England in the early 1990s. The idea was not to identify threats to national security and to deal with them; rather, it was to reduce the routine volume crimes that had been on a long-term upward trajectory. Kent Police believed that the collection and analysis of information on offenders and their associates could inform targeted enforcement activities that would prevent criminal behaviour by disrupting it. Since that time intelligence-led policing has become influential, not just on policing in the UK but also globally.

Though, as already noted, it was the events of 9/ll that spurred the Americans to believe they needed to improve their intelligence capabilities at all levels in the interests of improving homeland security. The Americans have also recognized, following the Kent model, that this may be a way of countering local crime activities. Likewise, the language and methods of intelligence-led policing have been taken up in other countries too (for example, Australia, Canada and parts of western Europe).

Intelligence-led policing enjoys a high level of surface plausibility. If offenders can be caught, disrupted in their activities or incapacitated, their ability to offend will be stifled. The Gunpowder Plot example serves to illustrate this. Generalizing the intelligence-led approach to policing, in which overall preventive effects can be expected and demonstrated, is, however, problematic. There are few examples where the outcomes are as clear as those achieved in 1606. One recent British case that came to court in 2007 relates to plans by a group of Islamic extremists to detonate a large fertilizer-based bomb, which were thwarted following fairly large-scale intelligence operations using a variety of covert means to track the offenders, link them and assemble the evidence required to bring those involved to justice at a point where the plans were so far advanced that the size and nature of the major crime event forestalled were obvious. It is clear that many lives will have been saved. Statistical evidence of the overall beneficial effects in relation to more routine offending has, however, been harder to find.

Intelligence failures are more conspicuous than successes, of course. The covert nature of criminal and terrorist behaviour, the need to build plausible pictures on the basis of limited information, the inevitable ceiling to the resources available to check on and follow up leads and the absence of public debate to help probe and correct misconceptions all clearly mean that there are substantial risks of intelligence errors. In addition to this, smarter criminals and terrorist groups may well be involved in systematic efforts to disinform the authorities.

The National Intelligence Model is the major vehicle through which intelligence-led policing is being delivered in the UK. As with the versions of intelligence-led policing being developed in the USA and Australia, this incorporates elements of problem-oriented policing and community policing. These have rather different histories and rationales from intelligence-led policing. They are associated with more broadly based preventive strategies, which may include social and situational methods as well as enforcement, depending on analytic findings relating to a specific presenting problem. These approaches to policing also require the involvement of non-enforcement organizations and community bodies, as well as enforcement agencies.

Nick Tilley

Related entries

Community policing; Compstat; Covert policing; Criminal investigation; Entrapment; Fraud and policing; National Intelligence Model (NIM); Neighbourhood policing; Problem-oriented policing; Serious Organized Crime Agency (SOCA); Tasking and co-ordinating groups (TCGs).

Key texts and sources

Audit Commission (1993) *Helping with Enquiries: Tackling Crime Effectively.* London: HMSO.

Bureau of Justice Assistance (2005) *Intelligence-led Policing: The New Intelligence Architecture.* Washington, DC: US Department of Justice.

Ratcliffe, J. (2003) *Intelligence-led Policing: Trends and Issues in Crime and Criminal Justice.* Canberra: Australian Institute of Criminology.

Tilley, N. (2003) 'Community policing, problem-oriented policing and intelligence-led policing', in T. Newburn (ed.) *Handbook of Policing.* Cullompton: Willan Publishing.

See also Association of Chief Police Officers' *Guidance on the National Intelligence Model* (http://www.acpo.police.uk/asp/policies/Data/nim2005.pdf) for a business model based on intelligence-led policing.

INTERAGENCY POLICING

Interagency policing refers to partnership arrangements that generate internal organizational change and collaboration aimed at providing social control, maintaining security and achieving community safety (Crawford 1998). These partnership arrangements exist between private, public and voluntary organizations and the community.

During the 1980s, the Conservative government placed a clear responsibility for the increasing crime rate squarely on the shoulders of the Police Service. This era represented a period when the police were focused fundamentally on crime fighting and reactive policing (Newburn 2002). The lack of effective partnership practice with other agencies was reflected in the 1991 Morgan Report that argued for a lead agency to co-ordinate efforts, with the creation of local structures on a statutory basis. This report generated interest and change in local authorities and was an important framework for the Crime and Disorder Act 1998. This Act provided the legislative backing necessary to ensure that local authorities and the Police Service worked in partnership with public, private and voluntary agencies to avoid the lack of direction and impact that partnership arrangements had experienced in the past. It was this legislation that underpinned partnership working by placing statutory responsibility on local authorities and the Police Service to design, implement and evaluate strategies aimed at reducing crime and disorder (Home Office 1991). When Labour was elected in 1997, the Crime and Disorder Act 1998 signalled a clear change in strategy, focusing on proactive partnerships aimed not just at crime but also at the causes of crime.

The rationale behind interagency approaches argues that the police cannot have sole responsibility for crime and that the resources and intelligence from a range of agencies can be pooled together and used more effectively (Phillips 2002). This information can be used for evidence-based practice, to identify the best agency to address particular challenges and to create what the government has termed 'joined up' thinking (Home Office 2001a). The chief officer and local authority are tasked with designing and implementing short and long-term policies aimed at crime reduction. The tensions of the past, however, have not been totally eradicated: working in partnership is difficult because of the conflicts created by a clash of organizational cultures and because of power relations between agencies (Newburn 2002). This conflict of organizational goals has also been heightened due to the introduction of new public management, bureaucracy and performance targets (Newburn 2002). Agencies have targets that are generated by the Home Office and their own organization, in addition to joint agency goals that need to be achieved (Home Office 2001a). Therefore, although interagency policing is developing partnership collaboration and working arrangements between agencies, there are still significant barriers to achieving further improvements. The creation of common goals, the use of seconded staff and appropriate resources are some of the challenges that need to be resolved for interagency partnerships to achieve their true potential (Rogers 2006).

Steve Tong

Related entries

Best value; Crime and Disorder Act 1998; Crime reduction; New public management (NPM); Police performance indicators.

Key texts and sources

Crawford, A. (1998) *Crime Prevention and Community Safety: Politics, Policies and Practices*. London: Longman.

Newburn, T. (2002) 'Community safety and policing: some implications of the Crime and Disorder Act 1998', in G. Hughes *et al.* (eds) *Crime Prevention and Community Safety: New Directions*. London: Sage.

Phillips, C. (2002) 'From voluntary to statutory status', in G. Hughes *et al.* (eds) *Crime Prevention and Community Safety: New Directions*. London: Sage.

Rogers, C. (2006) *Crime Reduction Partnerships*. Oxford: Oxford University Press.

INTERNATIONAL ASSOCIATION OF CHIEFS OF POLICE (IACP)

The International Association of Chiefs of Police (IACP) is a USA-based association of chiefs of police, predominantly representing the chiefs of US police forces. It has a long history of seeking to foster the development of policing and police practice in the USA and beyond.

Founded in 1893, the International Association of Chiefs of Police's (IACP) goals are:

to advance the science and art of police services; to develop and disseminate improved administrative, technical and operational practices and promote their use in police work; to foster police cooperation and the exchange of information and experience among police administrators throughout the world; to bring about recruitment and training in the police profession of qualified persons; and to encourage adherence of all police officers to high professional standards of performance and conduct

(www.iacp.org).

The IACP has several thousand members from the police chiefs across the USA and a substantial membership across the world.

In the USA, the IACP has been influential in developing and disseminating policing practice in a number of ways. Its *Police Chief* magazine is key reading material for the 14,000 or so police chiefs from the huge range of departments across the states. It has been involved, with the Federal Bureau of Investigation, in the development of standards for areas such as fingerprint identification, crime scene investigation, unified crime recording and the use of force. It provides training programmes and access to web-based materials. Its conferences are a key part of the annual cycle of business for US police chiefs in somewhat the same way as the Association of Chief Police Officers' conferences are for the UK.

The IACP has been influential in the UK and outside the USA in a number of ways. First, its annual conference has, at various times, attracted key UK-based and European senior officers seeking to learn from developing practice in the USA. Key examples of this were the spread of 'policing by objectives' in the early 1980s and problem-oriented policing in the late 1980s and 1990s. The latter was also influenced by the Police Executive Research Forum, which represents primarily the larger USA police departments and which runs its 'Town hall forums' at the IACP's conferences. The IACP has also been influential through its training programmes, notably on police ethics and on the police use of force. It was the IACP that developed the standards for the use and deployment of the TASER (the electrical stun weapon that has been deployed in a number of jurisdictions, including the UK, as a less lethal weapon). The IACP's guidance has been widely borrowed as 'good practice'.

However, it is important not to overstate the USA influence on UK policing. Even with the TASER guidance, there has been a clear recognition in the UK that USA guidance in this area comes against a very different environment in the use of force. As Jones and Newburn (2007) have demonstrated, US to UK policy and practice transfer is much less substantial and more complex than is sometimes asserted.

Peter Neyroud

Related entries

Association of Chief Police Officers (ACPO); Police Executive Research Forum (PERF).

Key texts and sources

Jones, T. and Newburn, T. (2007) *Policy Transfer and Criminal Justice: Exploring US Influence over British Crime Control Policy.* Milton Keynes: Open University Press.

The IACP's website (**www.iacp.org**) is a good source on the IACP and on police practice generally.).

INTERNATIONAL POLICE CO-OPERATION

International police co-operation encompasses activities and structures designed to assist the police forces and agencies of different states to tackle criminality that crosses international borders more effectively. Such co-operation can also assist police professional development in the participating states.

It has always been recognized that some forms of criminality cannot be effectively tackled by national police services responding in isolation. Contemporary problems most frequently cited in this context are those of drug and people trafficking. Indeed, the problem of people trafficking led to an international conference in Paris as far back as 1902. That conference resulted in the 1904 International Agreement for the Suppression of White Slave Traffic. Initially signed by 12 European countries, its provisions were also recognized and adhered to by other countries, including the USA. The first real initiative to create an international police organization was taken at the First Congress of International Criminal Police in Monaco in 1914. However, despite its name, it was a meeting dominated by politicians and diplomats as opposed to police professionals. In 1923 the organization now known as Interpol was founded – the International Criminal Police Commission.

Operational international assistance is primarily concerned with establishing the means whereby intelligence can be exchanged and, where appropriate, exploited to a degree that results in criminals being put before the courts of the relevant jurisdiction. No one country or police service has a monopoly on professionalism or innovation, and truly professional services invariably seek to capitalize on the experience and expertise of other forces, regardless of national boundaries. Certain forces or agencies have historically been seen as setting the standard for others to aspire to, and the USA's Federal Bureau of Investigation (FBI), for example, has consciously sought to influence policing globally by a deliberate policy of outreach. Senior international police officials are encouraged to attend courses organized by the FBI. These courses not only foster friendships between international counterparts but they also encourage common approaches to particular problems.

It should be noted that police co-operation is not automatically or inherently a benign activity and that, historically, there have been examples of international police co-operation which have been designed to suppress political opposition. Interpol is today a respected and much used mechanism for police co-operation but, during the Second World War, it was subverted by Nazi Germany for its own purposes. International police co-operation must be governed by appropriate agreements and legal frameworks that provide for appropriate political oversight and adherence to ethical standards.

Paul Kernaghan

Related entries

Covert policing; Federal Bureau of Investigation (FBI); Human trafficking; Intelligence analysis (previously crime analysis); Interpol; National Intelligence Model (NIM); National security; Organized crime; Terrorism; Transnational policing.

Key texts and sources

Bresler, F. (1992) *Interpol.* London: Sinclair-Stevenson. See also the National Criminal Justice Reference Service's website (http//www.ncjrs.gov/policing/int63.htm).

INTERPOL

Interpol is an international force established in the early 1920s. It was originally known as the International Criminal Police Commission.

In the growing and increasingly complex terrain of international police co-operation, Interpol has the longest-standing arrangement. Originally established in Vienna in 1923 under the banner of the International Criminal Police Commission (ICPC), its membership has grown from 19 to 180 member countries. The ICPC all but ceased to exist over the course of the Second World War but was refounded in 1946 under a Belgian initiative and its headquarters relocated to Paris. In 1956, the commission's statutes formally changed its name to the 'International Criminal Police Organization – Interpol', or just Interpol as it is popularly known. Interpol's involvement in anti-terrorist activity was established in 1985 with the creation of a specialized group, the Public Safety and Terrorism Subdirectorate. Its structure was further rationalized by the creation of a separate European unit, the European Liaison Bureau, in the late 1980s.

Interpol was never intended as an operational police force. It was designed as a clearing-house for information and intelligence between participating police forces and as a network forum for senior officers or a 'policeman's club' (Anderson 1989: 43). Interpol's aims are summarized in Article 2 of its constitution:

(a) to ensure and promote the widest possible mutual assistance between all criminal police authorities within the limits of the laws existing in the different countries and in the spirit of the 'Universal Declaration of Human Rights';

(b) to establish and develop all institutions likely to contribute effectively to the prevention and suppression of ordinary law crimes

(cited in Hebenton and Thomas 1995: 64).

Under Article 5 of its constitution, the supreme governing body of Interpol is the General Assembly, comprising delegates appointed by each member country. The General Assembly meets annually and is responsible for all decisions related to policy, resources, working methods, finances and activities. A 13-member Executive Committee elected by the General Assembly meets three times a year to monitor policy decisions. Interpol's permanent presence is the General Secretariat, based since 1989 in Lyon. The offices are open round the clock, operating Interpol's Command and Co-ordination Centre, and they house officials from more than 80 countries. Each member country maintains a national central bureau (NCB). The NCBs act as the designated contact point for the General Secretariat, regional offices and other member countries requiring assistance with overseas investigations and the location and apprehension of fugitives (**www.interpol.int/public/icpo/ default.asp**).

Interpol currently has five priority crime areas: 1) fugitives; 2) public safety and terrorism; 3) drugs and organized crime; 4) trafficking in human beings; and 5) financial and hi-tech crime. Its core function is the circulation of information between NCBs on what are known as 'international notices' (colour coded as red, blue, green, yellow, black and orange).

Two major problems have generally been identified with Interpol. First, because of its perceived failing in tackling terrorist crime adequately in the 1970s, European states made other arrangements, notably the establishment of the Trevi group (the platform for the launch later of Europol). Secondly, there have been persistent concerns about the security and efficiency of Interpol's communications network. These have been allayed, if not entirely dispelled, by developments in information technology (for example, a new database, the Interpol Criminal Information System, in 1998 and, in 2002, the launch of the I-24/7 web-based communication system, improving access for member countries to Interpol's multiple databases).

Yet, despite improvements in organizational structure, Walker maintains that Interpol remains the 'paradigm case of an *inter*national police organisation' that has 'never challenged the statist prerogative in police operations and lacks the legal, symbolic and material resources to be anything other than parasitic on national police authorities' (2003: 117). Because of these restrictions, and in the light of wider developments, Interpol's predominance in the international policing scene has been largely superseded.

Mario Matassa

Related entries

Covert policing; Europol; International police co-operation; Transnational policing.

Key texts and sources

Anderson, M. (1989) *Policing the World: Interpol and the Politics of International Police Co-operation.* Oxford: Clarendon Press.

Hebenton, B. and Thomas, T. (1995) *Policing Europe: Co-operation, Conflict and Control.* London: Macmillan.

Walker, N. (2003) 'The pattern of transnational policing', in T. Newburn (ed.) *Handbook of Policing.* Cullompton: Willan Publishing.

Interpol's website is at **http://www.interpol.int/**.

INVESTIGATIVE INTERVIEWING

The investigative interviewing approach emphasizes the importance of gathering ethically as much reliable information as possible from interviewees (e.g. suspects) rather than coercing responses from them (e.g. confessions).

Until fairly recently, little was known about the quality of police interviews with suspects, witnesses and victims. Only 20 years ago was legislation brought in requiring that all police interviews with suspects be fully recorded (e.g. on audio tape) in England and Wales. What the tape recordings revealed in several studies published in the early 1990s was that most police officers were poor interviewers. The few studies that have been published regarding other countries' police interviewing (where tape recording is not usually required) have come to similar conclusions.

This general ineptitude should not be surprising. Such police officers had only received limited training in interviewing, and what training they did receive (if any) was not based on systematically acquired knowledge (e.g. research) of, and scientific theories about, human behaviour and the mind, but on anecdotes and professionals' varied opinions.

In England and Wales this lack of skill led to the publication of Home Office Circular 22/92 (*Principles for Investigative Interviewing* – see Williamson 2006: 153). It had became apparent that the police's former emphasis on interviewing suspects to obtain confessions had been a cause of problems. For example:

- Appeal courts had decided in some cases that confessions obtained in interrogations that were coercive could not be deemed reliable or voluntary and therefore that miscarriages of justice had occurred (and the relevant prison inmates were released).
- There had been many retractions of confessions once the interrogatory pressures were no longer present.
- There was a lack of information that could or could not corroborate some confessions.

Therefore, the circular recommended that the phrase 'investigative interviewing' from then on be adopted to emphasize that the main aim of police interviews with suspects is to gather reliable information (i.e. the same aim as for interviews with witnesses and victims).

The investigative interviewing approach emphasizes that quality information is likely to be obtained if:

- resources are purposely devoted to planning interviews properly and in fully preparing for them;
- the interviewee (e.g. a suspect) can be engaged in a meaningful conversation with the interviewer;
- the interviewee is enabled and encouraged in a way that complies with the law to provide his or her account of what took place/what he or she knows;
- challenges are then skilfully made concerning aspects of the account the suspect provides;
- an accurate and comprehensive review is provided by the interviewer at the end of each interview (or each part of a long interview) of what the interviewee has said so that errors and confusions can be cleared up and so that the interviewee knows he or she is being/has been listened to; and
- the interviews are formally and properly evaluated (electronically recording them makes such evaluation much more likely).

This approach has been devised for crimes the police routinely investigate and it notes that coercion is likely to cause reactance (i.e. those who may be willing to divulge information may decide not to because of the attempted coercion).

Ray Bull

Related entries

Criminal investigation; Forensic and investigative psychology.

Key texts and sources

Milne, R. and Bull, R. (1999) *Investigative Interviewing: Psychology and Practice.* Chichester: Wiley (a second edition is in preparation).

Williamson, T. (ed.) (2006) *Investigative Interviewing: Rights, Research and Regulation.* Cullompton: Willan Publishing.

J

'JUDGES' RULES'

> The 'Judges' Rules' provided guidance to police officers about conduct that was considered appropriate to the performance of their duties when questioning, detaining and arresting suspects.

The 'Judges' Rules' were originally introduced in 1912 by judges of the King's Bench Division. Periodically updated, the rules were last revised in 1964 as *Practice Note (Judges' Rules)* by judges of the Queen's Bench Division. In introducing this revised edition, Lord Parker said: 'These rules…are designed to secure … that only answers and statements which are voluntary are admitted in evidence against their maker and to provide guidance to police officers in the performance of their duties.' Appendix A, which was provided before this revised edition of the rules, included the principle:

> *(e) that it is a fundamental condition of the admissibility in evidence against any person, that it shall have been voluntary, in the sense that it has not been obtained from him by fear of prejudice or hope of advantage, exercised or held out by a person in authority, or by oppression.*

This principle was stated to be 'overriding and applicable in all cases', and 'Within that principle the Judges' Rules [are] put forward as a guide to police officers conducting investigations'. The rules have now been superseded by codes of practice that were introduced pursuant to the Police and Criminal Evidence Act 1984.

The rules were rules of practice for police officers and others involved in the questioning, detention and arrest of suspects. Although seen not as rules of law but only rules of conduct, failure to comply with the rules could result in evidence being deemed inadmissible (see *R* v. *May*). An example of procedural requirements is in relation to the caution. Rules II and III (now replaced by paras. 10 and 16 of Code C in the codes of practice) provided:

> II. *As soon as a police officer has evidence which would afford reasonable grounds for suspecting that a person has committed an offence, he shall caution that person or cause him to be cautioned before putting to him any questions, or further questions, relating to that offence…*
>
> III. *(a) Where a person is charged with or informed that he may be prosecuted for an offence he shall be cautioned…*
>
> *(b) It is only in exceptional cases that questions relating to the offence should be put to the accused person after he has been charged or informed that he may be prosecuted.*

The rules were of particular importance in relation to confession evidence. Any breach of the rules might, but would not necessarily, result in the confession being inadmissible on the basis that it was not provided voluntarily. The breach merely served to enable a submission to be made that judicial discretion be exercised and a confession that would otherwise be deemed admissible should be excluded. In reality, where a relatively minor technical breach of the rules occurred, the courts were reluctant to exclude the evidence. Further, if the breach did not directly relate to, or have an effect on, the issue of whether or not the confession was voluntary, the courts would allow the confession evidence. In *R* v. *Prager*, the Court of Appeal considered the rules within the broad obligation to consider the admissibility of evidence – in particular, confession evidence. Subsequently, judicial discretion was to be exercised acknowledging this broad obligation, taking account not only of any breach of the rules but also of any breach of the principles that accompanied the rules and relevant Home Office guidelines.

Larry Mead

Related entries

Caution; Evidence; Police and Criminal Evidence Act 1984 (PACE).

Key texts and sources

Halsbury's Laws of England (3rd edn). London: Butterworths (Vol. 10, 470–3, para. 86).
Practice Note (Judge's Rules) [1964] 1 WLR 152.

L

LEADERSHIP

> Leadership is the ability to influence and combine individuals and resources effectively to achieve objectives that would otherwise be impossible.

The Police Service is one of those rare organizations in which everyone from the newest recruit to the highest rank understands that, from the moment he or she chooses to serve, he or she accepts the leadership responsibility that goes along with this. This is particularly applicable to police officers who are formally responsible to society for upholding the law, but everyone in the Police Service, regardless of rank, grade or role, faces this leadership challenge and exercises leadership at one of five defined levels, each of which leads to the next.

Over the past 30 years, however, there have been regular concerns about police performance and police leadership, and also a number of attempts to improve quality in this area (some of the more notable criticisms include HMIC 1999b; Macpherson 1999). At the national level, a number of bodies have been established, including, in 2001, the Police Leadership Development Board. The increasing emphasis given to such issues could be seen in the National Policing Plan for 2003–6 (Home Office 2002c), which stated that '[s]trong police leadership [was] central to delivering improvements in police performance and therefore to reducing crime and the fear of crime'.

The definition of leadership above captures the essence of the whole model. It is not simply about the leader 'taking command'; nor is it about managing resources effectively and providing supervision. It combines both these things with the extra ability to influence others by deft of personality, by setting a positive example and by supporting others to help them deliver more than they might otherwise have felt capable of doing. It is a more 'democratic' style of leadership that involves the team in the decision-making process and that respects the views and abilities of others but that still provides the vision, drive and direction to harness this collective purpose towards common goals.

There is no single right way to 'do leadership'. The transformational style of leadership is *more likely* to result in a higher performing, better motivated team than other styles. This is a style that sees the role of leaders as being the development of the organization and the delivery of performance through motivating, stimulating and developing their teams to achieve goals. It is, in effect, a more democratic style of leading. The use of other styles of leadership, however, is of paramount importance if the leader is to be truly an 'all-round' effective leader. In that respect the *ability* to lead in a transformational way is paramount, but this must be coupled with a situational awareness and a knowledge of how other styles can be used effectively. Anyone who has been connected with policing knows that the role is one which, on occasions, necessitates rapid, decisive and, at times, robust command and control. There is no contradiction in being able to manage such a situation effectively and yet have a transformational style.

Ethical and effective police leadership must also embody the core values of personal awareness, personal integrity and a passion for achievement, as identified in the Police Leadership Qualities Framework. A new tool designed to help all police leaders to begin or to continue to become an effective leader, this provides an extension of the Integrated Competency Framework and it is the basis for a doctrine of British police leadership. It sets out what it is the

Police Service believes about leadership in terms of its constituent elements of styles, values, ethics, standards and competences, and it lays out what everyone, whether an operational leader or chief constable, should aspire to become as a means to improving police leadership.

Jenny Deere

Related entries

Association of Chief Police Officers (ACPO); Forensic and investigative psychology; Rank structure; Stephen Lawrence Inquiry; Training (police).

Key texts and sources

Gibson, A. and Villiers, P. (2006) *Leading for those we Serve – The Police Leadership Qualities Framework.* Bramshill: Centrex Leadership Academy for Policing.
HMIC (1999) *Managing Learning.* London: HMIC.

LEGITIMACY

In the policing context, legitimacy is the rightful exercise of authority or the rightful use of power.

Legitimacy is a key concept in political and social theory, bound up with power, authority and force. Legitimacy is associated with the rightful exercise of authority or the rightful use of power. In liberal democratic societies, those in authority, including the police, have valued the importance of legitimating their power. There are several reasons for this. First, the police exercise power over others – the state delegates to them the 'monopoly of the legitimate use of physical force' (Weber cited in Gerth and Wright Mills 1948: 78). This power is significant in its consequences for citizens, who can be deprived of their liberty. In liberal democracies, such power requires justification.

Secondly, to be effective, policing requires a measure of consent, and the legitimacy of the British police has traditionally been justified by claims of policing by consent, which was devel-

oped through the policies adopted by the founders of the 'New Police' in 1829 (Reiner 2000: ch. 2). Thirdly, the police play a role in the mediation of social conflict, which inheres in them a political role in that policing decisions and actions are 'concerned with the allocation of a significant public good' (Loader 1996: 37). In a democratic society, an institution fulfilling such roles must justify the trust placed in it and the powers delegated; the institution requires legitimation.

There is also a more prosaic reason why it benefits the police to seek legitimacy – namely, that if police power is legitimated, it facilitates the task of discharging policing functions. A police service which is accepted by the policed as just and rightful is more likely to have positive relations with communities and more likely to secure the co-operation and consent of citizens – this in itself can contribute to the effectiveness of policing. While it is clearly simplistic to equate effectiveness with legitimacy, there is a reciprocal connection between the two.

Police legitimacy is central to the study of policing and has been considered in relation to, *inter alia*, the legal and political arrangements for police accountability (Jefferson and Grimshaw 1984) and policing and democracy (Alderson 1984: chs. 12 and 13; Loader 1996). General discussions of police legitimacy tend to draw on Weberian influences of 'legal' legitimacy and a belief in the need for consent. Reiner (2000: 9), for example, argues that, for policing to be accepted as legitimate, 'the broad mass of the population, and possibly even some of those who are policed against, accept the authority, the lawful right, of the police to act as they do, even if disagreeing with or regretting some specific actions'. More specific studies have considered the multiple dimensions of police legitimacy. For example, Mawby (2002) examined police legitimacy using Beetham's (1991) framework, which analyses legitimacy through the criteria of 1) 'conformity to established rules'; 2) the existence of 'shared beliefs'; and 3) evidence of 'expressed consent'. Such an approach enables the capture of the complexity of police legitimacy.

Rob C. Mawby

Related entries

Bail; Ethics in policing; Force (police use of); Independent advisory groups; Models of policing; Public attitudes to the police.

Key texts and sources

Mawby, R.C. (2002) *Policing Images: Policing, Communication and Legitimacy.* Cullompton: Willan Publishing.

Reiner, R. (2000) *The Politics of the Police* (3rd edn). Oxford: Oxford University Press.

LESS LETHAL WEAPONS

'Less lethal weapons' include weapons and technologies that, when used together with appropriate tactics, are designed to induce compliance in pursuit of a legitimate policing aim without a substantial risk of serious or permanent injury or death to the subject to whom they are applied.

The UN Basic Principles on the Use of Force and Firearms by Law Enforcement Officials, adopted in September 1990, states that governments and law enforcement agencies should equip law enforcement officials with various types of weapons and ammunition that would allow for a differentiated use of force and firearms. It also encouraged the development of 'non-lethal incapacitating weapons' for use in appropriate situations.

However, the greatest impetus to research into less lethal options, for use by the British Police Service, was the publication in September 1999 of the report of the Independent Commission on Policing for Northern Ireland (the Patten Commission). Recommendations 69 and 70 of that report required research into a potentially less lethal alternative to the existing baton round and that a broader range of public-order equipment be made available to the police. As a consequence, a UK-wide steering group was established to lead a research programme to address these issues. The Home Office Scientific Development Branch then conducted extensive research into commercially available technologies, based upon an operational requirement established by the Association of Chief Police Officers in June 2001.

Some technologies were found worthy of greater consideration and medical evaluation. Such an evaluation was conducted by the Defence Scientific Advisory Council sub-committee on the Medical Implications of Less Lethal Weapons (DOMILL). One such technology was the taser, which then underwent a successful operational trial and was subsequently authorized for operational use in September 2004, when specified criteria are met.

In June 2001, the Home Office granted authority for the operational deployment of the L21A1 baton round as a less lethal option in situations where conventional firearms were authorized for use. Following work by the steering group, a potentially less injurious alternative to the L21A1 was developed by the Defence Science and Technology Laboratory. After an evaluation by DOMILL and after Home Office authority had been granted, the attenuating energy projectile was brought into operational use in June 2005. Other technologies currently authorized for use by the Police Service, following extensive research, testing and evaluation, are the chemical incapacitants CS (chlorobenzylidene malononitrile) and PAVA (pelargonic acid vanillylamide), and the water cannon.

With all these technologies, the desired intent is to control and then neutralize a threat. While the actual outcome with some may, on occasions, be lethal, this is less likely than through the use of more conventional firearms. Appropriate tactics are therefore necessary when using these technologies to ensure that their effectiveness is maximized.

The Home Office Code of Practice on Police use of Firearms and Less Lethal Weapons has imposed controls in respect of the availability and introduction of less lethal weapons by the police (see Force (police use of)). In order to develop an international consensus on operational needs, as these apply to minimal force options and less lethal technologies, an International Law Enforcement Forum has now been established.

Martyn Perks

Related entries

Firearms (police use of); Force (police use of); Patten Report; Technology and policing.

Key texts and sources

See the following websites:
http://www.unhchr.ch/html/menu3/b/h_comp43.htm
http://www.nio.gov.uk/index/nio-publication.htm
   (less lethal)

---

http://scienceandresearch.homeoffice.gov.uk/hosdb/
   publications-2/weaponry-publications
http://www.westmercia.police.uk/publications/
   acpopoliceuseoffirearms.htm
http://police.homeoffice.gov.uk/news-and-
   publications/publication/operational-policing/
   useoffirearms.pdf
http://www.ilef.org
http://www.ilef.nldt.org/publications.html

M

MASS PRIVATE PROPERTY

The term 'mass private property', which was originally coined by Clifford Shearing and Philip Stenning (1981), refers to property which, although privately owned, depends for its economic viability on the fact that the general public are routinely invited on to it.

The concept of 'mass private property' has mainly been used to explain the significant growth of private policing, especially in urban areas, during the last decades of the twentieth century. The term refers to property which, although privately owned, depends for its economic viability on the fact that the general public are routinely invited on to it. Despite its private ownership, it thus has characteristics commonly associated with public places.

The quintessential example of mass private property is the large suburban shopping mall. Other examples are sports and recreational stadiums and centres, holiday resorts, entertainment centres, hotel complexes and, increasingly since the late 1990s, airports and other transport terminals. Such property proliferated particularly in North America during the 1960s and beyond, but can now, in the era of economic globalization, be found to a greater or lesser extent in almost every country in the world.

For a variety of reasons, the typically corporate owners of such property commonly prefer to have it privately policed, either by employing their own 'in-house' security personnel or by contracting for them from a commercial security company. In the first place, having policing done by one's own employees gives an owner greater freedom to determine and control policing policies and practices, so that they reflect the owner's particular commercial or other institutional interests. Policing by the public police cannot usually be controlled in this way, as they are sworn to police in the broader 'public interest'. Secondly, the private provision of such policing is often less expensive and more efficient. Thirdly, many mass private property owners feel that the visible presence of public police on their property may make their businesses less attractive to potential customers.

The enclosed nature of much mass private property allows private policing to be undertaken without the 'free rider' problem, whereby neighbouring property owners who are not paying for the policing may nevertheless benefit from it (Spitzer and Scull 1977: 23–4). Also, the fact that such property is privately owned means that private police can have the benefit of the particular legal powers of the property owners for whom they work (such as trespass laws and the power to deny entry without having to justify doing so) to do policing. Furthermore, constitutional rights, such as freedom of movement, association and speech, which apply to public access to and use of publicly owned places, typically do not apply on privately owned property, which gives property owners greater rights to control behaviour on it.

The great proliferation of mass private property in recent years, and the extent to which public life increasingly takes place on it, has led both courts and legislators to consider whether these citizens' rights should be extended to it so as to limit the extent to which they can be trumped by the traditional rights of private property owners, particularly through the activities of private police who act as their agents.

Similar to mass private property in many of these respects are other forms of 'common' (Von Hirsch and Shearing 2000) or 'communal' (collectively owned) property, such as gated communities, private housing estates and recreational clubs (e.g. golf clubs), that are, for similar reasons, often policed privately rather than by the public police (Kempa *et al.* 2005).

Philip Stenning

Related entries

Plural policing; Private policing.

Key texts and sources

Shearing, C. and Stenning, P. (1981) 'Modern private security: its growth and implications', in M. Tonry and N. Morris (eds) *Crime and Justice: An Annual Review of Research. Vol. 3.* Chicago, IL: University of Chicago Press.
Spitzer, S. and Scull, A. (1977) 'Privatization and capitalist development: the case of the private police', *Social Problems*, 25: 18–29.

MEDIA AND POLICING

While the police and the media have always had a close relationship, in recent times the media have become even more closely involved with policing. The media now set policing agendas and priorities, act as a resource in investigations and often report on policing operations as they happen.

The police and media have been important to each other ever since the inception of modern policing. Crime stories are perennially prominent in the mass media. This makes the media strongly dependent on police co-operation, enabling the police to become primary definers of news about crime. The police have also sought to cultivate the media as a crucial source of their legitimation. In late modernity, the media have become even more closely intertwined with policing. A complex of technological, social and cultural changes means that the media increasingly constitute policing processes, rather than just representing them after the event. In an era in which security and law and order are major concerns, the media frame policing agendas and priorities, act as an investigative resource and frequently report on policing operations as they happen.

Media representations of policing have been a perennial source of concern. The police have frequently complained that they are presented in an unfavourable light. On the other hand, there has been anxiety that the law-and-order framework informing much media representation of crime and policing threatens popular support for democratic ideals of the rule of law. The balance between supportive and critical representations of policing has varied over time, but a constant theme has been 'police fetishism' – the portrayal of the police as the vital 'thin blue line' protecting people against crime and chaos.

Media and policing before the Second World War

The media played a significant role in the nineteenth-century police struggle for legitimation in the face of the widespread opposition to their establishment. Popular literature was a key arena. The police memoirs genre was imported from France in the 1830s and 1840s. Charles Dickens 'virtually appointed himself patron and publicist to the Detective Department' of Scotland Yard, according to Ian Ousby's history of detective stories (1976: 65–6).

On the other hand, music-hall songs and cartoons in newspapers or magazines frequently highlighted police incompetence and corruption. In the early twentieth century, the cinema was often criticized for glamourizing crime and for lampooning the police. Before the Second World War, crime stories usually portrayed the police as comic or corrupt, and hardly ever had police heroes.

Police and media since the Second World War

During the late 1940s the police began to be featured for the first time as heroic figures in popular fiction. This was symbolized by two of the most popular series on early television: *Dixon of Dock Green* in Britain and *Dragnet* in the USA, each part of a broader wave of very positive representations.

After the late 1960s, however, policing became an increasingly controversial political issue.

Media stories increasingly featured negative or controversial aspects of policing. The major corruption scandals at Scotland Yard during the 1970s were triggered initially by revelations in *The Times* about a bent 'firm within a firm'. During the 1970s and 1980s, media stories (news and fiction) increasingly highlighted policing malpractice and failures: miscarriages of justice, racism, sexism, abuse of powers, declining detection rates and violent public-order tactics. During the early 1990s there emerged a consensus between the political parties around a shared framework of tough law and order. Although stories of police wrongdoing continued to feature in the media, the main focus shifted to concern and criticism about failures in police effectiveness in providing public security.

Content analyses of media representations suggest they offer a predominantly positive image of policing, though to a declining extent. The overall picture is of the police as effective guardians of the public against serious threats. The media concentrate on serious violent and sexual offences, and mainly feature crimes that are successfully cleared up. The high news value of stories of official wrongdoing lead even the most law-and-order-oriented media assiduously to seek out stories about police corruption, causing considerable anxiety to the police themselves. But the potentially delegitimating impact of corruption stories has traditionally been neutralized by presenting them in a 'one bad apple' framework, emphasizing that the police as a whole should not be condemned because of rogue individuals. As the number of 'bad apples' seemed to multiply in the 1970s, this became increasingly implausible. An alternative legitimating framework, the reform narrative, became more prominent, in which widespread problems are acknowledged but the emphasis is on the official reform strategy. More recently, as the politics of law and order became increasingly dominant, police abuse has often been legitimated as the lesser or even a necessary evil in the fight against fearful threats – the 'Dirty Harry' or 'noble cause corruption' narratives.

The predominantly supportive media image of policing is only in part a result of law-and-order ideology, however. It also owes much to the professional sense of what constitutes a 'good story' (news or fiction) for the public. Narratives about serious violent crimes, ultimately resolved by reliable guardians of public security, provide vivid drama and vicarious, often voyeuristic, thrills, but also offer an ultimate resolution of tensions, reassurance and moral closure. Practical exigencies lead to producers of crime news or entertainment often requiring the cooperation of the police or courts as reliable and safe sources. Thus the police often become 'primary definers' of crime stories.

None the less, media representations since the late 1960s have become increasingly negative about police effectiveness and integrity. In television programmes, for example, the 1950s *Dixon of Dock Green* image of the police as paragons of virtue was succeeded by the more ambiguous *Z-cars* and, ultimately, in the 1970s by the antithesis of Dixon, *The Sweeney*, presenting the police as tough, sometimes deviant, thief-takers. In the 1980s these poles were synthesized by *The Bill*, offering an all-round characterization of different elements of policing. But since the 1980s TV series have offered an ever more explicit exploration of police problems, including corruption, racism and sexism.

The overall representation of policing remains overwhelmingly positive about its fundamental effectiveness and integrity, even though procedural and personal deviance are more frequently represented. The media still reproduce police fetishism, celebrating the police as a bedrock imperative of security and order, even if they sometimes must dirty their hands to deal with increasingly virulent threats.

Robert Reiner

Related entries

Corruption (police); Dixon of Dock Green; Fear of crime; Legitimacy; Public attitudes to the police.

Key texts and sources

Leishman, F. and Mason, P. (2003) *Policing and the Media.* Cullompton: Willan Publishing.

Mawby, R.C. (2002) *Policing Images.* Cullompton: Willan Publishing.

Reiner, R. (2003) 'Policing and the media', in T. Newburn (ed.) *Handbook of Policing.* Cullompton: Willan Publishing.

MENTALLY DISORDERED OFFENDERS

A narrow definition of a mentally disordered offender would be someone who falls within the diagnostic criteria set out in s. 1 of the Mental Health Act 1983 and who has been convicted of a criminal offence. However, in practice, the term is frequently applied in a more liberal fashion.

The term 'mentally disordered offenders' has a number of potential meanings (Peay 2007). First, it means people who have a mental disorder who have also committed a criminal offence, usually of a trivial nature. A proportion of these may never be convicted but, rather, are diverted to mental health services at an early stage in the criminal justice process. Secondly are offenders who develop a mental disorder after conviction. While some of these people will be unknown to the psychiatric services, others will be known but are, none the less, dealt with primarily as offenders until the point of sentencing, when their mental state may result in a hospital disposal under the Mental Health Act 1983 rather than a penal disposal.

Thirdly are people with serious mental disorders that either prevent them from entering a valid plea at trial or result in them being found not guilty. Both such occurrences are rare, and it is technically inappropriate to describe such individuals as offenders since they have not been found culpable. When people are found unfit to plead, they may nevertheless be held to have committed the *actus reus* of an offence – that is, they are found to have done the act – even though their mental state does not permit a full trial to go ahead. In these circumstances, 'offenders' may be given a hospital disposal or dealt with in the community. In the even rarer cases where 'offenders' are found not guilty by reason of insanity (as per the *M'Naghten* case of 1843), they are truly not offenders since they have been acquitted. However, in these circumstances the courts have the power to send such individuals to hospital for treatment, to give them a community disposal or to discharge them altogether.

Police involvement with mentally disordered offenders is likely to arise primarily in two contexts (Littlechild and Fearns 2005); first, in the community and, secondly, at the police station. In the community, the police will be required to exercise their discretion in relation to any individual found in a public place who appears to the officer to be 'suffering from mental disorder and to be in immediate need of care and control'. Under s. 136 of the Mental Health Act 1983, the officer may, 'if he thinks it necessary to do so in the interests of that person or for the protection of other persons', remove the individual to a 'place of safety' where he or she may be detained for up to 72 hours in order for an assessment to be undertaken with a view to making any necessary arrangements for that individual's treatment or care. Such arrangements may entail compulsory admission to a psychiatric hospital under s. 2 or s. 3 of the 1983 Act. This constitutes a diversionary power since it may be used even where an individual is believed to have committed a criminal offence. In so doing, an officer may short-circuit a process whereby offenders will otherwise be sent to hospital following a criminal conviction because of their psychiatric needs at the point of sentence.

The police may also be called upon to execute a warrant under s. 135 of the 1983 Act to search for and remove a person from any place where it is believed that the individual is suffering from mental disorder and needs to be removed to a 'place of safety' because he or she is being ill-treated, neglected or is otherwise unable to care for him or herself, with a view to making arrangements for his or her treatment or care. In executing such a warrant an officer needs to be accompanied by an approved social worker and a registered medical practitioner. In both instances of such community involvement, a 'place of safety' includes, but is not limited to, the police station and any health service hospital.

At the police station, the police have particular responsibilities to safeguard the interests of mentally disordered people, whether as suspects or witnesses, under Code C of the Police and Criminal Evidence Act 1984. This makes considerable demands on the police since it requires them not only to be alive to the definition of what constitutes mental disorder under s. 1 of the Mental Health Act 1983 but also necessitates that they institute all the protections and additional rights to which the mentally vulnerable are entitled, including the right to have an appropriate adult present during questioning (Code C, para 1.4) in the presence of even a suspicion of mental disorder. While the police cannot be expected to be expert diagnosticians, the threshold for triggering the need for an appropriate adult is set sufficiently low, in the context of a complex relationship between offending and mental disorder (Prins 2005), for the question to be asked: why it is that an appropriate adult is not invariably present during interrogation? While the opportunities for diversion at this point are considerable (Vaughan *et al.* 2001), the practice of diversion indicates that many people with mental health needs are being inappropriately processed by the criminal justice system because of a failure to identify their needs at the police station and to divert them appropriately.

Since mentally disordered offenders are to be found throughout both the mental health and criminal justice systems (and, in particular, in institutional contexts such as prisons, secure units and special hospitals), it is inevitable that the police will have contact with them in a variety of different guises. Similarly, police involvement with such bodies as multi-agency public protection panels, established with a supervisory role in respect of those who pose a risk of serious harm to the public, will bring the police into contact with other bodies and professionals with differing responsibilities and ethical obligations in respect of the mentally vulnerable. Since it will not always be immediately evident that offenders have mental health needs or that patients have committed offences not necessarily brought to the attention of the prosecuting authorities, the police need to be aware of the considerable and varied demands on their professionalism that such individuals pose, and the implications of their presence for routine police practices.

Jill Peay

Related entries

Caution; Discretion; Police and Criminal Evidence Act 1984 (PACE); Warrants.

Key texts and sources

Littlechild, B. and Fearns, D. (eds) (2005) *Mental Disorder and Criminal Justice: Policy, Provision and Practice.* Lyme Regis: Russell House Publishing.
Peay, J. (2007) 'Mentally disordered offenders, mental health and crime', in M. Maguire *et al.* (eds) *The Oxford Handbook of Criminology* (4th edn). Oxford: Oxford University Press.
Prins, H. (2005) *Offenders, Deviants or Patients?* (3rd edn). London: Taylor & Francis.
Vaughan, P., Kelly, M. and Pullen, N. (2001) 'The working practices of the police in relation to mentally disordered offenders and diversion services', *Medicine, Science and the Law*, 41: 13–20.
See also the Crown Prosecution Service's web page on mentally disordered offenders (http://www.cps.gov.uk/legal/section3/chapter_a.html).

METROPOLITAN POLICE/NEW POLICE

The Metropolitan Police/New Police came into being when the Metropolitan Police Act 1829 replaced London's parochial systems of law and order with a centralized force accountable to the Home Secretary. The new force's role was to prevent crime in the city through rigorous patrolling.

The year 1829 is generally associated with the emergence of the New Police in England. Here, the introduction of the Metropolitan Police Act (under the stewardship of Robert Peel) brought police reform to London, replacing the city's localized, parochial systems of law and order (administered by parish constables and watchmen) with a full-time, centralized force of officers accountable to the Home Secretary. Policing of the Metropolitan District was placed in the hands of a body of 3,000 men, whose stated role was to prevent crime through rigorous patrolling. While scholars generally concur that the emergence of the New Police was a key moment in the development of law enforcement in England, their interpretations of why this change took place have varied considerably. Broadly speaking, there are three approaches to understanding this history: the traditional/Whig version, revisionist accounts and, most recently, a more nuanced body of work. Each of these is outlined in turn below.

During the 1820s, the Home Secretary, Robert Peel, agitated for an overhaul of the existing system of policing within the capital, arguing that increasing crime statistics highlighted the failure of the old parochial forces of law and order to cope with new crime threats borne out of industrialization and urban expansion. Traditional policing histories (often referred to as Whig or orthodox accounts) have echoed the rhetoric of contemporary commentators such as Peel, presenting the introduction of the New Police as a natural and progressive process warranted by the state of existing arrangements. Thus, following the claims of police reformists, Whig historians have argued that, by the nineteenth century, the old system of policing was outdated and unable to cope with a rising tide of crime. As Critchley (1967) has noted, parish officers were incapable of performing their duties since the job attracted those who were infirm, incompetent and often corrupt. In addition, the localized and segmented nature of parish arrangements was seen to limit the ability of forces to offer a consistent service or effective response to crime. Whig historians have also emphasized the significant improvements made to the policing of the capital following 1829 when the introduction of a new force of officers, appointed under strict regulations, ensured that men were younger, healthier and of better character than their predecessors. The new Metropolitan force was, they argue, more effective at preventing crime and disorder, and the success attributable to this new body of officers is evidenced both in the rapid dissipation of opposition to the New Police and in the subsequent extension of the Metropolitan model throughout the country (Emsley 1996: 248).

Whig interpretations of the emergence of the New Police have been heavily criticized by modern scholars for being oversimplistic and linear. In accepting, at face value, the social and political rhetoric of eighteenth and nineteenth-century commentators, Whig historians have assumed that the development of policing was a natural and progressive process, necessitated by modernization, and ultimately successful. In consequence, traditional accounts of policing have glossed over the complexities of this area of history.

From the 1970s, traditional histories of policing came under increasing scrutiny from those who offered a revisionist interpretation of the development and function of policing. In contrast to Whig accounts, revisionist histories have placed nineteenth-century policing development within a broader framework of changing class and power structures. For revisionist scholars, the massive changes wrought by industrialization and urbanization had a significant impact on traditional class relationships, both at a real and perceived level. For instance, alongside the rapid growth of cities (such as London), increasing class segregation and coalescence, together with the disintegration of established deferential ties, rendered traditional mechanisms of class control increasingly outmoded (Reiner 2000: 24–5). In an environment where the relationship between class and crime was already firmly established (Emsley 2005), this dual process magnified society's perceived 'dangerous classes' and fuelled the fears of middle-class elites about the physical and moral threat posed by an increasingly visible and unregulated working-class population. For revisionists, it is against this backdrop that the introduction of the New Police can be understood. In these accounts, the establishment of a centralized force, under the 1829 legislation, was a move to counteract this threat. When considered through this historical lens, the New Police were an instrument of class coercion, attempting to instil bourgeoisie moral values into the lifestyles of the lower orders. As Storch (1976) has argued, the New Police were 'domestic missionaries' charged with controlling such activities as drinking and gambling – behaviours that were morally undesirable in a middle-class value system. Thus, the hub of police attention was on lower-class communities and, through the idiom of crime prevention, focused on many of the popular activities, practices and pastimes of this social group (Storch 1975).

By placing the emergence of policing in a framework of class and power, revisionist accounts provided a more sophisticated examination of this history than those given in traditional explanations. Nevertheless, like the orthodox school, revisionism has been criticized for its unilinear and deterministic approach (Reiner 2000). As critics have noted, revisionist accounts have wrongly assumed both that there was unified agreement among the propertied classes concerning the need for and nature of changes to policing arrangements, and that these imagined intentions were subsequently achieved in the outcomes of police reform. Furthermore, in their accounts of the introduction of the New Police, revisionist histories have typically overstated the overt class-control function of the police, the singularly oppositional nature of working-class responses to their presence and the persistence of that opposition (Reiner 2000: 45). As critics have noted, this is a rather 'one-sided' interpretation of the development and implementation of policing that has overlooked many of the intricacies of this history.

As a growing body of research has explored the dynamics of English police reform, a more nuanced history has emerged, throwing 'considerable doubt on the comfortable verities of orthodox and revisionist historians' (Taylor 1997: 4) and, in contrast, emphasizing the complex mix of social, economic and political influences that shaped reform (Emsley 1996; Taylor 1997). Such accounts have evidenced the range of influences on the development of the New Police, creating a more multidimensional understanding of this history. For instance, local studies have demonstrated the considerable variety of contemporary debate that contributed to the nature and form of policing. As historians now recognize, such 'diversity, dissension and debate' have underlined the erroneousness of generalization (in whatever form) and have emphasized that 'there was

nothing inevitable about the form of policing that was to develop in nineteenth-century England' (Taylor 1998: 73).

John Locker

Related entries

Beat; Bow Street 'Runners'; Colonial policing; Constabulary independence; Criminal investigation department (CID); Hue and cry; Patrol; Peel, Sir Robert; Politics (police involvement); Rank structure; Rowan and Mayne.

Key texts and sources

Critchley, T.A. (1967) *A History of Police in England and Wales.* London: Constable (Whig account).
Emsley, C. (1996) *The English Police: A Political and Social History.* London: Longman (nuanced account).
Storch, R. (1975) 'The plague of the blue locusts: police reform and popular resistance in northern England, 1840–57', *International Review of Social History*, 20: 61–90 (revisionist account).
Storch, R. (1976) 'The policeman as domestic missionary: urban discipline and popular culture in northern England, 1850–80', *Journal of Social History*, 9: 481–509 (revisionist account).
See also the websites of the Metropolitan Police (http://www.met.police.uk/) and the Metropolitan Police Federation (http://www.metfed.org.uk/).

MILITARY POLICING

Military policing refers to a policing agency that relies primarily on access to physical force in order to maintain social order and that is characterized by military-style structures and discourse in its internal relationships.

There are four common usages of the term military policing. First, it is used institutionally to describe the practice of most national armed forces to employ specialized units primarily, though not exclusively, to deal with internal disciplinary matters – for example, the Royal Military Police and the US Military Police

Corps. Such police operate in a controlled environment with a population subject to a host of disciplinary requirements not available in civil policing work (Bayley and Shearing 2001). Secondly, generically, it is used to describe the minor, external military actions of certain nation-states against small-scale threats to their national well-being. For example, in the 1930s, the British state used its air force to suppress local communities in Kurdistan, describing that bombing as a military policing action. Thirdly is paramilitary policing – the practices of localized armed groups to enforce social order in their own communities. Paramilitary policing has been used to describe, among other examples, the policing of Republican areas by the Irish Republican Army in Northern Ireland in the latter part of the twentieth century. Finally, military policing is used criminologically to distinuish low-level order maintenance (such as community policing) from armed state police practices designed to enforce internal sovereignty. Lea and Young (1984) use the concept of military policing to refer to the form of policing that occurs when relationships between the police and community break down.

Historically, the origins of the last form of military policing lie in the concept of a 'low' police and a 'high' police (Brodeur 1983). In Napoleonic France, the Police Minister distinguished between policing functions concerned with the social order of the streets (incivilities such as prostitution or neighbour disputes) and policing in defence of the state. This is a precursor to the modern-day distinction between community policing and military policing.

A military policing agency is characterized by the following features:

- It is a close-knit, distinct group that perceives of the citizenry as a population to be controlled on behalf of the central state rather than by the criminal law.
- Control is based primarily on coercion rather than on consent.
- Its police officers – in the British colonial tradition – are drawn from a population different from the citizens being policed.
- Force is readily used as the first resort – from the collation of intelligence on suspect populations, to a reliance on firearms.

Many continental police forces are military in nature, often acting in partnership with a second tier of locally recruited, more consensual agencies. These range from the French gendarmerie to the Italian carabinieri. Similarly, each state in Brazil has a Polícia Militar do Estado. These are uniformed gendarmerie forces in charge of patrolling and preventing crime, and they are the principal police forces of the state. They are structured in the same way as the military forces and, until recently, some Brazilian states' military police were even equipped with tanks and artillery. A second tier of civil police (polícia civil) is in charge of criminal investigation.

Mike Brogden

Related entries

Colonial policing; Models of policing; Paramilitary policing; Peace support operations (the police contribution).

Key texts and sources

Brodeur, J.-P. (1983) 'High policing and low policing: remarks about the policing of political activities', *Social Problems*, 30: 507–20.

Brogden, M.E. (1982) *The Police: Autonomy and Consent.* London: Academic Press.

Lea, J. and Young, J. (1984) *What is to be Done about Law and Order?* Harmondsworth: Penguin Books.

See also the websites of the Royal Military Police (http://www.army.mod.uk/rmp/) and the Defence Police Federation (http://www.dpf.org.uk/).

MINISTRY OF JUSTICE

The Ministry of Justice is a new ministry that brings together the functions of the Department for Constitutional Affairs with a number of responsibilities previously held by the Home Office, including the National Offender Management Service, sentencing and youth justice.

One of the most significant parts of governmental reorientation affecting criminal justice was announced in early 2007. The Prime Minister, using the Royal Prerogative which allows for administrations to be reconfigured at will, announced that, as of May 2007 a new Ministry of Justice was to be created and that this new department would take over the staff and responsibilities of the Department for Constitutional Affairs (what formerly had been the Lord Chancellor's Department), together with a host of functions historically the responsibility of the Home Office. These latter include the Prison and Probation Services, now largely amalgamated as the National Offender Management Service, criminal law and sentencing, youth justice, the Parole Board and the Office for Criminal Justice Reform. The slimmed-down Home Office retains responsibility for security and for policing, crime reduction, drugs (though with some overlap with the Department of Health), immigration and asylum, identity and passports. As a result, Gibson (2007a: 15) observes, the new ministry 'draws together various strands of activity under a broad remit that can be labelled "justice matters" and "constitutional affairs"'.

This was a swift piece of reorganization by any Whitehall standards. The former Lord Chief Justice, Lord Woolf, was critical of the apparent speed of reform, saying that any rearrangement of the 'checks and balances' of the constitution should be considered very carefully. 'We should work it out beforehand', he suggested, 'and not wait until we have created the change and then somehow or other try to scramble to get it into place.' He was particularly critical of the absence of parliamentary debate on the matter and said that he was also concerned about disturbing the traditionally close relationship between the Lord Chancellor and the judiciary as a result of the extension of the remit of the Ministry of Justice.

Although the pace of change was remarkable, the prospect of such a split had been mooted for some time. Indeed, the Labour Party committed itself to just such a separation of responsibilities in its 1992 general election manifesto. Moreover, looked at in international context, the new arrangements are far from novel. Many European countries have separate ministries of justice and ministries of the interior/internal affairs. Indeed, the separation of those parts of government concerned with security, on the one hand, and with justice and the imposition of punishment, on the other, is one of the major expectations of new member states joining the Council of Europe. At one level, therefore, the changes are only bringing Britain into line with other European nations. Indeed, for many commentators, the separation of policing matters from criminal justice policy more generally is a positive development and one that is long overdue.

Rob Canton and Tim Newburn

Related entries

Accountability and governance; Association of Chief Police Officers (ACPO); Home Office; Politics (police involvement).

Key texts and sources

Gibson, B. (2007a) *The New Ministry of Justice: An Introduction.* Winchester: Waterside Press.
Gibson, B. (2007b) *The New Home Office: An Introduction.* Winchester: Waterside Press.
The Ministry of Justice's website is at http://www.justice.gov.uk/. See also the Home Office's website (http://www.homeoffice.gov.uk/). The news story containing Lord Justice Woolf's remarks ('Woolf fears Home Office reforms') is available online at http://news.bbc.co.uk/1/hi/uk_politics/6586437.stm.

MODELS OF POLICING

Models of policing attempt to classify the police systems of different countries. To produce such a typology of police systems, the underlying principles of the police in different societies must be evaluated and compared.

The nature of 'the police' varies markedly between countries and over time. For example, the model that emerged in the UK and the USA in the nineteenth century differed from the centralized, autocratic arm of state authority that preceded it on continental European (Chapman 1970) and, while the cross-national interchange of ideas in recent years has resulted in police structures and methods from one country being imported to others, there are still stark contrasts.

Comparing police systems in different countries can be done in a variety of ways. One is to focus on countries separately and to identify the core features of their policing systems in the context of their social and political systems, subsequently classifying them according to a typology (Mawby 1990; Findlay and Zvekic 1993). An alternative approach is to identify different models that apply to groups of countries. For example, we might distinguish between Anglo-American police, policing on continental Europe, communist/post-communist police, colonial police and the type of police that has emerged in the Far East (Mawby 1999). The main weakness of these approaches is that there are often as many differences within countries or between countries in a model as there are between alternative models, a point made forcefully by Anderson and Killingray (1991, 1992) in the context of a colonial police system. Equally, there are often variations within a country. For example, in Canada marked variations exist between the centralized Royal Canadian Mounted Police and local urban and provincial police (Mawby 1999). A third approach entails focusing on the core features of the police and identifying ideal-type police systems – for example, a control-dominated system and a community-oriented system.

A control-dominated system is one where the main function of the police is to maintain order; where the population generally fails to recognize the legitimacy of the state and its agents, the police. In such societies, the police may carry out a range of administrative tasks on behalf of the state, but rarely provide a public service that addresses the welfare needs of the community. The police is consequently generally organized and managed centrally and has many paramilitary qualities.

In complete contrast, a community-oriented system is one where the main function of the police is to provide a public service that addresses the wider needs of the community. Maintaining order is important, but the emphasis is more on crime as symptomatic of community problems than an affront to author-

ity. Such a model assumes that the police is accorded considerable legitimacy by local communities. The police is consequently generally organized and managed locally, and barriers between the police and public are minimized.

The control-dominated system can be identified with traditional policing on continental Europe, with the policing established in the colonies by Britain and its European neighbours and with policing in communist Europe. Raymond Fosdick, for example, who worked as an administrator with the New York Police Department, toured Europe at the beginning of the twentieth century. His text, published in 1915 and subsequently reissued (1969), contrasted the centralized, militaristic, control-oriented police systems he found there with the situation in England and the USA. This notion of a 'police state' (Chapman 1970) formed the basis for the development of policing in Russia and, subsequently, its satellites in eastern Europe (Shelley 1997). This system of policing was characterized by a centralized and militaristic uniformed police subordinate to the secret police; an emphasis on maintaining political order rather than tackling conventional crime; and a close link between the police and the Communist Party, with minimal public or legal accountability.

The other police system that has been consistently recognized in the literature as control dominated is the colonial model. For example, Britain created a type of policing for its empire that was appropriate for the control of a subjugated population, where the needs of economic imperialism required a politically controlled paramilitary force prioritizing public order (Cole 1999). Colonial police may be characterized as centralized and militaristic (for example, armed and living as units in barracks); as prioritizing public order tasks; and as deriving their legitimacy from their colonial masters rather than the indigenous population. Additionally, given the difficulties occupying powers have had in recruiting loyal and reliable police officers, a common tactic was to recruit from either indigenous minorities or from other colonies, on the basis that such groups would be less likely to form allegiances with local people against the interests of the occupying power.

While identifying a control-dominated model may be useful, it should not blind us to the fact that most countries associated with it differ in a number of respects. For example, although British colonial authority was centralized in London, in different countries the police system was often regionally based and officers were not always issued with firearms. On continental Europe, there were also considerable variations. For example, the Dutch system was neither overtly militaristic nor excessively centralized and, while countries such as France, Spain and Italy traditionally had control-dominated police systems, in each case the maintenance of at least two police forces ensured that no one institution achieved sufficient power to threaten government.

The task of assigning specific police systems to a community-oriented model is even more difficult. Although this may be the type of democratic policing to which many of us aspire, it is difficult to nominate any one country as even approaching it (Mawby 1990; Brogden 1999). In England and Wales, for example, often eulogized as the home of 'community policing', modern systems of policing emerged at least in part as a means of maintaining order in the midst of working-class protest and, in many cases, police were recruited from rural areas to work in the cities, undermining the claim that they were local citizens in uniform. In the USA, where police systems have been traditionally locally based, personnel have been recruited locally and officers have engaged in a wide range of 'non-crime' responsibilities, the image of the police as a militaristic body charged with fighting the 'war' against crime is equally pervasive. Elsewhere, Bayley's (1976) early presentation of the Japanese police as community based and welfare oriented has been severely undermined (Miyazawa 1992; Aldous 1997; Leishman 1999).

It may, therefore, be that the key strengths of specifying control-dominated and community-oriented models centre around understanding the underlying principles of the police in different societies and in evaluating changes.

Rob I. Mawby

Related entries

Colonial policing; Community policing; Legitimacy; Military policing; Paramilitary policing.

Key texts and sources

Findlay, M. and Zvekic, U. (eds) (1993) *Alternative Policing Styles: Cross-cultural Perspectives.* Boston, MA: Kluwer.
Mawby, R.I. (ed.) (1999) *Policing across the World: Issues for the Twenty-first Century.* London: UCL Press

MURDER

Murder is a common law offence involving the intentional killing of one person by another.

Murder is one of the oldest offences known to the law and is one of the three offences classified by the Home Office as homicide. The other two are the offences of manslaughter (where someone is unlawfully killed but without the intent required in murder) and infanticide (where a mother intentionally kills her child under one year old while she is suffering from the effects of childbirth).

Homicide has generated a great deal of case law that influences the way courts interpret evidence in such cases. For example, intent or 'malice aforethought' is a defining characteristic of murder. In practice it is difficult to prove what is in an offender's mind when he or she kills, and so a legal construct has developed which holds that the term is 'a mere arbitrary symbol, for the malice may have in it nothing really malicious and need never be really aforethought' (Kenny cited in Smith and Hogan 1996: 356). This means that a mercy killing (where there is no malice) could be held to be malicious, and a spontaneous assault (where there is no intention to kill) could be held to be 'malice aforethought'. Such legal constructs mean that, in many cases, the difference between murder, manslaughter and infanticide can turn on the slightest of facts or their interpretation. Because of this, the police initially investigate every suspicious death as murder and only consider the alternatives once all the evidence is available.

Homicide is an infrequent event. There are generally well below 900 homicides in England and Wales each year and, although numbers have increased slightly over the medium term, the risk of being a victim of homicide has remained relatively stable at around 1.35 per 100,000 population. An HM Inspectorate of Constabulary (HMIC) survey of ten police forces found that the level of risk varied. The highest rate was in the Metropolitan Police area, with 2.3 homicides per 100,000, and the lowest was in Derbyshire Constabulary, which was 0.8 (HMIC 2000b: 104). These are relatively low rates by international standards. Of the 28 countries listed by Richards (1999: 29), Norway had the lowest (0.9 homicides per 100,000), England and Wales had the sixth lowest and South Africa had the highest at 58.9.

It is generally agreed that some homicides remain undiscovered. This occurs for two reasons. First, some offenders dispose of bodies in ways that make their discovery unlikely. Secondly, the cause of death or the circumstances in which it occurred are sometimes misinterpreted as being from natural or accidental causes rather than homicide. The scale of undiscovered homicides is unknown, but the case of Harold Shipman, a general practitioner who is estimated to have murdered 215 of his patients over a 20-year period, is illustrative of the problem.

Although infrequent, homicide is generally considered by the public to be among the most serious of crimes, and so the police place a high priority on its successful investigation. National policy and practice in its investigation is developed by the Association of Chief Police Officer's Homicide Working Group, and this is published to the service in the *Murder Investigation Manual* (2006) and in the *Journal of Homicide and Major Incident Investigation*. Each force maintains a number of senior investigating officers (SIOs) who lead all homicide investigations. They are trained on the Senior Investigating Officers Development Programme, and are accredited at level three of the Professionalizing Investigation Programme. All forces have a capacity to establish a major incident room using the Home Office Large Major Enquiry System (HOLMES) computer system, and this is generally the hub of an investigation. Because homicide is relatively infrequent, forces have traditionally established temporary teams to investigate it by drawing officers from other duties. This generally led to a dip in investigative performance in relation to other types of crime and meant that officers assigned to its investigation may have been relatively inexperienced. To counter this, some forces have established full-time teams to investigate all homicide and major incidents, generally known as major incident teams.

Not all homicides are difficult to solve. Many are the outcome of spontaneous criminal violence, such as child abuse, domestic violence or public disorder. In these cases the levels and frequency of the violence may be chronic, but the death itself is rarely planned. Such offences often generate large amounts of information and offenders may not even try to avoid detection. They are usually solved quickly. In a minority of cases offences are planned, and this enables offenders to minimize the amount of information they generate. They can also frustrate investigations by taking action after the event, such as cleaning scenes, disposing of evidence or intimidating witnesses. As with other types of crime, witnesses are important in determining the outcome of homicide investigations. Most spontaneously provide information to the police but, where they do not, because they are intimidated or for other reasons, the police find it difficulty to make progress. Homicides where little information has been generated or where offenders or witnesses inhibit its transmission to the police can be among the most difficult of all crimes to investigate.

This wide variation in the circumstances in which homicide is committed and in the behaviour of offenders and witnesses means that no two investigations are the same. There is, therefore, no single 'best way' of investigating a homicide. In many cases the identity of the suspect is known at an early stage; if not, success depends largely on investigators correctly interpreting the circumstances in which the homicide has been committed and selecting the most appropriate investigative techniques to locate information. A high value is therefore placed on the abilities of SIOs. But the low frequency of homicide and high variability in the circumstances in which it is committed mean that even the most experienced SIO is unlikely to have encountered all types. SIOs, therefore, seek to harness the skills and experience of all those working on the case, which includes investigators and such experts as forensic scientists, pathologists and behavioural scientists. However, it is widely acknowledged that the key to success in most cases is motivating those with information about the killing to pass it on to the police.

Peter Stelfox

Related entries

Child abuse; Crime; Crime scene examiners (CSEs); Criminal investigation; Critical incidents; Stephen Lawrence Inquiry.

Key texts and sources

Brookman, F. (2005) *Understanding Homicide.* London: Sage.

HM Inspector of Constabulary (2000) *Policing London.* London: HMIC.

Innes, M.R. (2003) *Investigating Murder: Detective Work and the Police Response to Criminal Homicide.* Oxford: Oxford University Press.

Richards, P. (1999) *Homicide Statistics. House of Commons Research Paper* 99/56. London: House of Commons Library.

Smith, Sir J. and Hogan, B. (1996) *Criminal Law* (8th edn). London: Butterworths.

N

NATIONAL INTELLIGENCE MODEL (NIM)

The National Intelligence Model (NIM) is the business process for policing in the UK. It provides a common basis for gathering and analysing information and for using this to adopt a problem-solving approach to reducing crime and disorder, to law enforcement and to community reassurance.

The value of gathering, collating and disseminating information about crimes and those believed to be involved in them has always been recognized within the Police Service. But systems to do this were often organized solely to support the local investigation of crime, were focused on the collection of data rather than its analysis and used systems that varied from force to force (and even between units in the same force). Under these conditions, intelligence often had a high tactical value, but it was difficult to use it for any strategic purpose or to apply it to areas other than criminal investigation.

In the 1990s police forces started to adopt more proactive methods of crime management following the Audit Commission's (1993) report, *Helping with Enquiries: Tackling Crime Effectively* and early experiments in intelligence-led policing in Kent (John and Maguire 2007: 210). These highlighted the strategic potential of intelligence and the possibility of using it as the basis for all police activity. In 2000, the National Intelligence Model (NIM) was introduced by the National Criminal Intelligence Service to bring standardization to the process. While the benefits of a national system were widely acknowledged, NIM was not implemented consistently throughout the country

and so, in 2005, the Home Secretary used powers under the Police Reform Act 2002 to introduce national standards. These are contained in the Home Office's (2005b) *Code of Practice on the National Intelligence Model* and The Association of Chief Police Officers' *Guidance on the National Intelligence Model* (ACPO 2005a).

NIM describes a response to crime and disorder at three levels:

- *Level 1*: local crime and disorder that can be addressed at the basic command unit (BCU) or small force level. This can extend down to neighbourhoods in circumstances where forces have devolved decision-making to that level.
- *Level 2*: cross-border issues affecting more than one BCU or affecting more than one force or a region.
- *Level 3*: crime that requires a response on a national and international scale.

There is considerable discussion within policing about how meaningful the three levels are in practice. The levels reflect the organizational division of police and other agencies rather than reflecting the way in which crime is committed or the degree of social harm it causes. Thus, while offences such as burglary in dwelling houses are likely to be considered a priority at level 1, it is unlikely to feature as an issue at level 2 or 3. As a consequence, it is argued, those who travel across force or national boundaries to commit crimes that are not considered a priority for agencies working at level 2 or 3 can operate in an intelligence gap – which means that their activities are effectively un-policed.

At the heart of NIM is the concept of decision-making based on the production of intelligence products, enabling rational decisions about priorities, tactics and the identification of success factors. This decision-making is formalized in the tasking and co-ordination process. Tasking and co-ordination groups (TCGs) are charged with considering the response to threats at each of the three levels specified in NIM.

In order to feed the TCG process, NIM describes the identification and use of information sources, which may encompass a range of information obtained by covert and overt means. It then provides a systematic means for the recording (based on an intelligence requirement) of the information required to address the various policing problems prioritized by the TCG. This information is subject to research, development and analysis.

This analysis is used to produce one of the four standard intelligence products:

- Strategic assessments.
- Tactical assessments.
- Subject profiles.
- Problem profiles.

From these products the strategic TCG identifies its priorities (contained in a control strategy) and, at a tactical level, the TCG will take the priorities identified to develop tactical resolutions, which are the individual actions mounted in support of the strategy. Finally, an operational review takes place to identify the effectiveness of the operation or tactic, useful intelligence and any lessons that could inform future operations or delivery plans. This cycle enables policing (through the TCG process) to respond to the changing environment by identifying new priorities and by collecting intelligence to develop strategic and tactical options to address them.

By providing a common system, NIM enables intelligence to be shared between the three levels described in the model and between different agencies, such as the Serious and Organized Crime Agency and HM Revenue & Customs. The principles of NIM have also been adopted by many crime and disorder reduction partnerships to enable them to prioritize and manage business.

The effectiveness of NIM depends on the quality of information feeding decision-making. Too narrow a view of requirements (for example, based exclusively on performance targets) results in an inadequate intelligence picture, which impacts on the TCG's ability to identify problems and take effective action. Equally, a lack of clear requirements results in too much low-quality information, and the system can become overloaded, making it impossible to see the wood for the trees. Overcoming these problems depends on policing developing a better organizational memory: information should be transferred from officers' heads into systems that can be searched and where links can be identified. This will encourage them to share useful information and to make them more discriminating about inputting low-quality information. This agenda was given added impetus by the shortcomings in police information management identified by the Bichard Inquiry and described in the Home Office's (2005a) *Code of Practice on the Management of Police Information* and ACPO's (2006a) *Guidance on the Management of Police Information*.

Giles Herdale and Peter Stelfox

Related entries

Criminal investigation; Detectives; Home Office; Hotspots; Intelligence analysis (previously crime analysis); Intelligence-led policing; Neighbourhood policing; Tasking and co-ordinating groups (TCGs).

Key texts and sources

ACPO (2005) *Guidance on the National Intelligence Model.* Wyboston: NPIA (available online at http://www.acpo.police.uk/asp/policies/Data/nim2005.pdf).
ACPO (2006a) *Guidance on the Management of Police Information.* Wyboston: NPIA.
ACPO (2006b) *Practice Advice on Tasking and Co-ordination.* Wyboston: NPIA.
Home Office (2005a) *Code of Practice on the Management of Police Information.* London: Home Office.
Home Office (2005b) *Code of Practice on the National Intelligence Model.* London: Home Office.

John, T. and Maguire, M. (2007) 'Criminal intelligence and the National Intelligence Model', in T. Newburn *et al.* (eds) *Handbook of Criminal Investigation.* Cullompton: Willan Publishing.

More information about NIM and other developments in the field of intelligence-led policing can be found at the following websites:

www.acpo.police.uk

www.npia.police.uk

www.homeoffice.gov.uk

NATIONAL POLICING IMPROVEMENT AGENCY (NPIA)

Established under the Police and Justice Act 2006, the National Policing Improvement Agency (NPIA) was set up to support the Police Service in England Wales by providing expertise in key areas. These include information and communications technology; support for information and intelligence sharing; core police processes; managing change; and recruitment and national training.

Support for the police was traditionally provided by the Home Office through a number of agencies which had evolved over many years. Their number and the fact that they were known by their initials or acronyms prompted one Home Secretary to describe them as a 'vast alphabet soup' (Home Secretary's speech to the Association of Chief Police Officers' annual conference 2005). They came to be viewed as unco-ordinated and overlapping, and so the National Policing Improvement Agency (NPIA) was established to streamline this structure. It replaced two of the largest agencies, the Central Police Training and Development Authority (Centrex) and the Police Information Technology Organization, and it incorporated some of the functions of others. Under the Police and Justice Act 2006, it has statutory objectives to:

- develop good practice in policing;
- provide expert support to the police service;
- carry out a national threat assessment for police forces;
- share international understanding of policing issues; and
- provide national information and communications technology, procurement and training support.

It became operational on 1 April 2007 and is a non-departmental public body under the Home Office. This means that, while it is funded by the Home Office, its day-to-day operations are independent of it. This independence was further underlined when the Home Secretary stated that it is to be a police-led organization. The first director is a serving chief constable, and the deputy director is also a police officer. Both are members of the Association of Chief Police Officers (ACPO). Governance of the organization is through a board with a chairperson appointed by the Home Secretary. Other members of the board represent ACPO, the Association of Police Authorities and the Home Office, and two are independent. The board must publish an annual plan describing how it is to meet the objectives. This plan is subject to extensive consultation, both within and outside the Police Service, and it seeks to reflect a consensus on the priorities for improving policing.

NPIA staff are drawn from a wide range of backgrounds. Many are police officers seconded from their forces to the agency for periods of between three and five years. Others come from industry, government departments and the education sector. The main focus of the NPIA's work is policing improvement in England and Wales, but it has officers on secondment from forces in Scotland and Northern Ireland and collaborates with relevent bodies in those countires on some initiatives.

Bringing a wide range of functions into one organization will streamline the way support is provided to the Police Service and has the potential to lead to cost savings. It also creates an organization that will be highly influential in the direction policing takes in the future.

For the first time in the UK, outside the specialist areas of organized crime, the NPIA creates a national body for policing, interestingly paralleled by the creation of the Scottish Police Services Agency at the same time. Their creation marks an open recognition of the need for some key services – national training, procurement, technology and infrastructure – to be run centrally. In the case of the NPIA, there is a more fundamental shift to recognize the need for the Police Service to have a Police Service-led and owned body that supports the implementation of major changes across policing. The NPIA has also taken policy responsibility for large areas of policing out of the centre of the Home Office, which, therefore, requires the NPIA to have a close relationship with ministers as well as with the Police Service.

Peter Stelfox

Related entries

Doctrine; Home Office; Police and Justice Act 2006; Rank structure; Training (police).

Key texts and sources

The NPIA's website is at http://www.npia.police.uk/. See also the Home Office's web page on the NPIA (http://police.homeoffice.gov.uk/police-reform/policing-improvement-agency/).

NATIONAL SECURITY

The protection of a state's safety is usually the task of one or more specialist institutions that are concerned with the disruption and prevention of undesirable activities that threaten national security. These institutions are often less concerned with law enforcement and criminal prosecutions.

'National security' is an essentially contested concept, not only intellectually but also on the political plane. Since it is regarded as being of overriding importance, other moral and political considerations are generally regarded as subordinate in the event of conflict (for a critical analysis of the concept, see Buzan 1991; Lustgarten and Leigh 1994: ch. 1). Moreover,

institutions and officials tasked with the preservation of national security (most notably, the Security Service, or MI5, and Government Communications Headquarters – the signals intercept body) are often granted unique powers and legal immunities. As the term implies, they have always been agents of national government, and in states which follow the Westminster constitutional model, were, until the 1980s, creatures of the Royal Prerogative, accountable (if at all) to the executive branch only. Legal limitations on their work are of equally recent origin. The consequences may be, and often have demonstrably been, severe and unnecessary damage to political freedom and wider human rights.

Traditionally, by contrast, state policing in western common-law jurisdictions has been predominantly local, tied constitutionally in various ways to territorial subdivisions and financed by them. It has also been orientated around the law, primarily directed at the arrest and prosecution of those committing specific offences, or using the open-ended flexibility of much criminal law as the source of discretion to invoke it in particular circumstances for the purpose of maintaining order. To oversimplify somewhat, but only somewhat, national security institutions have acted pre-emptively and outside the judicial system, whereas the police have worked reactively within a legal framework whose purpose is prosecution and the sanction of offenders and which is staffed by members of a judicial system consciously independent of other branches of government.

This ideal-typical model is increasingly obsolete. Perhaps the most significant trend in the last 15 years has been the *convergence* of function, method, structure and even modes of accountability, in relation to institutions of national security and policing. There have been three primary drivers of this convergence. One has been a reorientation of the goals of criminal justice policy, largely carried through by the Labour government since 1997. Crime prevention and an ill-defined 'community safety' and 'reassurance' function (analogous in their plasticity and vagueness to 'national security') have assumed much greater importance. Although crime prevention has been part of the police mission since the first instructions issued to the Metropolitan Police in 1829 (Scarman 1981), this was understood to mean the establishment of a physical presence as a deterrent, rather like a live scarecrow. Prevention now means the interdisciplinary collection and exchange of information between police and other state agencies, such as schools and social services, especially about young people who may not have committed, and certainly have not been prosecuted for, any offence. The statutory requrement that each local authority establishes a youth offending team is a prime example. Another is the creation and increasing use of anti-social behaviour orders, imposing restrictions on those who have not been tried, let alone convicted, by any criminal process. Although the police have long been recognized as a 'secret social service' (Punch and Naylor 1973), they are now taking over the roles, and often the vocabulary, of social workers, though always backed by powers of legal coercion. A second factor, whose influence was felt even earlier, is the growth of '-led' policing.

Perhaps most important in furthering the convergence, although operating on a very different plane, has been the increasing concentration on 'terrorism', a term that itself has expanded worrying in scope in recent years. Here the main techniques are extended electronic and visual surveillance, the cultivation and use of informants, and an emphasis on building up intelligence databases and networks – with disruption and prevention rather than prosecution being the primary aims. Informants apart, these practices have historically been the province of MI5 and only secondarily of the police, and their new primacy has changed the way the most sensitive area of policing is conceived and carried out. Conversely, in addition to a new 'lead' role in relation to terrorism, national security institutions were, in 1996, given an unprecedented statutory competence in relation to 'serious crime', and MI5 personnel have appeared as prosecution witnesses in several criminal trials.

These developments are reflected in changes in organization and accountability. The Home Office identification of three levels of criminality, ranging from local (level 1) to national and international (level 3), may be seen as a rational response to the world of global communications and the internationalization of crime in which we now live. It also reflects the proliferation of international police co-operation and, in particular, the emergence of European Union policing institutions and criminal competences. However, it has also led to the complete removal of a major element of policing activity from local institutions. The recently established Serious Organized Crime Agency (SOCA) replaces the National Crime Squad and National Criminal Intelligence Service, both of which had previously drawn most of their employees from officers seconded from local forces, and which reported to a service authority that contained at least limited local representation. SOCA will employ thousands of its own people who will have their own career structure and will report directly to, and be requred to follow the strategic priorities set by, the Home Secretary. The non-executive chair of the agency is Sir Steven Lander, the previous Director-General of MI5. That service reported the 'suspension' of its work in the field of serious crime once SOCA became operational. All local connection has disappeared; in effect, local governance institutions now deal only with police activities at a local and sometimes regional level. It remains to be seen whether such territorially based distinctions can work in practice. Drug commerce, in particular, has both international and highly localized, almost chaotic, dimensions. And it is widely recognized that any effective anti-terrorist strategy must be grounded in good relations with local communities, which alone can yield the intense knowledge of the activities of individuals or groups that are at most loosely affiliated to international organizations.

Moreover, it would be mistaken to ignore the depth of feeling among councillors and other public representatives that policing requires local accountability. The Home Office made precisely that error when, in 2005, it announced a programme of major amalgamations, which would have led to the disappearance of nearly half the present English and Welsh forces. Strong local opposition persuaded a new Home Secretary, John Reid, to abandon the policy in July 2006.

Laurence Lustgarten

Related entries

Community safety; Human trafficking; Police Service of Northern Ireland (PSNI); Politics (police involvement); Serious Organized Crime Agency (SOCA); Special branch (SB); Terrorism.

Key texts and sources

Buzan, B. (1991) *People, States, and Fear* (2nd edn). London: Longman.

Gill, P. (2000) *Rounding up the Usual Suspects?* Aldershot: Ashgate (chs 7–10).

Lustgarten, L. and Leigh, I. (1994) *In from the Cold: National Security and Parliamentary Democracy.* Oxford: Oxford University Press (ch. 1).

See also MiS's website (**http://www.mi5.gov.uk/**).

NEIGHBOURHOOD POLICING

Neighbourhood policing seeks to increase interaction with the public in defined geographical areas and, as such, shares common ground with community policing. The term 'neighbourhood policing' is currently preferred by the government, in part in recognition that individuals can belong to several communities while living in a single neighbourhood (Innes 2005) and also to underline a difference in the mechanisms through which outcomes are intended to be delivered.

Neighbourhood policing is expected to lead to increased public confidence and reduced crime and anti-social behaviour through tackling local priorities in partnership with the public, whereas the community policing model set out by Alderson in the 1970s suggested that crime reduction would follow increased police legitimacy delivered through a whole-force effort to improve community relations (Tilley 2003). Confusingly, the term 'neighbourhood policing' was used in the

1980s to describe a Metropolitan Police Service project to improve community relations through foot patrol, flexibility, community feedback and training to improve police attitudes to the public.

During the 1990s, the whole-force, problem-oriented approach to community policing, typified by the Chicago Alternative Policing Style, became highly influential and was widely adopted in the USA despite implementation problems. By contrast, community policing in England and Wales became increasingly organizationally and culturally marginalized. New impetus was eventually provided for a geographical approach focused on public priorities by reassurance policing, informed by the signal crimes perspective (Innes 2005). The ensuing Home Office evaluation of the Association of Chief Police Officers (ACPO)-led National Reassurance Policing Programme (NRPP) identified the key constituents of activity on the ground that were required to deliver outcomes at neighbourhood level – police visibility, which would enable community engagement to determine public priorities, which could then be tackled through joint problem-solving with partners and the public.

Government plans for neighbourhood policing set out in *Building Communities, Beating Crime* (Home Office 2004a) drew on the NRPP and other international and UK local policing models. The white paper put forward the view that community policing in the UK, while it could potentially reassure the public, had lacked the targeting and problem-solving focus required to reduce crime. The National Intelligence Model (NIM) was proposed as the means to support the analysis and targeting of resources on priority problems required by neighbourhood policing. An ACPO team was commissioned to develop the programme and to provide intensive implementation support. In 2005, the government committed to establishing neighbourhood policing teams in every neighbourhood by 2008, supported by police community support officers.

The key features of neighbourhood policing set out in the white paper and in ACPO documents are supported by evidence of 'what works' and what leads to implementation failure:

- Dedicated resources to avoid abstracting officers to duties outside neighbourhoods.

- Community engagement to identify and address priority problems.
- Stronger partnership working arrangements and mechanisms to target resources at local priorities, such as joint tasking and co-ordination groups through NIM.
- Organizational and cultural change to support the emphasis on local problem-solving.

While the meaning and origin of the term are open to question (Innes 2005), neighbourhood policing can be understood as an attempt to bring together key features of community policing, problem-oriented policing and intelligence-led policing (Tilley 2003).

Rachel Tuffin

Related entries

Community policing; Community support officers (CSOs); Intelligence-led policing; National Intelligence Model (NIM); Problem-oriented policing; Reassurance policing.

Key texts and sources

Innes, M. (2005) 'Why "soft" policing is hard: on the curious development of reassurance policing, how it became neighbourhood policing and what this signifies about the politics of police reform', *Journal of Community and Applied Social Psychology*, 15: 156–69.

Tilley, N. (2003) 'Community policing, problem-oriented policing and intelligence-led policing', in T. Newburn (ed.) *Handbook of Policing*. Cullompton: Willan Publishing.

See also ACPO's neighbourhood policing web page (**http://www.neighbourhoodpolicing.co.uk/**), Community Engagement in Policing's website (**http://www.communityengagement.police.uk/**), the Home Office's neighbourhood policing web page (**http://police.homeoffice.gov.uk/community-policing/neighbourhood-police**) and the Home Office Research, Development and Statistics Directorate's publications web page (**http://www. homeoffice. gov.uk/rds/pubsintro1.html**).

NEIGHBOURHOOD WARDENS

Neighbourhood wardens are municipal policing auxiliaries who provide a visible and semi-official presence in residential areas, undertaking a range of neighbourhood management activities aimed at community development.

Closely allied to the government's Neighbourhood Renewal agenda, the arrival in 2001 of neighbourhood wardens greatly increased the number of municipal, estate-based warden schemes operating in the UK. Neighbourhood wardens were a policy response of the Social Exclusion Unit to the problems afflicting Britain's most socially and economically marginalized areas. In the context of increasing fear of crime and social polarization, coupled with the decline in secondary social control occupations (Jones and Newburn 2002) and the perceived withdrawal of community-focused police patrols in residential areas, neighbourhood wardens were seen as a means by which local communities could be provided with regular access to a familiar and visible figure of authority. The policy drew inspiration from the positive experiences of the Dutch *Stadswacht* scheme of 'city wardens', which employed the long-term unemployed to perform a range of supervisory roles without recourse to formal powers (Hauber *et al.* 1996). Similarly, neighbourhood wardens act as an intermediary between informal and formal modes of social control. While they may gain police accreditation status and thus be empowered to issue fixed-penalty notices for minor acts of anti-social behaviour, their powers are mostly informal and are derived from their personality and identity traits (Crawford and Lister 2004).

In 2000 the government established the Neighbourhood Wardens' Unit to deliver the Neighbourhood Wardens' Programme, investing £91 million in 245 'neighbourhood', 'street' and 'street crime' warden schemes between 2000 and 2006. These different schemes fulfil similar roles, albeit the latter two extend their activities beyond residential areas. Local councils, housing associations and multi-agency partnerships have established a comparable number of neighbourhood warden schemes, many of which appear to have been stimulated by the Crime and Disorder Act 1998. As central government funding of warden schemes was mostly for an initial period of three and half years, their long-term sustainability has been a key concern. Indeed, many have folded either as a result of the time-bounded nature of their funding or, in some instances, as a result of local funding being switched to finance other 'community-orientated' forms of policing, such as community support officers.

Given that most neighbourhood warden schemes aim to build community cohesion and to improve the 'liveability' of public spaces, they tend to have a breadth of functions. These usually include monitoring social housing stock and tenancy management; maintaining the physical environment by early reporting of visible signs of disorder, such as graffiti and criminal damage; facilitating community development, fostering intergroup understanding and supporting vulnerable and excluded groups; and preventing crime and disorder, dealing with neighbourhood disputes and reducing fear of crime (Crawford et al. 2005a). Visible patrol, liaising with residents and engaging in partnership work with housing managers, local police and a range of other service-providing agencies are therefore prominent aspects of the role.

The breadth of functions in warden schemes, however, raises some potentially problematic issues for their success. First, it risks diversifying the focus of warden schemes to such an extent that they become pulled in different directions by competing interests in a community. This may result in the activities of wardens being determined by those residents with the greatest capacity to assert their priorities over those of more marginalized residents. Secondly, the 'policing' activities of wardens, such as enforcing evictions and collecting information on anti-social behaviour, may stymie the extent to which they are able to foster trust with residents and engage all parts of the community. This queries not only the extent to which formal powers should be conferred on wardens but also more broadly the collaborative nature of their

relationships with the police. Clearly, wardens should not be viewed solely through a policing lens. The extent to which wardens are able to balance the tensions that emerge through the diversity of the role is a crucial consideration if they are to generate social capital and thus further community well-being (Crawford and Lister 2004).

Stuart Lister

Related entries

Anti-social behaviour; Community policing; Patrol; Plural policing; Reassurance policing.

Key texts and sources

Crawford, A. (2006) 'Fixing broken promises? Neighbourhood wardens and social capital', *Urban Studies*, 43: 957–76.

Office of the Deputy Prime Minister (2004) *Neighbourhood Wardens Scheme Evaluation.* London: ODPM.

See also the Communities and Local Government's neighbourhood wardens web page (**http://www. neighbourhood.gov.uk/page.asp?id=567**) and the Home Office's crime reduction web page on neighbourhood wardens (**http://www. crime reduction.gov.uk/crpinit/crpinit11.htm**).

NEIGHBOURHOOD WATCH

Neighbourhood Watch is a range of programmes based on the idea of crime prevention through citizen surveillance.

Neighbourhood Watch programmes include such things as block watch, home watch, citizen alert and apartment watch in residential areas, and boat watch, farm watch and park watch in non-residential areas. The idea of Neighbourhood Watch grew out of a movement in the USA to promote the greater involvement of citizens in the prevention of crime. One of the first recorded programmes in the USA was a scheme established in Seattle in 1973, and one of the first in the UK was a scheme set up in

Cheshire in 1982. It is estimated that over a quarter of all households in England and Wales are members of Neighbourhood Watch schemes.

Neighbourhood Watch is often implemented as part of a crime prevention package. The typical package is often referred to as the 'big three' and includes Neighbourhood Watch, property marking and home security surveys. Some programmes include a fourth or fifth element, such as citizen patrols, educational programmes or victim support services. Neighbourhood Watch schemes vary in terms of the size of the area covered. One of the smallest schemes was the 'cocoon' Neighbourhood Watch programme in Rochdale in England, which covered just one dwelling and its immediate neighbours. One of the largest was the Manhattan Beach Neighbourhood Watch scheme in Los Angeles, covering a population of over 30,000 residents.

The most frequently recorded mechanism by which watch programmes might reduce criminal behaviour is through residents looking out for suspicious activities and reporting these to the police. This might reduce crime by deterring potential offenders from committing offences or by improving the police's ability to catch them. Other proposed methods are reducing the opportunities for offending or increasing informal social control. The vast majority of programmes identify residential burglary as the sole or most important target crime of Neighbourhood Watch. Other offences mentioned include street robberies, auto thefts and vandalism.

It is still unclear whether Neighbourhood Watch actually works in reducing crime. One review of the literature on the effectiveness of Neighbourhood Watch programmes looked only at evaluations with the strongest research designs and concluded: 'The oldest and best-known community policing program, Neighborhood Watch, is ineffective at preventing crime' (Sherman *et al.* 1997: 353). Another systematic review of evaluations used meta-analytic techniques to determine the effectiveness of Neighbourhood Watch and concluded that, overall, it was associated with reductions in crime (Bennett *et al.* in press).

Overall, Neighbourhood Watch has been described as the largest single organized crime prevention activity ever. However, the reviews of the literature on the effectiveness of Neighbourhood Watch have produced mixed results. One explanation is that programmes vary in their structure and operation. Another is that the evaluations vary in their ability to determine outcome effectiveness. One of the challenges for the future is to find out under what conditions Neighbourhood Watch works.

Trevor Bennett

Related entries

Burglary; Community policing; Crime prevention (situational and social); Private policing.

Key texts and sources

Bennett, T.H., Holloway, K. and Farrington, D.P. (in press) 'Does Neighbourhood Watch reduce crime? A systematic review and meta-analysis', *Journal of Experimental Criminology*.

Sherman, L.W., Gottfredson, D.C., MacKenzie, D.L., Eck, J., Reuter, P. and Bushway, S. (1997) *Preventing Crime: What Works, What Doesn't, What's Promising*. Washington, DC: US Office of Justice Programs.

See also the website of Neighbourhood Watch (http://www.neighbourhoodwatch.uk.com/) and the Home Office's web page on Neighbourhood Watch (http://www.crimereduction.gov.uk/nbhwatch.htm).

NEW PUBLIC MANAGEMENT (NPM)

The term 'new public management' (NPM) was originally coined by Christopher Hood in the early 1990s to describe a series of developments that had taken place to transform public administration from its traditional bureaucratic model of the postwar period and that were increasingly apparent in the western world (Hood 1991).

The phenomenon of new public management (NPM) was, from the outset, also variously labelled as 'public sector managerialism' (Pollitt 1993), 'market-based public administration' (Lan and Rosenbloom 1992) and 'entrepeneurial government' (Osborne and Gaebler 1992), and was generally regarded as representing a new model (or paradigm shift) for public administration.

As Hood (1991: 7) himself recognized, 'there is no single accepted explanation or interpretation of why NPM coalesced and why it caught on'. However, more than anything, its advent was seen to reflect a widening perception in governmental circles that the conventional model of administration was not working as well as was desired and a response to the growing challenge to the traditions and values on which that model had been based. Worsening economic conditions in the mid-1970s provided the opportunity for New Right economics to take root in governmental thinking. A fierce critique of the state as a burden on the economy and on individual enterprise and of the inherent inefficiency in service provision of public bureaucracies therefore developed. The solution, the argument ran, was to manage the public sector more like business – and so the essence of NPM was established.

Christopher Hood (1991) captured this essence in his description of seven doctrines:

1. *Hands-on professional management in the public sector*: implying sharper accountability through more 'active, visible, discretionary control of organisations from named persons at the top' (1991: 4).
2. *Explicit standards and measures of performance*: implying the setting of clear goals and performance targets and the more thorough monitoring of achievements against them.
3. *Greater emphasis on output controls*: implying more orientation to the results and correspondingly less preoccupation with the procedures and inputs involved.
4. *A shift to disaggregation of units*: implying the breaking up of the monolithic bureaucracies into a series of manageably sized units, each operating as a distinct budget (or cost) centre.
5. *A shift to greater competition in the public sector*: implying more contracting out and public tendering processes, using rivalry as a key to better standards and lower costs.

6. *A stress on private sector styles of management practice*: implying a shift from the traditional public service ethos, the adoption of more flexibility in hiring and rewarding personnel and the adoption of other methods and techniques used in the private sector to incentivize efficiency and effectiveness.
7. *A stress on greater discipline and parsimony in resource use*: implying a fresh emphasis on cost-cutting, stronger resistance to union demands, limitations on compliance costs and a commitment to the ethic of value for money and 'doing more with less'.

The extent to which these various doctrines were evident in practice in both different public services and different countries around the world was the subject of much debate, and most analysts of the phenomenon of NPM acknowledged its inherent complexities and, indeed, its contradictions. There was also a recognition of its evolving character, with some commentators (for example, Davis 1997) arguing that the development of 'contractualization' that was experienced by some public services (e.g. the National Health Service in the UK) itself represented a progression to a separate model in its own right. Similarly, Raine and Willson (1995b) argued in the context of the criminal justice sector that the growing interest in partnership and collaborative working between agencies also represented a new public organizational model. More generally throughout the 1990s there was also a growing recognition of the development of the NPM model in the direction of a consumerist doctrine, with the contemporary public service agenda becoming increasingly absorbed with issues of customer service, quality, marketing and the notion of 'choice' – ideas that were, at best, implicit, and certainly not explicitly captured, in Hood's original typology of a decade earlier.

Particularly in UK policing, early signs of NPM were to be found in the Conservative government's Financial Management Initiative of the early 1980s and in the various circulars that followed (e.g. Home Office Circulars 114/83 and 106/88), designed to promote greater efficiency and productivity and the application of market principles (McLaughlin and Muncie 1993).

Subsequently, the Sheehy and Posen Inquiries, and the Labour government's further emphasis on managerial reform, strengthening accountability and performance improvement (alongside its various policy reforms in pursuit of crime reduction), all left a significant legacy of greatly increased central control in the service. Indeed, in 2005, the same managerial agenda largely underlay the government's plans for a regionalization of policing by amalgamations of neighbouring forces (plans that were only abandoned when a new Home Secretary bowed to the intense opposition that had grown up in various quarters).

In public services more generally, the phenomenon of NPM has absorbed and preoccupied the public administration academic community, and a sizeable literature has been compiled that examines and critiques its impact across the public sector around the world. Hughes (1998: 78) summarizes the complexity of the debate by highlighting the key weaknesses of the NPM model:

1. The questionable basis of the economics of managerialism.
2. The potentially poor fit of the private sector model for a public service context.
3. The limits of a neo-Taylorist preoccupation with scientific management and measurement.
4. The failure to take account of the political nature of public services.
5. Difficulties in making public servants publicly accountable, as the model demanded.
6. Shortcomings in the capability of the bureaucracy to implement the model effectively.
7. Inadequate clarity about exactly what the managerial model demanded beyond the generalities of performance measurement, incentives and programme budgeting etc.

His overall assessment was that, in essence, the managerialist agenda was quite simple: 'that governments provide scarce resources to public programmes and wish to know that public ends are being served in an efficient and effective manner' (1998: 78). His general conclusion was that the NPM model 'contains some valid points but is unconvincing, or at least unproven' and that the ensuing debate had usefully raised important questions about the role of the public service and of government in society:

> *Managerialism does not mean usurpation of government by technocrats, a reduction in accountability or a diminution of democracy. All the managerial changes do is allow for public purposes to be carried out in a more efficient, cost-effective way, by providing more and better information to those making decisions*
>
> (1998: 79).

Hughes has also predicted that the entrepreneurial trend established under NPM will continue and that public servants will become more innovation minded in relation to the supply of services, and with much less emphasis on direct governmental provision. One sure sign of the prospects for this scenario is the ongoing fascination of governments around the world with private finance and privatization programmes.

John Raine

Related entries

Community safety; Consultation; Crime and Disorder Act 1998; Crime reduction; Interagency policing; Rank structure.

Key texts and sources

Hughes, O. (2003) *Public Management and Administration* (3rd edn). Basingstoke: Macmillan.
McLaughlin, K., Osborne, S. and Ferlie, E. (eds) (2002) *New Public Management: Current Trends and Future Prospects*. London: Routledge.

O

OFFENDER PROFILING

> Offender profiling comprises a range of techniques (mainly psychology based) for inferring the characteristics of offenders from crime scene behaviours in order to assist in the prioritizing of suspects and lines of inquiry.

The term 'offender profiling' entered common parlance in the 1970s, with the development of the Behavioural Science Unit (BSU) at the Federal Bureau of Investigation (FBI) Academy in the USA. Representatives of the BSU claimed that behavioural information gleaned from the crime scene could be used 'Like a fingerprint, [where] the crime scene can be used to aid in identifying the murder' (Ressler *et al.* 1986).

In the UK, based largely on David Canter's recommendation for a more scientific approach (1995), there is greater recognition of the need for developing multiple strands of research to test the reliability of drawing such inferences about criminal characteristics from crime scene actions. (Canter assisted the Surrey Police in the case of John Duffy, one of the offenders in the 'railway rapist' case.) Specifically, Alison *et al.* (2002) questioned the feasibility of the FBI's claim of drawing direct 'one to one' relationships between how an offender acts and his or her background characteristics (i.e. age, socio-economic status, marital status and personality). They suggested that researchers more closely examine the multifarious situational pathways that can effect how any given criminal event emerges.

Historically, many authors have argued for a distinction between so-called 'clinical and statistical' and 'inductive and deductive' approaches, with various key figures in the field inappropriately categorized (and indeed polarized) into one or other camp. For example, Paul Britton, the psychologist who controversially drew up a profile in the Wimbledon Common murder investigation that was roundly criticized in court, by the popular press and by several academic psychologists, has been classified as representing a 'clinical' approach. In contrast, David Canter has often been portrayed as an exemplar of the 'statistical approach'. Such extreme views do not really reflect the current picture of contemporary approaches, which are based on a combination of evidence-based research, case-based analysis and close collaboration with the inquiry team in trying to appreciate the situation-specific features of the crime (see Alison *et al.* 2004).

In the UK at least, a more moderate view of what is possible in profiling has emerged, in which 'profilers' are one small part of a very large picture of the investigation. Thus, in recent years, there has been less focus on individual 'profilers' as representing competing camps and, rather, greater recognition of a broader definition of offender profiling. The contemporary view recognizes that advisers can contribute to DNA intelligence-led screens, risk assessments, interview advice, linking crimes, media strategy and a plethora of other domains in which an understanding of psychological principles can assist an inquiry team in understanding the offender and prioritizing lines of inquiry. In recognition of this wider remit and in an effort to distance the discipline from its largely intuitive but hyperbolic claims, practitioners have adopted the term 'behavioural investigative advice'. In the UK this has led to an accredited list of profilers and a more robust method of screening and evaluating contributions from advisers.

Although there is no doubt that the UK boasts some of the highest professional standards of behavioural science contributions, based largely on an almost wholly exclusively UK-based research agenda, there is very little to assist senior investigating officers in evaluating how to act on the advice contained in such reports. Recent work, conducted by Alison and his colleagues in collaboration with the behavioural investigative advisers at Bramshill, is now beginning to emerge that has begun to address this question, and greater academic efforts are being invested in understanding the range of possible contributions from behavioural support and the most effective methods for utilizing such advice (see http://www.liv.ac.uk/University/scieng/psychology/ccir/).

Laurence Alison

Related entries

Crime mapping; Forensic and investigative psychology; Geographic(al) profiling.

Key texts and sources

Alison, L. (2005) *The Forensic Psychologist's Casebook: Psychological Profiling and Criminal Investigation.* Cullompton: Willan Publishing.

Alison, L., Bennell, C., Mokros, A. and Ormerod, D. (2002) 'The personality paradox in offender profiling: a theoretical review of the processes involved in deriving background characteristics from crime scene actions', *Psychology, Public Policy and Law*, 8: 115–35.

Canter, D. (1995) *Criminal Shadows: In the Mind of the Serial Killer.* London: HarperCollins.

Ressler, R., Burgess, A., Douglas, J., Hartman, C. and D'Agostino, R. (1986) 'Murderers who rape and mutilate', *Journal of Interpersonal Violence*, 1: 273–87.

ORGANIZED CRIME

Article 2 of the UN Convention against Transnational Organized Crime (2000) defines an organized criminal group as 'a structured group of three or more persons, existing for a period of time and acting in concert with the aim of committing one or more serious crimes or offences ... in order to obtain, directly or indirectly, a financial or other material benefit.'

Since the 1960s, an increasing diversity of criminal groups has augmented the more traditional forms of organized crime, such as those represented by the Mafia and similar groupings. Motorcycle and youth gangs and black, Asian and Hispanic crime groups have expanded in the USA and elsewhere. Terrorist groups are also routinely involved in international crime, especially drugs and trafficking in arms. Many of these groups are international in the sense that they operate in several jurisdictions. However, whether we should describe them as 'transnational' (in the sense that they transcend every jurisdiction) is debatable.

We can properly use the term 'enterprise crime' to describe many of the activities of organized crime. The activities of enterprise crime are on the same continuum as those of legitimate business but operate beyond prescribed legal limits. For example, offering 'security' by means of protection rackets is an illicit form of security provision. Dealing in prohibited goods is an illicit form of trading. The main enterprise activities of organized crime groups include trafficking in drugs and people. The worldwide demand for heroin, cocaine and cannabis provides an important vehicle for criminal groups to make large profits. People smuggling for economic and other reasons is an illicit form of immigration. Trafficking in women and children to feed the sex industry is also increasing. Both types may involve force or coercion.

Not all organized crime involves 'gang-related' activity. White-collar and corporate crime often amounts to organized crime. Fraud of all kinds, including fraud against supranational bodies such as the EU, is widespread. The profits from such activities are huge. Because much organized crime is actually business crime, there is an increased blurring of the line between legitimate and illicit business. Criminal groups use money laundering extensively to convert the proceeds of crime into legitimate assets. International efforts against money laundering to 'follow the money' are necessary to stem the tide of activity in this area.

New forms of organized crime have become evident in Europe and elsewhere. These often involve collaboration between groups, such as the Mafia, triads, indigenous criminal groups and international drugs producers. Since the political changes of the late 1980s, organized crime in Russia and eastern and central Europe has expanded rapidly. However, despite the evident collaboration, it is difficult to prove that a kind of *Pax Mafioso* or merger exists between these groups. Globalization has also facilitated the growth of organized crime emanating from and preying upon the developing world. The rapid growth of the economies of China and India may pose new problems in this field.

Measures for policing organized crime operate at the national and international levels. In the UK, in addition to the role of police forces in combating organized crime, the Serious and Organized Crime Agency (SOCA) brings together police, customs and intelligence officers to deal with serious cases and to form links with agencies abroad. The security services have increasingly become involved in this field, especially where there are links with terrorism. The expansion of the Europol mission provides a means of combating organized crime across Europe. International conventions, especially those relating to drugs and to the seizure of criminal assets, help to tackle the problems of organized crime internationally.

Alan Wright

Related entries

Drugs and policing; Human trafficking; Serious Organized Crime Agency (SOCA); Transnational policing; Victim and witness support.

Key texts and sources

Lyman, M. and Potter, G.W. (2004) *Organized Crime* (3rd edn). Upper Saddle River, NJ: Pearson.

Wright, A. (2006) *Organised Crime*. Cullompton: Willan Publishing.

SOCA's website is at **http://www.soca.gov.uk/**. A useful bibliographic database is available online at **http//www.yorku.ca/nathanson/search.htm**. See also the Home Office's web page on organized and international crime (**http://www.homeoffice. gov.uk/crime-victims/reducing-crime/organised-crime/**) and the Office of Public Sector Information's website for the Serious Organized Crime and Police Act 2005 (**http://www.opsi. gov.uk/ACTS/acts2005/20050015.htm**).

P

PARAMILITARY POLICING

> Paramilitary policing is a descriptive and/or pejorative characterization of the style, organization, weaponry and tactics of policing that likens it to the military.

The characterization of policing as 'paramilitary' is rarely value neutral, for it is assumed to be the polar opposite of civil and/or democratic policing. This reflects the liberal model of policing in which the state's monopoly of force is entrusted to two custodians: on the one hand the military, who use the maximum permissible force against enemy combatants and, on the other, the police, who are expected to use the minimum of force sufficient to subdue suspected criminals. Paramilitary policing dissolves this distinction and is rhetorically associated with such concepts as 'police states', 'army of occupation', etc.

Descriptively, paramilitary policing means police operating ancillary to the military. Less strictly, it has come to mean adopting military characteristics (e.g. uniforms, command structure, weaponry, etc.); more accurately, it means *quasi-military*. In this sense, many contemporary police forces are paramilitary. European gendarmeries have both civil and military responsibilities; many of them are or have been both police forces in times of peace and light infantry in times of war. Typically, gendarmes are accountable through ministries of defence rather than ministries of the interior. Historically, colonial police were organized in similar ways, albeit that, throughout the British Empire, there was an aspiration to adopt a civil policing style, but this was repeatedly frustrated by the need to repress insurgencies. However, both the Royal Canadian Mounted Police and New Zealand Police made the successful transition from paramilitary to civil policing.

'Paramilitary policing' often refers to a *style* of policing: one that relies on force to repress popular resistance. Heavily armed special weapons and tactics (SWAT) and/or riot police are most likely to earn the sobriquet of being 'paramilitary'. SWAT officers are heavily armed compared with other officers and are indistinguishable from military special forces that perform similar duties (e.g. hostage rescue). Riot squads, whether military or police, use similar equipment and tactics, and critics argue that even defensive equipment (e.g. shields) can lend the police an appearance of invincibility.

These apparent similarities disguise important differences between the police and military. For example, the ubiquitous Heckler and Koch MP5 (used by military special forces and SWAT squads) is marketed to police forces as *semi* rather than *fully* automatic. The assumption that weaponry will inevitably be used aggressively is also questionable. For example, McPhail *et al.* (1998) document how, during a period in which 'paramilitary' riot control became more available, public order policing in the USA replaced 'escalated force' with 'negotiated management' (a transition found elsewhere; della Porta and Reiter 1998). This was also a period during which many police forces worldwide embraced 'community policing'.

The debate between Waddington (1987, 1991, 1993a) and Jefferson (1987, 1990, 1993) concluded in agreement that the difference between them lay in the perspective each took. As a top-down method of repressing crime and disorder, paramilitary policing has advantages over traditional methods but, from the bottom up this is likely to be experienced as repressive and can engender antagonism.

P.A.J. Waddington

Related entries

Colonial policing; Force (police use of); Military policing; Models of policing; Police Service of Northern Ireland (PSNI); Vigilantism.

Key texts and sources

Jefferson, T. (1990) *The Case against Paramilitary Policing.* Milton Keynes: Open University Press.

Kraska, P.B. (ed.) (2001) *Militarising the American Criminal Justice System: The Changing Roles of the Armed Forces and the Police.* New York, NY: NYU Press.

Waddington, P.A.J. (1991) *The Strong Arm of the Law.* Oxford: Clarendon Press.

PATROL

Patrol is 'the backbone of policing' (Cordner 1989: 60), with various studies estimating that the majority of police resources are devoted to foot and vehicle patrol activities.

Through patrol duties the police perform a number of broad functions, including the prevention and detection of criminal behaviour, the management of public order problems and traffic occurrences, and the provision of assistance to the public (Horton 1989: 33). However, the detail of patrol work is difficult to define precisely because it 'is determined almost entirely by what the public asks the police to do' (Bayley 1994: 16).

The activity of patrol is embedded within the historical development of policing and grew out of early changes to the machinery of law and order in medieval England. During the thirteenth century, legislation required that all towns create a 'watch' for the purpose of maintaining order at a local level, and residents were periodically required to serve as unpaid watchmen in their area. The primary function of the watch was to patrol the streets at night, with the power to question and detain suspicious or disruptive persons (Rawlings 2003: 45). Particularly from the eighteenth century the watch was gradually professionalized as the role of patrolling the streets became a salaried activity, financed through local rates. Indeed, by the nineteenth century some areas had established very effective patrol services (Paley 1989). In addition, from the mid-eighteenth century, in London, patrol activities were gradually expanded through the development of a variety of additional, centrally funded initiatives. Most famously, the Bow Street horse and foot patrols were established to police the highways and suburban areas around the capital, adding another layer of patrol provision.

While 1829 saw the reorganization of law and order across London (and subsequently throughout England), patrol continued to be a central function of the duties of the New Police. Following the introduction of the Metropolitan Police Act 1829 a force of 3,000 uniformed officers was established in the capital to prevent crime – a task that, in theory at least, was to be achieved through the deterrent effect of rigorous beat patrolling. This development saw some notable changes to the nature of patrolling, such as alterations to the geography of patrol routes and a more intensive focus on daytime patrols (Paley 1989). Nevertheless, order maintenance continued to be a central facet of patrol. Thus, the daytime patrol activities of the New Police were closely tied to the enforcement of order in public places – a task that was accomplished through the regulation of those (mainly) working-class groups who congregated on the streets (Emsley 1996: 152). Indeed, patrol was (and has remained) a key instrument through which the police were brought into regular contact with their 'property' (Reiner 2000: 93).

Traditional methods of beat patrol remained central to policing delivery throughout (and beyond) the first half of the twentieth century (Newburn 2003a: 85). However, in response to issues such as the proliferation of motor transport, particularly after 1945, the police use of vehicles in service delivery increased. This, in turn, was reflected in changes to the nature and characteristics of patrolling, with many walking beats being replaced or supplemented by motorized patrols. The introduction of 'unit beat policing' during the 1960s is one such example of this movement (Emsley 1996: 176).

The activity of patrol remains a central component of modern policing systems and (particularly in respect of calls for a more wholehearted return to walking beats) is an enduring theme in popular discourses about the preferred future direction of policing (Bowling and Foster 2002: 989).

John Locker

Related entries

Beat; Bow Street 'Runners'; Civilianization; Community support officers (CSOs); Neighbourhood policing; Neighbourhood wardens; Neighbourhood Watch; Plural policing; Reassurance policing; Roads (policing of); Special Constabulary; Specialist squads; Stop and search; Unit beat policing (UBP).

Key texts and sources

Cordner, G.W. (1989) 'The police on patrol', in D.J. Kenney (ed.) *Police and Policing: Contemporary Issues.* New York, NY: Praeger.
Emsley, C. (1996) *The English Police.* London: Longman.

PATTEN REPORT

The Patten Report, which was published in September 1999, was a result of the 1998 Good Friday Agreement reached in Belfast. Its recommendations led to the formation of the new Police Service of Northern Ireland.

The Independent Commission on Policing for Northern Ireland was a product of the agreement reached in Belfast on Good Friday 1998 between political parties in Northern Ireland and the British and Irish governments. It was chaired by former British Cabinet minister, Chris Patten. Some of the other seven commissioners had extensive knowledge and experience of policing.

Detailed policing principles and terms of reference were set out in the Good Friday Agreement (GFA). The objective was the creation of a police service appropriate to post-conflict circumstances. One requirement was that the service should become more representative – by 1998 only 8 per cent of Royal Ulster Constabulary (RUC) officers were Roman Catholics, whereas Catholics made up over 40 per cent of Northern Ireland's population. Another was that the service should become more accountable to the community, adequate accountability having been a problem during the years of active terrorism and serious civil disorder. Yet another was the aim that policing be delivered in partnership with the community at all levels. And stress was laid on the need for delegation of authority within the police, which had also been difficult during the emergency.

The commission conducted wide-ranging consultations. These included numerous public meetings all over Northern Ireland and listening to the views of officers serving at all levels in the RUC. The commission reported in September 1999. It made 175 recommendations, the vast majority of which were widely welcomed, particularly in police circles.

The Chief Constable was to be accountable for his or her performance and that of the police to a powerful Policing Board, the majority of whose members were to be drawn from among the representatives of the main political parties in the Northern Ireland Assembly, a legislative body envisaged in the GFA. Although the Chief Constable would retain operational responsibility, the board was to be empowered to call for reports on all aspects of police activity, including operational matters and, where appropriate, to initiate follow-up inquiries. Police performance was to be measured against the board's policing plan and a variety of other indicators designed to achieve best practice and best value. At district command level, partnerships were to be established with local people designed to enable police performance in each district to be assessed publicly and to encourage local communities to share responsibility for policing with the police. Measures were proposed designed to free district commanders from the straitjacket of hierarchical bureaucracy endemic in the conventional policing model and to give them the flexibility to deploy their resources as they should see fit. The report committed the new 'Police Service of Northern Ireland' to new standards of ethics and human rights.

The more controversial proposals included the recommendation that, for a 10-year period, Catholics and non-Catholics should be recruited from a pool of eligible applicants on a 50/50 basis. Another was that the RUC be renamed and rebadged to remove references to the British state. Thus the Police Service of Northern Ireland (PSNI) came into existence. Today, the proportion of Catholics in the police is approaching three times that of the RUC and is rising steadily towards equivalence with the proportion of Catholics in the population as a whole.

In spite of the failure of other institutions envisaged in the GFA to take root, the Policing Board and district policing partnerships have been established, and the Patten reforms are generally judged to have been a success, the PSNI currently enjoying a high level of confidence in both communities.

Peter Smith

Related entries

Accountability and governance; Ethics in policing; Force (police use of); Less lethal weapons; Police Service of Northern Ireland (PSNI).

Key texts and sources

Independent Commission on Policing in Northern Ireland (1999) *A New Beginning: Policing in Northern Ireland. The Report of the Independent Commission on Policing in Northern Ireland* (the Patten Report). Belfast: Independent Commission on Policing in Northern Ireland.
See also Ulster University's 'Conflict archive on the Internet' web page on the Patten Report summary of recommendations (http://cain.ulst.ac.uk/issues / police/patten/recommend.htm) and the Northern Ireland Office's web page on the Patten Report (http://www.nio.gov.uk/index/faq/niofaq-policing.htm).

PEACE SUPPORT OPERATIONS (THE POLICE CONTRIBUTION)

A peace support operation is an operation that impartially makes use of diplomatic, civil and military means, normally in pursuit of UN charter purposes or principles, to restore or maintain peace. Such operations may include conflict prevention, peacemaking, peace enforcement, peacekeeping, peace-building and/or humanitarian operations. The contribution of the police to achieving domestic peace and stability is increasingly recognized as vital.

The end of the Cold War was the catalyst for major changes in both international relations and the role of armed forces. The old order of two competing politico-military blocks was swept away, to be replaced by a world of widespread disorder. The number and complexity of peacekeeping missions undertaken by the UN since 1989 have grown dramatically. Indeed, 'peacekeeping' has been superseded by the term 'peace support operations', which embraces the reality of all those activities designed to prevent conflict and regenerate or sustain fragile states. A world of international disputes has become one where the main threat arises from intra-state conflict.

New capabilities are required to sustain or regenerate fragile states and, increasingly, there has been a recognition by politicians and diplomats that domestic order is a prerequisite for prosperity and development generally. The rule of law, complemented by effective policing, is a key constituent of any nation or society. Thus policing has become a central pillar of many peace support operations.

Peace support operations are widely thought to be confined to peace enforcement and post-conflict reconstruction scenarios. However, ideally, peace support operations should also be mounted in countries at risk of instability, where a limited assistance effort might well avert widespread conflict.

The exact nature of the police contribution to peace support operations will vary from mission to mission. It must be relevant to the needs of the country in question and be integrated into the overall mission's goals and plan of operations. It should be noted that the term 'police' is a broad one in the international context, with some countries' police forces having constitutional links with their ministries of defence and deploying capabilities not regarded in the UK as police matters. The challenge in such missions is to ensure that contributing countries provide contingents that are mutually compatible and that, together, can provide a service that meets the needs, above all, of the local population.

The police contribution to peace support missions not only addresses the immediate needs of the conflict area but also, by tackling issues of lawlessness, impacts positively on international crime, including terrorism. British police officers have made significant contributions in recent years to peace support operations in Bosnia-Herzegovina, East Timor, Iraq, Kosovo and Sierra Leone.

Paul Kernaghan

Related entries

National security; Terrorism; Transnational policing.

Key texts and sources

Ministry of Defence (2004) *The Military Contribution to Peace Support Operations. Joint Warfare Publication* 3-50 (2nd edn). London: Ministry of Defence.

PEEL, SIR ROBERT

As Home Secretary, Sir Robert Peel was responsible for the introduction in London in 1829 of the new Metropolitan Police Force (the 'Peelers').

Robert Peel was born the son of a wealthy cotton manufacturer in Lancashire, in 1788. Educated at Harrow and Oxford, he began to work towards a career in law but, under his father's influence, he entered the House of Commons in 1809 as a member of a Tory government. In 1817, his strong opposition to catholic emancipation made him a national figure. As a result, he was elected MP for Oxford University. Working under Lord Liverpool, Peel helped to direct the military operations against the French, and was rewarded with an appointment as Chief Secretary for Ireland. However, the lengthy and tiring frequent trips between Dublin and London took their toll. He resigned in 1818 and held no office until he became Home Secretary in 1822. Peel relied on expert advice throughout his time in office, so that he always appeared and, indeed, was well prepared whenever he spoke in the House. He passed eight pieces of legislation between 1822 and 1827 that changed and/or consolidated the criminal law and repealed more than 250 outdated laws. As a result of this programme of large-scale reform of the legal system, George Canning thought that Peel was 'the most efficient Home Secretary that this country ever saw'. In 1822 Peel proposed that a House of Commons Select Committee under his chairmanship should investigate the policing of London. However, the committee reported that an effective system of policing could not be reconciled with a free society. Peel left government when Canning became Prime Minister in 1827, but his second spell as Home Secretary in the Duke of Wellington's government allowed him to return to the topic of policing. In 1829 he introduced the new Metropolitan Police Force, which became known (for obvious reasons) as the 'Peelers'.

His time in government was again cut short when Wellington was replaced by Earl Grey in 1830. In opposition, he became leader of the Tories and, in 1834, on the dissolution of Grey's administration, he became Prime Minister. He argued for gradual reforms while preserving traditions. With the support of the Whigs, Peel's government was able to pass some important bills. However, he was constantly being outvoted in the House of Commons and, on 8 April 1835, he resigned. In August 1841 Peel was once again invited to form a Conservative administration, and he spent the following decade trying to govern Ireland through the tragic period of the

Irish potato famine in 1845. Peel realized that the only way to avert starvation was to remove the duties on imported corn but, although the Corn Laws were repealed in 1846, the policy split the Conservative Party and Peel was forced to resign. Four years later, Peel was badly injured after falling from his horse, and he died on 2 July 1850.

Barry Godfrey

Related entries

Colonial policing; Metropolitan Police/New Police; Rowan and Mayne.

Key texts and sources

Gash, N. (1985) *Mr Secretary Peel: The Life of Sir Robert Peel to 1830.* London: Longman.
Gash, N. (1986) *Sir Robert Peel: The Life of Sir Robert Peel after 1830.* London: Longman.

PLURAL POLICING

Plural policing refers to the patchwork of policing provision and authorization – involving a mix of the police, municipal auxiliaries, commercial security and the activities of the citizenry – that is replacing the idea of the police as the monopolistic guardians of public security.

'Plural policing' refers simultaneously to the growing mix of public, parochial and private forms of policing and to a shift in the focus of policing studies away from a preoccupation with the professional state police towards a broader concern with social regulation, law enforcement and order maintenance conducted by a plethora of formal and informal actors and systems of control. It is both *a new way of looking at policing*, which is no longer police centred, and *a new set of things to look at* – namely, the growing role of the non-state sector. Conceptually, policing is unshackled from its association with what the police alone do. The state-centred thinking that dominated social sciences largely blinded policing research from understanding the governing

capacities of diverse forms of extra-state regulation. There is growing recognition that the police are only a small element in society's total policing endeavours and acknowledgement that new providers and authorizers of security have emerged. Contributing to this reorientation of policing studies, Johnston and Shearing have articulated an approach that proceeds from the theme of 'security governance', defined as 'the property of networks rather than as the product of any single centre of action' (2003: 148). They deliberately accord no conceptual priority to the state in order to highlight the range of governmental intersections that exist and the relationships between them. The precise nature of policing arrangements and the role of various contributors are matters for empirical inquiry. Importantly, this perspective challenges us to think critically about the distinctiveness of state action and the possibilities of private and parochial forms of governance. It directs attention to the diverse tasks undertaken by non-state security agents and the complex interactions and relations between different providers.

Much focus has concentrated on the visible face of policing and the array of patrol and guarding agents employed in diverse spheres of social life. This includes neighbourhood wardens on housing estates, concierges in apartment blocks and offices, private security guards in shopping and retail outlets, door supervisors or 'bouncers' in bars and nightclubs, stewards at entertainment venues, park police in open spaces and recreational areas, street wardens and city-guards in town centres and traffic wardens patrolling the streets – all of whom impact upon public security in routine, but essential, ways. Non-state policing agents also provide investigation services, including private detectives, debt collectors and bailiffs. Much of this activity engenders little public scrutiny as cases often do not end up in court, largely because the commercial objectives of private investigations are not necessarily compatible with prosecution. Policing can also feature as a secondary or ancillary task in many occupations, as diverse as teachers, taxi-drivers and landlords. Given the salience of concerns over insecurity and behaviour, security-related tasks may become more widespread and explicit. Increasingly, citizens are also enlisted as active 'partners' against crime and anti-social behaviour. A further dimension of plural policing has seen the embedding of security features or technologies into the built environment. Policing here becomes part of the architecture through security designs, surveillance and situational crime prevention. Technological developments promoted by the commercial sector have driven an expansion in the manufacture, sale and installation of electronic and physical equipment.

Research has shown that different forms of plural policing deploy divergent styles, tools and techniques and are often informed by different understandings of problem-solving. These are not always reducible to public/private distinctions, but the strategies of commercial security tend to be driven more by the business imperatives of security, with an emphasis on instrumental thinking over moral ordering traditionally associated with the police. Commercial policing has tended to prioritize loss prevention and risk reduction rather than the prosecution of offenders. Consequently, in the contemporary mixed economy of security with its complex division of labour and blurred boundaries, public values coalesce around, and collide with, private or parochial interests.

Analogous plural policing developments are to be found in diverse societies, albeit with specific inflections (Jones and Newburn 2006). In the UK, a number of dynamics driving pluralization are noteworthy:

- *The changing nature of land use and property relations*: on the one hand, tracts of public space have been transferred into private ownership; on the other hand, privately owned places have taken on a decidedly public character. These 'quasi-public spaces' are privately owned places open for public access and use (for example, shopping malls, airports and leisure centres). Not least given the need to maximize profits, private corporations have preferred to determine and control their own security in relation to their own needs. Consequently, in 'mass private property', the public are routinely policed by private security and through powers vested in private property. The extent to which the growth of 'mass private property' has the same relevance in the

UK, compared with North America, is questionable. Nevertheless, it highlights that dynamics driving change often lie outside government activity in civil society.

- *The growth of private security*: figures suggest that, in the UK, there are somewhere between 300,000 and 600,000 people employed in the private security industry. The number working in the security guarding sector more than doubled between 1988 and 2004 (http://www.bsia.co.uk/industry. html). Numerically, private security employees now outnumber their police counterparts. However, this growth has not necessarily come at the expense of the police, whose numbers have also increased, notably over the last decade.

- *The limited capacity of the police to meet public demands*: despite growing police numbers, inflated public demand (notably increasing emergency calls) and managerial pressures have made it difficult for the police to attend to the proactive tasks associated with community patrols that the public want. Under managerialist pressures to measure performance, as a means of improving it, professional policing throughout the 1990s narrowed to reactive crime fighting, neglecting the less tangible elements of public reassurance. This mismatch left many looking for alternative providers of locally responsive policing. This 'patrolling vacuum' was exacerbated by the post-war decline in institutions of secondary social control and intermediaries, such as park keepers, train guards and bus conductors.

- *The commercialization of the police*: since the mid-1990s the police have been able to charge more widely for goods and services that they previously provided without charge, including the contracting out of police officers. Increasingly, police forces have exploited this freedom as a means of income generation. More generally, managerial reforms have required the police to open up much of their work to external commercial and internal civilian providers.

- *Local government involvement in security matters*: as local authorities have assumed greater responsibility for community safety, notably in the light of the Crime and Disorder Act 1998 (the Act not only places a duty on all local authorities to work with the police and other partners in local crime and disorder reduction partnerships, but it also requires local authorities to consider the crime and disorder implications of all their activities and decisions (s. 17)), they have sought to assert greater control over the form and direction of local policing endeavours. One manner in which this has expressed itself has been through the funding of additional security patrols from the private sector, police or directly provided and managed in the guise of neighbourhood or street wardens.

There has also been a pluralization within the police organization. The specialization of policing tasks advanced by a workforce modernization agenda has seen the idea of the omni-competent constable give way to different skills-related activities, with different entry points, training requirements and career trajectories. Some of these specialist posts have been opened up to civilian staff. The most notable example has been the introduction of '(police) community support officers' (CSOs) as a new breed of employee dedicated to patrol and with limited powers. Government plans to increase CSO numbers to 16,000 by March 2008 will radically reshape the face of front-line policing. Freed from many of the pressures that serve to abstract constables from contractual arrangements, CSOs will furnish the police with a significant capacity to address the 'patrolling vacuum' and to compete with the private sector in the additional security market. Moreover, given the short-term government funding arrangements to encourage CSO expansion, external income generation from local authorities, housing associations and businesses will increasingly become a significant part of future plans.

The importance of policing beyond the police has been acknowledged in recent policy debates through reference to the notion of the 'extended police family' (Crawford and Lister 2004). This also reflects recognition that, if harnessed in the furtherance of public safety, the total activities of members would amount to more than the sum of the parts. Implicitly, there is an admission that the level of co-ordination between members of the plural policing family has been poor. British research supports this picture of a fragmented patchwork (Crawford *et*

al. 2005b). It suggests that the mixed economy has developed in an uneven manner. Relations between policing providers vary considerably, from effective co-production through partnerships to mutual indifference and rivalry. All too often, relations are poorly organized and co-ordinated, suffer duplication of effort and are marked by competition and mistrust.

As well as questions about effectiveness and co-ordination, pluralization raises important normative and ethical considerations regarding the interests served by security networks, the social implications of differential access to policing resources and how robust forms of governance and regulation are to be secured to ensure plural policing is delivered in accordance with democratic values of justice, equity, accountability and effectiveness. Bayley and Shearing (1996: 585) provocatively claimed: 'Future generations will look back on our era as a time when one system of policing ended and another took its place.' There is some debate over the epochal nature of recent trends, the novelty of pluralization and the precise empirical mix of plural policing (Jones and Newburn 2002). Nevertheless, it has become harder and less appropriate to think of policing solely in terms of what the police do.

Adam Crawford

Related entries

Community support officers (CSOs); Mass private property; Private policing.

Key texts and sources

Bayley, D. and Shearing, C. (1996) 'The future of policing', *Law and Society Review*, 30: 585–606.
Crawford, A. and Lister, S. (2004) *The Extended Policing Family.* York: Joseph Rowntree Foundation.
Crawford, A., Lister, S., Blackburn, S. and Burnett, J. (2005) *Plural Policing: The Mixed Economy of Visible Patrols in England and Wales.* Bristol: Policy Press.
Johnston, L. and Shearing, C. (2003) *Governing Security.* London: Routledge.
Jones, T. and Newburn, T. (2002) 'The transformation of policing?', *British Journal of Criminology*, 42: 129–46.
Jones, T. and Newburn, T. (eds) (2006) *Plural Policing: A Comparative Perspective.* London: Routledge.

POLICE ACT 1964

The Police Act 1964 is one of the most important pieces of legislation affecting policing. Arising out of the Royal Commission on the Police established in 1960, the Act created the tripartite structure of police accountability.

The Police Act 1964 was a response to the perceived need for changes in the existing system of policing and included many recommendations made by the Royal Commission on the Police, which reported in 1962. The Royal Commission was considered necessary to clarify a number of issues, including concerns arising from 'two perennial conflicts: between local and central control on the one hand, and between professional autonomy and democratic governance on the other' (Walker 2000: 67). The Act was also an attempt to bring a degree of national consistency to what had developed into a patchwork of forces of varying shapes and sizes (Oliver 1997: 14).

The Act established the 'tripartite structure' of police accountability, the current system of holding the 43 police forces of England and Wales accountable. This remains the fundamental basis of police governance. The tripartite system distributes responsibilities between the Home Office, the local police authority and the chief constable of the force. Chief constables were given 'direction and control' of their forces, police authorities were responsible for maintaining an 'adequate and efficient' police force and the Home Secretary had a variety of supervisory and co-ordinating functions, including the promotion of police efficiency (Marshall 1965: 96–101; Mawby and Wright 2003: 185). Although the Act separated power, it reinforced that of the Home Office and chief constables at the expense of the local police authorities and contained much 'studied ambiguity' concerning the relative influence of each of the three parties (Jones 2003: 608). Legislation since the 1964 Act, including the Police and Magistrates' Courts Act 1994, the Police Act 1996 and the Police Reform Act 2002, has endorsed the tripartite arrangements, though not always to universal approval as power has tended to move towards the centre.

While the Police Act 1964 is principally referenced in terms of defining the tripartite structure, its effect was far-reaching in other areas, including the following:

- *Amalgamations*: provisions within the Act for the amalgamation of police forces led to a significant restructuring of policing in England and Wales. In 1966 a programme began to reduce the number of forces outside London from 117 to 49; later, under the Local Government Act 1972, these 49 were reduced to 41.
- *Her Majesty's Inspectorate of Constabulary (HMIC)*: Section 38 of the Act specified the inspectors' role and gave them the power to inspect and report to the Home Secretary on the efficiency and effectiveness of police forces.
- *Police complaints*: the Act made provision for the formal recording and investigation of complaints against police officers. Although this did not introduce an independent complaints system, s. 50 required local police authorities and HMIC to keep themselves informed as to how individual forces were dealing with complaints.

In addition, the Act, *inter alia*, extended the jurisdiction of individual constables beyond their local forces to the whole of England and Wales; gave authority for chief officers to enter into collaborative arrangements, thereby making possible regional crime squads; and gave statutory recognition to 'common services', which included the Police Staff College, district training centres and forensic science laboratories.

Rob C. Mawby

Related entries

Accountability and governance; Chief constables; Civil liability; Home Office; Police authorities; Police Reform Act 2002; Royal Commission on the Police (1962).

Key texts and sources

Marshall, G. (1965) *Police and Government*. London: Methuen (Chapter 7 is an account of the passage of the bill through Parliament and discusses the main provisions of the Act. Appendix B is an extract of the Act's main sections).

See also the UK Statute Law Database's website for the text of the Police Act 1964 (http://www.statute law.gov.uk/content.aspx?LegType=All+Legislation &PageNumber=1&NavFrom=3&parentActiveText DocId=1845813&activetextdocid=1846048).

POLICE AND CRIME STANDARDS DIRECTORATE (P&CSD)

The Police and Crime Standards Directorate (P&CSD) aims to maintain standards of excellence in policing and in initiatives that strive to ensure community safety. It is part of the Crime Reduction and Communtiy Safety Group within the Home Office.

The Police and Crime Standards Directorate (P&CSD) focuses on performance through assessments of policing and community safety. Each unit in the directorate has responsibility for different aspects of the performance management cycle. The Performance Framework and Assessment Unit develops tools that measure and analyse data on a regional and national level. The Policing and Community Safety Performance and Policy Unit formulates policy according to these analyses. Constant feedback is provided from the operational delivery units to those that measure and review performance to ensure that targets are appropriate and optimal. Quality assurance of data is of prime importance, as it is analysed and disseminated to central government, police forces, partnerships and other delivery agencies, providing the definitive Home Office view on performance analysis used by all partners.

The Partnership Performance Support Unit ensures that the desired performance outcomes are delivered on a regional and national level. It works with the government offices in England and the Welsh Assembly government to bring about sustained improvements in the contribution of local partnerships. It identifies specific development needs, provides practical tailored support packages and carries out intensive engagements where required. A national support framework is being developed, comprising a range of skilled service providers working with partnerships to deliver high-quality, tailored support. The unit also promotes effective good practice by crime reduction practitioners, by means of information services, such as the crime reduction website and the Improving Performance through Applied Knowledge project.

The Police Standards Unit provides intensive support to police forces and basic command units to help them meet the desired levels of performance. National programmes include Automatic Number Plate Recognition and Tackling Violent Crime. The latter entails working closely with areas to reduce more serious violence. The unit also manages national initiatives designed to improve operational effectiveness and national campaigns on such issues as alcohol enforcement and domestic violence. Other work involves the continuing development of forensic science techniques, using new technologies to solve 'cold cases' (for example, in rape cases).

The Offender-based Interventions Unit targets drug-misusing offenders and prolific offenders, to break the cycle of criminal behaviour. The aim is to address the underlying causes of offending, thereby reducing crime and reoffending. Such work includes the Prolific and Other Priority Offenders programme – a national scheme involving the police, probation, prisons, youth offending teams and other community partners. Those offenders who cause most damage to their communities are identified to ensure that they receive tailored interventions to tackle their offending behaviour, backed up with the promise of a swift return to the courts if they continue to offend. There is also the Drug Interventions Programme, which aims to identify the drug-misusing offenders already in the criminal justice system and to encourage them into treatment and wider support. As the drugs strategy states, everyone can win: drug-misusing offenders get help through treatment and support, communities suffer less crime and the taxpayer saves money as criminal justice costs are reduced.

Paul Evans

Related entries

Audit Commission; Home Office.

Key texts and sources

See the following websites:

http://www.homeoffice.gov.uk/about-us/
 organisation/directorate-search/crcsg/pcsd/

http://www.crimereduction.gov.uk/

http://www.drugs.gov.uk/drug-interventions-
 programme/

http://police.homeoffice.gov.uk/about-us/police-
 crime-standards/

POLICE AND CRIMINAL EVIDENCE ACT 1984 (PACE)

The Police and Criminal Evidence Act 1984 (PACE) is the principal legislation on police powers, supplemented by seven codes of practice.

The Police and Criminal Evidence Act 1984, known as PACE, had its origins in the report of the Royal Commission on Criminal Procedure. The subject is one that notoriously bristles with hotly disputed issues. The Chairman of the royal commission, Sir Cyril Philips, a historian and former Vice chancellor of London University, managed to get his fellow commissioners to agree a report that was unanimous on almost all its recommendations.

The royal commission was established in 1977 by the Callaghan Labour government. It reported in 1981 to Mrs Thatcher's Conservative government. The aim of the report was to strike the right balance between the interests of the defendant and the interests of the prosecution. When it was published, the report was denounced as too prosecution minded by the political left and the civil liberties lobby, but most of the other important interest groups –

the lawyers, the police, the judiciary and magistrates – gave it a broadly favourable reception. The Home Office quickly moved to prepare a bill based on the commission's proposals.

In November 1982, the first PACE bill was introduced into the Commons by the then Home Secretary, William Whitelaw. But this bill did not became law. Its progress through Parliament was stopped by the May 1983 general election. The bill that eventually passed was a revised version introduced in October 1983 by the new Home Secretary, Leon Brittan.

Both bills were strongly contested by the Labour Opposition. The committee stage in the Commons was the longest on record. The government made innumerable amendments. After Royal Assent in October 1984, it took more than another year before the Act was activated. This was mainly because the police required time to prepare. Every police officer in the country was supposed to have four days' training on the new system. This was unavoidably a lengthy process. Also in 1985, an immense amount of police time was absorbed in dealing with the miners' strike. The Act went live as from 1 January 1986. It has therefore been in force for more than 20 years. The fierce debates over the contents of the first and second PACE bills have long been forgotten. The Runciman Royal Commission on Criminal Justice, which sat from 1991 to 1993, received something approaching a thousand submissions. Not one questioned the basic structure and role of PACE.

Since Royal Assent in 1984, there have been literally hundreds of further amendments. A few (such as DNA evidence and identification procedures based on video recording) were the result of technological developments. Most just reflected the seemingly endless, year-on-year extension of the scope and reach of police powers. A few topics that were originally in the Act were later removed into other legislation – documentary hearsay evidence and complaints against the police are the most important examples. PACE powers given to the increasingly important body of civilian community support officers were placed in the Police Reform Act 2002. But almost all legislation on police powers is in PACE.

Most of the Act applies only to England and Wales. Northern Ireland has its own separate, almost identical legislation copied from the original and adapted to the province. Scotland has its own quite separate legislation.

The Philips Royal Commission recommended that the Home Office prepare codes of practice to accompany the Act. This recommendation was accepted, and the codes have become an integral and, indeed, central part of the PACE package. Originally there were four codes: Code A on stop and search; Code B on entry and search of premises and the seizure of evidence; Code C on the detention, treatment and questioning of suspects; and Code D on the tape recording of interviews with suspects. Three more codes were added later – Code E on identification procedures (1988); Code F on the visual recording of interviews (2003); and Code G on arrest (2006).

The booklet containing the codes (with index) now runs to 244 pages. It can be bought from the Stationery Office. The booklet format includes a CD version. The codes can also be found on a Home Office website (see below). The Home Office circulates drafts of new codes and of proposed amendments to relevant interest groups and individual experts. The final text has to be approved by both Houses of Parliament. New versions of the codes were approved by Parliament in 1991, 1995, 2003 and 2006. Copies of the current version of the booklet are provided to police officers free of charge.

Partly, the codes restate the provisions of the Act in less formal language; partly, they consist of rules elaborating those provisions in more detail. Technically, the codes are not law. A breach of the codes by the police cannot give rise to either criminal or civil proceedings against the officers concerned, and police disciplinary proceedings for such breaches are virtually unheard of. It might seem, therefore, that the codes are not of much importance. This impression is mistaken. The codes are one of the reasons for the success of PACE.

One reason is that the courts have a discretion to exclude evidence obtained when there has been a breach of the codes. The evidence does not even have to be caused by the breach.

If there has been a breach that the court regards as serious – say, in wrongfully denying the suspect access to a solicitor or in failing to keep the required detention records – evidence, such as a confession, may be held to be inadmissible, even though the breach of the rules did not cause or even contribute towards the confession. Whether the court applies this discretion is unpredictable, but it happens sufficiently often to be a factor in maintaining the authority of the codes.

Even more crucial is that, from the start, police at management level accepted that the codes represent the ordinary, routine way of carrying on police business. The fact that the codes are extremely detailed, leaving little room for discretion, is part of the reason that, operationally, they are treated by the police as their rule book. Unsurprisingly, the level of compliance with the four codes that relate to the suspect in the police station (Codes C, D, E and F) is better than with Codes A and B (affecting operations in the street or on premises), that are less subject to monitoring and supervision. (Code G is a hybrid. While an arrest normally takes place outside the police station, the arrested person must then be taken to a police station, at which point the PACE rules on detention take effect.)

Of all the provisions of PACE, probably the most important is s. 78, which gives the court the discretion to exclude evidence if the judge considers that 'the admission of the evidence would have such an adverse effect on the fairness of the proceedings that the court ought not to admit it'. When the first (William Whitelaw) bill was introduced into Parliament, this topic was not even mentioned. There still was no reference to it in the mark II (Leon Brittan) version introduced after the 1983 general election. It was only inserted in the very last stages as a government revision of an amendment first moved in the House of Lords by Lord Scarman. It is ironic that the section that is by far the most frequently used in the courts was included in the bill as a late afterthought.

At the time the Act became law, the pundits were sceptical whether the section would make much impact. Pre-PACE, the judges had shown themselves generally indulgent to the reception of illegally or improperly obtained evidence. Why would s. 78 cause them to change their approach? The pundits, however, were wrong. Not that judges are easily persuaded to penalize the prosecution by excluding evidence or quashing a conviction because of some improper conduct by the prosecution, but they have often given decisions grounded in principle that emphasize the importance of the rules over pragmatic considerations based on the familiar slogans of the 'war on crime'.

The detailed provisions of the Act and of the codes will go on developing and altering, but it looks as if this legislation will remain a permanent part of the system. PACE reflects the community's best effort at doing what the Philips Royal Commission envisaged in its 1981 report – striking the balance between the competing values, on the one hand, of law enforcement and, on the other hand, of safeguarding both the ordinary citizen and the suspect from the overbearing power of the state. The tension between those values cannot be avoided. It is in the nature of the operation of the criminal justice system.

Michael Zander

Related entries

Discretion; Evidence; 'Judges' Rules'; Police powers.

Key texts and sources

Zander, M. (2005) *The Police and Criminal Evidence Act 1984* (5th edn). London: Sweet & Maxwell (esp. pp. 521–656).

See also the Home Office's policing web page for the codes of practice (http://www.police-homeoffice. gov.uk/operational-policing/powers-pace-codes/ pacecodes.html).

POLICE AND JUSTICE ACT 2006

The Police and Justice Act 2006 is a piece of legislation that introduces a number of police reforms, as well as adding further measures relating to anti-social behaviour as part of the Labour government's 'Respect' action plan. It is a multifaceted Act that covers such areas as police training, local police authority membership and powers, fixed-penalty notices and the activities of crime and disorder reduction partnerships.

The Police and Justice Act 2006 established the National Policing Improvement Agency. Replacing Centrex (the body hitherto responsible for police training and development), the Police Information Technology Organization and a number of other bodies, the task of the new agency is to identify and disseminate good practice, to assist police forces to deliver major national priorities and to provide operational policing support.

The Act also made a number of changes to the composition and method of appointment of members of police authorities. The Police and Magistrates' Courts Act 1994 had reformed police governance and accountability, in particular introducing what have become known as 'independent members' (i.e. members who are not drawn from the local authority because of their role as magistrates). There was much criticism of the original means by which such members were appointed (Jones and Newburn 1997). The 2006 Act abolishes the separate category of magistrate members of police authorities, though magistrates may still participate as independent members.

The Act also amends the powers available to police authorities, in particular including introducing a new overarching duty to hold the chief officer to account for the exercise of his or her functions and those of persons under his or her direction and control. It also brought to a conclusion an ongoing review of the Crime and Disorder Act 1998 and made a number of important changes to the work of crime and disorder reduction partnerships. The major changes include the following:

- The removal of the requirement to audit communities every three years.
- Local three-year community safety plans will be refreshed every year.
- The s. 17 duty on local authorities to consider the crime and disorder implications of all their decisions is extended to include anti-social behaviour, substance misuse and behaviour that adversely affects the environment.

The Act makes a number of amendments to existing anti-social behaviour legislation. These include extending the range of agencies that can enter into parenting contracts and apply for parenting orders beyond youth offending teams and local education authorities to include other parts of the local authority, such as housing officers and anti-social behaviour co-ordinators, as well as registered social landlords. It also reinforced certain aspects of what are known as anti-social behaviour injunctions (ASBIs), which enable social landlords to apply for injunctions to prohibit anti-social behaviour that affects the management of their housing stock, including allowing those the ASBI is designed to protect not to be named on the order.

Finally, the Act introduces a wide variety of other amendments across a range of criminal justice and policing activities:

- Creating a standard set of powers available to all community support officers.
- Amending the Police and Criminal Evidence Act 1984 to allow the police to stop and search any person or vehicle in any area of an airport, where they have reasonable grounds to suspect that criminal activity has taken place or is about to take place.
- Giving chief constables the power to accredit trading standards officers with the power to issue penalty notices for disorder.
- Extending the conditional caution scheme to provide for punitive conditions (such as the payment of a financial penalty; unpaid work for a period not exceeding 20 hours; or attendance at a specified place for a period not exceeding 20 hours) to be attached, in addition to the reparative and rehabilitative conditions already in existence, as well as introducing a power of arrest for breach of a conditional caution.

Tim Newburn

Related entries

Accountability and governance; Anti-social behaviour; Community support officers (CSOs); Crime and Disorder Act 1998; Crime prevention (situational and social); Crime reduction; Police authorities; Police Reform Act 2002.

Key texts and sources

As yet there are no published guides to this legislation. The Act itself is available at the Office of Public Sector Information's website (**http://www.opsi.gov.uk/acts/acts2006/20060048.htm**).

POLICE AND MAGISTRATES' COURTS ACT 1994

The Police and Magistrates' Courts Act 1994 reformulated the powers and relationship of the three partners which exercised responsibility for police affairs – the Home Office, police authorities and chief constables. This Act (whose key aims were incorporated into the Police Act 1996) forms the basis for the contemporary system of control and accountability of policing.

The Police Act 1964 established a three-way (or tripartite) division of responsibilities for police affairs. However, there were a number of imperfections with the 1964 legislation. The apportionment of responsibilities lacked precision, which led to a series of clashes during the early 1980s in which some police authorities challenged the ability of chief officers to set priorities for their forces. Although the Home Office tended to support embattled chief constables in that period, central government became increasingly restless with the way in which policing was delivered.

Morgan (1989) discusses the influence exerted by new public management on the Police and Magistrates' Courts Act 1994. Earlier attempts to ensure that the Police Service provided good value for money had failed to secure this objective, and the 1994 legislation sought to promote it by readjusting the relationship between the three partners exercising responsibility for police affairs to ensure that, henceforth, the Home Office could exercise a dominant role.

The Act enabled the Home Secretary to set 'national objectives' (the term 'ministerial priorities' was later used) that each of the 43 police forces in England and Wales were required to deliver. Thus, henceforth the Home Secretary rather than chief constables would determine police force priorities. Performance indicators accompanied these national objectives so that the extent to which forces had attained these requirements could be assessed. The Act also introduced cash-limited budgets for police forces to enhance central control over expenditure. Simplified procedures were put in place to enable the Home Secretary to amalgamate forces, and police authorities were reconstituted as free-standing corporate bodies divorced from the structure of local government. Their key role is to draw up an annual costed local policing plan that incorporates the Home Secretary's national objectives with local objectives and that contains performance indicators and a statement of finance available to meet these targets. This provides them with an instrument with which they can hold their chief officer accountable for the way in which policing is delivered locally.

The composition of police authorities was also amended by the 1994 Act. The key innovation was the introduction of independent members, who were designed to provide for local representation that went beyond that afforded by councillors and magistrates. Initially it was proposed that these would be chosen by the Home Secretary, but the view that this would transform them into Home Office 'placemen' resulted in their appointment by regional shortlisting panels, with the Home Secretary making the final choice. Although a Home Office review (2004g) argued that the independent members have 'brought considerable added value to authorities in the range of their expertise and have also added crucially to the geography, gender and balance' of police authorities, their presence has been criticized on the basis of increasing the 'democratic deficit' in the composition of these bodies.

The 1994 Act introduced a number of innovations into policing. Loveday (1994, 1995) refers to the increased central direction of the Police Service. A particular problem was politicization – the concern that the police could be used as an instrument to advance the political concerns of the government. However, Jones and Newburn (1997) point to the consensual manner in which key stakeholders have fashioned mutually agreed national objectives. Additionally, although chief officers lost their ability solely to determine the priorities for their forces, they were given an enhanced degree of freedom over personnel and financial matters.

Peter Joyce

Related entries

Accountability and governance; Chief constables; Consultation; Home Office; Police Act 1964; Police authorities; Politics (police involvement); Royal Commission on the Police (1962); Sheehy Inquiry.

Key texts and sources

Home Office (2004) *Review of the Selection and Appointments Process of Independent Members of Police Authorities.* London: Home Office.

Jones, T. and Newburn, T. (1997) *Policing after the Act: Police Governance after the Police and Magistrates' Courts Act 1994.* London: Policy Studies Institute.

Loveday, B. (1994) 'The Police and Magistrates' Courts Act', *Policing*, 10: 221–33.

Loveday, B. (1995) 'Reforming the police: from local service to state police?', *Political Quarterly*, 66: 141–56.

See also the Office of Public Sector Information's website (**http://www.legislation.gov.uk/acts/acts 1994/Ukpga_19940029_en_1.htm**) for the text of the Police and Magistrates' Courts Act 1994.

POLICE AUTHORITIES

> Police authorities are independent bodies consisting of locally elected and independent members. They have an immediate responsibility for holding the chief constable accountable for policing the area, for policing strategy, for the police budget and for local consultation.

Police authorities were created by the Police Act 1964. Despite pressures of later legislation, this Act continues to provide the core element of contemporary police governance in England and Wales. Police authorities are seen as the third arm of the tripartite structure of police authorities, chief constables and the Home Secretary. This structure was originally designed to permit local governance of the police, but the Police Act 1964 shifted responsibility for policing governance away from local government towards chief constables and the Home Secretary.

Following the Police and Magistrates' Courts Act 1994 and the Police Act 1996, police authorities currently consist of seventeen members, of which nine are local councillors, five are independent members and three are magistrates. However, given their size, a number of metropolitan police authorities have slightly larger memberships. More significant, perhaps, are the responsibilities exercised by these bodies. As with much else in the police authority ambit, these responsibilities diminished when the day-to-day management of the force was made the responsibility of the chief constable. Currently, police authorities are required to set the force's strategic direction and to hold the chief constable to account on behalf of the local community.

Police authorities also have an ongoing responsibility for the police budget and decide how much council tax (the police precept) should be raised for local policing. With significant shifts in central grants over recent years, the police precept may be highly locally charged. This can lead local communities to question whether they receive value for money from their police force, when police precepts rise but there is no corresponding increase in visible policing.

The police authority's role has, however, been circumscribed by the Police Act 1996. Under this Act, the chief constable now determines what the police authority may spend and also the number of officers it may employ. The unusual situation of the service provider exercising control over the ostensible service purchaser is perhaps unique to public administration in Britain. It does, however, provide an interesting example of the extent to which the Home Office has sought to protect the Police Service from the perceived dangers of local political pressure or from interference in operational policing matters. Chief constables have also proved adept in extending the definition of what constitutes 'operational policing', which has increased their discretion in how these powers are exercised.

The relationship between police authorities and chief officers changed rather abruptly, however, with the arrival of a new Home Secretary committed to driving up police performance. As a result of the shooting of an innocent man in Hastings and the subsequent decision of the Chief Constable of Sussex to promote one of the officers involved, in 2001 David Blunkett drastically altered the policing governance landscape by forcefully exercising the Home Office powers in the tripartite arrangement. One consequence of this action was the early retirement of the Chief Constable of Sussex in the interests of police force efficiency.

The government response was the Police Reform Act 2002, which gave the Home Secretary the power to intervene directly in underperforming police forces. Before the Home Secretary intervened, however, the Act provided that HM Inspectorate of Constabulary (HMIC) should first submit a report to the relevant police authority. The police authority and chief officer were thus given immediate responsibility for taking remedial action to improve police performance. The protection provided by this Act was subsequently removed by the Police and Justice Act 2006, which gives the Home Secretary the power to intervene in an underperforming police force without there first being a report from HMIC. The Act also extends the Home Secretary's powers to intervene in underperforming police authorities and to direct them both to improve their performance.

Under the Police and Justice Act 2006, police authorities have also been given the responsibility to hold the chief constable to account for the exercise of his or her functions. The Act also significantly alters the composition of police authorities. Magistrate members no longer form a separate category of membership, the number of independent members being increased proportionately and their appointment simplified. The legislation also ends the requirement placed on police authorities under the Police Act 1996 to seek the agreement of chief officers for staffing levels. The government has, however, recognized that this has undermined police authorities' independence, while also inhibiting their ability to hold chief officers to account.

The changes to the tripartite system brought about by recent legislation mean that police authorities and chief constables are now both subject to centrally determined targets, measures and objectives. These are now the responsibility of HMIC and the Police Standards Unit based at the Home Office. The government's determination to centralize control of the police was exemplified in the HMIC report, *Closing the Gap* (2005b), which provided a springboard for subsequent police force mergers. The proposed mergers highlighted the loss of confidence in the Association of Chief Police Officers (ACPO) of many police authorities. With ACPO personnel having close links with the Home Office, the association seemed ready to accept the inevitability of police force mergers (Godfrey 2006). A number of police authorities actively opposed the merger programme under the Campaign for Local Policing, while two police authorities were prepared to seek judicial review rather than accept the merger plan. The government's decision in 2006 not to merge forces justified this resistance and served to resurrect and reinvigorate the role of the police authority in national policing governance.

Barry Loveday

Related entries

Accountability and governance; Chief constables; Consultation; Home Office; Police Act 1964; Police and Justice Act 2006.

Key texts and sources

Godfrey, J. (2006) *None of the Above: Lessons Learned from the Police Force Structure Debate*. Lewis: Sussex Police Authority.

Loveday, B. and Reid, A. (2003) *Going Local: Who should Run Britain's Police?* London: Policy Exchange.

Reiner, R. (2000) *The Politics of the Police* (3rd edn). Oxford: Oxford University Press.

See also the Association of Police Authorities' website (http://www.apa.police.uk/apa).

POLICE CULTURE

Police culture (or subculture) refers to the mix of informal prejudices, values, attitudes and working practices commonly found among the lower ranks of the police that influences the exercise of discretion. It also refers to the police's solidarity, which may tolerate corruption and resist reform.

Like any occupation, police officers share informal knowledge, values and attitudes that inform their working practices, especially the exercise of discretion. The principal elements of the police culture found among the lower ranks in many jurisdictions include conservative authoritarian attitudes; prejudice on the basis of gender, race and sexuality; peer group defensive solidarity; masculinity; suspicion and cynicism; and resistance to reform (especially that motivated by liberal values). This informal culture is now widely recognized as a malign influence that needs to be removed in order to improve policing.

The cultural dimension of policing was the focus of many pioneering texts on policing (e.g. Westley 1953; Skolnick 1966; Wilson 1968b; Reiss 1971; Cain 1973; Manning 1977; Bittner 1990) that revealed the murky world in which policing was not done 'according to the book' but through the invisible exercise of discretion. Formal procedures designed to protect suspects were found to be routinely subverted to ensure conviction, and cynicism about the criminal justice system to extend to tolerating misconduct and protecting wrongdoers behind a 'blue curtain' of solidarity. Later research confirmed the tenacity and near-universality of this culture (Holdaway 1979; Punch 1979; Smith and Gray 1983; Fielding 1988; Brewer 1990a; Brogden and Shearing 1993; Chan 2003a). The concept has become such a conceptual commonplace that it is increasingly invoked to explain a wide range of police misconduct, from sexism in the workplace to brutality towards suspects.

Skolnick (1966) located the imperatives that produced police culture in two structural contingencies of police experience: authority and danger. For instance, the police must be alert to threats to their physical safety and to come to regard African-Americans as 'symbolic assailants'. Expanding on this, Holdaway (1983) pointed to the obligation that police officers feel to come to firm conclusions in fluid and confused circumstances, which encourages prejudicial stereotyping. Kleinig (1996) identifies the anomic nature of policing, in which officers are duty bound routinely to transgress normal standards of conduct by intruding into privacy, deceiving those suspected of crime (see also Manning 1977) and using force (possibly lethal). This functional nature of police culture has been highlighted by how officers during the IRA (Irish Republican Army) insurgency in Northern Ireland avoided the stress arising from the threat of violence (Brewer 1990b) and by how humour is used to insulate them from such potentially distressing experiences as dealing with corpses (Young 1995).

The source of this culture lies with the informal influence of peers, especially during the officer's early experience of patrol. Typically, the 'rookie' is advised to forget everything taught during training and to learn how policing is really done on the street. The loyalty of rookies to their peer group is often tested by exposing them to minor misconduct and by enticing them into committing minor infractions (such as 'easing' in 'tea-holes'; Cain 1973), before inducting them into more serious and systematic wrongdoing. Peers are also a source of excuses that neutralize moral and legal deviancy (Kappeler *et al.* 1994).

While widely accepted and employed in research and commentary, some conceptual and empirical issues arise concerning police culture. First, the concept of 'police culture' is almost invariably applied to the lower uniformed ranks. It is increasingly recognized, however, that other ranks and specialists have divergent and even antagonistic cultures. Detectives are much more individualistic and competitive than the characteristic culture allows. 'Street cops' do not trust 'management cops' (Reuss-Ianni and Ianni 1983). As the plethora of police *cultures* expands, there is the danger that they can be invoked at will to explain anything untoward. For example, Kraska (2001) sees special weapons and tactics (SWAT) squads in the USA as succumbing to a 'warrior culture', whereas the Independent Police Complaints Commission has criticized armed British police as infected with an excessive 'culture of caution' (Glass 2005).

A much more profound debate exists, however, over what 'culture' is and how it operates. Many researchers implicitly regard it as a competing set of norms or rules, but Shearing and Ericson (1991) conceptualize culture in an entirely different and less deterministic way. They argue that all cultures are conveyed through dramatic narratives and tropes that give meaning to events, but do not necessarily prescribe action.

There are also doubts about the connection between culture and behaviour. While Terrill *et al.* (2003) detect a relationship, other research suggests that situational factors far eclipse the personal dispositions of officers when dealing with incidents (Sherman 1980; Worden 1996). Waddington (1999a) argues that canteens (and other 'backstage' locations) are distinctive venues in which officers indulge in an 'oral culture' only tenuously linked to operational experience.

While it is often assumed that police values and attitudes are distinctive, the evidence for this is equivocal (for a summary, see Waddington 1999a). Chan (1997) argues that culture cannot be divorced from the context within which officers work (e.g. the racism of the Australian police owes much to the colonial origins of the country and its police). Her research following recruits through training found that it was first-hand experience of police work on the streets that transformed the attitudes of recruits (Chan 2003a).

Police culture is widely regarded as a subversive, illiberal and malign obstacle to reform that can be changed as an act of will. Wilson (1968a) regards this as an intellectually lazy 'bad men' theory that pathologizes rather than explains police conduct. When policy is promoted vigorously, this can change even the most ingrained habits, as witnessed with respect to police shootings in the USA (Reiss 1980; Fyfe 1982; Sherman 1983). On the other hand, policy that is divorced from the wider social realities in which policing is performed fares poorly (Chan 1997).

'Police culture' is a normative as well as descriptive and analytical construct. As Chan (1996: 110) observed: 'Police culture has become a convenient label for a range of negative values, attitudes, and practice norms among police officers'.

P.A.J. Waddington

Related entries

Black police associations; Community and race relations; Corruption (police); Criminal investigation department (CID); Discretion; Ethics in policing; Gender and policing; Institutional racism; Stephen Lawrence Inquiry.

Key texts and sources

Bittner, E. (1990) *Aspects of Police Work.* Boston, MA: Northeastern University Press.
Chan, J. (1996) 'Changing police culture', *British Journal of Criminology*, 36: 109–34.
Manning, P.K. and Van Maanen, J. (eds) (1978) *Policing: A View from the Street.* New York, NY: Random House.
Punch, M. (1983) *Control in the Police Organization.* Cambridge, MA: MIT Press.
Waddington, P.A.J. (1999b) *Policing Citizens.* London: UCL Press.

POLICE EXECUTIVE RESEARCH FORUM (PERF)

The Police Executive Research Forum (PERF) is a not-for-profit membership agency established in 1976. It aims to promote and develop the delivery of a professional police service to its membership by challenging traditional ideas and encouraging innovation.

The Police Executive Research Forum (PERF) was established in the USA in 1976 as a not-for-profit agency devoted to the improvement of policing and the advancement of professionalism. It aims to challenge traditional ideas of policing in an open and constructive manner. PERF is a membership organization supported by senior police officers across the USA and currently contributes to the development of policing through research, debate and teaching. In addition to its 'general' members, who lead the larger police agencies, PERF welcomes 'subscribing' members from smaller agencies, from academics working in the criminal justice field and from those with a professional interest in criminal justice issues from other agencies and jurisdictions.

PERF is governed by a president, elected by the membership (currently Chief William J. Bratton from the Los Angeles Police Department), and a board of directors (one of whom is the Commissioner of the Metropolitan Police in London). They are collectively responsible for the appointment of the executive director, who manages the organization and its 30 full-time staff, all of whom are based in Washington, DC. It is funded through modest contributions from members, as well as government grants and contracts and partnerships with private foundations and other agencies.

PERF was influential in the development of problem-oriented policing (POP) in the USA. An early publication describes one of the best known POP projects, carried out in Newport News and reported by Eck and Spelman (1987). This project led to the now widely used acronym SARA (scanning, analysis, response and assessment), which is seen as a fundamental element of POP. Goldstein's (1990) seminal work on POP was also supported by the US National Institute of Justice as part of its support to PERF.

From 1993 to 2003, PERF was responsible for the organization of the US POP conference, which was the largest gathering of police staff interested in POP in the world. It also established (in 1993) the Herman Goldstein POP Award which recognizes outstanding contributions to the development of POP from agencies and individual officers. This annual competition continues today under the direction of the US Community Oriented Policing (COPS) Office and it has a UK equivalent, the Tilley Award, which is run along similar lines.

PERF encourages research into policing issues and publishes results in areas felt to be topical and relevant to the professional development of its membership. Since 1976 these have covered a wide spectrum of interests, including community policing, problem-solving and a range of issues related to police management, leadership and protection. Much of its recent research has been supported by the US National Institute of Justice or the US COPS Office.

The use of force and police accountability are two particular issues of constant concern to police executives in the USA. Reflecting this, PERF has recently established a Center on Force and Accountability, which aspires to identify emerging trends, to conduct research, to provide technical assistance and to be seen as the first port of call for information on these issues.

In addition to an annual conference and other meetings, PERF runs a series of training sessions – perhaps two each year in the summer – in collaboration with the University of Boston. These Senior Management Institute for Police sessions are intensive, three-week courses aimed at mid to upper-level officers and concentrate on offering management training comparable with that offered to private sector corporations.

PERF makes available a wide range of publications on policing issues, including books, guidance documents and manuals, through its website.

Gloria Laycock

Related entries

Accountability and governance; Force (police use of); Problem-oriented policing.

Key texts and sources

Eck, J. and Spelman, W. (1987) *Problem Solving: Problem-oriented Policing in Newport News.* Washington, DC: Police Executive Research Forum.
Goldstein, H. (1990) *Problem-oriented Policing.* London: McGraw-Hill.
PERF's website is at http://www.policeforum.org/.

POLICE FEDERATION

The Police Federation represents the views of police officers up to the rank of chief inspector in connection with all matters affecting the welfare and efficiency of the Police Service.

The Police Federation emerged out of industrial action undertaken by police officers in 1918 and 1919. In 1913 the National Union of Police and Prison Officers (NUPPO) was formed to put forward their concerns on a range of issues that included pay, war bonuses and pensions. Abortive discussions on these issues resulted in a police strike in London in 1918, which the government settled by conceding all main NUPPO demands save recognition of the union. A committee chaired by Lord Desborough was also established to consider police pay in provincial forces. This resulted in the Police Act 1919. A key aim of this measure was to outlaw NUPPO. Accordingly, the 1919 Act established the Police Federation as a statutory body to represent the interests of police officers. The legislation made it illegal for a police officer to join any union that was concerned with seeking to influence police pay, pensions or conditions. The federation was thus a staff association rather than a trade union, and its members were unable to engage in strike action.

There are three separate Police Federations – the Police Federation of England and Wales, the Scottish Police Federation and the Police Federation for Northern Ireland. In England and

Wales, each force has a full-time representative and a joint branch board that consists of representatives drawn from the three ranks it represents (constables, sergeants and inspectors/chief inspectors). Every three years the branch boards elect a central committee for each of these three ranks, and the federation's executive branch and policy-making body is a joint central committee drawn from representatives from the individual central committees. The joint central committee elects the federation's national officers, including the chair, general secretary and treasurer.

That the role of the federation in England and Wales is to represent its members in all matters affecting welfare and efficiency – save issues affecting promotion and discipline – was reiterated in the Police Act 1996. The key concerns of the federation are with pay, allowances, hours of duty, leave and pensions. Much work of this nature is conducted in the Police Negotiating Board, whose remit covers the entire UK. The federation is also consulted on the formulation of police regulations and performs a number of services for its members in connection with such matters as providing advice and representation for disciplinary hearings and employment tribunals and offering financial and debt-counselling services.

Fielding (1990) argued that, initially, police officers failed to warm to the new organization and that the imminence of its introduction resulted in a second police strike in 1919, which involved officers from London, Liverpool and Birmingham. However, the influence it was accorded grew after 1945 when it added campaigning and lobbying roles to its original functions. Its ability to undertake these functions was much aided by the resources at its disposal, which have enabled it to sponsor MPs, employ press and publicity staff, fund its own journal, *Police*, and mount campaigns.

It embarked on campaigns that sought to promote ideas (especially in connection with law and order during the 1970s) and to resist proposals that were felt to be disadvantageous to its members (such as the 1993 Sheehy Report regarding police management and the Police Reform Act 2002's proposals regarding police pay and conditions) (McLaughlin and Murji 1998). It also provided a rank-and-file police

perspective on current issues affecting the service, voicing opposition to the role performed by the Police Complaints Authority in 1989, seeking to resurrect the patrol function of policing in 1996 and expressing concern about the Macpherson Report (especially his views on institutional racism) in 1999. Although Savage *et al.* (2000) argue that the federation is a permanent part of the police policy network, it performs its role primarily as an outsider group, seeking to secure influence by mobilizing public opinion behind its concerns.

Jan Berry

Related entries

Politics (police involvement); Sheehy Inquiry.

Key texts and sources

Fielding, N. (1990) *The Police and Social Conflict: Rhetoric and Reality.* London: Athlone.

Judge, A. (1968) *The First Fifty Years: The Story of the Police Federation.* London: Police Federation.

Judge, A. and Reynolds, G. (1968) T*he Night the Police Went on Strike.* London: Weidenfeld & Nicholson.

Savage, S., Charman, S. and Cope, S. (2000) *Policing and the Power of Persuasion.* London: Blackstone Press.

The Police Federation's website is at **http://www.polfed.org/**. See also the Metropolitan Police Federation's website (**http://www.metfed. org.uk/**).

POLICE NATIONAL COMPUTER

The Police National Computer is a national information system available to the police, criminal justice agencies and a variety of other non-policing organizations. It holds comprehensive details of people, vehicles, crimes and property on its database which can be electronically accessed all day, every day. It is increasingly becoming a powerful tool for investigating crime and supporting operational policing. It is maintained and delivered by the National Policing Improvement Agency.

The Police National Computer is a national system that supports the Police Service in the UK. It was designed in the late 1960s and started operation in the mid-1970s. It has been substantially upgraded over the 40 years, including, particularly, a major upgrade in the mid-1990s when all the details of criminal records were added after being converted from the microfiche records that had been kept in Scotland Yard.

The Police National Computer is available 24 hours a day, 365 days a year. Its functionality includes the following:

- Criminal names and records database.
- Missing and wanted persons database.
- QUEST (Querying Using Enhanced Search Techniques). QUEST enables users to search the names database to identify suspects. They can do this using gathered information, such as physical description and personal features.
- VODS (Vehicle Online Descriptive Search). VODS allows users to search the vehicles database by such search criteria as registration, postcode and colour details to narrow the list to potential suspect vehicles.
- ANPR (Automatic Number Plate Recognition). ANPR is used to take a visual image of a number plate. The Police National Computer devices will scan thousands of numbers each hour, alerting the police to any that are of interest.
- Property – the Police National Computer can search for items that are lost and found, such as firearms, trailers, plants and animals.

- CRIMELINK is an enhanced, web-based version of the Comparative Case Analysis Tool (CCA), which can be used to solve serious serial-type crimes by searching for similarities in incidents, thus helping investigators to identify patterns and links.

The Police National Computer is used by all police forces in England, Wales, Scotland and Northern Ireland and by over 60 other criminal justice and law enforcement organizations. Each force has specially trained personnel using the Police National Computer.

Over nearly 40 years, the system has grown to embrace many technological advances, incorporating advice from the government and policing bodies, as well as from in-house and industry technical experts. It has developed from a record-keeping service to a sophisticated intelligence tool. Recent additions include the Violent and Sex Offender Register (ViSOR), as well as the national firearms register. Technology is now enabling the move towards mobile data. By using Airwave (the digital radio system in use in all UK police forces), police officers will increasingly be able to access the Police National Computer through hand-held devices.

While a vital tool, the Police National Computer has been criticized on a number of counts. First, there have been concerns about the accuracy of criminal record data on the system. These concerns have arisen because of the problems of timeliness in getting court results on to the system. Secondly, there has been an increasing debate about the 'surveillance society' and the extent of the state's record keeping about citizens, which led to two inquiries in 2007, one by the Home Affairs Committee of the House of Commons and one by the House of Lords. As Neyroud and Disley (forthcoming) suggest, the Police National Computer, like the other developing technologies that support policing (including biometric identification systems such as the DNA Database), need to have proper, transparent governance, and careful steps must be taken to ensure continuing public support.

Peter Neyroud

Related entries

Bichard Inquiry; National Policing Improvement Agency (NPIA).

Key texts and sources

Chan, J.B.L. (2003) 'Police and new technologies', in T. Newburn (ed.) *Handbook of Policing.* Cullompton: Willan Publishing.

Neyroud, P.W. and Disley, E. (forthcoming) 'Technology and policing: implications for fairness and legitimacy', *Policing: An International Journal*, 2.

See also the National Policing Improvement Agency's website (**www.npia.police.uk**).

POLICE PERFORMANCE INDICATORS

Police performance indicators are quantitative measures, typically expressed as a rate or percentage, used to assess the achievement of targets or comparison over time/with peers. They are used internally as management information and by the Home Office and others as part of a central monitoring regime for police performance.

Effective organizations measure their performance to assess how well they are doing and to identify opportunities for improvement. For decades, success in policing terms was measured simply but crudely by levels of crime and detection rates. By the 1980s, public sector reform emphasized the three 'E's – economy, efficiency and effectiveness – and generated interest in measurement. Additionally, rising crime rates prompted senior officers to declare that crime figures were actually performance measures for *society* rather than for the police alone. In the early 1990s, the Audit Commission began publishing annual tables of police performance indicators (PIs). A decade later, these have been replaced by Home Office-published statutory PIs, which are increasingly comprehensive in coverage.

PIs turn statistics into measurements of comparison and achievement of targets. For example, a force reports that the burglary detection rate is 24 per cent. To pass the 'so what?' test, we need to know: is this better than last year's performance? How does it compare with rates achieved by peer forces? Has it met the target set? PIs have limited explanatory value but they do prompt action – why performance has declined or how other forces secure better results.

The main types of PI capture inputs, processes, outputs and outcomes; of these, the most valued are outcome PIs, which reflect the impact that policing has on communities – for example, less fear of crime and disorder. Some areas of policing are more amenable to measurement than others, arousing concern that 'what gets measured gets done'. Of vital importance is that PIs – especially those that attract national attention – reflect priority areas. They *do* skew behaviour, which is beneficial if that behaviour is directed appropriately and managed within a robust supervisory framework. Otherwise, officers striving to meet PIs around arrests or other processes may act without integrity and undermine public confidence.

Initially, PIs predominantly measured hard-edged issues such as crimes, detections, response times or the percentage of crime scenes yielding forensic retrievals. The advent of mass survey techniques has introduced a wealth of 'soft' PIs based on the user experience (e.g. satisfaction with the way that an incident was dealt with) which instil confidence that PIs can be part of a balanced performance framework. But the use of PIs is fraught with problems of definition, attribution (can the police claim success for reducing the number of incidents of anti-social behaviour in a town centre, or is the extension of CCTV the key?) and interpretation. Rigour has been introduced by principles of good measurement (Home Office 2004e) that limit the use of national PIs to those that meet strict acceptance criteria. One is that PIs must be directionally unambiguous – for instances of recorded burglary, the fewer the better. But if forces proactively encourage fuller reporting of hate crime and domestic violence, do high levels mean success?

Balance is also critical in respect of the range of PIs – policing is complex, and some key activities are hidden from view. It is easy to record a homicide and the ensuing outcome (usually, a detection), but how best to capture the success of efforts to *prevent* homicides? Volume crime is measurable by the simple counting of incidents, but the criminal activities of organized criminal networks – drugs traffickers, counterfeiters, etc. – are less tractable. Problematically, efforts to tackle criminality with a high risk of public harm may be 'outscored' by large volume but relatively low risk incidents.

In summary, PIs are an essential part of the landscape for performance improvement but must be set within a coherent framework and treated with caution.

Kate Flannery

Related entries

Best value; Clear-up rates; Consultation; Crime and Disorder Act 1998; Police and Magistrates' Courts Act 1994; Rank structure; Repeat victimization; Roads (policing of); Zero-tolerance policing (ZTP).

Key texts and sources

Audit Commission (1990) *Effective Policing. Police Paper* 8. London: Audit Commission.
Collier, P.M. (2006) 'In search of performance and priorities: police PIs', *Public Money and Management*, 26: 165–72.
Home Office (2004) *Managing Police Performance: A Practical Guide to Performance Management.* London: HMSO.
See also the Home Office's police web page for performance assessment methods (**http://police. homeoffice.gov.uk/performance-and-measurement/ assessment-methods/**) and for answers to frequently asked questions on performance assessment and measurement (**http://police.home office.gov.uk/performance-and-measurement/ performance-assessment/faqs/**).

POLICE POWERS

> Police powers are conferred on the police so that they can perform their law enforcement functions. In the UK, police powers have been established in an *ad hoc* way through Acts of Parliament and the common law. In modern times, the greatest rationalization of this *ad hoc* provision of police powers occurred with the passing of the Police and Criminal Evidence Act 1984.

Policing in any society requires that its operatives are given powers over the citizenry in order to enforce the law. The sources and the extent of these powers vary significantly depending upon which state one addresses. In the UK, police powers are derived from Acts of Parliament and the common law. These have developed in a piecemeal manner, particularly since the enactment of the Metropolitan Police Act 1829. Many statutes conferring various powers on the police have been passed since that date that have subsequently been amended or repealed, and common law judgments have proliferated accordingly.

The greatest single rationalization of police powers in modern times occurred through the enactment of the Police and Criminal Evidence Act 1984 (PACE). This Act constituted an attempt to consolidate many statutory police powers and powers under the common law into a more codified framework in order to promote greater clarity and accountability. PACE was largely motivated by the recommendations of the Royal Commission on Criminal Procedure that was convened in response to increasing concerns regarding a number of policing issues.

Very soon after the Royal Commission reported its recommendations, some of these concerns erupted in a particularly violent manner. This manifested as the inner-city riots during the summer of 1981, where many urban areas were subjected to serious disorder. A significant proportion of the protestors were from ethnic minorities who complained about poor social and economic conditions, as well as police harassment. The main focus of their discontent was centred on police powers of stop and search.

In response to increasing levels of street crime, particularly in places such as Brixton in south London, the police adopted a saturation strategy and deployed large numbers of police officers on the streets. This led to many young black males being routinely stopped and searched, which led to the perception of racist conduct on the part of the police. This was one of several issues addressed by the Scarman Report (1981) that inquired into the causes of the Brixton disorders.

Part I of PACE addressed this particularly contentious aspect of police powers by providing a statutory framework that empowered the police to effect stops and searches in public, while creating a greater level of accountability as to how this power was to be used. The latter is largely enshrined in the PACE codes of practice that now apply to the bulk of police powers. These codes accompany PACE and endeavour to clarify many of its key provisions. One of its many purposes is to provide guidance to the police as to when stopping and searching suspects is justified. This is based on the concept of 'reasonable grounds to suspect' that certain items will be found on the suspect or in a vehicle. However, since the introduction of PACE, s. 60 of the Criminal Justice and Public Order Act 1994 and ss. 43–46 of the Terrorism Act 2000 have created police powers to stop and search even where there is no *individual* suspicion of the persons concerned. These powers may only apply where prior authorization has been made by a senior police officer in order to prevent incidents of serious violence or acts of terrorism, respectively.

Other police powers under PACE and the codes of practice include entry and search of premises, as well as the seizure of any evidence found there; powers to make arrests; and the detention of persons in police custody, including their questioning and treatment. Although PACE constitutes the biggest single source of police powers, it is not the only source. As indicated above regarding stop and search, various powers are conferred upon the police by other statutes, some of which were enacted over a hundred years ago. The sources of police powers are therefore a complex patchwork of legislation as well as the common law.

The provisions under PACE regarding the *general* powers of the police to enter and search premises, with or without a warrant, are also subject to numerous safeguards, augmented by the codes of practice. This also applies to the seizure of evidence discovered during these searches. Police powers to enter and search premises with or without warrant for specialized tasks, such as drug enforcement or anti-terrorism, can be found under the Misuse of Drugs Act 1971 and the Terrorism Act 2000, respectively.

Police powers of arrest without warrant are nearly all contained under s. 24 of PACE. The police may arrest anyone committing or about to commit an offence, or where there are reasonable grounds for suspecting either. This arrest power may also apply where an offence has been committed and the suspect is guilty of it, or where there are reasonable grounds to suspect this. If the police have reasonable grounds to suspect that an offence has been committed in the first place, they may arrest anyone whom they have reasonable grounds to suspect is guilty of it. However, these summary powers of arrest may be exercised only where there are reasonable grounds for believing that any of the following conditions are fulfilled: to enable the suspect's name and/or address to be ascertained; or to prevent the suspect from suffering physical injury or causing physical harm to him or herself or another person, or causing loss of or damage to property, or committing an offence against public decency, or causing an unlawful obstruction of the highway. There are three other conditions – namely, to protect a child or other vulnerable person from the suspect; to allow the prompt and effective investigation of the offence or the suspect's conduct; or to prevent the suspect from absconding. These arrest powers are also subject to the codes of practice under PACE.

The detention, treatment and questioning of persons held in police custody involve the use of numerous police powers that, in turn, are subject to many constraints imposed under PACE and the codes of practice. These include limits on detention time, the searching of suspects, the taking of photographs, fingerprints and body samples, the recording of interviews, and drug testing, to name but a few. Police *duties* rather than *powers* in respect of the general treatment of detained persons are exhaustively covered under the codes of practice. Among other things, these stipulate certain minimum standards regarding the conditions under which detainees are held, as well as a host of other rights to which they are entitled.

As seen above, although PACE is the main focus in terms of *general* police duties, specialized law enforcement operations often work under the framework of other legal sources. A further example includes the Public Order Act 1986 that enables the police to deal with a range of offences against public order, as well as to take preventative measures. Another is the Regulation of Investigatory Powers Act 2000 that is generally addressed to covert policing. Among other things, this is concerned with the interception of communications, covert surveillance, undercover officers and informants, as well as the investigation of electronic data protected by encryption. The use of these powers is also subject to a number of safeguards, including the provision of the codes of practice under the Act. Anti-terrorism legislation is a further source of police powers that is used in specific circumstances, as well as a host of other statutes that empower the police to act in response to a number of different situations.

The role of the common law in the exercise of police powers has diminished significantly since the introduction of PACE. The main common law power that has survived to date is the power to deal with, or prevent, a breach of the peace. The concept of preserving the Queen's (or King's) peace is a very ancient one that has given rise to a number of powers exercisable by those in authority. In *R* v. *Howell* and more recent cases, a breach of the peace has been broadly defined as imminent or occurring violence, or damage to property. The police (and ordinary citizens) may arrest a person who is threatening or causing a breach of the peace. Alternatively, they may temporarily restrain that person until he or she calms down. Apart from enabling the arrest or restraint of such persons, this common law power also allows entry into private property for the purpose of preventing or dealing with a breach of the peace. However, this power should be exercised with great care and in a proportionate manner, as held by the European Court of Human Rights in *McLeod* v. *United Kingdom*. Although this power overlaps with certain provisions under PACE, such as in s. 17, as well as public order legislation, this common law power continues to have a useful application. This was acknowledged by the House of Commons during its scrutiny of the Serious Organized Crime and Police Bill when it thwarted an attempt by the government to repeal this power.

It is important to note that the Human Rights Act 1998 has made a significant impact on the exercise of police powers. One example has already been cited above, namely *McLeod* v. *United Kingdom*. Since the Act came into force, all public bodies, including the police, have a duty to comply with the European Convention on Human Rights and Fundamental Freedoms. Also, the courts in this country are under a duty to take into account the previous decisions of the European Court of Human Rights when making their own judgments.

The creation of the extended police family (see Plural policing) and the Serious Organized Crime Agency has produced new dimensions regarding the exercise of police powers. Part 4, Chapter 1 and Schedules 4 and 5 of the Police Reform Act 2002 created the extended police family that consists of community support officers, investigating officers, detention officers and escort officers. All these officers are civilians who have been given a range of police powers in order to fulfil specified roles. As they are not police officers, their duties are largely governed by the menu of powers available to them under the Police Reform Act. In addition, the Act enables suitable civilians performing community safety functions to be accredited with a limited range of law enforcement powers. The Serious Organized Crime and Police Act 2005 has taken civilianization further and enables the powers and duties of custody officers to be exercised by civilians known as 'staff custody officers'. This Act has also created the Serious Organized Crime Agency, whose officers may be designated the powers of a constable or immigration officer, or the customs powers of an officer of HM Revenue and Customs. Furthermore, under s. 8 of the Prison Act 1952, prison officers employed by HM Prison Service, when on duty, have all the powers and privileges of a constable.

Leonard Jason-Lloyd

Related entries

Anti-social behaviour; Arrest; Civilianization; Civil liability; Discretion; European Convention on Human Rights (ECHR); Police and Criminal Evidence Act 1984 (PACE); Warrants.

Key texts and sources

Clark, D. (2004) *Bevan and Lidstone's 'The Investigation of Crime: A Guide to the Law of Criminal Investigation'* (3rd edn). Oxford: Oxford University Press.
English, J. and Card, R. (2005) *Police Law* (9th edn). Oxford: Oxford University Press.
Jason-Lloyd, L. (2005) *An Introduction to Policing and Police Powers* (2nd edn). London: Cavendish Publishing.
Sampson, F. (2005) *Blackstone's Police Manual. Volume 4. General Police Duties 2006.* Oxford: Oxford University Press.
Zander, M. (2005) *The Police and Criminal Evidence Act 1984* (5th edn). London: Sweet & Maxwell.
See also the Home Office's web page on police powers (**http://www.homeoffice.gov.uk/police/powers/**).

POLICE PROPERTY

Police property refers to those elements of society who are believed to pose a threat to the general good order of the community but are not necessarily breaking the law. They are perceived to be of low social status, with little or no economic or political power, and are considered by the dominant majority as 'problematic and distasteful' (Reiman 1992: 118).

The term 'police property' was first coined by Cray (1972: 11), but is now most associated with Lee (1981: 53–9). It was originally used in relation to discriminatory policing practices in the USA but quickly entered the lexicon of the wider literature on police occupational culture or 'cop culture' (Reiner 2000) and has now become so accepted that it is frequently used without attribution.

Those termed 'police property' share some characteristics with the 'dangerous classes' (Silver 1967) or the 'underclass' (Crowther 2000), but it is important to realize that it could also include others who may be regarded as problematic, including, for example, the young and members of immigrant communities.

Lee (1981) suggests that the powerful in society are prepared to allow the police a free rein to deal with any problems associated with such lower-status groups, as long as it is done effectively and without attracting unfavourable attention from the media or other concerned organizations. The police role in society is to maintain order but, as Waddington (1999b) points out, it is not to maintain order *per se* but, rather, to maintain a *particular* order, and it is the powerful in society who are able to determine what is and is not socially acceptable.

The police are empowered to use their authority to deal with the problematic elements of society: those who are regarded as dangerous, threatening, unruly or disreputable. In dealing with this 'police property', they are not restricted to the use of the law to maintain order but, rather, to 'using the law as one resource among others' (Reiner 2000: 93). The guiding principles that inform the police are not restricted to the law as written but also include an understanding of the norms and social values that are to be upheld and the circumstances in which they are to be imposed. The police, therefore, may feel perfectly justified in moving on groups of young people congregating in the street or other public areas, in evicting the homeless rough-sleeper from a shop doorway or in using the discriminatory and sometimes unlawful 'stop and search' powers against certain sections of the community.

The problem for the police is that the attribution of the status 'police property' is not fixed. It is a social construct and, although it may contain some relatively stable elements, it is reflective of the dominant culture at any particular time.

Therefore the police have to be constantly alert to the nuances of changing social and behavioural conventions when performing their duties, for failure to do so creates the potential for challenges to their legitimacy, resulting in disorder and disobedience rather than order and stability.

Douglas Sharp

Related entries

Discretion; Legitimacy; Patrol; Police culture.

Key texts and sources

Lee, J.A. (1981) 'Some structural aspects of police deviance in relation to minority groups', in C. Shearing (ed.) *Organisational Police Deviance.* Toronto: Butterworths.
Reiner, R. (2000) *Politics of the Police* (3rd edn). Oxford: Oxford University Press.
Waddington, P.A.J. (1999) *Policing Citizens.* London: UCL Press.

POLICE REFORM ACT 2002

The Police Reform Act 2002 followed directly from the government white paper entitled *Policing for a New Century: A Blueprint for Reform* (Home Office 2001b), which was published in December 2001. The aim of the white paper and the Police Reform Bill which followed was 'to outline a radical programme of police reform'.

Some sections of the Police Reform Bill were greeted with hostility from within the Police Service and were either modified or abandoned, but what emerged as the Police Reform Act in July 2002 nevertheless remained significant. The overriding effect was to continue the process of the redistribution of power and responsibility within the tripartite structure of chief constable, local police authority and the Home Secretary, towards the Home Secretary.

The Act required the Home Secretary to publish a *National Policing Plan*, which set out the government's strategic priorities for the Police Service together with a series of measurable objectives and targets. In addition, the Home Secretary was empowered to make regulations to govern police procedures and practices and to publish mandatory codes of practice for police forces and local police authorities.

Local police authorities were required to publish a three-year action plan to address the priorities set out in the national plan, and both police authorities and police forces were subject to a more robust system of inspection by HM Inspectorate of Constabulary (s. 3). In the event of a critical report, the Home Secretary had the power to direct that the police authority should take 'such remedial measures as may be specified' (s. 4). The role of the Home Secretary was further extended by providing powers to direct a local police authority to require a chief constable to retire or resign on the 'grounds of efficiency and effectiveness' (s. 30(2)).

The Act also contained significant provisions for policing and the investigation of complaints against police officers. The notion of the extended police family was enhanced by providing powers to chief constables to designate persons employed by a police authority or acting under the direction and control of the chief constable in a range of specified roles with limited powers. The highest profile of these is the uniformed police community support officer, who provides a visible presence on the streets in order to control low-level anti-social behaviour and to provide reassurance to the general public. The Police Complaints Authority was abolished and replaced by the Independent Police Complaints Commission (IPCC). As its title suggests, the IPCC was established as an independent body to undertake investigations into complaints made by members of the public into the conduct and actions of persons serving with the police.

The overall effect of the Act was to continue the process of centralization that had begun in the mid-1990s. Nevertheless, it did not go so far as to dismantle the structure of the tripartite relationship of police governance established by the Police Act 1964 and therefore maintained elements of local accountability which lie at the heart of the British model of policing.

Douglas Sharp

Related entries

Anti-social behaviour; Civilianization; Community support officers (CSOs); Doctrine; Independent Police Complaints Commission (IPCC); National Intelligence Model (NIM); Police authorities; Police powers; Rank structure.

Key texts and sources

Home Office (2001) *Policing for a New Century: A Blueprint for Reform.* London: HMSO.

See also the Office of Public Sector Information's website (http://www.opsi.gov.uk/acts/acts2002/20020 030.htm) for the text of the Police Reform Act 2002.

POLICE SERVICE OF NORTHERN IRELAND (PSNI)

The Police Service of Northern Ireland (PSNI) was established in November 2001 as successor to the Royal Ulster Constabulary (RUC).

The Police Service of Northern Ireland (PSNI) arose from the recommendations of the Independent Commission on Policing (1999) whose report (commonly known as the Patten Report) outlined a series of measures to develop policing structures in Northern Ireland that could command widespread community support in the aftermath of decades of political violence.

The difficulties surrounding policing in Northern Ireland were (and are) immense, and ultimately arose from the disputed nature of the state and the role of the police in securing that state. The largely Protestant Unionist and Loyalist communities sought to maintain Northern Ireland's position within the UK, while the largely Catholic Nationalist and Republican communities opposed the continuation of this political framework. These political differences were mirrored in attitudes to and experiences of the police. Since the foundation of the state in 1922, the Royal Ulster Constabulary (RUC) had performed a dual role of state security and crime prevention/service provision. For Unionists/Loyalists, the RUC represented a crucial line of defence against Republican aggression and a key marker of the political character of the state; for Nationalists/Republicans, the RUC was also viewed as a key symbol of the state, albeit a discriminatory state that denied full political participation to non-Unionists. From the late 1960s until the paramilitary ceasefires of 1994, Northern Irish society was enmeshed in violent conflict between Republican paramilitary organizations, their Loyalist counterparts and the security forces of the state. The establishment of the PSNI was an important step in the protracted conflict-resolution process that ensued.

Although the PSNI mirrored the RUC in many respects, it operated within a greatly different institutional framework for the governance of policing. Key changes included the establishment of a Police Ombudsman to investigate complaints against the police, a Policing Board to provide oversight of police policy, a network of district policing partnerships in local authority areas and an Oversight Commissioner to monitor implementation of the agreed reforms.

The main difficulties for the PSNI arose from the historical legacy of the RUC and from the continuing difficulties of policing a society marked by profound political division. Although the PSNI was a 'new' organization, at its inception it was composed entirely of RUC personnel, and the controversies that had dogged the RUC raised equal questions of the PSNI, especially allegations of collusion between the security forces and Loyalist paramilitaries. Furthermore, although the 1998 Belfast Agreement had outlined a framework for conflict resolution in terms of new political structures, police reform, prisoner release and other issues, this was a deeply contested process. The declaration in July 2005 by the Provisional Irish Republican Army (the main Republican paramilitary organization) that it was formally ending its activities and subsequent confirmation that it had decommissioned its arsenal of weapons did provide further evidence that a final agreement would be reached. Nevertheless, after several brief periods of office, by the end of 2006 the devolved government in Northern Ireland was still suspended, and Sinn Féin (the main Republican political party) had yet to endorse the PSNI, although it appeared closer than ever to doing so.

Securing the support of Nationalists/ Republicans against this uncertain background proved problematic, but efforts to increase Catholic recruitment were successful. In 2006, the PSNI comprised some 7,500 officers in the regular force, a further 680 officers in the full-time reserve (due to remain in office until March 2008), nearly 1,000 part-time officers and 3,200 civilian staff. The Patten Report had proposed a generous voluntary severance package to assist in downsizing the force from the 13,000 officers the RUC had comprised during the 1990s, to facilitate increased Catholic recruitment and to provide an exit strategy for officers unwilling to countenance the new structures of policing. By 2006, over 2,400 officers had left under this scheme. The Patten Report had recommended that, for a period of 10 years, the PSNI should recruit on the basis of a 50:50 ratio of Catholics and 'other', and implementation of this policy changed the force's composition considerably. In 2001, Catholics comprised 8.3 per cent of the regular force and, by April 2006, this had risen to 19.5 per cent. Over the same period, the proportion of female officers increased from 13 to 20.5 per cent of the force.

The transition from the RUC to the PSNI generated considerable challenges for operational policing. The clearance rate for recorded crime dropped from 30.2 per cent in 1999–2000 to 20.1 per cent in 2001–2, although by 2005–6 it had climbed back to 30.6 per cent. The retirement of a significant number of experienced officers generated severe organizational strain. Public complaints about levels of routine patrols and crime prevention activities also undermined the PSNI's efforts to situate 'policing with the community' at the heart of its activities, although that situation improved as levels of violence and disorder declined.

Public opinion towards the PSNI reflects the contested political background of Northern Ireland. Although a majority of both Catholics and Protestants are satisfied that the PSNI treats the public as a whole fairly, the differences in their assessments of policing are marked. For instance, one omnibus survey conducted in 2006 found that Protestant respondents are considerably more likely than Catholics to rate the police as treating everyone fairly (74 and 55 per cent, respectively) and equally (70 and 51 per cent, respectively).

Despite considerable optimism surrounding many aspects of the reform agenda, the full potential of these measures will require a level of political stability that has not yet been reached. Nevertheless, the case of Northern Ireland highlights two issues of particular significance. First, it demonstrates the pivotal role of police reform in processes of conflict resolution. Secondly, it is an important case study in assessing the potential of a nodal model for the governance of security (although the Patten Report's recommendations on this were not implemented in full). The international significance of both these issues will ensure that developments in Northern Ireland continue to feature in wider debates about the future of policing.

Aogán Mulcahy

Related entries

Code of conduct/ethics; Patten Report.

Key texts and sources

Independent Commission on Policing (1999) *A New Beginning: Policing Northern Ireland* (the Patten Report). Belfast: HMSO.

Mulcahy, A. (2006) *Policing Northern Ireland: Conflict, Legitimacy and Reform.* Cullompton: Willan Publishing.

The Northern Ireland Policing Board's website is at **http://www.nipolicingboard.org.uk/**. See also the Office of the Oversight Commissioner's website (**http://www.oversightcommissioner.org/**), the Office of the Police Ombudsman of Northern Ireland's website (**http://www.policeombudsman. org/**) and the PSNI's website (**http//:www.psni. police.uk/**).

POLICE SUPERINTENDENT'S ASSOCIATION (PSA)

> The Police Superintendent's Association (PSA) is the representative body for all superintending ranks in Home Office forces in England and Wales, the Civil Nuclear Constabulary and the British Transport Police.

The Police Superintendent's Association (PSA), established by the Police Act 1964 as a staff association, has three main objectives. To:

1. lead and develop the Police Service to improve the quality of its service delivery to local communities;
2. influence practice, policy and decision-making at chief officer and government level; and
3. provide appropriate support and advice to members to maintain and improve the professional status of the rank and to enjoy constitutionally the rights of consultation, participation and negotiation on all matters relating to the duties, responsibilities, welfare and efficiency of the members and the Police Service, other than in respect of promotion affecting individuals.

The members of each force of the rank of superintendent form a branch of the association, and the branches are organized into a five-district structure. Two representatives from each district make up the PSA's policymaking body, the National Executive Committee (NEC). There are also three reserved places on the NEC representing the interests of female, black and minority ethnic and lesbian, gay, bisexual and transgender members. NEC members in turn lead the organisation's business areas, which formulate responses to consultation documents and research core areas of work in support of the above objectives.

The PSA works in two distinct areas. It is a pressure group for change on policing issues as well as a traditional staff association, looking after the working conditions of its members. It achieves the former (which has become a much more significant part of its work in the last decade) by lobbying and utilizing the media, while also being a mandatory consultee for the government. It safeguards and seeks to improve the working conditions of its members through the use of the established negotiating machinery, primarily the Police Negotiating Board and the Police Advisory Board for England and Wales.

The President and Vice-president are elected positions, and they represent the PSA on a number of government steering groups and committees. The National Secretary and Deputy Secretary are appointed positions, and they conduct negotiations on issues affecting pay and conditions through the Police Negotiating Board. The President and Vice-president also undertake the media-facing role for the association being contributors to all forms of media, both broadcast and print. The PSA also has a widely developed panel of 'friends' who offer guidance and support to members who are under scrutiny and who can negotiate on their behalf with the other parties concerned in the investigation.

Rick Naylor

Related entries

Politics (police involvement).

Key texts and sources

The PSA publishes a magazine three times a year, and regular updates affecting officers appear on the association's website (**www.policesupers.com**). The PSA's rules, objectives, policies and position statements can also be found at this website.

POLICING

> Policing involves organized order maintenance, peace keeping, rule or law enforcement, crime investigation and prevention, and other forms of investigation and associated information brokering, which may involve the conscious exercise of coercive power.

There is considerable disagreement about how to define 'policing'. Much academic work in this area has focused on the sociology of *the* police rather than on poli*cing*. The term 'police' has come largely to be used as a means of talking about state organizations employed specifically to maintain order and control crime, and much of the early academic literature talked of policing as if it were indistinguishable from those activities undertaken by the police. However, in recent decades the rise of private security and other policing bodies has clearly illustrated the limitations of such an approach.

Much early sociological writing focused on the nature of the police role and on police culture. In the UK, work by Michael Banton in the 1960s, Maureen Cain in the 1970s and David Smith and Policy Studies Institute colleagues in the 1980s (Smith and Gray 1985) established the template for much that followed. One of the most important and long-lasting observations about the police – that the police officer is primarily a 'peace officer' rather than a 'law officer' – is to be found at the very beginning of Banton's path-breaking, *The Policeman in the Community* (1964). Some of the work that followed examined the nature of the police 'function', with various contributors focusing on the relative importance of 'order maintenance', 'crime control' and what Punch and Naylor (1973) called the 'secret social service' aspects of policing.

Moving beyond a concern with the different functions of policing, an alternative approach has considered the legal capacity that the police bring to their activities. In this regard it is the work of Egon Bittner that has been most important. Following Max Weber's original insight, Bittner begins from the position that it is the police service's role as the institution wielding legitimate force on behalf of the state that really sets it apart. In a famous passage he argued (1974) that:

> The police are empowered and required to impose or, as the case may be, coerce a provisional solution upon emergent problems without having to brook or defer to opposition of any kind, and that further, their competence to intervene extends to every kind of emergency, without any exceptions whatever. This and this alone is what the existence of the police uniquely provides, and it is on this basis that they may be required to do the work of thief-catchers and of nurses, depending on the occasion.

For Bittner, then, it is the capacity the officer brings to any eventuality that distinguishes what he or she does. In his own distinctive formulation: 'The policeman, and the policeman alone, is equipped, entitled and required to deal with every exigency in which force may have to be used, to meet it.'

In recent times, however, a number of developments have served to reorient academic attention towards policing activities beyond those of agents in the employment of the state – not least the rapid expansion of the private security industry. As a result, a significant body of work has emerged that has explored and analysed private policing, together with the activities of a range of hybrid bodies and regulatory agencies that go to make up what is now generally referred to as the system of plural policing.

In this context, the work of Clifford Shearing and Philip Stenning has been hugely important, not least a short piece they wrote on the policing of Disney World (1987). Here they drew attention to the multiple and subtle ways in which social control is managed informally and yet effectively. Disney World, they argued, was in many ways the exemplar of modern corporate policing. Visitors are not policed by uniformed agents of the state but, rather, 'trouble is anticipated and prevented. Opportunities for disorder are minimized by constant instruction, by physical barriers which severely limit the choice of action available and by the surveillance of omnipresent employees who detect and rectify the slightest deviation'.

In some respects the shifting focus in academic research from a preoccupation with *the police* outwards to *policing* involves something of a return to an older conception of 'police'. In the eighteenth century, it referred to the activities involved in the more general well-being of the population, as well as to a broad range of administrative functions (though in the main such activities were not conducted by professionals).

However, the danger in allowing the definition of policing to become too broad is that we lose sight of the distinction between policing and social control activities. Policing is not the same as social control and would become a meaningless term if used in this way. Teachers and parents, for example, both exercise considerable social control. However, neither are usefully understood as policing in any formal sense. Rather, as suggested above, any useful definition must combine some sense of the functional characteristics and coercive capacity involved in policing, together with a recognition that these must be viewed as a core or defining element of the role. Such a definition can encompass the activities of an HM Revenue and Customs investigation department, private detectives, health and safety inspectors, bouncers and closed-circuit television operators, among many others, as well as the work of those employed by constabularies.

Nevertheless, there is a developing argument in the criminological literature that views the term 'policing' as being inadequate to capture either the range or complexity of current arrangements. Such work proposes instead the use of the phrase 'security governance', the intention of which is to shift the focus away from the preoccupation with the state, which, it is argued, is inherent in the term 'policing'.

Tim Newburn

Related entries

Legitimacy; Plural policing; Police culture; Police powers; Private policing; Security.

Key texts and sources

Bittner, E. (1974) 'Florence Nightingale in pursuit of Willie Sutton: a theory of the police', in H. Jacob (ed.) *The Potential for Reform in Criminal Justice.* Newbury Park, CA: Sage (reprinted in Newburn, T. (ed.) (2004) *Policing: Key Readings.* Cullompton: Willan Publishing).

Johnston, L. and Shearing, C. (2003) *Governing Security.* London: Routledge.

Jones, T. and Newburn, T. (1998) *Private Security and Public Policing.* Oxford: Clarendon Press (ch. 1).

Shearing, C.D. and Stenning, P. (1987) 'Say cheese! The Disney order that is not so Mickey Mouse', in C.D. Shearing and P. Stenning (eds) *Private Policing.* Thousand Oaks, CA: Sage.

POLITICS (POLICE INVOLVEMENT)

There are two dimensions to the political involvement of policing: the police response to political actions and ideas, and their attempt to exercise influence over police policymaking.

The involvement of the police in crowd situations entails interventions in extra-parliamentary political activities conducted through such means as demonstrations, direct action and industrial disputes (see Public order). A more specialized form of political involvement, however, has been charted by Bunyan (1977), who discussed 'political policing'. When policing was reformed in the early decades of the nineteenth century, there was considerable concern that it should not monitor political activity. None the less, the Police Service did scrutinize political organizations (such as the National Political Union of the Working Classes and the Chartists) in an *ad hoc* way. A more formalized development occurred in 1883 in consequence of the violence of Irish nationalism. A bombing campaign mounted by the Fenians on mainland Britain resulted in the formation within the Metropolitan Police Criminal Investigation Department of the Special Irish Branch, which sought to counter their activities mainly through the surveillance of political militants.

The word 'Irish' was subsequently dropped from the title of this police squad, whose activities became broader and directed against a wide range of political groups that were perceived to threaten the well-being of the state and the life and safety of its citizens. These initially included foreign immigrant groups (who were identified with anarchism) and, at the beginning of the twentieth century, the suffragettes and industrial militants. Subsequently, attention was focused on the Communist Party (which was formed in 1920) and organizations such as the Campaign for Nuclear Disarmament that were perceived to be influenced by it. In the Cold War era the information gathered on individuals by Special Branch was used in the process of positive vetting, which was designed to ensure that those associated with organizations of this nature did not secure employment in sensitive areas of government work. Initially, Special Branch existed within the Metropolitan Police but, following reorganization initiated in 1961, all police forces established squads of this nature, which were formally under the control of their respective chief constables.

The rivalry between Britain and Germany at the beginning of the twentieth century led to a further development in political policing. In order to thwart the spying activities of Germany, a new organization, the Security Service or MI5, was set up in 1909. It was controlled by the Home Secretary, although the organization enjoyed a considerable degree of operational freedom. Initially, MI5 operated under a cloak-and-dagger existence. It lacked statutory basis until the enactment of the Security Service Act 1989 and its recruitment was largely through the 'old boy' network until the open recruitment of graduates was introduced in 1995.

The main function of MI5 was to counter subversion. This term was defined by the Security Services Act 1989, which referred in particular to protecting national security 'against threats from espionage, terrorism and sabotage, from the activities of agents of foreign powers and from actions intended to overthrow or underline parliamentary democracy by political, industrial or violent means'. It has also been argued that the agency has mounted operations against democratically elected governments. Walsh (1982) and Wright (1987), for example, alleged that Labour governments and politicians were on the receiving end of MI5 activities during the 1970s.

MI5's main role is to gather intelligence through a range of methods that include intercepting mail and telephone communications, planting bugs and utilizing informants, but it has also been accused of mounting operations. Milne (1995) detailed the role allegedly played by an MI5 informant in the National Union of Miners' headquarters during the 1984–5 miners' dispute whose role included undertaking actions designed to destabilize the union. Some limitations have subsequently been imposed on the activities of MI5, the most important of which was the need for ministers to sign warrants to authorize activities such as planting bugging devices. This procedure was set out in the Security Services Act 1989 and, latterly, MI5 activities were controlled by the Regulation of Investigatory Powers Act 2000.

The Police Service itself also acts in a political capacity by engaging in activities to influence the police policymaking agenda. This role is promoted by four key bodies – the Association of Chief Police Officers (ACPO), the Police Federation, the Police Superintendent's Association (PSA) and the National Black Police Association.

The origins of ACPO date from the formation of the County Chief Constables' Club in 1858 and the Chief Constables' Association of England and Wales in 1896, which represented the chief officers of urban forces. These two bodies amalgamated in 1948 to form ACPO, and the Royal Ulster Constabulary was incorporated in 1970. The organization adopted company status in 1997. It consists of the most senior ranks of the Police Service (assistant chief constable and above) which numbered 312 in 2005.

During the nineteenth century the chief constables' organizations did little more than facilitate social contact between its members. However, the role of ACPO in the twentieth century became broader, seeking to promote the effectiveness, efficiency and professional interests of the Police Service and to safeguard the individual and collective interests of its members. In 1996 these two functions were separated, with the newly formed Chief Police Officers' Staff Association becoming responsible for dealings with the Police Negotiation Board on issues related to its members' salaries and conditions of service. This meant that, henceforth, ACPO could concentrate on the development of police policy, both in the sense of influencing the activities pursued by individual forces (a role that had formerly been hindered by the doctrine of constabulary independence) and by seeking to influence the content of centrally directed police policy (a function that was aided by its position as an 'insider' group in the Whitehall corridors of power).

Key changes to the position of ACPO in policymaking during the 1990s have been discussed by Savage et al. (2000), who argued that its previous 'sporadic' influence over the police agenda developed as the consequence of the emergence of a 'corporacy' (or cohesiveness) among ACPO members. This has been attributed as the product of a number of circumstances that included the negative views of senior officers to the government's reform agenda of the 1990s – the Sheehy Report (1993), the Police and Magistrates' Courts Act 1994 and the Posen Inquiry (1995) into police core and ancillary functions – which enhanced the level of ACPO campaigning.

The concerns of rank-and-file police officers are voiced by a different organization, the Police Federation. This body emerged as the consequence of the police strikes of 1918 and 1919 that were organized by the National Union of Police and Prison Officers. The resultant Police Act 1919 forbade police officers to join trade unions but set up the Police Federation as a statutory advisory body to represent the views of police officers (now up to the rank of chief inspector) on all matters related to their welfare and efficiency. Its work included negotiating on pay and conditions of service and it is consulted on the formulation of police regulations.

The Police Federation has (like ACPO) evolved from a staff association into an organization that seeks to exert influence on police and criminal justice policy. Unlike ACPO, it mainly performs this role from outside the corridors of power – a role that was developed after 1955 when it was granted the ability to levy a subscription from its members in order to conduct campaigning.

Initial federation campaigns were concerned with such issues as police pay and support for the death penalty, but a watershed in its political role occurred during the 1970s when increases in crime and the negative views held by some left-wing politicians towards the police prompted the federation to seek more vigorously to influence public opinion. These campaigns were documented by McLaughlin and Murji (1998) and witnessed the use of lobbying techniques allied with such methods as press advertising to appeal directly to the public over the heads of senior police officers and the government.

The federation's 1975 law-and-order campaign has been described by McLaughlin and Murji (1998) as 'the crucial moment of overt politicisation'. The target of this campaign were the liberal reforms promoted during the 1960s, which it depicted as the root of the contemporary crime problem, and it aimed to mobilize the silent majority in favour of tougher law-and-order policies. This campaign ran alongside a further one designed to increase police pay, which challenged the government's incomes policy.

The Conservative Party enthusiastically endorsed many of the federation's demands. Although there were some differences of opinion (on issues such as the Police and Criminal Evidence Act 1984), a good relationship was struck between police and government during the 1980s, which led to the perception of the service being politicized in the sense of acting to further the government's objectives rather than serving society. This perception climaxed during the 1984–5 miners' dispute when the image of 'Maggie's boot boys' was raised in connection with the robust policing utilized during that strike.

The relationship between the federation and the Conservative government was adversely affected by the Conservative reform agenda of the 1990s. This prompted the federation to adopt aggressive lobbying and campaigning techniques and to become willing to work with other groups to oppose these initiatives. This led to the federation becoming more influential – one early product of which was the virtual abandonment of Sheehy's proposals affecting rank-and-file policing.

A third body seeking to influence the policing agenda is the Police Superintendent's Association (PSA). This was set up in 1920 to represent superintendents and chief superintendents. Initially, the PSA was seen as little more than a senior officers' dining club, but Savage et al. (2000) have referred to the more significant (if intermittent) role on policing and criminal justice policy that it subsequently achieved on issues that included the imposition of gun controls in the wake of the 1996 Dunblane shootings.

A final development affecting police involvement in political activities was the formation of the National Black Police Association to represent police officers from minority ethnic communities. The origins of this organization lie in the formation of the London Black Police Association in the Metropolitan Police Service in 1994, which became a national organization in 1998. The role of this body has extended beyond the articulation of the interests and concerns of minority ethnic officers in police forces in England and Wales (especially racial discrimination in the service and the consequent high wastage rate of minority ethnic officers). This campaigning role was developed in 2006 when the National Black Police Associations of the UK and USA hosted the first 'International education and training' conference in Manchester, one aspect of which was a march by delegates through Moss Side, which aimed to reach out to local communities.

Peter Joyce

Related entries

Association of Chief Police Officers (ACPO); Black police associations; National security; Police Federation; Police Superintendent's Association (PSA).

Key texts and sources

Bunyan, T. (1977) *The History and Practice of the Political Police in Britain.* London: Quartet Books.
McLaughlin, E. and Murji, K. (1998) 'Resistance through representation: "storylines", advertising and Police Federation campaigns', *Policing and Society*, 8: 367–99.
Savage, S., Charman, S. and Cope, S. (2000) *Policing and the Power of Persuasion.* London: Blackstone Press.

PORNOGRAPHY (CHILD)

While deviant sexual interests have for centuries found their expression in forms that have been labelled 'pornography', in the last two decades the production, distribution and possession of sexually abusive images of children have emerged as a rapidly growing problem, due in large measure to the expansion of information and communications technologies.

The last 20 years have witnessed a shift in cultural attitudes as greater freedom of access to pornography has democratized sexual gratification. 'Adult' pornography has been normalized to the extent that, when rock star Pete Townshend faced allegations of downloading abusive images of children in 2003, he said he was not a paedophile but had used adult porn all his life. In an era in which 'lads' mags' have brought sexually explicit images of women to the mainstream publishing world, Townshend's revelation was barely commented on in the UK media.

Law enforcement reflects this changing technological and cultural landscape and, while the production and distribution of sexually explicit images of adults no longer constitute a policing priority, the launch of the Child Exploitation and Online Protection (CEOP) Centre in 2006 underlines the UK police's commitment to stemming the global Internet trade in child pornography. At a local level, however, the decentralized nature of policing in England and Wales means a lack of standardization and varying levels of commitment to combating the problem (Jewkes and Andrews 2005). When the government set up the National Hi-tech Crime Unit (NHTCU) in 2001, £10 million of the £25 million start-up costs was earmarked for the provision of at least two specialist officers in every force. However, some forces struggled to recruit suitable applicants and, even on major investigations such as Operation Ore, some investigators reported they were inadequately trained for the task (Jewkes and Andrews 2005). Unable to cope with the demands made upon it, therefore, the NHTCU was wound down in 2006 and absorbed into the Serious and Organised Crime Agency, which has a broader remit than simply online crimes.

In some countries a different approach is taken to 'policing' Internet child pornography. For example, in New Zealand, the Censorship Compliance Unit (CCU) in the government's Department of Internal Affairs claims a higher success rate than many police forces who may give cybercrime a low priority compared with 'real world' offences. Because the CCU is responsible for investigating a relatively narrow range of offences it has developed a proactive strategy based on specialist intelligence and technical expertise (Jewkes and Andrews 2007). This is the approach CEOP hopes to emulate: undercover officers have set up fake websites and pose as children in chatrooms to lure paedophiles; investigators employ powerful face recognition software to match images and to trace abusers, victims and locations; the centre aims to establish a permanent presence in countries with such problems as sex tourism (initially Cambodia) and will work with local police to identify offenders; and officers are working with the computer industry to develop new products and services that prevent children from being exposed to abuse. In addition, a website allowing victims of paedophiles to report their experiences to CEOP claimed its first success in June 2006 when a Nottinghamshire man who had groomed several young girls in chatrooms was convicted and sentenced to nine years in prison.

Yvonne Jewkes

Related entries

Cybercrimes; Europol.

Key texts and sources

Jewkes, Y. and Andrews, C. (2005) 'Policing the filth: the problems of investigating online child pornography in England and Wales', *Policing and Society*, 15: 42–62.

Jewkes, Y. and Andrews, C. (2007) 'Internet child pornography: international responses', in Y. Jewkes (ed.) *Crime Online.* Cullompton: Willan Publishing.

PRIVATE POLICING

Private policing refers to 'policing' activities that are authorized and/or directly undertaken by non-state bodies and that promote explicitly 'private' interests rather than a more general conception of the public interest.

It is now generally recognized that norm enforcement, peacekeeping and other activities undertaken by state *police* institutions are a subset of a broader range of *policing* functions authorized and undertaken by a variety of state, commercial, voluntary and community bodies. These are themselves a subset of the wider framework of social controls. A useful definition of policing must be specific enough to capture the distinctive features of policing within the diffuse mesh of formal/informal social controls in society, but at the same time general enough to include the range of activities undertaken by, or on behalf of, non-state bodies. The most helpful working definitions to date have focused on relatively organized manifestations of regulation and norm enforcement. For example, Johnston's (2000: 10) definition of policing as 'a purposive strategy involving the initiation of techniques which are intended to offer guarantees of security to subjects' provides a basis for consideration of the full range of policing bodies and activities. Definitional discussions about policing have arisen, in part, from a growing criminological focus on the law enforcement, crime prevention and order maintenance activities undertaken by individuals and organizations other than state police forces.

Studies of private policing have included various investigation and regulatory bodies attached to national and local government, forms of patrol provision provided by local municipalities and even the activities of functionally or spatially specialized police forces, such as the British Transport Police (Johnston 1992; Button 2002). Although this has provided a helpful corrective to the previous exclusive focus on state constabularies, it can also be misleading. For example, many of the agencies included under this broader usage – such as municipal patrollers, health and safety investigators and environmental health officers – are clearly 'public' in so far as they are delivered by state functionaries and funded (at least in part) by taxation revenue (Jones and Newburn 1998). However, 'private policing' may be understood as those policing activities authorized and/or directly undertaken by non-state bodies, promoting explicitly 'private' interests rather than a more general conception of the public interest. This covers the range of policing activities undertaken under the rubric of commercial security, including prevention and surveillance services undertaken by 'contract' security firms and those provided 'in-house' by specialist security employees of commercial companies. It also includes the less formalized activities undertaken in communities on a voluntary basis, such as the activities of Neighbourhood Watch schemes and some forms of vigilantism (Johnston 1996). In some jurisdictions, private policing can be undertaken by public officials (for example, when contractual arrangements allow the hiring of public police officers to undertake private security functions).

There is widespread agreement that certain forms of private policing have expanded enormously in importance over the past 30 years or so. Commercial provision of security – including guarding, the provision of security hardware and technology and private investigatory services – has grown substantially in the UK in recent decades, and there is strong evidence suggesting similar trends across many parts of the globe (Jones and Newburn 2006). Various factors have contributed to such developments, including growing demands for policing services outstripping the resources of public providers, the policies of privatization and contracting out as part of governmental reform programmes, the growing privatization of urban space and broader structural changes in contemporary industrial societies that have contributed to growing perceptions of insecurity. In addition to the proliferation of policing providers, there has been an expansion of authorizers of security functions (Bayley and Shearing 2001). This reflects a more fundamental shift in governance, with the growth of domains of non-state governments that not only employ security provision themselves but also determine the nature of the order to be upheld, decide the rules that are necessary to do this and shape the ways in which compliance is achieved (Shearing 2006). However, much literature on policing continues to give conceptual priority to state institutions and obscures the important role played by non-state forms of governance. A number of authors have suggested that the concept of 'nodal governance' best captures the way in which not only policing but also governing in general is now undertaken in contemporary societies (Johnston and Shearing 2003; Wood and Dupont 2006).

The expansion of private policing has stimulated vigorous normative debate about the future of policing. On the one hand, it has been argued that some forms of private policing have a number of dysfunctional effects. In particular, concerns have been raised about the standard of service provided by private policing and about the perceived lack of public accountability of individuals exercising policing powers in support of private ends. It is also suggested that privately organized policing exacerbates social divisions and that such polarization further increases feelings of insecurity. Thus, for example, there has been a long-standing literature on the need to provide effective forms of regulation of the commercial security sector and to bring the broader network of security providers under the direction and control of democratic institutions (Loader 2000). On the other hand, some authors have argued that the growth of private policing demonstrates the importance of moving beyond conceptions of policing that privilege state-centric arrangements. On this view, non-state forms of security provision and governance provide an important opportunity to develop more equitable and effective forms of security provision in local communities (Shearing 2006). The arguments of these writers suggest that we need to facilitate the participation of less advantaged groups in security markets and enable them to develop their own locally designed forms of private governance (Wood and Dupont 2006). Although private policing clearly plays an increasingly important role in policing generally, it is important not to underplay the continuing importance of state-organized arrangements. In response to the 'nodal governance' writers, some commentators have argued that state policing should be viewed as something more than 'one node among many' (Crawford 2003). A number of authors have provided compelling arguments in favour of retaining a conception of policing as a social good, and one which should be promoted and organized – if not always directly delivered – by democratically accountable collective political institutions (Loader and Walker 2001).

Trevor Jones

Related entries

Community safety; Cybercrimes; Mass private property; Plural policing; Policing; Transnational policing.

Key texts and sources

Crawford, A. (2003) 'The pattern of policing in the UK: policing beyond the police', in T. Newburn (ed.) *Handbook of Policing*. Cullompton: Willan Publishing.

Johnston, L. (2000) *Policing Britain: Risk, Security and Governance*. London: Longman.

Jones, T. and Newburn, T. (1998) *Private Security and Public Policing*. Oxford: Clarendon Press.

Wood, J. and Dupont, B. (eds) (2006) *Democracy, Society and the Governance of Security*. Cambridge: Cambridge University Press.

PROBLEM-ORIENTED POLICING

Problem-oriented policing includes the full range of crime and non-crime issues that fall to the police. It adopts a critical, analytic and evidence-based approach to the classification of specific problems, to the identification of conditions producing and reproducing those problems, and to the selection of whichever ethical responses might be put in place by the police or other parties to remove, reduce or ameliorate them.

Problem-oriented policing was devised by Herman Goldstein, an American professor of law at the University of Wisconsin, Madison, who had previously been an adviser to the Chicago Police Department. The idea was first mooted in an article published in 1979, which was then developed in more detail with examples in a book published in 1990 (Goldstein 1990).

Goldstein was critical of American policing at the time for its inattention to community concerns, for its preoccupation with process over outcome, for its focus on individual incidents and for the ineffectiveness of its standard responses. Goldstein instead emphasized the importance of identifying and understanding specific police-relevant patterns of problem behaviour and of devising responses that could lead to sustainable falls in the level, severity or impact of the problem. Problems are not confined to crime but may include a wide range of issues (for example, missing children, noisy parties, barking dogs, demonstrations, suicides and false burglar alarms). Responses often include the transference of responsibility to bodies better placed than the police to deal effectively with the identified problem in the long run. For Goldstein, enforcement is a means, not an end, in policing. The police are there to identify and address effectively specific police-relevant problems by whatever ethical means are available. While police enforcement may sometimes be needed, this will not always be the case and will seldom be sufficient for effective longer-term solutions.

Initial experiments in problem-oriented policing took place in the Metropolitan Police Service and Surrey Constabulary, as well as in various American police agencies. The most influential early work was that in Newport News, Virginia. It was here that the influential SARA process was devised. This refers to 'Scanning, Analysis, Response and Assessment'. Scanning comprises an exploration of the specific patterned issues the police are being asked to address. Analysis includes efforts to understand the conditions producing the problem pattern and the failures hitherto to deal with it by existing means. Response refers to the measure or suite of measures put in place to deal with the problem in the light of the analysis. Assessment tries to garner evidence to establish whether or not the problem has been dealt with effectively, what lessons have been learnt and whether additional efforts are needed. The SARA process is now used in most efforts to structure problem-oriented policing wherever it is attempted. Critics have suggested that the SARA process can often be undertaken in rather a simple-minded four-step manner. In practice, in order to find ways of dealing effectively with persistent problems, it is generally necessary to return to scanning, analysis and response in a recursive process where problem definition, problem understanding and strategies to address the problem are refined increasingly over time.

A heuristic device used in much problem-oriented work has been the problem analysis triangle (PAT). The three sides refer to the victim, offender and location. PAT is used to focus analysis on what each element is contributing to the specific problem pattern. Attention then turns to identifying practical measures that can be taken to address relevant aspects of whichever is most open to intervention. PAT has clear affinities with routine activities theory, according to which all predatory crimes require a likely offender, a suitable target and the absence of a capable guardian. Removal of any one of these essential conditions means the crime cannot take place. Though not focused exclusively on crime problems, PAT makes use of a similar logic.

In Britain there are few, if any, police services where problem-oriented policing has not been attempted. It sits well with policies aiming to reduce crime and to introduce neighbourhood policing. Both stress the identification of local problems and priorities. Both focus on finding effective responses to problems that do not depend on continuing enforcement activities by the police. Both stress partnership with the community and other local agencies. Indeed, the term 'problem-oriented partnership' is often preferred to 'problem-oriented policing' in view of the shared local responsibilities for identifying and dealing with local crime and disorder issues that are enshrined in the Crime and Disorder Act 1998.

The theory of problem-oriented policing has almost universally been found compelling, yet it has been found in practice to be very tricky to implement. Difficulties have been found both organizationally and technically. Organizationally, cultural resistance, cynicism, crude performance management regimes, staff turnover, lack of trained analysts and interagency hostilities, for example, have all obstructed the successful and sustained implementation of problem-oriented policing and partnership. Technically, poor problem formulation, limitations in data availability and quality, weaknesses in analysis, dependency on traditional responses and an absence of independent evaluation have all characterized much that has been undertaken in the name of problem-oriented policing and partnership. Much problem-oriented work has lacked the sharp focus, ambition and scope for transferable lesson-learning promised in Goldstein's original vision. It has tended, on the one hand, to have been confined to *ad hoc* means of dealing with small-scale and one-off problems and, on the other, to take loosely defined wide-ranging issues that include numerous specific problems that require separate attention.

Notwithstanding implementation shortcomings, there are many examples of successful problem-oriented work in the UK as well as the USA. Moreover, there is an increasing number of informed guides to ways of dealing with specific problems, of exemplars of previous effective problem-oriented work and of tools for analysis and evaluation. Most of these are available through the Center for Problem-oriented Policing at http://popcenter.org/.

Nick Tilley

Related entries

Crime prevention (situational and social); Intelligence-led policing; Neighbourhood policing.

Key texts and sources

Bullock, K., Erol, R. and Tilley, N. (2006) *Problem-oriented Policing and Partnerships.* Cullompton: Willan Publishing.

Goldstein, H. (1990) *Problem-oriented Policing.* New York, NY: McGraw Hill.

Knuttson, J. (ed.) (2003) *Problem-oriented Policing: From Innovation to Mainstream. Crime Prevention Studies* 15. Cullompton: Willan Publishing.

The Center for Problem-oriented Policing website is at **http://popcenter.org/**. See also the Home Office's

Neighbourhood Watch web page on problem-oriented policing (http://www.crimereduction.gov.uk/neighbourhoodwatch/nwatch03f.htm) and the Home Office's web page on problem-oriented policing (http://www.crimereduction.gov.uk/fearofcrime0208.htm).

PROFESSIONALIZATION

> Professionalization has traditionally been used in the Police Service as shorthand for improved training and continuing professional development. Though still central to professionalization, more recently the term has come to be used to describe a wider set of developments aimed at improving practitioner's capacity to carry out their roles and of assuring their competence to do so.

Professionalization includes both continuing professional development and a broader set of issues. These include the following:

- The establishment of performance criteria, such as those contained in the National Occupational Standards.
- The development of doctrine that sets out the policy, business processes and practice individuals need in order to police.
- The establishment of knowledge management systems aimed at making relevant bodies of knowledge and good practice available to practitioners.
- The development of accreditation schemes, such as the Professionalization of Investigation Programme, to develop and accredit practitioners.

Developments such as these focus on individual practitioners as a means of bringing about improvements in service delivery. This distinguishes them from other ways of bringing about change, such as the development of organizational policy and improved business systems, although these things are obviously closely connected.

There was a period in the evolution of policing when it was generally believed that police work was so straightforward that all the competences, specialist knowledge and practice needed to carry it out could be possessed by all practitioners: a belief that was embodied in the concept of the omni-competent constable. Whether such individuals ever truly existed is open to debate, but the wide social, legal and policy roles now played by the Police Service, together with the complexity of the society it polices, mean that no single individual can posses the knowledge required to address every issue. Professionalization enables the Police Service to respond to these changes by facilitating the development of distinct professional practices for different functional areas of policing.

Professionalization has not been the result of a managed process. Each of its elements has tended to develop independently in response to specific changes in the policing environment and has been absorbed into policing incrementally. As a result, not all areas of policing have been subject to the same level of professionalization. Areas of high organizational risk, such as firearms operations, the command of sporting events and other senior command functions, have tended to be professionalized first, but all areas of policing are now moving in a similar direction. A key driver in this has been the Police Service's focus on performance management and, in particular, the Workforce Modernization Programme, which seeks to match skills and abilities more closely to business needs. Professionalization has been used as a way of supporting such initiatives by defining performance criteria, by targeting training and by accrediting competence.

So far, professionalization has provided the Police Service with a means of responding to changes in the policing environment, of managing high-risk functions and of promoting performance improvements. However, it represents a fundamental change in the way in which the service uses its human resources, and these may not yet have been fully acknowledged. An increasingly professionalized workforce will need to be managed differently from the traditional non-specialist model on which many police human resources practices are based. For example, those who have invested time and effort into professional development and accreditation are unlikely to view an officer's position in the management hierarchy as evidence of professional competence or to accept that he or she should be moved from one post to another simply to match operational needs.

The continued success of the professionalization of the Police Service is likely to rest on how senior managers respond to such challenges.

Peter Stelfox

Related entries

Association of Chief Police Officers (ACPO); Chief constables; Civilianization; Community support officers (CSOs); Ethics in policing; HM Inspectorate of Constabulary (HMIC); Training (police).

Key text and sources

Stelfox, P. (2007) 'Professionalising investigative processes', in T. Newburn *et al.* (eds) *Handbook of Criminal Investigation.* Cullompton: Willan Publishing.

See also the Home Office's policing web page on Professionalizing the Investigation Process (http://police.homeoffice.gov.uk/operational-policing/investigation/professional-investigation-pip/).

PROSTITUTION

Prostitution is a social institution shaping and regulating the exchange of sex for money or other economic benefits. It is a term that indicates not only the way that sex is sold but also the wider social, political, ideological and economic conditions that structure the ways the exchange takes place, the conditions of existence for those involved and its regulation.

There have been over 200 years of empirical and theoretical study of prostitution. The key debates contained in these writings concentrate on three main questions: Why do people (mainly women) prostitute? What are the 'problems' of prostitution? What should be done about those problems? In common with criminological theorizing, early writers focused on determining the specific characteristics of individuals in order to explain their involvement in prostitution. More latterly, however, feminist scholarship has come to dominate thinking about prostitution. Feminists have focused on the relationship between individuals in prostitution and broader socio-economic conditions.

Opening up the debate in the UK, McLeod (1982) pointed to the interconnections between women's general socio-economic position in society and their involvement in prostitution by arguing that many women turn to prostitution as a means of resisting economic dependency on, and relative poverty to, men. Using the same logic, others have argued that involvement in prostitution is a form of gendered sexual violence, both in relation to the regularity of physical and sexual violence, that women in prostitution suffer and, more broadly, in terms of the commodification of women's sexuality (O'Connell Davidson 1999; Phoenix 2001).

Throughout the 1980s and 1990s, academic and campaigning debates became increasingly polarized around the question of consent: whether sex workers choose to sell sex and/or whether experiences of victimization, exploitation by partners (or pimps) or poverty compel sex workers into prostitution. Despite such polarization, writers nevertheless agreed that sex workers face much higher risks of sexual violence and rape than other women and are routinely and regularly discriminated against by the police. This means that UK street-working sex workers have been under-protected by the police for the crimes committed against them and over-policed for their prostitution-related offences.

There are four different policing responses to prostitution: negative regulationism, decriminalization, abolition and legalization. Traditionally, the UK has pursued negative regulationism in which only the 'more disruptive' aspects of prostitution have been regulated (i.e. the visibility of street prostitution). However, since 2000, policy changes in the UK have shifted, and there is a detectable abolitionist agenda that is not geared to managing prostitution but, rather, to abolishing it. Here, the police in conjunction with voluntary and statutory welfare services work together to compel women to seek help for their personal and social welfare problems and thus to exit prostitution. With these policy changes, academic focus has turned from earlier, polarized theoretical discussions to the recognition of the lack of human rights, the absence of safety and social inequalities experienced by those in sex work.

Joanna Phoenix

Related entries

Broken windows; Dispersal orders; Human trafficking; Sexual Offences Act 2003 (SOA); Sexual offences/sexual violence.

Key texts and sources

Campbell, R. and O'Neill, M. (eds) (2006) *Sex Work Now.* Cullompton: Willan Publishing.

O'Connell Davidson, J. (1999) *Prostitution, Power and Freedom.* Cambridge: Polity Press.

Phoenix, J. (2001) *Making Sense of Prostitution.* London: Palgrave.

Sanders, T. (2005) *Sex Work: Risky Business.* Cullompton: Willan Publishing.

The Association of Chief Police Officers' guidelines for dealing with exploitation and abuse through prostitution (*Policing Prostitution*) are available online at http://www.nswp.org/pdf/UKACPO-PROST-0410.PDF. The Home Office's document, *A Coordinated Prostitution Strategy*, is available online at http://www.homeoffice.gov.uk/documents/ProstitutionStrategy.pdf?view=Binary.

PUBLIC ATTITUDES TO THE POLICE

It is essential to monitor public attitudes to the police closely. If the Police Service fails to command public confidence, public co-operation with the police may be jeopardized. In the long run, if the police as an institution fails to command legitimacy, public compliance with the law may be threatened.

The belief was widespread 50 years ago that the British police were the best in the world. Since then, public support for the police has declined, though the police remain more highly regarded than other parts of the criminal justice system, such as prison officers, probation officers, youth justice workers, magistrates and judges. They are also more highly regarded than civil servants, NHS managers, trade unionists, business leaders and, notably, politicians and journalists.

The main sources of information about public attitudes to the police are national surveys (such as the British Crime Survey) and polls carried out by survey companies such as MORI and Gallup. It is useful to distinguish between public opinion about the *effectiveness* of the police, public opinion about the *fairness and integrity* of the police and the views of police users about the *quality of service* they receive.

Effectiveness

The British Crime Survey indicates a long-run decline in public satisfaction with police effectiveness. This could in part reflect the fact that the UK is becoming a less deferential society (and showing less approval to a range of institutions). It could also reflect the fact that, for most of the last half-century, crime has actually been rising. Curiously, however, the fall in public confidence has been steepest since 1995, when crime began to *fall*. The failure of public opinion to become more positive in response to falling crime has been called the 'reassurance gap', and recent policing policy has attempted to narrow this gap by more responsive forms of policing. There are some signs that ratings of the police are now improving.

Fairness

The proportion of the population who think that police malpractice *never* occurs has fallen over the last 25 years. On the other hand, the proportion thinking that malpractice *often* occurs has remained the same – or even declined slightly. Currently, four fifths of the population in England and Wales believe that the police respect the rights of suspects, and two thirds think they treat witnesses well. Black people are less likely than those from other ethnic groups to say that the police respect the rights of suspects. A much larger proportion of Londoners in 2000 thought that the police treated minority ethnic groups unfairly than did in 1981.

Ratings of experience of the police

Long-run trends in satisfaction among victims are downwards. For example, 68 per cent of victims were satisfied in 1992, compared with 58 per cent in 2004–5, according to the British Crime Survey. Trends have been steady since 2000, however, with a quarter of victims in England and Wales being very satisfied and a further third fairly satisfied. A persistent source of dissatisfaction is the lack of follow-up information about incidents: while most feel they do not wait unreasonably long for the police to attend and that the police show sufficient interest and energy when they turn up, under a third feel they are kept adequately informed.

The British Crime Survey shows that around one in six of the population has felt 'really annoyed' with a police officer in the last five years. The figure has been stable over the last few years. Those most likely to have felt really annoyed tend to be from minority ethnic groups and to be young adults.

Understanding public attitudes towards the police

In contrast to most parts of the criminal justice system, large proportions of the population have some contact with the police. Just under a third of adults contact the police for some reason or other in the course of a year, and one in five is approached by the police for various reasons. Bearing in mind that friends and family swap experiences of the police, direct or indirect contact is likely to be a very important driver of opinion. At the same time, both the news and entertainment media are likely to have a large effect. For example, the reporting of the findings of the Macpherson Inquiry (1999) into the death of Stephen Lawrence will certainly have had a marked impact both on Londoners' views of the police and on the views of those who live elsewhere. The sensational reporting of crime figures is also likely to have an effect.

The importance of winning the 'hearts and minds' of the population – through various forms of community policing – has been recognized by senior police for many years, but other priorities sometimes disrupt styles of policing that are most likely to win public support. The most recent variant of community policing is neighbourhood policing. This emerged from the reassurance policing pilot. It involves small, geographically based teams of police officers and police community support officers, who are expected to get to know their local population, policing the neighbourhood in a way that is responsive to public preferences. It remains to be seen how successful this strategy will be in reversing the decline in ratings of the police.

Mike Hough

Related entries

Legitimacy; Media and policing; Neighbourhood policing; Reassurance policing.

Key texts and sources

Allen, J., Edmonds, S., Patterson, A. and Smith, D. (2006) *Policing and the Criminal Justice System – Public Confidence and Perceptions: Findings from the 2004/05 British Crime Survey. Home Office Online Report* 07/06. London: Home Office (available online at **http://www.homeoffice.gov.uk /rds/pdfs06/rdsolr0706.pdf**).

Hough, M. (2007) 'Policing London, twenty years on', in A. Henry and D. Smith (eds) *Transformations in Policing.* Aldershot: Ashgate.

Roberts, J. and Hough, M. (2005) *Understanding Public Attitudes to Criminal Justice.* Maidenhead: Open University Press.

A survey conducted on behalf of the Home Office by MORI to gauge public confidence in the criminal justice system is available online at **http://www. home office.gov.uk/rds/pdfs04/r221.pdf**.

PUBLIC ORDER

Public order policing is distinguished by its relatively large-scale deployment of officers in group formations subject to superior command and control. It is easily visible to the media. When it is used, force is more likely to be directed at groups rather than individuals.

Public order policing is distinguished by its scale: it is usually associated with large numbers of officers deployed in squads dealing with large gatherings of members of the public. However, scale is continuous – minor public order incidents are frequent and involve handfuls of police officers dealing with small crowds (e.g. at entertainment venues late at night). These encounters enjoy the same 'low visibility' as many other policing tasks.

Large-scale public order operations attract most attention because they are publicly visible. They may be pre-planned or spontaneous and cover a broad spectrum of circumstances: political protests, community disorder, celebrations, sporting events, terrorist atrocities and disasters. Central to all of them is the requirement to mobilize and deploy numerous officers, sometimes calling upon mutual aid from neighbouring police forces. Pre-planned operations deploy officers in advance. Spontaneous operations involve mobilizing and redeploying those officers who are already on duty. It is standard procedure for police forces to have a mobilization plan for rapid response to unforeseen events.

The most controversial public order operations involve those where people are explicitly exercising their democratic right to freedom of speech. They may oppose or support a political, ethical or religious cause, or may seek to promote or resist the interests of sections of the population (e.g. pickets). Unlike other policing tasks, those who are policed are not suspects but virtuously engaged in civic and political participation. They are moral equals with the police, deserving protection as well as control. Allegations of police heavy handedness are likely to receive sympathetic attention from the media (Waddington 1995).

The police are deployed in formations (e.g. police support units), but may also involve specialist officers, most notably mounted and traffic officers, riot squads, intelligence officers, etc. In Britain, there is a nationally prescribed command structure:

- *Gold* is responsible for the strategy and for 'slow time' decisions (e.g. the refreshment and replenishment of the officers deployed).
- *Silver* is responsible for the tactical implementation of the strategy through 'fast time' decisions.
- *Bronze* is responsible for territory or functions and deploys resources in accordance with Silver's tactics.

Public order operations are wrongly associated with forceful policing. Many operations involve little or no use of force, simply marshalling crowds. Even volatile political protests are often policed through 'negotiated management' (McPhail *et al.* 1998). What characterizes most public order operations is the priority given to maintaining order rather than enforcing the law.

P.A.J. Waddington

Related entries

Anti-social behaviour; Force (police use of); Less lethal weapons; Models of policing; Patrol; Police powers; Politics (police involvement).

Key texts and sources

della Porta, D., Petersen, A. and Reiter, H. (eds) (2006) *The Policing of Transnational Protest.* Aldershot: Ashgate.

della Porta, D. and Reiter, H. (eds) (1998) *Policing Protest: The Control of Mass Demonstrations in Western Democracies.* Minneapolis, MN: University of Minnesota Press.

HMIC (1999) *Keeping the Peace: Policing Disorder.* London: HMSO.

Waddington, P.A.J. (2003) 'Policing public order and political contention', in T. Newburn (ed.) *Handbook of Policing.* Cullompton: Willan Publishing.

See also the Home Office's policing web page on public order (**http://police.homeoffice.gov.uk/operational-policing/crime-disorder/public-order.html**).

R

RACIALLY MOTIVATED OFFENDING

> The Police Service has generally failed to provide an adequate response to racially motivated offending. Key to efforts to improve provision has been the widespread adoption of the following definition, taken from the Macpherson Report (1999): 'A racist incident is any incident which is perceived to be racist by the victim or any other person.'

The paucity of the police response to racially motivated offending has been a recurring motif in the 'tale of failure' (Scarman 1981) that has characterized police relations with minority ethnic communities. While high-profile racist attacks sometimes receive considerable media coverage, the more common characteristic of racially motivated offending is that it is 'low level' and – if an event were taken in isolation – is a type of incident that is unlikely to be treated seriously by the police. Bowling's (1998) research into racist crime in London showed that the Police Service has tended to react to discrete incidents and so has been ill-equipped to provide an adequate response to racist offending that is experienced by victims as a *process* of sustained minor episodes.

A related problem has been that officers have tended to 'define out' racist motivation from offences and have sought to reclassify them as 'ordinary' offences and thus marginalize what victims often regarded as central characteristics of their experience. Once the context of racism is removed from many incidents, the nature of the offence is likely to seem much less severe, and an overwhelmingly white Police Service has usually failed to grasp the cumulative impact of racist offending on individual victims and minority ethnic communities more broadly.

Various legislative and policy changes have been made in an effort to tackle these failings, and there are grounds to suggest these have had some success. The Crime and Disorder Act 1998 introduced enhanced punishments for a new category of 'racially aggravated' offences. Existing offences (assault, criminal damage, theft and so on) were rewritten such that cases that were 'aggravated' by 'racial' factors were subject to more serious tariffs. Crucially, prosecutors did not have to prove that such offences were *motivated* by racism, only that there was some element of racism associated with them. Case law has subsequently established that the use of racist epithets (for example, during the commission of an offence) – even if not a motivating factor – can be sufficient grounds to establish 'racial aggravation'. The number of racially and religiously aggravated offences recorded by the police has risen steadily in recent years: from 30,113 in 2001–2 to 37,028 in 2004–5. Some 36 per cent of these offences were 'cleared up' in 2004–5, a greater proportion than the 30 per cent of comparable offences that were not racially or religiously aggravated.

In order to reduce the tendency to 'define out' racism, a new definition of a racist incident was introduced following a recommendation of the Macpherson Report. Police services should now record an incident in this way if the victim, a witness or any other person claims that it was racist. No longer is it for the police officer to decide if an incident is characterized in these terms. It seems highly likely that this is one reason why the number of recorded incidents has also risen: Home Office statistics indicate that 57,902 racist incidents were recorded by the police in England and Wales in 2004–5. In 1997–8 the comparable figure was 13,936. It seems likely that these increases reflect a greater rate of reporting rather than a rise in the number of offences. In part this is a reflection of the huge focus on the policing of racially motivated offending that has occurred in the wake of the Stephen Lawrence Inquiry (Macpherson 1999). A review of the impact of the inquiry on the Police Service suggested that it had contributed to a significant improvement in the recording and monitoring of racially motivated offending (Foster *et al.* 2005).

Mike Rowe

Related entries

Black police associations; Crime; Crime and Disorder Act 1998; Hate Crime; Independent advisory groups; Institutional racism; Repeat victimization; Stephen Lawrence Inquiry; Victim and witness support.

Key texts and sources

Bowling, B. (1998) *Violent Racism: Victimisation, Policing and Social Conflict.* Oxford: Clarendon Press.
Foster, J., Newburn, T. and Souhami, A. (2005) *Assessing the Impact of the Stephen Lawrence Inquiry. Home Office Research Study* 294. London: Home Office.
Scarman, L. (1981) *The Brixton Disorders.* London: Home Office.

RACIAL PROFILING

Racial profiling decribes the contentious practice that is sometimes adopted by the police and other law enforcement agencies of focusing investigations on individuals selected only on the basis of their racial characteristics.

'Profiling' offenders is not in itself contentious; it is part of the routine activities of the police and other law enforcement agencies. They will typically take the details of a suspected offender from a victim or witnesses, one of these details may be the suspect's race. Racial profiling is rather different and starts with the observation, for example,

that street robbers are more likely to be young black males (which, in parts of the UK, is the case). It goes on to argue that, on this basis, young black males are likely to be street robbers (which is not the case) and targets them for increased police attention – for example, stop-and-search activities. This practice is based on the fallacy that, because offenders of type A are disproportionately of race B, then anyone of race B is likely to be an offender of type A. Operating on this basis leads to police attention being directed at a potentially large number of individuals who are not offenders and who then resent (for good reason) the unwelcome police attention directed at them.

This practice became known in the USA as DWB – driving while black – which is obviously not an offence but which led to a disproportionate number of police officers stopping young black males when driving vehicles for no other reason than their race. DWB has been subject to even greater criticism following the terrorist attacks in the USA on 11 September 2001 when people of Middle Eastern origin were targeted for police attention, again for no other reason than their racial appearance.

In September 2006, the International Association of Chiefs of Police released their report, *Protecting Civil Rights: A Leadership Guide for State, Local, and Tribal Law Enforcement,* which deals with many aspects of promoting respect of citizens' civil liberties by law enforcement officials, including racial profiling. The first of five recommendations in regard to racial profiling was to design policies prohibiting the practice. Almost every state in the USA now collects data on police stops and searches either on a mandatory or voluntary basis, which is intended to ensure this practice does not occur.

The words 'racial profiling' have not been in quite such common use in the UK but, in essence, the concerns amount to the same issue – the extent of disproportionality in attracting police attention on the basis of race. This has been a frequent research theme and was given greater emphasis following the murder of Stephen Lawrence, a young black man whose death and its subsequent investigation by the Metropolitan Police led to considerable criticism. The report of the Stephen Lawrence Inquiry (Macpherson 1999) led to the observation that the police were stopping and searching young black males to a disproportionate extent and, although acknowledging the complex reasons for this, it concluded that the Metropolitan Police investigation was hampered by institutional racism. In 2000 HM Inspector of Constabulary called for research to be carried out to explore the issue of racial profiling. The conclusion of a programme of research from the Home Office was that it probably does not happen to a significant extent, although the arguments are indeed complex and there is no room for complacency (Miller *et al.* 2000).

Gloria Laycock

Related entries

Institutional racism; International Association of Chiefs of Police (IACP); Offender profiling; Stephen Lawrence Inquiry; Stop and search.

Key texts and sources

HMIC (2000) *Policing London – Winning Consent: A Review of Murder Investigations and Community Race Relations Issues in the Metropolitan Police.* London: HMSO.

Macpherson, Sir W. (1999) *The Stephen Lawrence Enquiry: Report of an Inquiry by Sir William Macpherson of Cluny* (Cm 4262-I). London: HMSO.

Miller, J., Quinton, P. and Bland, N. (2000) *Police Stops and Searches: Lessons from a Programme of Research. Briefing Note.* London: Home Office Research Development and Statistics Directorate.

RANK STRUCTURE

Rank structure refers to the hierarchical organization of police forces.

Police forces are organized hierarchically. The rank structure established for the new Metropolitan Police in 1829 has essentially remained intact across the police forces of England and Wales, though with the addition of intermediate ranks in the Metropolitan and City of London Police. The Metropolitan Police was established (beneath two commissioners) with a hierarchical rank structure of superintendents, inspectors, sergeants and constables. The superintendent and inspector titles were taken from the old parochial and public office systems (Ascoli 1979: 85), while the office of constable was long established and provided some continuity with older forms of policing. Only the title of sergeant, taken from the army, added a militaristic taint. The general duties of each rank were laid out by the first two commissioners, Charles Rowan and Richard Mayne, in the *General Instructions* issued to all members of the new force in September 1829. The rank structure currently existing in forces is as shown in Table 1.

In Table 2 the distribution of officer numbers across the ranks is laid out. From this it can be seen that most officers (77 per cent) fall within the lowest rank of constable. The table also shows the under-representation of female and minority ethnic officers across all ranks.

This organizational structure faced increasing criticism during the 1990s, prompting the Sheehy Inquiry, which examined the rank structure, remuneration framework and the terms and conditions of service of police officers. Its final report tackled perceived internal management deficiencies and recommended a flatter rank structure, fixed-term appointments, performance-related pay and the abolition of allowances and perks (Sheehy 1993).

Sheehy recommended dispensing with the ranks of chief inspector, chief superintendent and deputy chief constable. There followed a period when the ranks of chief superintendent and deputy chief constable were no longer used, but both have since been resurrected. In recent years, criticisms of the quality of police supervision and leadership have remained persistent. These have run hand in hand with the development of a performance culture that has become an increasingly prominent aspect of policing (see New public management (NPM); Police performance indicators). This has implications for the recruitment, training and promotion of police officers.

Table 1 The Police Service rank structure

	Provincial and Metropolitan forces	The Metropolitan Police Service	City of London Police
The federated ranks			
Practitioners	Constable	Constable	Constable
Supervisors	Sergeant	Sergeant	Sergeant
Managers	Inspector	Inspector	Inspector
	Chief inspector	Chief inspector	Chief inspector
The superintending ranks	Superintendent	Superintendent	Superintendent
Middle managers	Chief superintendent	Chief superintendent	Chief superintendent
The Association of Chief Police Officers (ACPO) ranks			
Strategic managers	Assistant chief constable	Commander	Commander
	Deputy chief constable	Deputy assistant commissioner	Assistant commissioner
	Chief constable	Assistant commissioner	Commissioner
		Deputy commissioner	
		Commissioner	

Source: Mawby and Wright (2003)

Table 2 Distribution of police officers by rank (at 31 March 2007)

Rank	Total police strength	Female	Minority ethnic
ACPO ranks	216	27	7
Chief superintendent	496	50	13
Superintendent	1,044	101	25
Chief inspector	1,913	230	52
Inspector	7,115	933	172
Sergeant	22,037	3,321	639
Constable	109,554	28,515	4,612
Totals	142,374[1]	33,177[1]	5,520[1]

Note: 1. Because of rounding there is an apparent discrepancy between this total and the sums of the constituent items.

Source: Bullock and Gunning (2007).

All officers enter the Police Service at the lowest rank of constable. Successful applicants spend two years as probationary officers, completing their training. Until recently probationer training was undertaken residentially at regional centres, but this has been replaced by the Initial Police Learning and Development Programme (IPLDP), following its successful piloting during 2004.

Under the IPLDP, training is provided in the force and community where officers will be working. In order for officers to progress through the ranks, they must pass the sergeants' and inspectors' examinations (OSPRE or, in full, the Objective Structured Performance Related Police Promotion Exam), which test for knowledge of the law and for management and supervisory aptitude. They

235

must then be successful in interview. Promotion to senior posts above the rank of inspector depends on successful assessment. To achieve the ACPO ranks of assistant chief constable and above, superintendents and chief superintendents must first prepare a detailed application to the Senior Police National Assessment Centre (Senior PNAC). This must be endorsed by senior managers, who provide confirmation that candidates are ready to operate at ACC/commander level. Candidates who subsequently pass the Senior PNAC assessment (a four-day process) proceed to attend the seven-week Strategic Command Course (SCC), designed by Centrex (the working name of the Central Police Training and Development Authority, which became part of the National Policing Improvement Agency in 2007).

Officers who pass the SCC are able to apply for assistant chief constable posts advertised by local police authorities, which devise their own interview and assessment policies, drawing on guidance provided by the Home Office (the most recent being Home Office Circular 60/02, *Chief Officer Recruitment*). The Police Reform Act 2002 has delegated ministerial approval of candidates to HM Chief Inspector of Constabulary, who chairs a panel to consider candidates' suitability. It has become commonplace at ACPO level for police authorities to offer fixed-term contracts of between four and seven years.

While all police officers begin as constables, there has been a recurring debate concerning direct entry to the higher ranks and, to a lesser extent, accelerated promotion schemes (for example, the current Police High Potential Development Scheme which was introduced in 2002), which aim to recruit fast-tracking high achievers. On the one hand it is argued that it is necessary for prospective chief constables to walk the beat for two years and to have practised policing in order that they can understand and lead a police force. This view is becoming increasingly difficult to justify and, on the other hand, it is argued that the multi-tiered rank system discourages ambitious, able graduates and that a chief constable post is more suited to an experienced professional person with a knowledge of business and finance, strategy and management, than to a practising police officer.

Rob C. Mawby

Related entries

Metropolitan Police/New Police; New public management (NPM); Police performance indicators; Recruitment; Rowan and Mayne; Sheehy Inquiry; Training (police).

Key texts and sources

Mawby, R.C. and Wright, A. (2003) 'The police organisation', in T. Newburn (ed.) *Handbook of Policing.* Cullompton: Willan Publishing.

The Home Office policing web page provides general information on career development (**http://police. homeoffice.gov.uk/training-and-career-development/**).

REASSURANCE POLICING

Reassurance policing is an accessible and responsive approach to policing that targets visible crime and disorder with the aim of improving public confidence in the police not only by making people safer but also by making them *feel* safer.

The idea of reassurance policing has been attributed to US academic, Charles Bahn. He posited (1974: 340) that one function of police patrol was 'citizen reassurance – the feeling of security and safety that a citizen experiences when he sees a police officer or police patrol car nearby'. He went on to argue the case for highly visible, locally known police officers patrolling at prominent locations 'to offer the greatest reassurance to the most people' (1974: 344). Reassurance policing subsequently became something of an all-encompassing term that was difficult to distinguish from the equally hard to define catch-all concept of community policing.

In England and Wales, the issue of public reassurance came to the fore during the 1990s when, despite falls in recorded crime, the perception remained among many people that crime was rising. This disparity was described by HM Inspectorate of Constabulary as 'the reassurance gap' (2001). Reassurance has subsequently featured prominently in the Home

Office's police reform programme, and successive national policing plans have directed the Police Service to reassure the public through high-visibility, accessible policing.

Reassurance policing was tested as an operationalizational concept through the Home Office's National Reassurance Policing Programme (NRPP) between April 2003 and April 2005. Two police force areas trialled reassurance policing, before its launch in 16 pilot sites across eight police forces. The approaches adopted in the NRPP sites drew on the signal crimes perspective and community policing models, and included the following:

- Targeted policing activity and problem solving to tackle the particular crimes and disorder that matter in neighbourhoods.
- Community involvement in identifying priorities for action and then in tackling them.
- The presence of visible, accessible and locally known authority figures in neighbourhoods, particularly police officers and community support officers (Tuffin *et al.* 2006: 4).

The Home Office evaluation found that the NRPP had a positive effect on crime levels, perceptions of crime and feelings of safety, and on confidence in the police (Tuffin *et al.* 2006). These reported positive outcomes and the lessons learnt from the NRPP are being fed into the national roll-out of neighbourhood policing.

While some commentators contend that reassurance policing is yet another repackaging of community policing, others have argued that the NRPP approach to reassurance policing was genuinely different in that it involved research as a central element of the programme, focused on signal crimes and was theoretically underpinned to an unprecedented extent (Innes 2006: 15).

Rob C. Mawby

Related entries

Anti-social behaviour; Community support officers (CSOs); Fear of crime; National Intelligence Model (NIM); Neighbourhood policing; Plural policing; Public attitudes to the police; Signal crimes.

Key texts and sources

Policing and Society (2006) Special issue: 'Reassurance and the "new" community policing', Vol. 16, no. 2.

Tuffin, R., Morris, J. and Poole, A. (2006) *An Evaluation of the Impact of the National Reassurance Policing Programme. Home Office Research Study* 296. London: Home Office Research, Development and Statistics Directorate (available online at http://www.homeoffice.gov.uk/rds/pdfs06/hors296.pdf).

See also the Home Office's crime reduction website (http://www.crimereduction.gov.uk/policing05.htm and http://www.crimereduction.gov.uk/policing17.htm) and the Home Office Research, Development and Statistics Directorate's website (http://www.homeoffice.gov.uk/rds/reassurance.html). The Home Office report, *National Reassurance Policing Programme: A Ten-site Evaluation (Findings* 273) is available online at http://www.homeoffice.gov.uk/rds/pdfs06/r273.pdf.

RECRUITMENT

The quality and effectiveness of the police service could be said to start with recruitment. This should be a process that attracts the best qualified individuals for the next phase in the process – that of selection.

Every person who enters the Police Service in England and Wales currently does so at the rank of constable, although there is a school of thought that suggests different entry scales at the various rank structures may be the way of the future.

Until April 2003, police forces had variable selection criteria, which meant that, for example, different forces required different standards from recruits, such as height and eyesight. However, there are now national recruitment standards that have removed minimum and maximum height requirements while also introducing a minimum age limit for recruitment (18 years). There is no upper age limit. Applicants to the police have to satisfy the following criteria:

- Applicants must be a British citizen, an EU/EEA national or Commonwealth citizen or foreign national with no restrictions applicable on their length of stay in the UK.

- While there are currently no formal educational requirements, applicants must pass written and numeracy tests as part of a structured assessment day.
- Applicants must also pass a 'job related' fitness test.

Suitable candidates can apply to any force in the country that has vacancies and is recruiting.

It has been argued by O'Malley (1997) that, historically, the police have recruited individuals with an 'apprenticeship' type approach, with members beginning as recruits and spending a considerable time at the lower level before progressing to specialisms of any kind. This process tended to ensure that only like-minded individuals from similar backgrounds were recruited and groomed for future positions, thereby perpetuating the process. There is now evidence that this approach has changed to ensure that individuals are recruited from a wider, culturally diverse background, and that following their two-year probationary period they can specialize at an early stage in their career.

Any police service should be representative of the public it serves. At present, there are 142,374 full-time or equivalent police officers in England and Wales. This total had increased steadily for several years, but it is anticipated that, in the current political climate, it will continue to decrease in the foreseeable future with the greater use of police community support officers as part of the extended policing family. Of the total number of police officers, 5,520 are classed as minority ethnic police officers. For that reason, in 1998 the then Home Secretary published local and national targets for the increased recruitment of minority ethnic staff within the Police Service. Practical approaches, such as conducting targeted recruitment campaigns, working with local community organizations and running familiarization and access courses, are all seen as a positive step to encouraging minority ethnic recruitment. However, these approaches have to compete with the fact that minority ethnic police officers are sometimes unwilling to recommend the Police Service to potential recruits because of some of their experiences in the job.

Colin Rogers

Related entries

Community support officers (CSOs); Constables; Rank structure.

Key texts and sources

O'Malley, P. (1997) 'Politics and postmodernity', *Social and Legal Studies: An International Journal*, 6: 363–81 (reprinted in Newburn, T. (ed.) (2004) *Policing: Key Readings*. Cullompton: Willan Publishing).

Further details of police recruitment for England and Wales can be found at http://www.policecould you.co.uk/.

REGULATION OF INVESTIGATORY POWERS ACT 2000 (RIPA)

The Regulation of Investigatory Powers Act 2000 (RIPA) was the first piece of legislation to provide a comprehensive regulatory structure governing the interception of communications, access to communications data, covert surveillance, the use of informants and other covert human intelligence sources, and the decryption of encrypted material.

The Regulation of Investigatory Powers Act 2000 (RIPA) replaced the Interception of Communications Act 1985 and amended but did not repeal the Police Act 1997 (Part III) and the Intelligence Services Act 1994. It is accompanied by a number of RIPA codes of practice (issued under RIPA, ss. 71 and 72), including the Covert Human Intelligence Sources Code and the Covert Surveillance Code, and the government is consulting on an Acquisition and Disclosure of Communications Data Code. In addition, a large number of regulations have been issued under the statute.

Chapter I of Part I makes it unlawful to intercept public postal communications and communications by a public or private telecommunications service in the course of their transmission unless authorized under the Act. It also creates a tort where a communication is intercepted in the course of its transmission by means of a private telecommunications system by, or with the consent of, a person having the right to control the operation or use of that system. Lawful interception may be carried out without a warrant in certain circumstances set out in ss. 3 and 4. Other interceptions are only lawful if carried out in accordance with a warrant issued by the Secretary of State (s. 5). Controversially, s. 17 imposes severe restrictions on the disclosure and use in evidence of warranted interceptions. Chapter II of Part I governs access to communications data and authorizes the Secretary of State to designate certain persons to authorize access to or disclosure of communications data, provided certain conditions are satisfied.

Part II regulates covert surveillance and the conduct and use of covert human intelligence sources (CHIS). The level of, and grounds for, authorization for covert surveillance depends upon whether it is 'intrusive surveillance' (essentially covert surveillance carried out in relation to anything taking place on residential premises or a private vehicle, but subject to exceptions) or 'directed surveillance' (other forms of covert surveillance carried out for the purposes of a specific investigation or operation) (s. 26). CCTV and other forms of general surveillance are thus excluded from regulation by the Act. There is no limitation on the evidential use of the product of covert surveillance. The definition of a CHIS means that it includes both informants and police officers acting undercover if their activities are carried out in a manner calculated to ensure that the subject(s) of surveillance is unaware that it is or may be taking place (s. 26(7)–(10)).

Part III governs the power to demand that encrypted material be rendered intelligible, or that a key be handed over to enable it to be decrypted. Part IV creates a supervisory structure in relation to powers exercised under the Act and provides for the appointment of an Interception of Communications Commissioner and other commissioners, who must report annually.

Ed Cape

Related entries

Covert policing; Evidence; Police powers.

Key texts and sources

Cape, E. (ed) (2005) *Current Law Statute Guide: RIPA 2000, Related SIs and Codes of Practice.* London: Sweet & Maxwell.
Harfield, C. and Harfield, K. (2005) *Covert Investigation.* Oxford: Oxford University Press.
See also the Home Office's RIPA updates website (**http://security.homeoffice.gov.uk/surveillance/ripa-updates/?version=1**) and the Office of Public Sector Information's website (**http://www.opsi.gov.uk/Acts/acts2000/20000023.htm**) for the text of RIPA.

REPEAT VICTIMIZATION

Repeat victimization refers to the repeated criminal victimization of a person, place, vehicle or target, however defined. 'Virtual' repeats can occur when a target is victimized because it has similar characteristics to one that was previously (successfully) victimized. Policing uses knowledge of repeat victimization to allocate resources where they are most needed.

Policing needs strategies that allocate its resources efficiently. Preventing repeat victimization is a strategy that allocates resources according to risk. It is an effective means of 'getting the grease to the squeak' (Hough and Tilley 1998). It allows a drip-feeding of crime prevention effort to crimes as they occur so that it does not place undue strain on police resources. It means the police can 'empower' victims, including business owners, via advice and assistance on avoiding further crime: officers give tangible and practical help rather than 'tea and sympathy'.

Some types of crime seem intuitively likely to be repeated. These include domestic violence, child abuse and racial attacks. But repeat victimization occurs for all manner of crimes, such as assaults and robberies, commercial burglaries, fraud, computer crimes, e-commerce crimes, stalking, elder abuse, shoplifting, vandalism and break-ins to pharmacies, schools and other hot targets, to name but a few. Murder cannot be repeated but it can be preceded by attempts. There is even emerging evidence that terrorist attacks recur against the same targets and certainly as 'virtual' repeats against targets with similar characteristics.

Some victims and targets are particularly crime prone. The British Crime Survey has shown (Pease 1998: 3) that, while: 16 per cent of the UK population experience property crime, 2 per cent experience 41 per cent of it, and that, while 8 per cent of the UK population experience personal crime, 1 per cent experiences 59 per cent of it. Repeat victimization often occurs quickly, but the risk declines with time. This means crime prevention effort should be mobilized and put into place as soon as possible – preferably within 24 hours. But this also means that resources might be temporarily focused on one risky target then reallocated to another.

The same offenders often commit repeat victimization. This is particularly so if they have learnt that it is easy or rewarding to commit crime against that target. Not surprisingly, bank robbers return if they got away with a lot of cash the first time around. Burglars come back for items they could not carry first time around, or they wait a while to plunder replacements bought with insurance. Street robbers target the same victims who walk that way to work each day, and school bullies quickly learn who lets them get away with it. Yet this is also why preventing repeat victimization is less likely to result in displacement, because offenders are unexpectedly 'interrupted' and cannot simply switch to an equally attractive target.

Following an innovative project in the Kirkholt area of Rochdale in the 1980s which prevented repeat burglaries by 'all locally appropriate means', the Home Office undertook a series of studies of repeat victimization. The research programme and the way it tied into policing policy and practice have been detailed by Gloria Laycock, who was responsible for much of the impetus. In the mid-1990s, all UK police forces were obliged to develop strategies to prevent repeat victimization, and this was integrated into police performance indicators (see Laycock 2001; Laycock and Farrell 2003). Basic command unit-level police managers can use repeat victimization as a performance indicator, and the strategy allocates resources to high crime areas as a matter of course (rather than using an indicator such as poverty or other area characteristics as a basis for policing strategy). Preventing repeat victimization can also help generate common goals and positive work between the police and other agencies since, with the possible exception of offenders who are victimized, work to assist victims is universally lauded.

The 'trigger' to allocate resources to prevent repeat victimization is when a crime is reported. Hence it does not require data analysis to introduce the strategy. Research, however, needs to be cautious in measuring repeat victimization because it is often hidden or understated in police records. For example, if only 50 per cent of mobile phone thefts are reported to police, then only 25 per cent of two-time victims will show up in police data, and only 12.5 per cent of three-time victims (assuming for simplicity here that other things are equal). And while police IT systems are improving hand over fist, it is still not always easy to trace the history of events involving the same persons and/or locations.

The risk of repeat victimization increases with further victimization. A three-time victim is more likely to experience a fourth victimization than a one-time victim is a second. This led to the introduction of graduated police responses. A project in Huddersfield pioneered the 'Olympic System', whereby first-time victims received a bronze response, two-time victims received a silver response and victims of three or more crimes received a gold response. The gold response was the most sophisticated, requiring the most cost and resources but, in turn, promising the greatest preventive returns. The graduated response is a further refinement of the allocation of resources according to risk.

Through the notion of repetition or the fact that crime always clusters, thinking about repeat victimization has now become integrated with other ways of focusing police resources. Repeat victimization can generate and overlap with hotspots. It is more likely to be committed by serious prolific offenders and overlaps with the targeting of valuable 'hot products', such as SatNavs, PDAs and mobile phones. Under the umbrella of repeats, police crime prevention strategies have the potential to become increasingly focused and, in turn, efficient.

Efforts to prevent repeat victimization should work alongside other police strategies and crime prevention efforts. Identifying which crime prevention tactics should be put in place can be the trickiest aspect – we may know where and when we want to prevent crime, but knowing how to do that is a separate question that cannot be tackled here. In short, however, the strategy of repeat victimization remains in its infancy. To date it has not been adequately exploited in relation to many types of crime, and so its potential as a policing strategy remains underdeveloped.

Louise Nicholas and Graham Farrell

Related entries

Burglary; Child abuse; Crime mapping; Domestic violence; Hotspots; Racially motivated offending.

Key texts and sources

Bridgeman, C. and Hobbs, L. (1997) *Preventing Repeat Victimisation: The Police Officers' Guide. Police Research Group Paper.* London: Home Office (available online at http://www.homeoffice.gov.uk/rds/pdfs2/ah310.pdf).

Lamm Weisel, D. (2005) *Analyzing Repeat Victimization: Problem-oriented Guide for Police. Problem-solving Tools Series* 4. Washington, DC: COPS/US Department of Justice (available online at http://www.popcenter.org/Tools/PDFs/Repeat Victimization.pdf).

Pease, K. (1998) *Repeat Victimisation: Taking Stock. Crime Prevention and Detection Series* 90. London: Home Office (available online at www.homeoffice.gov.uk/rds/prgpdfs/cdp90bf.pdf).

The Home Office's repeat victimization crime reduction toolkit is available online at http://www.crimereduction.org.uk/toolkits/rv00.htm.

RESTORATIVE JUSTICE/ RESTORATIVE CAUTIONING

Restorative justice encompasses the values, aims and processes that have as their common factor attempts to repair the harm caused by criminal behaviour. Its core values include mutual respect; the empowerment of all parties involved in the process; accountability; consensual, non-coercive participation and decision-making; and the inclusion of all the relevant parties in dialogue (although the issue of the non-coercion of offenders is not without contention).

The inclusion of victims as active parties is a primary aim of many restorative schemes, although it is difficult to achieve in practice. Hence there is disagreement over what it means to participate, with some arguing that participation can be indirect – through a mediator, for example, or through a representative at a meeting. Restorative processes should hold offenders accountable by requiring them to explain how they think their actions might have affected others. Through dialogue it is hoped that victims' feelings of anger or fear towards 'their' offender, or crime more generally, will be alleviated, and that offenders will experience genuine remorse and develop a greater sense of victim empathy.

Restorative justice in English policing has its roots in the renowned 'effective cautioning' scheme that began in Wagga Wagga, New South Wales, Australia and aimed to caution juvenile offenders according to restorative principles. The Wagga Wagga model's main influences were the New Zealand system of family group conferences and the criminological theory of 'reintegrative shaming' (Braithwaite 1989). The latter argues that the best way to control crime is to induce a sense of shame in offenders for their actions while maintaining respect for them as people (to condemn them as bad people might push them towards deviant identities, commitments or subcultures). It further posits that this kind of reintegrative shaming is best achieved by exposing offenders to the emotionally charged opinions of those whom they most care about, such as parents, partners and friends.

While most Australian jurisdictions ultimately rejected police facilitation in favour of community mediators (the New Zealand conferencing model), other jurisdictions, particularly in the UK and the USA, that subsequently adopted restorative cautioning have tended to use the Wagga Wagga police-led scripted model. Most English police forces introduced restorative justice into their cautioning processes and, following the establishment of youth offending teams, more broadly into their youth justice processes, under the Crime and Disorder Act 1998 and the Youth Justice and Criminal Evidence Act 1999. More recently still, the conditional caution includes reparative or restorative conditions stipulated by the police and approved by the Crown Prosecution Service (Criminal Justice Act 2003, Part 3, ss. 22–27).

Police cautioning before the advent of restorative justice had remarkably little legislative intervention or oversight. There was little training, supervision or expectation of consistency for the police who delivered cautions, and empirical research suggests that they were often short and perfunctory, but could also be demeaning and punitive. This changed with restorative justice, which brought with it a full training programme, covering not just how to deliver a caution following a detailed script but also the theoretical justifications for each question and statement included in that script. An accreditation scheme and a number of high-profile academic evaluations of existing schemes followed. This research suggests that a transformation of cautioning practices has been effected that is remarkable in its scope and intensity and that includes a commitment to broader community involvement, procedural fairness and the use of a coherent criminological theory.

Restorative cautioning embraces multiple aims, including the lessening of the fear of crime and a strengthening of a sense of community, the reintegration of offenders back into legitimate, law-abiding communities and the repair of relationships damaged by crime. However, the primary concerns of policymakers and government have been the reduction of crime and the satisfaction of victims. Notwithstanding examples of poor implementation of the model in some schemes, research makes clear that victims who meet with offenders in the presence of other affected parties are much more likely to feel that they had experienced a fair and inclusive process than those who do not. Indeed, a consistent picture of high aggregate victim satisfaction with police-led processes emerges from the research across jurisdictions. There is, however, little evidence to suggest that restorative cautioning results in a statistically significant reduction (or increase) in reoffending. A series of randomized, controlled trials showed that police-led restorative cautioning has been associated with increases as well as decreases in repeat offending, with results varying according to socio-legal context, offence type and the characteristics of the offender (although meta-analyses of empirical projects suggest that, when restorative cautioning is carried out properly, it can have positive benefits on reoffending rates).

Over the last decade, the police have been more heavily involved in restorative justice than other criminal justice agencies, whether as police officers cautioning adults or as officers seconded to youth offending teams delivering youth justice interventions. In this respect they have expanded their previously minimal involvement in sentencing because restorative cautioning presupposes that the offender has acknowledged responsibility for an offence. It should not be concerned with fact-finding, which has traditionally been the focus of police work, but with an appropriate response to an admitted offence. Consequently, there has been unease about whether police facilitation places too much power in their hands and whether restorative justice expands their punitive function and opens up possibilities of police abuse of power. The literature has some, albeit not many, examples of such abuses, with a few police facilitators using the caution further to investigate the offender and sometimes even his or her friends or family, while others dismiss legitimate complaints about fellow police officers. Some are reported to be less than reintegrative in their approach, lapsing into stigmatizing language and behaviours. There are also concerns that the police management of restorative cautioning could contribute to net-widening (there was some evidence of this in the Northern Ireland pilot schemes).

Although constraints on police facilitation and due process safeguards for defendants can do a great deal to reassure those sceptical of police involvement, principled criticisms of police facilitation are not easy to dismiss. In particular, the argument that there should be a separation of powers between the key stages of the criminal process is persuasive. It is clearly problematic to have one agency having so much power and control over a criminal process, from arrest to punishment, especially when that agency has a strained relationship with certain, often disadvantaged communities. However, there are similar principled objections to the involvement of other state agencies in the facilitation of restorative processes (social workers, for example, tend to be offender focused rather than balanced in their approach), and entirely community-based schemes offer none of the protections of a state-based system.

There are pragmatic reasons for police involvement: they have the political backing, the resources and apparently the support from victims and offenders. There are also benefits to the police of their involvement in restorative justice in terms of transforming police culture, if only for those officers directly involved. However, with restorative justice now firmly embedded in the criminal justice process, the time may have come to acknowledge that these justifications are insufficient; that there needs to be a new and viable alternative. Specialist teams of professional restorative justice facilitators are one possibility. Quasi-judicial facilitators would, like stipendiary magistrates, bring professional independence to the process and have none of the cultural baggage or professional agendas of other state agents.

Carolyn Hoyle

Related entries

Caution; Victim and witness support; Youth and policing.

Key texts and sources

Braithwaite, J. (1989) *Crime, Shame and Reintegration.* Cambridge: Cambridge University Press.
Johnstone, G. (2003) *A Restorative Justice Reader: Texts, Sources, Context.* Cullompton: Willan Publishing.
Johnstone, G. and Van Ness, D. (2007) *Handbook of Restorative Justice.* Cullompton: Willan Publishing.
Roche, D. (2003) *Accountability in Restorative Justice.* Oxford: Oxford University Press.
See also the websites of the Restorative Justice Consortium (http://www.restorativejustice.org.uk/), Restorative Justice Online (www.restorativejustice.org/), Real Justice (www.realjustice.org/index.html) and the Home Office's crime reduction website (http://www.crimereduction.gov.uk/criminaljusticesystem12.htm).

RIGHT OF SILENCE

The right of silence is the right to remain silent when questioned pre-trial and the accused's right to remain silent at trial. The right to silence remains but is now subject to the Criminal Justice and Public Order Act 1994.

The right of silence applies to accuseds at trial and to suspects being questioned pre-trial. Prior to the Criminal Evidence Act 1898, an accused was incompetent to give evidence on his or her own behalf. It was therefore only subsequent to this Act that recognition of a 'right' of silence in court and issues related to a failure to testify truly emerged. Section 1(a) of this legislation gave the accused a general right to testify in criminal cases. The accused could give evidence only 'on his own application' and so became a competent but not a compellable witness. Section 1(b) prohibited any comment from the prosecution on the accused's failure to give evidence. The right of a suspect to remain silent when questioned by a police officer was recognized at common law, and information on this right is specifically communicated to suspects when cautioned – uncertainty had arisen in the past regarding the issue of such silence forming the basis for adverse inferences.

Subsequent legislation has been introduced that some view as being too favourable to the accused and, while the right of silence has never been specifically granted in legislation, it is clearly recognized. It is now the Criminal Justice and Public Order Act 1994 (ss. 34–38) that applies. This Act preserves the rule that an accused is competent, not compellable, to give evidence. However, the Act further provides that 'proper' inferences may be drawn from an accused's silence. Section 34(1)(a) and (b) acknowledges an individual's right to silence pre-trial, both before being charged when questioned under caution and subsequent to being charged. In the event that the party questioned remains silent, adverse inferences against the suspect are permitted under this statute. It was in consequence of this section that the wording and length of the caution were changed. Section 35(2) states:

> the court shall, at the conclusion of the evidence for the prosecution, satisfy itself (in the case of proceedings on indictment with a jury, in the presence of the jury), that the accused is aware that the stage has been reached at which evidence can be given for the defence and that he can, if he wishes, give evidence, and that, if he chooses not to give evidence, or having been sworn, without good cause refuses to answer any questions, it will be permissible for the court or jury to draw such inferences as appear proper from his failure to give evidence or his refusal, without good cause to answer any questions.

Acts of Parliament do in some instances remove the right to silence (e.g. the Official Secrets Act 1989, s. 6, which provides that it is an offence to withhold evidence from a duly authorized officer of the police). The comment of Lord Mustill in R v. *Director of Serious Fraud Office* that 'The legislature has not shrunk, where it has seemed appropriate, from interfering to a greater or lesser degree with the immunities grouped under the title of the right to silence' is suggestive perhaps of significant intrusion. The right of silence, however, remains, albeit now subject primarily, but not exclusively, to the Criminal Justice and Public Order Act 1994.

Larry Mead

Related entries

Caution; Defendants; Evidence.

Key texts and sources

O'Reilly, G.W. (1994) 'England limits the right to silence and moves towards an inquisitorial system of justice', *Journal of Criminal Law and Criminology*, 85: 402–52.
Starmer, K., Strange, M. and Whitaker, Q. (2001) *Criminal Justice, Police Powers and Human Rights.* Oxford: Oxford University Press.

ROADS (POLICING OF)

Roads policing aims to encourage compliance with traffic laws and to facilitate the security and safety of all road users.

The year 2005 marked a milestone for British roads policing in that a national Roads Policing Strategy was issued jointly by the Association of Chief Police Officers (ACPO), the Department for Transport and the Home Office, underlining the government's joined-up approach and commitment to roads policing, the latter of which has occasionally been questioned. This strategy outlines five key elements that define in broad terms what roads policing should comprise, namely: denying criminals the use of the roads; reducing road casualties; tackling the threat of terrorism; reducing the anti-social use of the roads; and enhancing public confidence and reassurance by patrolling the roads. In practice, the role of roads policing is wide, including the uncovering of criminal networks, road safety education of the public, collision investigation, traffic management, automatic number plate recognition (ANPR) support for armed operations and regular patrolling for motoring and non-motoring offences. The terms 'roads policing' and 'traffic policing' tend to be used interchangeably, although ACPO favours the former as this is broader and deals with the safety of all road users rather than just traffic violation enforcement (HMIC 1998: 15).

In the early 1990s many forces decentralized with specialist traffic units dissolved and dedicated traffic officers moved to divisional command within basic command units, where such officers tend to be used for tasks additional to roads policing. This makes counting the numbers of traffic officers difficult, but the general trend is clear and downward. For example, HM Inspector of Constabulary (1998: 10, 12) noted that designated traffic officers fell from 15–20 per cent of force strength in 1966 to 7 per cent in 1998. Since then and until 2004, the numbers of sworn officers with traffic as a main function fell overall, though they picked up in 2005 (Hansard 20 December 2005: Col. 2905W; 11 November 2005: Col. 853W), while support staff numbers have risen considerably (Hansard 10 January 2005: Col. 364W).

The government's response to the Transport Select Committee's (2006) report on roads policing and technology (House of Commons Transport Committee 2007) noted that roads policing was a responsibility of all police officers, that any officer could enforce road law and that it was a matter for individual chief police officers to decide deployment of their resources. Indeed, different aspects of the traffic policing role have been taken on by an array of civilian agencies to 'free up' the time of sworn officers for core enforcement duties, although this has not stopped public calls for more 'traffic cops' in place of automated enforcement technology.

Nowadays, the Highways Agency supplies traffic officers (HATOs) with responsibility for managing and monitoring traffic flow on motorways and trunk roads and at collision sites; the Vehicle Operator Services Agency conducts compliance checks, particularly of commercial and foreign vehicles; community support officers have increased powers under the Serious Organized Crime and Police Act 2005 to direct traffic; special constables play a support role to roads police officers; and traffic wardens from local authorities can enforce recently decriminalized offences, such as parking, junction box and bus lane infringements.

Other new agencies supporting the roads police are the Vehicle Crime Intelligence Service and the Vehicle Surveillance Police Agency, which targets major road and mainstream crime. Partnership working is also prominent in roads policing, with local links forged with safety camera partnerships and crime and disorder reduction partnerships.

While the Home Office retains responsibility for roads policing, the key task of road casualty reduction is encharged to the Department for Transport. This bifurcation of responsibility could be implicated in the commonly perceived, long-standing insufficient prioritization of roads policing on government and policing agendas (e.g. HMIC 1998: 15–17; Gaventa 2005: 7, 15). For instance, the three-year National Policing Plan for 2005–8 makes specific mention of roads policing in only one paragraph, and seemingly not all forces have adopted the Roads Policing Strategy (House of Commons Transport Committee 2007: 7). However, after many years without a core performance indicator in regard to roads policing, one has been introduced to complement the government's national target of a 40 per cent reduction in killed and serious injured road casualties (KSIs) by 2010. This is Statutory Performance Indicator 9a: the number of KSIs per 100 million vehicle kilometres travelled.

There is a thriving European context to roads policing that is currently addressing huge annual road casualty rates and high levels of offending and crashes by non-resident drivers using roads in other member states. In 2001 the EU set a target to halve annual road deaths from a base rate of 40,000 by 2010, and in 2004 it reserved the right for binding legislation should progress falter towards that target. An EU consultation in 2006 confirmed this fear, which led the European Transport Safety Council, backed by the European Traffic Police Network , to support a European-wide directive. Research estimates indicate that up to 14,000 European lives would be saved annually through best enforcement practice for the 'big three' of speeding, drink-driving and seat-belt use. However, political will for a joined-up approach may be lacking among individual member states, such as Britain, that are reluctant to harmonize with European drink-drive maxima.

Automated enforcement technology is designed to strengthen the efficiency and effectiveness of roads policing rather than to supplant it, yet achieving a balance satisfactory to all may prove challenging. Speed camera and red-light camera technology has been in use in Britain since 1993 and, while many lives have been saved through encouraging compliance at camera sites (e.g. Gains *et al.* 2005: 2), much controversy has been generated. There has been majority public support for speed cameras since their inception (Gains *et al.* 2005), yet accumulating numbers of drivers with penalty points, the perception of fixed-penalty fines generating 'easy money' for the authorities and reports of many drivers escaping prosecution through identification problems could risk the erosion of public support.

The capabilities of ANPR technology prompted the Home Office to invest £32.5 million in 2006 for its development. It works by high-visibility intercept teams stopping vehicles whose details register a 'hit' on one or more linked databases operated nearby. It thus removes discretion from stopping individual drivers and results in far higher arrest rates than achieved by regular patrols (e.g. Metropolitan Police Authority 2005). Importantly, it detects 'invisible' vehicles and drivers with inadequate documentation who otherwise escape prosecution, and can lead to the arrest of wanted offenders. However, concerns are raised by the long-term storage capabilities of data gathered by ANPR, and automated enforcement technology in general cannot yet detect bad driving offences.

The perceived value and significance of roads policing seem finally to be on the upturn, with increasing recognition being given to it by senior police and government. The realization of a strong relationship between motoring offending and mainstream offending (e.g. Rose 2000) has elevated the intelligence value of roads policing and has led to a prioritizing of the objectives of 'denying criminals use of the road' and 'tackling the threat of terrorism'. Moreover, a recent evaluation of enforcement studies concluded that increasing the level of traffic policing does reduce crash, casualty and violation rates, although establishing the exact relationship between policing levels and outcome is not straightforward (Elliott and Broughton 2004).

Claire Corbett

Related entries

Anti-social behaviour; Patrol; Plural policing; Police performance indicators; Reassurance policing.

Key texts and sources

ACPO/Department for Transport/Home Office (2005) *Roads Policing Strategy.* London: ACPO/DfT/Home Office (available online at **http://www.acpo.police.uk/asp/policies/Data/acp_dft_ho_rp_strat_jan05.pdf**).

Corbett, C. (2003) *Car Crime.* Cullompton: Willan Publishing.

Gaventa (2005) *Policing Road Risk: Enforcement, Technologies and Road Safety.* London: Parliamentary Advisory Council for Transport Safety.

House of Commons Transport Committee (2007) *Roads Policing and Technology: Getting the Right Balance: Government Response to the Committee's Tenth Report of Session 2005–06* (HC 290). London: HMSO.

The Department for Transport *Roads Policing Strategy* is available online at **http://www.dft.gov.uk/pgr/road safety/drs/roadpolicingcommitment**. See also the Home Office's policing web page on roads policing (**http://police.homeoffice.gov.uk/operational-policing/road-traffic.html**).

ROWAN AND MAYNE

Lieutenant-Colonel Sir Charles Rowan KCB (c. 1782–1852) and Sir Richard Mayne KCB (1796–1868) were the original Joint Commissioners of the Metropolitan Police.

Charles Rowan was born in Country Antrim of Scottish-Irish ancestry. He had a distinguished military career, joining the army as an ensign in 1797 and rising to the rank of Lieutenant-Colonel at the time of his resigning his commission in 1822. Richard Mayne also hailed from Ireland, being born in Dublin. He followed a legal rather than military career, being called to the Bar in 1822. He was a successful lawyer and, in 1829, he applied to become one of the Joint Commissioners of the Metropolitan Police. He was accepted and became both the longest-serving commissioner and the youngest-ever appointed in the history of the organization.

The two men, although possessing dissimilar personalities, became lasting friends and together organized and developed the Metropolitan Police over a period of 21 years. They began on 7 July 1829, soon moving into new offices at 4 Whitehall Place (later known as Scotland Yard), with Rowan living in an apartment over the offices. Despite only having little over three months to create the new police force, the Joint Commissioners successfully recruited, equipped and trained 1,011 men (895 constables, 88 sergeants, 20 inspectors and 8 superintendents), ceremonially swearing in the New Police on 16 September 1829. Rowan brought his military experience into play with the creation of a divisional beat system, modelled on military practice. However, both Rowan and Mayne argued against the military-style uniform that Peel had originally favoured. They realized that the New Police needed to appear to be part of the community it served, rather than a continental gendarmerie. Mayne contributed his legal expertise to the creation of the force, being the chief architect of the *General Instruction Book*, the 'bible' of the police force, in which the powers and legal standing of police constables were both prescribed and proscribed.

In 1850 Rowan retired He died two years later and was given a glowing obituary by *The Times*: 'No individual of any rank or station could be more highly esteemed or loved when living, or more regretted in death'. Mayne continued, first remaining as Joint Commissioner with another ex-military man, Captain William Hay, who died in 1855, and then continuing as sole Commissioner until his own death in 1868. Despite facing growing criticism about his leadership style and his handling of the Hyde Park Riots in 1866 (where he was forced to call in military assistance), Mayne remained throughout a dedicated servant of the Metropolitan Police and received a posthumous appreciation from Queen Victoria: 'Her Majesty believes him to have been a most efficient head of the police, and to have discharged the duties of his important situation most ably and satisfactorily in very difficult times'. Mayne is rather less well known for introducing 'The Knowledge' route-memorizing requirement of hackney-cab

drivers in 1851, following numerous complaints that the drivers often did not know how to reach their destinations.

David J. Cox

Related entries

Beat; Metropolitan Police/New Police; Rank structure.

Key text and sources

Fido, M. and Skinner, K. (1999) *The Official Encyclopaedia of Scotland Yard.* London: Virgin.
See also the Metropolitan Police history web page (www.met.police.uk/history/).

ROYAL COMMISSION ON THE POLICE (1962)

The Royal Commission on the Police (1962) was established to investigate the complex and ill-defined system of police governance that had developed in Britain. The commission's report led to the foundation of the tripartite structure of police governance (i.e. the Home Office, police authorities and chief constables), which remains largely in place today.

The Royal Commission on the Police (1962) (also known as the Willink Commission after its Chairman, Sir Henry Willink), was established in 1959. The terms of reference were:

to review the constitutional position of the police throughout Great Britain, the arrangements for their control and administration and, in particular, to consider:

(1) *the constitution and function of local police authorities;*

(2) *the status and accountability of members of police forces, including chief officers of police;*

(3) *the relationship of the police with the public and the means of ensuring that complaints by the public against the police were effectively dealt with;*

(4) *the broad principles which should govern the remuneration of the constable, having regard to the nature and extent of police duties and responsibilities and the need to attract and retain an adequate number of recruits with the proper qualifications.*

The fundamental reason for the establishment of the commission was a concern that the piece-meal way in which policing had developed in Britain had created a complex and ill-defined system of police governance which, through a series of scandals, had led to serious concerns about police accountability. A further reason was the inability of the police to recruit and retain sufficient officers to deal with the problems of escalating crime and increasing road traffic as the country became more prosperous after the Second World War.

The first priority of the commission was to address the issue of police pay and, in November 1960, it produced an interim report that went beyond the original remit to establish 'broad principles' and recommended a formula which substantially increased police salaries. Despite concerns that the commission had exceeded its terms of reference, the recommendation was accepted and the new pay scales were immediately introduced.

In reviewing the constitutional position of the police, the commissioners considered a recommendation to restructure the 125 forces that then existed in England and Wales to form one national police force. After deliberation they 'preserved the idea of local forces but these were to be brought under more effective central control' (Oliver 1997: 8) through a restructured system of local police authorities and the establishment of the 'tripartite structure' of police accountability. The tripartite structure allocated specific roles to the Home Office, the police authority and the chief constable, but failed to set down detailed responsibilities.

The final report was presented to the government in May 1962 and contained a total of 111 recommendations. The government and Parliament accepted the majority of the proposals and published a Police Bill in November 1963, which received Royal Assent the following May as the Police Act 1964.

The importance of the royal commission cannot be underestimated, for it established the system of police governance that remained unaltered for 30 years and, despite substantial modification following the Police and Magistrates' Courts Act 1994, the Police Act 1996 and the Police Reform Act 2002, it still provides the foundations for the organization and control of policing in England and Wales at the beginning of the twenty-first century.

Douglas Sharp

Related entries

Accountability and governance; Chief constables; Constabulary independence; Home Office; Independent Police Complaints Commission (IPCC); Police Act 1964; Police authorities.

Key texts and sources

Critchley, T.A. (1967) *A History of Police in England and Wales.* London: Constable.

Emsley, C. (1991) *The English Police.* Harlow: Addison Wesley Longman.

Walker, N. (2000) *Policing in a Changing Constitutional Order.* London: Sweet & Maxwell.

S

SCARMAN INQUIRY

> The Scarman Inquiry resulted in a landmark report that was focused on a particular series of urban disorders in London in 1981, but the reports came to exert a wide influence over the general direction of British policing during the decades that followed.

The Scarman Inquiry into the 1981 Brixton disorders established an agenda for policing in Britain that continues to be influential a quarter of a century later. The report, published at the end of 1981, was the result of a public inquiry established in the aftermath of the disturbances. If, as cynics sometimes suggest, politicians establish public inquiries in order to push problematic topics into the long grass, that was not the outcome on this occasion. Although there was some opposition from sections of the Police Service to Scarman's analysis and recommendations, his prescriptions came to be widely endorsed and were established as the 'orthodox analysis of the police role for all Chief Constables' (Reiner 2000: 75).

The Brixton disorders were not the first of the urban riots of the 1980s – others had taken place a year previously in Bristol – and they were not the most serious in terms of death, injury or destruction. They did, however, become iconic, epitomizing urban crisis, decay and revolt, and a synonym for troubled police–community relations. The disorders occurred over the weekend of 10–12 April 1981 and followed a week-long police initiative (Operation Swamp) designed to tackle burglary and robbery. The operation entailed 'flooding' the streets with officers instructed to stop and search, on the basis of surveillance and suspicion, as many people as possible. Some 943 people were stopped, more than half of whom were black and two thirds were aged under 21.

While police stop-and-search practices and the suggestion that they have a disproportionate impact on some minority ethnic communities have continued to be a controversial topic, in the early 1980s the 'sus' laws continued to give officers almost a free hand to stop and search. The black community had grounds for the widely held view that officers abused their position and used their powers in a racist way. The extent of the concern was illustrated by Greaves (cited in Benyon 1984: 67):

> So apprehensive had some parents become that their children might be charged as suspected persons that they either kept them indoors, particularly after dark, or arranged for them to be escorted by an adult if they had to be out. For example, parents would take turns to meet a group of children and escort them to their houses from the youth club.

It was in this context that the efforts of two police officers to assist an injured black youth attracted a crowd, which became hostile as police support arrived, further escalating tensions. Violence eventually erupted: although on a relatively minor level that evening, it reignited the following afternoon and the Saturday evening saw events that Scarman (1981: 1) described in the following terms:

> the British people watched with horror and incredulity … scenes of violence and disorder in their capital city, the like of which had not previously been seen in this century in Britain. In the centre of Brixton, a few hundred young people – most, but not all of them, black – attacked the police on the streets with stones, bricks, iron bars and petrol bombs, demonstrating to their

fellow citizens the fragile basis of the Queen's peace ... These young people, by their criminal behaviour – for such, whatever their grievances or frustrations, it was – brought about a temporary collapse of law and order in the centre of an inner suburb of London.

In the aftermath of the disorders, Lord Scarman, a senior judge, was appointed to conduct an inquiry into the circumstances of the disorders and the police response. Scarman had conducted similar inquiries into earlier unrest, such as that between police and anti-fascist protestors in Red Lion Square in London in 1974, and he held hearings into the Brixton unrest at Lambeth Town Hall in June and July 1981 and visited community groups and police organizations across the country. The subsequent report provided a compelling account of events and a series of recommendations relating to policing and to social policy more generally. Perhaps the central contribution of the report was its insistence that the disorders could only be understood against the particular context of social deprivation, political marginalization and economic disadvantage. An inflexible and militaristic style of policing, with poor public engagement, exacerbated the situation and made worse tensions and pressures but did not solely create them. Scarman's insistence that socio-economic, political and cultural factors lay behind the 'riots' provided a very different perspective from that which was predominant in much of the national press and was expressed by Conservative government ministers. In the aftermath of further unrest in July 1981 in, *inter alia,* Toxteth, Moss Side and Handsworth, Prime Minister Margaret Thatcher rejected suggestions that poverty was a cause of disorder and argued that nothing 'would condone the violence that took place ... One must totally condemn it' and that 'it is totally inexcusable and unjustifiable' (Benyon 1984: 5). Other politicians and commentators suggested that the riots were the result of a sinister conspiracy. The plotters – sometimes portrayed as anarchists, sometimes as left-wing subversives – had

been identified, the media (often citing police sources) claimed, touring the affected areas on motorcycles and manufacturing petrol bombs (Benyon 1984). Scarman found no evidence that the disorders were premeditated or planned, although he did suggest that there may have been an element of 'media contagion' that helped to spread disorders to towns and cities across the country. Reiner (2000: 145) argued that the 'law and order' analysis of the disorders in Brixton and elsewhere in 1981 was predominate in the immediate aftermath of each incident of unrest. However, in the longer term, Scarman's emphasis that the disorders were caused by a combination of the failure of social policy, the decline of the inner cities and inflexible policing came to be established as a powerful contra-discourse (Reiner 2000: 146).

Many of Scarman's recommendations relating to policing (for example, on training, the role of community policing, lay visitors to police stations, discipline and stop and search), established an agenda for the following decade. That some of the problems he identified were reiterated almost 20 years later in the Lawrence Inquiry suggests both that the reforms Scarman advocated were crucial and that they had not been effectively implemented.

Mike Rowe

Related entries

Community policing; Consultation; Discretion; Force (police use of); Independent advisory groups; Institutional racism; Police powers; Racially motivated offending.

Key texts and sources

Benyon, J. (ed.) (1984) *Scarman and After: Essays Reflecting on Lord Scarman's Report, the Riots and their Aftermath.* Oxford: Pergamon Press.

Keith, M. (1993) *Race, Riots and Policing: Lore and Disorder in a Multiracist Society.* London: UCL Press.

Reiner, R. (2000) *The Politics of the Police* (3rd edn). Oxford: Oxford University Press.

Scarman, Lord (1981) *The Brixton Disorders.* London: HMSO.

SCHENGEN

> Schengen is an agreement, covering a number of European countries, whose aim is to establish an area uninhibited by border controls, thus providing the conditions for the freedom of movement of people and goods.

The Schengen Convention was signed in June 1990 and came into effect on 26 March 1995. The original agreement (named after the town in Luxembourg where it was signed) was signed on 14 June 1985 by Belgium, France, Germany, Luxembourg and the Netherlands. Italy joined in 1990, Spain and Portugal in 1991 and Greece in 1992. The Schengen *acquis* now covers all EU member states with the exception of the UK and Ireland (Denmark has signed the agreement but can choose within the EU framework whether or not to apply any new decisions), in addition to two non-EU countries, Norway and Iceland. The Amsterdam Treaty on the EU, which came into force on 1 May 1999, incorporated the set of measures adopted under the Schengen umbrella into the EU's legal and institutional framework.

The convention abolished the checks at internal borders of the signatory states while simultaneously creating and strengthening a single external frontier, where checks for all signatories were to be standardized with a common set of rules. Integral to the establishment of an area of free travel are a series of compensatory measures designed to enhance police co-operation. Among the main rules adopted by the Schengen members are the following:

- The removal of checks on persons at common EU internal borders.
- A common set of rules applying to people crossing EU external frontiers, regardless of the EU country in which that external frontier is situated.
- The separation at air terminals and, where possible, at seaports of people travelling within the Schengen area from those arriving from countries outside the Schengen area.

- The harmonization of rules regarding conditions of entry and visas for short stays.
- Co-ordination between administrations on surveillance of borders.
- The definition of the role of carriers in the fight against illegal immigration.
- Enhanced police co-operation (including the rights of cross-border surveillance and hot pursuit).
- The strengthening of judicial co-operation through a faster extradition system and the transfer of the enforcement of criminal judgments.
- The creation of the Schengen Information System (SIS).

At the heart of policing arrangements was the perceived need for a system to facilitate the rapid exchange of information between signatories. The SIS was set up to allow police forces and consular agents to access data on specific individuals (i.e. criminals wanted for arrest or extradition, missing persons, third-country nationals to be refused entry and persons to be submitted to discreet surveillance or specific checks for the prevention of threats to public safety, etc.) and on goods that have been lost or stolen. By 2002 it was reported that some 10 million people were listed on the SIS, in addition to 1.3 million convicted and suspected criminals flagged on its alert system (cited in Lewis 2005: 106). The second-generation SIS is currently under development and was due to be in operation by March 2007.

Although the UK and Ireland remain outside Schengen, the UK requested in March 1999 to participate in police and legal co-operation in criminal matters, in the fight against drugs and in the SIS. The request was approved in May 2000. Ireland made a similar request in June 2000, which was granted in February 2002.

Mario Matassa

Related entries

Constabulary independence; International police co-operation; Surveillance; Transnational policing.

Key text and sources

Lewis, N. (2005) 'Expanding surveillance: connecting biometric information systems to international police cooperation', in E. Zureik and M.B. Salter (eds) *Global Surveillance and Policing: Borders, Security, Identity*. Cullompton: Willan Publishing.

SCOTLAND (POLICING)

Scottish policing has a long history and tradition, with the Glasgow Police coming into being in 1800, almost 30 years before the Metropolitan Police. Despite being often subsumed under the title of 'British' policing, there are significant differences to policing in Scotland, not least that it functions within a context of Scots law and criminal procedure different from that in England and Wales.

Scotland has eight territorial police forces based on the regions created by local government reorganization in 1975. Although these local government units have now disappeared, the names remain in the force titles: Central Scotland, Dumfries and Galloway, Fife, Grampian, Lothian and Borders, Northern, Strathclyde and Tayside. Strathclyde is by far the largest force, covering half of Scotland's area and population and employing almost half the country's 16,000 police officers. The three smallest forces – Central Scotland, Dumfries and Galloway, and Northern – each employ fewer officers than an average Strathclyde division. This contrast, with its implications for both resources and specialist capabilities, has led to some debate about whether or not the current structure best meets the demands of modern policing.

There are also several common police services that provide central support and specialist assistance on a national basis. These are the Scottish Police College, which provides elements of probationer and in-service training, the Scottish Criminal Record Office, which includes the Scottish Fingerprint Service and Disclosure Scotland, and the Scottish Police Information Strategy, dealing with computer information systems. Slightly apart from these, though still a central service, is the Scottish Crime and Drugs Enforcement Agency (SCDEA). The SCDEA began in 2001 with an emphasis on interrupting drug supplies into the country. The Police, Public Order and Criminal Justice (Scotland) Act 2006 redefined the organization to focus on serious organized crime, hi-tech crime and anti-terrorism activities. It differs from other common services in being more involved in operational policing, and it now has the capacity to recruit its own officers directly.

The cornerstone of policing in Scotland remains the Police (Scotland) Act 1967, which defines the role of the constables of the police force as 'to guard, patrol and watch so as – (i) to prevent the commission of offences; (ii) to preserve order; and (iii) to protect life and property'. The limitations of this as a statement of purpose in recent times is increasingly obvious as its focus on the individual constable, its emphasis on reactive policing and its open-ended definition of policing functions have not kept pace with changing circumstances. Police forces in Scotland have to balance the efficient deployment of officers for both public reassurance and specialist activities, to develop more proactive approaches to ensuring community safety and crime reduction and to prioritize workloads through technological means, such as call management systems or by delegating certain roles to other groups, such as community wardens. None the less, Scottish policing remains committed to a community policing model that seeks to allocate some officers specifically to communities as community constables, to develop community involvement in local organizations, such as schools and community councils, and to ensure a rapport with communities that actively promotes their co-operation with the police. Maintaining this model is increasingly difficult in the face of resource constraints and new priorities (in particular, the extraction of community officers to other tasks).

The governance and accountability of policing in Scotland are based on the traditional tripartite structure. The central government element is fulfilled by the Scottish Executive created by the Scotland Act 1998 as part of the devolution settlement. The Justice Minister within the executive has responsibility for the police and broadly exercises the powers and duties previously carried out by the Secretary of State for Scotland, although in a more active fashion than was ever true of Westminster government. At the local government level, police boards consist solely of elected councillors nominated from the constituent councils that comprise joint board areas. These boards carry out the traditional role of making senior appointments and ensuring that resources are available to their forces, but they are increasingly expected to undertake an independent monitoring function in relation to efficiency and best value in forces. In practice this task has proved difficult for them to fulfil. A similar arrangement applies to common police services through the new Police Services Authority, comprising executive nominees, police board chairs and police representatives.

The idea of 'constabulary independence' is vested in the role of the chief constable, who has the sole responsibility for controlling and directing police operations. This includes the management of increasing numbers of civilian support staff, who now constitute over one third of police employees in Scotland. There are, however, an increasing number of constraints on individual chief constables, partly because of the amount of national legislation, policies and 'new' accountabilities (such as target-setting and auditing activities) promoted by the Scottish Executive and its agencies, partly because of the increased tendency of corporate bodies such as the Association of Chief Police Officers in Scotland (ACPOS) to develop common policies to which all forces adhere, and partly because of the more assertive role carried out by HM Inspectorate of Constabulary (HMIC) for Scotland as the executive's main advisers on policing. In Scotland, where historically the police have never played any part in prosecutions, the role of the chief constable is also subject to the power of the Lord Advocate and local procurators fiscal to direct the police in relation to the investigation of crime.

The police in Scotland have considerable discretion in the exercise of their powers, balanced by the right of the public to complain. Chief constables are responsible for dealing with complaints in their own areas, and police authorities have a statutory duty to be informed of this. HMIC includes a lay inspector with a specific role in overseeing how complaints are handled by forces. However, it can be argued that this does not constitute a fully independent complaints system, and a new post of Police Complaints Commissioner for Scotland was introduced in 2006 to review the way in which forces deal with complaints.

Ken Scott

Related entries

Accountability and governance; Community policing; Discretion.

Key texts and sources

Donnelly, D. and Scott, K.B. (2002) 'Police accountability in Scotland. 1. The "new" tripartite system. 2. "New" accountabilities', *Police Journal*, 75: 1–12, 56–66.
Donnelly, D. and Scott, K.B. (eds) (2005) *Policing Scotland.* Cullompton: Willan Publishing.
The annual reports of HMIC for Scotland are available online at **http://www.scotland.gov.uk/Topics/Justice/Police/15403/3431**. See also ACPOS's website (**http://www.acpos.police.uk/**) and **http://www.scottish.police.uk/** for links to other relevant websites.

SECURITY

> Security is a term now regularly invoked in connection with an array of phenomena, ranging from a generalized sense of well-being, to the activities of private policing bodies, all the way to the general territory of protecting the nation-state from outside threats – namely, national security.

The term 'security' derives from the Latin *securus* (without care) and *securitas* (freedom from anxiety or fear). Until relatively recently, security was not an especial focus of criminological attention. However, the term is now deployed in a variety of circumstances to refer both to a state of mind (a feeling of well-being or assurance, or its reverse, a feeling of *insecurity*) and to a range of activities, including:

- the use of physical security measures, such as locks, bolts and alarms;
- the protection against victimization afforded by the activities of both public policing and private security agencies and, indeed, the growing trade in security as a commodity; together with
- those activities undertaken in the name of protecting the nation-state and its citizens from 'external threats' – generally captured by the term 'national security'.

The ubiquitousness of the term in contemporary life, and some of the variety of ways in which it is deployed, can be seen by the fact that the first of the Home Office's seven published objectives in 2007 was to 'help people feel secure in their homes and local communities' and the sixth was to 'secure our borders, and control migration for the benefit of our country'. Nevertheless, it is, as Zedner (2003) notes, 'a slippery concept'. As she goes on to point out, at its most abstract it may be taken to refer to either a negative or a positive presence – something that we have and value, or something that we lack and desire. The politicization of crime and its control in recent decades has been accompanied by apparently increasing concern about safety and security. In turn, a market in security has developed, comprising a range of commodities such as alarms, closed-circuit television and other apparatus of surveillance, as well as 'manned security' in the form of a variety of private security operatives, from guards to nightclub bouncers (Hobbs *et al.* 2003).

The growing visibility of privatized security arrangements and personnel is argued to be one of the distinguishing features of our late modern social environment (Jones and Newburn 1998). A number of influential authors have argued that policing is being transformed and restructured in the modern world (e.g. Bayley and Shearing 2001). There has been some debate over the nature of this change, and how it is to be understood and conceptualized. A

growing literature has focused on different elements of this process of change, including:

- the emergence and spread of transnational policing bodies (Sheptycki 2000);
- changes in the organization and goals of police work;
- the rise of a proactive, risk-oriented mentality; and
- the gradual emergence of a significantly more complex policing division of labour (Jones and Newburn 1998).

Bayley and Shearing (2001) refer to this process as one of 'multilateralization'. One of the consequences is that the state is increasingly seen as being only one of a number of 'auspices' of policing, alongside private governments (Shearing 2006) and citizens. This is so substantial a shift away from the traditional state-centred view of policing that a number of authors – most notably Clifford Shearing – have argued that we should now be talking about the 'governance of security' rather than policing (Johnston and Shearing 2003).

Despite the terminology, this new literature has largely ignored matters that might generally fall under the rubric of 'national security' – though it is important to note that the meaning of the term 'national security' is far from straightforward (Buzan 1991). Although the 'new policing' debate challenges the existing scholarly preoccupation with the police at the expense of private sector sources of security provision, it has yet to devote much attention to those forms of governance that are involved in the security of the state itself – what Brodeur (1983) has characterized as 'high policing' – whether this is done by security agencies or law enforcement bodies. Growing concerns about national security since the September 2001 attacks in New York and Washington, DC and, closer to home, in London in July 2005 are beginning to change this, and the disciplinary boundaries between political science, international relations and sociology/criminology are beginning to break down in this area. This is an area of scholarship in which there is likely to be very considerable expansion in the near future.

In terms of policing, invoking national security tends often to involve appeals for the creation, or justifying the use, of extraordinary powers of both coercion (including the use of military might) and intrusion (including the use of secret intelligence). Moreover, the end of the Cold War and the rise of international terrorism have led to the emergence of what some observers now refer to as the 'new security agenda'. Concerns about the new terrorism have begun to reshape the governance of domestic security generally and policing more particularly (Shearing 2006). Arguably, these changes may lead to something of a blurring of the roles of the police, the military and the security agencies, as well as something of a blurring of the boundary between international security and domestic concerns of order maintenance (Buzan *et al.* 1998). In part, such blurring may occur as matters that were previously seen as straightforwardly in the policing domain, or more broadly as public policy issues, increasingly come to be viewed through the lens of (national) security. Furthermore, they open up the possibility that extraordinary powers, introduced in order to combat threats perceived to be especially unusual, gradually become part and parcel of everyday policing activity.

Tim Newburn

Related entries

Fear of crime; Human rights; National security; Plural policing; Special branch (SB); Terrorism.

Key texts and sources

Bayley, D.H. and Shearing, C. (2001) *The New Structure of Policing: Description, Conceptualization and Research Agenda.* Washington, DC: National Institute of Justice.

Shearing, C. and Stenning, P. (1981) 'Modern private security: its growth and implications', in M. Tonry and N. Morris (eds) *Crime and Justice: A Review of Research.* Chicago, IL: University of Chicago Press.

Zedner, L. (2003) 'The concept of security: an agenda for comparative analysis', *Legal Studies*, 23: 153–76.

SERIOUS ORGANIZED CRIME AGENCY (SOCA)

Established by the Serious Organized Crime and Police Act 2005 and operational from 1 April 2006, the Serious Organized Crime Agency (SOCA) is an amalgamation of the National Crime Squad, the National Criminal Intelligence Service, the former HM Customs & Excise, the organized trafficking investigation section of HM Immigration Service and the organized crime section of MI5.

Envisaged to become more than the sum of its parts (Hansard (Lords) 5 April 2005: col. 60), the Serious Organized Crime Agency (SOCA) is the culmination of an evolution in collaboration that began with the regional crime squads merging to form the National Crime Squad in 1998.

SOCA's statutory functions are as follows (Serious Organized Crime and Police Act 2005, ss. 2 and 3):

- Preventing and detecting serious organized crime.
- Contributing to the reduction of such crime in other ways and to the mitigation of its consequences.
- Gathering, storing, analysing and disseminating information relevant to the prevention, detection, investigation or prosecution of offences, or the reduction of crime in other ways or the mitigation of its consequences.

Ministers have robustly asserted that SOCA 'is not a police force' intended solely to undertake traditional investigations. Although some operations may result in prosecution, SOCA will also seek to disrupt and dismantle organized crime groups and markets (Hansard (Commons) 11 January 2005: cols 9, 32-35, 38 and 43).

The public conceptual origins of SOCA were articulated in a 2004 white paper outlining three strategic principles for a new UK response to organized crime:

- The reduction of criminal profits (asset recovery).

- The disruption of criminal markets and businesses.
- The increase of risk of prosecution/conviction for major criminals.

The white paper identified five critical success factors in the new strategy, of which two were the creation of a new organized crime agency to bring a new clarity of approach, with enhanced capabilities and skills, and a radical improvement in the use of intelligence throughout the system.

A new, intelligence-led agency was seen as the solution to interagency rivalry between the police, customs and MI5 made worse, the government conceded, by competing performance indicators (Hansard (Commons) 11 January 2005: cols 35 and 66). Uniting different organizational cultures with a legacy of animosity is a significant challenge to SOCA's management.

Also of concern is SOCA's relationship with local forces. Both the regional crime squads and the National Crime Squad supported local police operations, and local police authorities were represented in the oversight structures of these bodies. There is no such representation on the SOCA board, which is dominated by Home Office appointees. Concerns prevail that SOCA will concentrate on transnational criminality. The consequential sub-national, cross-border void may have to be filled by the recreation of the regional crime squads.

Clive Harfield

Related entries

Accountability and governance; Cybercrimes; Drugs and policing; National security; Organized crime; Police powers; Transnational policing.

Key texts and sources

Harfield, C. (2006) 'SOCA: a paradigm shift in British policing', *British Journal of Criminology*, 46: 743–71 (available online at **http://bjc.oxfordjournals. org/cgi/rapidpdf/az1009v1**).

Home Affairs Committee (1995) *Organized Crime: Third Report* (HC Session 1994–95, 18-I). London: HMSO.

Home Office (2004) *One Step Ahead: A 21st Century Strategy to Defeat Organized Crime* (Cm 6167). London: HMSO.

See also SOCA's website (**http://www.soca.gov.uk/**).

SEXUAL OFFENCES ACT 2003 (SOA)

> The Sexual Offences Act 2003 (SOA) is the most important reform of sexual offences legislation to date, signifying a substantial reform of sexual offences legislation in ways that more closely reflect women and children's experiences of sexual violence.

The Sexual Offences Act 2003 (SOA) represents the most fundamental reform of sexual offence legislation in the UK to date. Prior to this, the law on sexual violence was based on the piecemeal introduction of legislation in response to a series of moral panics that occured throughout the nineteenth and twentieth centuries. So, for instance, the raising of the age of consent to 16 years old was, arguably, the result of the 'Maiden tribute to modern Babylon' series of articles by W.I. Stead in the *Pall Mall Gazette* in which he claimed that young girls from across Britain were being sold into prostitution. The Sexual Offences Act 1956 was an attempt to consolidate these various piecemeal amendments, and it created the legal framework that shaped the policing of sexual offences throughout the latter half of the twentieth century.

Feminist campaigning and scholarship at the end of the twentieth century were successful in demonstrating the lack of justice that victims of sexual violence obtained. As a result of this, in 1999 the newly elected New Labour government convened a wide-reaching and detailed review of sexual offences in England and Wales. The terms of the review were to make recommendations that would provide a legal framework that would be clear and coherent and that would offer protection to individuals, enable the appropriate punishment of perpetrators and be fair and non-discriminatory. The result was *Setting the Boundaries* (Home Office 2000), which was followed by the government white paper, *Protecting the Public* (Home Office 2002b). The Sexual Offences Bill was introduced in January 2003, and it received Royal Assent in November 2003.

The key features of the SOA are that it addresses a number of criticisms concerning how sexual violence had been dealt with previously. Of significance, the SOA:

- defines consent;
- broadens the definition of sexual assault by redefining 'sexual' to mean anything that is done with a sexual intent or that any reasonable person would understand to be sexual;
- provides a framework of only three sexual offences (rape, assault by penetration and sexual assault);
- outlaws any and all sexual contact between or with children;
- gender neutralises all sexual offences; and
- appreciably increases the punitive response to all sexual offences (in many cases from up to two years' imprisonment as the maximum punishment to up to fourteen years or life).

While the SOA signifies a substantial reform of sexual offences legislation in ways that more closely reflect women and children's experiences of sexual violence, there is some debate about whether it will, in practice, offer justice and protection. More, there is also some discussion in academic circles as to whether, through the careful deployment of a rhetoric of victimhood, the SOA signifies a considerable extension of social control in the area of sexuality (Phoenix and Oerton 2005).

Joanna Phoenix

Related entries

Prostitution; Sexual offences/sexual violence.

Key texts and sources

Home Office (2000) *Setting the Boundaries*. London: HMSO.
Home Office (2002) *Protecting the Public*. London: HMSO.
See also the Office of Public Sector Information's website (http://www.opsi.gov.uk/ACTS/acts2003/20030042.htm) for the text of the SOA.

SEXUAL OFFENCES/SEXUAL VIOLENCE

Sexual offences are offences that relate specifically to sex and sexual activity. Sexual violence, however, is a term used to signify any bodily harms or violation that have a sexual component and that may (or may not) be recognized in law or statute.

In the UK, the final decades of the twentieth century saw significant changes to how academic communities and government discussed rape and other forms of sexual violence. The success of a predominantly feminist narrative about sexual violence transformed thinking and practice, not just within the UK but arguably across the globe. Prior to this and throughout most of the nineteenth and twentieth centuries, thinking about rape and sexual violence was dominated by a male-constructed medical and legal model in which sexual offences were primarily about sex, were relatively rare events and in which women's sexuality was constituted as passive and men's as aggressive. Sexual violence was thereby understood as the 'regrettable' result of some men's sexual excesses or perversion. By the end of the twentieth century, feminist campaigners and scholars, grass roots organization and a burgeoning feminist research literature systematically challenged these myths. New voices claimed that rape and sexual violence are routine, daily acts of violence, power and aggression are not about sex *per se* but about the maintenance of patriarchal power as expressed at the personal level and the social level through discriminatory legal frameworks that offer women little protection or justice. Within academic communities, feminist scholars turned their attention to analysing both the legal framework and the criminal justice response to sexual violence. The critique centred on three problems: definition, prevalence and the lack of justice accorded to victims.

Until 1976 there was no statute definition of rape. Instead, common law defined it as 'unlawful sexual intercourse with a woman without her consent, by force, fear or fraud'. With the

Sexual Offences (Amendment) Act 1976, rape was defined as unlawful sexual intercourse with a woman that knowingly or recklessly took place without her consent. The feminist challenge to this definition was four-fold. First, the definition focused on one particular sexual activity (penile penetration of a vagina) to the exclusion of other types of sexual violation (such as forced oral sex or penetration by objects). Secondly, it placed the burden of proof on the victim to prove that she did not consent. Thirdly, until 1994 it excluded married partners or men. Fourthly, the mechanistic, narrow definition did not resonate with the experiences of women as recorded in the research literature. Simply, the legal framework belied the social realities of many women's lives, in which pressurized and coerced sex were regular occurrences (Kelly 1988). Research literature showed that rape and sexual violence were much more common than once thought. So, in 2002, the British Crime Survey suggested that 1 in 20 women had been raped and that, in 1999, 61,000 women had been raped. Yet Home Office official statistics for 2002–3 reported only 12,293 women raped.

Rape and other forms of sexual violence have an extremely high attrition rate, even though there is some contention about the exact rate. Most studies place that rate well below 10 per cent of the reporting rates. Harris and Grace (1999), for example, found that only 6 per cent of cases originally reported as rape resulted in a conviction of rape – that the Crown Prosecution Service (CPS) or the police had discontinued 65 per cent. Others noted that, while the numbers of women coming forward to make complaints of rape had dramatically increased in the last quarter of the twentieth century, the attrition rate also increased, despite the reforms to police practice in the last two decades of that century.

Throughout the 1990s there were also a series of qualitative studies that shed some light on the social processes that make rape and sexual violence one of the crimes with the lowest reporting rate and the highest attrition rate. These studies confirmed that the prosecution of rape and other sexual offences hinged on the degree to which the CPS felt that a case was 'winnable' (and by

that it is meant that the case closely mirrored the myth of the virtuous woman being raped by a stranger) and on 'extra-legal' factors, such as the extent to which the victims conformed to very limited stereotypes of 'respectable femininity' (Temkin 1987; Lees 2002). This body of literature indicated that, for many victims of sexual violence, pursuing a prosecution through the criminal justice system meant her sexual choices and morality were open to scrutiny and, with that, victims reported experiencing a secondary, symbolic victimization.

The combination of insights offered by the burgeoning feminist scholarship and research and the specific issue campaigns produced the impetus for changing both the procedures for dealing with sexual violence (and most particularly rape) and the law itself. There have been year-on-year reforms to practice. Key has been the introduction of specially trained police officers and rape suites (now called sexual assault referral centres) throughout the UK, whose aim is to create a less intimidating and more supportive atmosphere for victims. But the pressure for reform found its ultimate expression in the legal reforms contained in the Sexual Offences Act 2003 (SOA). This Act altered the legal framework for sexual violence in three ways. Firstly, it replaced the earlier mechanistic definition of sexual offences with a more 'subjectivist' approach. Whereas once the law defined rape very specifically, the SOA defines it as any penile penetration of any orifice without consent. A new offence of assault by penetration now covers all non-penile non-consensual penetration. Similarly, the raft of specific sexual assaults (buggery, indecent assault and so on) has been replaced by one offence of sexual assault that is defined as any non-consensual touching that is sexual in nature. This 'subjectivist' approach is also noted in the definition of 'sexual'. 'Sexual' means anything that any reasonable person would consider sexual or that is done with a sexual intent. Secondly, the SOA gender neutralizes all offences. In this way, a regulatory framework that is based on sexual harm committed against anyone has superseded a century of legislation that specified exactly what *men* could and could not do to *women*. Finally, in regards to rape, the SOA introduces for the first time in UK history a statute definition of consent and, importantly, it reverses the burden of proof by requiring the accused to demonstrate actively the steps he took to obtain consent.

Joanna Phoenix

Related entries

Attrition; Crime; Dangerous offenders and dangerousness; Domestic violence; Gender and policing; Pornography (child); Prostitution; Sexual Offences Act 2003 (SOA); Victim and witness support.

Key texts and sources

Harris, J. and Grace, S. (1999) *A Question of Evidence: Investigating and Prosecuting Rape in the 1990s. Home Office Research Study 196.* London: Home Office.

Kelly, L. (1988) *Surviving Sexual Violence.* Cambridge: Polity Press.

Lees, S. (2002) *Carnal Knowledge: Rape on Trial.* London: Women's Press.

Phoenix, J. and Oerton, S. (2005) *Illicit and Illegal: Sex, Regulation and Social Control.* Cullompton: Willan Publishing.

Temkin, J. (1987) *Rape and the Legal Process.* London: Sweet & Maxwell.

See also the Child and Woman Abuse Studies website (http://www.cwasu.org/) and the Home Office's crime reduction website (http://www.crime reduction.gov.uk/sexual/sexual23.htm and http://www.crimereduction.gov.uk/sexual/sexual22.htm).

SHEEHY INQUIRY

The Sheehy Inquiry was established to examine the rank structure, remuneration and working conditions of the Police Service in England and Wales, Scotland and Northern Ireland and to recommend any appropriate changes.

The Sheehy Inquiry was announced by the Home Secretary at a Police Federation conference in May 1992. Its terms of reference were: 'To examine the rank structure, remuneration, and conditions of the police service in England and Wales, in Scotland and in Northern Ireland, and to recommend what changes, if any, would

be sensible.' It was chaired by Sir Patrick Sheehy, the chairman of BAT industries, and its other members were John Bullock (Joint Senior Partner, Coopers & Lybrand), Professor Colin Campbell (Vice Chancellor, Nottingham University), Eric Caines (Director of Personnel, NHS) and Sir Paul Fox (former Managing Director, BBC Television). It was intentional that none of the members of the inquiry had any experience of policing.

The inquiry eventually reported on 1 July 1993 (Sheehy 1993), just two days after the publication of a white paper on police reform. It made 272 recommendations in all, designed, it was suggested, to 'reward good performance and penalise bad'. Some of the major recommendations included the following:

- New recruits to the police to be hired on 10-year fixed-term contracts, which would be considered for renewal subsequently every five years.
- The abolition of the ranks of deputy chief constable, chief superintendent and chief inspector.
- The introduction of a severance programme to enable the termination of the contracts of up to 5,000 middle-ranking and senior officers.
- The introduction of performance-related pay, with up to 30 per cent of the salaries of chief constables and their assistants being linked to performance-related bonuses.
- The reduction of starting pay and the linking of pay rates to non-manual private sector earnings.
- The ending of many forms of overtime payment and the freezing of housing allowances.

Reactions varied. The Police Federation argued that the recommendations would remove the vocational aspect of the work, turning it into a 'job like any other job', a sentiment echoed by the Police Superintendent's Association, who suggested that recruitment, retention and motivation would all be hit by the proposals. No doubt elements of the Sheehy Inquiry recommendations would always have been controversial. However, tensions were exacerbated by the fact that the recently published white paper on police reform had also recommended a number of far-reaching measures, including the radical reform of local police authorities and introducing national league performance tables – measures that were eventually incorporated into the Police and Magistrates' Courts Act 1994.

In the main the proposals contained in both the Sheehy Inquiry report and the white paper were discussed together by the national press and, indeed, this is largely how they should be seen. They were both part of a long-term centralizing trend in British policing, although both also bore the hallmarks of the increasing managerialism that was affecting most public services. Few of Sheehy's recommendations were implemented or implemented in the manner the inquiry intended. Nevertheless, they did bring about a number of important changes, not least the introduction of fixed-term contracts and performance-related pay for senior officers and the, albeit slight, flattening of the police organizational hierarchy.

Tim Newburn

Related entries

New public management (NPM); Politics (police involvement); Rank structure; Recruitment.

Key texts and sources

Sheehy, Sir P. (1993) *Inquiry into Police Responsibilities and Rewards.* London: HMSO.

SIGNAL CRIMES

Signal crimes are criminal incidents that act as warning signals to people about threats to their security and that have a disproportionate impact on the way people think, feel or act.

The signal crimes perspective (SCP) is closely associated with the work of Martin Innes (University of Surrey) and has informed the development of reassurance policing and neighbourhood policing. The perspective examines how crimes and disorders are perceived and rendered meaningful by people in their everyday lives, and it helps to shape their reaction to

them. The SCP is held in contrast to the broken windows thesis, which holds that disorders lead to more serious crime.

Drawing on symbolic interactionism and semiotics, a central feature of the SCP is that crimes and disorders are inherently communicative and 'send signals' to people about potential risks to their security (Innes 2004b). Not all crimes and disorders hold the same 'signal value': some matter more than others and affect people in different ways and at different times. This helps explain why some homicides generate widespread public reaction, but not others. Crucially, the public are seen to draw a fairly fluid distinction between crimes and disorders, and the events that have a cognitive, affective or behavioural effect will not necessarily be the same as those traditionally prioritized by the police (for example, graffiti or litter may be more salient than a series of burglaries in the neighbourhood).

Whereas 'signal crimes' refer to criminal incidents (and could include major crimes), 'signal disorders' are physical and social disorders that communicate risk. Together, these are referred to as 'signal events'. 'Control signals' are acts of social control that are intended to shape people's perceptions, such as high-visibility foot patrol. Their impact, however, will not always be to make people feel safer, and they could trigger unease.

Unlike other approaches, the SCP outlines a formal methodology to identify the signals from 'background noise' through the analysis of people's talk about crime and disorder. The patterns that emerge are seen as a way of targeting the activities of the police and partner agencies. It is argued that, in tackling these signals, the police will have a disproportionate impact on public confidence and fear of crime by generating reassurance. This idea was central to the Association of Chief Police Officers (ACPO)-led and Home Office-evaluated National Reassurance Policing Programme, which focused on identifying and tackling local public priorities. Empirical research was also carried out in parallel to expand the initial signal crimes concept.

Criticism has tended to focus on reassurance policing rather than the SCP that informed it and which is concerned more about explaining social reaction to crime and disorder. Loader (2006) has argued that people's views are unlikely to be entirely benign and may not reflect a rational assessment of risk, and that some people may lack sufficient social capital to be heard by the police. A focus on people's perceptions of risk may also divert attention away from more objective, less visible risk factors. Others have also expressed concern that the subtleties around signal crimes were lost with implementation of reassurance policing.

Paul Quinton

Related entries

Fear of crime; Neighbourhood policing; Reassurance policing.

Key texts and sources

Innes, M. (2004) 'Signal crimes and signal disorders: notes on deviance as communicative action', *British Journal of Sociology*, 55: 335–55.
Loader, I. (2006) 'Policing, recognition and belonging', *Annals of the American Academy of Political and Social Science*, 605: 201–21.
See also ACPO's neighbourhood policing web page (http://www.neighbourhoodpolicing.co.uk/).

SKILLS FOR JUSTICE

Skills for Justice is the sector skills council covering all employers, employees and volunteers working in the UK justice system. Sector skills councils are independent, UK-wide organizations (Skills for Justice is a company limited by guarantee) licensed by the Secretary of State for Education and Skills. Skills for Justice works with justice sector organizations across England, Wales, Northern Ireland and Scotland to identify the skills, priorities and actions required for workforce development.

Skills for Justice has its origins in a collaboration between three former national training organizations (NTOs): the Community Justice NTO, the Custodial Care NTO and the Police Skills and Standards Organization. To these were added a number of other member organizations, including court services, Customs and Excise and the Crown Prosecution Service.

Skills for Justice's primary responsibility is to provide the support necessary to enable the justice sector to identify its current and future learning needs, to engage more effectively with learning providers in order to meet these needs with high-quality development programmes, and to link the acquisition of learning to reputable and valued qualifications.

Skills for Justice's activities can be broadly divided into four programmes:

- Engaging with and influencing employers, government departments, devolved administrations and all key partners.
- Understanding and articulating clearly the current and future skills needs of those working in the justice sector.
- Developing tools and services to improve the skills of the workforce, and working with employers, learning providers and individuals.
- Implementing practical solutions to improve the skills of the workforce, and working with employers, learning providers and individuals.

One of the major areas of activity undertaken by the organization is to develop National Occupational Standards (NOSs) for the major employers in the justice sector. These NOSs describe competent performance in terms of outcomes and are used to support individual and organizational development and quality assurance, as well as providing benchmarks of good practice. NOSs also form the basis of qualifications, most commonly National Vocational Qualifications (NVQs) and Scottish Vocational Qualifications (SVQs). Other qualifications promoted by Skills for Justice include the following:

- Apprenticeships (for 16–24-year-olds), equivalent to GCSE level, which incorporate an NVQ to Level 2.
- Advanced apprenticeships, equivalent to A-levels, incorporate an NVQ to Level 3.
- Foundation degrees (two years' full time or three years' part time).
- A Diploma in Probation Studies.
- 14–19 diplomas, a flexible qualification that combines theoretical and practical learning with functional skills in English, mathematics and ICT.

In relation to policing, the most significant development is the Integrated Competency Framework (ICF). The ICF is a series of national standards and guidelines that are intended to enable police forces and individual officers and staff members to improve the quality and consistency of performance and behaviour in jobs throughout the Police Service.

The ICF is made up of three strands:

- National Competency Framework.
- National Occupational Standards.
- National Performance and Development Review.

The intention is that the ICF can be used to plan training needs, to compile job descriptions, to assist in recruitment, to monitor and assist staff development, and to improve performance.

Tim Newburn

Related entries

Ethics in policing; Professionalization.

Key texts and sources

Full details of the activities of Skills for Justice can be found on its website (**http://www.skillsforjustice.com/default.asp?PageID=1**). Details of the Integrated Competency Framework are available online at **http://www.skillsforjustice.com/template01.asp?pageid=35**. Links to community justice organizations can be found at **http://www.skillsforjustice.com/template01.asp?PageID=142**.

SPECIAL BRANCH (SB)

'Within the police service, Special Branches play a key role in protecting the public and maintaining order. They acquire and develop intelligence to help protect the public from national security threats, especially terrorism and other extremist activity, and through this they play a valuable role in promoting community safety and cohesion ... Special Branch exists primarily to acquire intelligence, to assess its potential operational value, and to contribute more generally to its interpretation.' (Home Office 2004d: para. 18).

In the mid-nineteenth century, the Metropolitan Police Service (MPS) had, within its Criminal Investigation Department, specialist detective teams investigating Irish and, not least, Irish-American extremists, using covert infiltration pioneered, not uncontroversially, in 1833 by one Sergeant Popay.

In 1883 the MPS established a more formal structure, the Special Irish Branch, to investigate the activities of Fenian terrorists undertaking a bombing campaign in London. As the unit's responsibilities expanded to include all state-threatening subversion, the activities of other foreign anarchists and the policing of ports of entry, so it came to be known as Special Branch (SB). In the 1960s and 1970s, shire police forces set up their own SB departments. Outside metropolitan forces these were generally small, nothing like as complex as the MPS SB, although the Irish terrorist campaign on the UK mainland during the 1970s and political unrest in the 1970s and 1980s saw an expansion of SB capacity across the UK.

SB currently has responsibility for counter-terrorism (the primary role); the close protection of royalty and VIPs; security at ports; and community safety and counter-extremism. SB also assists and works closely with MI5 and MI6 in their statutory duties regarding national security protection. The links that force SB departments can forge with community policing significantly enhance the intelligence capability of the national agencies.

SB work has had a longer history of national co-ordination than other forms of policing. The Association of Chief Police Officers produced national terms of reference in 1970 and, in 1987, the first National Co-ordinator of Ports Policing was appointed. The head of MPS SB became the first National Co-ordinator for Investigation of Irish Republican Terrorism in 1990, before the Security Service (MI5) assumed lead responsibility for gathering intelligence on Irish terrorism in 1992.

Home Office-issued national guidelines for SB work in 1994 were updated in 2004 following a thematic inspection of SB by HM Inspector of Constabulary (2003a) in the aftermath of the heightened security threat following the al-Qaeda terrorist attacks of 9/11.

SB officers have no special powers or privileges but operate within the same legal and discipline framework as other police officers and staff and are equally accountable for their actions.

The Popay incident, together with SB's former role in counter-subversion and the policing of dissent (e.g. the CND movement), have led civil libertarians to describe SB as Britain's political police, a perception robustly rejected by SB and anti-terrorist specialists. The counterterrorist priority has been recently re-emphasized with the creation of regional SB intelligence cells and the merger of MPS SB (SO12) with the MPS Anti-terrorist Branch (SO13) in the new Counterterrorist Command (SO15).

John Grieve

Related entries

National security; Politics (police involvement); Terrorism; Transnational policing.

Key texts and sources

Bunyan, T. (1976) *The Political Police in Britain*. London: Friedman.
Doherty, R. (2004) *The Thin Green Line: A History of the Royal Irish Constabulary GC, 1922–2001*. Barnsley: Pen & Sword.
Mason, G. (2004) *The Official History of the Metropolitan Police*. London: Carlton.
Statewatch (2003) *Special Branch more than Doubles in Size* (special report). London: Statewatch.
See also the Metropolitan Police's special branch web page (**http://www.met.police.uk/so/special_branch.htm**).

SPECIAL CONSTABULARY

The Special Constabulary is the volunteer section of the British police. Special constables are unpaid uniformed police officers who have full police powers and are under the direct control of their respective chief officer.

Special constables are normal members of the local community who are sworn in as unpaid, fully warranted police officers, undertaking operational policing roles with similar powers to their regular, paid colleagues. Their powers cover their own police force area, along with the areas of surrounding contiguous police forces. Special constables normally contribute a minimum of 200 hours of service each year and receive out-of-pocket travelling and subsistence allowances. Some overseas police services have police volunteers equivalents (Gill and Mawby 1990), often termed 'auxiliary' police officers. Others have a part-time policing section commonly termed 'reserves', who are fully paid for services undertaken while on duty and are obliged to perform duties when required to do so.

The first recorded statutory recognition of the concept of the 'special constable' can be traced to the Poor Relief Act 1662, which permitted two justices of the peace to appoint temporary constables. The term 'temporary' later became 'special' by virtue of the Special Constables Act 1820, this Act thereby becoming the first piece of statutory legislation specifically dealing with the appointment of special constables. Many official sources of information erroneously cite the Special Constables Act 1673 as being the first enactment for the appointment of special constables. In fact, no such Act has ever existed. The most commonly referred to Act of Parliament dealing with the establishment of the Special Constabulary is the Special Constables Act 1831 that followed the Metropolitan Police Act 1829, which itself established the Metropolitan Police Service (Seth 1961).

The Second World War saw the numbers of special constables increase, and many constables were appointed into the role by virtue of powers conferred by the Special Constables Act 1914. The Special Constables Act 1923 provided for the continued appointment of special constables due to their effectiveness during the Second World War. The role and provision of the Special Constabulary were made permanent under the Police Act 1964, and many modern regulations and legislative provisions emanate from this. Over this period, the role of the Special Constabulary changed from being one of an emergency police reserve, deployed in times of civil unrest and emergency, to that of a peacetime, additional resource, used for assisting regular paid police officers in crime prevention activities. Special constables perform a wide range of operational policing roles, ranging from community policing activities, anti-social patrols and traffic regulation to community visibility roles, and there have been various attempts to rebrand them in recent years (Southgate *et al.* 1995). Their role is governed by the discretion of each chief police officer, who has the authority to deploy and target special constables towards specific tasks. Most special constables patrol with either an experienced special constable or a regular police officer.

The last 10 years has seen an increase in the amount of policy changes dealing with an array of such issues as conditions of appointment and the payment of allowances. In 2003, the Home Office introduced the 'Capacity building fund', which provides financial assistance to police forces with the intention to increase the recruitment numbers of special constables. In 2005, the Police Federation of England and Wales rejected the concept of offering membership to special constables.

The numbers of special constables have steadily decreased since the early 1920s, when they peaked at around 128,000 officers (Gill and Mawby 1990). Many reasons are cited for this reduction, including low morale, changes in family circumstances, other voluntary sector opportunities and a general reduction in service tenure. In March 2006, the total number of special constables in the 43 police forces of England and Wales was 13,179 officers (Clegg and Kirwan 2006). While the larger metropolitan/city-type police forces have the greater numbers of special constables, the smaller rural-type forces have numbers of specials ranging from approximately

10 to 35 per cent of their regular police officer strength. The gender and ethnic composition of the Special Constabulary is far more balanced than that of the regular Police Service.

Special constables are constitutionally unique. They form a valued part of the plural policing mix (Crawford *et al.* 2005b) and are an embodiment of the active community volunteer (Gill and Mawby 1990). However, while the 'multilateralization of policing' (Bayley and Shearing 1996) has generally increased the diversity of those employed in policing, the growth in plural policing as a whole is not reflected in the Special Constabulary.

Mark Harron and Rob I. Mawby

Related entries

Plural policing; Police Act 1964; Roads (policing of).

Key texts and sources

Clegg, M. and Kirwan, S. (2006) *Police Service Strength, England and Wales, 31 March 2006. Home Office Statistical Bulletin* 13/06. London: Home Office (available online at **www.homeoffice. gov.uk/rds/pdfs06/hosb1306.pdf**).

Gill, M.L. and Mawby, R.I. (1990) *A Special Constable: A Study of the Police Reserve.* Aldershot: Ashgate.

The Home Office policing web page on special constables is at **http://specials.homeoffice.gov.uk/**. See also **http://www.policespecials.com/** – the website for special constables.

SPECIALIST SQUADS

Specialist squads are created to provide particular expertise in defined areas of policing. They provide a unified approach to particular problems and vary in size and scope. Being specialists within the generalized police organization, they can be disbanded when their remit is met and their staff absorbed back into the police population.

Throughout the development of the modern police there has been a need to establish specialist squads to tackle emerging policing problems.

A major driver for this has been the need for a more efficient and effective use of scarce, and costly, resources. The effort required to tackle certain types of criminal and certain forms of criminality is beyond the capacity of the patrol officer to deliver, and thus requires special measures. This is reflected in the types of squads most prevalent in police forces: the drug squad, fraud squad, child protection unit and intelligence bureau (Morgan *et al.* 1995: 2). Their remit is to tackle the least visible or most organized criminals (Maguire 2003: 374), and their perceived success in doing so often leads to the emergence of other, more transient, squads that focus on particular categories of offenders ('persistent', 'travelling', 'serious', etc.) involved in more conventional crimes, such as robbery, burglary and vehicle theft.

The aim of squads is to focus on the criminal, not the crime. The patrol section will react to the crime, take a report and investigate the crime (this runs the risk of deskilling patrol officers who are left to deal with the tasks that no one else in the organization wants to handle). Squads concentrate instead on identifying the 'criminal' and gathering 'intelligence' about their illicit activities with an emphasis on obtaining the evidence necessary to arrest and convict them for their criminal lifestyle, rather than for any single offence. This 'proactive' approach to police work can lead to longer-term investigations targeting the activities of criminals and criminal gangs who are adept at concealing their methods and the proceeds of their dealings. Outside specialists are often brought in to squads to help track finances or to interrogate high-tech equipment where the skills are not to be readily found within the police. This can make squad life look attractive to outsiders: their high-profile arrests and unconventional methods have an appeal that is often exaggerated by fictional dramatizations of their work.

The collection of criminal intelligence does, however, lead squad detectives into direct social contact with offenders, which is an unconventional occurrence for most police officers. This can be through the recruitment of informants or as 'undercover' operatives and presents many ethical risks to the individual and the organization. It was unfortunate that, throughout the 1970s and 1980s, some squad members adopted the popularized 'squad' persona and drifted into corrupt behaviour, which resulted in several scandals. The intervention of the Metropolitan Commissioner, Sir Robert Mark, under 'Operation Countryman', following allegations of police corruption and the disbanding of the West Midlands Serious Crime Squad by their Chief Constable, Geoffrey (now Lord) Dear, brought an end to the specialist squad carte blanche. Criminal intelligence gathered from 'informants' remains at the heart of the activities of squads, but there is now an important 'firewall' brought in by the expansion of intelligence bureaux. These squads feed intelligence into other squads and are prevented from taking part in any operational initiatives, thereby creating a 'sterile corridor' between the informant and the resulting police activity.

Stan Gilmour

Related entries

Corruption (police); Covert policing; Intelligence analysis (previously crime analysis).

Key texts and sources

Maguire, M. (2003) 'Criminal investigation and crime control', in T. Newburn (ed.) *Handbook of Policing.* Cullompton: Willan Publishing.
Morgan, J., McCulloch, L. and Burrows, L. (1995) *Central Specialist Squads: A Framework for Monitoring and Evaluation.* London: Home Office.

STEPHEN LAWRENCE INQUIRY

The Stephen Lawrence Inquiry into the failed police investigation of the racist murder of Stephen Lawrence, a young black man, in south London in 1993, began in 1997 and published its findings in 1999. The inquiry (chaired by Sir William Macpherson) received widespread publicity and support – its recommendations being endorsed by the British government and senior police officers – and it succeeded in bringing the policing of racist violence from the periphery to the centre of law-and-order policy in Britain.

The Stephen Lawrence Inquiry is evaluated in terms of its impact on police reform and the law, and in terms of the subsequent criticisms of the inquiry. The inquiry arose from a long-standing campaign by the victim's parents, Doreen and Neville Lawrence, to seek justice for their son's murder, yet no one has been convicted of the murder. Announcing a string of initiatives and changes in policy and the law since the inquiry, the government both reflected and led changes in the ways that racist violence came to be popularly perceived.

Macpherson claimed to have uncovered a litany of police actions and attitudes towards the murder victim, his accompanying friend, the victim's parents and in the conduct of the murder investigation that revealed – perhaps unwitting – racist assumptions among the investigating officers. From the very beginning – the arrival of police officers at the murder scene – insensitive, unsympathetic, suspicious and stereotyping assumptions, attitudes and actions were conveyed by police officers. The underlying message of Macpherson was that, because the victim was black, this disqualified him in the eyes of the police from being considered an innocent victim of a racist murder, deserving of a proper and urgent murder investigation to catch the killers. Macpherson concluded that the investigation was marred by incompetence, a failure of leadership and 'institutional racism'. It was the use of the term 'institutional racism' as an overall explanation for these failures that subsequently courted most controversy. The term referred to the ways in which collective police organizational processes, attitudes and behaviour could unwittingly discriminate against and disadvantage minority ethnic people.

The inquiry's 70 recommendations included measures that would make the policing of racism far more central to police priorities than it had been, that would increase the powers of HM Inspectorate of Constabulary, simplify and clarify the definition of a racist incident, improve the care for witnesses and the families of victims, encourage a presumption in the Crown Prosecution Service that prosecution of racist crimes is in the public interest and improve the training of police officers in racism awareness.

Macpherson has been criticized on a number of counts, not least because of the methodological difficulty of grounding the concept of institutional racism in an investigation of a single incident of a failed murder inquiry. Whether or not the inquiry was logically entitled to infer the existence of institutional racism from the details of a single case, and whether that term was appropriately applied to individual instances of police conduct, the political ramifications for the police have been considerable (Dennis *et al.* 2000). Before addressing the criticisms, it is necessary to consider what the inquiry achieved. In 1999 the police adopted Macpherson's definition that 'any incident which is perceived to be racist by the victim or any other person is racially motivated'. Following Macpherson's recommendation, the Race Relations (Amendment) Act 2000 brought the police and criminal justice system within the laws prohibiting racial discrimination. Previously the police were exempt. Other changes in the law include the Crime and Disorder Act 1998, which introduced into law the concept of racially aggravated offences in relation to violence, harassment, public order and criminal damage. Of most significance, the main impact of Macpherson has been to have greatly increased the reporting of, and the willingness of the police to record, incidents as racist.

Turning to the impact and criticisms of the inquiry, Home Office research on the working of these new laws (Burney and Rose 2002) suggests that knowledge about (and application of) the new laws and reporting systems is uneven, and that extensive under-reporting and distrust of the police continue to be a problem. As a result of the inquiry, some police officers were anxious about racist crimes, while others seemed genuinely committed to dealing with them. Foster *et al.* (2005; see also Docking and Tuffin 2005) concluded that there had been significant improvements in policing hate crimes across a range of police activities, including recording, the conduct of murder investigations, liaison with families of victims of murder, consultation with local communities and the excision of racist language from the Police Service. These developments, however, were found to be uneven across police forces, and the continuing greatest difficulty was understanding the nature of, and designing responses to, the problem of 'institutional racism' within policing. Significantly, many officers felt the inquiry to have been unfair, and their anger and resentment focused on the use of the term 'institutional racism'. Officers felt that this term implied that there was extensive racist behaviour in the police. Officers felt under greater and more intense scrutiny, with the greatest anxiety reserved for stop and search, in which they were afraid of being accused of racism.

Academic criticism has focused on the inquiry's overly narrow institutional analysis, arguing that this ignored the wider context and the nature of racist violence. The inquiry did not address how the motivations of perpetrators might be understood, which raises questions about the appropriate ways of tackling violence. The label of institutional racism describes rather than explains police racism, blaming a restrictive police occupational culture despite policies that flow from this description having a long history of failure. Besides, officers' cultural beliefs do not necessarily translate into action on the streets. The label denies personal responsibility, generates impotence and resentment and does not tell us *which* institutional processes encourage racism. It fails to locate the causes of racism in relations between the police and economically and politically powerless groups, including minority communities. Finally, supporters of laws against racist crimes – that these crimes be punished more severely – face criticism that such exemplary punishment

erodes a fundamental human right of thought and opinion, however abhorrent.

Colin Webster

Related entries

Hate crime; Institutional racism; Police culture; Racially motivated offending; Stop and search; Victim and witness support.

Key texts and sources

Foster, J., Newburn, T. and Souhami, A. (2005) *Assessing the Impact of the Stephen Lawrence Inquiry. Home Office Research Study* 294. London: Home Office.
Iganski, P. (ed.) (2002) *The Hate Debate: Should Hate be Punished as a Crime?* London: Profile Books.
Rowe, M. (ed.) (2007) *Policing beyond Macpherson: Issues in Policing, Race and Society.* Cullompton: Willan Publishing.
Webster, C. (2007) *Understanding Race and Crime.* Maidenhead: Open University Press.
Copies of the Macpherson Report can be obtained from **http://www.archive.official-documents.co.uk/document/cm42/4262/4262.htm**. See also the Black Information Link web page on Stephen Lawrence for links to other documents (**http://www.blink.org.uk/subsections.asp?grp=14**) and the *Guardian* web page on the Stephen Lawrence Inquiry (**http://www.guardian.co.uk/lawrence/0,,179674,00.html**).

STOP AND SEARCH

Stop and search is the legal discretionary power that allows the police in public places to stop citizens, either on foot or in vehicles, in order to interrogate and search them.

Stop and search is one way of describing the virtually ubiquitous legal power afforded to police worldwide to intrude into citizens' privacy in order to establish their true identities. The precise powers enjoyed by the police vary according to the legal context in which they are exercised. For example, in jurisdictions where citizens are required routinely to carry official identification documents, the police are usually granted the power to check compliance. Societies that guard the rights of citizens usually require officers to have reasons for suspecting an individual before they can legally stop him or her. In reality, such curbs on unnecessary intrusion are ineffective because 'suspicion' is open to considerable interpretative licence. For example, was a person acting 'furtively'? Was the manner in which a vehicle was being driven indicative that the driver was intoxicated? Since, by its nature, stop and search is routinely conducted by lone officers on patrol, it epitomizes 'low visibility' discretion (Goldstein 1960).

Stop and search is often a controversial power that has attracted accusations that it is used in a discriminatory fashion, reflecting police cultural stereotyping rather than patterns of offending. Certainly, this and similar powers are used selectively against young men, especially those of low social status and particularly from marginalized ethnic and racial groups. This disproportionality has become a political cause célèbre in various jurisdictions. In the USA, Canada and Australia, for example, it is described as 'racial profiling' and colloquially referred to as 'walking/driving while black'. However, there is a reasonably close correspondence between the general pattern of offending among sections of the population and the pattern of stop and search (Smith and Gray 1983; Weatherburn *et al.* 2003). Moreover, the likelihood that a given stop and search will reveal offences ('the hit rate') tends to remain much the same, irrespective of the group membership of the person stopped. When group rates of stop and search are compared, not with the profile of the local resident population but with those in public places and, therefore, 'available' for stop and search, differences tend to reduce or disappear entirely (Miller and MVA 2000; Waddington *et al.* 2004).

Stop and search seems to be more effective than other policing tactics in reducing criminality, especially when carefully targeted against clearly identified 'hotspots' (Moore 1980; Sherman 1990; Sherman *et al.* 1997; Sherman 2000). It is equally apparent that it breeds a lower estimation of the police among those who have been subjected to it. This seems largely to reflect the manner in which the stop and search

is conducted (Southgate and Ekblom 1985; Skogan 1990, 1994; Bucke 1997; Mirrlees-Black and Budd 1997; Yeo and Budd 2000; Clancy *et al.* 2001; Jansson 2006).

P.A.J. Waddington

Related entries

Community support officers (CSOs); Police and Criminal Evidence Act 1984 (PACE); Police powers; Police property; Racial profiling; Scarman Inquiry; Stephen Lawrence Inquiry; Youth and policing.

Key texts and sources

Bowling, B. and Phillips, C. (2001) *Racism, Crime and Criminal Justice.* Harlow: Longman.
Smith, D.J. and Gray, J. (eds) (1983) *Police and People in London. Vols 1–4.* London: Policy Studies Institute.
Waddington, P.A.J. (1999) *Policing Citizens.* London: UCL Press.

STREET CRIME

'Street crime' would appear to constitute a descriptive term for all offences perpetrated in the street, but it has a more restricted meaning: the offences of robbery, attempted robbery and snatch theft from a person, irrespective of location (Smith 2003). Street crime is also widely known as 'mugging' or 'jacking'.

Research has shown that forms of street crime are a perennial feature of all societies. In the UK, one can trace the history of street crime from the outlaws of the Middle Ages to the highwaymen of the seventeenth century. As towns and cities grew in size, so did the numbers of street crimes and street criminals. Pickpockets, for example, were originally known as nippers or cutpurses because they cut the belts on which purses were worn. By the seventeenth century these terms had been replaced with those of the 'gonalph' or 'buzzer'. The highwayman was also known as the Toby man, the land pirate or the gentleman of the road. The trade they practised was called 'highway service' (robbery). The street robber was also known in the nineteenth century as a 'rampsman' (derived from the term 'rampage') or mugger.

The term 'mugger' has an interesting history. It appears to have developed in London in the nineteenth century, where it is mentioned in the novel *A Child of Jago*, by Arthur Morrison in 1896. The term then disappears from use in the UK but surfaces as a description of the urban street robber in the USA, where it is used specifically to designate black street criminals. By the late 1970s the term had been reimported to its country of origin and was being used widely by the media to identify what was presented as a new folk devil – the black urban mugger.

Given that robbery is a trade that hinges for its success on mobilizing force to separate a victim from his or her possessions, it might appear strange to imagine the street robber in any other terms than as a folk devil incarnate. It is in this image, as an anonymous violent predator, that they are typically thought of today. The historical record, however, attests to a figure who by no means has always been thought of in negative terms. As Hobsbawn's (2000) investigation of the social bandit demonstrates, many societies at one time or another have produced street robbers, many of whom were accorded a folk hero status. The myths of Robin Hood exemplify this image, as do the celebratory myths surrounding figures such as the bushwhacker Ned Kelly in Australia and the outlaw Jessie James in the USA. In class-divided societies characterized by oppressive and exploitative ruling regimes, the audacious street robber constituted a figure with which many people could vicariously empathize. Indeed, as the myths that coalesce around figures such as Robin Hood, Ned Kelly and Jessie James show, myths about the robber constitute in part founding myths about national identity.

While pervasive and perennial, the street criminal has not attracted much criminological attention. For the political right, the street robber was theorized as a member of a mal-socialized underclass (Murray 1990) – a street predator produced by permissive women heading single-parent families from which father figures were absent. Driven by drugs and devoid of moral consciousness, the street robber was viewed as a creature defective and different from law-abiding citizens.

Rejecting the idea that British society was confronting a rising tide of street crime perpetrated by black muggers in the 1970s (as the media were arguing), Hall *et al.* (1978) sought to establish why the moral panic that surrounded street crime emerged and, as part of this, tried to understand why the term mugger was being applied. The result of this inquiry was published as *Policing the Crisis*. Rejecting the idea that there was a real rise in street crime, Hall *et al.* saw the moral panic as a scapegoating mechanism, with young black males performing the role of a scapegoat in a deeply racist capitalist society that was engulfed in wider economic and political crisis. Far from recognizing that the crisis was about capitalism, the focus of social concern was displaced away from the economic base to the ideological superstructure, where the crisis was condensed into a narrative about black muggers. The term had been reapplied from its American setting to describe what had been constructed as a moral panic about a victimized white community.

More recent explanations about street crime have rejected the idea that the street robber is alienated from the norms and values of mainstream society, and they reject, too, the idea that the robber is mal-socialized (see Hallsworth 2005). Street robbers from this perspective are, like other young people, over-socialized into the mores and consumption rituals of consumer society. Street robbery, as such, is a means by which consumption desires may be assuaged by those who do not possess the capacity to consume what they have been seduced to desire legitimately. Why some engage in this form of 'flawed consumption' while most do not, however, is dependent on processes of differential association coupled with deficits in the control effort. Far from being a problem posed by social outcasts who are defective, the street robber is thus very much a product of the free market society that produced him or her.

Simon Hallsworth

Related entries

Anti-social behaviour; Broken windows; Dispersal orders; Racial profiling; Youth and policing.

Key texts and sources

Hall, S., Critcher, C., Jefferson, T., Clarke, J. and Roberts, B. (1978) *Policing the Crisis: Mugging, the State and Law and Order*. London: Macmillan.

Hallsworth, S. (2005) *Street Crime*. Cullompton: Willan Publishing.

Hobsbawn, E. (2000) *Bandits*. London: Weidenfeld & Nicolson.

Murray, C. (1990) *The Emerging British Underclass*. London: Institute for Economic Affairs.

Smith, H. (2003) *The Nature of Street Robbery*. Home Office Research Study 254. London: Home Office.

See also the Home Office's crime reduction web page on street crime (**http://www.crimereduction.gov. uk/streetcrime/streetcrime01.htm**) and the Home Office's web page on robbery and street crime (**http://www.homeoffice.gov.uk/crime-victims/ reducing-crime/robbery/**).

SURVEILLANCE

Surveillance is any collection and processing of personal data, whether identifiable or not, for the purposes of influencing or managing those whose data have been garnered.

Britain's Information Commissioner, Richard Thomas, expressed concerns in 2004 that the country risks 'sleepwalking into a surveillance society' as more and more information about people is collected and circulated. As David Lyon (2001: 2), who provided the above definition of surveillance, explains: 'It is hard to find a place, or an activity, that is shielded or secure from some purposeful tracking, tagging, listening, watching, recording, or verification device' (2001: 1). Thus, today, credit card transactions, mobile phone calls, uses of the Internet, call centre contacts and journeys between (and increasingly within) countries are among the countless routine actions providing data trails that can be linked to individuals. As the Surveillance Studies Network has observed, 'these systems represent a basic, complex infrastructure which assumes that gathering and processing personal data is vital to contemporary living' (2006: 5).

Surveillance is a central aspect of law enforcement. According to Ericson and Haggerty (1997), contemporary police work is increasingly about information gathering and communication and less about coercion, and these authors propose we should now think of the police primarily as 'knowledge workers'. Advances in communication technologies, such as personal radios, electronic mail, mobile data terminals and computer-aided dispatch, transformed policing in the twentieth century, and information technology is now indispensable to the development of problem-oriented and intelligence-led policing strategies.

One of the most visible transformations in British policing in the last 20 years has been the proliferation of closed-circuit television (CCTV) systems in towns and cities, enabling surveillance of a locality, the alerting of law enforcement agencies when incidents arise and the provision of information as officers arrive at the scene. Such systems are now so prominent across both public and private spheres that one's image may be captured on CCTV several hundred times a day (Surveillance Studies Network 2006). Yet while overt public surveillance serves criminal deterrence as well as detection functions, the police also rely on covert strategies to detect crime, including undercover operations and the use of technical surveillance devices and informers.

The IT infrastructure of the police also includes national and local information systems, of which the most central is the Police National Computer (PNC), a database holding details of persons, vehicles, crimes and property. It includes information on people convicted, cautioned or recently arrested, as well as links to the National DNA Database, the National Automated Fingerprint Identification System, the Automatic Number Plate Recognition Database and the Violent Offender and Sex Offender Register, and a Facial Images National Database, incorporating facial recognition software, is currently in development. In the case of major crime inquiries and disasters, generated information is managed through HOLMES 2 – a national investigation management system. At the local level, many police forces have invested in geographic information systems for the purposes of crime analysis, to display the local spatial distribution of crime.

Globally, networks of policing and surveillance now enable countries' national police and intelligence agencies to share data with each other, as well as customs and immigration departments, travel operators, consulates and private surveillance organizations (Lyon 2001). International police organizations, such as Interpol and Europol, play a central role in the transnational exchange of police information with, for example, Interpol's I-24/7 police communications system enabling its national central bureaux – maintained by each member country – to access each others' national databases for information on wanted persons, suspected terrorists, DNA profiles and fingerprints, and stolen property (including travel documents, vehicles and works of art). For EU countries, Europol fulfils similar functions, and a Europol computer system facilitates the sharing of similar information and intelligence. In addition, the Schengen Information System (SIS) provides the 15 EU countries prior to May 2004, together with Norway and Iceland, with a shared governmental database containing alerts on wanted persons, missing persons and persons required for court appearances (including witnesses); requests for information on serious offenders and linked vehicles; and stolen vehicles, trailers, firearms, identity documents and registered banknotes. Through the ongoing Home Office-funded Sirene UK programme, access to the SIS is soon to be provided to the British police via the PNC.

Border controls are another important aspect of transnational policing surveillance. As part of Britain's ongoing efforts to enhance its border security, an e-Borders Programme is now underway to facilitate the recording of every traveller's arrivals and departures and the immigration statuses of migrants to Britain to check passenger details against interagency 'watchlists' of those posing potential security threats and to expand the use of biometric passports and visas. The growth in travel associated with increased international tourism and overseas working presents enormous challenges in the monitoring of borders, yet as Lyon notes, 'more subtle forms of illegal activity cross borders silently and invisibly in cyberspace' (2001: 97), and the detection of electronic transfers of funds that may be associated with terrorist financing, money laundering or fraud is an area urgently requiring new forms of policing and surveillance.

Britain's transnational surveillance infrastructure also includes the work of national security agencies, of which Britain has three: the Secret Intelligence Service, often referred to as MI6, the Security Service, often referred to as MI5, and the Government Communications Headquarters. These services gather intelligence at home and overseas by means of espionage, the interception of communications and interagency co-operation.

The concerns implicit in the Information Commissioner's remarks about the rise in social surveillance are associated most strongly with privacy and data protection, including the risks of gathered data being incorrect or falling into the wrong hands. Thus, as state surveillance has expanded in the post-9/11 environment, so too has organized resistance to such practices, through monitoring and campaign groups such as Statewatch, Liberty and Privacy International, as well as the more impromptu practice of 'sousveillance': the redirecting of surveillance technologies towards those in authority (Mann *et al.* 2003). A famous example is Los Angeles resident George Holliday's videotaping of the police assault on Rodney King, whom the officers had stopped for a traffic violation, leading to their trial (but not conviction) and international condemnation of the police brutality that Holliday had exposed. As surveillance tools such as the Internet and camera phones proliferate, there is an increasing capacity for citizens and communities to manage their own security, as well as to turn the scrutiny back on those watching them.

Alison Wakefield

Related entries

Covert policing; Cybercrimes; National security; Schengen; Security; Technology and policing; Transnational policing.

Key texts and sources

Lyon, D. (2001) *Surveillance Society: Monitoring Everyday Life*. Buckingham: Open University Press.
Surveillance Studies Network (2006) *A Report on the Surveillance Society*. Wilmslow: Information Commissioner's Office.

T

TASKING AND CO-ORDINATING GROUPS (TCGs)

Tasking and co-ordinating groups (TCGs) provide a common system for managing police and law enforcement resources. They are therefore central to intelligence-led policing and have been adopted by all police forces in the UK.

Tasking and co-ordinating groups (TCGs) are the means by which the police and law enforcement managers apply the various elements of the National Intelligence Model (NIM) to their area of responsibility. This can be at any of the three NIM levels: level 1, which is local; level 2, which is force and regional; or level 3, which is national and international.

At whatever NIM level they are held, the composition of TCGs is flexible. This enables them to cater for the unique features of the area or the specific remit of a particular agency. They are generally led by someone from the command team and consist of those who manage resources, those who have responsibility for delivering operational plans, intelligence managers and analysts. Commanders are also likely to invite representatives of those partner agencies that can contribute to the resolution of policing problems. These problems need not be exclusively crime related. Depending on the NIM level at which the TCG is operating, they may encompass anything within the wide strategic remit of the police or law enforcement agencies.

TCGs have both a strategic and a tactical purpose. The strategic purpose has four elements:

1. Considering the strategic assessment carried out under NIM to identify the problems facing the area or the agency.

2. Setting a strategy to address the problems (known as a control strategy).
3. Identifying the intelligence needed to implement the control strategy (known as the intelligence requirement).
4. Prioritizing the resources needed to implement the control strategy.

These strategic-level meetings take place every six months and are reviewed every three. The control strategy, together with the associated intelligence requirements and resource priorities, provide a high-level plan to address policing or law enforcement problems in the area. The tactical purpose of the TCG is to put this plan into operation. In order to do this at tactical level, the TCG meets every fortnight to instigate and manage the operational activity needed to achieve the aims in the control strategy. The principal mechanism for doing this is the tactical assessment, which monitors levels of crime and other relevant incidents, identifies operational opportunities and monitors operational outcomes.

TCGs are central to intelligence-led policing. They have been adopted by all police forces in the UK and so provide a common system for managing police and law enforcement resources. Furthermore, the concept of managing policing activity through a structured process such as the NIM has gathered widespread acceptance, and it is not uncommon to hear the term TCG used to describe operational management in general. In some police forces TCGs are the sole means by which operational activity is managed. Other forces still have separate TCG and performance management mechanisms, many of which are based on the Compstat model. It seems likely that future developments in the TCG process will increasingly focus on bringing these two processes together.

Peter Stelfox

Related entries

Intelligence analysis (previously crime analysis); National Intelligence Model (NIM); Neighbourhood policing.

Key texts and sources

John, T. and Maguire, M. (2004) *The National Intelligence Model: Key Lessons from Early Research. Home Office Online Report* 30/04. London: Home Office (available online at http://www. homeoffice.gov.uk/rds/pdfs04/rdsolr3004.pdf).

TECHNOLOGY AND POLICING

Technology is the application of scientific knowledge to produce a desired result.

The applications of technology to policing are evident on at least seven dimensions.

Organizational maintenance

Like most organizations in modern society, police organizations rely on technology for day-to-day maintenance. In addition to communications, discussed below, personnel records, pay systems, transport and a myriad of other routine functions are facilitated by technology.

Communications

Technology, particularly the advent of digital technology, has revolutionized communications, both within the police organization and between the police and the public it serves. The police are able to disseminate information more quickly and efficiently than ever before.

Intelligence

The police are the custodians of vast amounts of information. Digital technology, in particular, lends itself to the storage, retrieval and collation of data.

Surveillance

A range of technologies provides an unprecedented capacity to exercise surveillance over people, places and commodities. These include closed circuit television (CCTV), which may be conbined with biometric technology to identify particular individuals or anomalous patterns of movement. X-rays, magnetic resonance imagery, thermal sensors, technologies of sound and light detection, global positioning and radio-frequency identification technologies all have law enforcement applications.

Restraint

The non-lethal restraint of aggressive or suicidal individuals has been a persistent challenge to the police. A variety of technologies have been developed for use in such circumstances. Most common is oleoresin capsicum spray. Tasers are used to immobilize a target with an electrical charge. Nets can be used to envelop a target. Other technologies include fog or foam for use in confined spaces, as well as adhesives that, when sprayed at the feet of an individual, can literally stop him or her in his or her tracks. Vehicles may be immobilized by physical or electronic means.

Self-protection

Technological innovations can reduce the physical risks that arise in certain policing situations. Robots or remote-controlled devices may be useful in disarming or disposing of actual or suspected explosive devices. Body armour can reduce the risk of injury by firearms or sharp instruments. Firearms are being developed so that they may be fired only by an authorized user – a design that can prevent the police from being attacked with their own weapons.

Investigation

Arguably the most dramatic developments in technology as they affect policing may be seen in forensic science. Applications abound, from crime scene anaylsis to DNA profiling.

Notwithstanding the tremendous benefits they confer, technologies have their downside. They may be expensive to acquire and difficult to maintain. The ease of communications may cause the police to become overloaded with information and unable to meet citizens' expectations.

Technologies of restraint may detract from traditional policing skills. Capsicum spray is no substitute for good interpersonal relations. The art of observation can wither if one relies on the automated matching of images. Police vehicles confer mobility but may inhibit face-to-face interaction with members of the public.

Technology continues to advance, increasing in capacity and decreasing in cost. It will continue to assist policing along each of the dimensions identified above. Nevertheless, the police are well advised to avoid the uncritical embrace of technology. Some technologies may be excessively costly, while others may be ineffective or may produce adverse, unintended consequences. Some technologies are regarded by the public as threatening or unnecessary, and their perceived abuse may detract from police legitimacy.

Whenever feasible, open public discussions about new applications of technology to policing should precede their introduction. Ideally, the rigorous evaluation of pilot programmes and tools should take place before full implementation.

Peter Grabosky

Related entries

Covert policing; Cybercrimes; DNA profiling; Fingerprints; Forensic investigation; Home Office Large Major Enquiry System (HOLMES); Less lethal weapons; National Policing Improvement Agency (NPIA); Plural policing; Roads (policing of).

Key texts and sources

Chan, J.B.L. (2001) 'The technological game: how information technology is transforming police practice', *Criminology and Criminal Justice*, 1: 139–59.

Marx, G.T. (2005) 'Seeing hazily, but not darkly, through the lens: some recent empirical studies of surveillance technologies', *Law and Social Inquiry*, 30: 339–99.

See also the Home Office's policing web page on technology and equipment (**http://police.homeoffice. gov.uk/operational-policing/bichard-implementation/technology-equipment/?version =2**) and the Home Office's web page on science and technology (**http://www.homeoffice.gov.uk/science-research/using-science/police-science-tech/**). The Justice Technology Information Network website (**http://www.nlectc.org/**) provides links to other sites, and the Association of Chief Police Officers' website (**http://www.acpo.police. uk/policies.asp**) provides links to policies.

TERRORISM

'Terrorism' is most commonly used to describe 'revolutionary' or sub-state violence for political ends. Terrorists seek to raise – through the 'propaganda of the deed' – public consciousness of their own cause and also to provoke their state opponents into over-reaction and public alienation.

An authoritative definition of terrorism is elusive. The label is often pejoratively ascribed in order to denigrate an opponent and to bolster the legitimacy of counter-force. The effect might be summed up in the common aphorism, 'one man's terrorist is another man's freedom fighter'. In line with this political indeterminacy, there is no single agreed definition in international law, but in UK law, a definition of terrorism is set out in s. 1 of the Terrorism Act 2000. It involves serious violence against a person or endangering another's life, serious damage to property, creating a serious risk to public health or safety, or seriously interfering with, or disrupting, an electronic system. These activities should be designed to influence the government or an international governmental organization or to intimidate the public, and should be made for the purpose of advancing a political, religious or ideological cause.

In contemporary usage, 'terrorism' most commonly describes 'revolutionary' or sub-state violence for political ends. The terrorists seek, from a position of military and political weakness, to raise (through the 'propaganda of the deed') public consciousness of their own cause and also to provoke their state opponents into overreaction and public alienation. The most effective proponents of revolutionary terrorism since 1945 have been nationalist groups, such as the Irish Republican Army in Northern Ireland, but political violence has also been deployed by political radicals such as the Red Army Faction (or Baader-Meinhof Group) in Germany. More recently, al-Qaeda, which perpetrated the attacks on 11 September 2001, has been interpreted as expressive of a new postmodern cause and format of terrorism. Its campaign represents a clash of civilizations and the rejection of 'western' modernity, while it operates through loose international networks. Nevertheless, though the emphasis in politics and law is nowadays on sub-state violence, it should be realized that far more powerful and destructive in history has been state terrorism. The term 'terrorism' was first coined to describe the excesses of French revolutionaries after 1789, the terror tactics of which were practised by Hitler and Stalin on a scale that was vaster than any sub-state campaign since 1945.

The policing of terrorism is characterized by two important features. The first is that policing is based around complex and wide-ranging special legislation that emphasizes intelligence gathering and early intervention in order to combat the anticipatory risk of terrorism. Some provisions have the objective of bolstering the criminal justice system in one of three ways: by augmenting policing powers (such as allowing for detention following arrest for up to 28 days; Terrorism Act 2000, s. 41, as amended); by altering criminal justice processes (such as through the abolition of juries in the 'Diplock' courts in Northern Ireland under Part VII of the Terrorism Act 2000); and by instituting loosely worded criminal offences that catch the early stages of attacks (such as the possession of materials under the Terrorism Act 2000, s. 57, or the Terrorism Act 2006, s. 5) or the encouragement or 'glorification' of terrorism (Terrorism Act 2006, s. 1). Other special laws have even offered administrative alternatives to criminal justice. Most controversial of all was detention without trial of foreign terror suspects, which operated under Part IV of the Anti-terrorism, Crime and Security Act 2001 between 2001 and 2005. This policy ended after being condemned as discriminatory by the House of Lords in *A* v. *Secretary of State for the Home Department*. It has been replaced by the imposition through 'control orders' under the Prevention of Terrorism Act 2005 of severe conditions on liberty and private life. Many of these provisions are considered to be draconian and threatening to human rights but are, none the less, said to be justified not only because of the threat of terrorism but also to avoid the compromise of sensitive sources and techniques which might flow from the need to

put evidence into open court during a prosecution under 'normal' laws. They are therefore subject to an exceptional amount of scrutiny by Parliament (with many reports by select committees) and by an independent reviewer (currently Lord Carlile of Berriew).

There is also a growing body of special international law about terrorism that shapes, to some extent, domestic law, including offences about attacks on diplomats and civilians, the taking of hostages and the hijacking of aircraft, and wide-ranging measures against the financing of terrorism. Following 9/11, the UN established the Counter-terrorism Committee to oversee implementation. At EU level, intergovernmental co-operation is evidenced by measures on data exchange and extradition without exception for political causes.

The second feature relevant to the policing of terrorism is that the seriousness of the threat of terrorism and its specialist nature have long shaped policing organizational change in the UK. Within the Metropolitan Police, a Special Branch was formed in 1883 to respond to the then Irish bombing campaign. Now, the pressures of terrorism have sparked the reorganization of local police special branches into regional clusters, as well as the regional co- ordination of ports policing. In 2006, the Metropolitan Police formed the Counter-terrorism Command (SO15), which has merged its special branch with the more operational Anti-terrorist Branch that had been established in the 1970s in response to Irish terrorism. The new command links intelligence analysis and development with investigations and operational support activity. Corresponding counter terrorism units are being formed in some regions, building on the formation of anti-terror units in 2005. Terrorism policing also heavily engages the Security Service which, since 1992, has become the prime intelligence-gathering agency. Anti-terrorism work now consumes the bulk of its resources, and its budget and personnel have substantially increased since the 9/11 attacks. Its Joint Terrorism Analysis Centre, formed in 2003, handles threat intelligence assessment and reports upwards to ministers. The process of specialization is further reflected in the Crown

Prosecution Service which, in 2005, founded a Counter-terrorism Division.

Clive Walker

Related entries

Arrest; Dangerous offenders and dangerousness; Europol; Human rights; Interpol; National security; Organized crime; Peace support operations (the police contribution); Police powers; Special branch (SB).

Key texts and sources

Duffy, H. (2005) *The 'War on Terror' and the Framework of International Law.* Cambridge: Cambridge University Press.

HMIC (2003) *A Need to Know: HMIC's Thematic Inspection of Special Branch and Ports Policing.* London: HMIC.

Home Office (2004) *Counter Terrorism Powers* (Cm 6147). London: HMSO.

Home Office (2006) *Countering International Terrorism: The United Kingdom's Strategy* (Cm 6888). London: HMSO.

Privy Counsellor Review Committee (2003–4) *Anti-terrorism, Crime and Security Act 2001 Review: Report* (HC 100). London: HMSO.

Walker, C. (2002) *The Anti-terrorism Legislation.* Oxford: Oxford University Press.

Walker, C. (2006a) 'Clamping down on terrorism in the United Kingdom', *Journal of International Criminal Justice,* 4: 1137–51.

Walker, C. (2006b) 'Intelligence and anti-terrorism legislation in the United Kingdom', *Crime, Law and Social Change,* 44: 387–422.

Wilkinson, P. (2000) *Terrorism versus Democracy.* London: Frank Cass.

See also the following websites: UK Resilience (a Cabinet Office service) for information on emergencies arising from terrorism and for links to other sites (**http://www.ukresilience.info/emergencies/terrorism.aspx**); the Centre for the Study of Terrorism and Political Violence (**http://www.st-andrews.ac.uk/intrel/research/cstpv/**); the Home Office (including reports by Lord Carlile) (**http://www.homeoffice.gov.uk/security/**); the Metropolitan Police (**http://www.met.police.uk/so/counter_terrorism. htm**); the Security Service (MI5) (**http://www.mi5.gov.uk/output/Page545. html**); the UN Counter-terrorism Committee (**http://www.un.org/sc/ctc/**); and the US Department of State (**http://www.state.gov/s/ct/**).

TRAINING (POLICE)

From didactic, regimented training delivery methodologies and a fragmented, decentralized organization, the training of police officers in England, Wales and Northern Ireland has gone through several metamorphoses in the last 50 years.

Street riots took place in the late 1970s and early 1980s in cities in England. As a result, an eminent judge, Lord Scarman, whose report criticized the police handling of the incidents, chaired a public inquiry that concluded that improvements should be made to police training. Although further reforms to police training were made in the 1980s, the image and reputation of the British Police Service were further tarnished during the 1990s. This brought into question the effectiveness of the current approach to police training and, as a result, police training underwent various high-level scrutinies and reports: the Stubbs Report (1999b) and HM Inspector of Constabulary's and the Home Secretary's conclusions. Hitherto, police training had been centrally directed through the Police Training Council via 'Centrex' – the national police training body. Although a central police college was to be retained, along with new national occupational standards (NOSs) detailed in the integrated competency framework, generally training was to be devolved to local police forces, including the training of recruits. The National Policing Improvement Agency (NPIA) has responsibility for specialist police training; learning and development (supporting training and learning throughout the Police Service); the Leadership Academy (open leadership development programmes for police managers and international delegates); and the Examinations and Assessment Unit (recruitment, selection and assessment processes). The NPIA also identifies, develops and promotes policing best practice through the 'doctrines' it produces; it also has legal obligations to develop draft regulations and codes commissioned by the Home Secretary.

All other forms of technical police training are devolved to local police forces and their training schools, although there are some centres of excellence providing specific types of training. Under the latest training reforms, police forces have been encouraged to form partnerships with local training providers and higher education institutes to deliver training in a cost-effective and high-quality manner. All police staff are subject to continuous professional development requirements through the 'Skills for justice' NOS, which is administered through the Professional Development Review (PDR) continuous process. The NOS has a more detailed 'Integrated competency framework' that contains 12 behavioural competencies in three areas of 'Leadership', 'Working with others' and 'Achieving results'. Each competency has a title, an overall definition and two or three categories. Each category represents a different complexity, and has a definition and a number of positive behavioural indicators attached to it. Each of the 12 behaviours has a set of negative indicators.

Also, research by Skills for Justice (conducted to ascertain the main tasks, responsibilities, functions, knowledge and skills required of police employees) was then used to build 'activity libraries' – actual work carried out by the practitioners. This has been built into the PDR process to enable individuals to identify their own training and development needs.

Alan Beckley

Related entries

Civilianization; Community support officers (CSOs); Firearms (police use of); HM Inspectorate of Constabulary (HMIC); National Policing Improvement Agency (NPIA); Professionalization; Rank structure; Scarman Inquiry.

Key texts and sources

English, J. (2003) *Police Training Manual*. London: McGraw-Hill.

Neyroud, P. and Beckley, A. (2001) *Policing, Ethics and Human Rights*. Cullompton: Willan Publishing.

See also the Home Office's policing web page on training and development (**http://police.homeoffice. gov.uk/training-and-career-development/**).

TRANSNATIONAL POLICING

> Transnational policing is any form of policing that traverses or transcends the boundaries of the nation-state.

Transnational policing takes numerous forms: travelling abroad to search for fugitives; identifying nationals killed in natural disasters; sharing intelligence by fax, phone or computer; posting a permanent police 'liaison officer' in a foreign city; or attending international conferences and training events.

Globalization is transforming policing. Even local police commanders are becoming 'globally aware', recognizing that international trade in illegal drugs and guns, for example, can profoundly affect local crime. The police must also liaise with visiting foreign police officers and those resident in their cities. In many small states, the work of domestic police officers involves constant communication and co-operation with overseas counterparts. In response to the growth of international co-operation, national policing is being strengthened and expanded. The newly created Serious Organized Crime Agency (SOCA), for example, has national responsibility and a global reach. Supranationally, regional policing structures (e.g. Europol, TREVI and Schengen) and regional associations of police chiefs, training courses, conferences and exchange programmes create new opportunities for communication and co-operation among both 'street' and 'management cops'. Interpol, headquartered in Lyon, supports a global computer network facilitating the distribution of 'notices' seeking information about unidentified bodies or missing persons and requests for the arrest of wanted persons.

Police officers have travelled overseas since the origins of policing. The British colonial system is a precursor of contemporary transnational policing. Built on the model of the Royal Irish Constabulary, officers were despatched across the Empire to create constabularies, many of which retain their 'Royal' title today. During the Cold War, the British government created networks of regional special branch officers to share intelligence on 'subversives'. British police regularly travel overseas to undertake investigations or to provide assistance to other forces and to UN peacekeeping operations.

The 'patchwork quilt' of transnational policing (Sheptycki 1995) extends far beyond the traditional 'blue uniformed' police. For example, HM Customs & Excise has long had a role in policing illegal drugs: first enforcing the flow of opium from India to China in the 1800s and now attempting to control the flow of heroin and cocaine into the UK. Drug liaison officers (DLOs) were first posted overseas in the mid-1980s, with an office in Karachi expanding rapidly into a network of 113 officers across 30 countries in Europe, South America, the Caribbean, the Indian subcontinent and southeast Asia. The DLO network is now incorporated, together with HM Customs & Excise enforcement, the National Crime Squad, the National Criminal Intelligence Service and immigration enforcement, into SOCA, positioning the new agency as the UK's transnational policing capacity. As a hybrid police–intelligence agency, SOCA also has close links with territorial policing, the Security Service (MI5) and the Secret Intelligence Service (MI6).

In the eighteenth-century, federal marshals travelled from the USA to neighbouring Mexico, the Bahamas and Canada in pursuit of fugitive slaves and, in the 1920s, to enforce the prohibition of alcohol (Nadelmann 1993). US police have frequently travelled to Europe to learn about new policing techniques and to form international associations. The USA has also extensively funded police training, equipment and information communications technology since the 1970s. The Drugs Enforcement Agency has the most expansive reach, but there are numerous globally mobile US agencies, such as the Bureau of Alcohol, Tobacco and Firearms, the US Treasury Department and the Federal Bureau of Invesgtation (FBI), as well as 'big-city police' such as Miami Dade and the New York Police Department. Similarly, Australian police officers are based throughout southeast Asia and the Pacific rim, while the Royal Canadian Mounted Police has 35 liaison officers in 25 countries. There are at least 40 foreign police liaison officers based in London.

The key driver of transnational policing is the belief that domestic police forces (e.g. a UK shire constabulary) have insufficient knowledge of serious organized crime or the capacity to respond to the threat that it poses. At the same time, the 'governance of crime' is globalizing with the advent of international criminal law and the International Criminal Court. Transnational policing is facilitated by international agreements – such as the UN Conventions on Narcotic and Psychotropic Drugs (1988) and Transnational Organized Crime (2000) – which stimulate co-operation, joint operations and the use of 'special investigative techniques', such as undercover operations and 'controlled delivery'.

Legal and administrative structures have been created to facilitate bilateral and multilateral co-operation. For example, mutual legal assistance treaties underpin co-operation among law enforcement officers in the collection of evidence. While national sovereignty generally prevents police officers having coercive powers outside their geographical jurisdiction, they collect and share intelligence and can request a foreign police authority to arrest and question a suspect. The example best known in the UK was the FBI-ordered arrest of Derek Bond in South Africa in February 2003. Mr Bond was released after three weeks in custody after it transpired that he was an innocent British pensioner who had the misfortune of having his identity stolen by an American criminal wanted by the FBI.

The forces of globalization seem likely to increase the demand for transnational policing (Sheptycki 2000, 2003). However, numerous unresolved issues remain. It is unclear to whom 'globally mobile' cops should be accountable and how we should assess their effectiveness, ensure that their intelligence is accurate and reliable and that any mistakes are remedied quickly. Few 'due process' mechanisms exist to protect the rights of those accused from afar. We know little about the transnational role of the private security industry or about the links with military and secret intelligence agencies. While the goal of transnational policing is to provide public protection, new challenges emerge as intrusive and coercive powers extend beyond the boundaries of the nation-state.

Ben Bowling

Related entries

Colonial policing; Europol; Federal Bureau of Investigation (FBI); Interpol; Schengen; Serious Organized Crime Agency (SOCA); Special branch (SB).

Key texts and sources

Nadelmann, E. (1993) *Cops across Borders.* University Park, PA: Pennsylvania State University Press.

Sheptycki, J. (1995) 'Transnational policing and the makings of a postmodern state', *British Journal of Criminology*, 35: 613–35.

Sheptycki, J. (ed.) (2000) *Issues in Transnational Policing.* London: Routledge.

United Nations (2000) *United Nations Convention against Transnational Organised Crime* (available online at www.un.org).

See also the websites of the International Association of Chiefs of Police (http://www.theiacp.org/) and Interpol (http://www.interpol.int/).

U

UNIT BEAT POLICING (UBP)

Unit beat policing (UBP) was a system of geographical policing that comprised the 24-hour motorized patrolling of a specified area, within which two 'area constables' were responsible for the day-to-day policing of sub-areas, supported by a designated detective constable.

In 1967 the Home Office issued a circular, *Police Manpower, Equipment and Efficiency*, which encouraged police forces to adopt a new system of geographical policing. The system originated from a scheme devised in 1965 by Lancashire Constabulary to police the town of Kirkby. In this high-crime, under-policed town, the 11 foot beats were amalgamated into five motorized beats, each patrolled 24 hours each day by 'panda' cars. The mobile officers kept in touch with each other and with their local station through the use of personal radios. The chief constable claimed the scheme reduced crime, increased detections and was popular with his officers and the public.

The Home Office monitored the Kirkby scheme and modelled an updated version that was introduced in 1966 in Accrington. This became the template for unit beat policing (UBP) that was implemented nationally. Twelve foot beats were changed to four motorized patrol areas covered 24 hours each day by a panda car. Each motorized beat also had two area constables, each working flexible hours within a personal geographical area of responsibility (rather than walking a beat with fixed points; see Beat). Each motorized beat also had a designated detective constable, and another detective acted as a collator and disseminator of information passed on by the patrol officers. In this way UBP was intended to be policing by a team of officers who spent as much time as possible working their area.

The rationale for introducing UBP was that it was a response to the national shortage of police officers and the pressure to make the best use of existing resources. In addition, the value of traditional foot patrol was being questioned: beat officers felt undervalued, and the foot patrol system was failing to provide the policing services required by the public. The Home Office planned that the new system would overcome the shortage of police officers through increased efficiency and would improve police relations with the public through a swifter response to their calls for assistance and by officers working closer to communities. The new role, it was hoped, would also alleviate the low status and morale of beat officers.

Although the Home Office oversaw the Accrington scheme, no formal evaluation was published prior to the recommendation that UBP should be implemented nationally; in fact there existed scant evaluation research to support UBP's effectiveness (Weatheritt 1986: 45). Nevertheless, by the early 1970s, UBP had become the standard urban policing method across England and Wales. However, in 1975 a Home Office study reported inadequate implementation of UBP (Comrie and Kings 1975), and the system has since been widely discredited for introducing an overly reactive 'fire brigade' policing style (Baldwin and Kinsey 1982: 29–36; Reiner 2000: 60). Despite the initial high hopes for UBP, taking police officers off the beat and putting them in cars is regularly cited as the catalyst for the breakdown of the police–public relationship. It is somewhat ironic that UBP came to be held popularly responsible for exacerbating the perceived policing weaknesses that it was intended to alleviate and for critically damaging the traditional relationship between the beat officer and the public.

Rob C. Mawby

Related entries

Beat; Patrol.

Key texts and sources

Home Office (1967) *Police Manpower, Equipment and Efficiency: Reports of Three Working Parties.* London: HMSO.

Weatheritt, M. (1986) *Innovations in Policing.* London: Croom Helm.

V

VICTIM AND WITNESS SUPPORT

Past concerns about the indifference of the police to the well-being of victims and about the general lack of police support for witnesses are now being addressed via a range of initiatives that require the police to be more proactive in their interactions with victims and witnesses.

Much of the attention given to the interactions between the police, victims and witnesses has focused on poor police practices and negative experiences. Studies of police responses to domestic violence frequently revealed a failure to take victims concerns seriously, while victims of sexual assault often received unsympathetic treatment at the hands of male investigating officers. Victims of racist crimes often experienced similar forms of indifference or hostility with rank-and-file officers often dismissing such crimes as not worthy of investigation and being unwilling to ascribe a racial motive to an attack even if this was the victim's belief. Witnesses, too, have often failed to receive supportive treatment from the police and have largely been taken for granted by the criminal justice system more generally.

Since the early 1990s, however, there have been significant practical and policy changes aimed at improving the relationships between the police, victims and witnesses. Following Home Office recommendations, police forces have appointed domestic violence officers with a specific remit to support and reassure victims of violence between intimates. Rape examination suites and the use of female officers in dealing with victims of sexual assault have helped address concerns that rape victims often

experience a 'second victimization' during the reporting process. The racist murder of Stephen Lawrence in 1993 and the subsequent inquiry chaired by Sir William Macpherson have also acted as important catalysts in changing the way police handle victims of racist crimes. The Macpherson Report (1999) urged the police to train victim/witness liaison officers and highlighted the need for family liaison officers to provide a victim's family with information about a crime and its investigation.

Recent legislation has reinforced this growing recognition of the victim-centred duties of the police. Under the Crime and Disorder Act 1998 the police must seek the views of victims when deciding whether to issue a 'reprimand' or 'warning' to young offenders. The Youth Justice and Criminal Evidence Act 1999 has established a framework for police-facilitated restorative justice in cases involving young offenders, whereby a victim can meet with the offender as part of a process of the offender taking responsibility for his or her behaviour and making reparation to the victim. More recently, the Domestic Violence, Crime and Victims Act 2004 established the Code of Practice for Victims of Crime (replacing the Victims Charter) which identifies a range of obligations for the police, including ensuring that victims can access local support services, identifying vulnerable or intimidated victims, assigning a family liaison officer to any relatives where a victim has died and notifying victims about criminal proceedings and the bailing of suspects.

Overlapping with these victim-centred developments have been several initiatives aimed at increasing police support for witnesses within the criminal justice system. The No Witness, No Justice Programme is a partnership between the Crown Prosecution Service and the Association of Chief Police Officers that aims to deliver a new model of witness care in which the police assess the needs of a witness when he or she is first interviewed and then provide continued support and information via a witness care officer from the time a suspect is charged, through to the witness's appearance at court and the immediate post-court period.

Furthermore, growing concerns about vulnerable and intimidated witnesses (VIWs) have resulted in legislation introducing 'special measures' for VIWs in the courtroom, including screens to shield the witness from the accused and the public gallery, video-recorded evidence and live television links. Given their responsibility for initially identifying VIWs, the police have a crucial role as the main 'gatekeepers' to these special measures.

In the most serious cases of witness intimidation, where the lives of witnesses and their family may be at risk, many police forces have established specialist witness protection programmes with officers trained to manage the secure and permanent relocation of witnesses and their families away from their home area and, if necessary, to provide them with new identities. Until the Serious Organized Crime and Police Act 2005 such witness protection programmes were not governed by any specific legal framework, but now, if the police want to make use of witness protection in organized crime investigations, they must adhere to strict eligibility criteria for witnesses and their families. The availability of protection will depend on the nature of the risks witnesses face, the financial costs of protecting them, their ability to adjust to their change in circumstances (given the disruption caused by relocation) and the importance of their testimony.

For the police, the key benefits of protection programmes are that responsibility for protecting witnesses is taken away from the limited resources of an investigating team and, because witness protection officers have no connection with the cases witnesses are involved in, the police are less likely to be accused of coaching a witness by defence teams during a trial.

To what extent are these initiatives improving the relationships between the police and victims and witnesses? Research in this field is limited, but there is some encouraging evidence to show that victims and witnesses provided with police support are not only positive in their assessment of the police but are also likely to be more satisfied with their involvement in the criminal justice process more generally. Nevertheless, important challenges remain. In cases of sexual assault, for example, there are often fundamental tensions between the welfare needs of the victim who is trying to deal with a traumatic experience and the focus of the police on establishing her veracity as a complainant and identifying and apprehending the offender. Similarly, for witnesses placed on protection programmes, there may be tensions between the short-term needs of the police to ensure vital evidence can be presented in court and the ability of the police to address the longer-term welfare issues arising from the relocation of witnesses and their families.

Nick Fyfe

Related entries

Crime and Disorder Act 1998; Domestic violence; Racially motivated offending; Restorative justice/restorative cautioning; Sexual offences/sexual violence; Stephen Lawrence Inquiry.

Key texts and sources

Fyfe, N. (2001) *Protecting Intimidated Witnesses.* Aldershot: Ashgate.

Hoyle, C. and Young, R. (2003) 'Restorative justice, victims and the police', in T. Newburn (ed.) *Handbook of Policing.* Cullompton: Willan Publishing.

Office of Criminal Justice Reform (2005) *Code of Practice for Victims of Crime.* London: Office of Criminal Justice Reform.

See also the websites of Victim Support, an independent charity that helps people to cope with the effects of crime (**http://www.victimsupport. org.uk/**), and Respect, a government strategy aimed at tackling bad behaviour (**http://www. respect.gov.uk/article.aspx?id=9130**).

VIGILANTISM

> Vigilantism is the use (or threatened use) of force by private citizens with the object of exerting control over crime or social disorder.

Vigilantism is an enigmatic concept. The term is popularly used to describe acts in which citizens 'take the law into their own hands' in order to deter criminality and/or to punish criminal wrongdoing. Yet, such popular definitions are fraught with difficulty. For example, while vigilante groups commonly act against criminal infractions, the latter is by no means a necessary condition for vigilante mobilization. Thus, in the nineteenth century, the 'Bald Knobbers' of Missouri punished criminal wrongdoing but also undertook 'morally sanctimonious vigilance' (Burrows 1976: xv) against those who partook of liquor, gambling or prostitution. More recently, 'punishment squads' in Northern Ireland have acted not only against local burglars and 'joyriders' but also against members of Republican and Loyalist paramilitary organizations who failed to 'toe the line'. There is, therefore, considerable dispute among those writers who have explored the phenomenon of vigilantism as to its precise character: whether or not it is inherently violent, conservative, extra-legal, organized and directed only towards criminal acts; whether it can be undertaken by agents acting on behalf of the state (such as the police) as well as by private citizens; and whether it is a genuine social movement or a mere social reaction (see Brown 1975; Burrows 1976; Rosenbaum and Sedeberg 1976; Bowden 1978; Abrahams 1987; Culberson 1990).

Some writers caution against stretching the concept of vigilantism to accommodate everything from crime-oriented 'vigilante' groups to members of bodies such as the Ku Klux Klan (see Marx and Archer 1976). By contrast, others use the concept to describe a wide range of apparently heterogeneous behaviours, the most extreme example being Rosenbaum and Sedeberg's (1976) depiction of vigilantism as 'establishment violence' – any form of violent behaviour undertaken in defence of establishment values. However, equating vigilantism with 'establishment violence' produces a concept that encompasses everything and therefore nothing. In response to this – and with the aim of facilitating empirical study – Johnston (1996: 232) has proposed a criminological definition of vigilantism. According to that definition, vigilantism:

> is a social movement giving rise to premeditated acts of force – or threatened force – by autonomous citizens. It arises as a reaction to the transgression of institutionalized norms by individuals or groups – or to their potential or imputed transgression. Such acts are focused upon crime control and/or social control and aim to offer assurances (or 'guarantees') of security both to participants and to other members of a given established order.

By defining vigilantism as a form of voluntary (autonomous) citizenship (i.e. one lacking state support or legitimacy), Johnston both rejects the concept of 'state vigilantism' (cf. Rosenbaum and Sedeberg 1976) and draws a distinction between vigilante acts and similar acts committed by commercial security agents (cf. Sharp and Wilson 2000). For a recent attempt to explore vigilante–police relations in one locality drawing on this definition, see Williams (2005). Finally, readers may note that some of the richest analysis of vigilantism comes, not from criminologists, but from historians (Brown 1975) and from anthropologists (e.g. Abrahams 1987, 1998).

Les Johnston

Related entries

Neighbourhood Watch; Private policing.

Key texts and sources

Abrahams, R. (1998) *Vigilant Citizens: Vigilantism and the State*. Cambridge: Polity Press.
Johnston, L. (1996) 'What is vigilantism?', *British Journal of Criminology*, 36: 220–36.

VOLUME CRIME

Volume crimes are those crimes that are widely experienced and that make up a high proportion of all crime.

In practice, volume crime has generally been taken to refer to domestic and non-domestic burglary and to theft of and theft from motor vehicles. These offences yield quick returns to offenders and are generally committed when the victim or any other witnesses are out of sight. Detection rates and hence risks to offenders are low. The lowest rate of detection relates to theft from motor vehicles. Taking account of non-reports of crime, an offender will be sentenced in only 1 in 190 offences committed in England and Wales. The low risk faced by the offender in relation to volume crimes presumably partly explains why large numbers of them are committed.

For more than a quarter of a century, from 1969 to 1996, volume crimes accounted consistently for about half of all recordable offences in England and Wales. The peak was reached in 1992 when they made up 52 per cent of recorded crime. Since that time absolute numbers have fallen dramatically, as has the percentage of all crime represented by them. By 2004–5 the four types accounted collectively for only 25 per cent of all crime:

- In 1992 there were 705,934 recorded domestic burglaries, representing 12.6 per cent of all recorded crime. In 2004–5 there were 318,921 offences, representing only 5.7 per cent of recorded crime.
- In 1992 there were 646,733 recorded non-domestic burglaries, representing 11.6 per cent of all recorded crime. In 2004–5 there were 358,061 offences, representing 6.4 per cent of recorded crime.
- In 1992 there were 585,501 recorded thefts of motor vehicles, representing 10.5 per cent of all recorded crime. In 2004–5 there were 230,729 offences, representing 4.1 per cent of recorded crime.
- In 1992 there were 961,340 recorded thefts from motor vehicles, representing 17.2 per cent of all recorded crime. In 2004–5 there

were 496,681 offences, representing 8.9 per cent of recorded crime.

Similar patterns of fall are revealed for domestic burglary and theft of and theft from vehicles in victimization surveys. Equivalent information is not available for non-domestic burglary, which is not measured in regular victimization surveys.

Policy attention has tended to focus on the detection and prevention of domestic burglary as the crime type having the most direct effect on victims in terms of loss and personal impact. Vehicle crime has received some but less attention as a crime experienced by individuals, but with less harm to them than domestic burglary. Non-domestic burglary, which includes a wide range of targets including commercial premises, public buildings and buildings detached from residences, has received least policy attention. It is striking, nevertheless, that there have been marked falls in all types. Moreover, similar patterns of fall in these volume crime types have been experienced in many other industrialized countries also. It is not clear why they have taken place, but the generality of the falls casts doubt on the importance of the role played by any particular government or agency. The somewhat steeper fall in England and Wales between 1992 and 2004–5 in numbers of domestic rather than non-domestic burglaries (55 per cent v. 45 per cent), however, may in part be a function of the greater level of official attention devoted to the former compared with the latter.

Nick Tilley

Related entries

Burglary; Crime prevention (situational and social); Crime reduction; Crime scene examiners (CSEs); Criminal investigation; Forensic investigation; Geographic(al) profiling; Hotspots; Intelligence-led policing; Police performance indicators.

Key texts and sources

Tilley, N., Robinson, A. and Burrows, J. (2007) 'The investigation of high-volume crime', in T. Newburn *et al.* (eds) *Handbook of Criminal Investigation*. Cullompton: Willan Publishing.

Walker, A., Kershaw, C. and Nicholas, S. (2006) *Crime in England and Wales, 2005/6. Home Office Statistical Bulletin* 12/06. London: Home Office.

See also **www.acpo.police.uk/asp/policies/Data/ volume_crime_manual.doc** for the Association of Chief Police Officers' *Investigation of Volume Crime Manual* and the Home Office Research, Development and Statistics Directorate's web page on investigating volume crime (**http://www. homeoffice.gov.uk/rds/ivcrime1.html**).

WARRANTS

A warrant is a written authority, usually addressed to the police or to a named individual or organization, to carry out some action.

There are six types of warrant in practice:

- *Arrest*: to arrest a named individual or containing a description of an individual who should be arrested and placed before the court.
- *Commitment*: to arrest and detain a named individual and convey him or her to prison.
- *Distress*: to seize personal goods and property from a person who has defaulted on paying fines.
- *Ejectment*: to eject persons from named premises to effect possession of the premises; this type of warrant is normally addressed to bailiffs, although the police may be asked to attend to prevent a 'breach of the peace'.
- *Non-payment of fine*: a warrant to collect money from a named individual or, in default, place before the court.
- *Search*: to enter premises, search for specified property or items and seize the property which is to be used in evidence to prove/disprove a criminal offence.

Procedurally, all warrants must be in the possession of the police officer (or the person to whom they are addressed) when they are executed, except in the case of the arrest warrant. Although the application to a magistrate or judge for a warrant to carry out one of the above actions is a legally recognized method of obtaining evidence to investigate criminal offences, over the last 30 years the police have been given wide-ranging powers to investigate offences, enter, search premises and seize property without the necessity to 'swear out' a warrant. Warrants are granted once a police officer, on oath, has established to the satisfaction of the judge or magistrate that there is evidence of reasonable suspicion to justify the action. More commonly, police officers will now use self-granted statutory powers of entry, search and seizure given to them under legislation such as the Police and Criminal Evidence Act 1984 (PACE).

The two most common types of warrant that police officers will encounter during day-to-day policing activities are the arrest and the search warrant. Warrants of arrest may be issued by magistrates and the Crown court where the statute containing the suspected criminal offence and the powers of the court allows. Arrest warrants may also be granted to secure the attendance of a witness at court or where a defendant fails to appear at court after summons. When executing warrants of arrest, police officers should take great care to check that the details contained in the documents are correct and that they apply to the individual suspect. There are also a number of rules relating to the power of police officers to execute warrants forwarded from jurisdictions in other countries with different legal systems.

Search warrants are usually obtained from the court under the statute covering the suspected criminal offence. The availability and scope of this provision are contained within the wording of the statute. The police powers to search and seize under warrant are also covered by several sections of PACE and, if the provisions of the sections are not complied with, the search will be rendered unlawful.

Alan Beckley

Related entries

Arrest; Mentally disordered offenders; Police and Criminal Evidence Act 1984 (PACE); Police powers; Regulation of Investigatory Powers Act 2000 (RIPA).

Key texts and sources

Beckley, A. (2000) *Human Rights: The Guide for Police Officers and Support Staff.* Goole: The New Police Bookshop.

Hutton, G. and Johnston, D. (2001) *Blackstone's Police Manual: Evidence and Procedure.* London: Blackstone.

Sampson, F. (2000) *Blackstone's Police Manual: General Police Duties.* London: Blackstone.

YOUTH AND POLICING

> Children and young people come to the attention of the Police Service in a number of different guises: victims, witnesses, suspects and offenders. The emphasis in this entry rests on the relations between the police and young people as suspects and offenders.

Public anxieties relating to juvenile delinquency, disorder and youth crime can be traced back to pre-industrial seventeenth-century society, whereas more recognizably 'modern' concerns originated and consolidated throughout the nineteenth century. The terms 'hooligan' and 'yob' (backslang for 'boy') each emerged in the late 1800s. Both expressions were widely used to describe young members of 'street gangs' in the burgeoning urban centres and developing cities of industrial Britain. Furthermore, a report compiled by the Howard Association on juvenile offenders in 1898 addressed the common concern that young people were becoming increasingly unruly, requiring more rigorous control. Indeed, many criminologists, sociologists and social historians have observed that policing young people, far from being a distinctive characteristic of modern times, has a much longer history; it is more accurately conceived as a perennial feature of industrial society rather than a present-day aberration.

Equally, historical analyses reveal that relations between the police and identifiable groups of young people (especially working-class males) are frequently characterized by tension and strain, particularly in the public sphere. It is the city centre, the shopping precinct, the bus station, the street corner, the local park – places of particular significance for young people

'hanging around' – where police–youth relations are shaped and defined. Numerous research studies have disclosed proactive patterns of policing public space, often underpinned by suppositions that groups of young people comprise a latent criminal presence and/or a threat to social order.

It is important to locate the police–youth relation in historical context and to acknowledge its complexities, controversies and contested forms. It is equally important to note that the comparatively low age of criminal minority or criminal responsibility in UK jurisdictions effectively means that expectations of the police – with regard to 'controlling' children and young people – are greater than those found elsewhere. Indeed, UK jurisdictions hold children to be criminally responsible at conspicuously young ages: 8 in Scotland and 10 in England and Wales and Northern Ireland. Other countries prefer to delay the formal 'criminalization' of the young, and there is significant variation in the age of criminal minority (for example, 12 in Canada, the Netherlands and Turkey; 13 in France; 14 in Germany, Italy, Japan, New Zealand and Spain; 15 in Denmark, Finland, Norway and Sweden; and 18 in Belgium and Luxembourg). In other words, young people in the UK enter the orbit of the criminal justice system significantly earlier than their counterparts in most other western jurisdictions.

It follows that, once a child has reached the age of 8 or 10 in the UK, the police are vested with various statutory duties, powers and responsibilities. In England and Wales, for example, the Police and Criminal Evidence Act 1984 empowers a police officer to stop and search a child or young person for stolen or prohibited articles if the constable has 'reasonable grounds' to believe he or she will find such an article as a result of the search. The same legislation also authorizes various powers of arrest, detention, questioning/interviewing under warrant, fingerprinting, photographing and charging, whereas the Bail Act 1976 provides for the granting or withholding of bail. The most significant legislation with regard to policing young people in England and Wales, however, is the Crime and Disorder Act 1998.

The Crime and Disorder Act 1998 is an extraordinarily wide-ranging statute substantially, although not exclusively, weighted towards 'tackling' youth crime, youth disorder and 'anti-social behaviour'. It is of particular significance with regard to the police–youth relation because it shifts the prime responsibility for crime prevention from the police to a police–local authority partnership. In this sense it provides statutory expression to the recommendations contained in the report of the Morgan Committee. The Morgan Committee was established in 1990 to consider multiagency partnership approaches to 'crime prevention', and it formally reported in 1991. The Morgan Report observed that the term 'crime prevention' leant itself to narrow interpretation, implying that the police were solely responsible. The committee preferred the concept of 'community safety', arguing that it is open to wider application, thus encouraging greater participation from a number of key agencies in the 'fight against crime'. The Crime and Disorder Act 1998 applied this principle by imposing new duties on local authorities – in partnership with the police and other agencies – to reduce and ultimately prevent crime. The emphasis on 'joining up' services has since become a central feature of youth crime and disorder reduction strategies.

The provisions of the Crime and Disorder Act 1998 have served to establish new national and local structures in order to prevent youth crime, disorder and anti-social behaviour. At the national level the legislation established an executive non-departmental public body: the Youth Justice Board for England and Wales. The board principally has responsibility for advising the Home Secretary on the operation of the youth justice system, monitoring performance,

establishing standards and supporting new practice initiatives. At the local level the Act has required local authorities (principally social services and education departments) to provide and co-ordinate appropriate services to 'tackle' youth offending in their area in partnership with the police, the Probation Service and the regional health authorities. Such arrangements have been operationalized through the creation of multi-agency youth offending teams (YOTs) in all areas of England and Wales.

The infrastructure of the youth justice system in England and Wales has expanded very substantially since the implementation of the Crime and Disorder Act 1998 in April 2000. YOTs are sizeable organizations, and the logic of youth crime prevention and community safety has penetrated the breadth of locally delivered services. Furthermore, 'youth disorder' and anti-social behaviour have been systematically factored into the preventive imperative, resulting in a considerable extension of 'system reach'. Early intervention predicated upon 'risk factors' and intensive intervention directed at 'persistent young offenders' are defining features of the 'new youth justice'. This is aptly expressed in the Association of Chief Police Officers' (ACPO) strategy for children and young people: 'never too early and never too late.'

Alongside YOTs a further range of structures and initiatives has developed in order to address – directly or indirectly – youth crime, disorder and anti-social behaviour, including Connexions, education and health action zones, intensive supervision and surveillance schemes, 'On track', 'Positive activities for young people', 'Positive futures', youth inclusion programmes, youth inclusion and support panels, safer schools partnerships and 'Sure Start', together with a range of mentoring schemes and parenting interventions. The interagency partnership principle applies across the board, and the Police Service is involved – to a greater or lesser extent – with many if not all of these schemes. The interventionist interagency policing thrust of policy and practice is invariably presented in benign terms. The ACPO strategy, for example, defines the objective as 'working with partners to … enable those children and young people at greatest risk to be identified at the earliest opportunity'. Alternative interpretations adopt a more circumspect and critical perspective, however, emphasizing the counterproductive tendencies of 'labelling' and stigmatization and raising concerns about criminalization, surveillance and potential human rights violations. Indeed, the question of policing children and young people in modern times assumes broad, opaque and certainly contested forms.

Perhaps the most controversial feature of the youth–police relation applies to the question of differential or selective policing. Police services throughout the world generally claim that their primary function is to prevent crime, to bring offenders to justice and to protect the law-abiding majority in a way that treats all sections of the community equally. Historical analyses of youth and policing, however, reveal that interventions are invariably mediated through the structural relations of social class, 'race' and gender. Furthermore, research evidence provides that identifiable groups of young people (male, working-class, black and minoritized youth) disproportionately experience unfavourable and discriminatory modes of police attention and intervention.

The history of the youth–police relation comprises continuity, change, complexity and contestation. The future of policing young people will almost certainly be characterized by further challenges and tensions. The Police Foundation is currently developing a major international initiative on the policing of children and young people to complement work being undertaken by the Council of Europe. The initiative will no doubt cast light on the size and nature of such challenges and tensions.

Barry Goldson

Related entries

Anti-social behaviour; Caution; Crime and Disorder Act 1998; Restorative justice/restorative cautioning.

Key texts and sources

ACPO (2003) *ACPO Strategy for Children and Young People*. London: ACPO.
Goldson, B. and Muncie, J. (eds) (2006) *Youth Crime and Justice*. London: Sage.
Loader, I. (1996) *Youth, Policing and Democracy*. London: Macmillan.
Muncie, J. (2004) *Youth and Crime*. London: Sage.
See also the Home Office's web page on youth crime (**http://www.homeoffice.gov.uk/crime-victims/ reducing-crime/youth-crime/**) and the Home Office Research, Development and Statistics Directorate's web page on youth crime statistics (**http://www.homeoffice.gov.uk/rds/youth justice1.html**).

Z

ZERO-TOLERANCE POLICING (ZTP)

> Zero-tolerance policing (ZTP) is a style of policing associated with the assertive policing of minor crime and disorder as a means of 'taking back the streets' and preventing and reducing the level of more serious crimes.

The term 'zero-tolerance policing' (ZTP) originates from the approach to the policing of New York adopted under the leadership of Mayor Rudolph Giuliani and directed by New York Police Department (NYPD) Commissioner William Bratton in the mid-1990s. Bratton and Giuliani were committed to tackling quality-of-life and public safety issues in New York and drew on the broken windows thesis – namely, that many small problems become a large problem and that small problems can cause more serious issues. They implemented a number of initiatives that collectively were described (though not by Bratton or Giuliani) as ZTP.

New York in 1993 was perceived as a dangerous high-crime city, and Giuliani (2002: 41–3) has recounted how, on becoming Mayor, he initiated an assertive policing approach. He describes how 'squeegee men' were notorious for their aggressive attitudes towards drivers in the city; they cleaned the windscreens of cars in slow traffic and then requested money for providing this unsolicited service. Operating commonly at bridges and tunnels, they gave a poor impression to people visiting and leaving the city. Hitherto, the police had felt the squeegee operators were not committing any offence. However, Giuliani and Bratton decided to prosecute them for the offence of jaywalking. The police duly targeted these 'jay walkers', issuing them with tickets and taking the

opportunity to check the details of each squeegee operator. This tactic found that many had outstanding warrants for violent and property crimes. Where this was the case, they were immediately arrested. If they became threatening, they were arrested. As a result of this crackdown, the squeegee problem reduced significantly within one month, producing visible improvements for those living in and visiting the city.

This type of police crackdown on a relatively minor problem resulting in quick and measurable results became the popular image of ZTP, which was taken up as a media-friendly slogan and advocated by commentators in different jurisdictions as an effective and popular policing approach. However, this example simplifies and misrepresents the full extent of the range of linked initiatives adopted in New York. As Bratton, Giuliani and academic writers (e.g. Weisburd *et al.* 2003) have pointed out, the changes to policing in New York were more comprehensive. The measures put in place included the following:

- The hiring of an additional 7,000 police officers (by Giuliani's predecessor in 1991).
- The restructuring and 're-engineering' of NYPD, including decentralization that returned power and accountability to the 76 precincts.
- The development of new crime control strategies and performance indicators. Perhaps most significantly, the adoption of Compstat, a process of collecting and analysing crime data on a daily basis to identify local and inter-precinct problems and patterns of crime and disorder. These data were used both in the precincts to manage the crime issues and also at regular Compstat meetings, held at headquarters, to which precinct commanders were

summoned and held to account for managing crime in their areas.

At the time that these initiatives were implemented, New York experienced significant reductions in crime. In the short term, during 1993–4 murders and robberies fell by 17.9 and 15.5 per cent respectively; in the longer term, between 1994 and 2001 overall crime reduced by 57 per cent, murders reduced by 66 per cent and shootings by 75 per cent. In 2002, there were 580 murders, which represented the lowest annual total for 40 years.

Given the apparent success of the measures adopted in New York, politicians and police officers from other jurisdictions visited NYPD on fact-finding missions and to ascertain whether transferable lessons existed. A lively debate took place that addressed the cases for and against the adoption of ZTP-type approaches in Britain (Dennis 1997; Weatheritt 1998). It was a debate that generated strong opinions; in the Cleveland policing area, the New York approach influenced the 'confident policing' style that was adopted initially in Hartlepool and later in Middlesbrough and which appeared to achieve popular support and reduced crime levels (Dennis 1997). In contrast, opponents of the ZTP approach criticized it as a return to 'hard policing' that disproportionately targeted the disadvantaged; an approach that tackled the symptoms rather than the causes of crime and disorder; and an approach that involved an unduly confrontational approach to management and was susceptible to abuse and rule bending (Pollard cited in Dennis 1997; Innes 1999). Critics have also questioned whether ZTP

was the causal factor in the crime reduction experienced in New York, citing other influences, including a record US prison population, the end of the crack-cocaine 'epidemic' and changing socio-democratic trends (Karmen 2004).

ZTP remains controversial. It is seen by some as a tough form of community policing (Bratton cited in Dennis 1997), by others as 'an iron fist in an iron glove' (Innes 1999) and by yet others as an 'imprecise term with different meanings for different people' (Pollard cited in Dennis 1997). Although the term retains a popular currency, by 2001 only one force in England and Wales, namely Cleveland, claimed to be deploying ZTP (Hale *et al.* 2004: 301).

Rob C. Mawby

Related entries

Anti-social behaviour; Broken windows; Community policing; Compstat; Crime reduction.

Key texts and sources

Dennis, N. (ed.) (1997) *Zero Tolerance: Policing a Free Society*. London: IEA Health and Welfare Unit.

Innes, M. (1999) 'An iron fist in an iron glove? The zero tolerance policing debate', *Howard Journal*, 38: 397–410.

Karmen, A. (2004) 'Zero tolerance in New York City: hard questions for a get-tough policy', in R. Hopkins Burke (ed.) *Hard Cop, Soft Cop: Dilemmas and Debates in Contemporary Policing*. Cullompton: Willan Publishing.

Weatheritt, M. (ed.) (1998) *Zero Tolerance: What Does it Mean and is it Right for Policing in Britain?* London: Police Foundation.

Appendix I

ABBREVIATIONS

The following list includes not only abbreviations used in this Dictionary but also many others found in common use in policing-related documentation.

AA	Alcoholics Anonymous/appropriate adult
ABC	acceptable behaviour contract
ABH	actual bodily harm
abs. dis.	absolute discharge
ACMD	Advisory Council on the Misuse of Drugs
ACPO	Association of Chief Police Officers
ACR	automatic conditional release
AD	absolute discharge
adj.	adjourned
AIDS	acquired immune deficiency syndrome
ANPR	automatic number plate recognition
AOABH	assault occasioning actual bodily harm
AP	accredited programme
APA	Association of Police Authorities
AR	arrest referral
ARO	alcohol-related offending
ASB	anti-social behaviour
ASBI	anti-social behaviour injunction
ASBO	anti-social behaviour order
ATF	(Bureau of) Alcohol, Tobacco and Firearms
AUR	automatic unconditional release
AVM	automated vehicle monitoring
BA	Bail Act 1976
BASW	British Association of Social Workers
BAWP	British Association for Women in Policing
BCS	British Crime Survey

BCU	basic command unit
BIO	bail information officer
BIS	Bail Information Scheme
BME	black and minority ethnic
BPD	Boston Police Department
BSIA	British Security Industry Association
BSU	Behavioural Science Unit
BTP	British Transport Police
BVPI	best-value performance indicator
CABX	Citizens' Advice Bureaux
CAD	computer-aided despatch
CAFCASS	Children and Family Court Advisory and Support Service
CAPS	Chicago Alternative Policing Strategy
CCA	crime-centred analysis/Comparative Case Analysis (tool)
CCC	community consultative committee
CCLO	Crown court liaison officer
CCO	conjunction of criminal opportunity
CCRC	Criminal Cases Review Commission
CCT	compulsory competitive tendering
CCTV	closed circuit television
C Ct	Crown court
CCU	Censorship Compliance Unit
C & D	crime and disorder
CDA	Crime and Disorder Act 1998
CDP	crime and disorder partnership
CDRP	crime and disorder reduction partnership
CDT	community drug team
CEA	crime environment analysis
CEOP	Child Exploitation and Online Protection
CEPOL	Collège européen de Police
CHIS	covert human intelligence source
CIA	Central Intelligence Agency
CID	criminal investigation department/Core Investigative Doctrine
CIDA	Concerted Inter-agency Drugs Action (Group)
CIRG	critical incident response group
CJ	criminal justice
CJIT	criminal justice integrated team
CJB	Criminal Justice Board
CJS	criminal justice system
CJSRU	Criminal Justice System Race Unit
CO	chief officer/clerical officer/community order
C of E	Council of Europe
conc.	concurrent (sentences)
con. dis.	conditional discharge
consec.	consecutive (sentences)
COPE	Citizen Oriented Police Enforcement (Unit)

COPS	Community Oriented Policing (Office)
CP	community punishment
CPO	community punishment order
CPOSA	Chief Police Officers' Staff Association
CPRO	community punishment and rehabilitation order
CPS	Crown Prosecution Service
CPT	child protection team
CPTED	crime prevention through environmental design
C & R	control and restraint
CRARG	Co-ordinated Response and Advocacy Resource Group
CRAVED	concealable, removable, available, valuable, enjoyable, disposable
CRC	(UN) Convention on the Rights of the Child
CRE	Commission for Racial Equality
CRO	community rehabilitation order
CRP	Crime Reduction Programme
CSA	Child Support Agency
CSE	crime scene examiner
CSI	crime scene investigator
CSIS	Canadian Security Intelligence Service
CSO	community support officer/community service officer/community service order
CSU	community safety unit
CVS	Commercial Victimization Survey
DAC	design against crime
DAT	drug action team
DCR	discretionary conditional release
D & D	drunk and disorderly
DfES	Department for Education and Skills
DIP	Drug Intervention Programme
DLO	drug liaison officer
DMSU	divisional mobile support unit
DoD	Department of Defence
DofEE	Department of Education and Employment
DoH	Department of Health
DPAS	Drug Prevention Advisory Service
DPC	death in police custody
DPP	Director of Public Prosecutions
DPPO	designated public places order
DRR	drug rehabilitation requirement
DSPD	dangerous and severe personality disorder
DSS	Department of Social Security
DTI	Department of Trade and Industry
DTO	detention and training order/drug treatment order
DTTO	drug treatment and testing order
DV	domestic violence
DVLC	Driver and Vehicle Licensing Centre
DWB	driving while black

DWP	Department of Work and Pensions
EAS	electronic article surveillance
EC	European Commission/European Community
ECHR	European Convention on Human Rights
ECtHR	European Court of Human Rights
ELO	European liaison officer
EM	electronic monitoring
ENP	European Network of Policewomen
FBI	Federal Bureau of Investigation
FIU	financial investigation unit
FLO	family liaison officer
FTA	failed to appear/attend
GBH	grievous bodily harm
GCHQ	Government Communications Headquarters
GFA	Good Friday Agreement
GIS	geographical information system(s)
GPA	Gay Police Association
GPS	global positioning system
HATO	Highways Agency traffic officer
HDC	home detention curfew
HIV	human immuno-deficiency virus
HMCIC	Her Majesty's Chief Inspector of Constabulary
HMCIP	Her Majesty's Chief Inspector of Prisons
HMI	Her Majesty's inspector of constabulary
HMIC	Her Majesty's Inspectorate of Constabulary
HMIP	Her Majesty's Inspectorate of Prisons/Probation
HMP	Her Majesty's prison
HMPS	Her Majesty's Prison Service
HMYOI	Her Majesty's young offender institution
HO	Home Office
HOCR	Home Office Counting Rules for Crime
HOLMES	Home Office Large Major Enquiry System
HOPNC	Home Office Police National Computer
HORU	Home Office Research Unit
HR	human resources
HRA	Human Rights Act 1998
HREOC	Human Rights and Equal Opportunity Commission
HSE	Health and Safety Executive
HVP	high-visibility policing
IACP	International Association of Chiefs of Police
IAG	independent advisory group
ICF	Integrated Competency Framework

ICPC	International Criminal Police Commission
ICPO	International Criminal Police Office/International Criminal Police Organization
ICT	information and communication technology
ICV	independent custody visitor
ICVS	International Crime Victim Survey
IDS	immigration detention standard
ILP	intelligence-led policing
IND	Immigration and Nationality Directorate
IPCC	Independent Police Complaints Commission
IPLDP	Initial Police Learning and Development Programme
IPP	imprisonment for public protection/indefinite (sentence for) public protection
IRA	Irish Republican Army
ISSP	Intensive Supervision and Surveillance Programme
IT	industrial tribunal/information technology/intermediate treatment
IWF	Internet Watch Foundation
JCC	joint consultative committee
JDI	Jill Dando Institute
JNC	joint negotiating committee
JNCC	joint negotiating and consultative committee
JP	justice of the peace
KSI	killed and seriously injured
KPI	key performance indicator
KPT	key performance target
LAGPA	Lesbian and Gay Police Association
LAPD	Los Angeles Police Department
LCC	London County Council
LCD	Lord Chancellor's Department
LCJB	Local Criminal Justice Board
LGBT	lesbian, gay, bisexual, transgender
LPU	local policing unit
LSC	Legal Services Commission
LSP	local strategic partnership
MAPPA	multi-agency public protection arrangement
MAPPP	multi-agency public protection panel
MARAC	multi-agency risk assessment conference
MDA	Misuse of Drugs Act 1971
MDO	mentally disordered offender
MDP	Ministry of Defence Police
MDT	mandatory drug testing
MIR	major incident room
MIRSAP	Major Incident Room Standardized Administrative Procedures
MO	modus operandi
MoD	Ministry of Defence

MoDP	Ministry of Defence Police
MPD	Metropolitan Police District/Metropolitan Police Department
MPS	Metropolitan Police Service
NAAG	National Association of Attorneys General
Nacro	National Association for the Care and Resettlement of Offenders
NAFIS	National Automated Fingerprint System
NAO	National Audit Office
NBPA	National Black Police Association
NCB	national central bureau
NCIS	National Crime Intelligence Service
NCJB	National Criminal Justice Board
NCPE	National Centre for Policing Excellence
NCRS	National Crime Recording Standards
NCS	National Crime Squad
NCVO	National Council for Vocational Qualifications
NCVS	National Crime Victimization Survey
NCWP	National Centre for Women and Policing
NDIU	National Drugs Intelligence Unit
NDNAD	National DNA Database
NDPB	non-departmental public body
NEC	national executive committee
NEO	no evidence offered
NFA	no fixed abode/no further action
NG	not guilty
NGO	non-governmental organization
NHS	National Health Service
NHTCU	National Hi-tech Crime Unit
NIJ	National Institute of Justice
NIM	National Intelligence Model
NOMIS	National Offender Management Information System
NOMM	National Offender Management Model
NOMS	National Offender Management Service
NOS	national occupational standard
NPFTC	National Police Firearms Training Curriculum
NPIA	National Policing Improvement Agency
NPM	new public management
NPS	National Probation Service
NRPP	National Reassurance Policing Programme
NSPCC	National Society for the Prevention of Cruelty to Children
NSPIS	National Strategy for Police Information Systems
NTO	national training organization
NTORS	National Treatment Outcome Research Study
NUPPO	National Union of Police and Prison Officers
NVQ	National Vocational Qualification
NW	Neighbourhood Watch
NYPD	New York Police Department

OA	output area
OAG	Office of the Attorney General
OASyS	offender assessment system
OB	offending behaviour
OBP	offending behaviour programme
OBPU	Offending Behaviour Programmes Unit
OCJR	Office for Criminal Justice Reform
OCU	operational command unit
ODPM	Office of the Deputy Prime Minister
OFA	outside the force area
ONS	Office for National Statistics
OPCS	Office of Population Census and Statistics
OPSR	Office for Public Sector Reform
OSPRE	Objective Structured Performance Related Police Promotion Exam
PACE	Police and Criminal Evidence Act 1984
PAT	problem analysis triangle
PBO	policing by objectives
PCA	Police Complaints Authority
PCCC	police community consultative committee
PCCG	police community consultative group
PCOJ	perverting the course of justice
P&CSD	Police and Crime Standards Directorate
PCSO	police community support officer
PCT	primary care trust
PD	personality disorder
PDO	potentially dangerous offender
PDR	Professional Development Review
PERF	Police Executive Research Forum
PI	performance indicator
PICTU	Police International Counter Terrorism Unit
PITO	Police Information Technology Organization
PMCA	Police and Magistrates' Courts Act 1994
PNAC	Police National Assessment Centre
PNC	Police National Computer
POA	problem-oriented approach/Prison Officers' Association
POLSA	police search adviser
POP	problem-oriented policing
PPAF	Policing Performance Assessment Framework
PPOs	prolific and other priority offenders
PPP	public–private partnership
PRT	Prison Reform Trust
PSA	Police Superintendent's Association/public service agreement
PSD	Petty Sessional Division
PSDB	Police Scientific Development Branch
PSI	Policy Studies Institute
PSNI	Police Service of Northern Ireland

PSSO	Police Skills and Standards Organization
PSU	Police Standards Unit
QUEST	Querying Using Enhanced Search Techniques
RAG	research and advisory group
RCCP	Royal Commission on Criminal Procedure
RCMP	Royal Canadian Mounted Police
RCS	regional crime squad
RCT	randomized control trial
RDS	Research Development and Statistics (Directorate)
RIC	remanded in custody
RIPA	Regulation of Investigatory Powers Act 2000
RJ	restorative justice
RO	referral order/reparation order
ROB	remanded on bail
ROR	risk of reoffending
ROTL	release on temporary licence
RSPCA	Royal Society for the Prevention of Cruelty to Animals
RUC	Royal Ulster Constabulary
RV	repeat victimization
SARA	Scanning, Analysis, Response and Assessment
SB	special branch
SBC	Scottish Business Crime (survey)
SCC	Strategic Command Course
SCDEA	Scottish Crime and Drugs Enforcement Agency
Sch. 1	Schedule 1 offence/offender
SCP	situational crime prevention/signal crimes perspective
SDVC	specialized domestic violence court
SEU	Social Exclusion Unit
SFO	Serious Fraud Office
SGC	Sentencing Guidelines Council
SIA	Security Industry Authority
SJC	standing joint committee
sine die	without a fixed date
SIO	senior investigating officer
SIRC	Security Intelligence Review Committee
SIS	Schengen Information System
SLA	service-level agreement
SMT	senior management team
SO	supervision order
SOA	Sexual Offences Act 2003
SOCA	Serious Organized Crime Agency
SOCO	scene of crime officer
SOB	suppression of burglary (unit)
SOTP	Sex Offender Treatment Programme

SSD	scientific support department
SSO	suspended sentence order
SSSO	suspended sentence supervision order
STAC	spatial and temporal analysis of crime
STC	secure training centre
STO	secure training order
SVQ	Scottish Vocational Qualification
SWAT	special weapons and tactics
T(A)DA	take and drive away
TCG	tasking and co-ordinating group
TIC	taken into consideration
TOIL	time off in lieu
TPI	Targeted Policing Initiative
TR	temporary release
TRG	tactical response group
TWOC	take without owner's consent
UBP	unit beat policing
UCB	unconditional bail
UKAEAC	United Kingdom Atomic Energy Authority Constabulary
UNCRC	United Nations Convention on the Rights of the Child
USI	unlawful sexual intercourse
VAP	violence against the person
VDT	voluntary drug testing
VED	Vehicle Excise Duty
ViSOR	Violent and Sex Offender Register
VIW	vulnerable and intimidated witness
VODS	Vehicle Online Descriptive Search
VSBRM	Violence, Sexual, Burglary, Robbery, Motoring
VSS	Victim Support Services/victim statement scheme
VWP	Voluntary Women Patrol
YI	youth inclusion
YIP	Youth Inclusion Programme
YJB	Youth Justice Board
YLS	Youth Lifestyle Survey
YOI	young offender institution
YOP	youth offender panel
YOS	Youth Offending Service
YOT	youth offending team
YTC	youth treatment centre
ZTP	zero-tolerance policing

Appendix II

POLICING TIMELINE

Some major events in the history of policing.

Date	Event
597	Conversion to Christianity leads to adoption of Christian Roman tradition of writing down laws.
690	Laws of Ine results in a shift from a codified *lex* to royal *edicta*.
871–99	Alfred develops the idea of the law becoming the aggressive weapon of the new state.
1066	The Norman Conquest, important as new conceptions of kingship were introduced regarding the Crown's duty to uphold law, order and justice.
1130	Henry I ordered every man of means over the age of 12 to be enrolled in a frankpledge.
1195	Richard I commissioned certain knights to preserve the peace in unruly areas. They were responsible for upholding the law and preserving the 'King's peace', and were known as the 'Keepers of the Peace'.
1215	Magna Carta, the most significant early influence on the extensive historical process that led to the rule of constitutional law.
1252	Royal Writ reiterated the role of constables, reinstated 'hue and cry' and established local watches to patrol parishes after dark.
1285	King Edward I passed Statute of Winchester which requested two constables in every hundred to prevent defaults in towns and highways.
1327	Act required that good and lawful men be appointed to every county to guard the peace. These individuals were referred to as 'conservators of the peace'/'wardens of the peace'.

1360	Some of the roles of constables taken over by justices of the peace.
1414	Parliament of Leicester enacted various measures to improve law and order.
1663	Watchmen employed in London; constitutes the first paid law enforcement body in the country.
1682	Edinburgh Town Guard formed to police the city and enforce the curfew; it was disbanded in 1817. It gained notoriety in 1726 when its Captain Porteous became the trigger for the Porteous Riots.
1714	Term 'police' first used in the United Kingdom with the appointment of 'Commissioners of Police to Scotland'.
1748	Henry and John Fielding take over Bow Street rotation office as resident magistrates, and introduce the Bow Street 'runners'.
1775	Marylebone Watch introduces three-tier command structure.
1785	Attempt to reorganize the policing of London by William Pitt the younger; the bill failed in Parliament.
1792	Middlesex Justices Act passed. Established seven police offices with permanent magistrates for London excluding the City.
1798	The Marine Police was established, based in Wapping. This was a localized force with a limited remit. Set up to protect merchandise at the Port of London. *Police Gazette* was first published around this time as *Hue and Cry*.
1800	Glasgow Police Act passed. This allowed the formation of the City of Glasgow Police, funded by taxation of local citizens. This was quickly followed by the setting up of similar police forces in other towns.
1812	A committee examined the policing of London.
1818	A committee examined the policing of London.
1820	Special Constables Act; allowed magistrates to recruit men as special constables.
1822	The Irish Constabulary Act; created the first organized police force in the British Isles.
1822	A committee examined the policing of London.
1829	Based on the committee's findings the Home Secretary, Robert Peel, introduced the Metropolitan Police Act 1829.

29 September 1829	The Metropolitan Police was founded.
1831	Special Constables Act 1831 dealt with the establishment of the Special Constabulary.
1835	Municipal Corporations Act 1835 reformed 178 boroughs. Obliged towns outside London to set up police forces.
1836	Royal Commission on a Rural Constabulary.
1839	County Police Act 1839 passed. The Act enabled justices of the peace in England and Wales to establish police forces in their counties.
1839	First county police force created, in Wiltshire.
1839	Metropolitan Police Act abolishes last 'old police'.
1840	County Police Act 1840 passed. Provided *inter alia* for the voluntary merging of borough police forces with county constabularies and the levying of a new 'police rate'.
1842	Within the Metropolitan Police a detective force was founded.
1842	The Parish Constables Act enabled professional superintending constables.
1848	The largest single deployment of special constables in order to counter the Chartists.
1850	The Parish Constables Act.
1856	County and Borough Police Act 1856 made county and borough police forces mandatory in England and Wales and subject to central inspection. By then around 30 counties had voluntarily created police forces.
1856	HM Inspectorate of Constabulary established.
1857	The General Police Act (Scotland) 1857 required each Scottish county and burgh to establish a police force, either on its own or by uniting with a neighbouring county.
1857	Police in England and Wales began to collate statistics on crime.
1860	By this year there were over 200 separate forces in England and Wales. In Ireland the Royal Irish Constabulary was created.
1877	The Turf Fraud scandal.
1878	The Metropolitan Police's Detective Department was reorganized and renamed the Criminal Investigation Department (CID).

1883	Special Irish Branch established in response to the Fenian terrorist threat; this later became known simply as Special Branch.
1890	The Police Act recommended that forces agreed to provide mutual aid in instances of popular disturbance and granted police officers a pension. The *Police Review* was founded around this time.
1913	National Union of Police and Police Officers (NUPPO) formed.
1914	Special Constables Act 1914 conferred powers to appoint people into the role of constable.
1914–1918	World War I; the police became unionized.
1918 and 1919	The police went on strike over pay and conditions.
1919	Police Act established the Police Federation. Set national rates of pay for police officers. This was brought about by the work of the Desborough Commission.
1923	Special Constables Act conferred powers to appoint people into the role of constable.
1936	Public Order Act granted new police powers in controlling demonstrations.
1946	Police Act 1946 passed. Abolished nearly all non-county borough police forces. This left 117 police forces.
1948	Association of Chief Police Officers of England and Wales joined as a unified body.
1948	Women accepted into Police Federation.
1948	Police Staff College created.
1950	'The Blue Lamp' is released, first introducing Dixon of Dock Green to the public.
1952	Oaksey Committee Report led to the formation of the Police Superintendent's Association.
1960	Royal Commission on the Police established.
1962	The first special course for accelerated promotion.
1964	Police Act created 49 larger forces and the tripartite arrangement of police accountability.
1967	'Unit beat policing' (UBP) introduced; encouraged more car patrols and fewer foot patrols.
1969	Establishment of Police National Computer.
1972	National Reporting Centre set up.

1976	Police Act established the Police Complaints Board.
1977	Members of Scotland Yard Obscene Publications Squad jailed for corruption.
1978	Operation Countryman set up to investigate police corruption.
1981	Royal Commission on Criminal Procedure (RCCP).
1981	Byford Inquiry, set up in response to Yorkshire Ripper murders.
1981	Scarman Inquiry, set up in response to Brixton riots.
1984–1985	Miners' strike.
1984	Police and Criminal Evidence Act 1984 (PACE).
1985	Prosecution of Offences Act provided for the establishment of the Crown Prosecution Service.
1986	The Crown Prosecution Service (CPS) established.
1987	British Association for Women in Policing founded.
1987	Hungerford shootings led to the creation of armed response vehicles.
1989	Operational Policing Review published.
1992	National Criminal Intelligence Service (NCIS) set up.
1993	Sheehy Inquiry. This was established to examine the rank structure, remuneration and working conditions of the police.
1993	Audit Commission Report, *Helping with Enquiries: Tackling Crime Effectively*.
1994	Police and Magistrates' Courts Act reformulated the powers/relationship of the three partners which exercised responsibility for police affairs.
1994	Intelligence Services Act.
1996	Police Act endorsed the tripartite arrangement of police accountability.
1997	Police Act set out functions of NCIS and created the Police Information Technology Organization (PITO).
1998	Glidewell Report (review of CPS).
1998	Crime and Disorder Act introduced various orders aimed at tackling crime and disorder.
1998	National Crime Squad set up.
1999	Macpherson Inquiry set up in response to the murder of Stephen Lawrence.

1999	Patten Report presented recommendations for the future of policing in Northern Ireland.
1999	Youth Justice and Criminal Evidence Act.
2000	Regulation of Investigatory Powers Act (RIPA).
2001	Police Service of Northern Ireland (PSNI) established.
2002	Police Reform Act introduced police community support officers (PCSOs).
2003	Bichard Inquiry set up in response to the Soham murders.
2003	Sexual Offences Act (SOA).
2004	Independent Police Complaints Commission comes into operation.
2005	Serious Organized Crime and Police Act established for the first time statutory responsibilities for crime and disorder on local authorities.
2005	7 July London bombings, followed by attempted bombings on 21 July and the subsequent shooting by police of Jean Charles de Menezes at Stockwell tube station.
2006	Serious Organized Crime Agency (SOCA) became operational. Provisions of the Serious Organized Crime and Police Act 2005 came into effect.
2006	Police and Justice Act established National Policing Improvement Agency.

References

Abrahams, R. (1987) 'Sungusungu: village vigilante groups in Tanzania', *African Affairs*, 86: 179–96.

Abrahams, R. (1998) *Vigilant Citizens: Vigilantism and the State*. Cambridge: Polity Press.

ACMD (2002) *The Classification of Cannabis under the Misuse of Drugs Act 1971*. London: Home Office.

ACMD (2006) *Pathways to Problems: Hazardous Use of Tobacco, Alcohol and other Drugs by Young People in the UK and its Implications for Policy*. London: COI.

ACPO (2000) *ACPO Guide to Identifying and Combating Hate Crime*. London: ACPO.

ACPO (2003a) *ACPO Strategy for Children and Young People*. London: ACPO.

ACPO (2003b) *Family Liaison Strategy Manual* (not published outside the Police Service).

ACPO (2005a) *Guidance on the National Intelligence Model*. Wyboston: NPIA (available online at **http://www.acpo.police.uk/asp/policies/Data/nim2005.pdf**).

ACPO (2005b) *Hate Crime: Delivering a Quality Service. Good Practice and Tactical Guidance*. London: ACPO (available online at **http://www.acpo.police.uk/asp/policies/Data/Hate%20Crime.pdf**).

ACPO (2005c) *Major Incident Room Standardised Administrative Procedures (MIRSAP)* (not published outside the Police Service).

ACPO (2005d) *National Call Handling Standards*. London: ACPO.

ACPO (2006a) *Guidance on the Management of Police Information*. Wyboston: NPIA.

ACPO (2006b) *Practice Advice on Tasking and Co-ordination*. Wyboston: NPIA.

ACPO (2006c) *Joining Forces: Drugs Guidance for Police Working with Schools and Colleges*. London: ACPO in association with the Home Office and the DfES.

ACPO/Department for Transport/Home Office (2005) *Roads Policing Strategy*. London: ACPO/DfT/Home Office (available online at **http://www.acpo.police.uk/asp/policies/Data/acp_dft_ho_rp_strat_jan05.pdf**).

ACPO/FSS/Audit Commission (1996) *Using Forensic Science Effectively*. London: HMSO.

ACPO/NPIA (2005) *Practice Advice of Core Investigative Doctrine*. Bramshill: NPIA.

Ainsworth, P. (2001) *Offender Profiling and Crime Analysis*. Cullompton: Willan Publishing.

Akdeniz, Y., Taylor, N. and Walker, C. (2001) 'Regulation of Investigatory Powers Act 2000. 1. BigBrother.gov.uk: state surveillance in the age of information and rights', *Criminal Law Review*, 73–90.

Alderson, J. (1984) *Law and Disorder*. London: Hamish Hamilton.

Aldgate, A. and Richards, J. (1999) 'The thin blue line', in A. Aldgate and J. Richards (eds) *Best of British*. London: Taurus.

Aldous, C. (1997) *The Police in Occupation Japan.* London: Routledge.

Alison, L. (2005) *The Forensic Psychologist's Casebook: Psychological Profiling and Criminal Investigation.* Cullompton: Willan Publishing.

Alison, L. (in press) *The Psychology of Critical Incident Management in Policing.* Cullompton: Willan Publishing.

Alison, L., Bennell, C., Mokros, A. and Ormerod, D. (2002) 'The personality paradox in offender profiling: a theoretical review of the processes involved in deriving background characteristics from crime scene actions', *Psychology, Public Policy and Law,* 8: 115–35.

Alison, L., West, A. and Goodwill, A. (2004) 'The academic and the practitioner: pragmatists' views of offender profiling', *Psychology, Public Policy and Law,* 10: 71–101.

Allen, J., Edmonds, S., Patterson, A. and Smith, D. (2006) *Policing and the Criminal Justice System – Public Confidence and Perceptions: Findings from the 2004/05 British Crime Survey. Home Office Online Report* 07/06. London: Home Office (available online at **http://www.home office.gov.uk/rds/pdfs06/rdsolr0706.pdf**).

Allen, R.J. (1976) 'The police and substantive rulemaking: reconciling principle and expediency', *University of Pennsylvania Law Review,* November: 62–117.

Anderson, D.M. and Killingray, D. (1991) *Policing the Empire: Government, Authority and Control, 1830–1940.* Manchester: Manchester University Press.

Anderson, D.M. and Killingray, D. (1992) *Policing and Decolonisation: Politics, Nationalism and the Police, 1917–1965.* Manchester: Manchester University Press.

Anderson, M. (1989) *Policing the World: Interpol and the Politics of International Police Co-operation.* Oxford: Clarendon Press.

Armitage, R. (2000) *An Evaluation of Secured by Design Housing within West Yorkshire. Home Office Briefing Note* 7/00. London: Home Office.

Ascoli, D. (1979) *The Queen's Peace.* London: Hamish Hamilton.

Ashbaugh, D. (1999) *Quantitative-qualitative Friction Ridge Analysis.* Boca Raton, FL: CRC Press.

Ashworth, A. (1998) 'Should the police be allowed to use deceptive practices?', *Law Quarterly Review,* 114: 108.

Ashworth, A. (2002) 'Re-drawing the boundaries of entrapment', *Criminal Law Review,* 161–79.

Ashworth, A. (2004a) 'Criminal Justice Act 2003. Part 2. Criminal justice reform – principles, human rights and public protection', *Criminal Law Review,* 516–32.

Ashworth, A. (2004b) 'Social control and "anti-social behaviour": the subversion of human rights?', *Law Quarterly Review,* 120: 263–91.

Ashworth, A. and Redmayne, M. (2005) *The Criminal Process.* Oxford: Oxford University Press.

Audit Commission (1990a) *Calling All Forces: Improving Police Communications Rooms.* London: HMSO.

Audit Commission (1990b) *Effective Policing. Police Paper* 8. London: Audit Commission.

Audit Commission (1991) *Reviewing the Organisation of Provincial Police Forces. Police Paper* 9. London: HMSO.

Audit Commission (1993) *Helping with Enquiries: Tackling Crime Effectively.* London: Audit Commission.

Audit Commission (2001) *Best Foot Forward: Headquarters' Support for Police Basic Command Units.* London: HMSO.

Audit Commission (2002) *Community Safety Partnerships: Learning from Audit, Inspection and Research.* London: Audit Commission.

Audit Commission (2003a) *Local Criminal Justice Boards: Supporting Change Management.* London: Audit Commission.

Audit Commission (2003b) *Victims and Witnesses: Providing Better Support.* London: Audit Commission.

Audit Commission (2006) *Neighbourhood Crime and Anti-social Behaviour: Making Places Safer through Improved Local Working.* London: Audit Commission.

Audit Commission and Wales Audit Office (2006) *Crime Recording 2005: Improving the Quality of Crime Records in Police Authorities and Forces in England and Wales.* London: Audit Commission.

Babington, A. (1999) *A House in Bow Street: Crime and the Magistracy, London 1740–1881* (2nd edn). London: Macdonald.

Bahn, C. (1974) 'The reassurance factor in police patrol', *Criminology,* 12: 338–45.

Baker, J.H. (1990) *An Introduction to English Legal History* (3rd edn). London: Butterworths.

Baldwin, R. and Kinsey, R. (1982) *Police Powers and Politics.* London: Quartet.

Bales, K. (2005) *Understanding Global Slavery: A Reader.* Berkeley, CA: University of California Press.

Banton, M. (1964) *The Policeman in the Community.* London: Tavistock.

Bartlett, R. (2000) *England under the Norman and Angevin Kings, 1075–1225.* Oxford: Oxford University Press.

Bayley, D.H. (1976) *Forces of Order: Police Behaviour in Japan and the United States.* Berkeley, CA: University of California Press.

Bayley, D.H. (1994) *Police for the Future.* Oxford: Oxford University Press.

Bayley, D.H. and Shearing, C.D. (1996) 'The future of policing', *Law and Society Review,* 30: 585–606.

Bayley, D.H. and Shearing, C.D. (2001) *The New Structure of Policing.* Washington, DC: US Office of Justice.

Beckley, A. (2000) *Human Rights: The Guide for Police Officers and Support Staff.* Goole: New Police Bookshop.

Beetham, D. (1991) *The Legitimation of Power.* London: Macmillan.

Bennett, T. (1998) *Drugs and Crime: The Results of Research on Drug Testing and Interviewing Arrestees. Home Office Research Study* 183. London: Home Office.

Bennett, T. (2000) *Drugs and Crime: The Results of the Second Development Stage of the NEW-ADAM Programme. Home Office Research Study* 205. London: Home Office.

Bennett, T.H., Holloway, K. and Farrington, D.P. (in press) 'Does Neighbourhood Watch reduce crime? A systematic review and meta-analysis', *Journal of Experimental Criminology.*

Benyon, J. (ed.) (1984) *Scarman and After: Essays Reflecting on Lord Scarman's Report, the Riots and their Aftermath.* Oxford: Pergamon Press.

Best, D., Sidwell, C., Gossop, M., Harris, J. and Strang, J. (2001) 'Crime and expenditure among polydrug misusers seeking treatment', *British Journal of Criminology,* 41: 119–26.

Bichard, Sir M. (2004) *The Bichard Inquiry Report (June 2004)* (HC 653). London: HMSO.

Bichard, Sir M. (2005) *The Bichard Inquiry: Final Report (March 2005).* London: HMSO.

Bittner, E. (1974) 'Florence Nightingale in pursuit of Willie Sutton: a theory of the police', in H. Jacob (ed.) *The Potential for Reform in Criminal Justice.* Newbury Park, CA: Sage (reprinted in Newburn, T. (ed.) (2004) *Policing: Key Readings.* Cullompton: Willan Publishing).

Bittner, E. (1990) *Aspects of Police Work.* Boston, MA: Northeastern University Press.

Blackburn, R. (1995) *The Psychology of Criminal Conduct: Theory, Research and Practice.* Chichester: Wiley.

Blair, I. (1998) 'Where do the police fit into policing?' Speech delivered to the Association of Chief Police Officers' conference, 16 July.

Blake, L. and Coupe, R.T. (2001) 'The impact of single and two-officer patrols on catching burglars in the act', *British Journal of Criminology*, 41: 381–96.

Blok, D. and Brown, J. (2005) *The Gendered Nature of Policing among Uniformed Operational Officers in England and Wales.* Guildford: University of Surrey.

Boba, R. (2005) *Crime Analysis and Crime Mapping.* London: Sage.

Bottoms, A.E. (1977) 'Reflections on the renaissance of dangerousness', *Howard Journal of Penology and Crime Prevention*, 16: 70–96.

Bottoms, A.E. and McClean, J. (1976) *Defendants in the Criminal Process.* London: Routledge.

Bowden, T. (1978) *Beyond the Limits of the Law.* Harmondsworth: Penguin Books.

Bowers, K.J., Johnson, S.D. and Pease, K. (2004) 'Prospective hot-spotting: future of crime mapping?', *British Journal of Criminology*, 44: 641–58.

Bowling, B. (1998) *Violent Racism: Victimisation, Policing and Social Conflict.* Oxford: Clarendon Press.

Bowling, B. (1999) 'The rise and fall of New York murder', *British Journal of Criminology*, 39: 531–54.

Bowling, B. and Foster, J. (2002) 'Policing and the police', in M. Maguire *et al.* (eds) *The Oxford Handbook of Criminology* (3rd edn). Oxford: Oxford University Press.

Bowling, B. and Phillips, C. (2001) *Racism, Crime and Criminal Justice.* Harlow: Longman.

Bowling, B., Phillips, C., Campbell, A. and Docking, M. (2004) *Policing and Human Rights.* Geneva: UN Research Institute for Social Development.

Boyne, G.A., Gould-Williams, J., Law, J. and Walker, R.M. (2001) 'The impact of best value on local authority performance', *Local Government Studies*, 27: 440–68.

Braithwaite, J. (1989) *Crime, Shame and Reintegration.* Cambridge: Cambridge University Press.

Brantingham, P.J. and Brantingham, P.L. (1981) *Environmental Criminology.* Prospect Heights, IL: Waveland Press.

Brantingham, P.J. and Faust, F.L. (1976) 'A conceptual model of crime prevention', *Crime and Delinquency*, 22: 284–98.

Bratton, W. (1997) 'Crime is down in New York City: blame the police' (reprinted in T. Newburn (ed.) (2005) *Policing: Key Readings.* Cullompton: Willan Publishing).

Bresler, F. (1992) *Interpol.* London: Sinclair-Stevenson.

Brewer, J.D. (1990a) *Inside the RUC.* Oxford: Clarendon Press.

Brewer, J.D. (1990b) 'Talking about danger: the RUC and the paramilitary threat', *Sociology*, 24: 657–74.

Bridgeman, C. and Hobbs, L. (1997) *Preventing Repeat Victimisation: The Police Officers' Guide. Police Research Group Paper.* London: Home Office (available online at http://www.home office.gov.uk/rds/pdfs2/ah310.pdf).

Bridges, L. (2002) 'The right to representation and legal aid', in M. McConville and G. Wilson (eds) *The Handbook of the Criminal Justice Process.* Oxford: Oxford University Press.

Brodeur, J.-P. (1983) 'High policing and low policing: remarks about the policing of political activities', *Social Problems*, 30: 507–20.

Brogden, M.E. (1982) *The Police: Autonomy and Consent.* London and New York, NY: Academic Press.

Brogden, M.E. (1999) 'Community policing as cherry pie', in R.I. Mawby (ed.) *Policing across the World: Issues for the Twenty-first Century.* London: UCL Press.

Brogden, M.E. and Shearing, C. (1993) *Policing for a New South Africa.* London: Routledge.

Brookman, F. (2005) *Understanding Homicide.* London: Sage.

Brooks, L.W. (2001) 'Police discretionary behaviour: a study of style', in R.G. Dunham and G.P. Alpert (eds) *Critical Issues in Policing* (4th edn). Prospect Heights, IL: Waveland.

Brown, J., Di Franco, C. and O'Neill, D. (2006) *The Well Conducted Constable.* Guildford: University of Surrey.

Brown, J., Hegarty, P. and O'Neill, D. (2006) *Playing with Numbers – a Discussion Paper on Positive Discrimination as a Means for Achieving Gender Equality.* Guildford: University of Surrey.

Brown, J. and Heidensohn, F. (2000) *Gender and Policing.* Basingstoke: Palgrave Macmillan.

Brown, M. and Pratt, J. (eds) (2000) *Dangerous Offenders: Punishment and Social Order.* London: Routledge.

Brown, R.M. (1975) *Strain of Violence.* New York, NY: Oxford University Press.

Bucke, T. (1997) *Ethnicity and Contacts with the Police: Latest Findings from the British Crime Survey. Home Office Research Findings* 59. London: Home Office.

Bullock, K., Erol, R. and Tilley, N. (2006) *Problem-oriented Policing and Partnerships.* Cullompton: Willan Publishing.

Bullock, S.K. and Gunning, N. (2007) *Police Service Strength, Home Office Statistical Bulletin* 13/07. London: Home Office.

Bunyan, T. (1976) *The Political Police in Britain.* London: Friedman.

Bunyan, T. (1977) *The History and Practice of the Political Police in Britain.* London: Quartet Books.

Bureau of Justice Assistance (2005) *Intelligence-led Policing: The New Intelligence Architecture.* Washington, DC: US Department of Justice.

Burney, E. (2005) *Making People Behave: Anti-social Behaviour, Politics and Policy.* Cullompton: Willan Publishing.

Burney, E. and Rose, G. (2002) *Racist Offences – how is the Law Working? The Implementation of the Legislation on Racially Aggravated Offences in the Crime and Disorder Act 1998. Home Office Research Study* 244. London: Home Office.

Burrows, W.E. (1976) *Vigilante.* New York, NY: Harcourt Brace Jovanovich.

Butler, G. (1999) *Inquiry into Crown Prosecution Service Decision-making in Relation to Deaths in Custody and Related Matters.* London: HMSO.

Butler, J. (2001) *Forensic DNA Typing: Biology and Technology behind STR Markers.* London: Academic Press.

Butler-Sloss, E. (1988) *Report of the Inquiry into Child Abuse in Cleveland.* London: HMSO.

Butterfield, R., Edwards, C. and Woodall, J. (2004) 'The new public management and the UK Police Service', *Public Management Review*, 6: 395–415.

Button, M. (2002) *Private Policing.* Cullompton: Willan Publishing.

Buzan, B. (1991) *People, States, and Fear* (2nd edn). London: Longman.

Buzan, B., Waever, O. and de Wilde, J. (1998) *Security: A New Framework for Analysis.* Boulder, CO: Lynne Rienner.

Bynum, T.S. (2001) *Using Analysis for Problem-solving: A Guidebook for Law Enforcement.* Washington, DC: COPS/US Department of Justice.

Cain, M. (1973) *Society and the Policeman's Role.* London: Routledge & Kegan Paul.

Campbell, R. and O'Neill, M. (eds) (2006) *Sex Work Now.* Cullompton: Willan Publishing.

Canter, D. (1995) *Criminal Shadows: Inside the Mind of the Serial Killer.* London: HarperCollins.

Canter, D. and Hodge, S. (2000) 'Criminals' mental maps', in L.S. Turnball *et al.* (eds) *Atlas of Crime.* Westport, CT: Oryx Press.

Canter, D. and Larkin, P. (1993) 'The environmental range of serial rapists', *Environmental Psychology*, 13: 63–9.

Cape, E. (2002) 'Assisting and advising defendants before trial', in M. McConville and G. Wilson (eds) *The Handbook of the Criminal Justice Process*. Oxford: Oxford University Press.

Cape, E. (2004) '50th anniversary article: the rise (and fall?) of a criminal defence profession', *Criminal Law Review*, 401–16.

Cape, E. (ed.) (2005) *Current Law Statute Guide: RIPA 2000, Related SIs and Codes of Practice*. London: Sweet & Maxwell.

Carmichael, S. and Hamilton, C.V. (1968) *Black Power: The Politics of Liberation in America*. London: Jonathan Cape.

Carrier, J. (1988) *The Campaign for the Employment of Women as Police Officers*. Aldershot: Avebury.

Cashmore, E. and McLaughlin, E. (eds) (1991) *Out of Order? Policing Black People*. London: Routledge.

Cassels, Sir J. (1994) *Final Report of the Independent Inquiry into the Role and Responsibilities of the Police*. London: Police Foundation/PSI.

Chainey, S. and Ratcliffe, J. (2005) *GIS and Crime Mapping*. Chichester: Wiley.

Chan, J.B.L. (1996) 'Changing police culture', *British Journal of Criminology*, 36: 109–34.

Chan, J.B.L. (1997) *Changing Police Culture: Policing in a Multicultural Society*. Cambridge: Cambridge University Press.

Chan, J.B.L. (2001) 'The technological game: how information technology is transforming police practice', *Criminology and Criminal Justice*, 1: 139–59.

Chan, J.B.L. (2003a) *Fair Cop: Learning the Art of Policing*. Toronto: University of Toronto Press.

Chan, J.B.L. (2003b) 'Police and new technologies', in T. Newburn (ed.) *Handbook of Policing*. Cullompton: Willan Publishing.

Chapman, B. (1970) *Police State*. London: Pall Mall Press.

Chatterton, M.R. (1979) 'The supervision of patrol work under the fixed points system', in S. Holdaway (ed.) *The British Police*. London: Edward Arnold.

Choo, A. (2006) *Evidence*. Oxford: Oxford University Press.

Clancy, A., Hough, M., Aust, R. and Kershaw, C. (2001) *Crime, Policing and Justice: The Experience of Ethnic Minorities. Findings from the 2000 British Crime Survey*. London: Home Office Research, Development and Statistics Directorate.

Clark, D. (2004) *Bevan and Lidstone's 'The Investigation of Crime: A Guide to the Law of Criminal Investigation'* (3rd edn). Oxford: Oxford University Press.

Clarke, R.V. (2005) 'Seven misconceptions of situational crime prevention', in N. Tilley (ed.) *Handbook of Crime Prevention and Community Safety*. Cullompton: Willan Publishing.

Clarke, R.V. and Eck, J. (2003) *Becoming a Problem-solving Crime Analyst in 55 Steps*. London: Jill Dando Institute of Crime Science, University College London (available online at **www.jdi.ucl.ac.uk**).

Clegg, M. and Kirwan, S. (2006) *Police Service Strength, England and Wales, 31 March 2006. Home Office Statistical Bulletin* 13/06. London: Home Office (available online at **www.home office.gov.uk/rds/pdfs06/hosb1306.pdf**).

Coid, J., Carvell, A., Kittler, Z., Healey, A. and Henderson, J. (2000) *Opiates, Criminal Behaviour, and Methadone Treatment*. London: Home Office.

Cole, B. (1999) 'Post -colonial systems', in R.I. Mawby (ed.) *Policing across the World: Issues for the Twenty-first Century*. London: UCL Press.

Cole, S. (2001) *Suspect Identities: A History of Fingerprinting and Criminal Identification*. Cambridge, MA: Harvard University Press.

Coleman, C. and Moynihan, J. (1996) *Understanding Crime Data: Haunted by the Dark Figure*. Milton Keynes: Open University Press.

Collier, P.M. (2006) 'In search of performance and priorities: police PIs', *Public Money and Management*, 26: 165–72.

Comrie, M.D. and Kings, E.J. (1975) *Study of Urban Workloads. Police Research Services Unit Report* 11/75. London: Home Office.

Cooper, C., Anscombe, J., Avenell, J., McLean, F. and Morris, J. (2006) *A National Evaluation of Community Support Officers. Home Office Research Study* 297. London: Home Office.

Corbett, C. (2003) *Car Crime.* Cullompton: Willan Publishing.

Corby, B. (2006) *Child Abuse: Towards a Knowledge Base.* Maidenhead: Open University Press.

Cordner, G.W. (1989) 'The police on patrol', in D.J. Kenney (ed.) *Police and Policing: Contemporary Issues.* New York, NY: Praeger.

Corre, N. and Wolchover, D. (2004) *Bail in Criminal Proceedings.* Oxford: Oxford University Press.

Cowley, R. and Todd, P. (2006) *The History of Her Majesty's Inspectorate of Constabulary: The First 150 years, 1856 to 2006.* London: Home Office.

Cox, D. (2003) '"A certain share of low cunning" – the provincial use and activities of Bow Street "Runners", 1792–1839', *ERAS Online Journal*, 5 (available online at **www.arts.monash.edu.au/eras/edition_5/coxarticle.htm**).

Crawford, A. (1997) *The Local Governance of Crime.* Oxford: Clarendon Press.

Crawford, A. (1998) *Crime Prevention and Community Safety: Politics, Policies and Practices.* London: Longman.

Crawford, A. (2003) 'The pattern of policing in the UK: policing beyond the police', in T. Newburn (ed.) *Handbook of Policing.* Cullompton: Willan Publishing.

Crawford, A. (2006) 'Fixing broken promises? Neighbourhood wardens and social capital', *Urban Studies*, 43: 957–76.

Crawford, A. (2007) 'Crime prevention and community safety', in M. Maguire *et al.* (eds) *The Oxford Handbook of Criminology.* Oxford: Oxford University Press.

Crawford, A., Blackburn, S., Lister, S. and Shepherd, P. (2004) *Patrolling with a Purpose: An Evaluation of Police Community Support Officers in Leeds and Bradford City Centres.* Leeds: Centre for Criminal Justice Studies Press, University of Leeds.

Crawford, A., Blackburn, S. and Shepherd, P. (2005a) *Filling the Void, Connecting the Pieces: An Evaluation of Neighbourhood and Street Wardens in Leeds.* Leeds: CCJS Press.

Crawford, A. and Lister, S. (2004) *The Extended Policing Family: Visible Patrols in Residential Areas.* York: Joseph Rowntree Foundation.

Crawford, A., Lister, S., Blackburn, S. and Burnett, J. (2005b) *Plural Policing: The Mixed Economy of Visible Patrols in England and Wales.* Bristol: Policy Press.

Cray, E. (1972) *The Enemy in the Streets.* New York, NY: Anchor Books.

Critchley, T.A. (1967) *A History of Police in England and Wales, 900–1966.* London: Constable.

Critchley, T.A. (1978) *A History of the Police in England and Wales.* London: Constable.

Croall, H. (1998) *Crime and Society in Britain.* London: Pearson.

Croall, H. (2001) *Understanding White Collar Crime.* Buckingham: Open University Press.

Cromwell, P.F., Olson, J.N. and Avary, D'A.W. (1991) *Breaking and Entering.* Newbury Park, CA: Sage.

Crowther, C. (2000) 'Thinking about the "underclass": towards a political economy of policing', *Theoretical Criminology*, 4: 149–68.

Culberson, W.C. (1990) *Vigilantism: Political History and Private Power in America.* New York, NY: Greenwood Press.

Davies, S. (1989) 'Streets ahead', *Police Review*, 10 November: 2277.

Davis, G. (1997) 'Implications, consequences and futures', in G. Davis *et al.* (eds) *The New Contractualism.* Basingstoke: Macmillan.

della Porta, D., Petersen, A. and Reiter, H. (eds) (2006) *The Policing of Transnational Protest*. Aldershot: Ashgate.

della Porta, D. and Reiter, H. (eds) (1998) *Policing Protest: The Control of Mass Demonstrations in Western Democracies*. Minneapolis, MN: University of Minnesota Press.

Dennis, N. (ed.) (1997) *Zero Tolerance: Policing a Free Society*. London: IEA Health and Welfare Unit.

Dennis, N., Erdos, G. and Al-Shahi, A. (2000) *Racist Murder and Pressure Group Politics: The Macpherson Report and the Police*. London: Civitas.

Department of Health (1999) *Working Together to Safeguard Children*. London: HMSO (available online at http://www.doh.gov.uk/quality5.htm).

Department of Health (2000) *Assessing Children in Need and their Families: Practice Guidance*. London: HMSO.

DfES (2004) *Drugs: Guidance for Schools*. London: DfES.

Dick, G. and Metcalfe, B. (2001) 'Managerial factors and organizational commitment: a comparative study of police officers and civilian staff', *International Journal of Public Sector Management*, 14: 111–28.

Di Nicola, A. (2005) 'Trafficking in human beings and smuggling of migrants', in P. Reichel (ed.) *Handbook of Transnational Crime and Justice*. Thousand Oaks, CA: Sage.

Ditchfield, J.A. (1976) *Police Cautioning in England and Wales*. London: HMSO.

Ditton, J. and Farrall, S. (eds) (2001) *The Fear of Crime. International Library of Criminology, Criminal Justice and Penology*. Aldershot: Dartmouth.

Ditton, J. and Innes, M. (2005) 'The role of perceptual intervention in the management of crime fear', in N. Tilley (ed.) *Handbook of Crime Prevention and Community Safety*. Cullompton: Willan Publishing.

Dixon, W. and Smith, G. (1998) 'Laying down the law: the police, the courts and legal accountability', *International Journal of the Sociology of Law*, 26: 419–35.

Docking, M. and Tuffin, R. (2005) *Racist Incidents: Progress since the Lawrence Inquiry. Home Office Online Report* 42/05. London: Home Office.

Dodd, T., Nicholas, S., Povey, D. and Walker, A. (2004) *Crime in England and Wales, 2003/2004. Home Office Statistical Bulletin* 10/04. London: Home Office.

Doherty, R. (2004) *The Thin Green Line: A History of the Royal Irish Constabulary GC, 1922–2001*. Barnsley: Pen & Sword.

Doig, A. (2006) *Fraud*. Cullompton: Willan Publishing.

Donald, I. and Wilson, A. (2000) 'Ram raiding: criminals working in groups', in D. Canter and L. Alison (eds) *The Social Psychology of Crime: Groups, Teams and Networks*. Dartmouth: Ashgate.

Donnelly, D. and Scott, K.B. (2002) 'Police accountability in Scotland. 1. The "new" tripartite system. 2. "New" accountabilities', *Police Journal*, 75: 1–12, 56–66.

Donnelly, D. and Scott, K.B. (eds) (2005) *Policing Scotland*. Cullompton: Willan Publishing.

Downes, D. (1977) 'The drug addict as a folk devil', in P. Rock (ed.) *Drugs and Politics*. New Brunswick, NJ: Transaction.

Duchaine, N. (1979) *The Literature of Police Corruption. Vol. II. A Selected, Annotated Bibliography*. New York, NY: John Jay Press.

Duffy, H. (2005) *The 'War on Terror' and the Framework of International Law*. Cambridge: Cambridge University Press.

Eck, J. and Spelman, W. (1987) *Problem Solving: Problem-oriented Policing in Newport News*. Washington, DC: Police Executive Research Forum.

Edmunds, M., Hough, M., Turnbull, P.J. and May, T. (1999) *Doing Justice to Treatment: Referring Offenders to Drug Services. Drug Prevention Advisory Service Paper* 2. London: Home Office.

Edmunds, M., May, T., Hough, M. and Hearnden, I. (1998) *Arrest Referral: Emerging Lessons from Research. Drugs Prevention Initiative Paper* 23. London: Home Office.

Edwards, A. and Stenson, K. (2004) 'Policy transfer in local crime control', in T. Newburn and R. Sparks (eds) *Criminal Justice and Political Cultures*. Cullompton: Willan Publishing.

Ekblom, P., Law, H. and Sutton, M. (1996) *Safer Cities and Domestic Burglary. Home Office Research Study* 164. London: HMSO.

Elliott, M. and Broughton, J. (2004) *How Methods and Levels of Policing Affect Road Casualty Rates. TRL Project Report* PR SE/924/04. London: Transport for London.

Emsley, C. (1991) *The English Police*. Harlow: Addison Wesley Longman.

Emsley, C. (1996) *The English Police: A Political and Social History* (2nd edn). London: Longman.

Emsley, C. (2005) *Crime and Society in England, 1750–1900* (3rd edn). Harlow: Longman.

English, J. (2003) *Police Training Manual*. London: McGraw-Hill.

English, J. and Card, R. (2005) *Police Law* (9th edn). Oxford: Oxford University Press.

Ericson, R. (1993) *Making Crime: A Study of Detective Work* (2nd edn). Toronto: Toronto University Press.

Ericson, R. and Haggerty, K. (1997) *Policing the Risk Society*. Oxford: Clarendon Press.

Evans, R. (1993a) *The Conduct of Police Interview with Juveniles. RCCJ Research Study* 8. London: Home Office.

Evans, R. (1993b) 'Evaluating young adult diversion schemes in the Metropolitan Police District', *Criminal Law Review*.

Evans, R. and Ellis, R. (1997) *Police Cautioning in the 1990s. Home Office RDS Research Findings* 52. London: Home Office.

Evans, R. and Wilkinson, C. (1990) 'Variations in police cautioning policy and practice in England and Wales', *Howard Law Journal*, 29: 155–76.

Ferraro, K. (2006) *Neither Angels nor Demons*. Boston, MA: Northeastern University Press.

Fido, M. and Skinner, K. (1999) *The Official Encyclopaedia of Scotland Yard*. London: Virgin.

Field, S. and Pelser, C. (1998) *Invading the Private: State Accountability and New Investigative Methods in Europe*. Aldershot: Ashgate.

Fielding, N.G. (1988) *Joining Forces: Police Training, Socialization, and Occupational Competence*. London: Routledge.

Fielding, N.G. (1990) *The Police and Social Conflict: Rhetoric and Reality*. London: Athlone.

Fijnaut, C. and Marx, G. (1995) *Undercover: Police Surveillance in Comparative Perspective*. The Hague: Kluwer.

Finch, E. (2003) 'What a tangled web we weave: identity theft and the Internet', in Y. Jewkes (ed.) *dot.cons: Crime, Deviance and Identity on the Internet*. Cullompton: Willan Publishing.

Finch, E. (2006) 'Stolen identity and the Internet', in Y. Jewkes (ed.) *Crime Online*. Cullompton: Willan Publishing.

Findlay, M. and Zvekic, U. (eds) (1993) *Alternative Policing Styles: Cross-cultural Perspectives*. Boston, MA: Kluwer.

Finney, A. (2006) *Domestic Violence, Sexual Assault and Stalking: Findings from the 2004/5 British Crime Survey. Home Office Online Report* 12/06. London: Home Office.

Fisher, A. (2001) *Critical Thinking: An Introduction*. Cambridge: Cambridge University Press.

Fisher, B. (2002) *Techniques of Crime Scene Investigation* (6th edn). Boca Raton, FL: CRC Press.

Fitzgerald, P. (1888/1972) *Chronicle of Bow Street Police Office: With an Account of the Magistrates, 'Runners' and Police*. London: Chapman & Hall (reprinted Montclair, NJ: Patterson Smith).

Flanagan, Sir R. (2007) *The Review of Policing: Interim Report*. London: Home Office.

Flint, J. (ed.) (2006) *Housing, Urban Governance, and Anti-social Behaviour*. Bristol: Policy Press.

Follett, M. (2006) 'Crime reduction', in E. McLaughlin and J. Muncie (eds) *The Sage Dictionary of Criminology*. London: Sage.

Fosdick, R.B. (1969) *European Police Systems* (2nd edn). Montelair, NJ: Patterson Smith.

Foster, J., Newburn, T. and Souhami, A. (2005) *Assessing the Impact of the Stephen Lawrence Inquiry. Home Office Research Study* 294. London: Home Office.

Fraser, J.G. (2000) 'Not science. Not support: forensic solutions to investigative problems', *Science and Justice*, 40: 127–30.

Freeman, M. (2002) *Human Rights*. Cambridge: Polity Press.

French, M.T., McGeary, K.A., Chitwood, D.D., McCoy, C.B., Inciardi, J.A. and McBride, D. (2000) 'Chronic drug use and crime', *Substance Abuse*, 21: 95–107.

Fyfe, J.J. (1982) Administrative intervention on police shooting discretion: an empirical examination', in J.J. Fyfe (ed.) *Readings on Police Use of Deadly Force*. Washington, DC: Police Foundation.

Fyfe, N. (2001) *Protecting Intimidated Witnesses*. Aldershot: Ashgate.

Gains, A., Nordstrom, M., Heydecker, B. and Shrewsbury, J. (2005) *The National Safety Camera Programme: Four Year Evaluation Report*. London: Department of Transport.

Garside, R. (2004) *Crime, Persistent Offenders and the Justice Gap. Discussion Paper* 1. London: Crime and Society Foundation.

Gash, N. (1985) *Mr Secretary Peel: The Life of Sir Robert Peel to 1830*. London: Longman.

Gash, N. (1986) *Sir Robert Peel: The Life of Sir Robert Peel after 1830*. London: Longman.

Gaventa (2005) *Policing Road Risk: Enforcement, Technologies and Road Safety*. London: Parliamentary Advisory Council for Transport Safety.

Gearty, C. (2007) *Civil Liberties*. Oxford: Oxford University Press.

Gerth, H.H. and Wright Mills, C. (eds) (1948) *From Max Weber: Essays in Sociology*. London: Routledge & Kegan Paul.

Gibson, A. and Villiers, P. (2006) *Leading for those we Serve – The Police Leadership Qualities Framework*. Bramshill: Centrex Leadership Academy for Policing.

Gibson, B. (2007a) *The New Ministry of Justice: An Introduction*. Winchester: Waterside Press.

Gibson, B. (2007b) *The New Home Office: An Introduction*. Winchester: Waterside Press.

Gill, M.L. and Mawby, R.I. (1990) *A Special Constable: A Study of the Police Reserve*. Aldershot: Ashgate.

Gill, P. (2000) *Rounding up the Usual Suspects?* Aldershot: Ashgate.

Gilling, D. (2005) 'Partnership and crime prevention', in N. Tilley (ed.) *Handbook of Crime Prevention and Community Safety*. Cullompton: Willan Publishing.

Giuliani, R. (2002) *Leadership*. London: Time Warner.

Glass, D. (2005) 'Lethal weapons', *Police Review*.

Gleeson, E. and Bucke, T. (2006) *Police Complaints: Statistics for England and Wales, 2004/05*. London: IPCC.

Godfrey, B. and Lawrence, P. (2005) *Crime and Justice, 1750–1950*. Cullompton: Willan Publishing.

Godfrey, J. (2006) *None of the Above: Lessons Learned from the Police Force Structure Debate*. Lewis: Sussex Police Authority.

Goldblatt, P. and Lewis, C. (eds) (1998) *Reducing Offending: An Assessment of Research Evidence on Ways of Dealing with Offending Behaviour. Home Office Research Study* 187. London: HMSO.

Goldsmith, A. (1991) *Complaints against the Police: The Trend to External Review*. Oxford: Clarendon Press.

Goldsmith, A. and Lewis, C. (eds) (2000) *Civilian Oversight of Policing: Governance, Democracy and Human Rights*. Portland, OR: Hart Publishing.

Goldson, B. and Muncie, J. (eds) (2006) *Youth Crime and Justice*. London: Sage.

Goldstein, H. (1990) *Problem-oriented Policing*. London: McGraw-Hill.

Goldstein, J. (1960) 'Police discretion not to invoke the criminal process: low visibility decisions in the administration of justice', *Yale Law Journal*, 69: 543–94.

Gossop, M., Marsden, J. and Stewart, D. (1998) *NTORS at One Year. The National Treatment Outcome Research Study. Changes in Substance Use, Health and Criminal Behaviour at One Year after Intake*. London: Department of Health.

Greene, J. (2000) 'Community policing in America: changing the nature, structure and function of the police', in J. Horney (ed.) *Criminal Justice 2000: Policies, Processes, and Decisions of the Criminal Justice System*. Washington, DC: US Department of Justice.

Grieve, J., Crego, J. and Griffiths, W. (2007) 'Critical incidents', in T. Newburn, T. Williamson and A. Wright (eds) *Handbook of Criminal Investigation*. Cullompton: Willan Publishing.

Gunn, J. (1982) 'Defining the terms', in J.R. Hamilton and H. Freeman (eds) *Dangerousness: Psychiatric Assessment and Management*. London: Gaskell.

Halachmi, A. (ed.) (2000) 'Symposium on value for money, best value and measuring government performance', *International Review of Administrative Sciences*, 66: 393–526.

Hale, C. (1996) 'Fear of crime: a review of the literature', *International Review of Victimology*, 4: 79–150.

Hale, C., Heaton, R. and Uglow, S. (2004) 'Uniform styles: aspects of police centralization in England and Wales', *Policing and Society*, 14: 291–312.

Hall, N. (2005) *Hate Crime*. Cullompton: Willan Publishing.

Hall, S., Critcher, C., Jefferson, T., Clarke, J. and Roberts, B. (1978) *Policing the Crisis: Mugging, the State and Law and Order*. London: Macmillan.

Hallsworth, S. (2005) *Street Crime*. Cullompton: Willan Publishing.

Hamilton-Smith, N. (2004) *The Reducing Burglary Initiative: Design, Development and Delivery*. *Home Office Research Study* 287. London: Home Office (available online at **www.home office.gov.uk/rds/pdfs05/hors287.pdf**).

Harfield, C. (2006) 'SOCA: a paradigm shift in British policing', *British Journal of Criminology*, 46: 743–71 (available online at **http://bjc.oxfordjournals.org/cgi/rapidpdf/az1009v1**).

Harfield, C. and Harfield, K. (2005) *Covert Investigation*. Oxford: Oxford University Press.

Harris, J. and Grace, S. (1999) *A Question of Evidence: Investigating and Prosecuting Rape in the 1990s. Home Office Research Study* 196. London: Home Office.

Hauber, A., Hofstra, B., Toornvliet, L. and Zandbergen, A. (1996) 'Some new forms of functional social control in the Netherlands and their effects', *British Journal of Criminology*, 36: 199–219.

Hebenton, B. and Thomas, T. (1995) *Policing Europe: Co-operation, Conflict and Control*. London: Macmillan.

Heidensohn, F. (1992) *Women in Control? The Role of Women in Law Enforcement*. Basingstoke: Palgrave Macmillan.

Hillyard, P. and Tombs, S. (2004) 'Beyond criminology?', in P. Hillyard *et al.* (eds) *Beyond Criminology: Taking Harm Seriously*. London: Pluto Press.

Hine, J. and Celnick, A. (2001) *A One Year Reconviction Study of Final Warnings*. Sheffield: University of Sheffield.

Hirschfield, A. (2005) 'Analysis for intervention', in N. Tilley (ed.) *Handbook of Crime Prevention and Community Safety*. Cullompton: Willan Publishing.

Hirschfield, A. and Bowers, K. (eds) (2001) *Mapping and Analysing Crime Data: Lessons from Research and Practice*. London: Taylor & Francis.

HMIC (1998) *Road Policing and Traffic: HMIC Thematic Inspection Report.* London: Home Office.

HMIC (1999a) *Keeping the Peace: Policing Disorder.* London: HMSO.

HMIC (1999b) *Managing Learning.* London: HMIC.

HMIC (2000a) *On the Record: Thematic Inspection Report on Police Crime Recording, the Police National Computer and Phoenix Intelligence System Data Quality.* London: HMIC.

HMIC (2000b) *Policing London – Winning Consent: A Review of Murder Investigations and Community Race Relations Issues in the Metropolitan Police.* London: HMSO.

HMIC (2000c) *Under the Microscope.* London: Home Office.

HMIC (2001) *Open All Hours: A Thematic Inspection Report on the Role of Police Visibility and Accessibility in Public Reassurance.* London: HMIC.

HMIC (2002a) *Getting Down to Basics: Emerging Findings from BCU Inspections in 2001.* London: HMIC.

HMIC (2002b) *Training Matters.* London: HMIC.

HMIC (2003a) *A Need to Know: HMIC's Thematic Inspection of Special Branch and Ports Policing.* London: HMIC.

HMIC (2003b) *Diversity Matters.* London: Home Office.

HMIC (2004) *Modernising the Police Service: A Thematic Inspection of Workforce Modernisation.* London: Home Office.

HMIC (2005a) *Annual Report, 2004–2005.* London: HMSO.

HMIC (2005b) *Closing the Gap.* London: HMIC.

Hobbs, D. (1988) *Doing the Business: Entrepreneurship, Detectives and the Working Class in the East End of London.* Oxford: Oxford University Press.

Hobbs, D., Hadfield, P., Lister, S. and Winlow, S. (2003) *Bouncers.* Oxford: Clarendon Press.

Hobsbawn, E. (2000) *Bandits.* London: Weidenfeld & Nicholson.

Holdaway, S. (1979) *The British Police.* London: Edward Arnold.

Holdaway, S. (1983) *Inside the British Police.* Oxford: Blackwell.

Holdaway, S. (1999) 'Understanding the police investigation of the murder of Stephen Lawrence: a mundane sociological analysis', *Sociological Research Online,* 4(1).

Holdaway, S. (2003) 'The final warning: appearance and reality', *Criminal Justice,* 3: 351–67.

Holdaway, S. and O'Neill, M. (2004) 'The development of black police associations in the UK', *British Journal of Criminology,* 44: 854–65.

Holdaway, S. and O'Neill, M. (2005) 'Institutional racism after Macpherson: an analysis of police views', *Policing and Society,* 16: 349–69.

Home Affairs Committee (1995) *Organized Crime: Third Report* (HC Session 1994–95, 18-I). London: HMSO.

Home Affairs Committee (1997) *Police Disciplinary and Complaints Procedures (First Report).* London: HMSO.

Home Affairs Committee (2002) *The Government's Drugs Policy: Is it Working?* London: HMSO.

Home Office (1967) *Police Manpower, Equipment and Efficiency: Reports of Three Working Parties.* London: HMSO.

Home Office (1983) *Manpower, Effectiveness and Efficiency in the Police Service* (Circular 114/83). London: Home Office.

Home Office (1991) *Safer Communities: The Local Delivery of Crime Prevention through the Partnership Approach* (the Morgan Report). London: Home Office.

Home Office (1992) *Principles for Investigative Interviewing (Circular 22/92).* London: Home Office.

Home Office (1995) *Core and Ancillary Tasks Review.* London: Home Office.

Home Office (2000) *Setting the Boundaries.* London: HMSO.

Home Office (2001a) *Criminal Justice: The Way Ahead* (Cm 5074). London: HMSO.

Home Office (2001b) *Policing for a New Century: A Blueprint for Reform* (Cm 5326). London: HMSO.

Home Office (2002a) *Chief Officer Recruitment* (Circular 60/02). London: Home Office.

Home Office (2002b) *Protecting the Public.* London: HMSO.

Home Office (2002c) *National Policing Plan, 2003–6.* London: Home Office.

Home Office (2003) *Tackling Distraction Burglary: A National Distraction Burglary Taskforce Report.* London: Home Office.

Home Office (2004a) *Building Communities, Beating Crime: A Better Police Service for the 21st Century* (Cm 6360). London: HMSO (available online at **http://police.homeoffice.gov.uk/police-reform/white-paper.html/**).

Home Office (2004b) *Counter Terrorism Powers* (Cm 6147). London: HMSO.

Home Office (2004c) *Deaths During or Following Police Contact: Statistics for England and Wales, April 2003 to March 2004.* London: HMSO.

Home Office (2004d) *Guidelines for Special Branch Work in the UK.* London: HMSO.

Home Office (2004e) *Managing Police Performance: A Practical Guide to Performance Management.* London: HMSO.

Home Office (2004f) *One Step Ahead: A 21st Century Strategy to Defeat Organized Crime* (Cm 6167). London: HMSO.

Home Office (2004g) *Review of the Selection and Appointments Process of Independent Member of Police Authorities.* London: Home Office.

Home Office (2005a) *Code of Practice on the Management of Police Information.* London: Home Office.

Home Office (2005b) *Code of Practice on the National Intelligence Model.* London: Home Office.

Home Office (2005c) *Use of Dispersal Powers* (available online at **http://www.together.gov.uk/article.asp?c=185&aid=3463**).

Home Office (2006a) *Countering International Terrorism: The United Kingdom's Strategy* (Cm 6888). London: HMSO.

Home Office (2006b) *Crime and Disorder Act Review* (available online at **http:www.crime reduction.gov.uk/partnerships60**).

Home Office (2006c) *Improving Call Handling – Good Practice Guide.* London: Home Office.

Home Office (2006d) *Rebalancing the Criminal Justice System.* London: Home Office.

Home Office (2006e) *Respect and Dispersal Powers.* London: Home Office.

Home Office (2006f) *Statistics on Race and the Criminal Justice System, 2005.* London: Home Office.

Home Office (2006g) *The Code of Practice for Victims of Crime: A Guide for Victims.* London: Office for Criminal Justice Reform.

Home Office Drug Strategy Unit (2002) *Updated Drug Strategy.* London: Home Office.

Homel, R. (2005) 'Developmental crime prevention', in N. Tilley (ed.) *Handbook of Crime Prevention and Community Safety.* Cullompton: Willan Publishing.

Hood, C. (1991) 'A public management for all seasons', *Public Administration*, 69: 3–19.

Hope, T. (1995) 'Community crime prevention', in M. Tonry and D. Farrington (eds) *Building a Safer Society. Crime and Justice: A Review of Research. Volume 19.* Chicago, IL: University of Chicago Press.

Hope, T. (2001) *Perspectives on Crime Reduction.* Aldershot: Ashgate.

Horton, C. (1989) 'Good practice and evaluating policing', in R. Morgan and D. Smith (eds) *Coming to Terms with Policing: Perspectives on Policy.* London: Routledge.

Hough, M. (2007) 'Policing London, twenty years on', in A. Henry and D. Smith (eds) *Transformations in Policing.* Aldershot: Ashgate.

Hough, M. and Maxfield, M. (2007) *Surveying Crime in the Twenty-first Century.* Cullompton: Willan Publishing.

Hough, M. and Mayhew, P. (1983) *The British Crime Survey: First Report*. London: HMSO.

Hough, M., McSweeney, T. and Turnbull, P. (2001) *Drugs and Crime: What Are the Links? Evidence to the Home Affairs Committee of Inquiry into Drug Policy*. London: DrugScope.

Hough, M. and Tilley, N. (1998) *Getting the Grease to the Squeak: Research Lessons for Crime Prevention. Crime Prevention and Detection Series* 85. London: Home Office (available online at **http://www.homeoffice.gov.uk/rds/pdfs05/cdps85.pdf**).

House of Commons Transport Committee (2007) *Roads Policing and Technology: Getting the Right Balance: Government Response to the Committee's Tenth Report of Session 2005–06* (HC 290). London: HMSO.

Hoyle, C. and Young, R. (2003) 'Restorative justice, victims and the police', in T. Newburn (ed.) *Handbook of Policing*. Cullompton: Willan Publishing.

Hucklesby, A. (1994) 'The use and abuse of conditional bail', *Howard Journal*, 33: 258–70.

Hucklesby, A. (1996) 'Bail or jail? The practical operation of the Bail Act 1976', *Journal of Law and Society*, 23: 213–33.

Hucklesby, A. (1997a) 'Court culture: an explanation of variations in the use of bail by magistrates' courts', *Howard Journal*, 36: 129–45.

Hucklesby, A. (1997b) 'Remand decision makers', *Criminal Law Review*, April: 269–81.

Hucklesby, A. (2001) 'Police bail and the use of conditions', *Criminal Justice*, 1: 441–64.

Hucklesby, A. (2002) 'Bail in criminal cases', in M. McConville and G. Wilson (eds) *The Handbook of the Criminal Justice Process*. Oxford: Oxford University Press.

Hucklesby, A., Eastwood, C., Seddon, T. and Spriggs, A. (2005) *The Restriction on Bail Pilots: Lessons for the First Six Months' Implementation*. London: Home Office.

Hucklesby, A. and Marshall, E. (2000) 'Tackling offending on bail: the impact of Section 26 of the Criminal Justice and Public Order Act', *Howard Journal*, 39: 150–70.

Hughes, G. (1998) *Understanding Crime Prevention: Social Control, Risk and Late Modernity*. Buckingham: Open University Press.

Hughes, G. (2004) 'Crime prevention, community safety and crime and disorder reduction', in J. Muncie and D. Wilson (eds) *Student Handbook of Criminal Justice and Criminology*. London: Cavendish.

Hughes, G. (2006) *The Politics of Crime and Community*. Basingstoke: Palgrave.

Hughes, O. (2003) *Public Management and Administration* (3rd edn). Basingstoke: Macmillan.

Hutton, G. and Johnston, D. (2001) *Blackstone's Police Manual: Evidence and Procedure*. London: Blackstone.

IACP (2006) *Protecting Civil Rights: A Leadership Guide for State, Local, and Tribal Law Enforcement* (available online at **http://iacp.org/documents/index.cfm?document_id=862&document_type_id=2&fuseaction=document**).

Iganski, P. (ed.) (2002) *The Hate Debate: Should Hate be Punished as a Crime?* London: Profile Books.

Inciardi, J.A. and Pottieger, A.E. (1994) 'Crack-cocaine use and street crime', *Journal of Drug Issues*, 24: 273–92.

Independent Commission on Policing in Northern Ireland (1999) *A New Beginning: Policing in Northern Ireland. The Report of the Independent Commission on Policing in Northern Ireland* (the Patten Report). Belfast: Independent Commission on Policing in Northern Ireland.

Independent Inquiry into the Misuse of Drugs Act 1971 (2000) *Drugs and the Law*. London: Police Foundation.

Innes, M. (1999) 'An iron fist in an iron glove? The zero tolerance policing debate', *Howard Journal*, 38: 397–410.

Innes, M. (2003) *Understanding Social Control: Deviance, Crime and Social Order.* Maidenhead: Open University Press.

Innes, M. (2004a) 'Reinventing tradition? Reassurance, neighbourhood security and policing', *Criminal Justice*, 4: 151–71.

Innes, M. (2004b) 'Signal crimes and signal disorders: notes on deviance as communicative action', *British Journal of Sociology*, 55: 335–55.

Innes, M. (2006) 'The public face of policing', *Criminal Justice Matters*, 63: 14–15.

Innes, M., Fielding, N. and Langan, S. (2002) *Signal Crimes and Control Signals: Towards an Evidence-based Framework for Reassurance Policing.* Guildford: University of Surrey.

Innes, M., Hayden, S., Lowe, T., MacKenzie, H., Roberts, C. and Twyman, L. (2004) *Signal Crimes and Reassurance Policing.* Guildford: University of Surrey.

Innes, M.R. (2003) *Investigating Murder: Detective Work and the Police Response to Criminal Homicide.* Oxford: Oxford University Press.

Innes, M.R. (2005) 'Why "soft" policing is hard: on the curious development of reassurance policing, how it became neighbourhood policing and what this signifies about the politics of police reform', *Journal of Community and Applied Social Psychology*, 15: 156–69.

IPCC (2005) *Annual Report, 2004/05.* London: IPCC.

Jacobs, J.B. and Potter, K. (1998) *Hate Crimes: Criminal Law and Identity Politics.* New York, NY: Oxford University Press.

Jansson, K. (2006) *Black and Minority Ethnic Groups' Experiences and Perceptions of Crime, Racially Motivated Crime and the Police: Findings from the 2004/05 British Crime Survey.* London: Home Office Research, Development and Statistics Directorate.

Jason-Lloyd, L. (2005) *An Introduction to Policing and Police Powers* (2nd edn). London: Cavendish Publishing.

Jason-Lloyd, L. (2006) 'Community support officers – an increasing grey area', *Justice of the Peace*, 170: 466.

Jefferson, T. (1987) 'Beyond paramilitarism', *British Journal of Criminology*, 27: 47–53.

Jefferson, T. (1990) *The Case against Paramilitary Policing.* Milton Keynes: Open University Press.

Jefferson, T. (1993) 'Pondering paramilitarism', *British Journal of Criminology*, 33: 374–81.

Jefferson, T. and Grimshaw, R. (1984) *Controlling the Constable.* London: Frederick Muller and the Cobden Trust.

Jeffries, C. (1952) *The Colonial Police.* London: Max Parrish.

Jenkins, R. (1996) *Social Identity.* London: Routledge.

Jewell, H.M. (1972) *English Local Administration in the Middle Ages.* Newton Abbot: David & Charles.

Jewkes, Y. (2003) 'Policing cybercrime', in T. Newburn (ed.) *Handbook of Policing.* Cullompton: Willan Publishing.

Jewkes, Y. and Andrews, C. (2005) 'Policing the filth: the problems of investigating online child pornography in England and Wales', *Policing and Society*, 15: 42–62.

Jewkes, Y. and Andrews, C. (2007) 'Internet child pornography: international responses', in Y. Jewkes (ed.) *Crime Online.* Cullompton: Willan Publishing.

John, T. and Maguire, M. (2004) *The National Intelligence Model: Key Lessons from Early Research. Home Office Online Report* 30/04. London: Home Office (available online at **http://www.homeoffice.gov.uk/rds/pdfs04/rdsolr3004.pdf**).

John, T. and Maguire, M. (2007) 'Criminal intelligence and the National Intelligence Model', in T. Newburn *et al.* (eds) *Handbook of Criminal Investigation.* Cullompton: Willan Publishing.

Johnson, S.D. and Bowers, K. (2004) 'The burglary as a clue to the future: the beginnings of prospective hot-spotting', *European Journal of Criminology*, 1: 237–55.

Johnson, S.D., Bowers, K. and Pease, K. (2005) 'Predicting the future or summarising the past? Crime mapping as anticipation', in M. Smith and N. Tilley (eds) *Launching Crime Science*. Cullompton: Willan Publishing.

Johnston, L. (1992) *The Rebirth of Private Policing*. London: Routledge.

Johnston, L. (1996) 'What is vigilantism?', *British Journal of Criminology*, 36: 220–36.

Johnston, L. (2000) *Policing Britain: Risk, Security and Governance*. London: Longman.

Johnston, L. (2005) 'From "community" to "neighbourhood" policing: police community support officers and the "police extended family" in London', *Journal of Community and Applied Social Psychology*, 15: 241–54.

Johnston, L. (2006) 'Diversifying police recruitment? The deployment of police community support officers in London', *Howard Journal*, 45: 388–402.

Johnston, L. and Shearing, C. (2003) *Governing Security: Explorations in Policing and Justice*. London: Routledge.

Johnstone, G. (2003) *A Restorative Justice Reader: Texts, Sources, Context*. Cullompton: Willan Publishing.

Johnstone, G. and Van Ness, D. (2007) *Handbook of Restorative Justice*. Cullompton: Willan Publishing.

Joint Parliamentary Committee on Human Rights (2004) *Deaths in Custody: Third Report. House of Lords Paper* 15, *House of Commons Paper* 137. London: HMSO.

Jones, T. (2003) 'The governance and accountability of policing', in T. Newburn (ed.) *Handbook of Policing*. Cullompton: Willan Publishing.

Jones, T. and Newburn, T. (1997) *Policing after the Act: Police Governance after the Police and Magistrates' Courts Act 1994*. London: Policy Studies Institute.

Jones, T. and Newburn, T. (1998) *Private Security and Public Policing*. Oxford: Clarendon Press.

Jones, T. and Newburn, T. (1999) 'Urban change and policing: mass private property reconsidered', *European Journal on Criminal Policy and Research*, 7: 225–44.

Jones, T. and Newburn, T. (2002) 'The transformation of policing', *British Journal of Criminology*, 42: 129–46.

Jones, T. and Newburn, T. (eds) (2006) *Plural Policing: A Comparative Perspective*. London: Routledge.

Jones, T. and Newburn, T. (2007) *Policy Transfer and Criminal Justice: Exploring US Influence over British Crime Control Policy*. Milton Keynes: Open University Press.

Jones, T., Newburn, T. and Smith, D.J. (1994) *Democracy and Policing*. London: Policy Studies Institute.

Judge, A. (1968) *The First Fifty Years: The Story of the Police Federation*. London: Police Federation.

Judge, A. and Reynolds, G. (1968) *The Night the Police Went on Strike*. London: Weidenfeld & Nicholson.

Justice (1998) *Under Surveillance: Covert Policing and Human Rights Standards*. London: Justice.

Kappeler, V.E., Sluder, R.D. and Alpert, G.P. (1994) *Forces of Deviance: Understanding the Dark Side of Policing*. Prospect Heights, IL: Waveland.

Karmen, A. (2004) 'Zero tolerance in New York City: hard questions for a get-tough policy', in R. Hopkins Burke (ed.) *Hard Cop, Soft Cop: Dilemmas and Debates in Contemporary Policing*. Cullompton: Willan Publishing.

Keith, M. (1988) 'Squaring circles? Consultation and "inner city" policing', *New Community*, 15: 63–77.

Keith, M. (1993) *Race, Riots and Policing: Lore and Disorder in a Multiracist Society*. London: UCL Press.

Kelling, G. (2005) 'Community crime prevention: activating formal and informal social control', in N. Tilley (ed.) *Handbook of Crime Prevention and Community Safety*. Cullompton: Willan Publishing.

Kelling, G. and Coles, C. (1996) *Fixing Broken Windows*. New York, NY: Free Press.

Kelly, L. (1988) *Surviving Sexual Violence*. Cambridge: Polity Press.

Kelly, L., Lovett, J. and Regan, L. (2005) *A Gap or a Chasm? Attrition in Reported Rape Cases*. London: Home Office.

Kempa, M., Stenning, P. and Wood, J. (2005) 'Policing communal spaces: a reconfiguration of the "mass private property" hypothesis', *British Journal of Criminology*, 44: 562–81.

Kempadoo, K. (ed.) (2005) *Trafficking and Prostitution Reconsidered: New Perspectives on Migration, Sex Work, and Human Rights*. Boulder, CO: Paradigm Publishers.

Kinchen, D. (1996) 'Out of time', *Police Review*, 1 November: 24–5.

Kind, S. (1987) 'Navigational ideas and the Yorkshire Ripper investigation', *Journal of Navigation*, 40: 385–93.

Kleinig, J. (1996) *The Ethics of Policing*. Cambridge: Cambridge University Press.

Knuttson, J. (ed.) (2003) *Problem-oriented Policing: From Innovation to Mainstream. Crime Prevention Studies* 15. Cullompton: Willan Publishing.

Kraska, P.B. (ed.) (2001) *Militarising the American Criminal Justice System: The Changing Roles of the Armed Forces and the Police*. New York, NY: NYU Press.

Kyle, D. and Koslowski, R. (2001) *Global Human Smuggling – Comparative Perspectives*. Baltimore, MD: Johns Hopkins University Press.

Lacey, N. (2002) 'Legal constructions of crime', in M. Maguire *et al.* (eds) *The Oxford Handbook of Criminology* (3rd edn). Oxford: Oxford University Press.

Laming, Lord (2003) *The Victoria Climbié Inquiry. Report of an Inquiry by Lord Laming*. London: Health and Home Department.

Lamm Weisel, D. (2005) *Analyzing Repeat Victimization: Problem-oriented Guide for Police. Problem-solving Tools Series* 4. Washington, DC: COPS/US Department of Justice (available online at **http://www.popcenter.org/Tools/PDFs/RepeatVictimization.pdf**).

Lan, Z. and Rosenbloom, D.H. (1992) 'Public administration in transition?', *Public Administration Review*, 52: 535–7.

Lawrence, R.G. (2000) *The Politics of Force: Media and the Construction of Police Brutality*. Berkeley, CA: University of California Press.

Laycock, G. (2001) 'Hypothesis-based research: the repeat victimisation story', *Criminal Justice: The International Journal of Policy and Practice*, 1: 59–82.

Laycock, G. and Farrell, G. (2003) 'Repeat victimization: lessons for implementing problem-oriented policing', in J. Knutsson (ed.) *Problem-oriented Policing: From Innovation to Mainstream. Crime Prevention Studies* 15. Monsey, NY: Criminal Justice Press.

Laycock, G. and Tarling, R. (1985) 'Police force cautioning: policy and practice', *Howard Journal*, 24: 81–92.

Lea, J.A. and Young, J. (1984) *What is to be Done about Law and Order?* Harmondsworth: Penguin Books.

Lee, J.A. (1981) 'Some structural aspects of police deviance in relation to minority groups', in C. Shearing (ed.) *Organisational Police Deviance*. Toronto: Butterworths.

Lee, M. and Punch, M. (2006) *Policing by Degrees*. Groningen: de Dondsrug Press.

Lees, S. (2002) *Carnal Knowledge: Rape on Trial*. London: Women's Press.

Leigh, A., Johnson, G. and Ingram, A. (1998) *Deaths in Police Custody: Learning the Lessons.* London: HMSO.

Leinen, S. (1984) *Black Police: White Society.* New York, NY: New York University Press.

Leipnik, M.R. and Albert, D.A. (eds) (2002) *GIS in Law Enforcement: Implementation Issues and Case Studies.* London: Taylor & Francis.

Leishman, F. (1999) 'Policing in Japan: east Asian archetype?', in R.I. Mawby (ed.) *Policing across the World: Issues for the Twenty-first Century.* London: UCL Press.

Leishman, F., Loveday, B. and Savage, S. (2000) *Core Issues in Policing* (2nd edn). Harlow: Pearson Education.

Leishman, F. and Mason, P. (2003) *Policing and the Media.* Cullompton: Willan Publishing.

Levi, M. (2003) 'Organised and financial crime', in T. Newburn (ed.) *Handbook of Policing.* Cullompton: Willan Publishing.

Lewis, N. (2005) 'Expanding surveillance: connecting biometric information systems to international police cooperation', in E. Zureik and M.B. Salter (eds) *Global Surveillance and Policing: Borders, Security, Identity.* Cullompton: Willan Publishing.

Liberty (2003) *Deaths in Custody – Reform and Redress.* London: Liberty.

Littlechild, B. and Fearns, D. (eds) (2005) *Mental Disorder and Criminal Justice: Policy, Provision and Practice.* Lyme Regis: Russell House Publishing.

Loader, I. (1996) *Youth, Policing and Democracy.* London: Macmillan.

Loader, I. (2000) 'Plural policing and democratic governance', *Social and Legal Studies*, 9: 323–45.

Loader, I. (2006) 'Policing, recognition and belonging', *Annals of the American Academy of Political and Social Science*, 605: 201–21.

Loader, I. and Mulcahy, A. (2003) *Policing and the Condition of England: Memory, Politics and Culture.* Oxford: Oxford University Press.

Loader, I. and Walker, N. (2001) 'Policing as a public good: reconstituting the connections between policing and state', *Theoretical Criminology*, 5: 9–35.

Loveday, B. (1994) 'The Police and Magistrates' Courts Act', *Policing*, 10: 221–33.

Loveday, B. (1995) 'Reforming the police: from local service to state police?', *Political Quarterly*, 66: 141–56.

Loveday, B. (2006a) 'Workforce modernisation: implications for the Police Service in England and Wales: evaluating HMIC Thematic Modernising of the Police Service', *Police Journal*, 79: 105–24.

Loveday, B. (2006b) *Size Isn't Everything: Restructuring Policing in England and Wales.* London: Policy Exchange.

Loveday, B. and Reid, A. (2003) *Going Local: Who should Run Britain's Police?* London: Policy Exchange.

Lustgarten, L. (1986) *The Governance of Police.* London: Sweet & Maxwell.

Lustgarten, L. and Leigh, I. (1994) *In from the Cold: National Security and Parliamentary Democracy.* Oxford: Oxford University Press.

Lyman, M. and Potter, G.W. (2004) *Organized Crime* (3rd edn). Upper Saddle River, NJ: Pearson.

Lyon, D. (2001) *Surveillance Society: Monitoring Everyday Life.* Buckingham: Open University Press.

MacGregor, S. (2000) 'The drugs–crime nexus', *Drugs: Education, Prevention and Policy*, 7: 311–16.

Macpherson, Sir W. (1999) *The Stephen Lawrence Enquiry: Report of an Enquiry by Sir William Macpherson of Cluny* (Cm 4262-I). London: HMSO.

Maguire, M. (2003) 'Criminal investigation and crime control', in T. Newburn (ed.) *Handbook of Policing.* Cullompton: Willan Publishing.

Maguire, M. and Corbett, C. (1991) *A Study of the Police Complaints System.* London: HMSO.

Maguire, M. and Norris, C. (1992) *The Conduct and Supervision of Criminal Investigations. Royal Commission on Criminal Justice Research Study* 5. London: HMSO.

Mann, S., Nolan, J. and Wellman, B. (2003) 'Sousveillance: inventing and using wearable computing devices for data collection in surveillance environments', *Surveillance and Society*, 1: 331–55.

Manning, P.K. (1977) *Police Work.* Cambridge, MA: MIT Press.

Manning, P.K. (1988) *Symbolic Communication: Signifying Calls and the Police Response.* Cambridge, MA: MIT Press.

Manning, P.K. and Van Maanen, J. (eds) (1978) *Policing: A View from the Street.* New York, NY: Random House.

Mars, G. (1982) *Cheats at Work: An Anthropology of Workplace Crime.* London: George Allen & Unwin.

Marshall, G. (1965) *Police and Government.* London: Methuen.

Marshall, G. (1987) 'Police accountability revisited', reprinted in T. Newburn (ed.) (2004) *Policing: Key Readings.* Cullompton: Willan Publishing.

Martin, S. (2000) 'Implementing best value: local public services in transition', *Public Administration*, 781: 232–45.

Martin, S., Davis, H., Bovaird, T., Downe, J., Geddes, M., Hartley, J., Lewis, M., Sanderson, I. and Sapwell, P. (2001) *Improving Local Public Services: Evaluation of the Best Value Pilot Programme.* Warwick: Warwick Business School.

Marx, G.T. (1988) *Undercover – Police Surveillance in America.* Berkeley, CA: University of California Press.

Marx, G.T. (2005) 'Seeing hazily, but not darkly, through the lens: some recent empirical studies of surveillance technologies', *Law and Social Inquiry*, 30: 339–99.

Marx, G.T. and Archer, D. (1976) 'The urban vigilante', *Psychology Today*, January: 45–50.

Mason, G. (2004) *The Official History of the Metropolitan Police.* London: Carlton.

Mason, P. and Leishman, F. (2003) *Policing and the Media.* Cullompton: Willan Publishing.

Mawby, R.C. (2002) *Policing Images: Policing, Communication and Legitimacy.* Cullompton: Willan Publishing.

Mawby, R.C. and Wright, A. (2003) 'The police organisation', in T. Newburn (ed.) *Handbook of Policing.* Cullompton: Willan Publishing.

Mawby, R.I. (1990) *Comparative Policing Issues: The British and American Experience in International Perspective.* London: Routledge.

Mawby, R.I. (ed.) (1999) *Policing across the World: Issues for the Twenty-first Century.* London: UCL Press.

Mawby, R.I. (2001) *Burglary.* Cullompton: Willan Publishing.

Mawby, R.I. (2003) 'Models of policing', in T. Newburn (ed.) *Handbook of Policing.* Cullompton: Willan Publishing.

Mawby, R.I. and Jones, C. (2006) 'Evaluation of a national burglary reduction initiative targeting older people', *Crime Prevention and Community Safety: An International Journal*, 8: 1–19.

May, T., Duffy, M., Warburton, H. and Hough, M. (2007) *Policing Cannabis as a Class C Drug: An Arresting Change?* York: Joseph Rowntree Foundation.

May, T., Warburton, H., Turnbull, P.J. and Hough, M. (2002) *Times They Are A-changing: Policing of Cannabis.* York: Joseph Rowntree Foundation.

McAlinden, A. (2001) 'Indeterminate sentences for the severely personality disordered', *Criminal Law Review*, 108–23.

McCartney, C. (2006) *Forensic Identification and Criminal Justice.* Cullompton: Willan Publishing.

McConville, M., Hodgson, J., Bridges, L. and Pavlovic, A. (1994) *Standing Accused: The Organisation and Practice of Criminal Defence Lawyers in Britain.* Oxford: Clarendon Press.

McConville, M., Sanders, A. and Leng, R. (1991) *The Case for the Prosecution.* London: Routledge.

McInnes, C. (1959/1992) *Absolute Beginners.* London: Allison & Busby.

McLagan, G. (2003) *Bent Coppers: The Inside Story of Scotland Yard's Battle against Police Corruption.* London: Weidenfeld & Nicholson.

McLaughlin, E. (2005a) 'Forcing the issue: new localism and the democratic renewal of police accountability', *Howard Journal of Criminal Justice,* 44: 473–89.

McLaughlin, E. (2005b) 'From reel to ideal: *The Blue Lamp* and the popular construction of the English "bobby"', *Crime, Media, Culture,* 1: 11–30.

McLaughlin, E. and Muncie, J. (1993) 'The silent revolution: market-based criminal justice in England', *Socio-legal Bulletin.*

McLaughlin, E., Muncie, J. and Hughes, G. (2001) 'The permanent revolution: New Labour, new public management and the modernisation of criminal justice', *Criminal Justice,* 1: 301–18.

McLaughlin, E. and Murji, K. (1998) 'Resistance through representation: "storylines", advertising and Police Federation campaigns', *Policing and Society,* 8: 367–99.

McLaughlin, K., Osborne, S. and Ferlie, E. (eds) (2002) *New Public Management: Current Trends and Future Prospects.* London: Routledge.

McLeod, E. (1982) *Women Working: Prostitution Now.* London: Croom Helm.

McPhail, C., Schweingruber, D. and McCarthy, J. (1998) 'Policing protest in the United States: 1960–1995', in D. della Porta and H. Reiter (eds) *Policing Protest: The Control of Mass Demonstrations in Western Democracies.* Minneapolis, MN: University of Minnesota Press.

McSweeney, T. and Hough, M. (2005) 'Drugs and alcohol', in N. Tilley (ed.) *Handbook of Crime Prevention and Community Safety.* Cullompton: Willan Publishing.

Metropolitan Police Authority (2005) *Automatic Number Plate Recognition Activity – Update Report* (available online at **http://www.mpa.gov.uk/committees/cop/2005/051202/05.htm?qs= 1&qu=automatic+number+plate+recognition&nh=&mc=3&sc=1&s=1&ar=&po=&fo= &lv=&dt=0&so=2&pg=3&hl=1**).

Miller, J. and MVA (2000) *Profiling Populations Available for Stops and Searches.* London: Policing and Reducing Crime Unit, Research, Development and Statistics Directorate, Home Office.

Miller, J., Quinton, P. and Bland, N. (2000) *Police Stops and Searches: Lessons from a Programme of Research. Briefing Note.* London: Home Office Research Development and Statistics Directorate.

Milne, R. and Bull, R. (1999) *Investigative Interviewing: Psychology and Practice.* Chichester: Wiley.

Milne, S. (1995) *The Enemy Within: The Secret War against the Miners.* London: Pan Books.

Ministry of Defence (2004) *Military Contribution to Peace Support Operations. Joint Warfare Publication* 3-50 (2nd edn). London: Ministry of Defence.

Mirrlees-Black, C. and Budd, T. (1997) *Policing and the Public: Findings from the 1996 British Crime Survey.* London: Home Office.

Miyazawa, S. (1992) *Policing in Japan: A Study on Making Crime.* New York, NY: State University of New York Press.

Moore, M.H. (1980) 'The police and weapon offences', *Annals of the American Academy of Political and Social Science,* 452: 22–32.

Moore, M.H. (2003) 'Sizing up Compstat: an important administrative innovation in policing', *Criminology and Public Policy,* 2: 469–94 (reprinted in Newburn, T. (ed.) (2005) *Policing: Key Readings.* Cullompton: Willan Publishing).

Morgan, H.B. (2004) *The Processing of Fingerprint Evidence after the Introduction of the National Automated Fingerprint Identification System (NAFIS). Online Report* 23/04. London: Home Office.

Morgan, J., McCulloch, L. and Burrows, L. (1995) *Central Specialist Squads: A Framework for Monitoring and Evaluation.* London: Home Office.

Morgan, R. (1989) 'Police accountability: current developments and future prospects', in M. Weatheritt (ed.) *Police Research: Some Future Prospects.* Aldershot: Avebury.

Mulcahy, A. (2006) *Policing Northern Ireland: Conflict, Legitimacy and Reform.* Cullompton: Willan Publishing.

Muncie, J. (2002) 'The construction and deconstruction of crime', in J. Muncie and E. McLaughlin (eds) *The Problem of Crime* (2nd edn). London: Sage.

Muncie, J. (2004) *Youth and Crime.* London: Sage.

Munday, R. (2005) *Evidence* (3rd edn). Oxford: Oxford University Press.

Murray, C. (1990) *The Emerging British Underclass.* London: Institute for Economic Affairs.

Nadelmann, E. (1993) *Cops across Borders.* University Park, PA: Pennsylvania State University Press.

National Audit Office (2004) *Facing Justice: Tackling Defendants' Non-attendance at Court.* London: National Audit Office.

National DNA Database Board (2006) *The National DNA Database Annual Report, 2004–2005.* London: HMSO.

Newburn, T. (1999) *Understanding and Preventing Police Corruption: Lessons from the Literature.* London: Home Office.

Newburn, T. (2002) 'Community safety and policing: some implications of the Crime and Disorder Act 1998', in G. Hughes *et al.* (eds) *Crime Prevention and Community Safety: New Directions.* London: Sage.

Newburn, T. (ed.) (2003a) *Handbook of Policing.* Cullompton: Willan Publishing.

Newburn, T. (2003b) 'Policing since 1945', in T. Newburn (ed.) *Handbook of Policing.* Cullompton: Willan Publishing.

Newburn, T. and Jones, T. (2002) *Consultation by Crime and Disorder Partnerships. Police Research Series Paper* 148. London: Home Office.

Newburn, T., Williamson, T. and Wright, A. (eds) (2007) *Handbook of Criminal Investigation.* Cullompton: Willan Publishing.

Neyroud, P.W. (2003) 'Policing and ethics', in T. Newburn (ed.) *Handbook of Policing.* Cullompton: Willan Publishing.

Neyroud, P.W. and Beckley, A. (2001a) *Policing, Ethics and Human Rights.* Cullompton: Willan Publishing.

Neyroud, P.W. and Beckley, A. (2001b) 'Regulating informers: the Regulation of Investigatory Powers Act, covert policing and human rights', in R. Billingsley *et al.* (eds) *Informers.* Cullompton: Willan Publishing.

Neyroud, P.W. and Disley, E. (forthcoming) 'Technology and policing: implications for fairness and legitimacy', *Policing: An International Journal,* 1.

Nickell, J. and Fischer, J.F. (1999) *Crime Science: Methods of Forensic Detection.* Lexington, KY: University Press of Kentucky.

Nutley, S. and Loveday, B. (2005) 'Criminal justice: tensions and challenges', *Public Money and Management,* 25: 263–314.

O'Connell Davidson, J. (1999) *Prostitution, Power and Freedom.* Cambridge: Polity Press.

Office of Criminal Justice Reform (2005) *Code of Practice for Victims of Crime.* London: Office of Criminal Justice Reform.

Office of the Deputy Prime Minister (2004) *Neighbourhood Wardens Scheme Evaluation.* London: ODPM.

Oliver, I. (1997) *Police, Government and Accountability* (2nd edn). London: Macmillan.

O'Malley, P. (1997) 'Politics and postmodernity', *Social and Legal Studies: An International Journal,* 6: 363–81 (reprinted in Newburn, T. (ed.) (2004) *Policing: Key Readings.* Cullompton: Willan Publishing).

O'Reilly, G.W. (1994) 'England limits the right to silence and moves towards an inquisitorial system of justice', *Journal of Criminal Law and Criminology,* 85: 402–52.

Ormerod, D. and Roberts, A. (2002) 'The trouble with Teixeira: developing a principled approach to entrapment', *International Journal of Evidence and Proof,* 6: 38.

Ormerod, D. and Roberts, A. (2003) 'The Police Reform Act 2003: increasing centralisation and contracting out crime control', *Criminal Law Review,* 141–64.

Osborne, D. and Gaebler, T. (1992) *Reinventing Government: How the Entrepreneurial Spirit is Transforming the Public Sector.* Reading, MA: Addison Wesley.

Osbourne, D. and Wernicke, S. (2003) *Introduction to Crime Analysis: Basic Resources for Criminal Justice Practice.* New York, NY: Haworth Press.

Ousby, I. (1976) *Bloodhounds of Heaven.* Cambridge, MA: Harvard University Press.

Paley, R. (1989) '"An imperfect, inadequate and wretched system?" Policing London before Peel', *Criminal Justice History,* 10: 95–130.

Parker, H. and Bottomley, T. (1996) *Crack Cocaine and Drug-crime Careers. Home Office Research Findings* 34. London: Home Office.

Pascoe, T. and Topping, P. (1997) 'Secured by design: assessing the basis of the scheme', *International Journal of Risk, Security and Crime Prevention,* 2: 161–73.

Pease, K. (1998) *Repeat Victimisation: Taking Stock. Crime Prevention and Detection Series* 90. London: Home Office (available online at **www.homeoffice.gov.uk/rds/prgpdfs/ cdp90bf.pdf**).

Peay, J. (2007) 'Mentally disordered offenders, mental health and crime', in M. Maguire *et al.* (eds) *The Oxford Handbook of Criminology* (4th edn). Oxford: Oxford University Press.

Pepper, I.K. (2005) *Crime Scene Investigation: Methods and Procedures.* Maidenhead: Open University Press.

Perry, B. (2001) *In the Name of Hate: Understanding Hate Crimes.* New York, NY: Routledge.

Phillips, C. (2002) 'From voluntary to statutory status', in G. Hughes *et al.* (eds) *Crime Prevention and Community Safety: New Directions.* London: Sage.

Phillips, C. and Bowling, B. (2007) 'Ethnicities, racism, crime, and criminal justice', in M. Maguire *et al.* (eds) *The Oxford Handbook of Criminology* (4th edn). Oxford: Oxford University Press.

Phillips, C. and Brown, D. (1998) *Entry into the Criminal Justice System: A Survey of Police Arrests and their Outcomes. Home Office Research Study* 185. London: Home Office.

Phillips, C., Considine, M. and Lewis, R. (2000) *A Review of Audits and Strategies Produced by Crime and Disorder Partnerships in 1999. Briefing Note* 8/00. London: Home Office.

Phoenix, J. (2001) *Making Sense of Prostitution.* London: Palgrave.

Phoenix, J. and Oerton, S. (2005) *Illicit and Illegal: Sex, Regulation and Social Control.* Cullompton: Willan Publishing.

Police Foundation (2000) *Drugs and the Law: Report of an Independent Inquiry.* London: Police Foundation.

Policing and Society (2006) Special issue: 'Reassurance and the "new" community policing', Vol. 16, no. 2.

Pollard, C. (1997) 'Zero tolerance: short-term fix, long-term liability?', in N. Dennis (ed.) *Zero Tolerance: Policing a Free Society.* London: IEA Health and Welfare Unit.

Pollitt, C. (1993) *Managerialism and the Public Services* (2nd edn). Oxford: Blackwell Business.

Posen, I. (1995) *Review of the Police Core and Ancillary Functions*. London: HMSO.

Pratt, J. (1997) *Governing the Dangerous: Dangerousness, Law and Social Change*. Sydney: Federation Press.

Prins, H. (2005) *Offenders, Deviants or Patients?* (3rd edn). London: Taylor & Francis.

Privy Counsellor Review Committee (2003–4) *Anti-terrorism, Crime and Security Act 2001 Review: Report* (HC 100). London: HMSO.

Punch, M. (1979) *Policing the Inner City*. London: Macmillan.

Punch, M. (1983) *Control in the Police Organization*. Cambridge, MA: MIT Press.

Punch, M. (2003) 'Rotten orchards: "pestilence", police misconduct and system failure', *Policing and Society*, 13: 171–96.

Punch, M. and Naylor, T. (1973) 'The police: a social service', *New Society*, 24: 358–61.

Raine, J.W. and Willson, M.J. (1994) 'Conditional bail or bail with conditions? The use and effectiveness of bail conditions.' Report to the Home Office (unpublished).

Raine, J.W. and Willson, M.J. (1995a) 'Just bail at the police station?', *Journal of Law and Society*, 22: 571–85.

Raine, J.W. and Willson, M.J. (1995b) 'New public management and criminal justice: how well does the coat fit?', *Public Money and Management*, 15: 35–40.

Raine, J.W. and Willson, M.J. (1996) 'The imposition of conditions in bail decisions', *Howard Journal*, 35: 256–70.

Rappert, B. (2002) 'Constructions of legitimate force: the case of CS sprays', *British Journal of Criminology*, 42: 689–709.

Ratcliffe, J. (2003) *Intelligence-led Policing: Trends and Issues in Crime and Criminal Justice*. Canberra: Australian Institute of Criminology.

Ratcliffe, J. (2004a) 'Crime mapping and the training needs of law enforcement', *European Journal on Criminal Policy and Research*, 10: 65–83.

Ratcliffe, J. (2004b) 'The hot spot matrix: a framework for the spatio-temporal targeting of crime reduction', *Police, Practice and Research*, 5: 5–23.

Ratcliffe, J. (ed.) (2004c) *Strategic Thinking in Criminal Intelligence*. Cullompton: Willan Publishing.

Rawlings, P. (2003) 'Policing before the police', in T. Newburn (ed.) *Handbook of Policing*. Cullompton: Willan Publishing.

Redner, P. and Duncan, S. (2004) 'Making the most of the Victoria Climbie Inquiry report', *Child Abuse Review*, 13: 95–114.

Reiman, J. (1992) *Justice and the Modern Moral Philosophy*. New Haven, CT: Yale University Press.

Reiner, R. (1991) *Chief Constables: Bobbies, Bosses or Bureaucrats?* Oxford: Oxford University Press.

Reiner, R. (1995) 'Counting the coppers', in P. Stenning (ed.) *Accountability for Criminal Justice: Selected Essays*. Toronto: University of Toronto Press.

Reiner, R. (2000) *The Politics of the Police* (3rd edn). Oxford: Oxford University Press.

Reiner, R. (2003) 'Policing and the media', in T. Newburn (ed.) *Handbook of Policing*. Cullompton: Willan Publishing.

Reiss, A.J. (1971) *The Police and the Public*. New Haven, CT: Yale University Press.

Reiss, A.J. (1980) 'Controlling police use of deadly force', *Annals of the American Academy of Political and Social Science*, 452: 122–34.

Reith, C. (1952) *The Blind Eye of History: A Study of the Present Police Era*. London: Faber.

Ressler, R., Burgess, A., Douglas, J., Hartman, C. and D'Agostino, R. (1986) 'Murderers who rape and mutilate', *Journal of Interpersonal Violence*, 1: 273–87.

Reuss-Ianni, E. and Ianni, F.A. (1983) 'Street cops and management cops: the two cultures of polic-
    ing', in M. Punch (ed.) *Control in the Police Organization.* Cambridge, MA: MIT Press.
Rhodes, R. (1997) *Understanding Governance: Policy Networks, Governance, Reflexivity and
    Accountability.* Buckingham: Open University Press.
Richards, P. (1999) *Homicide Statistics. House of Commons Research Paper* 99/56. London: House of
    Commons Library.
Roberts, J. and Hough, M. (2005) *Understanding Public Attitudes to Criminal Justice.* Maidenhead:
    Open University Press.
Roche, D. (2003) *Accountability in Restorative Justice.* Oxford: Oxford University Press.
Roe, S. and Man, L. (2006) *Drug Misuse Declared: Findings from the 2006/06 British Crime Survey.
    Home Office Statistical Bulletin* 15/06. London: Home Office.
Rogers, C. (2006) *Crime Reduction Partnerships.* Oxford: Oxford University Press.
Rose, G. (2000) *The Criminal Histories of Serious Traffic Offenders. Home Office Research Study* 206.
    London: Home Office.
Rosenbaum, H.J. and Sedeberg, P.C. (eds) (1976) *Vigilante Politics.* Philadelphia, PA: University of
    Pennsylvania Press.
Rossmo, D.K. (2000) *Geographic Profiling.* Boca Raton, FL, and London: CRC Press.
Rowe, M. (2004) *Policing, Race and Racism.* Cullompton: Willan Publishing.
Rowe, M. (ed.) (2007) *Policing beyond Macpherson: Issues in Policing, Race and Society.* Cullompton:
    Willan Publishing.
Royal Commission on Police Powers and Procedures (1929) *Report* (Cmd 3297). London: HMSO.
Royal Commission on the Police (1962) *Final Report* (Cmnd 1728). London: HMSO.

Salt, J. (2000) 'Trafficking and human smuggling: a European perspective', *International Migration,*
    38: 31–56.
Sampson, F. (2000) *Blackstone's Police Manual: General Police Duties.* London: Blackstone.
Sampson, F. (2005) *Blackstone's Police Manual. Volume 4. General Police Duties 2006.* Oxford:
    Oxford University Press.
Sampson, R.J. and Raudenbusch, S. (2001) *Disorder in Urban Neighbourhoods: Does it Lead to
    Crime? National Institute Research in Brief.* Washington, DC: US Department of Justice
    Office of Justice Programs, National Institute of Justice.
Sampson, R.J., Raudenbush, S.W. and Earls, F. (1997) 'Neighbourhoods and violent crime: a multi-
    level study of collective efficacy', *Science,* 277: 918–24.
Sanders, A. and Young, R. (2007) *Criminal Justice.* Oxford: Oxford University Press.
Sanders, T. (2005) *Sex Work: Risky Business.* Cullompton: Willan Publishing.
Santilla, P., Zappala, A., Laukannen, M. and Picozzi, M. (2003) 'Testing the utility of a geographical
    profiling approach in three rape series of a single offender: a case study', *Forensic Science
    International,* 131: 42–52.
Savage, S. (2007) *Police Reform: Forces for Change.* Oxford: Oxford University Press.
Savage, S., Charman, S. and Cope, S. (2000) *Policing and the Power of Persuasion: The Changing Role
    of the Association of Chief Police Officers.* London: Blackstone Press.
Scarman, Lord (1981) *The Brixton Disorders, 10–12 April 1981: Report of an Inquiry by Lord
    Scarman.* London: HMSO.
Seddon, T. (2006) 'Drugs, crime and social exclusion: social context and social theory in British
    drugs – crime research', *British Journal of Criminology,* 46: 680–703.
Seth, R. (1961) *The Specials.* London: Victor Gollancz.

Sharp, D. and Wilson, D. (2000) '"Household security": private policing and vigilantism in Doncaster', *Howard Journal*, 39: 113–31.

Shearing, C.D. (2000) '"A new beginning" for policing', *Journal of Law and Society*, 27: 386–93.

Shearing, C.D. (2006) 'Reflections on the refusal to acknowledge private governments', in J. Wood and B. Dupont (eds) *Democracy, Society and the Governance of Security*. Cambridge: Cambridge University Press.

Shearing, C.D. and Ericson, R.V. (1991) 'Culture as figurative action', *British Journal of Sociology*, 42: 481–506.

Shearing, C.D. and Stenning, P. (1981) 'Modern private security: its growth and implications', in M. Tonry and N. Morris (eds) *Crime and Justice: An Annual Review of Research. Vol. 3.* Chicago, IL: University of Chicago Press.

Shearing, C.D. and Stenning, P. (1987) 'Say cheese! The Disney order that is not so Mickey Mouse', in C.D. Shearing and P. Stenning (eds) *Private Policing*. Thousand Oaks, CA: Sage.

Sheehy, Sir P. (1993) *Inquiry into Police Responsibilities and Rewards* (Cm 2280.1). London: HMSO.

Shelley, L. (1997) *Policing Soviet Society: The Evolution of State Control*. London: Routledge.

Sheptycki, J. (1995) 'Transnational policing and the makings of a postmodern state', *British Journal of Criminology*, 35: 613–35.

Sheptycki, J. (ed.) (2000) *Issues in Transnational Policing*. London: Routledge.

Sheptycki, J. (2003) *In Search of Transnational Policing*. Aldershot: Avebury.

Sherman, L.W. (1978) *Scandal and Reform: Controlling Police Corruption*. Berkeley, CA: University of California Press.

Sherman, L.W. (1980) 'Causes of police behaviour: the current state of quantitative research', *Journal of Research in Crime and Delinquency*, 17: 69–99.

Sherman, L.W. (1983) 'Reducing police gun use: critical events, administrative policy, and organizational change', in M. Punch (ed.) *Control in the Police Organization*. Cambridge, MA: MIT Press.

Sherman, L.W. (1990) 'Police crackdowns: initial and residual deterrence', in M. Tonry and N. Morris (eds) *Crime and Justice: A Biannual Review of Research*. Chicago, IL: University of Chicago Press.

Sherman, L.W. (2000) 'Gun carrying and homicide prevention', *Journal of the American Medical Association*, 28: 1193–5.

Sherman, L.W., Gartin, P. and Buerger, M. (1989) 'Hot spots of predatory crime: routine activities and the criminology of place', *Criminology*, 27: 27–55.

Sherman, L.W., Gottfredson, D.C., MacKenzie, D.L., Eck, J., Reuter, P. and Bushway, S. (1997) *Preventing Crime: What Works, What Doesn't, What's Promising*. Washington, DC: US Office of Justice Programs.

Silver, A. (1967) 'The demand for order in civil society', in D. Bordua (ed.) *The Police*. New York, NY: Wiley.

Simpson, A.E. (1977) *The Literature of Police Corruption. Vol. I. A Guide to Bibliography and Theory*. New York, NY: John Jay Press.

Sinclair, G.S. (2006) *Colonial Policing and the Imperial Endgame, 1945–1980: 'At the End of the Line.'* Manchester: Manchester University Press.

Skogan, W.G. (1990) *The Police and the Public in England and Wales: A British Crime Survey Report*. London: Home Office.

Skogan, W.G. (1994) *Contacts between Police and Public: Findings from the 1992 British Crime Survey*. London: HMSO.

Skogan, W.G. (2003) *Community Policing: Can it work?* Belmont, CA: Wadsworth.

Skogan, W.G. (ed.) (2004) *Community Policing: Can it Work?* Belmont, CA: Thomson Wadsworth.

Skogan, W.G. (2006) 'Asymmetry in the impact of encounters with the police', *Policing and Society*, 16: 99–126.

Skolnick, J.H. (1966) *Justice Without Trial*. New York, NY: Wiley.

Smith, A. (2006) *Crime Statistics: An Independent Review, Carried out by the Crime Statistics Review Group for the Secretary of State for the Home Department*. London: Home Office (available online at **http://www.homeoffice.gov.uk/rds/pdfs06/crime-statistics-independent-review-06.pdf**).

Smith, D.J. (1986) 'The framework of law and policing practice', in J. Benyon and C. Bourn (eds) *The Police: Powers, Procedures and Proprieties*. Oxford: Pergamon Press.

Smith, D.J. and Gray, J. (eds) (1983) *Police and People in London. Vols 1–4*. London: Policy Studies Institute.

Smith, D.J. and Gray, J. (1986) *Police and People in London*. Aldershot: Gower.

Smith, G. (2006) 'A most enduring problem: police complaints reform in England and Wales', *Journal of Social Policy*, 35: 121–41.

Smith, H. (2003) *The Nature of Street Robbery. Home Office Research Study* 254. London: Home Office.

Smith, Sir J. and Hogan, B. (1996) *Criminal Law* (8th edn). London: Butterworths.

Snook, B., Canter, D. and Bennell, C. (2002) 'Predicting the home location of serial offenders: a preliminary comparison of the accuracy of human judges with a geographic profiling system', *Behavioural Sciences and the Law*, 20: 109–18.

Snook, B., Taylor, P.J. and Bennell, C. (2004) 'Geographic profiling: the fast, frugal and accurate way', *Applied Cognitive Psychology*, 18: 105–21.

Snook, B., Zito, M., Bennell, C. and Taylor, P. (2005) 'On the complexity and accuracy of geographic profiling strategies', *Journal of Quantitative Criminology*, 21: 1–26.

Social Exclusion Unit (2000) *Neighbourhood Wardens: Policy Action Team 6 Report*. London: Social Exclusion Unit.

South, N. (2007) 'Drugs, alcohol and crime', in M. Maguire *et al.* (eds) *The Oxford Handbook of Criminology* (4th edn). Oxford: Oxford University Press.

Southgate, P., Bucke, T. and Byron, C. (1995) 'Parish special constables', *Policing*, 11: 185–93.

Southgate, P. and Ekblom, P. (1985) 'Contacts between police and public: findings from the British Crime Survey', in K. Heal *et al.* (eds) *Policing Today*. London: HMSO.

Spitzer, S. and Scull, A. (1977) 'Privatization and capitalist development: the case of the private police', *Social Problems*, 25: 18–29.

Squires, P. and Stephens, D. (2005) *Rougher Justice: Anti-social Behaviour and Young People*. Cullompton: Willan Publishing.

Stallion, M. and Wall, D.S. (1999) *The British Police: Forces and Chief Officers, 1829–2000*. Bramshill: Police History Society.

Starmer, K. (1999) *European Human Rights Law: The Human Rights Act 1998 and the European Convention on Human Rights*. London: LAG.

Starmer, K., Strange, M. and Whitaker, Q. (2001) *Criminal Justice, Police Powers and Human Rights*. Oxford: Oxford University Press.

Statewatch (2003) *Special Branch more than Doubles in Size* (special report). London: Statewatch.

Stelfox, P. (2007) 'Professionalising investigative processes', in T. Newburn *et al.* (eds) *Handbook of Criminal Investigation*. Cullompton: Willan Publishing.

Stenning, P. (2006) 'The idea of the political "independence" of the police: international interpretations and experiences', in M. Beare and T. Murray (eds) *Police and Government Relations: Who's Calling the Shots?* Toronto: University of Toronto Press.

Stockdale, J.E. and Gresham, P.J. (1995) *Combating Burglary: An Evaluation of Three Strategies. Crime Detection and Prevention Series Paper* 59. London: Home Office.

Storch, R. (1975) 'The plague of the blue locusts: police reform and popular resistance in northern England, 1840–57', *International Review of Social History*, 20: 61–90.

Storch, R. (1976) 'The policeman as domestic missionary: urban discipline and popular culture in northern England, 1850–80', *Journal of Social History*, 9: 481–509.

Stubbs, Sir W. and McClure, R. (1999) *Report to the Home Secretary: The Organisation and Funding of Police Training in England and Wales: Guiding Principles*. London: Home Office.

Sunshine, J. and Tyler, T. (2003) 'The role of procedural justice and legitimacy in shaping public support for policing', *Law and Society Review*, 37: 513–48.

Surveillance Studies Network (2006) *A Report on the Surveillance Society*. Wilmslow: Information Commissioner's Office.

Taylor, D. (1997) *The New Police in Nineteenth-century England: Crime, Conflict and Control*. Manchester: Manchester University Press.

Taylor, D. (1998) *Crime, Policing and Punishment in England, 1750–1914*. London: Macmillan.

Taylor, J. (2004) *Crime against Retail and Manufacturing Premises: Findings from the 2002 Commercial Victimisation Survey. Home Office Findings* 259. London: Home Office.

Teers, R. and Bucke, T. (2005) *Deaths During or Following Police Contact: Statistics for England and Wales, 2004/5*. London: IPCC.

Temkin, J. (1987) *Rape and the Legal Process*. London: Sweet & Maxwell.

Terrill, W., Paoline, E.A. and Manning, P.K. (2003) 'Police culture and coercion', *Criminology*, 41: 1003–34.

Thomas, D.A. (2006) 'Sentencing: dangerous offenders – Criminal Justice Act 2003 – "significant risk of serious harm"', *Criminal Law Review*, 174–9.

Tilley, N. (ed.) (2002) *Analysis for Crime Prevention. Crime Prevention Studies* 13. Cullompton: Willan Publishing.

Tilley, N. (2003) 'Community policing, problem-oriented policing and intelligence-led policing', in T. Newburn (ed.) *Handbook of Policing*. Cullompton: Willan Publishing.

Tilley, N. (ed.) (2006) *Handbook of Crime Prevention and Community Safety*. Cullompton: Willan Publishing.

Tilley, N., Pease, K., Hough, M. and Brown, R. (1999) *Burglary Prevention: Early Lessons from the Crime Reduction Programme. Policing and Reducing Crime Unit, Crime Reduction Research Series Paper* 1. London: Home Office.

Tilley, N., Robinson, A. and Burrows, J. (2007) 'The investigation of high-volume crime', in T. Newburn *et al.* (eds) *Handbook of Criminal Investigation*. Cullompton: Willan Publishing.

Tombs, S. and Whyte, D. (2007) *Safety Crime*. Cullompton: Willan Publishing.

Tonry, M. and Farrington, D. (eds) (1995) *Building a Safer Society. Crime and Justice: A Review of Research. Volume 19*. Chicago, IL: University of Chicago Press.

Touche Ross Management Consultants (1987) *Review of Scientific Support for the Police. Volume III*. London: Home Office.

Tuffin, R., Morris, J. and Poole, A. (2006) *An Evaluation of the Impact of the National Reassurance Policing Programme. Home Office Research Study* 296. London: Home Office Research, Development and Statistics Directorate (available online at **http://www.homeoffice.gov.uk/rds/pdfs06/hors296.pdf**).

Turnbull, P.J., Hickman, M. and Fernandez, J.L. *et al.* (2007) *National Evaluation of Criminal Justice Integrated Teams: Summary*. London: Home Office (available online at **http://www.home office.gov.uk/rds**).

Tutt, N. and Giller, H. (1987) 'Manifesto for management: the elimination of custody', *Justice of the Peace*, 151: 200–2.

Tyler, T.R. (2004) 'Enhancing police legitimacy', *The Annals*, 593: 84–99.

United Nations (2000) *United Nations Convention against Transnational Organised Crime* (available online at **www.un.org**).

University of Nottingham (2006) *Work and Menopause*. Nottingham: University of Nottingham.

Van Dijk, J. and De Waard, J. (1991) 'A two-dimensional typology of crime prevention projects: with a bibliography', *Criminal Justice Abstracts*, 483–503.

Vaughan, P., Kelly, M. and Pullen, N. (2001) 'The working practices of the police in relation to mentally disordered offenders and diversion services', *Medicine, Science and the Law*, 41: 13–20.

Von Hirsch, A. and Shearing, C. (2000) 'Exclusion from public space', in A. Von Hirsch *et al.* (eds) *Ethical and Social Perspectives on Situational Crime Prevention*. Oxford: Hart Publishing.

Waddington, P.A.J. (1987) 'Towards paramilitarism? Dilemmas in policing civil disorder', *British Journal of Criminology*, 27: 37–46.

Waddington, P.A.J. (1991) *The Strong Arm of the Law*. Oxford: Clarendon Press.

Waddington, P.A.J. (1993a) *Calling the Police*. Aldershot: Avebury.

Waddington, P.A.J. (1993b) 'The "case against paramilitary policing" considered', *British Journal of Criminology*, 33: 14–16.

Waddington, P.A.J. (1995) 'Public order policing: citizenship and moral ambiguity', in F. Leishman *et al.* (eds) *Core Issues in Policing*. London: Longman.

Waddington, P.A.J. (1999a) 'Police (canteen) sub-culture: an appreciation', *British Journal of Criminology*, 39: 286–308.

Waddington, P.A.J. (1999b) *Policing Citizens: Authority and Rights*. London: UCL Press.

Waddington, P.A.J. (2003) 'Policing public order and political contention', in T. Newburn (ed.) *Handbook of Policing*. Cullompton: Willan Publishing.

Waddington, P.A.J., Stenson, K. and Don, D. (2004) 'In proportion: race, and police stop and search', *British Journal of Criminology*, 44: 889–914.

Walby, S. (2004) *The Cost of Domestic Violence*. London: DTI Women and Equality Unit.

Walker, A., Kershaw, C. and Nicholas, S. (2006) *Crime in England and Wales, 2005/06. Home Office Statistical Bulletin* 12/06. London: Home Office (available online at **http://www.home office.gov.uk/rds/pdfs06/hosb1206.pdf**).

Walker, C. (2002) *The Anti-terrorism Legislation*. Oxford: Oxford University Press.

Walker, C. (2006a) 'Clamping down on terrorism in the United Kingdom', *Journal of International Criminal Justice*, 4: 1137–51.

Walker, C. (2006b) 'Intelligence and anti-terrorism legislation in the United Kingdom', *Crime, Law and Social Change*, 44: 387–422.

Walker, N. (2000) *Policing in a Changing Constitutional Order*. London: Sweet & Maxwell.

Walker, N. (2003) 'The pattern of transnational policing', in T. Newburn (ed.) *Handbook of Policing*. Cullompton: Willan Publishing.

Wall, D.S. (1998) *The Chief Constables of England and Wales: The Socio-legal History of a Criminal Justice Elite*. Aldershot: Ashgate/Dartmouth.

Walsh, L. (1982) *CIA Infiltration of the Labour Movement*. London: Militant.

Weatherburn, D., Fitzgerald, J. and Hua, J. (2003) 'Reducing Aboriginal over-representation in prison', *Australian Journal of Public Administration*, 36: 65–73.

Weatheritt, M. (1986) *Innovations in Policing*. London: Croom Helm.

Weatheritt, M. (ed.) (1998) *Zero Tolerance: What Does it Mean and is it Right for Policing in Britain?* London: Police Foundation.

Weber, L. and Bowling, B. (2004) 'Policing migration: a framework for investigating the regulation of global mobility', *Policing and Society*, 14: 195–212.

Webster, C. (2007) *Understanding Race and Crime*. Maidenhead: Open University Press.

Weisburd, D., Mastrofski, S.D., McNally, A.M., Greenspan, R. and Willis, J.J. (2003) 'Reforming to preserve: Compstat and strategic problem solving in American policing', *Criminology and Public Policy*, 2: 421–56 (reprinted in Newburn, T. (ed.) (2005) *Policing: Key Readings*. Cullompton: Willan Publishing).

Westley, W.A. (1953) 'Violence and the police', *American Journal of Sociology*, 59: 34–41.

Whitfield, J. (2007) 'The historical context: policing and black people in post-war Britain', in M. Rowe (ed.) *Policing Beyond Macpherson*. Cullompton: Willan Publishing.

Wiles, P. and Costello, A. (2000) *The 'Road to Nowhere': The Evidence for Travelling Criminals. Home Office Research Study 207*. London: Home Office.

Wilkinson, P. (2000) *Terrorism versus Democracy*. London: Frank Cass.

Williams, J. (1985) 'Redefining institutional racism', *Ethnic and Racial Studies*, 8: 323–48.

Williams, J. (2000) 'The inappropriate adult', *Journal of Social Welfare and Family Law*, 22: 43–57.

Williams, K. (2005) '"Caught between a rock and a hard place": police experiences with the legitimacy of street watch partnerships', *Howard Journal*, 44: 527–37.

Williams, R. (2004) *The Management of Crime Scene Examination in Relation to the Investigation of Burglary and Vehicle Crime. Home Office Online Report*. London: Home Office.

Williamson, T. (ed.) (2006) *Investigative Interviewing: Rights, Research and Regulation*. Cullompton: Willan Publishing.

Wilson, J.Q. (1968a) 'Dilemmas in police administration', *Public Administration Review*, 28: 407–17.

Wilson, J.Q. (1968b) *Varieties of Police Behaviour: The Management of Law and Order in Eight Communities*. Cambridge, MA: Harvard University Press.

Wilson, J.Q. and Kelling, G. (1982) 'Broken windows', *Atlantic Monthly*, 249: 29–36, 38.

Wood, J. and Dupont, B. (eds) (2006) *Democracy, Society and the Governance of Security*. Cambridge: Cambridge University Press.

Wooten, J. (1991) *Royal Commission into Aboriginal Deaths in Custody*. Canberra: Australian Government Publishing Service.

Worden, R.E. (1996) 'The causes of police brutality: theory and evidence on police use of force', in W.A. Geller and H. Toch (eds) *Police Violence: Understanding and Controlling Police Abuse of Force*. New Haven, CT: Yale University Press.

Wright, A. (2006) *Organised Crime*. Cullompton: Willan Publishing.

Wright, P. (1987) *Spycatcher: The Candid Autobiography of a Senior Intelligence Officer*. New York, NY: Heinemann.

Wright Mills, C. (1959) *The Sociological Imagination*. New York, NY: Oxford University Press.

Yeo, H. and Budd, T. (2000) *Policing and the Public: Findings from the 1998 British Crime Survey.* London: Home Office.

Young, M. (1995) 'Black humour – making light of death', *Policing and Society*, 5: 151–68.

Zander, M. (2005) *The Police and Criminal Evidence Act 1984* (5th edn). London: Sweet & Maxwell.

Zedner, L. (2003) 'The concept of security: an agenda for comparative analysis', *Legal Studies*, 23: 153–76.

Index

Note: Words represented in **bold italics** indicate main dictionary entries